GED Quick Review

This review contains useful information about preparing for the GED. Be sure to read the book and take the practice tests before referring to this sheet. Review the information included here prior to entering the testing center, paying close attention to the areas where you think you need the most review. This review should not be used as a substitute for actual preparation; it is simply a review of important information presented in detail elsewhere in this book. ***Remember that you must secure this review with the rest of your personal belongings for the duration of testing in a location designated by the testing center.***

GENERAL TEST-TAKING STRATEGIES

1. Relax.
    - Don't panic if you are having a hard time answering some of the questions! You do not have to answer all the questions correctly to get a good score.
    - Take a few moments to relax if you get stressed during the test. Put your pencil down, close your eyes, take some deep breaths, and stop testing. When you get back to the test, you will feel better.
2. Do the easy stuff first.
    - You don't have to do the questions from each section in order. Skip the hard ones and come back to them later.
    - Keep moving so that you don't waste valuable time. If you get stuck on a question, move on!
3. Use the scratch paper.
    - Do the math! Draw pictures to help you figure out problems, and use the scratch paper to write down your calculations.
    - Note questions that you will need to come back to later.
    - Make notes on your scratch paper about the reading passages as needed.
4. Be aware of time.
    - Pace yourself. You learned in practice which questions you should focus on and which questions you should skip and come back to later if you have the time.
    - Time yourself with a nonbeeping watch. Do not rely on the proctor's official time announcements.
    - You have only a limited amount of time. Read and work actively through the test.
    - Stay focused. Ignore the things going on around you that you cannot control.
    - Check over your answers if you have time remaining.
5. Guessing.
    - There is no "guessing penalty," so leave no question unanswered!
    - As time is running out, quickly fill in one bubble on the answer sheet for each question you did not have time to read. Use the same bubble (1, 2, 3, 4, or 5) for every such guess.
    - Eliminate answer choices that you know are wrong. The more you can eliminate, the better your chance of getting the question right.
6. Changing your mind.
    - Do not second-guess yourself. Your first answer choice is more likely to be correct. If you're not completely comfortable with your first choice, write the question number on your scratch paper and come back to it later if you have time.
    - Change your answer only when you are sure that it's wrong.

MATH STRATEGIES

The GED Mathematics Test has two parts, each having 25 questions. On Part I, you ***may*** use the calculator provided to you. On Part II, you ***may not*** use a calculator. You will have 90 minutes to complete all 50 questions. Most questions are in multiple-choice format, but some are in alternate grid format. For these questions, you must fill in the digits of your numerical (decimal or fraction) answer on a separated grid, or you must fill in a circle corresponding to a point on the coordinate plane. Following are specific strategies for the Mathematics Test.

GENERAL MATH CONCEPTS

1. Specific formulas you will need to use are given to you in the test booklet.
2. In an equilateral triangle, all three sides have the same length, and all three angles have the same measure.
3. In an isosceles triangle, two sides have the same length.
4. The complete arc of a circle measures 360°.
5. A straight line measures 180°.
6. A prime number is any positive integer that can be divided only by itself and 1.
7. Squaring a negative number yields a positive result.
8. To change any fraction to a decimal, divide the numerator by the denominator.
9. To calculate the mean, or average, of a set of values, divide the sum of the values by the number of values in the set.
10. The median is the middle value of a list where the values are in either ascending or descending order.
11. A ratio expresses a mathematical comparison between two quantities. ($\frac{1}{4}$ or 1:4)
12. A proportion is an equation involving two ratios. ($\frac{1}{4} = \frac{x}{8}$ or $1:4 = x:8$)
13. When multiplying exponential expressions with the same base, add the exponents.
14. When dividing exponential expressions with the same base, subtract the exponents.
15. When raising one power to another power, multiply the exponents.
16. Remember the order of operations: PEMDAS (parentheses, exponents, multiplication and division [left to right], addition and subtraction [left to right]).

GENERAL MATH STRATEGIES

1. Draw pictures or create tables as necessary to help you figure out problems.
2. Look for a way to reason through the problem. Don't just go for your calculator.
3. When reading word problems, translate them into mathematical equations. ("Jenny has five more CDs than Amy" is equivalent to $J = A + 5$)
4. Paraphrase questions to make sure that you are answering what is asked.
5. Remember to estimate or "ballpark" answers when you can. It is sometimes possible to eliminate all but the correct answer choice without doing any actual math.

MULTIPLE-CHOICE-FORMAT QUESTIONS

1. Look at the format of the answer choices before you attempt to work through the problem. Remember that the answer choices will be in either ascending or descending order where appropriate.
2. Even if the format of the question is unfamiliar to you, read through it carefully. You might know how to solve the problem.

ALTERNATE-GRID-FORMAT QUESTIONS

1. There are no answer choices, so try to avoid careless mistakes when calculating your answers. Use the scratch paper—do not try to do the math in your head!
2. For numerical answers, write your answer in the boxes above the grid on the answer sheet, and then fill in the circles below.
3. Remember the following as you enter your answers:
   - Your answers can begin in any column.
   - Each grid has five columns.
   - The grid can accommodate only positive digits 1 through 9, and 0.
   - Your answers can be decimals or fractions, unless the question states otherwise.
   - If your answer is a mixed number (such as $1\frac{1}{2}$), you must covert it to an improper fraction (such as $\frac{3}{2}$) or a decimal (such as 1.5).
   - A question might have more than one correct answer. You will need to grid only one.
   - No answer may be a negative number.
4. For coordinate grid answers, before filling in a circle, carefully count the circles starting at the origin and moving along the x-axis, then count the circles starting at the origin and moving along the y-axis.

SOCIAL STUDIES STRATEGIES

The GED Social Studies Test includes 50 multiple-choice questions based on short reading passages, visuals (charts, graphs, maps, editorial cartoons), and combinations of reading passages and visuals. You will be given 70 minutes to complete the Social Studies Test. Although you do not have to know specific facts for the test, a basic understanding of U.S. history, world history, civics and government, economics, and geography is important. Following are specific strategies for the Social Studies Test.

1. Think critically about cause-effect relationships.
2. When reading charts, graphs, and maps, carefully read the measurement units and exactly what is being measured.
3. Many wrong answer choices may be eliminated because they are clearly irrelevant to the topic of the questions. Use the process of elimination extensively.
4. Try to predict an answer in your own words before looking at the answer choices. If an answer choice matches your prediction, it is most likely correct.
5. Paraphrase when you need to. Putting the question into your own words makes it easier to answer.
6. You do not have to do the questions in order. Skip the hard ones, mark the question numbers on your scratch paper, and come back to them later if you have time.

SCIENCE STRATEGIES

The GED Science Test includes 50 multiple-choice questions based on short reading passages. Questions are divided nearly equally between those that cover visual information and those that cover short reading passages. You will be given 80 minutes to complete the Science Test. Although you do not have to know specific facts for the test, a basic understanding of life science, earth and space science, and physical science is important. Following are specific strategies for the Science Test.

1. Think critically about cause-effect relationships.
2. Be sure to distinguish among facts, hypotheses, and opinions.
3. When reading charts, graphs, tables, and maps, carefully read the measurement units and exactly what is being measured.
4. Try to predict an answer in your own words before looking at the answer choices. If an answer choice matches your prediction, it is most likely correct.
5. Paraphrase when you need to. Putting a question into your own words makes it easier to answer. Sometimes science situations seem more complicated than they actually are. Before you become confused and frustrated, try to think about what you already know about how the universe, including living and nonliving things, behaves. Everyone has intuitive notions about concepts like gravity, nutrition, ecology, health, and so on.
6. You do not have to do the questions in order. Skip the hard ones, mark the question numbers on your scratch paper, and come back to them later if you have time.

WRITING STRATEGIES

The GED Language Arts, Writing Test consists of two parts. Part I includes multiple-choice questions covering the areas of organization (15% of questions), sentence structure (30%), usage (30%), and mechanics (25%). There are three types of questions in Part I: correction (45%), revision (35%), and construction shift (20%). You will be given 75 minutes to complete Part I. Part II includes a topic on which you must write an essay. You will be given 45 minutes to complete Part II.

Remember that you can take advantage of all 120 minutes given for the Writing Test! Move on to Part II as soon as you finish Part I, and if time remains after you finish Part II, you may return to work on Part I.

Following are specific strategies for the Reading Test.

CORRECTION QUESTIONS

1. Correction questions require you to identify an error.
2. Each question begins with a sentence and ends with the question "What correction should be made to sentence X?"
3. Answer choice (5) is always "no correction is necessary." Take this answer choice seriously.
4. Remember that when correcting sentences, simpler is usually better.

REVISION QUESTIONS

1. Revision questions ask you to identify the best revision for a part of a sentence, a whole sentence, a paragraph, the entire text, or the title.
2. If the underlined portion seems correct as it is within the sentence, mark choice (1) on your answer sheet. Take this answer choice seriously.
3. If the underlined portion does not seem correct, try to predict the correct answer. If an answer choice matches your prediction, it is most likely correct.
4. If your predicted answer does not match any of the answer choices, determine which of the selections is the clearest and simplest.

CONSTRUCTION SHIFT QUESTIONS

1. Construction shift questions assess your ability to detect wordiness or awkwardness in one or two sentences.
2. The sentence(s) might not be grammatically incorrect. However, they would benefit from a change in word order or by the addition or deletion of certain words.
3. Pay close attention to pronouns within sentences. They must all have a clear (unambiguous) antecedent (entity they refer to).
4. Try to predict the improved sentence. If an answer choice matches your prediction, it is most likely correct.
5. If your improved sentence does not correspond to any of the answer choices, work through the answer choices and select the one that seems most natural to you.

GED ESSAY

1. You will have 45 minutes to complete Part II (the essay). Use your time wisely.
2. Carefully read the prompt. Remember that an essay written off the topic will not be scored.
3. Spend about 10 minutes planning your essay. Create an outline to keep yourself on track.
4. Remember, there is no correct response—choose ideas that you can most strongly support with examples.
5. No matter what you write about the topic, make sure you have compelling reasons and examples to support it.
6. Try not to leave any holes in your logic. Make sure you consider whether anything in your essay would confuse someone reading it.
7. Do not worry about the number of examples included in your essay or the length of your essay; focus on the quality and cohesiveness of your ideas.

READING STRATEGIES

The GED Language Arts, Reading Test includes 40 multiple-choice reading comprehension questions that you will be given 65 minutes to answer. Following are specific strategies for the Reading Test.

1. Each excerpt is preceded by a "purpose question." The purpose question gives a reason for reading the material. Use these purpose questions to help focus your reading.
2. Read the questions first. Do not try to memorize—just get an idea of what you should be looking for.
3. Read each passage for topic, scope, and purpose. Then skim for structure. Try to isolate one topic word or sentence for each paragraph. The details will still be there when you need them. Don't spend precious time trying to "learn" them.
4. Do not stop on unfamiliar words the first time through. You may not need to know the meaning of a word to answer the questions. Remember that you will be rereading most of the passage as you work on the questions.
5. Read the question and the answer choices before making a selection. Answer the questions carefully, referring back to the passage as needed.
6. Try to predict an answer in your own words before looking at the answer choices. If an answer choice matches your prediction, it is most likely correct.
7. Paraphrase when you need to. Putting the question into your own words makes it easier to answer.
8. You do not have to do the questions in order. Skip the hard ones, mark the question numbers on your scratch paper, and come back to them later if you have time.

EXAM PREP

GED

Advantage Education

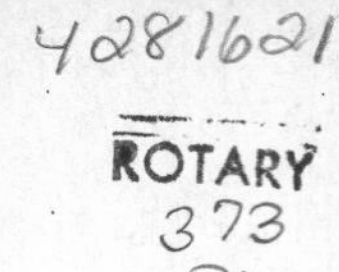

GED Exam Prep

ISBN-10: 0-7897-3658-6

ISBN-13: 978-0-7897-3658-1

Library of Congress Cataloging-in-Publication Data

Dulan, Steven W.

GED exam prep / Steven W. Dulan and Advantage Education.

p. cm.

Includes index.

ISBN 978-0-7897-3658-1 (pbk. w/cd)

1. General educational development tests—Study guides. 2. High school equivalency examinations—Study guides. I. Advantage Education (Firm) II. Title. III. Title: General educational development exam prep.

LB3060.33.G45D85 2007

373.126'2—dc22

2007010361

Printed in the United States of America

First Printing: April 2007

10 09 08 07 4 3 2 1

Trademarks

All terms mentioned in this book that are known to be trademarks or service marks have been appropriately capitalized. Pearson Education cannot attest to the accuracy of this information. Use of a term in this book should not be regarded as affecting the validity of any trademark or service mark.

Warning and Disclaimer

Every effort has been made to make this book as complete and as accurate as possible, but no warranty or fitness is implied. The information provided is on an "as is" basis. The author and the publisher shall have neither liability nor responsibility to any person or entity with respect to any loss or damages arising from the information contained in this book.

Bulk Sales

Pearson Education offers excellent discounts on this book when ordered in quantity for bulk purchases or special sales. For more information, please contact

U.S. Corporate and Government Sales
1-800-382-3419
corpsales@pearsontechgroup.com

For sales outside the United States, please contact

International Sales
international@pearsoned.com

ASSOCIATE PUBLISHER
David Dusthimer

ACQUISITIONS EDITOR
Betsy Brown

DEVELOPMENT EDITOR
Drew Cupp

MANAGING EDITOR
Patrick Kanouse

PROJECT EDITOR
Tonya Simpson

COPY EDITOR
Barbara Hacha

INDEXER
Ken Johnson

PROOFREADER
Linda Seifert

TECHNICAL EDITORS
Alan Tubman
Dan Powroznik

PUBLISHING COORDINATOR
Vanessa Evans

BOOK DESIGNER
Gary Adair

Contents at a Glance

Introduction 1

Part I: Getting Started

CHAPTER 1 Understanding the GED 9

CHAPTER 2 Diagnostic Test with Answers and Explanations 17

Part II: GED Testing Strategies

CHAPTER 3 Strategies to Get Your Best Score 85

Part III: Critical Thinking

CHAPTER 4 The Cognitive Domain of Bloom's Taxonomy 95

CHAPTER 5 Interpreting Graphical Information 97

Part IV: Language Arts, Writing

CHAPTER 6 About the Language Arts, Writing Test 107

CHAPTER 7 Overview of English Usage 111

CHAPTER 8 Grammar and Sentence Structure 125

CHAPTER 9 Effective Writing 143

CHAPTER 10 Writing Mechanics 153

CHAPTER 11 The GED Essay 169

CHAPTER 12 Language Arts, Writing Practice Questions and Answer Explanations 181

CHAPTER 13 Language Arts, Writing Terms 199

Part V: Language Arts, Reading

CHAPTER 14 About the Language Arts, Reading Test 205

CHAPTER 15 Prose Fiction 209

CHAPTER 16 Poetry 221

CHAPTER 17 Drama 229

CHAPTER 18 Prose Nonfiction 233

CHAPTER 19 Language Arts, Reading Practice Questions and Answer Explanations 243

CHAPTER 20 Language Arts, Reading Terms 257

Part VI: Social Studies

CHAPTER 21 About the Social Studies Test 265

CHAPTER 22 History of the World 267

CHAPTER 23 History of the United States 293
CHAPTER 24 Civics and Government 321
CHAPTER 25 Economics 333
CHAPTER 26 Geography 343
CHAPTER 27 Social Studies Practice Questions and Answer Explanations 353
CHAPTER 28 Social Studies Terms 371

Part VII: Science

CHAPTER 29 About the Science Test 381
CHAPTER 30 Life Science 383
CHAPTER 31 Earth and Space Science 399
CHAPTER 32 Physical Science 411
CHAPTER 33 Science Practice Questions and Answer Explanations 431
CHAPTER 34 Science Terms 449

Part VIII: Mathematics

CHAPTER 35 About the Mathematics Test 459
CHAPTER 36 Number Relationships 461
CHAPTER 37 Basic Operations 465
CHAPTER 38 Symbols and Figuring 471
CHAPTER 39 Decimals 477
CHAPTER 40 Fractions 485
CHAPTER 41 Statistics 493
CHAPTER 42 Percentages 499
CHAPTER 43 Probability 505
CHAPTER 44 Data Analysis 511
CHAPTER 45 Measurement 521
CHAPTER 46 Algebra 531
CHAPTER 47 Geometry 553
CHAPTER 48 Mathematics Practice Questions and Answer Explanations 571
CHAPTER 49 Mathematics Terms 587

Part IX: Full-Length Practice Tests

CHAPTER 50 Practice Test 1 with Answers and Explanations 595
CHAPTER 51 Practice Test 2 with Answers and Explanations 713

Part X: Appendixes

APPENDIX A	What's Next?	837
APPENDIX B	Calculator Directions	841
APPENDIX C	General Vocabulary List	845
APPENDIX D	Mathematics Formulas	855
APPENDIX E	Additional GED Resources	857
	Index	859

Table of Contents

Introduction 1

Using This Book 1
Using the Practice Tests 1
Scoring the Practice Tests 2
GED Training Schedules 3
GED Training Schedule 4
GED Emergency Plan 5
What's Next? 5

Part I Getting Started

Chapter 1:
Understanding the GED 9

What Is the GED? 9
Who Writes the GED? 9
How Do I Register for the GED? 9
Why Do the GED Tests Exist? 10
GED Scores 10
General Guidelines 10
Passing Scores 11
GED Agencies 11
Disabilities and the GED 14
What's Next? 15

Chapter 2:
Diagnostic Test with Answers and Explanations 17

Answer Sheets 19
Language Arts, Writing 23
Language Arts, Writing Part I 23
Language Arts, Writing Part II 35
Language Arts, Reading 35
Social Studies 44
Science 53
Mathematics Formulas 62
Mathematics 63
Mathematics, Part II 66
Language Arts, Writing Answers and Explanations 70
Part I 70
Part II 71

Language Arts, Reading Answers and Explanations . . . 72
Social Studies Answers and Explanations . . . 74
Science Answers and Explanations . . . 76
Mathematics Answers and Explanations . . . 79

Part II: GED Testing Strategies

Chapter 3:
Strategies to Get Your Best Score . . . 85

The Psychology of Testing . . . 85
Knowledge Versus Skills . . . 85
Practice to Perfect Your Skills . . . 86
Strategic Thinking . . . 86
Relax to Succeed . . . 87
Adrenaline Rush . . . 87
Suspense and Surprise . . . 88
Getting Ready to Take the GED . . . 89
Be Prepared . . . 89
Know Yourself . . . 89
Get Enough Rest . . . 89
Eat Right . . . 89
Listen to Music . . . 89
Taking the GED . . . 90
Do the Easy Stuff First . . . 90
Remember to Breathe . . . 90
Take Breaks . . . 90
Stay Calm . . . 91
Have a Plan of Attack . . . 91
Manage the Answer Sheet . . . 91
Be Aware of Time . . . 91
Changing Answers . . . 92
Guessing on the GED . . . 92
After the GED . . . 92
What's Next? . . . 92

Part III: Critical Thinking

Chapter 4:
The Cognitive Domain of Bloom's Taxonomy . . . 95

Knowledge . . . 95
Comprehension . . . 96
Application . . . 96
Analysis . . . 96

Synthesis 96
Evaluation 96
What's Next? 96

Chapter 5:
Interpreting Graphical Information 97

Interpreting Maps 97
Interpreting Tables 99
Interpreting Graphs 100
Line Graph 100
Circle Graph 101
Interpreting Editorial Cartoons 102
What's Next? 104

Part IV: Language Arts, Writing

Chapter 6:
About the Language Arts, Writing Test 107

Part I—Multiple Choice 107
Correction Questions 108
Revision Questions 108
Construction Shift Questions 109
Part II—Essay 110
What's Next? 110

Chapter 7:
Overview of English Usage 111

The Notion of "Standard English" 111
The Sentence 112
Parts of Speech 113
Nouns 115
Verbs 116
Agreement 117
Person 118
Number 118
Pronouns 122
What's Next? 124

Chapter 8:
Grammar and Sentence Structure 125

Traditional Grammar 125
Building from the Basic Sentence 126
Direct and Indirect Objects 126
Run-Ons 128

Combining Clauses 129
Tense 131
Voice 136
Parallel Structure 137
Modification 139
What's Next? 141

Chapter 9:
Effective Writing 143

The Paragraph 143
Logical Order 143
Pronoun Use 144
Word Choice 144
Redundant and Irrelevant Language 145
The Relationship Between Paragraphs 147
Common Mistakes 148
Too General 148
Too Emotional and Opinionated 148
Too Complicated 148
Risky Vocabulary 149
Poor Penmanship 149
Shaky Logic 149
Unsafe Assumptions 150
Too Conversational 150
Practicing Effective Writing 150
What's Next? 151

Chapter 10:
Writing Mechanics 153

Spelling 153
Homonyms 153
Contractions 158
Capitalization 160
Proper Names 160
Punctuation 161
Comma , ... 161
Apostrophe ' 163
Quotation Marks 163
Parentheses () 164
Colon : 165
Semicolon ; 165
Ellipsis 166

Hyphen - . . . 166
Dash — . . . 167
Underline Versus Italics . . . 167
What's Next? . . . 168

Chapter 11:
The GED Essay . . . 169
The Essay Prompt . . . 169
Your Essay Score . . . 170
Interpreting Your Score . . . 171
Skills Measured . . . 172
The Writing Process . . . 172
Steps to Writing Well . . . 172
Reasons to Write . . . 175
Revision and Editing . . . 175
Example Essays . . . 176
Example Essay, Score 1 . . . 176
Example Essay, Score 2 . . . 176
Example Essay, Score 3 . . . 177
Example Essay, Score 4 . . . 178
What's Next? . . . 179

Chapter 12:
Language Arts, Writing Practice Questions and Answer Explanations . . . 181
Answer Sheet . . . 182
Practice Questions . . . 183
Essay Topic . . . 193
Answers and Explanations . . . 195
Essay . . . 197
What's Next? . . . 197

Chapter 13:
Language Arts, Writing Terms . . . 199

Part V: Language Arts, Reading

Chapter 14:
About the Language Arts, Reading Test . . . 205
Format . . . 205
Scores . . . 206
Practice and Testing Strategies . . . 207
What's Next? . . . 207

Chapter 15:
Prose Fiction **209**

The Elements of Fiction 209
Analyzing Characters, Themes, and Points of View 215
Prose Style 216
What's Next? 220

Chapter 16:
Poetry **221**

Forms of Poetry 221
Hearing Poetry 222
Figurative Language 223
Interpreting Imagery, Symbolism, and Theme 224
Mood 227
What's Next? 228

Chapter 17:
Drama **229**

Dialogue and Stage Directions 229
Dramatic Structure 230
Analyzing Characters 231
What's Next? 232

Chapter 18:
Prose Nonfiction **233**

Forms of Nonfiction 233
The Author's Purpose and Tone 234
Cause and Effect 235
Comparing and Contrasting 237
Inference 238
Summarizing 239
What's Next? 241

Chapter 19:
Language Arts, Reading Practice Questions and Answer Explanations **243**

Answer Sheet 244
Practice Questions 245
Answers and Explanations 254
  Prose Fiction 254
  Poetry 254
  Prose Nonfiction 255
  Drama 256
What's Next? 256

Chapter 20:
Language Arts, Reading Terms 257

Part VI: Social Studies

Chapter 21:
About the Social Studies Test 265

Format and Content 265
What's Next? 266

Chapter 22:
History of the World 267

Prehistory 267
The Stone Age 267
Early Civilizations 268
Egypt 268
Ancient Greece and Rome 270
The Emergence of Religion 273
China 274
European Middle Ages 275
The Renaissance and the Enlightenment 276
The French Revolution 280
The Caribbean and Central America 283
The Industrial Revolution 283
New World Powers and World War I 284
The Bolshevik Revolution and Communism 287
World War II 288
The World After Global War 290
What's Next? 291

Chapter 23:
History of the United States 293

Native Peoples 293
Colonization 294
The Thirteen Original Colonies 294
Slavery 295
The American Revolution 295
The Revolutionary War 299
The First American Government 299
Westward Expansion 300
The Civil War and President Lincoln 301
From Noninterventionism to Imperialism 303
Industrialization and Immigration 304
The United States and World War I 305

Women and the Right to Vote . . . 305
The Great Depression . . . 306
The New Deal . . . 307
The Home Front During World War II . . . 308
The Korean War . . . 310
The Eisenhower Years . . . 310
President John F. Kennedy . . . 312
The Vietnam War . . . 314
The Nixon Years . . . 315
The Last Decades of the Twentieth Century and the Start of the Twenty-First Century 316
President Ford . . . 316
President Carter . . . 316
President Reagan . . . 317
President Bush (the Elder) . . . 317
President Clinton . . . 317
President Bush (the Younger) . . . 318
What's Next? . . . 319

Chapter 24:
Civics and Government . . . 321

Forms of Government . . . 321
The U.S. Government . . . 322
The Legislative Branch: Congress . . . 322
The Executive Branch: the President and Vice President . . . 323
The Judicial Branch: the Supreme Court and Lower Federal Courts . . . 325
Checks and Balances and the Legislative Process . . . 326
Constitutional Amendments . . . 327
The Electoral System . . . 328
The Role of the Citizen . . . 329
State and Local Government . . . 330
States . . . 330
Municipalities . . . 331
What's Next? . . . 332

Chapter 25:
Economics . . . 333

Elements of Production . . . 333
Supply and Demand . . . 334
Equilibrium . . . 335
Growth . . . 336
Inflation and Monetary Policy . . . 337
Measuring Growth . . . 337

The Role of the Government . . . 338
Capitalism . . . 339
Socialism . . . 339
Communism . . . 339
Money . . . 340
Fiscal Policy . . . 340
The Consumer . . . 341
What's Next? . . . 342

Chapter 26:
Geography . . . 343

The Earth . . . 343
Measuring the Earth . . . 345
Latitude and Longitude . . . 345
Time Zones . . . 346
Physical Geography . . . 347
Climate . . . 349
Demographics . . . 350
What's Next? . . . 351

Chapter 27:
Social Studies Practice Questions and Answer Explanations . . . 353

Answer Sheet . . . 354
Practice Questions . . . 355
Answers and Explanations . . . 367
What's Next? . . . 369

Chapter 28:
Social Studies Terms . . . 371

Part VII: Science

Chapter 29:
About the Science Test . . . 381

Format and Content . . . 381
What's Next? . . . 382

Chapter 30:
Life Science . . . 383

The Cell . . . 383
Genetics and DNA . . . 387
Organ Systems . . . 389
Nervous System . . . 389
Respiratory System . . . 390
Circulatory System . . . 391

Digestive and Excretory Systems 391
Skeletal and Muscular Systems 392
Endocrine System 392
Energy and Living Things 393
Classification of Organisms 393
Evolution 395
Ecology 396
What's Next? 397

Chapter 31:
Earth and Space Science 399

The Universe 399
Observation 400
Stars and Galaxies 400
The Solar System 401
Earth 404
Atmosphere 404
Hydrosphere 405
Biosphere 406
Lithosphere 407
What's Next? 409

Chapter 32:
Physical Science 411

Chemistry 411
The Atom 411
The Periodic Table 412
Chemical Reactions 414
Chemical Versus Physical Change 414
Compounds, Mixtures, and Solutions 415
Chemical Bonding 415
Acids and Bases 416
The Chemistry of Pollution 416
Physics 417
Mechanics 417
Energy 419
Simple Machines 419
Heat 421
Waves 423
Electromagnetic Radiation 425
Electricity and Magnetism 427
What's Next? 429

Chapter 33:
Science Practice Questions and Answer Explanations **431**

Answer Sheet 432
Practice Questions 433
Answers and Explanations 445
What's Next? 448

Chapter 34:
Science Terms **449**

Part VIII: Mathematics

Chapter 35:
About the Mathematics Test **459**

What's Next? 460

Chapter 36:
Number Relationships **461**

Place Value 461
The Number Line 461
Treating Positive and Negative Numbers 462
Practice Questions 463
Answers and Explanations 463
What's Next? 464

Chapter 37:
Basic Operations **465**

Addition and Subtraction 465
Multiplication and Division 465
Problem-Solving Strategies 466
Multistep Problems 466
Word Problems 466
Extra or Missing Information 467
Using Sketches and Diagrams 467
Practice Questions 468
Answers and Explanations 468
What's Next? 469

Chapter 38:
Symbols and Figuring **471**

Exponents and Square Roots 471
Parentheses 472
Order of Operations 472
Using Formulas 473
Practice Questions 473

Answers and Explanations 473
What's Next? 475

Chapter 39:
Decimals 477

Decimals Defined 477
Comparing Decimals 477
Rounding 478
Scientific Notation 478
Addition and Subtraction of Decimals 479
Multiplying and Dividing Decimals 479
Estimation 481
Practice Questions 482
Answers and Explanations 482
What's Next? 484

Chapter 40:
Fractions 485

Fractions Defined 485
Equivalent Fractions 485
Fractions and Decimals 486
Mixed Numbers and Improper Fractions 486
Comparing Fractions 486
Operations with Fractions 487
Addition and Subtraction of Fractions 487
Multiplication and Division of Fractions 488
Word Problems with Fractions 489
Practice Questions 489
Answers and Explanations 490
What's Next? 492

Chapter 41:
Statistics 493

Ratio 493
Rate 493
Proportion 494
Practice Questions 494
Answers and Explanations 495
What's Next? 497

Chapter 42:
Percentages 499

Percent Defined 499
Equivalent Percents, Ratios, and Decimals 499

Solving Percentage Problems . . . 500
Interest Calculations . . . 501
Practice Questions . . . 501
Answers and Explanations . . . 502
What's Next? . . . 504

Chapter 43: Probability . . . **505**
The Significance of 0 and 1 in Probability . . . 506
Dependent Probability . . . 506
Practice Questions . . . 507
Answers and Explanations . . . 508
What's Next? . . . 510

Chapter 44: Data Analysis . . . **511**
Mean and Median . . . 511
Charts and Tables . . . 512
Graphs . . . 513
Practice Questions . . . 514
Answers and Explanations . . . 516
What's Next? . . . 519

Chapter 45: Measurement . . . **521**
U.S. Customary Units . . . 521
The Metric System . . . 522
Unit Conversion . . . 523
Money . . . 524
Time . . . 525
Understanding Scale . . . 526
Practice Questions . . . 527
Answers and Explanations . . . 528
What's Next? . . . 530

Chapter 46: Algebra . . . **531**
Algebraic Expression . . . 531
Equations . . . 531
Common Word Problems . . . 532
Simplifying Algebraic Expressions . . . 533
Patterns . . . 534
Inequalities . . . 535

The Coordinate Plane . . . 536
Distance Between Two Points . . . 538
Linear Equations . . . 540
Slope of a Line . . . 541
Special GED Coordinate Grid Problems . . . 541
Multiplying Algebraic Expressions . . . 544
Factoring . . . 545
Practice Questions . . . 548
Answers and Explanations . . . 549
What's Next? . . . 551

Chapter 47:
Geometry . . . 553
A General Inventory of Geometric Concepts . . . 553
Points and Lines . . . 553
Angles . . . 554
Quadrilaterals . . . 554
Triangles . . . 555
Circles . . . 557
Derived 3-D Figures . . . 557
Side and Angle Relationships . . . 558
Similarity and Congruency . . . 559
Perimeter, Circumference, and Area . . . 560
Volume . . . 561
The Pythagorean Relationship . . . 561
Practice Questions . . . 563
Answers and Explanations . . . 565
What's Next? . . . 569

Chapter 48:
Mathematics Practice Questions and Answer Explanations . . . 571
Answer Sheet . . . 572
Practice Questions . . . 573
Mathematics Part II . . . 577
Answers and Explanations . . . 582
What's Next? . . . 586

Chapter 49:
Mathematics Terms . . . 587

Part IX: Full-Length Practice Tests

Chapter 50:
Practice Test 1 with Answers and Explanations **595**

Answer Sheets 597
Language Arts, Writing Test 597
Language Arts, Reading Test 597
Social Studies Test 598
Science Test 598
Mathematics Test 599
Mathematics Test (continued) 600
Language Arts, Writing Test 603
Writing, Part II 622
Language Arts, Reading Test 625
Social Studies Test 640
Science Test 659
Mathematics Formulas 672
Mathematics Test 673
Mathematics, Part II 678
Language Arts, Writing Answers and Explanations 684
Part I 684
Part II 687
Language Arts, Reading Answers and Explanations 688
Social Studies Answers and Explanations 692
Science Answers and Explanations 697
Mathematics Answers and Explanations 702
Part I 702
Part II 706

Chapter 51:
Practice Test 2 with Answers and Explanations **713**

Answer Sheets 715
Language Arts, Writing Test 715
Language Arts, Reading Test 715
Social Studies Test 716
Science Test 716
Mathematics Test 717
Mathematics Test (continued) 718
Language Arts, Writing Test 721
Writing, Part II 740
Language Arts, Reading Test 743
Social Studies Test 760

Science Test . . . 782
Mathematics Formulas . . . 796
Mathematics Test . . . 797
Mathematics, Part II . . . 803
Language Arts, Writing Answers and Explanations . . . 808
Part I . . . 808
Part II . . . 811
Language Arts, Reading Answers and Explanations . . . 812
Social Studies Answers and Explanations . . . 815
Science Answers and Explanations . . . 820
Mathematics Answers and Explanations . . . 824
Part I . . . 824
Part II . . . 829

Part X: Appendixes

Appendix A:
What's Next? . . . 837

GED and Employment . . . 837
GED and College . . . 838
GED and You . . . 839

Appendix B:
Calculator Directions . . . 841

Appendix C:
General Vocabulary List . . . 845

Appendix D:
Mathematics Formulas . . . 855

Appendix E:
Additional GED Resources . . . 857

General GED Information . . . 857
Language Arts Information . . . 857
Science Information . . . 857
Social Studies Information . . . 858
Math Information . . . 858
Additional Practice Tests . . . 858

Index . . . 859

About the Author

Since 1997, the faculty and staff of Advantage Education have been dedicated to providing effective and affordable test prep education in a variety of settings, including one-on-one tutoring via the Internet worldwide using Personal Distance Learning. The information and techniques included in this book are the result of Advantage Education's experience with test preparation for students at all levels over many years.

Join the thousands of students who have benefited from Advantage Education's instruction and coaching. Visit www.AdvantageEd.com for more information.

Acknowledgments

Advantage Education would like to thank Andrew Sanford, our lead researcher and writer, who worked tirelessly on this project. His commitment, attention to detail, and thoroughness were vital to the project's success.

Special thanks to Amy Dulan, Aishah Ali, Lisa DiLiberti, Kathy Matteo, Ryan Particka, Sasha Savinov, and Amanda Thompson for their hard work in making this project a success.

We Want to Hear from You!

As the reader of this book, *you* are our most important critic and commentator. We value your opinion and want to know what we're doing right, what we could do better, what areas you'd like to see us publish in, and any other words of wisdom you're willing to pass our way.

As an associate publisher for Pearson Education, I welcome your comments. You can email or write me directly to let me know what you did or didn't like about this book—as well as what we can do to make our books better.

Please note that I cannot help you with technical problems related to the topic of this book. We do have a User Services group, however, where I will forward specific technical questions related to the book.

When you write, please be sure to include this book's title and author as well as your name, email address, and phone number. I will carefully review your comments and share them with the author and editors who worked on the book.

Email: scorehigher@pearsoned.com

Mail: David Dusthimer
Associate Publisher
Pearson Education
800 East 96th Street
Indianapolis, IN 46240 USA

Reader Services

Visit our website and register this book at www.examcram.com/register for convenient access to any updates, downloads, or errata that might be available for this book.

Introduction

This book contains general information about the GED tests and includes chapters on each of the test subjects. It also contains a diagnostic test, a half-length practice test for each GED content area, two full-length GED tests, and specific-skill exercises throughout the text.

Using This Book

In a perfect situation, you will be reading this book at least several months before you take your actual GED tests. If that is not the case, you can still benefit from this book. If you do not have the time to thoroughly use the entire book, you should look at Part I, "Getting Started," and get through at least some of the questions on each section of Chapter 2, "Diagnostic Test." Then review Chapter 3, "Strategies to Get Your Best Score." Even just a few hours of study and practice can have a beneficial impact on your GED score.

EXAM ALERT

If you are reading this book only days before your GED tests, it is important to know that if your score is not acceptable, you can always retake the GED. Keep in mind, though, that rescheduling your GED testing date would be your best option at this point.

At the end of this introduction you will find scheduling hints to help you plan out your preparation. You should count backward from your GED test day and try to complete as many of the suggested activities as you can. If you have enough time between now and your GED testing date (at least three weeks, but preferably 12 to 18 weeks), you should work through this entire book. Some of the material should be used as practice, and some should be used as "dress rehearsal" material to get you ready for the whole experience of taking the GED tests. If you have less than three weeks, go to the GED Emergency Plan on page 5.

The students who increase their scores the most are the ones who put in consistent effort over time. Try to keep your frustration to a minimum when you are not doing as well as you had hoped over the course of your preparation. Similarly, try to keep yourself from becoming overconfident when you have a great day of practice testing.

Using the Practice Tests

The diagnostic test in Chapter 2 of this book is a simulated half-length GED. Take it as the first step in your test preparation program. It will help you to pinpoint areas of strength and weakness in your knowledge base and your skill set. Take it under realistic conditions. Time yourself strictly. You need to have an accurate picture of what your performance would be like if test day were today. Find out ahead of time if you will take all the tests in one day or over separate days; this varies by GED jurisdiction.

As you work with the practice tests, you should be aware that they are simulated exams. They are fairly accurate simulations written by experts. They contain some variations in style and a mix of question types. This is intentional so that you can get a taste of all the various formats and styles that can appear on a GED test. If you work through all the material provided, you can rest assured that there won't be any unwanted surprises on test day. However, you should keep your score results in perspective. Generally, students tend to score slightly higher on each successive practice test, although the truth is that GED tests are sensitive to factors such as fatigue and stress. So, the time of the day that you take the tests, your surroundings, and other variables in your life can have an impact on your scores. Don't get worried if you see some variations because of an off day or because the practice test exposed a weakness in your knowledge base or skill set. Just use the information that you gather as a tool to help you improve.

Use the suggestions in the training schedule at the end of this introduction to plan your study program. There will be times when you will want to work through some material without a time limit. The training schedule can help you decide when to switch the focus of your training from gaining knowledge to practicing skills, as well as when to make the shift to working on your timing.

Each practice question in this book has an explanation. You probably will not need to read all of them. Sometimes you can tell right away why you answered a particular question incorrectly. Everyone makes these "concentration errors" from time to time, and you should not worry when they occur. There is a good chance that your focus will be a little better on the real test as long as you train yourself properly with the aid of this book.

You should distinguish between those concentration errors and any issues of understanding or gaps in your knowledge base. If you have the time, it is worth reading the explanations for any of the questions that were challenging for you. Sometimes students get questions correct, but for the wrong reason or because they guessed correctly. While you are practicing, you should mark any questions that you want to revisit and be sure to read the explanations for them.

Scoring the Practice Tests

The tests in this book are simulations created by experts to replicate the question types, difficulty level, and content areas that you will find on your real GED test. The scoring worksheets provided for each test are guides to computing approximate scores. Actual GED tests are scored from tables that are unique to each test. The actual scaled scores depend on a number of factors, such as the number of students who take the test, the difficulty level of the items (questions and answer choices), and the performance of all the students who take the test. This means that "your mileage may vary." Do not get too hung up on your test scores on the practice tests in this book; the idea is to learn something from each practice experience and to get used to the "look and feel" of the GED.

The practice tests in this book are accompanied by scoring worksheets. Each scoring worksheet has formulas for you to work out an approximate scaled score for each section. (Your composite score can be computed by averaging your scaled scores from each test.)

A percentile rank will appear on your score report for each of the subject tests. This represents the percentage of a sample of graduating high school seniors who would have scored lower than you on the test. Remember that all test scores are just estimates of your knowledge and skills.

GED Training Schedules

The following pages include training schedules based on the amount of time that you have to prepare before your actual GED tests. The schedules are offered as guides to help you to stay focused on your preparation. You may modify the training schedules as necessary.

GED Training Schedule

- **At least 8 weeks before your GED**—Take the Diagnostic Test under actual test conditions. Time yourself strictly. Take the test in a place like the library, which approximates actual test conditions. Evaluate your results and pinpoint your areas of strength and weakness. Register for your GED test.
- **The first 4 to 6 weeks of training**—Don't worry about timing. Work through the exercises and half-length practice tests in this book at your leisure. Think about how the practice questions and reading passages are put together and study whatever other sources you need so that you can fill in any holes in your knowledge base.
- **2 to 3 weeks before your GED**—Using a full-length practice test, found in Part IX of this book, take your first "dress rehearsal" exam on the same day of the week and at the same time as you will take your GED. Time yourself as strictly as you did on your Diagnostic Test. Use the results to fine-tune the last part of your training. If you don't have your admission ticket yet (some jurisdictions may not require one), follow up with the GED Testing Service to make sure that your registration was processed properly.
- **1 to 2 weeks before your GED**—Take your second dress rehearsal full-length exam. If it doesn't go well, don't get too worried. Try to figure out what went wrong and review the explanations provided and the other relevant portions of this book. If it does go well, don't rest on your laurels. There is still time to consolidate your gains and continue to improve. Start planning a fun event for after your GED tests! (Remember that there is a good chance you will want a nap after your GED.)
- **2 to 5 days before your GED**—Make a practice run to the testing center. Figure out what you are going to wear on test day. Gather your materials together: your ticket (if necessary), pencils, black or blue pens, photo ID, and an analog watch. Adjust your sleep schedule so that you are able to wake up several hours before your test in order to be thinking clearly from the moment the test begins.
- **The day before your GED**—Do little or no practice or studying. Get a little physical activity so you fall asleep more easily and because the endorphins that you release to your brain help with stress management. Rest and relaxation are the order of the day. Make sure that you take care of your transportation needs and your alarm and/or wake-up call.
- **Test Day!**—Get up early. Eat a sensible breakfast. Read something to get you "warmed up." Bring your materials. Tear out and bring Appendix F, "Quick Review Sheet," and use it to remember your game plan for each section. Be on time. Follow the instructions of the test administrators. Avoid fellow test takers who are "stress monsters." Don't forget to breathe deeply and evenly, and don't tire yourself out with needless physical exertion such as tensing up your muscles while taking your GED. When the tests are finished, relax and try not to think about it until you get your score report.

GED Emergency Plan

If you have only a day or two before your GED, you should take the following steps. They are listed in order of priority, so you should do as many of them as you can before your test.

1. *Seriously consider rescheduling.* The GED is given many times each year at various testing centers. Rather than taking your tests with little or no preparation, you should look at the calendar and contact the GED Testing Service to inquire about future test days in your area.
2. *Relax.* Even if you don't have enough time to reschedule, you can get some useful information out of this book that will help you to pick up a few points that you might not have gotten otherwise.
3. *Take the Diagnostic Test.* There is a psychological theory called "Test Retest" that says that you should do a little bit better on a second test than a first test, even if you don't do any preparation in between. So, make the Diagnostic Test your first GED test. Time yourself strictly, and do it all in one sitting.
4. *Review the strategies in Chapter 3.* These are the high-yield test-taking strategies that will get you the most extra points on test day.
5. *Read through the content chapters.* The order should be the following:
    1. Language Arts, Reading (These are the least intuitive strategies.)
    2. Language Arts, Writing (This is possibly the most confusing format of the GED tests.)
    3. Mathematics (Skim through the stuff that you already know. Focus on the material that tends to confuse you.)
    4. Social Studies
    5. Science
6. *Practice.* Do as many practice questions as you can in your weakest area. Look at the explanations to gain a better understanding of how to approach the questions.
7. *Get some sleep.* Being well rested will have a bigger impact on your score than staying up all night "cramming." There is a significant skill component on this test. It is not all about knowledge, and you can't learn enough information to guarantee a higher score.

What's Next?

This book is divided into several parts, each dealing with a specific aspect of the GED. Part I provides some general information about the GED and how to register. It also includes the Diagnostic Test, which should allow you to assess your current readiness for the GED.

Part II covers the general test-taking strategies to help you maximize your GED scores, and Part III provides some insight into the critical thinking and interpretation skills tested on the GED.

Part IV deals with the Writing test, Part V deals with the Reading test, Part VI covers the Social Studies test, Part VII deals with the Science test, and Part VIII covers the Math test.

In Part IX, you will find two full-length GED practice tests, each of which covers all the content areas.

We've also included Appendixes in Part X with some additional useful information, such as a general vocabulary list, a list of mathematical formulae, calculator directions, and a Quick Review Sheet.

Congratulations on taking the first step toward improving your GED score!

PART I
Getting Started

Because you are reading this book, you probably intend to take the General Educational Development (GED) tests. Part I of this book contains background information on the administration of the GED and a diagnostic test to help you assess your present skill level.

Part I includes the following chapters:

Chapter 1 Understanding the GED

Chapter 2 Diagnostic Test with Answers and Explanations

1

CHAPTER ONE

Understanding the GED

This chapter is designed to give you a brief introduction to the General Educational Development (GED) tests, which are designed to measure the knowledge and understanding typically attained in high school.

What Is the GED?

The GED is a series of five tests, including a written essay, for adults who did not complete a traditional high school program. Over a period of 7 1/2 hours, you will take the following tests:

- Language Arts, Writing
- Language Arts, Reading
- Social Studies
- Science
- Mathematics

The GED is administered to assess and recognize the skills that you have learned in these areas, both during your years of formal education and outside of school. Jurisdictions across the United States and Canada use passing GED scores as the basis for granting high school equivalency credentials.

Who Writes the GED?

The GED is written and administered by the American Council on Education (ACE), an advisory group based in Washington, D.C., with more than 1,800 colleges, universities, and related organizations as members. ACE uses the GED to test for the basic skills that colleges and universities require of new students, and those that employers desire in their staff.

How Do I Register for the GED?

The GED is administered across the United States, U.S. territories, and Canada. The GED is available in English, Spanish, and French versions. (The Canadian edition of the GED includes social studies topics specific to Canada.) Your state, territory, or province has its own rules governing who may take the GED. For example, many states require you to be at least 19 years old. A list of contact phone numbers is included in Table 1.1 in the

"GED Agencies" section so you can speak to the right agency for your area. You can also speak with someone from the GED Testing Service directly at 1-800-62-MYGED (6-9433) to see whether you qualify to take the tests. Use this same number to locate a testing center and learn about fees, dates, and registration deadlines.

Why Do the GED Tests Exist?

The GED assesses high school level skills, making it possible for adults to prove their qualifications even if they do not have a high school diploma. Success on the GED opens doors to higher education (college, community college, vocational school), jobs and promotions (supervisory positions, pay-grade increases), and continued, lifelong learning.

GED Scores

You will receive a score for each of the five GED tests, as well as a total score, which is the average of your five individual, content-specific scores. In addition, you will receive a score for each of the five GED tests that compares you with all graduating high school seniors. This is called the percentile score.

General Guidelines

EXAM PREP Study TIP

If you are taking the GED for the first time, you will take all five subject tests. If you are retesting, the rules, fees, and scheduling of individual tests vary significantly across GED jurisdictions. Refer to your local GED agency (see Table 1.1).

Depending on who administers the GED, the five subject-area tests are given over one full day (normally a weekend day) or two or three partial days (normally weekday mornings or evenings). Make sure you choose a testing schedule that suits your needs when you register. There are scheduled short breaks between each test and a one-hour lunch break on longer days.

Administration of the GED is taken very seriously. Make sure you arrive at the testing center early (at least 30 minutes prior to the test). If you arrive late to testing, you will not be admitted. Leave enough time in the morning to account for unforeseen traffic delays, wrong turns, missed buses, and so on. At the testing center, you will first be required to fill out identification forms, a confidentiality agreement, and a demographics questionnaire. Some testing centers require you to attend a registration meeting before beginning testing. If this applies to you, be sure to have all the necessary documentation with you at that meeting.

GED administrators will examine your photo ID. Ideally, this would be a driver's license or state ID with a recent photo of you. If you have any doubts about how well your ID represents you, obtain a new one. If you want to use other forms of photo ID, be sure you meet the requirements of your local GED agency. Finally, your local GED agency might require additional forms of ID. Find out the current requirements ahead of time.

In some jurisdictions, GED administrators will take your photograph and videotape your test sessions. These are measures taken to protect the integrity of the test. In addition, you may not bring any unnecessary items into the testing room. Testing centers supply pencils, pens (which you must use for the essay), scratch paper, and the approved Casio fx-260 calculator. Any personal belongings you have will be secured until you are finished testing. Leave with the administrators anything that beeps! This includes digital watches and cellular phones. If they disturb the silence of the testing room, you risk being dismissed and having your test score voided. Many GED jurisdictions require you to wait a period of months before retesting following a dismissal.

Your scores are reported within a few weeks of testing. You must contact your local GED agency or testing center to receive a score report. The report may be obtained in person or in writing; no scores are given over the phone. Ask someone with your local GED agency about how to submit your scores to your state or province for high school equivalency certification.

Scores for the five tests in the GED series are reported separately and on a standard scale from 200 to 800. This score does not directly indicate the number of questions you answered correctly. The Language Arts, Writing Test has two parts, an essay and a multiple-choice section, and the reported score is a statistical combination of both parts.

Passing Scores

According to the GED Testing Service, the minimum passing score for each test is 410. The average of all five tests must be 450 to pass. Most jurisdictions use this standard passing-score requirement, but you should contact the agency in your area to be sure. A table of contact numbers follows in the next section. If you live outside of the United States, you should read about taking the GED in your country on the GED website, www.gedtest.org.

GED Agencies

Table 1.1 lists local GED agencies for all 50 states, U.S. territories and government institutions, and Canadian provinces.

TABLE 1.1 Local GED Agencies

United States		
State	**Agency**	**Phone**
Alabama	GED Testing Program, State Department of Postsecondary Education	334-353-4885
Alaska	GED Testing Program, Alaska Department of Labor and Workforce Development	907-465-4685
Arizona	Arizona State Department of Education	602-258-2410
Arkansas	Arkansas Department of Workforce Education	501-682-1978
California	State GED Office, California Department of Education	916-445-9438

(continues)

TABLE 1.1 *Continued*

United States		
State	**Agency**	**Phone**
Colorado	Colorado Department of Education	303-866-6942
Connecticut	Bureau of Adult Education and Nutrition Programs, State Department of Education	860-638-4151
Delaware	Department of Education	302-739-3743
District of Columbia	Adult Education, State Education Agency, University of the District of Columbia	202-274-7174
Florida	Bureau of Adult Programs, Florida Department of Education	850-245-9000
Georgia	Georgia Department of Technical and Adult Education	404-679-1621
Hawaii	Community Education Section	808-594-0170
Idaho	Department of Education	208-426-3284
Illinois	Illinois Community College Board	217-785-0123
Indiana	Division of Adult Education, Indiana Department of Education	317-232-0623
Iowa	Division of Community Colleges, Department of Education	515-281-3636
Kansas	Kansas Board of Regents	785-291-3038
Kentucky	Kentucky Adult Education, Council on Postsecondary Education	502-573-5114 ext. 102
Louisiana	Division of Family, Career and Technical Education, Louisiana Department of Education	504-342-3513
Maine	State Department of Education	207-624-6754
Maryland	Maryland State Department of Education	410-767-0168
Massachusetts	GED Office, Massachusetts Department of Education	781-338-6604
Michigan	Adult Education Office, Michigan Department of Career Development	517-373-1692
Minnesota	Minnesota Department of Education	651-582-8437
Mississippi	State Board for Community and Junior Colleges	601-432-6481
Missouri	State Department of Elementary and Secondary Education	573-751-1249
Montana	Office of Public Instruction	406-444-4438
Nebraska	Nebraska Department of Education	402-471-4807
Nevada	Office of Career, Technical, and Adult Education, Nevada Department of Education	775-687-9167
New Hampshire	Division of Adult Learning and Rehabilitation, State Department of Education	603-271-6699
New Jersey	New Jersey Department of Education	609-984-2420
New Mexico	State Department of Education	505-827-6531
New York	GED Testing, New York State Education Department	518-474-5906
North Carolina	North Carolina Community College System Office	919-807-7214
North Dakota	Adult Education and Literacy, North Dakota Department of Public Instruction	701-328-2393
Ohio	State Department of Education	614-466-1577
Oklahoma	State Department of Education	405-521-3321

(continues)

TABLE 1.1 *Continued*

United States		
State	**Agency**	**Phone**
Oregon	Oregon Department of Community Colleges and Workforce Development	503-378-8648 ext. 373
Pennsylvania	State Department of Education	717-783-3373
Rhode Island	Department of Education	401-222-8950
South Carolina	State Department of Education	803-734-8347
South Dakota	Department of Labor	605-773-3101
Tennessee	Tennessee Department of Labor and Workforce Development	615-741-7045
Texas	Texas Education Agency	512-463-9292
Utah	Utah State Office of Education	801-578-8356
Vermont	Career and Workforce Development, Vermont State Department of Education	802-828-0077
Virginia	Virginia Office of Adult Education, Department of Education	804-371-2333
Washington	State Board for Community and Technical Colleges	360-704-4321
West Virginia	GED Office, West Virginia Department of Education	304-558-6315
Wisconsin	Wisconsin High School Equivalency Program, Department of Public Instruction	608-267-2275
Wyoming	Wyoming Department of Workforce Services	307-777-7885
U.S. Territories		
Territory	**Agency**	**Phone**
American Samoa	GED Administrator, Government of American Samoa	684-633-5237
Guam	Guam Community College	671-735-5611
Marshall Islands	College of The Marshall Islands	692-625-3394
Micronesia	GED Administrator, Federated States of Micronesia National Government	691-320-2647
Northern Mariana Islands	Adult Basic Education Program, Northern Marianas College	670-234-5498
Palau	Bureau of Curriculum and Instruction, Ministry of Education	680-488-2570
Puerto Rico	Adult Education Services, Department of Education	787-759-6898 ext. 4567
Virgin Islands	Division of Adult Education, Department of Education	340-776-3484
U.S. Military, Government, and Others		
Institution	**Agency**	**Phone**
Federal Prisons	Federal Bureau of Prisons, Department of Justice	202-305-3808
U.S. Military and Coast Guard	Examination Programs, Defense Activity for Non-Traditional Education Support, Department of Defense	850-452-1063
Michigan Prisons	Michigan Department of Corrections	517-373-3642

(continues)

TABLE 1.1 *Continued*

Canada		
Province/ Territory	**Agency**	**Phone**
Alberta	Learner Assessment Branch, Alberta Learning	780-427-0010
British Columbia	Assessment Department, Ministry of Education	250-356-8133
Manitoba	GED Testing Program	204-325-1705
New Brunswick	NBCC Programs Branch, Department of Training and Employment Development	English: 506-453-8251 Français: 506-453-8238
Newfoundland and Labrador	Evaluation, Testing and Certification Office, Department of Education	709-729-2405
Northwest Territories	GED Testing Program, Department of Education, Culture and Employment	867-920-8939
Nova Scotia	GED Testing Service, Adult Education Division, Skills and Learning Branch, Nova Scotia Department of Education	902-424-3626
Nunavut	GED Testing Program, Deputy Minister for Education	867-975-5600
Ontario	Independent Learning Centre	416-484-2600 ext. 5134
Prince Edward Island	Literacy Initiatives Secretariat, Department of Education	902-368-6286
Québec	GED Testing Program	418-646-8363
Saskatchewan	GED Testing Program, Saskatchewan Learning	306-787-8131
Yukon Territory	GED Testing Program, Yukon College	867-668-8875

Disabilities and the GED

If you have a documented disability that could hinder your performance during normal GED testing, you might be entitled to accommodations. Accommodations are generally granted for people with the following diagnosed disabilities:

- Physical disabilities (vision, hearing, or mobility impairments)
- Learning disabilities (for example, dyslexia, dyscalculia, receptive aphasia, written language disorder)
- ADHD (Attention Deficit/Hyperactivity Disorder)
- Psychological disabilities (for example, bipolar disorder, Tourette's Syndrome)
- Chronic health issues

Accommodations may include, but are not limited to, the following:

- Audio edition of the test
- Braille edition of the test

- Large-print edition of the test (no documentation necessary)
- Vision-enhancing technologies
- Use of video equipment for candidates who must complete the Language Arts, Writing essay in sign language
- Use of a talking calculator or abacus
- Sign-language interpreter
- Use of a scribe
- Extended time; extra breaks
- Use of a private testing room
- One-on-one testing at a health facility

If you believe you are entitled to one or more accommodations, request the appropriate form from your local GED Testing Center: Learning Disabilities and/or Attention Deficit/Hyperactivity Disorder (Form L-15) or Physical Disabilities and Emotional or Psychological Disabilities (Form SA-001). Follow all the instructions carefully and submit the form well in advance of your test date so the GED Testing Service will have time to discuss your request with you.

What's Next?

The Diagnostic Test in Chapter 2 should be your next step. It will help you focus on areas of strength and weakness in your knowledge base and skill set. After you've assessed your current readiness for the GED, focus on the remaining chapters in the book to help you maximize your GED score.

CHAPTER TWO

Diagnostic Test with Answers and Explanations

This chapter will assist you in evaluating your current readiness for the GED. Make an honest effort to answer each question, then review the explanations that follow. Don't worry if you are unable to answer many or most of the questions at this point. The rest of the book contains information and resources to help you maximize your GED scores.

There are five separate sections on this test, including

- Language Arts, Writing, Part I and Part II
- Language Arts, Reading
- Social Studies
- Science
- Mathematics, Part I and Part II

Work on only one section at a time, and make every attempt to complete each section in the time allowed for that particular section. Carefully mark only one answer on your answer sheet for each question.

Your actual GED will contain approximately twice as many questions as this diagnostic test. Use this test to determine your areas of strength and weakness.

Mark your answers on the answer sheets on the following pages. Then compare your answers to the answers and explanations at the end of this chapter. Be sure to read through the explanations thoroughly. Identify and review topics you've consistently struggled with.

Answer Sheets

Language Arts, Writing Diagnostic Test

1. ① ② ③ ④ ⑤
2. ① ② ③ ④ ⑤
3. ① ② ③ ④ ⑤
4. ① ② ③ ④ ⑤
5. ① ② ③ ④ ⑤
6. ① ② ③ ④ ⑤
7. ① ② ③ ④ ⑤
8. ① ② ③ ④ ⑤
9. ① ② ③ ④ ⑤
10. ① ② ③ ④ ⑤
11. ① ② ③ ④ ⑤
12. ① ② ③ ④ ⑤
13. ① ② ③ ④ ⑤
14. ① ② ③ ④ ⑤
15. ① ② ③ ④ ⑤
16. ① ② ③ ④ ⑤
17. ① ② ③ ④ ⑤
18. ① ② ③ ④ ⑤
19. ① ② ③ ④ ⑤
20. ① ② ③ ④ ⑤
21. ① ② ③ ④ ⑤
22. ① ② ③ ④ ⑤
23. ① ② ③ ④ ⑤
24. ① ② ③ ④ ⑤
25. ① ② ③ ④ ⑤

Language Arts, Reading Diagnostic Test

1. ① ② ③ ④ ⑤
2. ① ② ③ ④ ⑤
3. ① ② ③ ④ ⑤
4. ① ② ③ ④ ⑤
5. ① ② ③ ④ ⑤
6. ① ② ③ ④ ⑤
7. ① ② ③ ④ ⑤
8. ① ② ③ ④ ⑤
9. ① ② ③ ④ ⑤
10. ① ② ③ ④ ⑤
11. ① ② ③ ④ ⑤
12. ① ② ③ ④ ⑤
13. ① ② ③ ④ ⑤
14. ① ② ③ ④ ⑤
15. ① ② ③ ④ ⑤
16. ① ② ③ ④ ⑤
17. ① ② ③ ④ ⑤
18. ① ② ③ ④ ⑤
19. ① ② ③ ④ ⑤
20. ① ② ③ ④ ⑤

Social Studies Diagnostic Test

1. ① ② ③ ④ ⑤
2. ① ② ③ ④ ⑤
3. ① ② ③ ④ ⑤
4. ① ② ③ ④ ⑤
5. ① ② ③ ④ ⑤
6. ① ② ③ ④ ⑤
7. ① ② ③ ④ ⑤
8. ① ② ③ ④ ⑤
9. ① ② ③ ④ ⑤
10. ① ② ③ ④ ⑤
11. ① ② ③ ④ ⑤
12. ① ② ③ ④ ⑤
13. ① ② ③ ④ ⑤
14. ① ② ③ ④ ⑤
15. ① ② ③ ④ ⑤
16. ① ② ③ ④ ⑤
17. ① ② ③ ④ ⑤
18. ① ② ③ ④ ⑤
19. ① ② ③ ④ ⑤
20. ① ② ③ ④ ⑤
21. ① ② ③ ④ ⑤
22. ① ② ③ ④ ⑤
23. ① ② ③ ④ ⑤
24. ① ② ③ ④ ⑤
25. ① ② ③ ④ ⑤

Science Diagnostic Test

1. ① ② ③ ④ ⑤
2. ① ② ③ ④ ⑤
3. ① ② ③ ④ ⑤
4. ① ② ③ ④ ⑤
5. ① ② ③ ④ ⑤
6. ① ② ③ ④ ⑤
7. ① ② ③ ④ ⑤
8. ① ② ③ ④ ⑤
9. ① ② ③ ④ ⑤
10. ① ② ③ ④ ⑤
11. ① ② ③ ④ ⑤
12. ① ② ③ ④ ⑤
13. ① ② ③ ④ ⑤
14. ① ② ③ ④ ⑤
15. ① ② ③ ④ ⑤
16. ① ② ③ ④ ⑤
17. ① ② ③ ④ ⑤
18. ① ② ③ ④ ⑤
19. ① ② ③ ④ ⑤
20. ① ② ③ ④ ⑤
21. ① ② ③ ④ ⑤
22. ① ② ③ ④ ⑤
23. ① ② ③ ④ ⑤
24. ① ② ③ ④ ⑤
25. ① ② ③ ④ ⑤

Mathematics Diagnostic Test

1. ① ② ③ ④ ⑤
2. ① ② ③ ④ ⑤
3.
4.
5. ① ② ③ ④ ⑤
6. ① ② ③ ④ ⑤
7. ① ② ③ ④ ⑤
8. ① ② ③ ④ ⑤
9. ① ② ③ ④ ⑤
10.
11. ① ② ③ ④ ⑤
12. ① ② ③ ④ ⑤
13. ① ② ③ ④ ⑤
14. ① ② ③ ④ ⑤
15. ① ② ③ ④ ⑤
16. ① ② ③ ④ ⑤
17. ① ② ③ ④ ⑤
18.

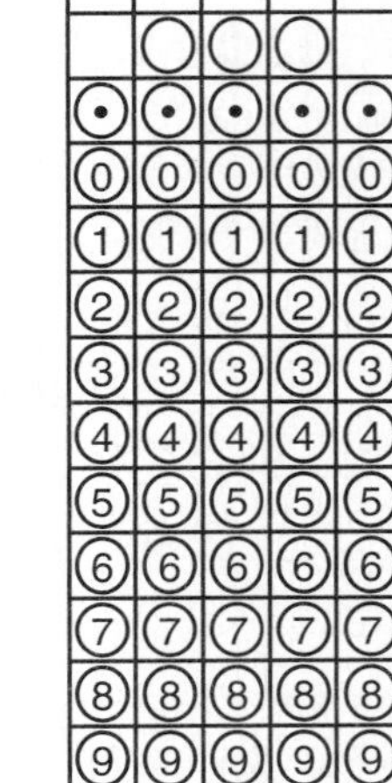

19. ① ② ③ ④ ⑤
20. ① ② ③ ④ ⑤
21. ① ② ③ ④ ⑤
22.

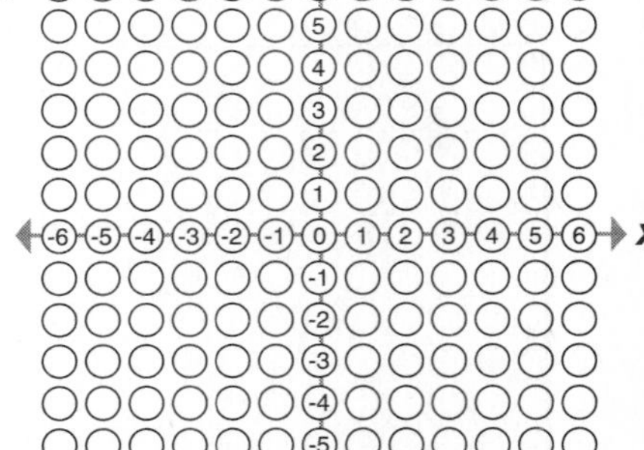

23. ① ② ③ ④ ⑤
24. ① ② ③ ④ ⑤
25. ① ② ③ ④ ⑤

Language Arts, Writing

Language Arts, Writing Part I

This diagnostic Language Arts, Writing Test has two parts, which must be taken consecutively. Part I consists of 25 multiple-choice questions that you have 38 minutes to complete. Part II tests your ability to write an essay about a topic of general interest. You will have 45 minutes to plan, write, and revise your essay. Just as with the actual GED, you may take advantage of the full time. If you finish Part I early, you may move on to Part II with the remaining time; likewise, if you finish your essay with time to spare, you may return to Part I.

Directions: Read all directions and questions carefully. Pick the single best answer, and answer every question. You will not be penalized for incorrect answers.

GO ON TO THE NEXT PAGE

Questions 1 through 8 refer to the following letter to a customer.

Civic Center Entertainment, Inc.

Mr. Paul Metzger
501 First Avenue NE
Arlington VA 22204

Dear Mr. Metzger:

(A)

(1) Everyone looks forward to a night of Falcons Hockey, so you certainly expected the service to be perfect. (2) Thank You for thinking of the Arlington Civic Center for your special night.

(B)

(3) Senior Banquet Manager Jeff Barnes handles the food, drink preparation and service in the Ambassador Suite. (4) I have trusted his skill and attention to detail for many important events. (5) Including a state dinner hosted by President Reagan.

(C)

(6) Jeff and I have reserved the Ambassador Suite for you for the Falcons game vs. the Hartford Flashes on December 20th at 7:30 p.m. (7) Within a few days he will contact you to confirm this reservation and answering any questions you may have. (8) If you have any additional questions or concerns, please call me. (9) Use my personal line printed on the enclosed business card.

(D)

(10) Your night of dining and hockey promises to be a memorable experience for you and your guests. (11) Everyone at Civic Center Entertainment hopes to serve you for your next important event.

Sincerely,

Emily Sorensen

Emily Sorensen
Vice-President, Guest Services

1. Sentence 1: **Everyone looks forward to a night of Falcons Hockey, so you certainly expected the service to be perfect.**

   Which is the best way to write the underlined portion of this sentence? If the original is the best way, choose option (1).

   (1) you certainly expected
   (2) you certainly expect
   (3) we certainly expected
   (4) you expected certainly
   (5) you will have certainly expected

2. Sentence 2: **Thank You for thinking of the Arlington Civic Center for your special night.**

   Which correction should be made to sentence 2?

   (1) change Thank You to Thank you
   (2) insert a comma after You
   (3) replace for with as
   (4) replace the with an
   (5) no correction is necessary

3. Sentence 3: **Senior Banquet Manager Jeff Barnes handles the food, drink preparation and service in the Ambassador Suite.**

   Which correction should be made to sentence 3?

   (1) change Banquet Manager to banquet manager
   (2) change handles to handling
   (3) replace food, drink with food and drink
   (4) insert a comma after preparation
   (5) insert is after Manager

4. Sentences 4 and 5: **I have trusted his skill and attention to detail for many important events. Including a state dinner hosted by President Reagan.**

   Which is the best way to write the underlined portion of this sentence? If the original is the best way, choose option (1).

   (1) events. Including a state
   (2) events: including a state
   (3) events, including a state
   (4) events including a state
   (5) events; a state

5. Sentence 6: **Jeff and I have reserved the Ambassador Suite for you for the Falcons game vs. the Hartford Flashes on December 20th at 7:30 p.m.**

   Which correction should be made to sentence 6?

   (1) change have to has
   (2) replace you with him
   (3) insert and after you
   (4) replace Falcons with Falcon's
   (5) no correction is necessary

6. Sentence 7: **Within a few days he will contact you to confirm this reservation and answering any questions you may have.**

   Which correction should be made to sentence 7?

   (1) change will contact to would contact
   (2) change to confirm to have confirmed
   (3) replace reservation and answering to reservation. Answering
   (4) change answering to answer
   (5) change may have to might be having

7. Sentences 8 and 9: **If you have any additional questions or concerns, please call me. Use my personal line printed on the enclosed business card.**

   The most effective combination of sentences 8 and 9 would includes which group of words?

   (1) call me, use my enclosed business card.
   (2) please enclose my personal line to call me.
   (3) please use my business card.
   (4) use my business card to call me.
   (5) please use my personal line, printed on the enclosed business card, to call me.

8. Sentence 10: **Your night of dining and hockey promises to be a memorable experience for you and your guests.**

   Which correction should be made to sentence 10?

   (1) replace promises with promise
   (2) replace your with you're
   (3) insert a comma after you
   (4) replace dining and hockey with dining hockey
   (5) no correction is necessary

GO ON TO THE NEXT PAGE

Questions 9 through 18 refer to the following memorandum.

MEMORANDUM

To: Ron, District Manager, Perfect Pizza

From: Matt, Night Supervisor, Perfect Pizza #104

Re: New Oven Proposal

Date: March 10, 2000

(A)

(1) The purpose of this memo is to propose a new oven purchase for the Perfect Pizza Restaurant #104 at 836 S. Main Street in Webberville.

(B)

(2) Our oven takes too long to bake pizzas the employees have all agreed. (3) The oven was designed originally to bake pizzas for a small number of people. (4) In the past three years, however, the number of Perfect Pizza customers growing. (5) We now has dine-in and delivery customers. (6) As a result, our customers have to wait, over 40 minutes for pizza. (7) Perfect Pizza, as it is, cannot keep up with such a large customer base. (8) The employees must keep increasing the wait time.

(C)

(9) I propose that we buy a new, larger oven. (10) The oven could bake more than just one pizza at a time. (11) This would cut down on the amount of baking time per pizza. (12) The oven could also bake each pizza faster.

(D)

(13) Perfect Pizza would be able to best meets the needs of its large customer base. (14) The wait time for both dine-in and delivery would be reduced. (15) In addition, Perfect Pizza will earn more profit because the restaurant will be able to serve more people.

(E)

(16) I look forward to discussing this proposal with you in more detail. (17) If you decide, to make this purchase I would be happy to assist in any way that I can. (18) Moreover, please consider a raise in salary for all of the employees here at Perfect Pizza.

GO ON TO THE NEXT PAGE

9. Sentence 1: **The purpose of this memo is to propose a new oven purchase for the Perfect Pizza Restaurant #104 at 836 S. Main Street in Webberville.**

   Which correction should be made to sentence 1?

   (1) insert a comma after Restaurant
   (2) insert a comma after memo
   (3) insert a semicolon after Restaurant
   (4) change Street to street
   (5) no correction is necessary

10. Sentence 2: **Our oven takes too long to bake pizzas the employees have all agreed.**

    If you rewrote sentence 2 beginning with As the employees have all agreed, the next word should be

    (1) our
    (2) oven
    (3) takes
    (4) too
    (5) long

11. Sentence 4: **In the past three years, however, the number of Perfect Pizza customers growing.**

    Which is the best way to write the underlined portion of this sentence? If the original is the best way, choose option (1).

    (1) growing.
    (2) grows.
    (3) have grown.
    (4) is growing.
    (5) has grown.

12. Sentence 5: **We now has dine-in and delivery customers.**

    Which correction should be made to sentence 5?

    (1) replace customers with customer
    (2) replace has with have
    (3) replace We with You
    (4) change now to recently
    (5) add a comma after dine-in

13. Sentences 9 and 10: **I propose that we buy a new, larger oven. The oven could bake more than just one pizza at a time.**

    The most effective combination of sentences 9 and 10 would include which group of words?

    (1) While I propose
    (2) oven, it could
    (3) Although I propose
    (4) oven, which could
    (5) oven, and could

14. Sentence 11: **This would cut down on the amount of baking time per pizza.**

    Which revision should be made to the placement of sentence 11?

    (1) move sentence 11 to the end of paragraph B
    (2) move sentence 11 to the end of paragraph C
    (3) move sentence 11 to the beginning of paragraph D
    (4) move sentence 11 to the beginning of paragraph E
    (5) remove sentence 11

The letter has been repeated for your use in answering the remaining questions.

MEMORANDUM

To: Ron, District Manager, Perfect Pizza

From: Matt, Night Supervisor, Perfect Pizza #104

Re: New Oven Proposal

Date: March 10, 2000

(A)

(1) The purpose of this memo is to propose a new oven purchase for the Perfect Pizza Restaurant #104 at 836 S. Main Street in Webberville.

(B)

(2) Our oven takes too long to bake pizzas the employees have all agreed. (3) The oven was designed originally to bake pizzas for a small number of people. (4) In the past three years, however, the number of Perfect Pizza customers growing. (5) We now has dine-in and delivery customers. (6) As a result, our customers have to wait, over 40 minutes for pizza. (7) Perfect Pizza, as it is, cannot keep up with such a large customer base. (8) The employees must keep increasing the wait time.

(C)

(9) I propose that we buy a new, larger oven. (10) The oven could bake more than just one pizza at a time. (11) This would cut down on the amount of baking time per pizza. (12) The oven could also bake each pizza faster.

(D)

(13) Perfect Pizza would be able to best meets the needs of its large customer base. (14) The wait time for both dine-in and delivery would be reduced. (15) In addition, Perfect Pizza will earn more profit because the restaurant will be able to serve more people.

(E)

(16) I look forward to discussing this proposal with you in more detail. (17) If you decide, to make this purchase I would be happy to assist in any way that I can.
(18) Moreover, please consider a raise in salary for all of the employees here at Perfect Pizza.

GO ON TO THE NEXT PAGE

15. Sentence 13: **Perfect Pizza would be able to <u>best meets the needs</u> of its large customer base.**

    Which is the best way to write the underlined portion of this sentence? If the original is the best way, choose option (1).

    (1) best meets the needs
    (2) best met the needs
    (3) met the needs better
    (4) meet better the needs
    (5) meet the needs best

16. Sentence 15: **In addition, Perfect Pizza will earn more profit because the restaurant will be able to serve more people.**

    Which correction should be made to sentence 15?

    (1) remove the comma after <u>In addition</u>
    (2) replace <u>will</u> with <u>would</u>
    (3) replace <u>restaurant</u> with <u>restaurants</u>
    (4) insert a comma after <u>profit</u>
    (5) no correction is necessary

17. Sentence 17: **If you <u>decide, to make this purchase</u> I would be happy to help out in any way that I can.**

    Which is the best way to write the underlined portion of this sentence? If the original is the best way, choose option (1).

    (1) decide, to make this purchase
    (2) decide to make, this purchase
    (3) decide, to make, this purchase
    (4) decide to make, this purchase
    (5) decide to make this purchase,

18. Which revision would improve the effectiveness of paragraph E?

    (1) remove sentence 16
    (2) remove sentence 17
    (3) remove sentence 18
    (4) move sentence 17 to the beginning of paragraph E
    (5) no revision is necessary

GO ON TO THE NEXT PAGE

Questions 19 through 25 refer to the following notice.

NOTICE: Steps to Successful Business Marketing

(A)

(1) HAVE A PLAN. (2) The most common marketing mistake is not having a plan. (3) A simple one- or two-page description of your customers; and what you'll do to get them to buy from you is sufficient.

(B)

(4) HAVE A BUDGET. (5) No matter how large or how small your marketing budget is, you must have one. (6) One of the basic principles in marketing is that you have to spend some money (though not necessarily a lot of money) in order to make money.

(C)

(7) UNDERSTAND THE VALUE OF A CUSTOMER. (8) Many business owners don't understand the lifetime value of a customer. (9) If a customer spends $10,000 with you over a year, and stays with you for an average of 10 years, with half of every $10,000 spent being profit, that means that every customer has a potential lifetime value of $50,000.

(D)

(10) HAVE A DATABASE OF CUSTOMER NAMES. (11) Get your customers' names in a database so you can contact them regularly. (12) This type of communication will encourage past customers to use your services or purchase your products again.

(E)

(13) UPSELL. (14) You should try to upsell every customer at the checkout counter if you're a retail business, or try to add additional services or offer longer-term contracts for your services if you're a service provider. (15) You can add hundreds or even thousands of dollars to you're business each year in this way.

(F)

(16) ASK FOR REFERRALS. (17) As simple as it may seem, this is one of the most overlooked and difficult strategies for small-business owners in employing. (18) Ask everyone who buys your product or service if they would give you the name of a friend or family member who could also use your product or service. (19) This way you'll be sure to have more customers every year. (20) Your net profits should increase.

GO ON TO THE NEXT PAGE

19. Sentence 3: **A simple one- or two-page description of your customers; and what you'll do to get them to buy from you is sufficient.**

    Which correction should be made to sentence 3?

    (1) replace of with by
    (2) remove the semicolon after customers
    (3) replace what you'll do with what one does
    (4) change to buy to to buying
    (5) no correction is necessary

20. Sentence 5: **No matter how large or how small your marketing budget is, you must have one.**

    Which is the best way to write the underlined portion of this sentence? If the original is the best way, choose option (1).

    (1) No matter how large or how small
    (2) No matter, whether large or small,
    (3) No matter how, large or small
    (4) No matter. How large or how small
    (5) No matter. If, how large or how small,

21. Sentence 8: **Many business owners don't understand the lifetime value of a customer.**

    Which revision should be made to the placement of sentence 8?

    (1) move sentence 8 to follow sentence 9
    (2) move sentence 8 to follow sentence 10
    (3) move sentence 8 to follow sentence 16
    (4) remove sentence 8
    (5) no revision is necessary

22. Sentence 11: **Get your customers' names in a database so you can contact them regularly.**

    If you rewrote sentence 11 beginning with To contact your customers regularly, the next words should be

    (1) getting their names in a database
    (2) you, by getting their names in a database
    (3) get their names in a database
    (4) and getting their names in a database
    (5) the database of names

23. Sentence 15: **You can add hundreds or even thousands of dollars to you're business each year in this way.**

    Which is the best way to write the underlined portion of this sentence? If the original is the best way, choose option (1).

    (1) you're business
    (2) you business
    (3) business
    (4) your business
    (5) it

24. Sentence 17: **As simple as it may seem, this is one of the most overlooked and difficult strategies for small-business owners in employing.**

    Which correction should be made to sentence 17?

    (1) remove the comma after seem
    (2) replace most with mostly
    (3) replace difficult with difficulty
    (4) change for to when
    (5) change in employing to to employ

25. Sentences 19 and 20: **This way you'll be sure to have more customers every year. Your net profits should increase.**

    The most effective combination of sentences 19 and 20 would include which group of words?

    (1) every year, if your
    (2) every year, but your
    (3) every year, and your
    (4) every year, finding your
    (5) every year, you may find your

Answers and explanations for this test begin on page 70.

GO ON TO: LANGUAGE ARTS, WRITING PART II

Language Arts, Writing Part II

The box on page 33 contains your assigned topic.

You must write on the assigned topic ONLY.

You will have 45 minutes to write on the assigned essay topic. (On a full-length test, if you have time remaining in this test period after you complete your essay, you may return to Part I of the Writing Test.)

Evaluation of your essay will be based on the following features:

- Well-focused main ideas
- Clear organization
- Specific development of your ideas
- Control of sentence structure, punctuation, grammar, word choice, and spelling

REMEMBER, YOU MUST COMPLETE BOTH THE MULTIPLE-CHOICE QUESTIONS (PART I) AND THE ESSAY (PART II) TO RECEIVE A SCORE ON THE LANGUAGE ARTS, WRITING TEST. To avoid having to repeat both parts of the test, be sure to do the following:

- Do not leave the pages blank.
- Write legibly in ink so that the essay readers will be able to read your handwriting.
- Write on the assigned topic. If you write on a topic other than the one assigned, you will not receive a score for the Language Arts, Writing Test.
- Write your essay on the lined pages of the answer sheets. Only the writing on these pages will be scored.

GO ON TO THE NEXT PAGE

Topic

Preparation is important for many actions and events. What was one situation in the past that you wish you had been better prepared for?

In your essay, identify what you wish you had been better prepared for and explain how your preparation could have been better. Use your personal observations, experience, and knowledge to support your essay.

Part II is a test to determine how well you can use written language to explain your ideas.

In preparing your essay, you should take the following steps:

- Read the **DIRECTIONS** and the **TOPIC** carefully.
- Plan your essay before you write. Use the scratch paper provided to make any notes and to organize your ideas. These notes will be collected but not scored.
- Before you finish your essay, reread what you have written and make any changes that will improve your essay.

Your essay should be long enough to develop the topic adequately.

An explanation of how to evaluate your writing on this test is found on page 71.

GO ON TO: LANGUAGE ARTS, READING

Language Arts, Reading

This diagnostic Language Arts, Reading Test consists of 20 multiple-choice questions that you have 33 minutes to complete. The questions assess your ability to analyze various short reading passages.

Each passage begins with a "purpose question" printed in all capital letters. These are not titles. They are intended to focus your reading and may help you grasp the meaning of the passages.

Some questions will reference certain lines of the passage by their numbers. For these, use the line numbers along the left side of the passage. Every fifth line is indicated, so find the number nearest the one you want and count up or down.

Directions: Read all directions and questions carefully. Pick the single best answer, and answer every question. You will not be penalized for incorrect answers.

GO ON TO THE NEXT PAGE

Questions 1 through 6 refer to the following poem.

HOW DOES A THUNDERSTORM AFFECT THIS PERSON?

The wind begun to rock the grass

The wind begun to rock the grass
With threatening tunes and low,—
He flung a menace at the earth,
A menace at the sky.

The leaves unhooked themselves from trees
And started all abroad;
The dust did scoop itself like hands
And throw away the road.

The wagons quickened on the streets,
The thunder hurried slow;
The lightning showed a yellow beak,
And then a livid claw.

The birds put up the bars to nests,
The cattle fled to barns;
There came one drop of giant rain,
And then, as if the hands

That held the dams had parted hold,
The waters wrecked the sky,
But overlooked my father's house,
Just quartering a tree.

"The wind begun to rock the grass" by Emily Dickinson, ©1891.

GO ON TO THE NEXT PAGE

1. What characteristic of the lightning is evident in lines 11–12: "The lightning showed a yellow beak, / And then a livid claw"?

   The lightning is

   (1) harmless
   (2) distant
   (3) beautiful
   (4) building
   (5) slow

2. What might the speaker mean when she says, "And then, as if the hands / That held the dams had parted hold" in lines 16–17?

   The rain

   (1) increased steadily over time
   (2) stopped as quickly as it started
   (3) increased stress on local water systems
   (4) devastated downstream areas
   (5) fell suddenly and heavily

3. What is the main effect of the lines "But overlooked my father's house / Just quartering a tree" (lines 19–20)?

   (1) to emphasize the danger of storms
   (2) to indicate that houses resist storms better than trees do
   (3) to reinforce that the speaker is afraid of storms
   (4) to link the father to the speaker's fear of storms
   (5) to clarify that storms cannot be controlled

4. How might the speaker react if she observed a powerful tornado while working in a farm field?

   The speaker might

   (1) shield her eyes from the destruction of property the tornado causes
   (2) ignore the tornado, not wanting to be distracted from work
   (3) glance quickly at the tornado, having become accustomed to them
   (4) tell her father to watch the tornado
   (5) stop and observe the powerful effects of the tornado

5. Emily Dickinson, the author of the poem, lived in rural New England during the 19th century. What evidence of her time period can be found in this poem?

   (1) Tight structure
   (2) Outdated technology
   (3) Social commentary
   (4) Dislike of harsh weather
   (5) Vivid imagery

6. As an adult, Emily Dickinson spent most of her time by herself at home. She never married and had no children. Of her hundreds of published poems, only seven appeared before her death. From her message in the poem and knowing these details about Emily Dickinson's life, which qualities best describe her?

   (1) Loving and sincere
   (2) Tormented and solitary
   (3) Serious and strong
   (4) Shy and mischievous
   (5) Light-hearted and childish

GO ON TO THE NEXT PAGE

Questions 7 through 11 refer to the following excerpt.

WHAT DOES BABBITT ADMIRE IN PEOPLE?

Babbitt's green and white Dutch Colonial house was one of three in that block on Chatham Road. To the left of it was the residence of Mr. Samuel Doppelbrau, secretary of an excellent firm of bathroom-fixture jobbers. His was a comfortable house with no architectural manners whatever; a large wooden box with a squat tower, a broad porch, and glossy paint yellow as a yolk. Babbitt disapproved of Mr. and Mrs. Doppelbrau as "Bohemian." From their house came midnight music and obscene laughter; there were neighborhood rumors of bootlegged whisky and fast motor rides. They furnished Babbitt with many happy evenings of discussion, during which he announced firmly, "I'm not strait-laced, and I don't mind seeing a fellow throw in a drink once in a while, but when it comes to deliberately trying to get away with a lot of hell-raising all the while like the Doppelbraus do, it's too rich for my blood!"

On the other side of Babbitt lived Howard Littlefield, Ph.D., in a strictly modern house whereof the lower part was dark red tapestry brick, with a leaded oriel [bay window], the upper part of pale stucco like spattered clay, and the roof red-tiled. Littlefield was the Great Scholar of the neighborhood; the authority on everything in the world except babies, cooking, and motors. He was a Bachelor of Arts of Blodgett College, and a Doctor of Philosophy in economics of Yale. He was the employment-manager and publicity-counsel of the Zenith Street Traction Company. He could, on ten hours' notice, appear before the board of aldermen or the state legislature and prove, absolutely, with figures all in rows and with precedents from Poland and New Zealand, that the street-car company loved the Public and yearned over its employees; that all its stock was owned by Widows and Orphans; and that whatever it desired to do would benefit property-owners by increasing rental values, and help the poor by lowering rents. All his acquaintances turned to Littlefield when they desired to know the date of the battle of Saragossa, the definition of the word "sabotage," the future of the German mark [currency], the translation of "*hinc illæ lachrimæ*," or the number of products of coal tar. He awed Babbitt by confessing that he often sat up till midnight reading the figures and footnotes in Government reports, or skimming (with amusement at the author's mistakes) the latest volumes of chemistry, archeology, and ichthyology.

Sinclair Lewis, excerpted from *Babbitt*, ©1922.

GO ON TO THE NEXT PAGE

7. When the narrator says, "They furnished Babbitt with many happy evenings of discussion" (lines 14–15), what is he suggesting about Babbitt?

   Babbitt is

   (1) happy about having different kinds of people as neighbors
   (2) happiest when he is in discussion with neighbors
   (3) so unhappy with his lifestyle that he prefers discussing the neighbors' lives
   (4) happy about having a lifestyle he sees as superior to his neighbors'
   (5) so unhappy he has a boring lifestyle compared to his neighbors

8. On the basis of Babbitt's reaction to Howard Littlefield revealed in this excerpt, how would Babbitt most likely act if he earned a college degree?

   He would probably

   (1) keep his degree a secret
   (2) tolerate other people more
   (3) demand that his employer increase his pay
   (4) insist that other people trust his statements
   (5) move to a better neighborhood

9. When the narrator says that Littlefield is "the authority on everything in the world except babies, cooking, and motors" (lines 28–30), he is implying which of the following?

   (1) Babies, cooking, and motors are not worthwhile subjects for Littlefield to learn.
   (2) Babies, cooking, and motors are too difficult for Littlefield to learn.
   (3) Babies, cooking, and motors are worthwhile subjects about which Littlefield has chosen not to learn.
   (4) Babies, cooking, and motors are not necessary subjects for Littlefield to know in his career.
   (5) Littlefield considers babies, cooking, and motors important subjects about which to learn.

10. Babbitt would probably identify which one of the following traits as being essential for belonging in the neighborhood?

   (1) unique taste
   (2) self-discipline
   (3) light-heartedness
   (4) open hostility
   (5) playfulness

11. Which of the following phrases is closest in meaning to the phrase "yearned over" in line 40?

   (1) admired
   (2) disregarded
   (3) sympathized with
   (4) thought about
   (5) forgot about

GO ON TO THE NEXT PAGE

Questions 12 through 15 refer to the following business document.

HOW MUST AN EMPLOYEE DEAL WITH ACCIDENTS?

MEMO

To: All Foundry Employees and Supervisors
Re: Emergency Procedures and Reporting Accidents

Several serious and unfortunate accidents have caused foundry management and other employees to reevaluate their workplace habits. Expect future communications regarding work procedures. In addition, management has determined that new accident-response measures must be implemented to minimize physical and financial costs to employees and the company caused by workplace accidents. Effective immediately, the following steps must be taken after every accident:

1. Where serious injuries or property damage are involved, care must be taken to leave the scene alone (unless this creates an unsafe situation) in order that:
    a. the cause of the accident and the extent of the damage incurred may be investigated; and
    b. damaged or defective equipment and machinery can be retained for inspection by insurance adjustors.
2. All accidents, dangerous incidents, and occupational diseases, however minor, must be reported at once using the attached report form. The immediate supervisor should complete the form, and then forward it to the Safety Office for review within 12 hours of the incident. When a victim is involved, the person completing the form should obtain the victim's signature, if possible. Where no injuries have been sustained, substitute the "name of victim" with the name of the person most closely involved with the incident.
3. As before, any accident resulting in injury to any employee or any accident which causes (in the opinion of the head of department) more than $100 damage to company property, or which stops production for longer than 15 minutes, requires that the affected employee or employees report to the Safety Office immediately for a drug screening.
4. No disciplinary action may be taken against any employee who pushes one of the red "ALL STOP" buttons on the foundry floor when he or she believes to have observed a hazardous situation. Similarly, all supervisors and management will maintain an "open door" policy regarding the reporting of potentially hazardous situations.
5. The Capital Equipment Department will increase the frequency of cleaning and painting machinery from monthly to bi-weekly. Yellow safety paint will be available to any employee who feels his or her workstation would benefit from some marking.
6. It is the responsibility of each head of department to ensure that the above procedure is being followed.

If assistance in completing the form is required, consult with the Human Resources Department or the Safety Office.

GO ON TO THE NEXT PAGE

12. Why must employees "leave the scene alone" (lines 7–8)?

    The scene will

    (1) create an unsafe situation
    (2) be cleaned up by professionals
    (3) help management assess the damage
    (4) cause a work stoppage
    (5) show employees the importance of safe workplace procedures

13. Who is responsible for reviewing accident report forms?

    (1) the employee involved
    (2) the head of the department involved
    (3) insurance adjustors
    (4) the Safety Office
    (5) the Human Resources Department

14. What is the meaning of "sustained" (line 17)?

    (1) suffered
    (2) maintained
    (3) withstood
    (4) validated
    (5) prevented

15. When would a person need to read this document?

    (1) when applying for a job at Foster Mining & Metals
    (2) after learning how to operate machinery
    (3) after retiring from Foster Mining and Metals
    (4) before being considered for promotion to a supervisor position
    (5) before beginning work at the Foster Mining and Metals foundry

GO ON TO THE NEXT PAGE

Questions 16 through 20 refer to the following excerpt from a play.

WHY DOES THE GIRL MISTRUST MEN?

[Enter from the door on the Right, a GIRL and a YOUNG OFFICER in khaki. The GIRL wears a discreet dark dress, hat, and veil, and stained yellow gloves. The YOUNG OFFICER is tall, with a fresh open face, and kindly eager blue eyes; he is a little lame. The GIRL, who is evidently at home, moves towards the gas jet to turn it up, then changes her mind, and going to the curtains, draws them apart and throws up the window. Bright moonlight comes flooding in. Outside are seen the trees of a little Square. She stands gazing out, suddenly turns inward with a shiver.]

YOUNG OFFICER: I say; what's the matter? You were crying when I spoke to you.

GIRL: *(With a movement of recovery)* Oh! nothing. The beautiful evening—that's all.

YOUNG OFFICER: *(Looking at her)* Cheer up!

GIRL: *(Taking off hat and veil; her hair is yellowish and crinkly)* Cheer up! You are not lonelee, like me.

YOUNG OFFICER: *(Limping to the window—doubtfully)* I say, how did you get into this? Isn't it an awfully hopeless sort of life?

GIRL: Yees, it ees. You haf been wounded?

YOUNG OFFICER: Just out of hospital to-day.

GIRL: The horrible war—all the misery is because of the war. When will it end?

YOUNG OFFICER: *(Leaning against the window-sill, looking at her attentively)* I say, what nationality are you?

GIRL: *(With a quick look and away)* Rooshian.

YOUNG OFFICER: Really! I never met a Russian girl. [The GIRL gives him another quick look] I say, is it as bad as they make out?

GIRL: *(Slipping her hand through his arm)* Not when I haf anyone as ni-ice as you; I never haf had, though. [She smiles, and her smile, like her speech, is slow and confining] You stopped because I was sad, others stop because I am gay. I am not fond of men at all. When you know—you are not fond of them.

YOUNG OFFICER: Well, you hardly know them at their best, do you? You should see them in the trenches. By George! They're simply splendid—officers and men, every blessed soul. There's never been anything like it—just one long bit of jolly fine self-sacrifice; it's perfectly amazing.

GIRL*: (Turning her blue-grey eyes on him)* I expect you are not the last at that. You see in them what you haf in yourself, I think.

YOUNG OFFICER: Oh, not a bit; you're quite out! I assure you when we made the attack where I got wounded there wasn't a single man in my regiment who wasn't an absolute hero. The way they went in—never thinking of themselves—it was simply ripping.

GIRL: *(In a queer voice)* It is the same too, perhaps, with—the enemy.

YOUNG OFFICER: Oh, yes! I know that.

GIRL: Ah! You are not a mean man. How I hate mean men!

YOUNG OFFICER: Oh! they're not mean really—they simply don't understand.

GIRL: Oh! You are a babee—a good babee aren't you?

[The YOUNG OFFICER doesn't like this, and frowns. The GIRL looks a little scared.]

GIRL: *(Clingingly)* But I li-ke you for it. It is so good to find a ni-ice man.

John Galsworthy, excerpted from *Defeat*, ©1921.

GO ON TO THE NEXT PAGE

16. What can the reader conclude about the girl from her statements in this excerpt?

    She

    (1) trusts men easily
    (2) feels sorry that the young officer was wounded
    (3) wishes to part ways with the young officer
    (4) approves of the war
    (5) remains cautious around men

17. Which of the following best explains why the girl likes the young officer more than other men she has met?

    (1) The young officer comforted her when she was sad.
    (2) She needs help with her English.
    (3) The young officer shares her interest in concerts.
    (4) She sympathizes with the injured young officer.
    (5) She prefers military men.

18. Which of the following best describes the girl and the young officer?

    (1) Employee and customer
    (2) Close friends
    (3) Brother and sister
    (4) Recent acquaintances
    (5) Nurse and patient

19. When the young officer exclaims, "By George!" (line 48), what does it indicate about his feelings?

    He is

    (1) amused by the war
    (2) surprised that the girl could speak poorly of men
    (3) angry at the enemy for their brutal tactics
    (4) thankful to the girl for keeping him company
    (5) astounded by the bravery of his comrades

20. In this excerpt, how does the author use the opening of the window?

    To develop

    (1) the girl's love of nature
    (2) the chilly yet romantic atmosphere
    (3) the girl's preference for cool over heat
    (4) the young officer's intimidation of the girl
    (5) the author's sympathy for injured soldiers

Answers and explanations for this test begin on page 72.

GO ON TO: SOCIAL STUDIES

Social Studies

This diagnostic Social Studies Test consists of 25 multiple-choice questions that you have 35 minutes to complete. You will have to draw upon some prior knowledge of history, civics and government, economics, and geography; however, you will not have to recall facts.

Directions: Choose the one best answer to each question.

GO ON TO THE NEXT PAGE

Questions 1 and 2 refer to the following chart:

World Population and Energy Consumption

Region	Population (Millions of People)	% of World Population	Energy Consumption (Million Tons of Oil Equivalent)	% of World Energy Consumption
Europe	784	12.5	2749	26.0
Middle East	177	2.8	446	4.2
Former USSR	286	4.6	962	9.1
China	1294	20.6	1426	13.5
Asia (excl. China)	2018	32.2	1224	11.6
North America	425	6.8	2701	25.5
Latin America	432	6.9	464	4.4
Africa	851	13.6	559	5.3
World	6268		10579	

1. According to the chart, what comparison can be made among the regions?

   (1) birth and mortality rates
   (2) probability of political stability
   (3) amount of economic activity
   (4) distribution of minerals
   (5) religious beliefs

2. What is the most probable reason for the level of energy consumption in North America and Europe when compared to the percentage of the world population that lives there?

   (1) They are located near large bodies of water.
   (2) They are highly developed countries.
   (3) Farming is the main activity in those regions.
   (4) They do not engage in manufacturing.
   (5) There are few automobiles in those regions.

3. According to the law of supply and demand, which of the following is most likely to occur when there is an unusually poor crop of apples, yet people want to buy more apples than they did the previous year?

   (1) The price of apples will increase.
   (2) Apple growers will demand tariff protection to prevent competition from foreign apple growers.
   (3) The incomes of apple growers will decrease.
   (4) The number of apple growers will decrease.
   (5) The cost of growing apples will increase.

GO ON TO THE NEXT PAGE

Question 4 refers to the following information.

During the Industrial Revolution in the United States, large urban areas offered new employment opportunities. At the same time, developments and improvements in farming technology reduced the need for farm workers.

4. Which of the following best explains why many people living in rural areas in the United States migrated to cities?

   (1) The weather conditions were harsher in rural areas.
   (2) Rural life was boring after several years.
   (3) The government forced people in rural areas to become urbanized.
   (4) People from rural areas moved to the cities to seek jobs.
   (5) People from rural areas had a wider social group.

Questions 5 through 7 refer to the following information.

Values are ideals and principles that people believe are important. Listed below are five cultural values held by some societies.

(1) Citizenship—Citizens should be well informed about and participate in the government.
(2) Work ethic—People should have an equal chance to be successful through hard work and determination.
(3) Tolerance—People should accept a wide variety of people, cultures, opinions, and traditions.
(4) Justice—People should be treated equally under the law.
(5) Compassion—People should show sympathy for and want to alleviate the distress of others.

5. Some governments set up constitutions that protect people's lives, liberty, and property.

   Which cultural value is protected when constitutions protect the rights of people to belong to the religion of their choosing?

   (1) citizenship
   (2) work ethic
   (3) tolerance
   (4) justice
   (5) compassion

6. Many workers came to North America to seek opportunities and jobs. Some came from places where success was determined solely by the class into which a person was born. They hoped to earn success through hard work.

   According to the definitions, which cultural value does this illustrate?

   (1) citizenship
   (2) work ethic
   (3) tolerance
   (4) justice
   (5) compassion

7. When people volunteer in soup kitchens and homeless shelters or conduct clothing and food drives, they are demonstrating which cultural value?

   (1) citizenship
   (2) work ethic
   (3) tolerance
   (4) justice
   (5) compassion

---

8. Which of the following is the most reasonable explanation for a shortage of a manufactured product on the market?

   (1) Most consumers find the product overpriced.
   (2) The producers overestimated the demand for the product.
   (3) An inexpensive substitute for the product is available.
   (4) Producers have not supplied enough of the product.
   (5) The product has limited uses.

GO ON TO THE NEXT PAGE

Questions 9 through 12 refer to the following different points of view.

SPEAKER A: Andrew Jackson was a true American hero. He courageously served in the Revolutionary War at the age of 13. He later went on to become a Major General in the U.S. Army, scoring a major defeat over the British in the Battle of New Orleans during the War of 1812. As president, Jackson worked for the "common man." He worked successfully to preserve the union during crises and expanded the nation westward.

SPEAKER B: Jackson was a brutal leader who assaulted our peaceful way of life. As a military commander and as president, he worked to steal Native American lands and undermine our ability to survive. He and others brought war and disease on our people. As president, Jackson signed the Indian Removal Act, which was enforced at our expense. Many of our ancestors suffered and died on the "Trail of Tears," a forced removal from our homeland.

SPEAKER C: Not all people are going to feel the same way about any historical figure. I think it is fair to say that Andrew Jackson was an important figure in American history. As the first "common man" president, he served as an example to others that anything is possible for those with talent and determination. Jackson helped establish universal white male suffrage in the United States, one part of a long chain of events that have made our country what it is today. Although he may have been a man of his time in the realm of minority rights, he was responsible for many important accomplishments.

9. What is the main issue that these three different points of view address?
   (1) reasons why Andrew Jackson became president
   (2) effects of Westward expansion
   (3) effects of Native American cultures on America
   (4) policies of American settlers and Native Americans
   (5) actions of Andrew Jackson

10. Which action would Speaker B most likely support?
   (1) enforcing the Indian Removal Act
   (2) Native Americans filing suit for the return of traditional lands
   (3) relocating Native Americans to urban centers
   (4) initiating war to regain lands lost while Jackson was president
   (5) honoring Jackson with a large landmark

11. On which do all speakers agree?

   Andrew Jackson

   (1) strengthened democracy in America
   (2) championed the common man
   (3) was a great moral leader
   (4) was an American hero
   (5) caused changes in America

12. What information would help most to prove the truth of Speaker C's statement that Jackson helped establish universal white male suffrage?
   (1) Not all white men were eligible to vote during Jackson's presidency.
   (2) By the end of Jackson's presidency, nearly all white men in the United States were eligible to vote.
   (3) Permitting white men to vote expanded democracy.
   (4) Native Americans were denied the right to vote under Jackson.
   (5) Jackson was a common man from middle-class roots.

13. Abraham Lincoln became convinced that emancipating the slaves in the U.S. South would help the Union during the Civil War. In 1862, President Lincoln issued the Emancipation Proclamation after a Union victory in battle. One goal of the order was to undermine the Confederate war machine. Additionally, the proclamation added another cause for which Union soldiers were fighting: liberty.

According to this information, what was one of Abraham Lincoln's reasons for issuing the Emancipation Proclamation?

(1) He wanted to anger white southerners.
(2) He wanted to weaken the Confederate Army.
(3) He hoped to gain support for the Confederate cause.
(4) He thought his political career would be helped.
(5) He favored unlimited Union power.

Questions 14 and 15 refer to the following advertisement:

America Behind the Wheel

1998. Technology Network will take you on an exploration of the industries that put America behind the wheel. Industries such as steel, coal, rubber, electronics, and, of course, automaking shaped industrial America and continue to influence modern life and culture. Leading historians, industrialists, and automobile enthusiasts discuss the history and economic roles of these industries in the past and present. *180 minutes total.*

15549HA.........3-video set.........$39.95

14. Which of the following best summarizes the content of the videos described in the advertisement?

(1) comments by automobile enthusiasts about U.S. history
(2) road tests of classic automobiles
(3) history and current status of major U.S. automakers
(4) historical role of the industries related to automobiles in U.S. society
(5) current trends in automaking

15. Based on the advertisement, what does Technology Network assume about the automotive industry?

(1) The automotive industry affected only a small part of society.
(2) The automotive industry is an important part of American society and culture.
(3) The automotive industry employs a large workforce.
(4) The automotive industry created several multimillionaires.
(5) The automotive industry does not affect other industries.

GO ON TO THE NEXT PAGE

Questions 16 and 17 refer to the following cartoon:

16. Which economic concept is the basis for this cartoon?

    (1) economic growth
    (2) fiscal policy
    (3) income and expenditure
    (4) gross national product
    (5) supply and demand

17. Lawmakers in a particular state proposed a law that would encourage construction of new homes.

    With which of the following statements would the cartoonist most likely agree?

    (1) Increase the number of new homes to encourage people to resettle in the state.
    (2) Mandate new home construction in areas of vacant land.
    (3) Take no action.
    (4) Do not build new homes when there is a surplus of existing homes.
    (5) Ban new home construction in the United States.

Question 18 refers to the following graph.

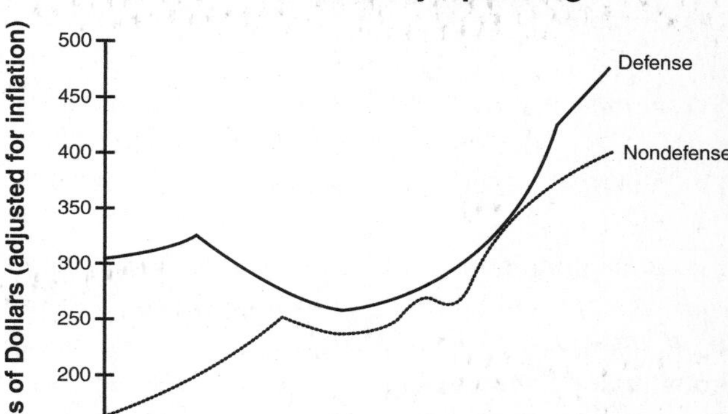

18. Based on the trends in discretionary spending shown in the graph, which of the following is likely in the decade immediately following the time shown in the graph?

    (1) Defense spending will increase, nondefense spending will decrease.
    (2) Defense spending and nondefense spending will both decrease.
    (3) Defense spending will decrease, nondefense spending will increase.
    (4) Defense spending and nondefense spending will both increase.
    (5) Defense spending and nondefense spending will both remain constant.

---

19. The writers of the Constitution had to compromise to please people from all the states. Which of the following is a conflict that arose between states with large populations and states with small populations?

    (1) The length of terms for the president and vice president
    (2) Whether seats in Congress should be equally assigned to every state or based on state populations
    (3) Whether the national government should provide for national defense
    (4) Whether the national government should tax heavily
    (5) The number of justices on the Supreme Court

GO ON TO THE NEXT PAGE

Questions 20 through 23 refer to the following table and information.

Common Forms of Government

Dictatorship	Absolute rule by leadership unrestricted by law, constitutions, or other social and political factors within the state. Rulers often gain power through control of the military.
Presidential republic	A representative, democratic system of government. The executive branch is elected separately from the legislative branch.
Parliamentary republic	A representative, democratic system of government. The executive branch of government depends on the direct or indirect support of the legislature, called parliament.
Absolute monarchy	A king or queen has the power to rule his or her country and subjects without limitation. Rulers ascend to power from royal family lines.
Parliamentary constitutional monarchy	A king or queen reigns with limited powers. Most or all decisions of government are made by elected representatives in the legislature, called parliament.
Single-party state	One political party forms the government, and no other parties are permitted to participate in elections. In most cases, parties other than the one in power are banned. The single-party system is often associated with dictatorship and communism.
Theocracy	A religious institution or leader governs. Civil rulers are leaders of the dominant religion, and governmental policies are either taken directly from, or are strongly influenced by, the teachings of the religion.

20. Throughout the history of the United Kingdom, the form of government has gradually been changed. The United Kingdom was once ruled by an absolute monarch, but several events over time led to a system in which the king or queen is largely a figurehead with real power exercised by an elected government.

    The government of the United Kingdom most closely resembles which of the following types?

    (1) absolute monarchy
    (2) parliamentary constitutional monarchy
    (3) parliamentary republic
    (4) dictatorship
    (5) theocracy

21. Most single-party states are communist states in which the ruling party puts forth Marxist socialist policies. In communist states, the state controls the economy and owns the means of production.

    Which of the following states is (or was) an example of a single-party state?

    (1) Florida
    (2) Canada
    (3) Soviet Union
    (4) Italy
    (5) France

22. Today, France is a parliamentary republic that has two leaders. The president is elected directly by the people, and the prime minister is elected by parliament.

    France's government is a mixture of which two types of government?

    (1) presidential republic and absolute monarchy
    (2) presidential republic and parliamentary republic
    (3) parliamentary republic and absolute monarchy
    (4) parliamentary republic and theocracy
    (5) dictatorship and theocracy

23. During the middle to late 1900s, many Latin American countries faced political instability. As a result, certain groups organized and took power. In several instances, military leaders used their political and social influence to seize authority. In command of the military, these leaders often eliminated opposition and ruled virtually without restriction.

    Such a government would likely be known as a

    (1) absolute monarchy
    (2) parliamentary constitutional monarchy
    (3) parliamentary republic
    (4) dictatorship
    (5) theocracy

GO ON TO THE NEXT PAGE

Question 24 refers to the following map.

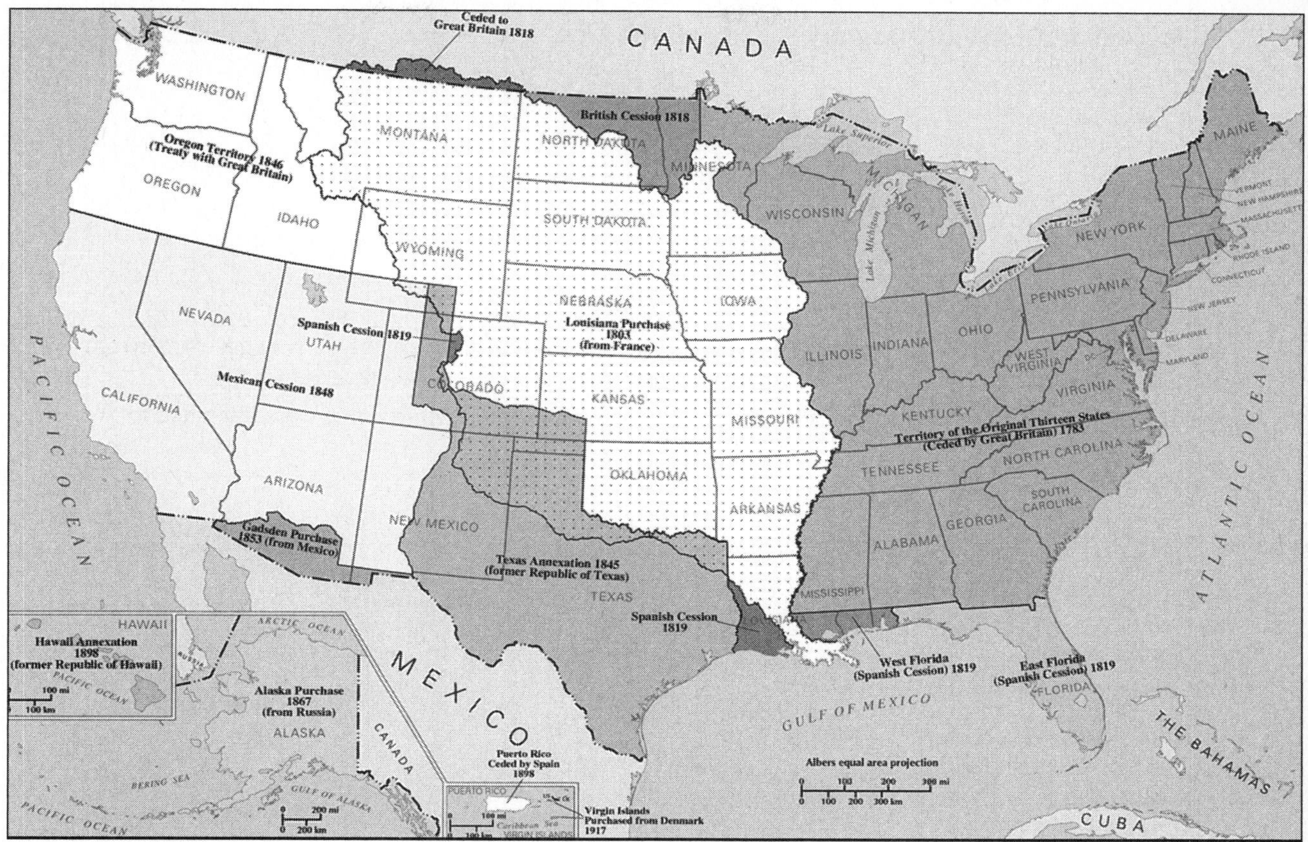

24. The territory of the United States has expanded many times since the country was created.

What conclusion about the territorial expansion of the United States can be drawn from the map?

(1) Florida was part of the original thirteen colonies.
(2) The border between Canada and the United States has never changed.
(3) Mexico once claimed territories that are now part of the United States.
(4) France once owned most of the present territory of the United States.
(5) Nevada was part of the Oregon Territory.

Question 25 refers to the following graph:

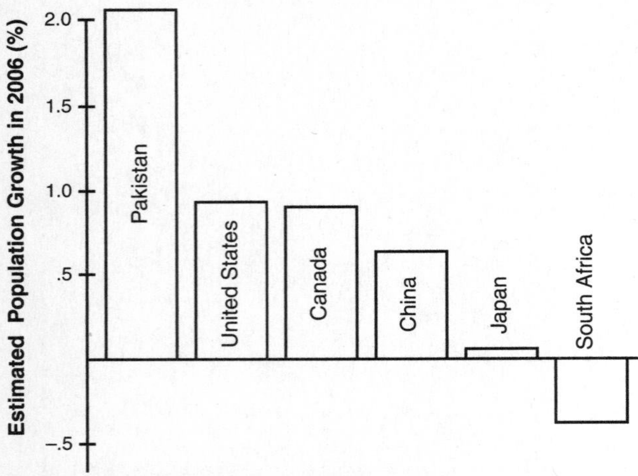

Source: CIA World Factbook, 2006

25. Which of the following statements about estimated population growth in 2006 is confirmed by the information provided?

    (1) Of the countries selected, Pakistan had the highest population.
    (2) Of the countries selected, China had the highest percentage of population growth.
    (3) The populations of the United States and Canada were almost equal.
    (4) The population of Japan was slowly decreasing.
    (5) China had a lower percentage of population growth than Canada had.

Answers and explanations for this test begin on page 74.

GO ON TO: SCIENCE

Science

This diagnostic Science Test consists of 25 multiple-choice questions that you have 40 minutes to complete. You will have to draw upon some prior knowledge of life science, earth and space science, and physical science; however, you will not have to recall facts.

Directions: Choose the one best answer to each question.

GO ON TO THE NEXT PAGE

1. A surfer is lying out on the beach. He knows about the harmful effects of the sun's ultraviolet radiation, so he applies sunscreen to his skin every three hours. What are some of the harmful effects of such ultraviolet rays?
   (1) damage to skin cells
   (2) light and heat energy
   (3) global warming
   (4) holes in the atmosphere's ozone layer
   (5) medical imaging

2. Jorge has always enjoyed watching the birds near his home. Lately he has not noticed his favorite type of bird that had once been plentiful in the area. Jorge also noticed that a new, much larger type of bird is living in the trees in which Jorge's favorite type of bird used to live. Which of the following statements is a possible hypothesis to explain why the larger birds have replaced Jorge's favorite birds near his home?
   (1) Larger birds consume available resources more quickly.
   (2) Smaller birds consume available resources more quickly.
   (3) Larger size helps the birds to compete more successfully for available resources.
   (4) Smaller size helps the birds to compete more successfully for available resources.
   (5) Flying faster helps the birds to compete more successfully for available resources.

3. A television is a telecommunication system for broadcasting and receiving moving pictures and sound over a distance.

   Which of the following concepts from physics does a television require for its development?
   (1) electrical conductivity
   (2) fluid dynamics
   (3) mechanics
   (4) quantum field theory
   (5) kinetic theory

4. Earthquakes result from a sudden, unpredictable release of stored energy that radiates seismic waves. Scientists can measure earthquakes in terms of location and magnitude.

   How can analyzing earthquakes help people?
   (1) Maps can be drawn.
   (2) Taller buildings can be constructed.
   (3) Dates and times of future earthquakes can be estimated.
   (4) Stronger transportation can be engineered.
   (5) Earthquakes can be documented for films.

5. When sugar is added to water, its molecules become dispersed, or dissolved, in the water. This process is called solvation. Solvation can occur only when the sugar molecules come into contact with the water molecules.

   What is one way to speed up the solvation process?
   (1) Use less sugar.
   (2) Use a different kind of sugar.
   (3) Stir the sugar into the water.
   (4) Add more water.
   (5) Use well water.

6. The world's energy needs are increasing each year. The Earth can replenish renewable energy sources naturally in a short period of time. Nonrenewable energy resources, however, cannot be re-created in a short period of time.

   Which of the following sources of energy is a nonrenewable energy resource?
   (1) solar power
   (2) hydro power
   (3) wind
   (4) oil
   (5) geothermal energy from inside the Earth

GO ON TO THE NEXT PAGE

7. Humans take in most of their daily calories from carbohydrates, fats, and proteins. Proteins and carbohydrates each give about four calories per gram, whereas fat gives about nine calories per gram.

   If a person wanted to consume the most calories per gram, what should he or she consume?

   (1) proteins
   (2) carbohydrates
   (3) fats
   (4) a mix of proteins and carbohydrates
   (5) bread

8. Heartburn occurs when a small amount of the acid from the stomach rises into the tube that carries food from the mouth to the stomach. Many people take antacids made from calcium carbonate to relieve the pain associated with heartburn.

   The pain is alleviated because the calcium carbonate

   (1) neutralizes the stomach acid
   (2) is contained in the stomach acid
   (3) repels acid
   (4) is an acidic substance
   (5) is taken with cold water

9. Steve knows that gold is denser than brass. Steve is given two discs identical in shape and size and is told that one is gold and one is brass. Steve compares the mass of the discs. Look at the pictures below.

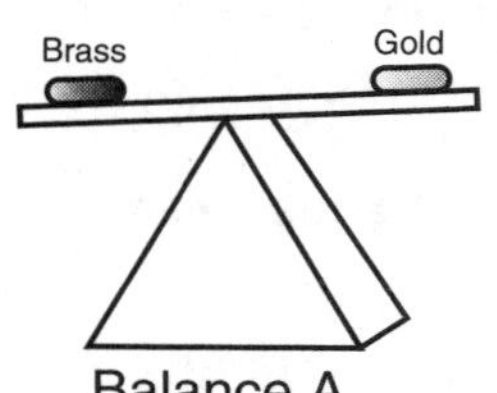

Balance A

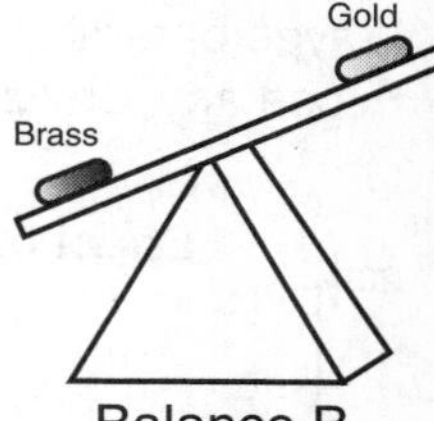

Balance B

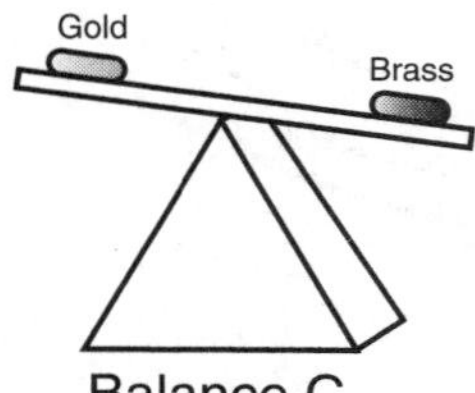

Balance C

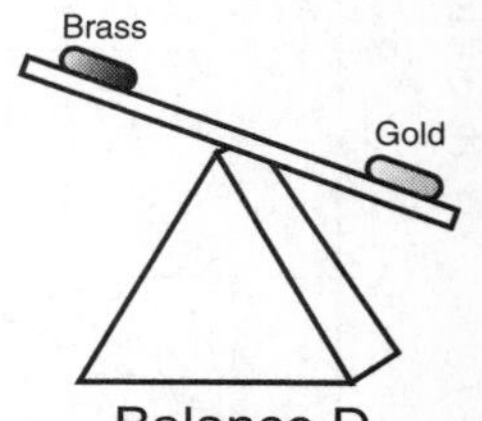

Balance D

   Which balance pictured above is correct?

   (1) balance A only
   (2) balance B only
   (3) balance C only
   (4) balance D only
   (5) both balances A and B

GO ON TO THE NEXT PAGE

10. Randall wants to grow larger orange trees. He is aware that several types of fertilizers are available. He decides to conduct an experiment with four different types of fertilizers. He begins with five rows of orange trees. On each of four rows he uses a different type of fertilizer. On the fifth row he does not use any fertilizer.

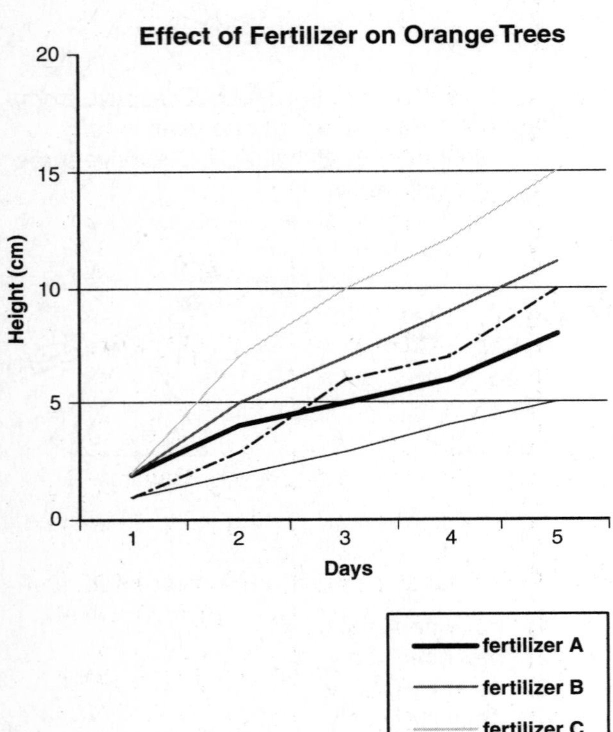

On this basis of this experiment, which fertilizer best supports the growth of Randall's orange trees?

(1) fertilizer A
(2) fertilizer B
(3) fertilizer C
(4) fertilizer D
(5) no fertilizer

11. Benzene is a colorless liquid that is toxic and highly flammable. Cyclohexane is used as a solvent and as a raw material in the production of nylon. Both benzene and cyclohexane are made up of carbon and hydrogen atoms.

Benzene

Cyclohexane

How does benzene's chemical structure differ from cyclohexane's chemical structure?

(1) by 1 carbon atom and 1 hydrogen atom
(2) by 2 carbon atoms and 2 hydrogen atoms
(3) by 1 carbon atom and 4 hydrogen atoms
(4) by 2 carbon atoms
(5) by 6 hydrogen atoms

GO ON TO THE NEXT PAGE

Questions 12 through 16 refer to the following information.

Chronic Wasting Disease (CWD) is a disease that has been found in deer and elk populations across North America. It has continued to trouble scientists and wildlife experts since its discovery in the late 1960s. Several of the features of CWD cause significant hurdles to scientists trying to control or eradicate the disease.

The origin of CWD is unknown and some speculate that it will never be possible to find out exactly how or when CWD arrived in North America. A disease of domestic sheep called *scrapie* has been recognized in the United States since 1947. Some scientists speculate that CWD evolved from this sheep disease. Although never proven, it is possible that deer came into contact with scrapie carriers on shared grazing lands or in captivity near the Rocky Mountains, where sheep grazing was prevalent.

On the other hand, CWD may be a spontaneous disease that occurred in the wild or in captivity. A disease that affects humans and is similar to CWD is thought to be spontaneous. This human disease affects approximately one out of every 1 million people per year. The hypothesis that CWD is spontaneous is unlikely to be verifiable, however.

Deer and elk with CWD demonstrate many strange behaviors. Deer or elk with CWD have been seen walking in repeated patterns. Slight head quivers were noticed in some animals. The sick deer and elk often congregate around water. They also may hold their heads and ears down. CWD-affected deer and elk eat less than healthy deer, and this semi-starvation leads to weakness. In the terminal stages of CWD, animals may have extreme salivation and drooling. Once these clinical signs appear, death is unavoidable. The life span of animals infected with CWD varies from a few days to about a year. Most deer or elk survive only three to eight weeks.

The longest an animal can survive with CWD is unknown. Studies have shown that deer in captivity can live more than 25 months. In the wild, it is harder to determine how long an animal could live with the disease. Among deer and elk residing in areas with an established CWD pattern, most natural cases occur when animals are two to seven years old. However, sometimes much older deer or elk can contract this disease.

12. Based on the passage, the infected animals do all of the following except:

    (1) walk in repetitive patterns
    (2) have slight head tremors
    (3) eat less than healthy animals
    (4) begin showing lesions on the body
    (5) congregate around water

13. Which of the following statements is **BEST** supported by the passage?

    (1) Most deer or elk with CWD survive from a few days to about one year.
    (2) Most deer or elk with CWD survive three to eight weeks.
    (3) Most deer or elk with CWD survive more than 25 months.
    (4) Most deer or elk with CWD survive two to seven years.
    (5) Most deer or elk with CWD survive one day.

14. The passage indicates that if an animal is showing clinical symptoms of CWD

    (1) the animal will have visible lesions that create thirst and drooling
    (2) the animal will likely die in less than a year
    (3) eating the animal will cause CWD in humans
    (4) the animal is between two and seven years old
    (5) the animal lives in the wild

15. Based on the information provided, it may be plausible to believe that CWD is connected to scrapie because

    (1) deer or elk may have come into contact with sheep infected by scrapie in the Rocky Mountain area.
    (2) scrapie and CWD were discovered by the same scientists during same time period.
    (3) sheep, deer, and elk have similar eating habits and digestive systems.
    (4) scrapie cannot be transmitted to any other animals except deer, elk, and cows.
    (5) sheep affected by scrapie show similar behaviors to deer and elk affected by CWD.

GO ON TO THE NEXT PAGE

16. According to the passage, an animal is in the terminal stages of CWD when it exhibits

    (1) grazing in the Rocky Mountains
    (2) continual thirst
    (3) circular walking patterns
    (4) excessive bleeding
    (5) extreme salivation and drooling

Question 17 refers to the following information and graph.

Evidence collected by an elementary school teacher and presented in the graph below compares the number of overweight children ages 5 to 10 in the teacher's school to the number of hours of television watched by the children per week.

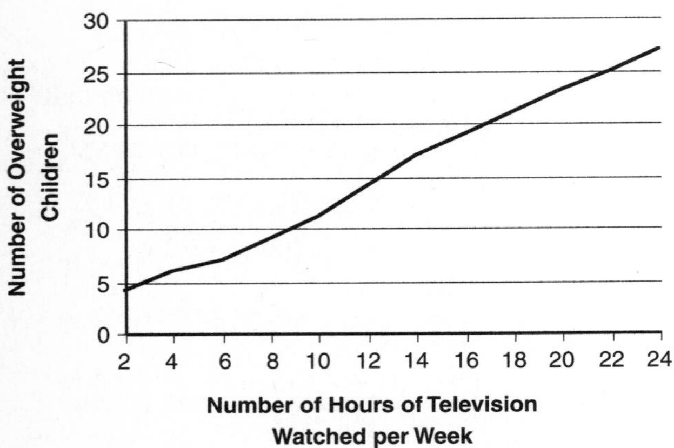

17. Which of the following represents the most appropriate conclusion to be drawn from the information presented?

    (1) Watching television might contribute to being overweight.
    (2) Television does not affect children as they grow older.
    (3) Watching television causes people to eat more food.
    (4) The number of overweight children is not related to the amount of television watched each week.
    (5) A larger number of small children are overweight compared to adults.

---

18. A mixture of water, oil, wood, and quartz is added to a container. The following table shows the average densities of these materials.

Material	Density (g/cm^3)
Water	1.0
Oil	0.9
Wood	0.6
Quartz	2.2

In which order, from top to bottom, would the materials be expected to settle in the container?

    (1) Water, oil, wood, quartz
    (2) Wood, oil, water, quartz
    (3) Quartz, water, oil, wood
    (4) Oil, water, quartz, wood
    (5) Oil, quartz, wood, water

19. Animal A has four digits on each foot joined by a thin layer of soft tissue called a web. Animal B has no toes on its foot but has a horny covering called a hoof. From the description of the feet of animals A and B, in which environment do these animals most likely primarily live?

    (1) animal A lives in the trees; animal B lives in the water
    (2) animal A lives on land; animal B lives in the water
    (3) animal A lives in the water; animal B lives in the trees
    (4) animal A lives in the trees; animals B lives in the trees
    (5) animal A lives in the water; animal B lives on land

20. A big factory dumps all its liquid waste into a nearby lake. Environmentalists claim that the total organism population in the lake will decrease because of the pollutants. The factory claims, however, that there will be no change in the total population of organisms in the lake.

    Which of the following statements about the lake, after the factory started to dump its waste, provides the best evidence to support the environmentalists' claim?

    (1) The fish population decreased.
    (2) The algae population increased.
    (3) Fungus started growing by the lake.
    (4) The population of all of the organisms decreased.
    (5) The population of all of the organisms increased.

21. Pairs of chromosomes are inside the nucleus of a cell. In each pair, one chromosome is from the egg cell, and one chromosome is from the sperm cell. If each human cell contains 23 chromosomes from the sperm cell, how many chromosomes are present altogether?

    (1) 2
    (2) 10
    (3) 23
    (4) 46
    (5) 50

Question 22 refers to the following information and diagram.

Marci placed a box at the top of a ramp, as shown in the diagram below. She expected the box to slide down the ramp, but it did not.

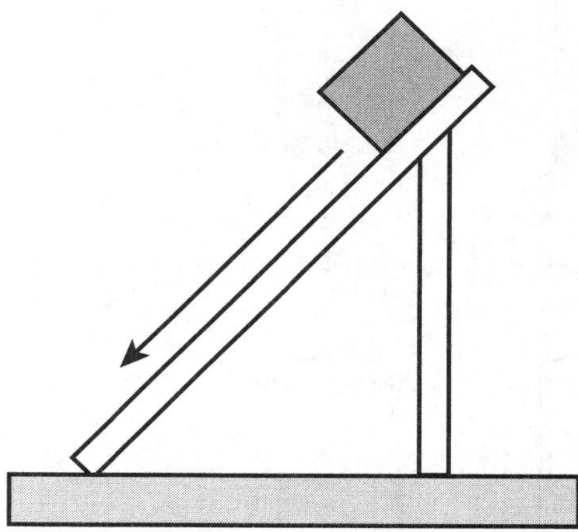

22. Which of the following best explains why the box did not slide down the ramp?

    (1) The ramp was too steep.
    (2) The force of gravity was greater than the force of friction.
    (3) The force of friction was greater than the force acting to move the box down the ramp.
    (4) The force of friction was weakened by the Earth's gravity.
    (5) The material that the ramp was made of was too smooth.

GO ON TO THE NEXT PAGE

23. George is measuring the volume of water in four different graduated cylinders. Look at the pictures below.

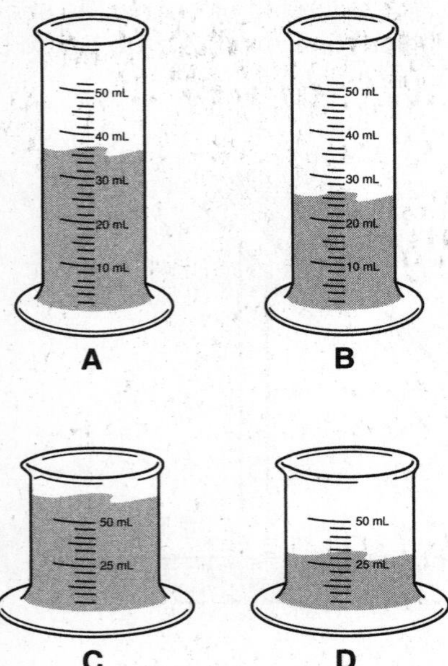

Which graduated cylinder(s) contain(s) the greatest amount of water?

(1) cylinder A only
(2) cylinder B only
(3) cylinder C only
(4) cylinder D only
(5) both cylinders A and D

24. If data shows that the average daily temperature on Earth is increasing, which of the following hypotheses would be supported?

(1) Levels of energy-trapping gases in the Earth's atmosphere are increasing.
(2) The amount of acid rain on Earth is increasing.
(3) More earthquakes are occurring each year on Earth.
(4) The Earth is moving closer to the sun.
(5) The Earth is running out of resources, such as oil and fresh water.

25. The water in the Earth's oceans is affected by the gravitational pull of the moon. The moon can pull water to an area to create "high tide." It can also pull water from an area to another to create "low tide." The graph below shows the high and low tide cycle for a certain Florida coastal city over a period of 24 hours.

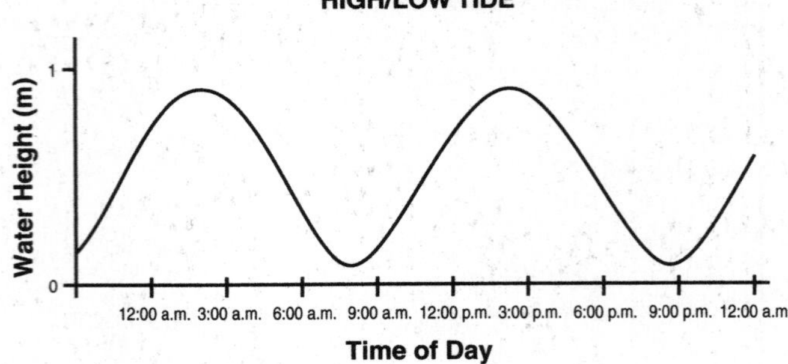

The last high tide occurred at approximately 2:30 p.m. What would be the best prediction for when the next high tide occurs?

(1) 6:30 p.m.
(2) 9:30 p.m.
(3) 12:00 a.m.
(4) 3:00 a.m.
(5) 9:30 a.m.

Answers and explanations for this test begin on page 76.

GO ON TO: MATHEMATICS

Mathematics Formulas

Area		
	Square	s^2
	Rectangle	$l \times w$
	Parallelogram	$b \times h$
	Triangle	$\frac{1}{2} \times b \times h$
	Trapezoid	$\frac{1}{2} \times (b_1 \times b_2) \times h$
	Circle	$\pi \times r^2$
Perimeter		
	Square	$4 \times s$
	Rectangle	$2 \times l + 2 \times w$
	Triangle	$\text{side}_1 + \text{side}_2 + \text{side}_3$
Circumference		
	Circle only	$2 \times \pi \times r$ OR $\pi \times$ diameter (diameter is two times the radius)
Volume		
	Cube [each face is a square]	s^3
	Rectangular solid	$l \times w \times h$
	Square pyramid [base is a square]	$\frac{1}{3} \times s^2 \times h$
	Cylinder [base is a circle]	$\pi \times r^2 \times h$
	Cone [base is a circle]	$\frac{1}{3} \times \pi \times r^2 \times h$
Coordinate Geometry		
	Distance between points; (x_1,y_1) and (x_2,y_2) are two points in a plane.	$\sqrt{(x_2 - x_1)^2 + (y_2 - y_1)^2}$
	Slope of a line; (x_1,y_1) and (x_2,y_2) are two points on the line.	$\frac{y_2 - y_1}{x_2 - x_1}$
Pythagorean Theorem		
	Determine the length of one side of a right triangle using the lengths of the other two sides; *a and b are legs; c is the hypotenuse (the side opposite the right angle).*	$a^2 + b^2 = c^2$
Measures of Central Tendency		
	Mean (average): *x* is a value and *n* is the total number of values for which you want a mean.	$\frac{x_1 + x_2 + \ldots + x_n}{n}$
	Median: begin with a set of values in numerical order.	The median is the middle value in a set with an odd number of values; halfway between (the average of) the two middle values in a set with an even number of values.
Rates		
	Simple Interest	principal (starting amount) × rate × time
	Distance	rate × time
	Total Cost	(number of units) × (price per unit)

GO ON TO THE NEXT PAGE

Mathematics

This diagnostic Mathematics Test consists of 25 questions. The test is divided into two parts. On Part I, questions 1–13, you may use a calculator. You have 23 minutes to complete Part I. On Part II, questions 14–25, you may not use a calculator. You have 22 minutes to complete Part II.

Directions: Choose the one best answer to each question.

Questions 1 and 2 refer to the following graph.

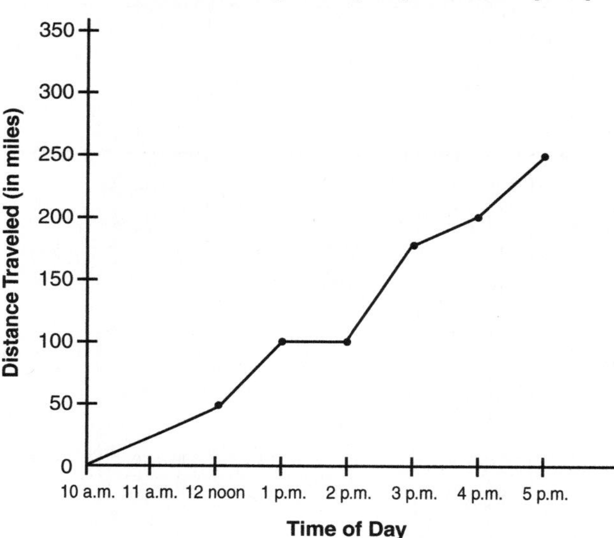

Movers from the Acme Moving Company delivered materials from a pick-up point to a delivery point. The graph represents the distance traveled from the pick-up point during the trip.

1. During which one-hour interval did the movers from Acme Moving Company travel at the fastest speed?
   (1) 10:00 a.m. to 11 a.m.
   (2) noon to 1:00 p.m.
   (3) 1:00 p.m. to 2:00 p.m.
   (4) 2:00 p.m. to 3:00 p.m.
   (5) 4:00 p.m. to 5:00 p.m.

2. At what average speed, in miles per hour (mph), did the movers travel between 10:00 a.m. and noon?
   (1) 50
   (2) 25
   (3) $12\frac{1}{2}$
   (4) $6\frac{1}{3}$
   (5) 4

3. A clothing store is receiving a shipment of 192 T-shirts that were packed in boxes of 16 T-shirts each. How many boxes should the store receive?

   Mark your answer in the circles in the grid on your answer sheet.

4. Randall deposited $2,500 in a bank account three years ago. Since then, the amount in the bank account has increased by 4%. In dollars, what is the amount of money in Randall's bank account now?

   Mark your answer in the circles in the grid on your answer sheet.

5. The base of the triangle below is 8 units long.

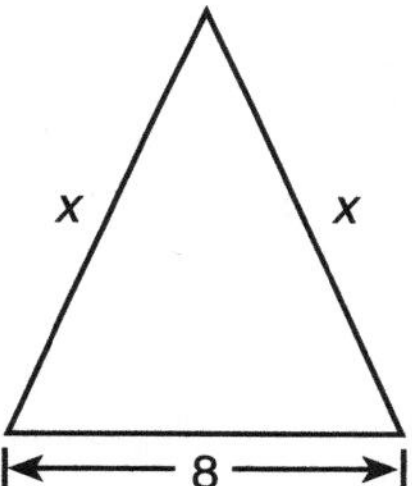

   If the length of x is $1\frac{1}{2}$ times the length of the base, what is the perimeter of the triangle?
   (1) 12 units
   (2) 24 units
   (3) 32 units
   (4) 36 units
   (5) 42 units

6. Andrea, who works at Dynamic Dry Cleaners, can clean dress shirts at a rate of 18 per hour. At 10:00 a.m. she receives an order to clean 99 dress shirts. If she works with a 45-minute break to eat lunch, at what time will she finish the job?
   (1) 11:45 a.m.
   (2) 12:15 p.m.
   (3) 2:45 p.m.
   (4) 3:30 p.m.
   (5) 4:15 p.m.

GO ON TO THE NEXT PAGE

Questions 7 through 9 refer to the following table.

Heat-Index Temperature

Air Temperature in °Fahrenheit

Relative Humidty (%)	80	85	90	95	100	105
90	86	102	119	141	168	199
85	85	99	115	136	161	190
80	84	97	112	131	154	180
75	84	95	109	126	147	171
70	83	93	106	122	141	163
65	82	91	103	117	135	155
60	82	89	100	114	129	148
55	81	88	98	110	124	141
50	81	86	96	107	119	135
45	80	85	94	104	115	129

The table above shows heat-index temperatures as a function of air temperature and relative humidity. It indicates the effect that relative humidity has on how a person senses the temperature. For example, suppose the air temperature is 90° F. If the relative humidity is 50%, then the temperature feels like it is 96° F, but 75% relative humidity makes the temperature feel like 109° F.

7. If the air temperature is 85° F and the relative humidity is 75%, what is the heat index temperature in degrees Fahrenheit?

(1) 95°
(2) 93°
(3) 91°
(4) 89°
(5) 85°

8. The makers of Polar Freeze air conditioners state that their deluxe model will cool a home in heat-index temperatures as high as 105° F. If the air temperature is 90° F, what is the highest relative humidity at which the Polar Freeze air conditioner can cool a home?

(1) 70%
(2) 65%
(3) 55%
(4) 50%
(5) 45%

9. The air temperature is 95° F and the relative humidity is 60%. If the relative humidity increases to 75% and the air temperature remains the same, by how many degrees does the heat-index temperature increase?

(1) 5°
(2) 7°
(3) 9°
(4) 12°
(5) 15°

---

10. What is the value of x in the diagram below?

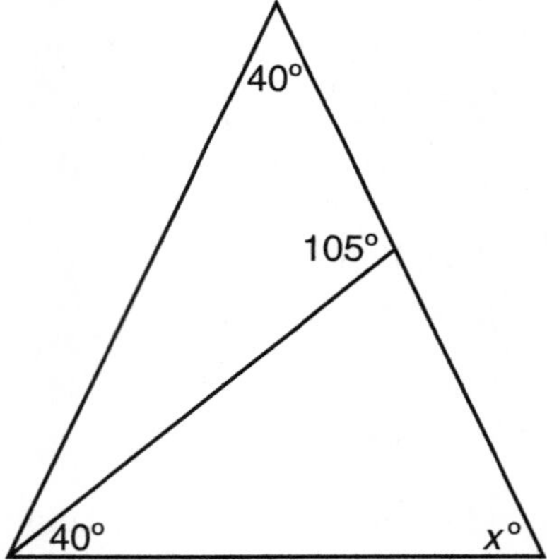

Mark your answer in the circles in the grid on your answer sheet.

GO ON TO THE NEXT PAGE

11. A school district's inventory indicated a total of 8,943 dry-erase markers. Robert mistakenly recorded a wrong amount by interchanging the digits for hundreds and ones. How many more dry-erase markers did Robert record than were actually counted?

    (1) 594

    (2) 549

    (3) 373

    (4) 119

    (5) 45

12. If $12.5 \times \frac{(12 - a)}{a} = 12.5$, what is the value of a?

    (1) 1

    (2) 2

    (3) 3

    (4) 6

    (5) 12

13. Highways currently run between three cities as follows: from Harrisville to St. Paul and from St. Paul to Cannonburg (as shown in the diagram below).

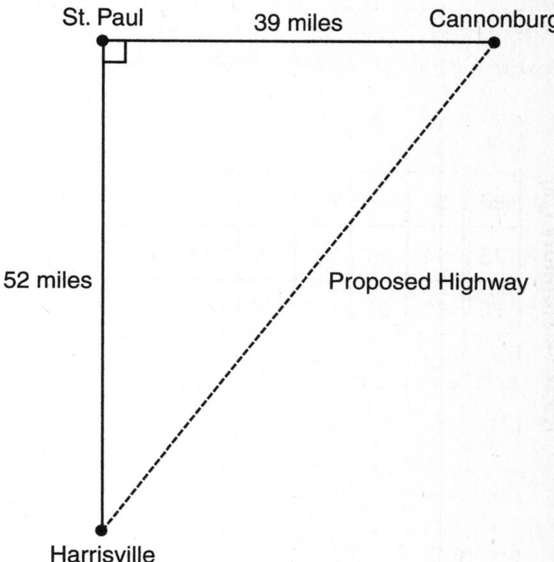

The Department of Transportation plans to build a direct highway from Harrisville to Cannonburg. In the department's report, what length, in miles, should be indicated for the proposed highway?

    (1) 54

    (2) 65

    (3) 73

    (4) 91

    (5) 102

GO ON TO: MATHEMATICS, PART II

Mathematics, Part II

Directions: You will have 22 minutes to answer questions 14–25. You may **NOT** use a calculator with these 12 questions. Choose the one best answer to each question.

Questions 14 and 15 refer to the following graph.

Portage Lake Marina Monthly Profits

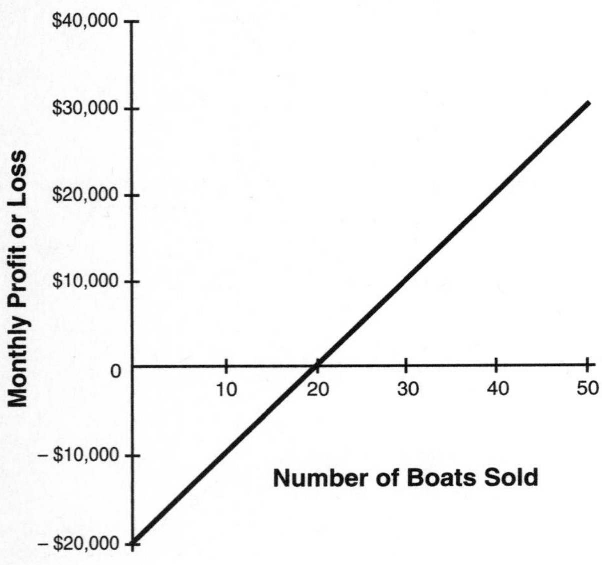

The expected monthly profit (or loss) that the Portage Lake Marina makes as a function of the number of boats sold that month is shown in the graph above.

14. The Portage Lake Marina has set this month's profit goal at $20,000. Based on the expected profit shown in the graph, what is the minimum number of boats that the marina must sell in order to reach its goal?
    (1) 10
    (2) 20
    (3) 30
    (4) 40
    (5) 50

15. What is the approximate monthly profit or loss (if negative) for the Portage Lake Marina if 25 boats were sold this month?
    (1) a profit of $15,000
    (2) a profit of $5,000
    (3) a profit of $1,000
    (4) a loss of $1,000
    (5) a loss of $5,000

16. In the diagram below, the measure of angle STR is 50°.

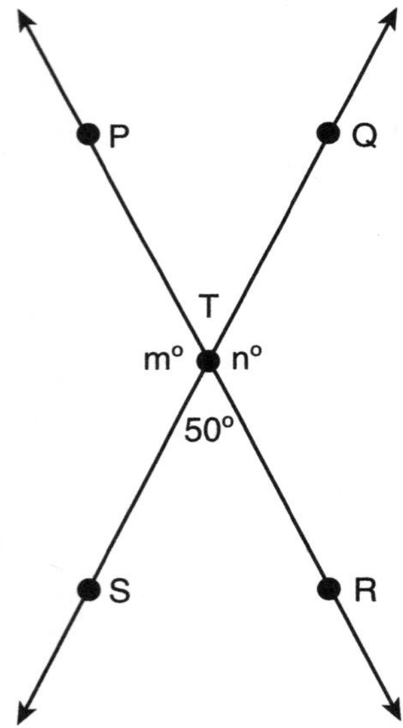

What is the value in degrees of $(m + n)$?
    (1) 100
    (2) 130
    (3) 260
    (4) 360
    (5) Not enough information is given.

GO ON TO THE NEXT PAGE

17. Joel wants to place a help-wanted advertisement in a local newspaper to find someone to mow his lawn and weed his garden. The newspaper charges $8 for the first 20 words and 5 cents per additional word. What would he pay for an advertisement that contained 31 words?

    (1) $3.10
    (2) $8.25
    (3) $8.30
    (4) $8.55
    (5) $9.55

18. The cost of Paulo's lunch totaled $11.00. He wants to leave a 15 percent tip for the server. In dollars, how much money should he leave as a tip?

    Mark your answer in the circles in the grid on your answer sheet.

19. Becky is asked to record the temperature of the greenhouse in which she works. During the time that she is recording, the temperature starts at 80° Fahrenheit (F), then decreases at a constant rate to 70°F during the first 10 minutes. After the temperature reaches the 70°F mark, it remains constant for one hour. It then increases to 95°F at the same rate at which it decreased. Which of the following graphs best represents the correct temperature cycle?

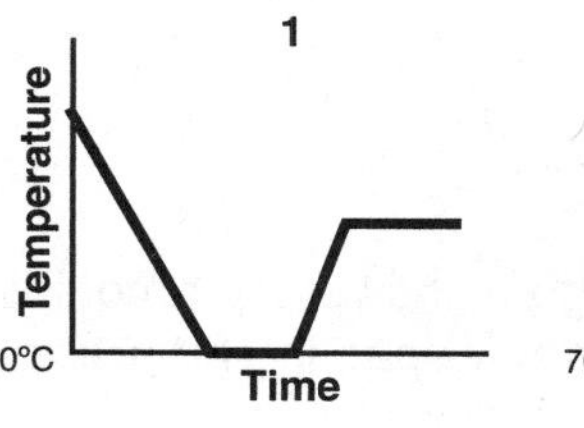

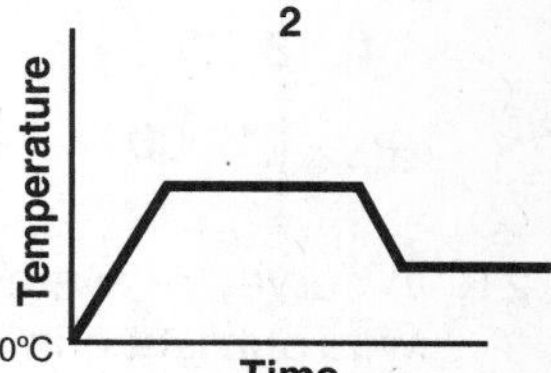

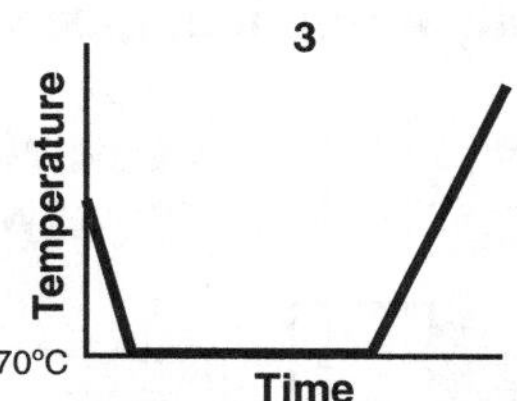

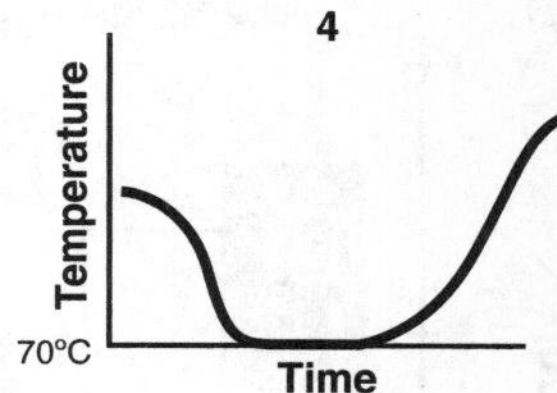

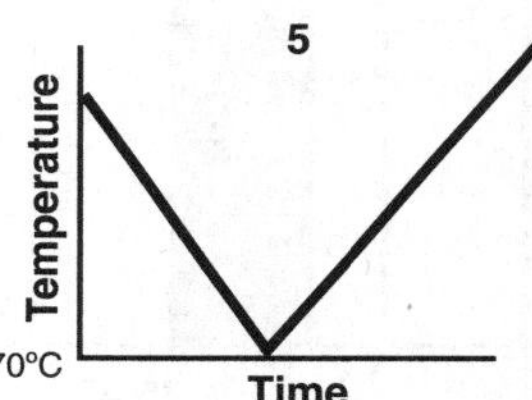

    (1) 1
    (2) 2
    (3) 3
    (4) 4
    (5) 5

20. After Darren sees his favorite baseball player hit the ball, it takes 2.84 seconds for Darren to hear the sound of the bat against the ball. Knowing that sound travels at 1,129 feet per second, which of the following would be the best estimate of the distance in feet between Darren and the baseball player?

(1) 20

(2) 500

(3) 800

(4) 3,000

(5) 11,000

21. A survey of average nightly sleep amounts was published in a newspaper. The article included the graph below.

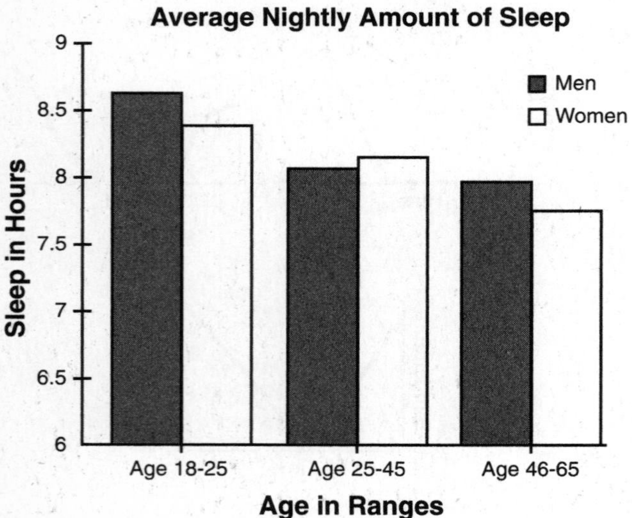

What is the approximate average nightly amount of sleep for women ages 46 to 65?

(1) 7.5 hours

(2) 7.75 hours

(3) 8.25 hours

(4) 8.5 hours

(5) 9.0 hours

22. Parts of the graphs of the linear functions

$$y_1 = -\frac{1}{2}x - 2 \quad \text{and} \quad y_2 = \frac{3}{2}x - 6$$

are shown on the coordinate plane grid below.

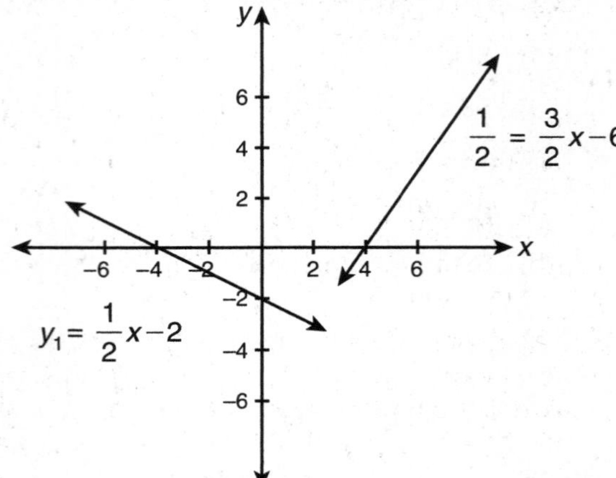

What is the point that is common to the graphs of both functions?

Mark your answer on the coordinate plane grid on your answer sheet.

23. Kevin's delivery service determines the cost of delivering a package with the following formula:

$$C = 12 + \frac{x^2}{10}$$

C is the cost (in dollars) for delivery and x is the largest dimension (in inches) of the package to be delivered. If Julie has a package that is 12 inches by 15 inches by 20 inches, what is the total amount that she would pay Kevin's service to deliver it?

(1) \$14

(2) \$24

(3) \$27

(4) \$52

(5) \$412

GO ON TO THE NEXT PAGE

24. A music store advertises a clearance sale that offers, "Take an additional 25% off the sale price." A CD that was originally $25.00 is on sale for $16.00. What is the clearance price?

    (1) $4
    (2) $8
    (3) $12
    (4) $16
    (5) $19

25. A licensed real estate assistant earns a monthly salary of $2,500 plus $500 for every house she helps to sell. If she earns a total of $4,000 in one month, in which of the following equations does x represent the number of houses she helped to sell that month?

    (1) $4000 = 2500 + 500x$
    (2) $4000 = 2500x + 500$
    (3) $2500 = 4000x + 500$
    (4) $500x = 4000 + 2500$
    (5) $x + 4000 = 2500 + 500$

Answers and explanations for this test begin on page 79.

END OF EXAMINATION

Language Arts, Writing Answers and Explanations

Part I

1. **The best answer is (2).** The simple present tense is appropriate here because the expectation of perfect service is ongoing.
2. **The best answer is (1).** In general, "thank you" should not be capitalized. Here, "Thank" should be capitalized because it is the first word of the sentence.
3. **The best answer is (3).** The last—or in this case, the only—two items in a series should be joined with "and." Use the comma to separate items in a list of three or more.
4. **The best answer is (3).** A comma should be used before phrases beginning with "including" that follow a noun ("events") and modify it.
5. **The best answer is (5).** The sentence is correct as written.
6. **The best answer is (4).** Parallel structure is required with verb phrases joined with "and." The infinitive form "confirm" and the gerund form "answering" do not match. Answer choice (4) changes the gerund to the infinitive.
7. **The best answer is (5).** This correction makes the most sense, considering that people enclose business cards with letters to give other people their phone numbers. The other answer choices either lack information or are awkwardly worded.
8. **The best answer is (5).** The sentence is correct as written.
9. **The best answer is (5).** The sentence is correct as written.
10. **The best answer is (1).** The next part of the sentence should be the subject of the main clause, "our oven," so the next word is "our."
11. **The best answer is (5).** This sentence needs a conjugated verb. The present perfect tense is correct because the action ("grow") began in the past and is still ongoing.
12. **The best answer is (2).** "We" is the first-person plural subject pronoun, so the verb cannot be in the third-person singular form.
13. **The best answer is (4).** When a sentence ends with the subject of the next sentence, the two sentences can usually be joined with a comma and some kind of "transition word." Here, the relative pronoun "which" stands in for the second subject, so it doesn't need to be repeated.
14. **The best answer is (5).** This sentence should be eliminated because sentence 12 restates the same information.
15. **The best answer is (4).** The sentence as it is written uses the third-person singular verb form "meets" when the bare verb "meet" is required. Answer choice (4) uses the correct verb form and correctly places the adverb immediately after the verb and before the long noun phrase "the needs of its large customer base."

16. **The best answer is (2).** Using the conditional "would" matches its usage in the first clause and in the previous two sentences.
17. **The best answer is (5).** The verb "decide" should not be separated from its predicate, "to make this purchase," by a comma. The whole "if" clause, however, should be separated from the main clause by a comma.
18. **The best answer is (3).** It is not appropriate to write a memo on one subject and then suddenly include unrelated information at the end.
19. **The best answer is (2).** This is not a correct use of the semicolon. Dependent clauses joined with "and" do not require punctuation before "and."
20. **The best answer is (1).** The phrase "no matter" should be followed by what it is that does not matter. No comma should be used. Using a period would create sentence fragments.
21. **The best answer is (5).** This sentence is in the appropriate place. It introduces a concept that the next sentence explains.
22. **The best answer is (3).** This is an example of sentence inversion with a slight change in the verb: "you can contact" becomes "to contact." The basic structure of the imperative (command) clause ("get their names…") should not be changed.
23. **The best answer is (4).** Answer choice (5) would be grammatical, but the pronoun "it" would not have a clear antecedent in context. The word "your" is the possessive pronoun between the homophones "your" and "you're," so it is correct before "business."
24. **The best answer is (5).** The infinitive form is used in phrases where the logical subject (distinguished from the grammatical subject, which requires a conjugated verb) is preceded by "for": "strategies for small business owners to employ," "dough for the baker to knead," "crib for the baby to sleep in," and so on.
25. **The best answer is (3).** The conjunction "and" is correct here because when used with a comma, it can indicate a cause-effect relationship; that is, profits rise because the number of customers increases.

Part II

Because grading the essay is subjective, we've chosen not to include any "graded" essays here. Your best bet is to have someone you trust, such as your personal tutor, read your essays and give you an honest critique. Make the grading criteria mentioned in Chapter 11, "The GED Essay," available to whoever grades your essays. If you plan to grade your own essays, review the grading criteria and be as honest as possible regarding the structure, development, organization, technique, and appropriateness of your writing. Focus on your weak areas and continue to practice to improve your writing skills.

Language Arts, Reading Answers and Explanations

1. **The best answer is (4).** The intensity of the lightning is increasing, or "building." The poem uses the metaphor "yellow beak" to describe the lightning, then strengthens the comparison using "livid claw." The word "livid" means the lightning had a deathlike color.
2. **The best answer is (5).** These lines use the imagery of a pair of hands supporting a dam to describe the rain. The rain is not literally held back by a dam, so answer choice (4) can be eliminated. Answer choice (5) is best because just as water would rush from a broken dam, the rain fell suddenly and heavily.
3. **The best answer is (1).** The poem personifies the storm; using the word "overlooked" suggests the storm had intended to spare the speaker's father's house, choosing to destroy the tree instead. These lines emphasize the danger of the storm because the personification suggests that the storm indeed had the power to destroy the house had it wanted to.
4. **The best answer is (5).** The poem has an even observational tone, indicating that the speaker is interested in stopping and watching the storm.
5. **The best answer is (2).** The poem includes the details of wagons on dusty streets. This indicates the setting predates widespread use of the automobile, whose production only began in the twentieth century. Also, the speaker feels the storm presented a danger to her father's house. Certainly, today's houses are built to withstand heavy thunderstorms, but they may not have been as sturdy in rural New England of the nineteenth century.
6. **The best answer is (2).** The fact that Emily Dickinson hardly published any of her poems suggests that she was either very timid or lacked confidence in their quality. Staying at home alone for most of her time shows that Dickinson probably suffered from some form of social anxiety, and preferred not to venture outside. The word "tormented" means "troubled," and "solitary" means "being alone."
7. **The best answer is (4).** The passage describes the neighbors (the Doppelbraus) in unfavorable terms—for example, mentioning "neighborhood rumors" and "obscene laughter." In lines 9–11, the passage says "Babbitt disapproved" of the neighbors. All this controversy fuels Babbitt's "happy evenings of discussion," the phrase indicating that in spite of his objections to the Doppelbrau's lifestyle, he enjoys gossiping about it.
8. **The best answer is (4).** In lines 51–56, the passage states that Littlefield "awed Babbitt by confessing" his intellectual reading habits. Littlefield is portrayed as conceited; nevertheless, Babbitt admires his appearance as intelligent. If Babbitt were to earn a college degree as Littlefield had, Babbitt would probably behave similarly to Littlefield, freely displaying his knowledge to the townspeople, expecting them to accept it as fact.
9. **The best answer is (3).** The mention of "babies, cooking, and motors" as subjects Littlefield does not know is an example of sarcasm on the part of the author, meaning that the author feels those subjects are very challenging but are usually considered beneath the concern of pompous intellectuals like Littlefield.

10. **The best answer is (2).** The phrase "too rich for my blood" in line 21 indicates that Babbitt values his strict, upright lifestyle. Answer choices (1), (3), and (5) may be eliminated because they reflect characteristics of the Doppelbraus, whose lifestyle Babbitt finds objectionable. Answer choice (4) is not supported by the passage.

11. **The best answer is (3).** Littlefield is defending the company before a group of civic leaders, so it would not make sense that he talks badly about employees. Eliminate answer choices (2) and (5). Answer choice (3) best reflects how Littlefield wanted the company to appear compassionate toward its employees.

12. **The best answer is (3).** The bullet points 1a. and 1b. explain why the scene must be left alone. Only answer choice (3) is supported.

13. **The best answer is (4).** Line 15 states that the complete forms must be forwarded "to the Safety Office for review."

14. **The best answer is (1).** If someone "sustains" injury, it means they "suffered" injury.

15. **The best answer is (5).** This document contains important procedures for all employees to follow inside the foundry facility. Important safety instructions would be issued prior to performing any work in the Foster Mining and Metals foundry.

16. **The best answer is (5).** In lines 37–38, the young officer asks the girl, "I say, is it as bad as they make out?" The girl replies, "Not when I [have] anyone as [nice] as you; I never [have] had, though." This indicates the girl has had bad experiences with men. Later in the dialog, the girl repeats the assertion: "Ah! You are not a mean man. How I hate mean men!" (lines 65–66). As she is spending time with the young officer, she continues to focus on her history of bad men. It makes sense, then, that she would be cautious around them. The other answer choices are not supported by the passage.

17. **The best answer is (1).** In lines 42–44, the difference between the young officer and other men is clearly defined by the girl: "You stopped because I was sad, others stop because I am gay. I am not fond of men at all." This proves the young officer impressed her with his compassion.

18. **The best answer is (4).** There is much evidence that the two were not previously acquainted. For example, the girl asks the young officer, "You [have] been wounded?" If she were in an extended relationship with the young officer, she would likely have known that fact; therefore, eliminate answer choices (2), (3), and (5). Answer choice (1) is not supported by the passage.

19. **The best answer is (5).** An exclamation is usually followed by a statement that explains it. Here, "By George!" is followed by the fact that impresses the young officer: how his comrades in arms sacrificed themselves in the trenches of warfare.

20. **The best answer is (2).** In the stage directions that set the scene (lines 1–13), the girl passes over turning on the heat ("the gas jet") to open the window instead. Moonlight enters the room, and before the dialog, she "suddenly turns inward with a shiver." These environmental details of cold and moonlight reinforce the mysterious, slightly uncomfortable mood in the scene.

Social Studies Answers and Explanations

1. **The best answer is (3).** By comparing population and energy consumption figures, you can determine how much energy is used per person. Generally, greater energy use per person corresponds with greater economic activity within a country.
2. **The best answer is (2).** Development in countries refers to the level of economic activity resulting in benefits to the citizens. "Developed countries" are characterized by high per capita (per person) gross domestic product and high per capita income. High per capita energy consumption is associated with developed countries.
3. **The best answer is (1).** According to the model of supply and demand, when supply decreases (here because of a reduced apple harvest) and demand remains the same or increases (as it does in this problem), the price increases.
4. **The best answer is (4).** If technology was reducing the number of farm jobs, some farm workers would have to find jobs elsewhere. Because cities offered many new job opportunities, people needing work resettled from rural areas to urban areas.
5. **The best answer is (3).** If a constitution recognizes the rights of citizens to belong to the religion of their choosing, it is demonstrating tolerance of people's different beliefs.
6. **The best answer is (2).** The question mentions "jobs" and "hard work," which specifically point to "work ethic."
7. **The best answer is (5).** The actions included in the question are examples of volunteering for charity. The meaning of "compassion" includes the ethic of helping to "alleviate the distress of others."
8. **The best answer is (4).** In basic economics, a shortage refers to a market condition where demand of a product exceeds supply of that product. If some consumers want to buy a product but cannot obtain one, this means that the product has not been supplied to the market in sufficient quantity.
9. **The best answer is (5).** The three paragraphs address different actions of Andrew Jackson. The other answer choices are too specific.
10. **The best answer is (2).** Speaker B criticizes the resettlement of Native Americans that Jackson authorized. The question asks what Speaker B would support, so you can eliminate answer choices (1), (3), and (5). Because the first sentence of the paragraph mentions "our peaceful way of life," answer choice (4) may be eliminated.
11. **The best answer is (5).** The other answer choices do not describe each of the three speakers' points of view. Speaker B, especially, would most likely object to all the incorrect answer choices.
12. **The best answer is (2).** If universal white male suffrage was fully implemented during the Jackson presidency, it is reasonable to believe that President Jackson had a role in helping to make it law.

13. **The best answer is (2).** The paragraph stating, "One goal of the order was to undermine the 'Confederate war machine,'" refers to the ability of the Confederate Army to make war with the Union.

14. **The best answer is (4).** The advertisement mentions many industries related to the manufacture of automobiles.

15. **The best answer is (2).** The advertisement says the videos discuss how the automotive industry continues "to influence modern life and culture."

16. **The best answer is (5).** The clue in this cartoon is the phrase "on the market." When you think about economic markets, think about the concept of supply and demand. Homes are difficult to sell when the supply of homes is too high or when demand for homes is too low.

17. **The best answer is (4).** The cartoonist would most likely disagree with any plan to encourage new home construction, which would increase the supply of homes in the market. To correct a market in which selling a home is difficult, supply of homes must instead be reduced or demand for homes must be increased.

18. **The best answer is (4).** Except for a few short downward trends near the beginning of the curves, each of the curves has a consistent upward trend. Therefore, you can reasonably predict that both defense spending and nondefense spending will increase into the future.

19. **The best answer is (2).** The structure of the U.S. Congress is a result of this compromise. The House of Representatives allocates its 435 seats according to population figures gathered by the census. The Senate, however, has two seats for each state, regardless of population. This is a measure to prevent the more populous states from dominating the legislative process.

20. **The best answer is (2).** Because the king or queen still reigns in the United Kingdom, the government is a monarchy. You can eliminate answer choices (3), (4), and (5). The second sentence indicates that the country is no longer ruled by an absolute monarch, so you can eliminate answer choice (1).

21. **The best answer is (3).** This question stem mentions "communist states." Among the answer choices, only the "Soviet Union" (now Russia) is an example of a communist country.

22. **The best answer is (2).** This question stem says that the French president is elected directly by the people and that the prime minister is elected by parliament. This means that the French system is a blend of presidential republic and parliamentary republic styles.

23. **The best answer is (4).** The question stem describes rule by one military leader, which can be described as a dictatorship. In addition, the table says the dictatorship is often secured through control of the military.

24. **The best answer is (3).** The map shows that the United States bought land "from Mexico" in the "Gadsden Purchase" of 1853. The darker-shaded territory is now part of the state of Arizona, which shares a border with Mexico.

25. **The best answer is (5).** The graph displays information only about the percentage of population growth. No data is given about the actual population of the selected countries; therefore, eliminate answer choices (1) and (3). The remaining answer choices require you to compare the bars on the graph. Because Canada experienced a greater percentage of population growth in 2006 than China did, answer choice (5) is confirmed.

Science Answers and Explanations

1. **The best answer is (1).** Sunscreen contains chemicals that deflect and absorb ultraviolet rays before they can cause skin damage. Answer choices (2) and (5) are incorrect because these answer choices are not harmful. Answer choices (3) and (4) are incorrect because these are not effects of ultraviolet radiation.
2. **The best answer is (3).** Jorge has noticed that near his home, a larger bird has replaced his favorite bird. This suggests that the larger size of the new bird is an adaptation that helps the bird to survive. Being better adapted to survive in nature depends on an organism's ability to compete successfully for limited resources, so answer choice (3) is correct. Answer choices (1) and (2) are incorrect because they do not answer the question. Answer choices (4) and (5) are incorrect because they are not supported by what Jorge has seen near his home.
3. **The best answer is (1).** A television requires electricity in order to work. The other answer choices are incorrect because the physics concepts are unrelated to the development of the television.
4. **The best answer is (4).** Scientists able to measure earthquakes' location and magnitude can then plot out trends in the data. Although answer choices (1) and (5) are true statements, they are not examples of helping people. Answer choice (2) is irrelevant. Answer choice (3) is untrue because the information in the question states that earthquakes are "unpredictable." Only answer choice (4) is an example of a helpful application of earthquake data.
5. **The best answer is (3).** In order to speed up the solvation process, more sugar molecules must come into contact with more water molecules. By stirring the sugar into the water, the sugar molecules are being spread around the water more quickly thus coming into contact with more water molecules. Answer choices (1) and (4) are incorrect because these would slow the solvation process down. Answer choices (2) and (5) are incorrect because they would not affect the solvation process.
6. **The best answer is (4).** The only answer choice that is a nonrenewable energy source is oil. The Earth cannot replenish oil naturally in a short amount of time. All the other answer choices are incorrect because they are renewable sources of energy.
7. **The best answer is (3).** If a person wanted to consume the most calories per gram, he or she would want to consume the material that contained the most calories per gram. Fat gives about nine calories per gram, which is more than both protein and carbohydrates. Therefore, a person wanting to consume the most calories per gram would want to consume fat. Answer choice (4) is incorrect because even if you mix carbohydrates and proteins, it would not equal fat's nine calories per gram.

8. **The best answer is (1).** Antacids reduce the pain associated with heartburn because they chemically neutralize the stomach acid that is causing the pain. Answer choice (2) is incorrect because if calcium carbonate (a base) was contained in the stomach acid, the acid would neutralize itself, and no additional medication would be needed. Answer choices (3) and (5) are incorrect because they would not affect a person's heartburn. Answer choice (4) is incorrect because if calcium carbonate were an acidic substance, it would make the pain worse.
9. **The best answer is (4).** If two objects with equal volume are compared, the object with greater density will have a greater mass. Because the discs are identical in shape and size, and because gold is denser than brass, the gold disc will have more mass than the brass disc. Therefore, the gold disc will tip the balance down.
10. **The best answer is (3).** The graph shows that the orange trees with fertilizer C grew the tallest. This shows that fertilizer C best supports the growth of Randall's orange trees. The other answer choices are incorrect because the orange trees did not grow as tall as the fertilizer C trees.
11. **The best answer is (5).** Benzene has six carbon atoms and six hydrogen atoms. Cyclohexane has six carbon atoms and 12 hydrogen atoms. The difference between each benzene and cyclohexane molecule is six hydrogen atoms.
12. **The best answer is (4).** The passage says that animals infected with CWD "have been seen walking in repeated patterns," "congregate around water," "eat less than healthy deer," and exhibit "slight head quivers." The only answer choice that is not mentioned in the passage is answer choice (4) ("begin showing lesions on the body").
13. **The best answer is (2).** The passage states at the end of the fourth paragraph: "Most deer or elk survive only three to eight weeks."
14. **The best answer is (2).** The passage says: "animals with CWD live variably from a few days to about a year." This implies that an animal already showing symptoms of CWD will probably not live more than one year.
15. **The best answer is (1).** The passage states at the end of the second paragraph: "it is possible that deer came into contact with scrapie carriers on shared grazing lands or in captivity near the Rocky Mountains, where sheep grazing was prevalent."
16. **The best answer is (5).** The passage states in the middle of the fourth paragraph: "In the terminal stages of CWD, animals may have extreme salivation and drooling."
17. **The best answer is (1).** According to the graph, as the number of hours of television watched per week increases, the number of overweight children also increases. This implies that with more hours of television watched, the probability increases that a child is overweight. Answer choice (1) is the best answer. Answer choices (2), (3), and (5) are incorrect because they are not related to the evidence presented by the teacher. Answer choice (4) is incorrect because the graph shows a correlation between amount of television watched and the number of overweight children.

18. **The best answer is (2).** When the mixture of water, oil, wood, and quartz is added to a container, the materials will settle in the container according to their densities. Materials with higher density settle toward the bottom of the container. Because wood has the least density, it will be on top.

19. **The best answer is (5).** Animal A has webbed feet. Animal B's feet are not webbed, but rather hooved. Therefore, it is most likely that animal A lives in the water and animal B lives on land.

20. **The best answer is (4).** The environmentalists claim that the total organism population in the lake will decrease. This refers to all the different plants, animals, fungi, bacteria, and so on that occupy the lake. If it was discovered that the population of each type of the organism decreased, the environmentalists' claim will be supported. Decrease in only certain species could potentially be compensated for by an increase in some other species; therefore, answer choices (1), (2), and (3) are incorrect.

21. **The best answer is (4).** Half of a human's genetic code is inherited from the father's sperm cell and half is inherited from the mother's egg cell. Because chromosomes occur in pairs, if a human cell contains 23 chromosomes from the sperm cell, it must also contain 23 chromosomes from the egg cell. Therefore, the human cell would contain 46 chromosomes altogether.

22. **The best answer is (3).** The box moves in the direction of the net force acting on the box. The box will slide down the ramp if the force required to move the box downward is greater than the friction force (resisting the motion). Because the box is not moving down the ramp, the force of friction must be greater than this downward force. Answer choice (3) is the best answer. Answer choices (1), (2), and (5) are incorrect because their conditions would cause the box to move down the ramp. Answer choice (4) is incorrect because gravity is constant.

23. **The best answer is (3).** Liquids can be measured using a graduated cylinder. Graduated cylinders are labeled at intervals to express the amount of liquid contained within the cylinder. Because graduated cylinder C contains more than 50 mL of water, it contains more than any of the other graduated cylinders. To answer this question successfully, remember to read the graduations (markings) on the cylinder. Ignore the illusion created by cylinders with different diameters.

24. **The best answer is (1).** If the levels of energy-trapping gases in the Earth's atmosphere were increasing, the energy level in the Earth's atmosphere would increase. Temperature is a measure of the average kinetic energy of molecules. If a substance has more energy, its temperature will be greater. Therefore, if energy is trapped in the Earth's atmosphere, temperature would increase. Answer choice (1) is the best answer. Answer choice (2), (3), and (5) are incorrect because they would not affect temperature. Answer choice (4) is incorrect because it is unlikely that the Earth would move closer to the Sun.

25. **The best answer is (4).** Because the tide cycle is regular, high tide occurs at regular intervals. According to the graph, high tide occurs roughly every 12 hours. The time 3:00 a.m. is about 12 hours after 2:30 p.m., so answer choice (4) is the best answer.

Mathematics Answers and Explanations

1. **The correct answer is (4).** To determine the one-hour interval in which the movers traveled at the fastest speed, calculate the miles traveled in the intervals. The interval in which the most miles are traveled is between 2 p.m. and 3 p.m. In that interval, the movers traveled 75 miles, making their speed 75 miles per hour. Another way to solve this problem is to find the interval in which the slope of the curve is steepest.

2. **The correct answer is (2).** To solve, divide the number of miles traveled during the given interval by the length of the interval. The graph shows that the movers traveled 50 miles between 10:00 a.m. and noon, which is a period of two hours. The average speed was therefore $\frac{50 \text{ mi}}{2 \text{ hr}}$, or 25 miles per hour.

3. **The correct answer is 12.** If 192 T-shirts are packed in boxes of 16 T-shirts each, then the number of boxes is 192 divided by 16, which is 12.

4. **The correct answer is $2,600.** To solve, first determine the value of 4% of the amount deposited in the account. To find 4% of $2,500, multiply $2,500 by the quantity .04 to get $100. The amount in the account is therefore $2,500 + $100, which equals $2,600.

5. **The correct answer is (3).** To solve, first determine the value of *x*. To do so, multiply the length of the base, 8 units, by $1\frac{1}{2}$ to get (8)(1.5), or 12 units. The perimeter of the triangle is the sum of the lengths of its three sides. Because two sides have a length of 12 units and the base is 8 units, the perimeter is 12 + 12 + 8, which equals 32 units.

6. **The correct answer is (5).** To solve, first calculate the time, in hours, it will take Andrea to clean 99 dress shirts at a rate of 18 dress shirts per hour. To calculate, divide 99 by 18 to get 5.5 hours, or 5 hours 30 minutes. Next, add in the 45 minutes that Andrea will take for lunch, bringing the time up to 6 hours 15 minutes. She starts the job at 10:00 a.m., so 6 hours 15 minutes later is 4:15 p.m.

7. **The correct answer is (1).** To solve, consult the chart by finding the value that lines up to the column for an air temperature of 85° F and the row for 75% relative humidity.

8. **The correct answer is (2).** To solve, consult the chart by finding the column for an air temperature of 90° F. Because the heat index must be less than 105° F for the Polar Freeze air conditioner to cool a room, find the highest relative humidity level at which the heat index is still less than 105° F. This occurs at the level of 65% relative humidity.

9. **The correct answer is (4).** To solve, first determine, by using the table, the heat index for an air temperature of 95° F at relative humidities of 60% and 75%. Then take the difference of the heat index values. At an air temperature of 95° F and a relative humidity of 60%, the heat index is 114° F. At an air temperature of 95° F and a relative humidity of 75 the heat index is 126° F. The difference in heat indexes is 126° F – 114° F, or 12° F.

10. **The correct answer is 65.** To solve, use the fact that the sum of the angles in a triangle is always 180°. The figure consists of three triangles: two smaller triangles that are contained within a larger triangle. To find *x*, treat it as an angle in the large triangle. From there, the values of the other angles of the large triangle can be used to compute the value of *x*. Before that can be done, however, the value of one of the angles in the large triangle must be found by summing the value of the unknown angle in the top small triangle with 40°. The unknown angle in the top small triangle is 180° – (105° + 40°) = 180° – 145°, which equals 35°. Therefore the value of *x* is 180° – (40° + 35° + 40°) = 180° – 115°, which equals 65°.

11. **The correct answer is (1).** If Robert mistakenly recorded a wrong amount by interchanging the digits for HUNDREDS and ONES, then he recorded the value 8,943 instead of 8,349. To find how many more erasers he recorded than were actually counted, subtract the value 8,349 from 8,943 , as follows: 8,943 – 8,349 = 594.

12. **The correct answer is (4).** To solve, first divide both sides of the equation by 12.5 to get $\frac{12 - a}{a} = 1$. Next, multiply both sides of the equation by *a* to get 12 - a = a. Adding a to both sides yields 12 = 2a. Dividing both sides by 2 yields a = 6.

13. **The correct answer is (2).** To solve, use the Pythagorean relationship, which states that in a right triangle with legs *a* and *b* and hypotenuse *c*, the lengths of the sides are related by the equation $c^2 = a^2 + b^2$. The proposed highway forms the hypotenuse of a right triangle with legs 52 miles and 39 miles long.

    $c^2 = a^2 + b^2$

    $c^2 = 52^2 + 39^2$

    $c^2 = 2{,}704 + 1{,}521$

    $c^2 = 4{,}225$

    (Calculate the square root of 4,225)

    $c = 65$

14. **The correct answer is (4).** To solve, locate the point on the graph that represents a $20,000 profit and determine the number of boats that must be sold at that point. This occurs at 40 boats on the graph.

15. **The correct answer is (2).** On the graph, the profit from selling 25 boats will be somewhere between the profit from selling 20 boats ($0) and the profit from selling 30 boats ($10,000). Because the graph appears to be increasing at a constant rate, the best approximation for the profit at 25 boats is $5,000.

16. **The correct answer is (3).** To solve, use the fact that the four angles in the diagram will add up to 360°. Also, angle PTQ has the same measure as angle STR because they are vertical angles, making the measure of angle PTQ = 50°. Therefore $m° + n° + 50° + 50° = 360°$, or $m + n = 360 - 100 = 260$.

17. **The correct answer is (4).** Because Joel's ad will contain 31 words, and the first 20 words are included in the $8 price, he will have to pay extra for 11 words. It is given in the problem that each additional word over the initial 20 costs 5 cents each, or $0.05 each. For the 11 extra words the cost is ($0.05)(11), which equals $0.55. The total cost of the ad is, therefore, $8.00 + $0.55 = $8.55.

18. **The correct answer is 1.65.** To find out how much a 15% tip is for a lunch that totaled $11, calculate 15% of $11. To do so, multiply $11 by the 0.15 : (11)(0.15). There are a couple of different ways to do the computation without a calculator. One way would be to do the longhand multiplication. Another way to solve would be to think of 15% as 10% plus 5%. Ten% of $11 is $1.10. To find 5% of $11, take half of 10% ($1.10). Half of $1.10 is $0.55. Therefore, 15% of $11 is $1.10 + $0.55, or $1.65.

19. **The correct answer is (3).** To solve, look at the graphs to determine which describes the scenario that is discussed in the question. The correct graph will be one that shows a decrease in temperature, followed by a period of constant temperature 6 times longer than the previous period of decrease (10 min. × 6 = 60 min. = 1 hr.), followed by an increase in temperature.

20. **The correct answer is (4).** The best way to solve this problem is to round the numbers given in the problem. The quantity 2.84 seconds equals about 3 seconds, and the quantity 1,129 feet per second equals about 1,000 feet per second. An estimate of the distance in feet between Darren and the source of the sound is, therefore, 3 × 1,000 feet, or 3,000 feet.

21. **The correct answer is (2).** To solve, consult the graph. The average nightly amount of sleep for women ages 46 to 65 is somewhere between 7.5 hours and 8.0 hours. The best approximation is 7.75 hours.

22. **The correct answer is**

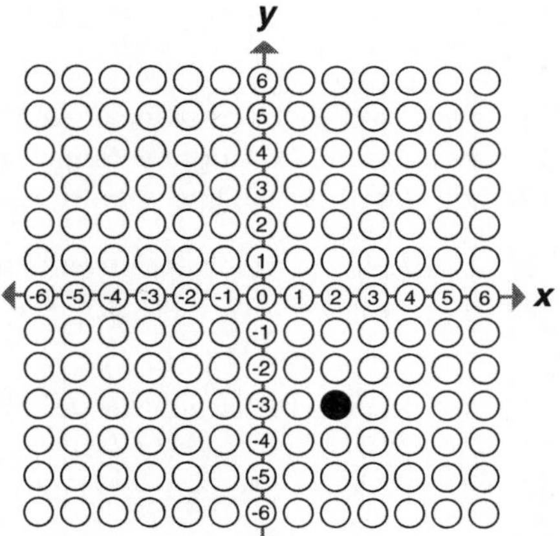

This question can be solved both graphically and algebraically. To solve graphically, continue the lines drawn in the graph until they intersect. They will intersect at the point (2, –3). To solve algebraically, use the fact that both equations are solved for y and set them equal to each other to get $-\frac{1}{2}x - 2 = \frac{3}{2}x - 6$.

From there solve for x and then substitute the value of x back into one of the initial equations to get the y-coordinate at which the lines intersect:

$$-\frac{1}{2}x - 2 = \frac{3}{2}x - 6$$

$$-2 = \frac{4}{2}x - 6$$

$$4 = 2x$$

$$2 = x$$

Substitute 2 for x in one of the original equations:

$$y = \left(-\frac{1}{2}\right)(2) - 2$$

$$y = -1 - 2$$

$$y = -3$$

Therefore, the point of intersection is $x = 2$ and $y = -3$, shown on the grid as point (2,–3).

23. **The correct answer is (4).** To solve, substitute 20 for x in the equation $C = 12 + \frac{x^2}{10}$. The result is $C = 12 + \frac{20^2}{10} = 12 + \frac{400}{10} = 12 + 40 = 52$.

24. **The correct answer is (3).** To solve, take 25% off of the quantity $16. To do so, recognize that 25% is the same as one quarter. One quarter of 16 is 4. To reduce the number 16 by 25%, subtract 4 from 16 to show that the clearance price of the CD was $12.

25. **The correct answer is (1).** The assistant earns a base monthly salary of $2,500 plus $500 for every house she helps to sell. The equation showing the relationship between the number of houses (x) she helped sell and the resulting month's salary of $4,000 is $4{,}000 = 2{,}500 + 500x$.

PART II

GED Testing Strategies

A major factor in determining your success on the GED is your set of test-taking skills. In this part of the book, you will review the skills that you can improve upon through practice to save time and energy and minimize mistakes when you take the GED tests.

Part II includes the following chapter:

Chapter 3 Strategies to Get Your Best Score

CHAPTER THREE

Strategies to Get Your Best Score

Now that you've assessed your strengths and weaknesses, it's time to take a look at some general test-taking strategies that should help you approach the GED with confidence. We'll start by discussing the importance of acquiring the skills necessary to maximize your GED score and finish with some tips on how to handle stress—before, during, and after the GED. Additional chapters in the book include strategies and techniques specific to each of the GED sections.

The Psychology of Testing

Cognitive psychologists, the ones who study learning and thinking, use the letters KSA to refer to the basic components of human performance in all human activities, from academics to athletics, from playing music to playing games. The letters stand for *knowledge*, *skills*, and *abilities*.

The GED measures a specific set of skills that can be improved through study and practice. You probably already understand this because you are reading this book. In fact, many thousands of students over the years have successfully raised their GED scores through study and practice.

Knowledge Versus Skills

The human brain stores and retrieves factual knowledge a little differently from the way it acquires and executes skills. Knowledge can generally be learned quickly and is fairly durable, even when you are under stress. You learn factual information by studying, and you acquire skills through practice. There is some overlap between these actions; you will learn while you practice, and vice versa. In fact, research shows that repetition is important for both information storage and skills acquisition.

As we just mentioned, repetition is necessary to acquire and improve skills: knowing *about* a skill, or understanding how the skill should be executed, is not the same as actually *having* that skill. For instance, you might be told *about* a skill, such as driving a car with a standard transmission, playing the piano, or typing on a computer keyboard. You might have a great teacher, have wonderful learning tools, and pay attention very carefully. You might *understand* everything perfectly. But the first few times that you actually attempt the skill, you will probably make some mistakes. In fact, you will probably experience some frustration because of the gap between your understanding of the skill and your ability to perform the skill.

Perfecting skills takes practice. When skills are repeated so many times that they can't be further improved, psychologists use the term *perfectly internalized skills*, which means that the skills are executed automatically, without any conscious thought. You need repetition to create the pathways in your brain that control your skills. Therefore, you shouldn't be satisfied with simply reading this book and then saying to yourself, "I get it." You will not reach your full GED scoring potential unless you put in sufficient time practicing as well as understanding and learning.

We hope that you will internalize the skills that you need for top performance on the GED so that you don't have to spend time and energy figuring out what to do during the introduction to the exam. We also hope that you will be well into each section while some of your less-prepared peers are still reading the directions and trying to figure out exactly what they are supposed to be doing. We suggest that you practice sufficiently so that you develop your test-taking skills, and, specifically, good GED test-taking skills.

Practice to Perfect Your Skills

While you practice, you should distinguish between practice that is meant to serve as a learning experience and practice that is meant to be a realistic simulation of what will happen on your actual GED tests.

EXAM✓**PREP**
Study**TIP**

It is important to note that you should not attempt any timed practice tests when you are mentally or physically exhausted. This will add unwanted stress to an already stressful situation.

During practice that is meant for learning, it is okay to "cheat." You should feel free to disregard the time limits and think about how the questions are put together; you can stop to look at the explanations in the back of the book. It is even okay to talk to others about what you are learning during your "learning practice." However, you also need to do some simulated testing practice, where you time yourself carefully and try to control as many variables in your environment as you can. Some research shows that you will have an easier time executing your skills and remembering information when the environment that you are testing in is similar to the environment where you studied and practiced.

You must be realistic about how you spend your time and energy during the preparation process. A psychological term, *cognitive endurance*, refers to your ability to perform difficult mental tasks over an extended period of time. Just as with your physical endurance, you can build up your cognitive endurance through training. As you prepare yourself for the GED, you should start off with shorter practice sessions and work up to the point where you can easily do one GED test section with no noticeable fatigue. Then work up to two sections, then three without a break, and so on.

Strategic Thinking

If you move on to higher education or improve your employment situation, you will likely experience stress from things such as family expectations, fear of failure, a heavy workload, increased competition, and difficult material. The GED tries to mimic this stress. The psychometricians (specialized psychologists who study the measurement of various aspects of the mind) who help design standardized tests use what they call "artificial stressors" to help determine how you will respond to that test.

The main stressor that the test makers use is the time limit. The time limits are set up on the GED so that many students must use all the time allowed.

Another stressor is the element of surprise. If you have practiced sufficiently, there will be no unpleasant surprises on test day. The GED is a very predictable exam. In fact, the introductory chapter of each subject area in this book tells you *exactly* how many questions of each type there are. A well-prepared test taker will know what to expect on test day.

Relax to Succeed

Probably the worst thing that can happen to a test taker is to panic. Research shows that predictable results occur when a person panics. When you panic, you can usually identify a specific set of easily recognizable symptoms, including sweating, shortness of breath, muscle tension, increased pulse rate, tunnel vision, nausea, lightheadedness, and in rare cases, even loss of consciousness. These symptoms are the result of chemical changes in the brain brought on by some stimulus. The stimulus does not have to be external. Therefore, you can bring on panic just by needlessly thinking about certain things.

Adrenaline Rush

The stress chemical in your body called *epinephrine*, more commonly known as *adrenaline*, brings on these symptoms. Adrenalin changes the priorities in your brain activity. It moves blood and electrical energy away from some parts of the brain and to others. Specifically, it increases brain activity in the areas that control your body and decreases blood flow to the parts of your brain that are involved in complex thinking. Therefore, panic makes a person stronger and faster—and less able to perform the type of thinking that is important on the GED. It is not a bad thing to have a small amount of adrenalin in your bloodstream because of a healthy amount of excitement about your exam. But you should take steps to avoid panic before and during your GED.

There is a theory that this ability to shift the brain's activities around on a moment's notice was very beneficial to our remote ancestors, providing a higher likelihood of survival and procreation. The set of physical and emotional responses that result from adrenalin's impact on the brain is known as the *fight or flight response*. It means that you become temporarily more ready to run fast to avoid danger or to confront physical situations such as an animal attack. The side effect of this change is that you are also temporarily less able to think clearly. In fact, there are true stories of people under the influence of adrenaline performing amazing feats of strength and speed that they probably would not have even attempted otherwise. So, panic makes a person stronger and faster, but less able to perform the type of thinking that is rewarded on a GED exam.

Adrenaline can be useful and even pleasurable in some situations. In fact, it is not a bad thing to have a small amount of adrenaline in the bloodstream because of a healthy amount of excitement about the exam. But it is something that you should control as much as possible before and during an exam.

Learn to recognize the symptoms of too much adrenaline: shortness of breath, rapid heartbeat, sweating, and so on. If you experience any of these symptoms before or during your exam, close your eyes and take some deep, calming breaths. This is a great way to refocus your energy and reduce your anxiety. Remember, if you practice sufficiently for your GED, you will be well prepared and should have no reason to panic.

Suspense and Surprise

Two of the most important stimuli for the release of adrenaline into the blood stream are suspense and surprise. This is well known to those who create haunted houses and horror movies. Suspense involves the stress that is present during the anticipation phase before an event that involves unknowns. Surprise occurs when you actually experience the unknowns. The speculation and wondering "what if…?" that you do before a big event can significantly increase stress and its effects on thinking patterns. There is also a sharper rise in adrenaline levels when you experience surprise, such as someone yelling "Boo!" behind you when you thought that you were home alone, or finding a question on an exam that looks unlike anything that you have ever seen before.

You can control both suspense and surprise by minimizing the unknown factors. The biggest stress-inducing questions are

- What do the GED writers expect of me?
- Am I prepared?
- How will I respond to the GED on test day?

EXAM PREP Study TIP

The goals of your preparation should be to learn about the tests, acquire the knowledge and skills that are being measured by the tests, and learn about yourself and how you respond to the different aspects of the exam.

If you spend some time and effort answering these questions by studying and practicing under realistic conditions before test day, you'll have a much better chance of controlling your adrenaline levels and handling the exam with no panic.

As you work through this book, you should make a realistic assessment of the best use of your time and energy so that you are concentrating on the areas that will yield the highest score that you can achieve in the amount of time you have remaining until the exam. This will result in a feeling of confidence on test day, even when you are facing very challenging questions.

You should also remember that you can retake the GED within just a few weeks of your initial test date. So don't worry if you fail one or all the subject tests your first time out.

Getting Ready to Take the GED

The guidelines in this section will help you to be as relaxed and confident as possible on test day.

Be Prepared

The Boy Scout Motto has been repeated for generations for a good reason: it works. The more prepared you feel, the less likely it is that you'll be stressed on test day. Do your studying and practice consistently during your training period. Be organized. Have your supplies and wardrobe ready in advance. Make a practice trip to the test center before your test day. Get a good night's sleep and eat a sensible breakfast the morning of your test day.

Know Yourself

This means to know your strengths and weaknesses on the GED as well as the ways that help you to relax. Some test takers like to have a bit of an anxious feeling that helps them to focus. Others are better off when they are so relaxed that they are almost asleep. You will learn about yourself through practice.

Get Enough Rest

Shakespeare described sleep as the thing that "knits the wraveled sleeve of care," meaning that the better rested you are, the better things seem. As you get fatigued, you are more likely to look on the dark side of things and worry more.

Eat Right

Sugar is bad for stress and brain function in general. Pouring tons of refined sugar into your system can create biological stress that has a negative impact on your brain chemistry. Adding a high concentration of caffeine, as many soda manufacturers do to their products, only magnifies the potential for a problem. If you are actually addicted to caffeine (that is, you get headaches when you skip a day), then consume no more than your regular amount.

Listen to Music

Some types of music increase measurable brain stress and interfere with clear thinking. Specifically, some rock, hip-hop, and dance rhythms, while great for certain occasions, can have detrimental effects on certain types of brain waves that have been measured in labs. Other music seems to help organize brain waves and create a relaxed state that is conducive to learning and skills acquisition.

Remember, you cannot listen to music during your GED, so do not listen to it during your practice tests.

Taking the GED

If you work through the material in this book and do some additional practice on Official Practice Tests, you should be more than adequately prepared for the GED. Use the tips in this section to help the entire testing process go smoothly.

Do the Easy Stuff First

You will have to get familiar with the format of each section of the GED so that you can recognize passages and questions that are likely to give you trouble. We suggest that you "bypass pockets of resistance" and go around those trouble spots rather than through them. It is a much better use of your time and energy to pick up all the correct answers that you can early on, and then go back and work on the tougher questions that you actually have a legitimate shot at answering correctly.

All the questions on a GED test are weighted equally, even though some of the questions are harder than others. You don't have to get all the questions right to get great GED scores. If you get sucked into a battle with a hard question while there are still other less-difficult questions waiting for you, you won't be doing yourself any favors. We often tell students that they should picture their GED test booklets sitting in a stack in a locked closet somewhere. Your book is there, waiting patiently for you. Within it are some questions that you are probably going to get wrong on test day. So when you see them, don't be surprised. Just recognize them and work on the easier material first. If time permits, you can always come back and work on the challenging problems in the final minutes before the proctor calls, "Time!"

This strategy is both a time-management and a stress-reduction strategy. The idea is to make three or four passes through the test section, always being sure to work on the easiest of whatever material remains.

Remember to Breathe

When humans get stressed, our breathing tends to get quick and shallow. If you feel yourself tensing up, slow down and take deeper breaths through your nostrils, exhaling through your mouth. This will relax you and probably get more oxygen to your brain so that you can think more clearly.

Take Breaks

It is a fact that you cannot stay focused intently on your GED for the entire time that you are in the testing center. You are bound to have distracting thoughts pop into your head, or there may be times when you simply cannot process the information that you are looking at. This is normal. What you should do is close your eyes, clear your mind, and then dig back into the test. This can all be accomplished in less than a minute. You could pray, meditate, or simply picture a place or person that helps you to relax. Try visualizing something fun that you have planned for right after your GED.

Stay Calm

Taking an important exam can certainly lead to stress. As part of the process of preparing thousands of people for standardized exams, we have seen a variety of stress reactions. These reactions range from a mild form of nervousness to extreme anxiety that has led to vomiting and fainting in a few cases. Most students deal fairly well with the stress of taking a test. Some students could even be said to be too relaxed in that they don't take the test seriously enough.

Have a Plan of Attack

The directions printed in this book (both in the chapters and on the Practice Tests) are very similar to the directions that you will find on your GED. It is important that you know how you are going to move through each portion of the exam. There is no time to formulate a plan of attack on test day. In fact, you should do enough practice so that you have internalized the skills necessary to do your best on each section and don't have to stop to think about what to do next.

Manage the Answer Sheet

Be sure to compare the question number in your test booklet with the question number on the answer sheet before you fill in the bubble sheet. You generally cannot circle your answer in the test booklet (or write in it at all), so be very careful when you fill in the bubbles on your answer sheet.

If you skip questions and come back to them later, be sure to jot down the question number on your scrap paper. That way, you can easily refer to the question in your test booklet after you've completed the other questions.

NOTE

If you have any questions regarding what is or is not acceptable when taking the GED, contact the testing center in your state.

Be Aware of Time

You really don't want it to be a surprise when the proctor yells, "Time!" on test day. Therefore, you are going to want to time yourself on test day. You should time yourself during at least some of your practice tests so that you get used to both the process and your timepiece. We suggest that you use an analog (not digital) watch. They generally are not set up to give off any annoying beeps that could get you in trouble with fellow test takers and your proctor on test day.

All that matters during the test is your test. All of life's other issues will have to be dealt with after your test is finished. You might find this mindset easier to attain if you lose track of what time it is in the outside world.

Changing Answers

You need to find out whether you are an answer changer or not—meaning, if you change an answer, are you more likely to change it *to* the correct answer or *from* the correct answer? You can learn this about yourself by doing practice exams and paying attention to your tendencies.

Guessing on the GED

Because there is no added scoring penalty for incorrect answers on the GED, you should never leave a bubble blank on your answer sheet. The answers are distributed fairly evenly across the tests, so you should always guess the same answer number if you are guessing at random. Decide what your random guessing number will be ahead of time to eliminate any additional stress on test day.

Of course, if you can eliminate a choice or two, or if you have a hunch, then this advice doesn't apply. Pick the best answer from those that remain after you have eliminated those choices that are clearly wrong, and then move on to the next question.

Some students worry if they notice long strings of same-position answers on their answer sheets. This does not necessarily indicate a problem.

After the GED

Most people find it easier to concentrate on their test preparation and on their GED exams if they have a plan for fun right after the test. You should plan something that you can look forward to as a reward to yourself for all the hard work and effort that you'll be putting into the test. Then, when the going gets tough, you can say to yourself, "If I push through and do my work now, I'll have so much fun right after the exam."

In the grander scheme of things, your success on the GED will lead to greater opportunities in higher education and the workplace. We have included an appendix called "What's Next?" in this book to address these opportunities in greater detail.

What's Next?

Chapter 4, "The Cognitive Domain of Bloom's Taxonomy," and Chapter 5, "Interpreting Graphical Information," contain information designed to help you understand the critical thinking skills necessary for GED success. The information found in those chapters can be applied to most of the sections on the GED.

PART III
Critical Thinking

Although some knowledge is necessary for the GED, the questions largely test your thinking skills. The specific types of reasoning skills on which GED questions are based come from a seminal work in educational psychology known as *Bloom's Taxonomy*. Many of the questions on the social studies, science, and mathematics tests assess the Bloom's Taxonomy skills using different kinds of graphics.

Part III includes the following chapters:

Chapter 4 The Cognitive Domain of Bloom's Taxonomy

Chapter 5 Interpreting Graphical Information

CHAPTER FOUR

The Cognitive Domain of Bloom's Taxonomy

Educational psychologist Benjamin Bloom's Taxonomy of Educational Objectives divides learning into three domains: *affective* (emotions), *psychomotor* (manipulation of objects), and *cognitive* (knowledge, comprehension, reasoning).* Questions on the GED tests are classified by level within the cognitive domain. Critical thinking skills at the high end of the domain require the skills at the low end. This chapter covers these cognitive levels, ranked from low to high.

Knowledge

Knowledge represents the accumulation of facts, terms, words, and basic concepts that you have learned throughout your life. For example, you know the fact that there are 24 hours in a day; you know your home address and telephone number, how to turn on the stove, and so on. Pieces of knowledge can be memorized. As a learner progresses beyond this cognitive level, increasing practice is necessary to develop more complex cognitive skills.

No GED questions are purely knowledge based. For example, the science test would not ask you how many moons Jupiter has or what the population of the United States is. Questions categorized in higher cognitive levels, however, will require you to apply some basic knowledge in a new way. This book will provide you with an overview of the basic writing, reading, social studies, science, and math knowledge expected of recent high school graduates.

EXAM ALERT

Although the GED tests your knowledge of certain subjects, it is primarily a skills test. You will be required to apply critical thinking skills when answering most of the questions on the GED.

*Taxonomy of Educational Objectives: The Classification of Educational Goals by a Committee of College and University Examiners. *Benjamin S. Bloom, ed., New York: Longmans, Green, 1956.*

Comprehension

Comprehension means being able to organize and compare elements of knowledge and then restate and summarize them. Comprehension can involve drawing conclusions from knowledge. For example, describing the plot of a book to a friend requires comprehension skills. The GED tests your ability to comprehend written passages, photographs, charts, graphs, diagrams, and political cartoons.

Application

Application is the skill of taking knowledge and applying it in a new context. For example, you should recognize that for a math question you can apply a certain formula. The GED measures your skill at applying ideas in different contexts—for example, by asking what a character in a passage might do in other circumstances based on what the character does in the passage.

Analysis

Analysis involves breaking down information into individual ideas and exploring the relationships between them. Motives and causes are identified. The GED tests your ability to distinguish fact from opinion or hypothesis, recognize unstated assumptions, identify cause-effect relationships, and compare, contrast, and conclude from evidence.

Synthesis

Synthesis involves production of unique communication by compiling information into hypotheses, theories, narratives, or essays. This is the primary skill associated with effective writing.

Evaluation

Evaluation is the skill of presenting and defending opinions, hypotheses, or judgments of quality and using internal evidence and external criteria. The GED tests your ability to judge the validity or accuracy of information or methods. You will have to examine evidence for hypotheses, conclusions, or generalizations; the role of certain values in belief systems and decision making; and logical fallacies within arguments.

What's Next?

Chapter 5, "Interpreting Graphical Information," provides tips on how to apply critical thinking skills to read the tables, charts, and graphs that appear on the GED.

CHAPTER FIVE

Interpreting Graphical Information

The GED includes many graphical representations of data. Their basic forms are described in this chapter. Graphical representations of figures in geometry are discussed in detail in Chapter 47, "Geometry."

Interpreting Maps

A map is a flat representation of a particular area of the earth. Because the earth is roughly spherical, flat maps are always slightly distorted. (Imagine trying to flatten an orange peel without tearing it.) The way the curvature of the earth is accounted for in a map is called the map's *projection*. For example, the Michigan precipitation map in Figure 5.1 is represented in Albers equal area projection.

Generally, maps include a *scale*, which defines the size ratio of the map to the real world. This is shown as a ratio (for example, Scale 1:35,000) or as a line with tick marks that enables the map reader to calculate distance with the help of a ruler. You can get more information on ratios in Chapter 41, "Statistics." Maps also contain a *legend*, which defines all the symbols and colors used in the map.

A *political map* shows imaginary boundaries, such as county lines and international borders, and marks political divisions, such as towns, cities, counties, states, and countries. Most *road maps* can be considered political maps. Road maps also include points of interest (museums, tourist attractions, and the like), important geographic features, and detailed markings of roadways (road names, exit numbers, different lines according to road type).

A *demographic map* shows information about people in a certain part of the world, such as population change or economic data. For example, census information would enable you to make a map using different colors to represent different population figures across counties in California.

A *topographical map* features the physical elements of an area of land. Detailed representations of elevation, soil types, landmarks, and bodies of water are particularly helpful for hikers or people planning new roads or construction through undeveloped land.

Complete the following exercise to test your knowledge of interpreting maps.

Interpreting Maps Exercise

Look over the map in Figure 5.1 and answer the following questions. The legend in Figure 5.1 indicates average annual rainfall levels in inches for Michigan.

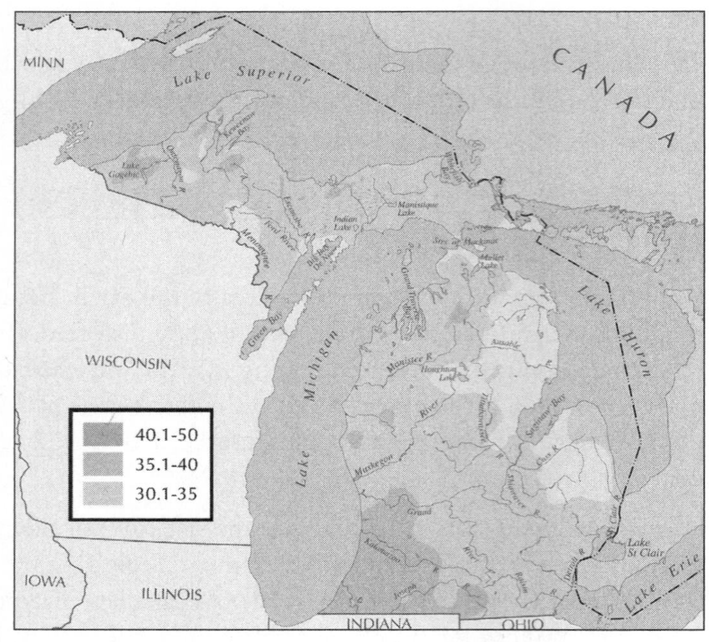

FIGURE 5.1 Average annual rainfall levels in inches for Michigan. (Source: U.S. Geologic Survey)

1. Does the shore of Lake Michigan or Lake Huron experience greater precipitation? ________________
2. Michigan shares a land border with which states? ________________
3. Describe the northernmost point in Michigan. ________________

Answers:

1. Lake Michigan (notice the darker colors indicating greater precipitation).
2. Ohio, Indiana, Wisconsin
3. A large island in Lake Superior (notice the "point" in the dashed international border between Michigan's upper peninsula and Canada).

Interpreting Tables

A *table* is an array of rows and columns for displaying data. Each intersection between a row and a column (called a *cell*) contains one item of data. You probably see tables every day—baseball statistics sheets, bus schedules, temperature forecasts for a group of cities, and so on. Usually, a graph plotted on the standard (x,y) plane can be created from the data in a table. Consider the example of a table in Table 5.1 and the bar graph generated from its data (see Figure 5.2).

TABLE 5.1 Lunches Sold, Daily Average

	1st Grade	2nd Grade	3rd Grade	4th Grade	*TOTAL*
Monday	46	56	54	50	206
Tuesday	43	55	57	49	204
Wednesday	41	54	58	51	204
Thursday	47	54	59	52	212
Friday	52	58	60	53	223
TOTAL	229	277	288	255	1049

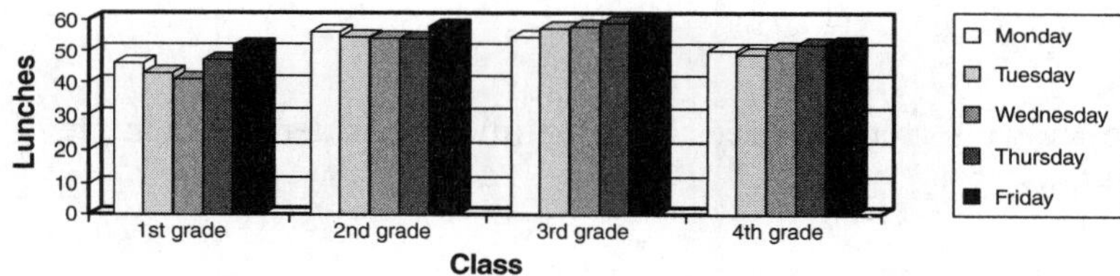

FIGURE 5.2 Lunches sold, daily average.

Interpreting Tables Exercise

Use Table 5.1 and the graph in Figure 5.2 to answer the following questions:

1. How many lunches are sold, on average, to the 1st grade class on Monday? __________
2. What is the greatest number of lunches sold on average to one class on any one day? __________
3. On what day of the week is the greatest number of lunches sold across all four grades? __________
4. Which grade shows increasing lunch purchases over the entire school week? __________

Answers:

1. 46
2. 60 (3rd grade on Friday)
3. Friday (223)
4. 3rd grade (notice how each day's average exceeds the previous day's average)

Interpreting Graphs

There are many kinds of graphs for displaying data. Their visual representation makes trends in data easier to perceive. Graphs have a title that describes the data and a legend (or key) that identifies what the differently colored or patterned segments represent. In the case of bar and line graphs, the horizontal and vertical axes are labeled. You saw how a bar graph was created from a table in the previous section. Now look at these different styles of graphs.

Line Graph

Line graphs are useful for showing trends, especially over time. Consider the example of a fictional stock chart in Figure 5.3.

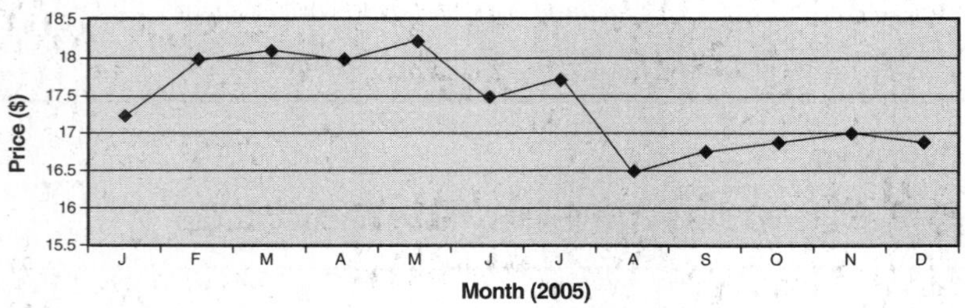

FIGURE 5.3 American Lollipop Co. stock, monthly price average.

Interpreting Line Graphs Exercise

Use the line graph in Figure 5.3 to answer the following questions.

1. In which month was the average stock price highest? __________
2. Over which two months did the average stock price decline the most? __________
3. What is the approximate difference in average price between February and August? __________

4. Between how many pairs of adjacent months did the average stock price decrease? ____________

Answers:

1. May (approximately $18.25)
2. July and August (approximately a $1.25 decline)
3. Approximately $1.50
4. (March to April, May to June, July to August, and November to December)

Circle Graph

Circle graphs (or pie charts) use different sized "wedges" to represent percentages or parts of the whole. The total of all the wedges must equal 100 percent. If the sample size is known, percentages represented by wedges may be used to calculate how much of the set belongs to a single category.

The circle graph in Figure 5.4 is an example of what you might encounter on your GED.

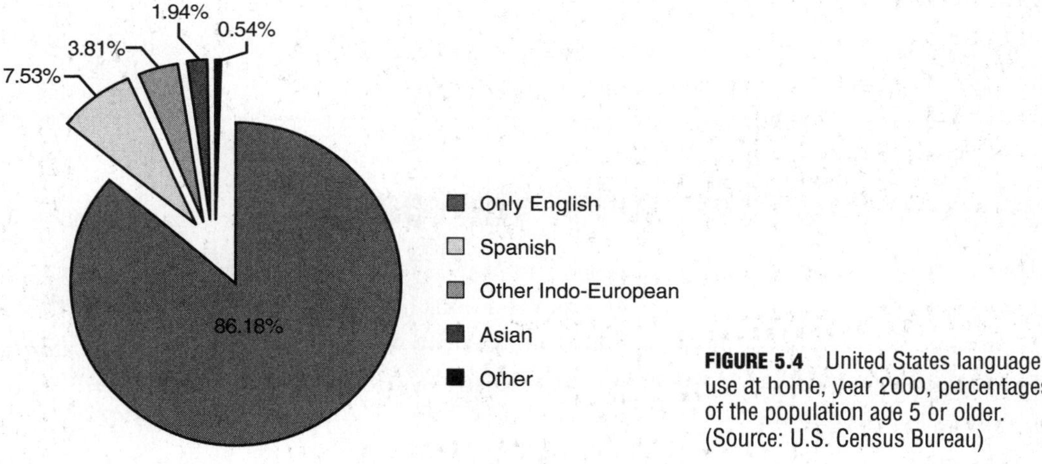

FIGURE 5.4 United States language use at home, year 2000, percentages of the population age 5 or older. (Source: U.S. Census Bureau)

Interpreting Circle Graphs Exercise

Use the circle graph in Figure 5.4 to answer the following questions. For questions 3 and 4, you will need the total population five years of age or older in the United States in the year 2000: 230,445,777.

1. What is the second-most popular language spoken at home in the United States? ______________________

2. What percentage of the U.S. population five years of age and older does not speak only English at home? ______________________

3. About how many people speak an Asian language at home in the United States? ______________________

4. About how many people do not speak only English at home in the United States? ______________________

Answers:

1. Spanish

2. 13.82% (*Two approaches:* Add the slices labeled "Only English," or subtract "Only English" from 100%.)

3. Approximately 4,470,648 (1.94% of total population: multiply 0.0194 by 230,445,777)

4. Approximately 31,847,606 (Use either process from question 2 to reach 13.82%; then use the process from question 3.)

Interpreting Editorial Cartoons

Editorial cartoons (or political cartoons) express the views of the cartoonist on a particular social or political issue or current event. Famous people are often portrayed with exaggerated features, which help the observer identify who is represented in the drawing. Like many creative works, editorial cartoons are rich in symbolism and often do not explicitly state the position of the cartoonist.

Famous symbols in American culture include the donkey for the Democratic Party, the elephant for the Republican Party, doves for peace, hawks for war, storks for birth, and vultures for death. Many cartoons use words as labels and dialog, but not all cartoons do. Consider the cartoon depicting Abraham Lincoln in Figure 5.5, which appeared in *Harper's Weekly* in 1860 just months before the U.S. presidential election.

FIGURE 5.5 Abraham Lincoln editorial cartoon. (*Harper's Weekly*, August 25, 1860)

Interpreting Editorial Cartoons Exercise

Use the editorial cartoon in Figure 5.5 to answer the following questions. Remember that the cartoon originally appeared just prior to the 1860 U.S. presidential election.

1. Who is the main figure in this cartoon? ______________________
2. What does the sign labeled "To the whirlpool" represent? ______________________
3. What does the man riding on the main figure's shoulders represent? ______________________
4. Why is the long rod labeled "Constitution"? ______________________

Answers:

1. Abraham Lincoln
2. Because Lincoln is walking a tightrope over water, the whirlpool literally represents the danger posed by the water if he were to fall in. Symbolically, the cartoonist portrays Lincoln taking a risky political course of action.
3. The black man on Lincoln's shoulders shows that the cartoonist saw Lincoln as a promoter of the black cause. In 1860, prior to Lincoln's election and the Civil War, slavery was widespread in the United States.

4. The rod labeled "Constitution" is how Lincoln is balancing on the tightrope. This indicates that Lincoln used the Constitution to support his views on the rights of black people in the United States.

What's Next?

The chapters that follow in Part IV provide an overview of the GED Language Arts, Writing Test, as well as a review of basic grammar and punctuation rules that are commonly tested on the GED. Be sure to carefully read each chapter if this is your weak area, and then complete the practice questions at the end of Part IV.

PART IV
Language Arts, Writing

This part of the book explains what the GED Language Arts, Writing Test involves and the basic writing and editing skills you need for success on this test. The Writing Test contains multiple-choice questions and an essay assignment.

Part IV includes the following chapters:

Chapter 6 About the Language Arts, Writing Test

Chapter 7 Overview of English Usage

Chapter 8 Grammar and Sentence Structure

Chapter 9 Effective Writing

Chapter 10 Writing Mechanics

Chapter 11 The GED Essay

Chapter 12 Language Arts, Writing Practice Questions and Answer Explanations

Chapter 13 Language Arts, Writing Terms

CHAPTER SIX

About the Language Arts, Writing Test

The GED Language Arts, Writing Test has two parts, which must be taken consecutively. Part I consists of 50 multiple-choice questions that you will be given 75 minutes to complete. Part II tests your ability to write an essay about a topic of general interest. You will have 45 minutes to plan, write, and revise your essay. The GED does permit you to take advantage of all 120 minutes allotted for the Language Arts, Writing Test, though. If you finish Part I early, you may move on to Part II with the remaining time; likewise, if you finish your essay with time to spare, you may return to Part I.

Part I—Multiple Choice

In Part I, you will read between six and nine short documents and answer multiple-choice questions about each document.

The questions test your knowledge of the following content areas:

- **Organization** (15% of questions)—Are the paragraphs and the sentences within them in logical order? What is the topic of the document or paragraph? How clear and cohesive is the document?
- **Sentence Structure** (30%)—Is the sentence a fragment? A run-on? Is there improper coordination and/or subordination? Is there a problem with the word order?
- **Usage** (30%)—Do the subject and verb agree? Do verb tenses match? Do pronouns match their antecedents?
- **Mechanics** (25%)—Pay attention to capitalization and punctuation. Is this a correctly formed possessive or contraction? You may have to choose among homonyms to correctly answer these questions.

We will provide more detailed information about each of the content areas in subsequent chapters in this book.

The documents on which you are tested will be of three types:

- Informational (for example, a description of a car's interior)
- Instructional (for example, steps for raising juicy tomatoes)
- Business-related (for example, an internal memo about customer service)

The questions about these documents will also be of three types:

- Correction (these questions make up about 45% of the Writing Test)
- Revision (these questions make up about 35% of the Writing Test)
- Construction shift (these questions make up about 20% of the Writing Test)

Correction Questions

Correction questions require you to identify an error. Each question begins with a sentence and ends with the question, "What correction should be made to sentence X?" Five answer choices are presented, which test all the content areas previously noted. Answer choice (5) is always "no correction is necessary."

Consider the following example of a correction question:

Example

Sentence 7: I was surprised, I could spend an entire evening with that strange little boy.

Which correction should be made to sentence 7?

1. Change was to is.
2. Remove the comma after surprised.
3. Change spend to spent.
4. Insert a comma after evening.
5. No correction is necessary.

The best answer is 2. No comma is necessary between the two clauses in this sentence.

Revision Questions

Revision questions ask you to identify the best revision for a part of a sentence, a whole sentence, a paragraph, the entire text, or the title. You must select the answer choice that would best replace the underlined portion in the sentence you are given. Answer choice 1 is always the same as the underlined portion. Choose answer choice 1 if no revision is necessary.

Consider the following example of a revision question:

Example

Sentence 10: There are many hazards on the job; including falling concrete.

Which is the best way to write the underlined portion of these sentences? If the original is the best way, choose option 1.

1. job; including
2. job including
3. job. Including
4. job and including
5. job, including

The best answer is 5. A phrase that modifies a noun phrase ("hazards on the job") using the word "including" should be set apart from the noun phrase with a comma.

Construction Shift Questions

Construction shift questions assess your ability to detect wordiness or awkwardness in one or two sentences. Although the sentence might be grammatically correct, it could benefit in clarity and conciseness from a change of word order or the addition or elimination of certain words.

Consider the following example of a construction shift question:

Example

Sentences 3 and 4: John arrived at Central Station by noon. He took a taxi.

The most effective combination of sentences 3 and 4 would include which group of words?

1. When John arrived
2. by noon, and he took a taxi
3. John took a taxi to arrive
4. By noon, John arrived
5. John, who arrived

The best answer is 3. This change would result in a single clear sentence: "John took a taxi to arrive at Central Station by noon."

Part II—Essay

In Part II, you will be given a topic about which you must write an essay. The topic addresses a common issue nearly every adult can speak to or write about, so it requires no special knowledge. You will have a total of 45 minutes in which to write your essay.

Information from the remaining chapters in Part IV, in combination with steady practice, will help you form a good, well-written essay.

What's Next?

The chapters that follow include information about the conventions of "Edited American English," which is the language tested on the GED. You will learn about grammar and sentence structure, basic writing mechanics, and how to write effectively.

CHAPTER SEVEN

Overview of English Usage

This chapter is designed to familiarize you with the conventions of standard written English, what the GED test makers call Edited American English (EAE). You will have a chance to review basic parts of speech, noun/verb agreement, pronouns, and formal elements of writing such as punctuation.

The Notion of "Standard English"

English is the fourth most widely spoken language in the world, behind Chinese, Hindi, and Spanish. As Great Britain expanded its empire, its troops and settlers brought British customs, culture, and language to the far reaches of the world.

A closer look at speech within the United States shows that English has great regional variation. One person might say "soda" and another one "pop," but the two native speakers certainly understand one another. A Michiganian may say, "Hey, you guys!" and a Texan, "Hey, y'all!" to represent the same thought. Some people choose to bicker about whose speech is right and whose is wrong, but modern linguists generally agree that dialects must not be compared to one another in terms of quality or purity. This notion is called *descriptivism*, which holds that each form of a language has legitimate, predictable grammar patterns that can be used to define the dialect. In spite of the reality of this natural evolution of language, some members of every society believe that efforts must be made to preserve the educated, literary form of their native tongue. This concept is called *prescriptivism*.

In some countries (France and Spain, for example), a body of intellectuals maintains a standard, prescriptive grammar manual and dictionary, which are notoriously conservative. Most countries, including the United States, do not maintain language academies as such. So what, then, is this so-called Standard English, or Edited American English (EAE)? It is the idealized form of the language that obeys traditional grammar rules identified by experts. This is the form of English you may read in a newspaper or hear on a nationwide nightly newscast. It avoids regional expressions, slang, and uncommon verb constructions. As the theory goes, by adhering to the rules of EAE, a speaker becomes as highly understandable as possible to the widest range of English speakers. People also regard EAE as a sign of education. You can go your whole life among friends and family speaking your native variety of English, but a solid knowledge of EAE is very important for school and the workplace. Of course, your success on the GED depends on your knowledge of EAE, too.

The Sentence

English, like most other languages in the world, has a writing system. In every one of these languages, the written word holds more tightly to the rules of traditional grammar than does the spoken word. A complete sentence must be grammatical and represent a coherent thought.

A sentence must have a *subject*; subjects are nouns, pronouns, or longer noun phrases. Consider the following example, which shows the subject in italic:

The fourth football game of the season was a total loss.

A sentence must have a *predicate*; predicates contain a verb with tense and, in general, describe the state of the subject or an action performed by the subject. Consider the following example, which shows the predicate in italic:

My brother *took out the trash*.

A sentence conveys a coherent thought. No information is left "dangling." Consider the following examples:

Good Sentence: The horses were in the corral.

(This sentence contains a subject and a predicate and conveys a complete thought.)

Bad Sentence: The horses were in the corral when suddenly.

(This sentence is not complete because you are never told what happens next.)

As long as a complete thought is being expressed, sentences can be quite short. Consider the following examples:

1. Dogs bark.
2. I am eating.
3. Who is it?
4. Run! (In commands, the subject "you" is implied.)

Sentences can also be quite long and employ a variety of punctuation to organize the information, as in the following examples:

1. When night falls, the lake takes on an eerie green color because of the unique mineral deposits found on its bottom.
2. Calling on his friends, our superhero finally succeeds in overcoming the villain who had so long laid siege to the town.

Building sentences will be addressed in more detail in Chapter 8, "Grammar and Sentence Structure."

Complete the following exercise to test your knowledge of basic sentence structure.

Sentence Structure Exercise

Identify whether the following items are complete sentences or sentence fragments. If the item is complete, circle the subject and the predicate. If the item is a fragment, rewrite it as a complete sentence, making any changes and additions you would like.

Example A: (Joe) (drives the speed limit). [complete sentence]

Example B: Soft ride on gravel. [fragment] *My car has a soft ride on gravel.*

1. Runs well. ________________
2. Sue is a cheerleader. ________________
3. Narrow highways in the mountains. ________________
4. The farmers harvest tomatoes in August. ________________
5. Completed the marathon. ________________

Possible Answers:

1. [fragment] (missing a subject) The car runs well. [complete sentence]
2. [complete] (Sue) (is a cheerleader).
3. [fragment] (missing a predicate) (Narrow highways in the mountains) (are difficult for most drivers to navigate). [complete sentence]
4. [complete] (The farmers) (harvest tomatoes in August).
5. [fragment] (missing a subject) (Amy) (completed the marathon in record time). [complete sentence]

Parts of Speech

All words are assigned a part of speech, which represents how the word is used in the sentence. Knowing the parts of speech will help you analyze and correct the reading passages and prepare the essay.

NOTE

It's not necessary to memorize the terms in this chapter. You should simply learn to apply them correctly in your writing.

Table 7.1 includes nine crucial parts of speech in English.

TABLE 7.1 Parts of Speech

Part of Speech	Description
Noun	A naming word: person, place, thing, and so on.
	Common nouns name something generally and are not capitalized.
	Proper nouns are given names, like those of people, pets, businesses, and specific geographic places; proper nouns are capitalized.
Verb	A word or phrase of action or state of being.
	Verbs have different forms according to tense and rules of agreement (discussed in detail later in this chapter).
Pronoun	A word that stands in for a noun.
	Pronouns must have a clear antecedent (what the pronoun represents).
	There is a limited set of pronouns. The most frequently used are the following:
	Subject pronouns: *I*, *you*, *he/she/it*, *we*, *they*
	Object pronouns: *me*, *you*, *him/her/it*, *us*, *them*
Determiner	A word that modifies a noun by expressing its reference, and sometimes quantity, in the context.
	Determiners are placed before a noun.
	There is a limited set of determiners, including the following:
	Articles*: a*, *an (indefinite)*; *the (definite)*
	Demonstratives: *this*, *that*, *those*, *these*
	Possessive determiners (sometimes called possessive adjectives): *his*, *her*, *its*, *my*, *our*, *your*, *their*
	Quantifiers: *some*, *all*, *every*, *each*, *many*, *few*
	Numerals: *one*, *two*, *fifty-eight*, *2,000*
	Ordinals: *first*, *second*, *forty-ninth*, *hundredth*
Adjective	A word that modifies a noun.
	In general, an adjective is found immediately before the noun it modifies: a *rainy* day.
	Many adjectives can be used as nouns when describing a group or class: The *Swiss* are friendly. I donate to the *poor*.
Adverb	A word that modifies a verb, an adjective, or another adverb.
	It may appear in several places in a sentence: I *quickly* ate my breakfast at the table. I ate my breakfast *quickly* at the table.
Preposition	A word that describes a physical or temporal relationship.
	There is a limited set of prepositions. Some common ones are *at*, *to*, *in*, *outside*, *within*, *after*, *around*, *under*, *of*, *for*.
Conjunction	A word that joins noun phrases or clauses.
	There is a limited set of conjunctions. The most common conjunctions are *and* and *but*.
Interjection	A word showing surprise or intense emotion.
	Interjections vary regionally and over time.
	Examples: *Gosh! Gee! Shucks! Ouch! Wow!*

Complete the following exercise to test your knowledge of important parts of speech.

Parts of Speech Exercise

Identify the part of speech of each of the words in the following sentences, and then mark it near the word. Use these common abbreviations: **n.** for noun, **v.** for verb, **pron.** for pronoun, **det.** for determiner, **adj.** for adjective, **adv.** for adverb, **prep.** for preposition, **conj.** for conjunction, and **interj.** for interjection.

Example:

I	especially	love	the	monkeys	at	the	zoo.
pron.	adv.	v.	det.	n.	prep.	det.	n.

1. Mark eats hotdogs with yellow mustard and relish.
2. My cat likes stalking mice.
3. Wow, that is an exceedingly large trout for this lake!

Answers:

1. n. v. n. prep. adj. n. conj. n.
2. det. n. v. v. n.
3. interj. pro. v. det. adv. adj. n. prep. det. n.

Nouns

Nouns are either *singular* (just one) or *plural* (more than one) in English. In most cases an "s" can be added to a singular noun to form a plural, or an "es" may be added when "s" creates an awkward pronunciation (usually after words ending in s, sh, ch, and x). Consider the following:

Singular/Plural
cat/cats
school/schools
class/classes
fox/foxes

Many nouns have irregular plural forms, as shown in the following examples:

Singular/Plural
ox/oxen
deer/deer
child/children

man/men
radius/radii
antenna/antennae

NOTE

The concept of singular versus plural is called *number* in grammar.

Nouns may mark possession using the apostrophe, as shown next:

- Singular nouns, add "apostrophe s":

  cat's meow

  John's knee

- Plural nouns with s, add an apostrophe:

  The champions' trophies

  The Johnsons' front yard

- Irregular plurals, add "apostrophe s":

  children's clothes

  oxen's labor

- To indicate joint possession, add "apostrophe s" to the last noun:

  Bill and Sue's apartment

- To indicate individual possession, add "apostrophe s" to all nouns:

  Brian's, Jason's, and Michael's wallets

Verbs

Verbs convey time as a part of their meaning. In addition to *agreement*, explained later, verbs are put in a form, or *conjugated*, according to *tense*, or when the action took place relative to when a sentence is spoken or written. Strictly speaking, there are three tenses: past, present, and future. For the traditional grammar reviewed in this book, however, the term *tense* takes on the properties of *aspect*. For example, for an action in the past, aspect describes at what point in the past or for how long in the past the action took place. Consider the following sentences:

Jordan drank the coffee.

This sentence is in simple past tense and suggests that Jordan has finished drinking the coffee.

Jordan was drinking the coffee.

Although this sentence is also in the past tense, it suggests that Jordan was in the process of drinking the coffee while something else was going on.

So, this combination of true tense and aspect carried on verbs creates the numerous grammatical tenses in English.

Complete the following exercise to test your knowledge of verbs.

Verb Exercise

Verbs are marked for past, present, or future. With multipart verb constructions (*have been writing*, *had visited*, and so on), the first verb, called an "auxiliary" or "helping" verb, carries past, present, or future. In the case of the future, the element "will," although not a verb itself, carries the tense information. In the sentences that follow, circle the word that carries tense and write whether it is past, present, or future on the line to the right.

Example A: I (will) be working on my homework all day. *future*

Example B: John (flew) to Hawaii yesterday. *past*

1. Sam was a difficult child. ________________
2. My sister runs fast. ________________
3. Interstate 75 extends from Michigan to Florida. ________________
4. I will be your partner on this project. ________________
5. I have won several pie-eating contests. ________________

Answers:

1. was/past
2. runs/present
3. extends/present
4. will/future
5. have/present

Agreement

In English, the subject and the verb in a sentence must match. You can think of this as a process of identifying the kind of subject a sentence has in terms of *person* and *number* and then matching the verb form to it.

Person

Grammatical person describes whether a subject is the speaker, the listener/reader, or something/someone else in the universe.

The terms *first person*, *second person*, and *third person* are used to make this distinction. Consider the following examples:

1. First-person subject: *I salute the flag.*
2. Second-person subject: *You met my teacher on Wednesday.*
3. Third-person subject: *Pluto has an irregular orbit.*

Number

Number describes whether a noun is singular or plural.

The six possible combinations of person and number result in six different sets of pronouns. Table 7.2 lists the sets of subject pronouns.

TABLE 7.2 Subject Pronouns

Person	Number	Subject Pronoun Set
First	Singular	I
	Plural	we
Second	Singular	you
	Plural	you
Third	Singular	he/she/it
	Plural	they

In the simple present tense, all verbs have regular conjugation except the two most common English verbs, "be" and "have." The person and number of the subject must match with the appropriate form of the verb in a sentence, as shown in Table 7.3.

TABLE 7.3 Subject/Verb Agreement

Person	Number	Simple Present Tense—Regular Verbs (add "s" only to third-person singular form)			Verb "be" *Simple present*	*Simple past*	Verb "have" *Simple present*	*Simple past*
First	Singular	I walk	I eat	I play	I am	I was	I have	I had
	Plural	we walk	we eat	we play	we are	we were	we have	we had
Second	Singular	you walk	you eat	you play	you are	you were	you have	you had
	Plural	you walk	you eat	you play	you are	you were	you have	you had
Third	Singular	he walks	he eats	he plays	he is	he was	he has	he had
		she walks	she eats	she plays	she is	she was	she has	she had
		it walks	it eats	it plays	it is	it was	it has	it had
	Plural	they walk	they eat	they play	they are	they were	they have	they had

Although conjugating verbs is very straightforward in the simple present tense, many irregulars exist among the past forms (the past participle and the simple past) of verbs. Many such irregular verb forms exist in English. They are used in forming *simple past* and *perfect* sentences, which are further explained in Chapter 8, "Grammar and Sentence Structure."

Consider the following examples of regular simple past forms that use the suffix *-ed* with the unconjugated verb:

- Simple present: *I walk to the store.*
- Simple past: *I walked to the store.*

Irregular simple past forms use a variety of suffixes and sometimes entirely different words, as shown in the following examples:

- Simple present: *I eat chicken sandwiches.*
- Simple past: *I ate chicken sandwiches.*
- Present perfect: *I have eaten chicken sandwiches.*

Even native speakers make mistakes with the irregular past forms of verbs. A good example is this common yet incorrect usage: *I have drank a half gallon of chocolate milk in one sitting*. The present perfect tense used here should be formed of the simple present "have" and the past participle of the verb "drink," which is "drunk" and not "drank." English has many irregular past forms. If you have any doubts, look up verbs in the dictionary. If no past forms are given, the verb has regular past forms (that is, add *ed*); otherwise, you will have to memorize the irregular forms.

The simple verb agreement table in this section uses the subject pronouns. When using expressed (spelled-out) subjects, it is important to match them with the correct verb form. A good test is to consider which pronoun would stand in for a subject. The same test can be used with all the different kinds of pronouns and the possessive determiners.

Complete the following exercise to test your knowledge of noun/pronoun agreement.

Noun/Pronoun Agreement Exercise

In the following sentences, if the subject and verb agree, rewrite the sentence replacing the subject with the appropriate subject pronoun.

Example: Laura skates very gracefully. *She skates very gracefully.*

If the subject and verb do not agree, rewrite the sentence with the correct form of the verb.

Example: Thunderstorms upsets many dogs. *Thunderstorms upset many dogs.*

1. California have great weather. ______________________
2. Maggie sprained her ankle. ______________________
3. Has all of you gotten gym memberships yet? ______________________
4. That doll are very bizarre. ______________________
5. Do restaurants in Europe charge sales tax? ______________________

Answers:

1. [subject and verb do not agree] California has great weather.
2. [subject and verb agree] She sprained her ankle.
3. [subject and verb do not agree] Have all of you gotten gym memberships yet?
4. [subject and verb do not agree] That doll is very bizarre.
5. [subject and verb agree] Do they charge sales tax?

NOTE

The subjects *California*, *Maggie*, *dolls*, and *restaurants* in the preceding exercise are so-called simple nouns because they are unmodified. Subjects are very often more complex, but it is the simple noun within the longer phrase that still controls person and number.

Table 7.4 includes examples of complex sentences.

TABLE 7.4 Complex Sentences

Sample Sentence	Complex Subject	Simple Subject	Subject Class	Applicable Pronoun
Twelve-pound bowling balls are difficult for me to control.	Twelve-pound bowling balls	balls	Third-person plural	"They"
Chocolate ice cream cones would be the perfect dessert.	Chocolate ice cream cones	cones	Third-person plural	"They"
Your poor work performance must not continue, Miss Scott.	Your poor work performance	performance	Third-person singular	"It"

Be careful with subjects that contain a conjunction. The conjunction "and" creates plurals, whereas the conjunction "or" does not, as shown in the examples in Table 7.5.

TABLE 7.5 Subjects with Conjunctions

Sample Sentence	Conjoined Nouns	Subject Class	Applicable Pronoun or Pronouns
Jonathan and I toured the science museum.	Jonathan (third-person singular); I (first-person singular)	First-person plural	"We"
Mark or Michelle will contact you about your reservation.	Mark (third-person singular); Michelle (third-person singular)	Third-person singular	"He or she"

Complete the following exercise to test your knowledge of compound sentences and noun/pronoun agreement.

Compound Sentences Exercise

Circle the entire noun phrase that constitutes the subject of the sentence, and then rewrite it using a pronoun in place of the subject.

Example A: (The chocolate-glazed donuts with the custard filling) are my favorite. *They are my favorite.*

Example B: (My younger brother Joe) is captain of a freighter. *He is captain of a freighter.*

1. Republican President George W. Bush was raised in Texas.

   ____

2. Miles Davis and John Coltrane made a great duo.

   ____

3. The red-colored cough syrup in the medicine cabinet upsets my stomach.

   ____

Answers:

1. Republican President George W. Bush/He was raised in Texas.
2. Miles Davis and John Coltrane/They made a great duo.
3. The red-colored cough syrup in the medicine cabinet/It upsets my stomach.

Modifying details, like the ones seen in the previous exercise, tend to separate the simple noun within a subject from the verb form that it controls. Reducing the proximity of simple subject and verb can cause agreement errors when speaking and writing. This is even more likely when so-called interrupting phrases include nouns of different person and/or number. The easiest way to make sure the subject and verb match is to imagine the sentence without the interrupting phrase, as shown in the examples in Table 7.6.

TABLE 7.6 Interrupting Phrases

Sample Sentence	Subject	Possible Trap	Sentence Without the Interrupting Phrase
Those twin sisters whose mother you met yesterday go to school downtown.	Those twin sisters (third-person plural)	"mother" is third-person singular.	Those twin sisters go to school downtown.
Joe, like Bill and Samir, prefers basketball to soccer.	Joe (third-person singular)	"Bill and Samir" is third-person plural.	Joe prefers basketball to soccer.
I, along with NASA scientists, have discovered a new lightweight plastic.	I (first-person singular)	"NASA scientists" is third-person plural.	I have discovered a new lightweight plastic.

Pronouns

Pronouns are small words that can replace nouns in a sentence, as long as the listener (or the reader) knows to whom or to what the pronouns refer. Imagine that you walk into work in the morning and the first thing your boss says to you is, "Thanks for doing *that* yesterday. I hate doing *that*." Sounds strange, doesn't it? The problem is that you don't already have in mind what "that" refers to. See how this alternative sounds: "Thanks for cleaning the copier yesterday. I hate doing *that*." Here, "that" refers to "cleaning the copier." After the boss mentions the longer phrase, a pronoun can then be used to represent it later in the dialog. The same is true in writing.

Table 7.7 introduces the personal pronouns in English, along with the possessive determiners, which tend to be grouped with these pronouns because of their similar properties.

TABLE 7.7 Personal Pronouns and Possessive Determiners

		Pronouns				Possessive
Person	Number	*Subject*	*Object*	*Reflexive*	*Possessive*	Determiners
First	Singular	I	me	myself	mine	my
	Plural	we	us	ourselves	ours	our
Second	Singular	you	you	yourself	yours	your
	Plural	you	you	yourselves	yours	your
Third	Singular	he/she/it	him/her/it	himself/herself/itself	his/hers/its	his/her/its
	Plural	they	them	themselves	theirs	their

There are also indefinite pronouns, which replace nouns without directly specifying which noun they replace. A finite (limited) set of indefinite pronouns exist, as shown in Table 7.8.

TABLE 7.8 Indefinite Pronouns

Singular	another, anybody, anyone, anything, each, either, everybody, everyone, everything, little, much, neither, nobody, no one, nothing, one, other, somebody, someone, something
Plural	both, few, many, others, several
Singular or plural	all, any, more, most, none, some

Whether an indefinite pronoun from the last row is singular or plural depends on whether the noun it is used with is singular or plural. Consider the following examples:

- Any horse is good enough for me.

  [Singular *any horse* and singular *is* match]

- Any soldiers with blisters on their feet need to break in their boots better.

  [Plural *any soldiers*, plural *their feet*, plural *their boots* match]

The most common error with indefinite pronouns is using *they*, *their*, or *them* to refer to a third-person singular entity whose gender is unknown. English does not have a gender-neutral third-person-singular set of pronouns for human beings. The various forms of *it* are gender-neutral but cannot be used with people, pets, ships, and other things to which humans assign gender. In these cases, it is usually best to reword the sentence to avoid the situation. Using just one gender may appear to show bias or sexism and phrases such as "he or she" usually come across as wordy. Consider the following examples:

- Sentence with pronoun/possessive determiner error:

  A nurse needs to care about *her* patients.

  Reason for error:

  Sexist language (there are men who are nurses)

  Corrected sentence:

  <u>Use the plural</u>: *Nurses* need to care about *their* patients.

- Sentence with pronoun/possessive determiner error:

  Each player will have one minute to make *their* move.

  Reason for error:

  Each player is singular; *their* is plural.

  Corrected sentence:

  <u>Use the plural</u>: *Players* will have one minute to make *their* moves.

  OR use the singular, <u>replacing *their*</u>: *Each player* will have one minute to make *a* move.

Complete the following exercise to test your knowledge of pronouns.

Pronoun Exercise

Rewrite the first three sentences using the correct pronouns in place of all nouns and noun phrases. Remember that if meaning is clear, a pronoun can appear more than once in a sentence and possibly refer to two different nouns. Rewrite the last three sentences using nouns and noun phrases of your choosing to replace all pronouns.

Note: Possessive phrases like "John's tree" may be simplified two ways, as "his tree" or simply "it." Experiment with both ways.

Example A: It was very important to us. [The championship was very important to Jeannette and me.]

Example B: John's soft hands with the ball let the Mustangs try difficult plays. *They let them try them.* OR *His soft hands with the ball let them try them.*

1. Jessica will not stay in the crib. ____________________
2. Extra-chunky peanut butter and grape jelly go on all of my toast. ____________________
3. You take success too seriously. ____________________
4. If I were him, I would give it back to her. ____________________
5. They are not going to burn it without it. ____________________
6. She asked him about ours. ____________________

Answers:

1. She will not stay in it.
2. They go on all of it.
3. You take it too seriously.
4. *For example:* If I were Joe, I would give the pink bicycle back to Sue.
5. *For example:* Bob and Carol are not going to burn the charcoal without the lighter fluid.
6. *For example:* The detective asked the suspect about our red pick-up truck.

What's Next?

The remaining chapters in Part IV cover additional rules governing standard written English. The GED will test your ability to apply these rules of grammar correctly.

CHAPTER EIGHT

Grammar and Sentence Structure

Like language itself, the field of linguistics is in a state of perpetual change. Among the most-changed notions in the recent study of language is what the term *grammar* should truly represent. For the GED, you are expected to know the principles of "traditional grammar," that is, morphology (how to assemble roots, prefixes, and suffixes into words) and syntax (how to assemble words into meaningful sentences). This book will not discuss the application of the term *grammar* in contemporary linguistics.

Traditional Grammar

Traditional English grammar stems from centuries of analysis of the original Western societies—ancient Greece and Rome. The rules and concepts of Ancient Greek and Latin have been used by scholars to build a framework for the English language. Traditional grammar determines what constitutes acceptable usage, which does not always coincide with whether a reader or listener fully understands what a writer or speaker intends to convey. Remember that no one speaks with traditional grammar all the time. It takes a concerted effort to maintain correct usage in speaking and writing.

Traditional rules are useful in teaching the language—especially writing in it—to children or nonnative speakers. It would be impractical to attempt to teach the unique dialect of each English-speaking region at any one moment in any one classroom. Teachers would have to learn new words, phrases, and syntax for every new situation. The challenge is that children speak differently from their parents, who speak differently from their parents, and so on. Language is always changing, across both time and territory, so traditional English grammar provides a standard that can be used universally, and it is much slower to change than any regional dialect rich in slang, colloquialism (informality), and fragments.

People learn their native dialect through socialization. Evidence shows that caregivers do not even have to correct their children's mistakes. Kids are excellent at assimilating grammar and vocabulary. What is not automatic, however, is a solid understanding of traditional grammar rules and what makes for quality speech and writing. These concepts require education, either in school or independently, followed by lots of practice. This is why knowing Standard English (what the GED calls Edited American English) makes people appear intelligent and well educated. It is knowledge that pays dividends throughout life.

Building from the Basic Sentence

As we mentioned in Chapter 7, "Overview of English Usage," the basic sentence must contain the following elements, and must represent a complete thought:

- A subject
- A predicate (the verbal information)

Sentences are composed of one or more clauses and, optionally, adjunct (additional) information. Clauses are composed of phrases and fulfill the requirements of the sentence as previously listed, and adjunct information modifies clauses. Adjuncts may be eliminated without making a sentence ungrammatical. Consider the following example:

> John is sleeping like a log.
>
> Clause: *John is sleeping*
>
> Adjunct: *like a log*

Every verb exists in a verb phrase, even if the verb is alone in the clause. Consider the following example:

> *Fluffy ate.*
>
> Verb phrase: *ate*
>
> Verb: *ate*
>
> *Fluffy ate her food.*
>
> Verb phrase: *ate her food*
>
> Verb: *ate*

The verb "eat" in these examples appears to have two usages. First, one could simply eat, that is, satisfy hunger by consuming food. Second, one could eat *something*, that is, chew and swallow it. This seemingly small distinction is important because it shows that one verb may have different usages associated with it, even if the meaning seems nearly the same. The fundamental difference between the two usages of "eat" lies in *constituency*, or the "needs" of the verb. The top usage of "eat" has only one need, a subject. All verbs have at least the subject constituent. The bottom usage of "eat" has two needs, a subject and a direct object (what was eaten).

Direct and Indirect Objects

The great majority of verbs in English have two constituents—a subject and either a direct object or an indirect object. A word or phrase is not a constituent if the sentence would still make grammatical sense without it. Table 8.1 breaks down the direct and indirect objects in a sample sentence.

TABLE 8.1 Direct and Indirect Object

The	shortstop	threw	the ball	to	the second baseman.
			direct object		*indirect object*

To find the direct object, ask yourself "what was thrown?" (the ball)

To find the indirect object, ask yourself "to whom was it thrown?" (the second baseman)

Following are examples of common usages of verbs and their constituency (subject and objects):

- **Give** (three constituents—subject, indirect object, direct object): I gave you the keys.
- **Fall** (one constituent—subject): John fell off his bike.
- **Write** (three constituents—subject, indirect object, direct object): Mike writes me letters.
- **Chop** (two constituents—subject, direct object): Chefs chop onions.

The simplest sentence (like those shown here) contains a subject correctly matched with a verb form whose constituents are all fulfilled.

Complete the following exercise to test your knowledge of subjects and objects:

EXAM PREP Study TIP

Sentences that lack either a subject or a verb are considered sentence fragments. Avoid sentence fragments in your writing.

Subjects and Objects Exercise

The following groups of words are fragments. Rewrite them to make complete sentences by adding the missing parts.

Example: As an adult, Joe has given. *As an adult, Joe has given lots of money to charity.*

1. Beats on a drum. ____________________
2. Bob goes to the zoo to see. ____________________
3. Mr. Smith teaches to the students. ____________________
4. Chef Robinson is boiling. ____________________
5. Give the ball! ____________________

Possible Answers:

1. beat/John [subject] beats on a drum.
2. see/Bob goes to the zoo to see the chimpanzees [direct object].
3. teach/Mr. Smith teaches Spanish [direct object] to the students.
4. boil/Chef Robinson is boiling lobster [direct object].
5. give/Give the ball to your brother [indirect object]!

Run-Ons

Run-ons are the combination of two or more clauses that should be separated with end punctuation. Strictly speaking, most run-ons are not ungrammatical; they are simply difficult to read because of their length and lack of necessary punctuation. Consider the following examples:

Run-on: *When I eat pizza, I get really bad indigestion, it's okay, though, because I know upset stomach runs in my family and I have to eat pizza because I love it.*

Correction: *When I eat pizza, I get really bad indigestion. It's okay, though, because I know upset stomach runs in my family. I have to eat pizza; I love it.*

The correction is much easier to read than the original run-on because the clauses are divided with end punctuation—periods and a semicolon.

A specific type of run-on is called a comma splice, which uses a comma to join clauses where end punctuation should be used. Consider the following:

Comma splice: *If you have the chance, drive over the Golden Gate Bridge, it's a beautiful landmark.*

Correction: *If you have the chance, drive over the Golden Gate Bridge. It's a beautiful landmark.*

Or: If you have the chance, drive over the Golden Gate Bridge; it's a beautiful landmark.

Use of punctuation is discussed in detail in Chapter 10, "Writing Mechanics."

Complete the following exercise to test your knowledge of run-on sentences:

Run-On Sentences Exercise

Rewrite these run-ons using appropriate punctuation.

Example: If you are in Philadelphia, try a cheese steak, they're really delicious. *If you are in Philadelphia, try a cheese steak. They're really delicious.*

1. Why are you talking to him, he's a mean man and yesterday he yelled at me. ____________________
2. Pandas eat bamboo, but if you feed them, they are willing to eat other things, they loved the fish I gave them. ____________________

Possible Answers:

1. Why are you talking to him? He's a mean man. Yesterday, he yelled at me. [Exclamation points could be used instead of periods, because this may be an excited statement.]
2. Pandas eat bamboo, but if you feed them, they are willing to eat other things. They loved the fish I gave them. [Again, this second statement could merit an exclamation point.]

Combining Clauses

Conjunctions are words that link words, phrases, or clauses. *Coordinating conjunctions* join elements of the same type: phrase with phrase, clause with clause, and so on. *Correlative conjunctions* join elements of the same type, but they are always used in pairs. *Subordinating conjunctions* are adverbs used to create dependency of one clause on the main clause. To avoid confusion with the part of speech "conjunction," adverbs used as subordinating conjunctions are often called "subordinators."

Following are examples of conjunctions and subordinators:

Coordinating Conjunctions

Coordinating conjunctions include *for*, *and*, *nor*, *but*, *or*, *yet*, *so*. The coordinating conjunctions in the following examples are italicized:

- I stayed inside, *for* I didn't bring my raincoat.
- John *and* Kristin are getting married.
- I didn't wash the dishes, *nor* did I vacuum the rug.
- I ate breakfast, *but* I skipped lunch.
- Snuff *or* blow out that candle.
- My kids hate the zoo, *yet* they love animals.
- The soup of the day was split pea, *so* I had a bowl.

Correlative Conjunctions

Correlative conjunctions include *both…and*, *not only…but also*, *either…or*, *neither…nor*, *whether…or*. The correlative conjunctions in the following examples are italicized:

- *Both* ketchup *and* mustard are essential hot dog condiments.
- *Not only* the Tigers *but also* the White Sox will make the playoffs.
- *Either* you hand over the money *or* I take you to court.
- *Neither* the employees *nor* the manager knows the combination to the safe.
- *Whether* you stay inside *or* go to the pool is no matter to me.

Subordinating Conjunctions

Subordinating conjunctions are not a limited set like the two types of conjunctions in the previous sections. Here are the most common ones arranged by their function:

- **Cause-effect**—as, because, in order that, now that, since, so
- **Condition**—even if, if, in case, only if, unless, whether or not
- **Opposition**—although, even though, though, whereas, while
- **Time**—after, before, since, until, when, while

Conjunctions and Commas

Coordinating conjunctions and subordinating conjunctions are preceded by a comma when introducing a clause. The exceptions are *because* and *if*, and *and*, which may be omitted only if the meaning is clear without it.

Complete the following exercise to test your knowledge of conjunctions:

Combining Clauses Exercise

In 1 through 5, fill in the blank with an appropriate conjunction (there may be more than one correct choice).

Example A: Reading this book is giving me a headache *because* I forgot my glasses.

In 6 through 8, write a sentence using the conjunction provided. Don't forget about the comma.

Example B: My brothers and I are all very slender, *but* my father is built like a tank.

1. This bread is expensive _______ the grain is special.
2. I was planning on a nice dinner, _______ I ordered a pizza instead.
3. It feels warm in the sun, _______ the thermometer reads 41°F.
4. _______you hate to exercise, you can lose weight.

5. _______Mark visits the Grand Canyon, he should take lots of photos.
6. *so*
7. *Neither…nor*
8. because

Answers:

1. because (no comma)
2. but, yet
3. but, yet, although, even though, though
4. Even though, Although, Though
5. When, If, While
6. *Example:* I sprained my ankle, so I went to the hospital.
7. *Example:* Neither Dr. Smith nor Dr. Lafleur will be available this afternoon.
8. *Example:* Because the water's so warm, I'll consider diving in.

Note: Use of some conjunctions is possible under very unusual readings, but they are not included here. For example, using "if" in question 1 would indicate that the bread sometimes, but not always, has special grain.

Tense

Although there are many tenses in English, forming each of them is generally simple. As defined earlier, the process of forming the proper tense is called *conjugation* of a verb. Each grammatical tense is used for a specific combination of tense (time) and aspect (duration).

The infinitive form of a verb is the particle "to" and the base form. Infinitives do not have tense properties, and they are used with many conjugated verbs (for example, *try to ski*, *learn to cook*).

Table 8.2 includes a list of verb tenses, along with some sample sentences. The last row of Table 8.2 shows how to use the verb *go* to form a kind of future tense.

TABLE 8.2 English Verb Tenses

		Positive Example	Negative Example	Question	What It Means
Past	Simple past	*I lifted weights yesterday.*	*We did not like t he play.*	*Did you see the accident?* [Note that a simple past form of "do" is used to form simple past questions.]	Action completed at a defined time in the past
	Past continuous	*John was reading the newspaper (when the telephone rang).*	*I was not at home (when you arrived).*	*Was it raining last week?*	Action or state ongoing or interrupted in the past; often used with background/setting information
	Past perfect	*I had already been to Canada (prior to my last trip).*	*They had not seen the Grand Canyon (before, so the helicopter tour was amazing).*	*Had we eaten all that candy (before we went on a diet)?*	Action that happened at a point in the past before another action
	Past perfect continuous	*We had been waiting at the airport for several hours (by the time our plane arrived).*	*She hadn't been skating more than four years (before she won her first competition).*	*How long had you been driving the car (before it overheated)?*	Expresses the duration of an action before another action in the past
	Habitual past	Using "used to": *I used to get an ice cream cone every Sunday.* Using "would": *When I was a little girl, I would dream about my wedding day.*	*I didn't used to be so skinny. When I was starting out as a receptionist, I wouldn't be very confident on the phone.*	*Did you used to be the principal of this school? In the 1950s, wouldn't you do bomb shelter drills a lot?*	Actions or states that were repeated or continuous in the past and which ended in the past

(continues)

TABLE 8.2 *Continued*

		Positive Example	Negative Example	Question	What It Means
Present	Simple present	*I eat cheese-burgers every Monday.*	*Sue does not sleep twelve hours per night.*	*Does Bob fish for trout?* [Note that a simple present form of "do" is used to form simple present questions.]	Current states of being; repetitive, habitual actions
	Present continuous	*Elizabeth is working this afternoon.*	*My dog is not chasing his tail.*	*Are you making popcorn?*	Currently ongoing actions; actions happening in the near future
	Present perfect	*The school has seen teachers come and go.*	*Mary has not tried oysters yet.*	*How long have you worked for the phone company?*	Expresses an action that began in the past and is ongoing; expresses an unspecified duration or repetition of an action in the past
	Present perfect continuous	*Mike has been working since yesterday morning.*	*Billy has not been fighting with his sister lately.*	*Have you been suffering from the flu?*	Expresses the duration of an action begun in the past and which is ongoing
Future	Simple future	*I will see you tomorrow.*	*Mark will have tea instead of coffee.*	*Will Reggie recognize the house?*	Actions in the future; future predictions and promises
	Future continuous	*Your flight will be taking off when I am going to bed.*	*You will not be studying French while you are in Spain.*	*Will you be finishing your degree in the summer of next year?*	Actions ongoing at a moment in the future

(continues)

TABLE 8.2 *Continued*

		Positive Example	Negative Example	Question	What It Means
	Future perfect	*We will have been married 20 years next August.*	*Bob will not have worked here two months when he gets fired today.*	*Will you have accomplished your goals by the end of the year?*	Actions in the past relative to a moment in the future
	Future perfect continuous	*I will have been working all day by the time you take over for me.*	*Mark will have been painting 10 years by the time he is eligible for promotion.*	*Will you have been flying at least 100 hours prior to the pilots' exam?*	Expresses the duration of an action up to a moment in the future
	Future using "going"	Relative to present: *I am going to eat breakfast before work.* Relative to past: *I was going to call you (before the game started).*	*I am not going to sit here any longer.* *I was not going to say anything (until you were rude to me).*	*Is Bob going to return my toolbox soon?*	Actions that will soon occur, relative to present time or a point in the past
Unreal Conditional	Past unreal conditional	*(If I had eaten breakfast,) I would not be hungry.*	*(If I had turned off the water,) the house would not have flooded.*	*If I had gone too, would you have gone to the movie?*	Hypothetical situations in the past
	Present unreal conditional	*I would run (if a dog came toward me).*	*I would have a second cup of coffee (if it would not give me jitters).*	*Would you go to the pharmacy for me?*	Hypothetical situations in the present or without a specific time
	Future unreal conditional	*My mom would quit her job next week (if she had a better offer).*	*Marcy would not sit at a table with John at tomorrow's wedding reception.*	*Would you go to the park with me if you got the day off?*	Hypothetical situations in the future

NOTE

The perfect and continuous forms can also be used with "would" to create conditionals.

Complete the following exercise to test your knowledge of tenses:

Verb Tense Exercise

In 1 through 5, fill in the blank with a correct form of the verb indicated. If more than one form seems appropriate, choose the one you think is best or most natural.

Example A: chat *Randy and Susan were chatting when they heard the explosion.*

In 6 through 10, the verbs are underlined. One or more verbs are not in the correct form based on the context. Rewrite the sentences using correct verb forms.

Example B: produce/simple present/much of the earth's oxygen/Forests *Forests produce much of the earth's oxygen.*

1. simmer

   The sauce ________ for an hour already.

2. inflate

   Dad ________ the inner tube after we get home.

3. exist

   Large dinosaurs ________ until about 65 million years ago.

4. chuckle

   The baby ________ continually since seven o'clock this morning.

5. wear

   My mother ________ a heavy coat on the way to last year's office party.

6. Joe will have been late for work yesterday.

   ____

7. Grizzly bears were eating salmon from the river by next week.

   ____

8. I am the best player on the team before breaking my leg.

   ____

9. The snow accumulation stopped by the time it reaches the rooftops.

   ____

10. For the past year, I will always take my lunch break at noon.

    ____

Answers:

1. has simmered, had simmered, has been simmering
2. will inflate

3. existed
4. has chuckled
5. wore
6. Joe was late for work yesterday.
7. Grizzly bears will be eating salmon from the river by next week
8. I was the best player on the team before breaking my leg. *OR* I had been the best player on the team before breaking my leg.
9. The snow accumulation stopped by the time it reached the rooftops.
10. For the past year, I have always taken my lunch break at noon.

Voice

If the subject of the sentence performs the action, the sentence is said to be in *active voice*. If the subject "receives" the action, the sentence has *passive voice*. The most common way to form the passive voice is with the verb "be" and a past participle. Consider the following examples:

Active voice

1. *Cats play with yarn.*
2. *The students took notes during the lecture.*

Passive voice

1. *Bridges are designed by engineers.*
2. *Garlic is included in the guacamole.*

Sometimes it is difficult to avoid the passive voice, particularly when the agent (who or what performs the action) is unknown or unimportant. Consider the following examples:

1. *Many soldiers were killed during World War II.*
2. *More than 75 percent of all the gold ever mined has been mined since the 1900s.*
3. *John was fired yesterday.*

In cases like these, revision with indefinite pronouns or some creative additions can create active voice:

1. *Fighting killed many soldiers during World War II.*
2. *Since the 1900s, people have mined more than 75 percent of all the gold ever mined.*
3. *Someone fired John yesterday.*

Complete the following exercise to test your knowledge of active and passive voice:

Active Versus Passive Voice Exercise

Identify whether the following sentences have active or passive voice. If a sentence has active voice, circle the subject and the verb. If it has passive voice, rephrase it in active voice.

Example A: These eggs were left by the Easter Bunny. *The Easter Bunny left these eggs.*

Example B: (Ketchup) (removes) tarnish from copper pots.

1. The center snaps the ball to the quarterback. ____________________
2. The flowers were sent by her boyfriend. ____________________
3. Bob was taught Spanish in high school. ____________________
4. The kitchen smells like maple syrup. ____________________
5. Linda was given a job in the mayor's office. ____________________

Answers:

1. (active) subject = *The center* verb = *snaps*
2. (passive) Her boyfriend sent the flowers.
3. (passive) Bob learned Spanish in high school.
4. (active) subject = *The kitchen* verb = *smells*
5. (passive) The mayor's office gave Linda a job.

Parallel Structure

Elements in a sentence that serve a parallel purpose should have parallel structure. When two adjectives modify the same noun, the adjectives should have similar forms. With lists, each element should have the same form. Also, in sentences with one expressed subject and multiple verbs, it is important to match the verbs. Consider the following examples:

- Sentence lacking parallel structure: *Our field trip included a visit* [noun] *to the art museum, talking* [gerund] *to a local artist, and a workshop* [noun] *on oil-painting techniques.*

Correction: *Our field trip included visiting* [gerund] *the art museum, talking* [gerund] *to a local artist, and attending* [gerund] *a workshop on oil-painting techniques.*

- Sentence lacking parallel structure: *Snowboarders are racing down the mountain then ride the chairlift back up.*

  Correction: *Snowboarders race down the mountain then ride the chairlift back up. OR Snowboarders are racing down the mountain then riding the chairlift back up.*

- Sentence lacking parallel structure: *Cowboys like to ride horses and singing campfire songs.*

  Correction: *Cowboys like riding horses and singing campfire songs. OR Cowboys like to ride horses and sing campfire songs.*

NOTE

In parallel constructions, it is not necessary to repeat the auxiliary verb, as in the second correction of the second sentence above, or the infinitive particle "to," as in the second correction of the third sentence above.

Complete the following exercise to test your knowledge of parallel structure:

Parallel Structure Exercise

Identify whether the following sentences have parallel structure. If a sentence has parallel structure, circle the parallel elements. If it lacks parallel structure, rewrite the sentence correctly. Note that there are usually several ways to create parallel structure in a sentence.

Example A: My dog's favorite hobbies are barking and licking.

Example B: I enjoy walking in the park, even if it is raining or snows. *I enjoy walking in the park, even if it is raining or snowing.* OR *I enjoy walking in the park, even if it rains or snows.*

1. On Sunday night, you are sure to find her asleep in her bed or watching television. ____________________
2. The boys love playing baseball, chewing bubble gum, and cheesy horror movies. ____________________
3. The judge prefers to fine defendants rather than sentencing them to jail time. ____________________

4. Cars are sliding all over the icy freeway and run into each other. ____________

5. Spice up your coffee with some chicory or a little mint syrup. ____________

Answers:

1. Correction: On Sunday night, you are sure to find her *sleeping* in her bed or watching television.
2. Correction: The boys love playing baseball, chewing bubble gum, and *watching* cheesy horror movies.
3. Correction: The judge prefers to fine defendants rather than *sentence* them to jail time.
4. Correction: Cars are sliding all over the icy freeway and *are running* into each other.
5. Parallel elements: *some chicory* (noun) and *a little mint syrup* (noun).

Modification

In grammar, modification means limitation or qualification. *Adjectives* modify nouns; *adverbs* modify verbs, adjectives, or other adverbs. Besides single words, longer phrases can modify words, phrases, and whole clauses.

Modifier phrases often use *that* or *which*, as shown below:

> *...the game <u>that the Tigers won</u>...*
>
> *...our house <u>that Dad built</u>...*
>
> *...the gravy, <u>which was delicious</u>,...*
>
> *...the humerus, <u>which is also called the funny bone</u>,...*

Special Modifiers

Which is used to give information about something in particular. *That* can be used the same way, but it's also used to pick one or more things from a greater set. Typically, *which* is used to denote a non-restrictive clause, and *that* is used to denote a restrictive clause, as shown in the following examples:

The dog, which I adopted at the pound, has become an important member of our family.

There is only one dog. The phrase "which I adopted at the pound" is a non-restrictive clause. It contains information that is not essential to the meaning of the sentence. Non-restrictive clauses are set apart from what they modify with a comma.

The dog that I adopted at the pound is the small brown and white dog.

There is only one dog OR there is a set of dogs and this one is the only one that was adopted at the pound. The phrase "that I adopted at the pound" is a restrictive clause. It provides essential information about the dog. Do not use commas with restrictive clauses.

Misplaced Modifiers

When using these modifier phrases, it is important to make sure that no ambiguity occurs in the sentence. Generally, the phrase should be set immediately following what it modifies, as shown next:

1. *There is a restaurant in the hotel lobby, which is very elegant.*

   The topic of the sentence is the restaurant, so there is ambiguity—what is elegant, the lobby or the restaurant?

2. *There is a restaurant, which is very elegant, in the hotel lobby.*

   Now it is clear that the restaurant is elegant.

Here are some more examples of misplaced modifiers:

1. *Josh had trouble deciding which college to attend at first*. (Did he really plan on attending more than one college?)

   Correction: *At first, Josh had trouble deciding which college to attend.*

2. *The young girl was walking her dog in a raincoat*. (Was the dog really wearing a raincoat?)

   Correction: *The young girl was in a raincoat walking her dog.*

   OR *The young girl in a raincoat was walking her dog.*

Dangling Modifiers

Another type of error is called *dangling modification*, in which phrases usually at the beginning of the sentence fail to refer logically to any word in the sentence.

Sentences can usually be corrected with little more than a change in word order. Consider the following example:

Dangling modification: *Making the varsity football team, Tim's dad could not be prouder of his son*. (Tim made the team, not his dad.)

Correction: *Tim's dad could not be prouder of his son who made the varsity football team.*

Sometimes the sentence needs more significant change, as in the following:

Dangling modification: *When eating in a restaurant, flies are especially annoying.* (People, not flies, eat in restaurants.)

Correction: *Flies are especially annoying for someone eating in a restaurant.*

Complete the following exercise to test your knowledge of modifiers:

Dangling Modifier Exercise

These sentences have misplaced modifiers. Rewrite the sentences without ambiguity.

Example: The note lay on the bed that Joe had been thinking about all day. *The note that Joe had been thinking about all day lay on the bed.*

1. The teacher recited poems for the students translated from Spanish.

   ____

2. Bob nearly ate a whole box of chocolates.

   ____

3. Joe's girlfriend is a tall French woman with long black hair weighing about 100 pounds.

   ____

Answers:

1. For the students, the teacher recited poems translated from Spanish. *(The students are not translated.)*
2. Bob ate nearly a whole box of chocolates. *(Bob did indeed begin eating but stopped before the box was empty.)*
3. Joe's girlfriend is a tall French woman who weighs about 100 pounds and has long black hair. *(The hair does not weigh 100 pounds.)*

What's Next?

Chapter 9 includes information on how to write effectively. You will learn the elements of good writing, such as structure, order, and word choice.

CHAPTER NINE

Effective Writing

Effective writing is well organized and focused. A good writer displays skill in structuring sentences and uses precise and relevant vocabulary. This chapter will focus on the elements of good, effective writing.

The Paragraph

Sentences are grouped into paragraphs, each representing a unique thought or line of reasoning. Each paragraph should have a topic sentence, which clearly defines the purpose of the paragraph. Consider the following paragraph:

> *Blue is certainly my favorite color.* All day, I find myself staring at the sky or the lake. The color seems to match anything—just consider denim jeans, the most popular pants in the world! Blue is the color of true indigo, a rare and alluring natural pigment. The blue backdrop in the American flag represents vigilance, perseverance, and justice.

The first sentence is the topic sentence, a notion that all the other sentences in the paragraph work together to support. Your topic sentence should clearly state the objective of the paragraph.

There is no absolute rule about how many sentences should make up a paragraph. The best test is to consider whether a topic is introduced and fully supported and keeps from straying to secondary or minor points. Paragraph length is also an important consideration. Readers struggle with a lot of little paragraphs or just a few very large ones, so be sure to vary the lengths of your paragraphs as you write.

Logical Order

Sentences within a paragraph should be arranged in an order that corresponds to time or mental reasoning.

Consider this example of poor logical order:

> During the mating season, male robins are characterized by dark black feathers on their heads. Robins can lay two sets of eggs in a season. The bird is commonly seen snatching worms from the earth to feed hatchlings. Soon, the females arrive to choose their mates and breed. They return to northern breeding grounds earlier than the females in order to compete with each other for the best nesting sites.

The following is the same series of sentences placed in a more logical order:

> During the mating season, male robins are characterized by brilliant black feathers on their heads. They return to northern breeding grounds earlier than the females in order to compete with each other for the best nesting sites. Soon, the females arrive to choose their mates and breed. Robins can lay two sets of eggs in a season. The bird is commonly seen snatching worms from the earth to feed hatchlings.

This paragraph could benefit from a topic sentence that unifies it, as shown in italic:

> *Early spring is a wonderful time to watch the mating rituals of the American robin.* During the mating season, male robins are characterized by brilliant black feathers on their heads. They return to northern breeding grounds earlier than the females in order to compete with each other for the best nesting sites. Soon, the females arrive to choose their mates and breed. Robins can lay two sets of eggs in a season. The bird is commonly seen snatching worms from the earth to feed hatchlings.

Pronoun Use

When composing paragraphs, pay close attention to pronouns. Use your best judgment to determine whether the reader will confuse the antecedent. Consider the following example:

> Larry and Chuck are my brothers. As kids, we would terrorize the neighborhood. During the summer, Larry, Chuck, and I would keep street hockey games going long into the evening. On the empty lot, he liked to build dirt ramps.

The antecedent of *he* in the last sentence could be either Larry or Chuck. One of those two names should be substituted for clarity.

Similarly, repetition of words can make writing dull, as shown in italics:

> The *tree* in my back yard was tall and gnarled. I marveled at that centuries-old *tree* every day as a kid. I wished the *tree* could tell stories about this land.

Other words could be substituted for *tree* to increase variety in the sentences, as follows:

> The *oak* in my back yard was tall and gnarled. I marveled at that centuries-old tree every day as a kid. I wished *that wise man* could tell stories about this land.

Figurative language, such as the personification of the tree in the last sentence of the previous example, makes reading more interesting. Avoid clichés, however, which are figures of speech that have lost their novelty because of overuse.

Word Choice

Be sure to explain the connection between the facts you are using and your conclusion. Don't assume that the reader will agree with your viewpoint regarding the significance of a given fact. For instance, imagine an essay about schools. A prejudicial statement in the essay, such as"...*which is merely a public school*," reveals the writer's bias and may not actually contribute to a convincing essay.

Consider "100%" words carefully. Words such as *every*, *everyone*, *all*, *entire*, *whole*, *none*, *no one*, *zero*, *always*, and *never* are absolute terms, which should generally be avoided. If you think critically about a topic, you usually find that there are likely exceptions, as shown next:

> It is always hot in Arizona.
>
> This cannot be true if Arizona has ever had cool weather.
>
> *Rephrase*: It is usually hot in Arizona.

> No doctor likes to reveal bad news.
>
> This cannot be true if there ever was a doctor who liked revealing bad news.
>
> *Rephrase*: Compassionate doctors do not like to reveal bad news.

EXAM ALERT

Watch for "100% words" within answer choices and question stems. These words can help you quickly eliminate incorrect answer choices.

Use *most* and *majority* carefully. These words mean "more than 50%" specifically, so be sure not to make overbroad statements. Consider the following examples:

> Most Americans like football.
>
> Certainly many Americans like football, but without specific data, it is impossible to know if football fans exceed half of the total population.
>
> *Rephrase*: Many Americans like football.

> A majority of the guests enjoyed the meal.
>
> Unless you know the specific number of guests who enjoyed the meal, you cannot assume that they number more than half, regardless of general impression.
>
> *Rephrase*: I believe a majority of the guests enjoyed the meal.

Redundant and Irrelevant Language

Good writing does not include information irrelevant to the topic of a sentence or paragraph. An effective paragraph conveys its information precisely and concisely. Many writers who strive to lengthen their work make the mistake of including redundant information. Consider the following paragraph:

> My first baseball game was *awesome* and *amazing*. My father bought us *third-row seats* along the first-base line *right by the wall*. I enjoyed all the action as I munched on nachos and a hotdog. *I like a lot of relish on my hotdogs*. Our team won the game, and I got to spend quality time with my dad. I would love to do it again.

Awesome and *amazing* are synonyms, meaning they have nearly the same meaning. One should be eliminated. *Third-row* means the *seats* are located near the wall at the edge of the field, making the phrase *right by the wall* unnecessary.

The sentence "*I like a lot of relish on my hot dogs.*" is irrelevant because the paragraph is about the writer's enjoyment of watching a baseball game, not the writer's choice of condiments.

Complete the following exercise to test your ability to write effective paragraphs.

Revising Paragraphs Exercise

Revise the following paragraph, paying attention to logical order of sentences and correcting mistakes, such as unclear pronouns, redundancy, and irrelevancy.

> While most varieties are native to warm tropical areas, orchids appear in every part of the world except Antarctica and dry desert areas. The orchid family comprises more species than any other family of flowering plants. Orchids even live beyond the Arctic Circle! The Arctic Circle is one of the major lines of latitude that divides the earth. Regardless of which side they're on, people seem powerfully drawn to the plants. Botanists, however, revere orchids for their highly evolved structures and physiology. Their diverse and beautiful flowers draw many people to collect the plants.

____

____

____

____

____

____

____

____

____

____

Possible Correction:

The orchid family comprises more species than any other family of flowering plants. Although most varieties are native to tropical areas, orchids appear in every part of the world except Antarctica and desert areas. Orchids even live beyond the Arctic Circle! Orchids' diverse and beautiful flowers draw many people to collect the plants. Botanists, however, revere orchids for their highly evolved structures and physiology. Regardless of which side they're on, people seem powerfully drawn to the plants.

The Relationship Between Paragraphs

Paragraphs must have a certain amount of independence from each other, yet they should have similar tone and style and provide the reader with a meaningful transition from one topic to the next.

For example, do not use a pronoun in one paragraph whose antecedent is in a previous paragraph, as shown next:

> ...John was an interesting fellow. I only knew him from one class in high school, but he instantly made an impression on me.
>
> The first time I met *him* was on the steps outside the building...

Replace *him* in the new paragraph with its antecedent, *John*.

Use "transition" words and phrases within and between paragraphs to introduce new topics or evidence. There are four basic categories of transition words. The following is a list of those categories along with some sample transition words:

- **Contrast:** but, however, on the other hand, conversely, alternatively, although, even though
- **Similarity:** likewise, similarly
- **Evidence:** since, because, in light of, first, second, third
- **Conclusion:** therefore, thus, as a result, so, it follows that, in conclusion

Observe how transition words are used to tie the following sentences and paragraphs together:

> Youth baseball pitchers are discouraged from practicing complicated pitches, *since* developing shoulders and elbows may not tolerate the powerful twisting and snapping action required to produce effective curveballs, screwballs, and the like. Little League Baseball, *however*, does not officially recognize any evidence that particular pitches lead to increased instances of injury *because* the only studies on the subject have been conducted with college-age or older pitchers.

On the other hand, evidence does exist that injury is minimized when the total number of pitches thrown by a young player is minimized. *As a result*, USA Baseball has issued recommendations for safe total-pitch counts according to player age.

Common Mistakes

Review these common errors that test takers make on the Language Arts, Writing Test essay. If you know what to avoid, you'll not only be a better writer, but you'll have a much easier time on the Language Arts, Writing multiple-choice test.

Too General

Effective writing uses specific examples. Think of the best teachers you have had. They tend to tell you the general concept that they are teaching and then give one or more specific, memorable examples. This strategy works because of the memorable examples.

If you are told that there is no progress without determination and hard work, you might accept the statement as true, and you may even remember it. However, you will have a much better chance of fully grasping the idea and remembering it later if you are given a specific example such as Thomas Edison, who tried thousands and thousands of different filament materials in his light bulbs before finally settling on one that gave acceptable light and lasted a reasonable period of time.

Too often, students make broad, general statements in their essays without giving any specific support. Make sure that you provide clear, simple examples of the general statements that you make.

Too Emotional and Opinionated

Although it is true that the stimulus will be asking you for an opinion, you should not make the entire essay about your feelings. You should state what your opinion is and then back up your opinion with well-reasoned logical support. Tell the reader *why* you feel the way you do rather than just telling *how* you feel.

For example, you should avoid a sentence such as "I think dress codes in schools is the worst idea in the world!" Instead, try "While some people believe that following a dress code will simplify a student's life, I disagree." Then, go on to offer examples of why you disagree.

Too Complicated

Many coaches and teachers have suggested that students apply the K.I.S.S. principle. Although a slightly less polite formulation exists, we'll explain K.I.S.S. as an acronym for "Keep It Short and Sweet." Do not use three words when one will do.

For example, write, "There are better proposals." Do not write, "I believe that I am correct when I state that the previously proposed solution to this complicated problem will be less than completely effective as compared to other potential solutions that have been brought forth recently."

The graders are not going to be blown away by your ability to use a dozen words to state a plain idea. They are going to be blown away if you are able to make your point cleanly and clearly. Furthermore, long, complicated sentences are more likely to contain errors.

Risky Vocabulary

If you are not sure what a word means, or whether it would be appropriate to your essay, don't use it. An otherwise good essay can be sunk by a word or two used incorrectly, which made the grader start to question the author's abilities.

For example, if you were grading an essay that contained the following sentence: "*High school students are often condemned for their kindness,*" you might know that the author meant to say, "*High school students are often commended for their kindness.*" As a grader, you would still have to note the error and take it into account in scoring the essay.

On the other hand, don't agonize over words while you write. The graders use the holistic method of judging an essay, which means they evaluate the entire essay as a whole. It is better to include a wrong word or two rather than write an incomplete essay because you have run out of time.

Poor Penmanship

As discussed in Chapter 11, "The GED Essay," the grader has to assign a score to your essay that depends on the grader's interpretation of the terms in the rubric (scoring guide). To help the grader interpret those terms in your favor when making judgment calls, you should write or print (depending on which will result in the most legible essay) as neatly as you can. Make it easy for the graders to find the good things about your essay that will allow them to give you all the points that your hard work deserves. Don't panic, however, because the essay readers will make a strong effort to interpret your penmanship.

Shaky Logic

The essay that you must write for the Language Arts, Writing Test is explanatory. It is an essay written with the purpose of describing something. The essay should have a conclusion about the topic and support for that conclusion.

Choose relevant examples that are connected to your topic in a direct way. One way to do this is to use examples that show a cause-effect relationship. For example, "*I really think I would enjoy teaching high school Spanish. Students are generally in a brighter mood in language classes. Happy students learn more, and through classroom learning they come to respect the teacher.*"

Although you may disagree with the conclusion of the preceding argument, the author clearly shows that there is a cause-effect connection between the evidence presented and the position that the author takes.

Unsafe Assumptions

There are two components to an assertion: evidence and conclusion.

Evidence leads to conclusions. You need at least two pieces of evidence to support one conclusion. So, if you only give one piece of evidence, you must be making an assumption. Logic professors refer to assumptions as "suppressed premises," which is just a fancy way to say "unstated evidence." If you leave too much of your evidence unstated, your argument starts to get weak.

For example, an essay states: "*Curfews are dangerous because what if I have to be somewhere after midnight?*" The reader immediately starts to wonder, "Where could you have to be so late? What would you be doing?" There are simply too many unanswered questions. If you happen to agree with the position that the writer is taking, you tend to "help" with the assumptions and provide your own examples and answers to the unanswered questions. You might read the previous statement and fill in an example from your own life or one that you would consider plausible. GED graders will not do that extra thinking work for you as they read your essay. You have to be aware of the completeness of your essay and try to minimize the unanswered questions.

Too Conversational

This essay is supposed to be an example of your command of Edited American English. Read the first sections of Chapter 7, "Overview of English Usage," and Chapter 8, "Grammar and Sentence Structure," for more information about why this is the case.

> **EXAM PREP Study TIP**
>
> When speaking, people tend to be more relaxed in their use of words, which can result in a blending of pronouns. You should avoid this in your writing. For example, if your essay starts out in the first person ("I"), stick to the first person throughout your essay.

Avoid the generic *you*: "*You could feel the tension in the room when Jeff had a pizza delivered to American History class.*" The pronoun does not actually mean "you, the reader." The person making that statement should have said, "*I could feel the tension…*" or "*We could all feel the tension…*"

In conversation we often try to be inclusive and gender neutral, although English has no third-person singular gender-neutral pronouns. *They*, *their*, *them*, and *theirs* must be used only as plurals in writing. Read more about choosing correct pronouns in Chapter 7.

The overall thing to keep in mind is that your essay needs to be a formal document. It is not appropriate to write in the same idiom that you use with friends in informal conversation.

Practicing Effective Writing

As noted earlier in this book, humans acquire skills through practice. Because the Language Arts, Writing Test Part II is a test of your writing skills, you should practice writing in order to score better. Specifically, you should practice the type of writing that is rewarded by the scoring rubric. The best way to make sure that you are on track is to have someone—whom you trust—with experience in this area give you specific feedback on the good and not-so-good parts of your practice essays. You can gain something by reading your own essays and comparing them to a rubric, but writers tend to develop blind spots when it comes to areas that need improvement in their own essays. It is always a good idea to get a fresh set of eyes to review your work. Anyone who has worked with high school teachers for any length of time can tell you that most of them would be delighted if a student came to them for help on a practice essay. It does not take long for an experienced grader to give feedback that can be immensely valuable to a student.

When assessing your own writing, set it aside for a day or two to regain some of the "freshness" of your perspective as a reader.

What's Next?

Chapter 10 introduces you to the mechanics of writing, including correct use of punctuation and capitalization. The GED will test your ability to apply these rules of grammar correctly.

CHAPTER TEN

Writing Mechanics

In speech, we use tone, pitch, loudness, and rhythm to guide the listener. These elements are unavailable to writers. Instead, spelling helps distinguish words from one other, and capitalization and punctuation help guide the reader through the information. Knowledge of these elements of mechanics will help you in the Language Arts, Writing Test.

Spelling

Although spelling is not directly tested on the GED, Part I of the Language Arts, Writing Test will assess your knowledge of possessives, homonyms, and contractions.

Read about forming possessives from nouns in Chapter 7, "Overview of English Usage."

Homonyms

For the purposes of the GED and this book, *homonyms* are words with different meanings that are pronounced the same, although not necessarily spelled the same. By this definition, a *homonym* ("same name") could also be called a *homophone* ("same sound"). It is important to note that because pronunciation varies regionally, some of these words may not be true homophones for you. Linguists often use the example of *marry*, *Mary*, and *merry*, which a great number of Americans pronounce exactly the same. Some speakers, such as natives of New York City, have a unique pronunciation of each of the three words.

Table 10.1 is a list, by no means exhaustive, of some of the most commonly confused English homonyms. Words can have many meanings beyond the common ones given here. Looking up words in the dictionary is a great way to boost your retention of vocabulary.

TABLE 10.1 Common Homonyms

Homonym	Meaning	Homonym	Meaning	Homonym	Meaning
accept	receive	**except**	excluding		
affect	produce change	**effect**	*(n.)*result; *(v.)*implement		
aisle	walkway	**isle**	island		
allowed	permitted	**aloud**	audible		
altar	raised platform in a church	**alter**	modify		
ate	past form of "eat"	**eight**	the number 8		
ball	round object	**bawl**	cry		
bear	large, furry mammal	**bare**	naked		
base	bottom	**bass**	a type of stringed musical instrument; low pitch		
billed	past form of "bill"	**build**	construct		
blew	past form of "blow"	**blue**	a type of color		
board	flat piece of wood	**bored**	not entertained		
brake	stop a car	**break**	fracture; pause in work		
buy	purchase	**by**	preposition with many usages	**bye**	goodbye
capital	investment money; city housing a government	**Capitol**	the building where the U.S. Congress meets		
cell	prison chamber; basic unit of life	**sell**	exchange for money		
cent	1/100th of a dollar	**scent**	aroma	**sent**	past form of "send"
chance	opportunity; luck	**chants**	songs		
chews	present form of "chew"	**choose**	select		
close	shut	**clothes**	clothing		
coarse	rough	**course**	class in school; path for racing		
creak	squeak	**creek**	small river		
days	periods of 24 hours	**daze**	confusion		
dear	cherished	**deer**	hoofed woodland mammal		
dew	water droplets	**do**	perform an action	**due**	owed

TABLE 10.1 *Continued*

Homonym	Meaning	Homonym	Meaning	Homonym	Meaning
facts	truths	**fax**	document sent via phone line		
fair	*(adj.)* equitable; *(n.)* festival	**fare**	price of a travel ticket		
fairy	mythical being, usually having magical powers	**ferry**	boat for passengers and/or cars		
find	locate	**fined**	penalized financially		
flour	baking ingredient	**flower**	*(n.)* reproductive part of a plant *(v.)* flourish		
for	preposition with many usages	**four**	the number 4	**fore**	at the front; verbal warning in golf
foreword	statement at the beginning of a book	**forward**	toward the front		
gene	division of DNA	**jean**	denim pant		
grease	slippery substance	**Greece**	European country		
groan	expression of disapproval	**grown**	past form of "grow"		
hair	outgrowth of the skin	**hare**	An animal similar to a rabbit		
hay	dry grass	**hey**	attention-getting interjection		
heal	repair a wound	**heel**	back of the foot		
hear	sense with the ears	**here**	in the present location		
hi	short for "hello"	**high**	elevated		
hoarse	having a raspy voice	**horse**	large hoofed mammal		
hole	empty space	**whole**	entire		
hour	60 minutes	**our**	belonging to us		
its	third-person possessive and possessive pronoun	**it's**	contraction of "it is"		
knight	medieval soldier on horseback	**night**	last part of the day		
knot	tie a rope	**not**	word of negation		
know	understand	**no**	word of rejection		
leased	rented	**least**	most minor		

(continues)

TABLE 10.1 *Continued*

Homonym	Meaning	Homonym	Meaning	Homonym	Meaning
loan	borrowed money	**lone**	only		
made	past form of "make"	**maid**	house cleaner		
mail	letters and packages	**male**	belonging to the masculine gender		
marry	wed	**Mary**	woman's first name	**merry**	happy
meat	flesh	**meet**	join; become acquainted		
mince	cut into very small bits	**mints**	breath-freshening candies		
missed	past form of "miss"	**mist**	fine spray		
morning	first part of the day	**mourning**	state of sorrow		
none	not one	**nun**	woman in a religious order		
one	the number 1	**won**	past form of "win"		
pail	bucket	**pale**	lacking color		
pear	a type of tree fruit	**pair**	two things grouped together	**pare**	remove in layers
patience	willingness to wait	**patients**	customers of a doctor		
piece	part	**peace**	lack of conflict		
plain	simple	**plane**	*(adj.)* flat; *(v.)* scrape flat; *(n.)* wood-shaving tool; *(n.)* short for "airplane"		
rain	liquid precipitation	**reign**	have power		
read	past form of "read"	**red**	a type of color		
right	correct; the direction of east when facing north	**write**	put words on paper		
road	path for automobiles	**rode**	past form of "ride"		
rose	a type of flower	**rows**	horizontal lines of objects; present form of "row"		
sail	*(n.)* sheet of cloth for catching wind; *(v.)* operate a sailboat	**sale**	transaction; period of reduced prices		

TABLE 10.1 *Continued*

Homonym	Meaning	Homonym	Meaning	Homonym	Meaning
scene	segment of an act in drama; situation	**seen**	past form of "see"		
sea	large body of water	**see**	sense with the eyes		
sew	stitch with thread	**so**	*(adv.)* very; cause-effect subordinating conjunction	**sow**	plant seeds
sole	single	**soul**	spirit		
son	male offspring	**sun**	star in the solar system		
stair	step for moving up or down	**stare**	look in a single direction		
steal	take without paying	**steel**	alloy of metals		
suite	ensemble of pieces of music; luxury hotel room	**sweet**	tasting of sugar		
their	third-person plural possessive	**there**	in an indicated location	**they're**	contraction of "they are"
threw	past form of "throw"	**through**	preposition with many usages		
to	preposition with many uses	**too**	in addition; exceedingly	**two**	the number 2
vary	change	**very**	to a high degree		
waist	area of the body around the hipbones	**waste**	undesirable byproducts		
wait	be in anticipation	**weight**	massiveness		
war	armed conflict	**wore**	past form of "wear"		
wear	put on the body	**where**	question-word of location	**ware**	article or good for sale
weak	lacking strength	**week**	7 days		
weather	atmospheric effects on earth	**whether**	Conjunction introducing alternatives		
which	question-word for choosing from a group; introduces modifier clauses	**witch**	magic woman		
wood	tree material	**would**	element for forming the conditional		
yore	times past	**your**	second-person possessive	**you're**	contraction of "you are"

Contractions

Contractions are formed by combining a noun or pronoun with a small, frequently used word. Forming contractions is possible only in specific cases, as shown next:

- Contraction with "am"

  I'm hungry.

- Contractions with "is"

  He's eating spaghetti.

  She's painting a waterfall.

  It's cold outside.

  Most singular nouns (third person): Mike's going crazy; The *subway's* closing at midnight tonight.

- Because contractions are motivated by the tendency to shorten common verb constructions, no contraction should be used that creates an awkward pronunciation or that is very close to the pronunciation of the component words themselves. Consider the following example:

  "The class's going to the art museum" is better as *"The class is going…* " (When in doubt, spell it out.)

- Contractions with "are"

  We're going to the mall.

  You're beautiful.

  They're too smart for their own good.

- Contractions with "not"

  Bob *can't* swim.

  I *couldn't* wash the car today.

  You *haven't* vacuumed the rug yet.

  Martha *hadn't* been able to run since her injury.

  Shouldn't you be studying tonight?

  I *wouldn't* pay that much for shoes.

  Won't you sing with me? ("will not")

  Isn't love grand?

  There *aren't* enough hours in the day.

  Bob *wasn't* eager to leave the party.

  You *weren't* happy to see your brother.

  This train *mustn't* stop.

- Contractions with the auxiliary verb "have" in present perfect or present continuous tense constructions (American English does not use contractions when "have" is the main verb.)

  I've been to Paris twice.

  You've asked me that question before.

  We've finally come to a conclusion

  They've forgotten all about us.

- Contractions with the auxiliary verb "has" in present perfect or present continuous tense constructions (American English does not use contractions when "has" is the main verb.)

  He's seen a lot of movies.

  She's been hollering all night.

  It's grown several feet this year.

  many singular nouns (third person): see "Contractions with is'" earlier.

- Contractions with auxiliary verb "had" in past perfect or past progressive tense constructions (American English does not use contractions when "had" is the main verb.)

  I'd locked the door before he could get in.

  You'd better turn on Channel 2.

  He'd been working as a janitor before his promotion.

  She'd been baking cookies since 9 a.m.

  We'd just finished pitching the tent when the rain started.

  They'd loaded the bases before the left fielder hit his double.

- Contractions with conditional element "would" or habitual past form with "would"

  I'd watch out for pickpockets on the subway if I were you.

  You'd take Joe's place in the event that he cannot attend.

  He'd ascend to stardom before age 8.

  She'd use a stool to reach the cupboards before she was tall enough.

  We'd sing songs every year at camp.

  They'd like an order of hot wings.

Using contractions is best avoided in formal writing, but you need to understand them to make sentence corrections in Part I of the Language Arts, Writing Test.

Capitalization

You will be tested directly on correct capitalization on the GED Writing Test, Part I. Following are some of the specific capitalization conventions that you should expect to be tested on.

Proper Names

Proper names are always capitalized. These are things called by a given name.

Following are examples of proper names:

- Lieutenant Commander Bobby Hernandez (people and their titles)
- Fido (pets)
- the *Titanic* (boats and ships—note that the names of ships are italicized when typed or underlined when written)
- the Louvre (buildings)
- Toronto, Ontario, Canada (cities, provinces/states/territories, countries)
- Japanese (languages and nationalities)
- *Of Mice and Men* (novels—note also that only the first and other significant words in titles are capitalized, and the whole title is italicized when typed or underlined when written)
- Market Street Bistro (businesses)
- Death Valley (specific geographic features/regions)
- Thursday, January 4, 2018 A.D. (days of the week, months, the abbreviations A.D. and B.C.)
- the Civil War (historical events)
- the Middle Ages (historical periods)
- New Year's Eve (holidays)
- Although not always proper names, acronyms are capitalized.

  CPR (cardiopulmonary resuscitation), AIDS (acquired immunodeficiency syndrome), NASA (National Aeronautics and Space Administration)

Be careful with family members, as shown in the following examples:

- Lowercase: "*I went sailing with my mom and dad last year.*"
- Capitalized: "*I went sailing with Mom and Dad last year.*"

In the first sentence, *mom* and *dad* are used as occupations because they are preceded by the possessive determiner *my*. In the second sentence, *Mom* and *Dad* are used as proper names.

Punctuation

At the very least, every sentence has end punctuation. This is either a period (.), a question mark (?), or an exclamation point (!). Other punctuation marks are used within sentences, as shown in the following sections.

The punctuation marks included in Table 10.2 are important to understand for essay writing. Other symbols exist, especially for use in mathematics or technical writing, but you are not expected to use them in either part of the Language Arts, Writing Test.

TABLE 10.2 Punctuation

.	period
?	question mark
!	exclamation point
,	comma
'	apostrophe
" "	double quotation marks
' '	single quotation marks
/	slash
( )	parentheses
:	colon
;	semicolon
...	ellipsis
-	hyphen
—	dash

Comma ,

The comma is used to divide specific units of meaning in the sentence. Some people find it helpful to think of the comma as a pause during reading, but it is important to remember that some sentences are better read without a clear pause, in spite of any intervening comma they may have. Remember that the comma must never be used to separate verbs from their constituents. Read about verb constituency in Chapter 8, "Grammar and Sentence Structure."

Following are examples of the proper use of commas:

- With coordinating conjunctions

  I would love to go to dinner, but I just ate.

  The travel agent confirmed our flight today, yet I feel something will go wrong with the reservation.

- After introductory clauses

  As the team captain, Kate knew how to motivate the other players.

  Whether in the United States or Canada, everyone should visit the Rocky Mountains.

- To set off nonrestrictive descriptive detail

  George Washington, the first U.S. president, led the fight against the British.

  Llullaillaco, the tallest of Argentina's volcanoes, last erupted in 1877.

- To set off transitional or parenthetical phrases

  That rope, in my opinion, is very strong.

  The new model, of course, is more expensive than the last one.

- To divide three or more items in a list

  When you go to the store, be sure to pick up eggs, flour, and ice cream.

  Cows, sheep, and chickens are important farm animals.

- With place names, dates, times, and numerals one thousand and greater

  Your cruise for two to London, England, departs June 20, 2008, at 4:30 PM.

  Payment of $132,642 is due within 30 days.

- With quotations

  Joe cried out, "How could you do such a thing?"

  "It was easy," Bob replied, "no thanks to you."

- To set off interjections

  Wow, that's a big fish!

  Darn, I had no idea that the store was closed.

Because you are more likely to be tested on correct comma placement than any other form of punctuation, we have included the following exercise.

Comma Exercise

Add the commas that are missing in the following sentences.

Example: Because of her experience Traci was elected class president.

Solution: Because of her experience, Traci was elected class president.

1. If you start a small restaurant be sure to consult with experts in commercial kitchen appliances sanitation and menu planning.
2. General Lee a commander of Confederate troops during the Civil War lost more than 10000 men at the Battle of Antietam.
3. The boat I believe is still under repair so we will have to wait to hear from the mechanic.
4. I was born in the small town of Clio Michigan December 2 1983.
5. Seeing the mess his son was making Richard called out to him "Stop smearing the spaghetti all over the table!"

Answers:

1. If you start a small restaurant, be sure to consult with experts in commercial kitchen appliances, sanitation, and menu planning.
2. General Lee, a commander of Confederate troops during the Civil War, lost more than 10,000 men at the Battle of Antietam.
3. The boat, I believe, is still under repair, so we will have to wait to hear from the mechanic.
4. I was born in the small town of Clio, Michigan, December 2, 1983.
5. Seeing the mess his son was making, Richard called out to him, "Stop smearing the spaghetti all over the table!"

Apostrophe '

Apostrophes are used to show missing letters in contractions and to create possessive forms of a word. Do not freely use the apostrophe with *s* to create plurals! The only widely accepted usages of the apostrophe to make plurals are with numerals and letters, as shown next:

- *Once you count off, the 1's meet here and the 2's meet across the hall.*
- *Be sure to cross your t's and dot your i's.*

Quotation Marks

Quotations marks have several uses, as shown next. Remember, in Edited American English, commas and periods go inside quotation marks, and semicolons and colons go outside, regardless of the punctuation in the original quotation. Question marks and exclamation points depend on whether the question or exclamation is part of the quotation or part of the sentence containing the quotation.

Double Quotation Marks ""

Double quotation marks are used to enclose a direct quotation, as in the following example:

Bob replied, "I don't have a sister!"

They are also used to mark a word as unusual, slangy, technical, foreign, and so on or to refer to the word itself, not the concept behind it, as shown next:

The first bicycle was known as a "velocipede."

Use double quotation marks to enclose titles, as shown next:

- Newspaper, magazine, and encyclopedia articles

  "Burst Water Main Creates Massive Sinkhole" by David Jones

- Television episodes

  The pilot episode of <u>Star Trek: The Next Generation</u> is called "Encounter at Farpoint."

- Poems

  "The Wreck of the Hesperus" by Henry Wadsworth Longfellow

- Essays

  "Here is New York" by E. B. White

- Short stories

  "The Tell-Tale Heart" by Edgar Allan Poe

- Plays of fewer than three acts

  "No Exit" by Jean-Paul Sartre

- Songs

  "The Battle Hymn of the Republic"

- Chapters within books

  "Common Household Stain Removers" on page 77

- Short musical compositions

  "Prelude Op. 28, No. 2" by Frederic Chopin

Single Quotation Marks ''

Use single quotation marks to perform any other functions of double quotation marks with words or phrases enclosed in double quotation marks, as in the following example:

> *"Do you know what he said to me?" Roger asked. "He said, 'You wash dishes too slowly.' Such nerve he has!"*

Parentheses ()

Use parentheses to enclose explanatory or secondary supporting details or inessential information, as shown next:

> *In addition to serving as class treasurer (during her junior year), she was also a National Merit Scholar.*
>
> *Alan visited the Football Hall of Fame (Canton, Ohio) during his summer vacation.*

Colon :

The colon has several functions, as shown next:

Use a colon to introduce a list:

We are required to bring the following items to camp: a sleeping bag, a pillow, an alarm clock, clothes, and personal care items.

Use a colon to introduce modifier information immediately after an independent clause:

Jennifer encountered a problem that she had not anticipated: a broken Internet link.

My sister suggested a great location: the park down the street from our house.

Use a colon to introduce direct quotations:

Captain John Paul Jones said: "I have not yet begun to fight."

Use a colon to end salutations in business correspondence:

Dear Mr. Smith:

Use a colon to introduce a subtitle:

Blaze: A Story of Courage

Semicolon ;

In Edited American English, the semicolon has two distinct purposes: to join two related independent clauses and to separate items in a list, as outlined next:

Use a semicolon to join closely related independent clauses when a coordinate conjunction is not used:

Jane starts a new job today; she is very excited.

I don't understand the directions; my teacher must explain them to me.

Use a semicolon with conjunctive adverbs to join independent clauses:

Skippy is interested in taking the class; however, it does not fit in his schedule.

My brother is very tall; in fact, he is the tallest person in our family.

Use a semicolon to separate coordinate ("equal") clauses when they are joined by transitional words or phrases:

My sister and I enjoyed the play; afterwards, we stopped for an ice cream cone.

(Compare with *My sister and I enjoyed the play, and afterwards, we stopped for an ice cream cone.*)

Betty often misplaces her keys; perhaps she should get a key locator.

(Compare with *Betty often misplaces her key, so perhaps she should get a key locator.*)

Use a semicolon to separate items that contain commas and are arranged in series:

The art museum contained some beautiful, old oil paintings; bronze, plaster, and marble statues; and colorful, abstract modern-art pieces.

My first meal at college consisted of cold, dry toast; runny, undercooked eggs; and very strong, acidic coffee.

Ellipsis ...

Use an ellipsis to indicate that a quotation has been abbreviated, as in the following example:

The Second Amendment to the U.S. Constitution says that "...the right...to keep and bear arms shall not be infringed."

Note that it is never appropriate to use the ellipsis when it would change the meaning of a quotation, as shown next:

John wished there was something he could do for the war and *John wished...for the war.*

Hyphen -

Writers often confuse the hyphen with the dash (the dash is wider/longer). Following are the appropriate uses of a hyphen:

Use a hyphen with compound modifiers, except those with *very* or *-ly* adverbs, that appear in adjective position before a noun:

Matt was a cold-hearted man.

John is a Chinese-American.

Use a hyphen with two-word names of numbers less than 99 and fractions:

What is two-thirds of two hundred twenty-eight?

Use a hyphen with prefixes that are used with new words or when a sound in a prefix would seem to make a different sound in combination with the start of the root:

After the inspection, I had to re-sandblast the beams.

I buy my produce from a growers' co-operative.

Use a hyphen to prevent a word with a prefix from being interpreted as a different word:

My favorite form of recreation is participating in Civil War re-creations.

Use a hyphen with people's compound last names:

Please welcome our speaker, Dr. Evelyn Jones-Whitman.

Use a hyphen to indicate spelling out loud or slow, deliberate pronunciation of a word:

I finally remembered how to spell that smelly black stuff: a-s-p-h-a-l-t.

John strained staring through his thick lenses, "Ka-la-ma-zoo-- Kalamazoo! We're almost there!"

Use a hyphen to show a strong link between two words or phrases (the slash (/) is also used this way):

Every American should read some of the Abraham Lincoln-Stephen Douglas debates.

Use a hyphen to connect numbers and words:

I will need a 40-foot ladder to complete this one-day paint job.

Dash —

Use a dash to mark a sudden break in thought or speech:

I feel a little drip—oh no, a pipe burst!

Also use a dash to set off parenthetical information with greater emphasis than when using parentheses:

Dr. Evans—a noted scientist and educator—spoke at our commencement ceremony.

The Homecoming float—cobbled together with wire and nails—teetered dangerously down the street.

Underline Versus Italics

In today's world of computers, italics (*slanted type like this*) has almost totally replaced the typographic function of the underline. Because italics cannot be easily done with handwriting (what you are expected to do for the GED essay), the underline must be used instead.

The following should be italicized in print and underlined when handwritten or typed on a device that cannot make italics:

Titles of major creative works and publications (see exceptions in "Double quotation marks usage" in this section), most often the following:

- Books

  <u>Catch-22</u> by Joseph Heller

- Movies

  <u>Apocalypse Now</u>, directed by Francis Ford Coppola

- Magazines/Journals

  Newsweek, published by Washington Post Company

  The Lancet, a British medical journal

- Newspapers

  USA Today, published by Gannett

- Musical compositions

  Beethoven's Ode to Joy

  Ballets, operas, plays of more than three acts, etc.

  Tchaikovsky's Swan Lake

- Musical albums

  Abbey Road by The Beatles

- Works of art

  The Last Supper by Leonardo da Vinci

- Websites

  Google

- Names of ships:

  Space Shuttle Challenger

  U.S. Navy aircraft carrier USS Ronald Reagan

- Foreign words (if you want, you can use double quotation marks instead):

  Michael is a baker par excellence.

  Before long, the big bowl of spaghetti was finito.

  The word cul-de-sac comes from the French, meaning "bottom of the bag."

- Words or phrases you want to emphasize:

  There's no way I'll be seen driving that car!

What's Next?

Chapter 11, "The GED Essay," reviews the skills necessary to write a successful GED essay, and includes the steps to writing well under timed conditions. You will also see some sample essay responses, both good and bad, so that you can learn what works and what to avoid in your writing.

11

CHAPTER ELEVEN

The GED Essay

As soon as you complete the Language Arts, Writing Test Part I, you may move on to Part II, the essay, even if time remains for Part I. If you are satisfied with your essay and time remains for it, you may work again on Part I until time expires. Unless you consistently finish Part I early on practice tests, you should count on only the allotted 45 minutes to plan, write, and review your essay.

The Essay Prompt

You are required to plan and write an explanatory essay on a given topic, called the prompt.

A GED essay prompt looks like this:

> **Writing, Part II**
>
> **Topic B**
>
> Skills can change over a period of time.
>
> Identify an important skill you have now but did not have in the past. Explain how you gained the skill and why it is important to you. Use your personal observations, experience, and knowledge to support your answer.
>
> Part II is a test to determine how well you can use written language to explain your ideas.
>
> In preparing your essay, you should take the following steps.
>
> 1. Read the **DIRECTIONS** and the **TOPIC** carefully.
> 2. Plan your essay before you write. Use the scratch paper provided to make any notes. These notes will be collected but not scored.
> 3. Before you turn in your essay, reread what you have written and make any changes that will improve your essay.
>
> Your essay should be long enough to develop the topic adequately.

Your GED essay topic will address a common issue nearly every adult can speak or write about, so it requires no special knowledge. Remember that writing is a skill that can be practiced and improved!

Time is rarely a problem for most students, and space is almost never a problem. (If you start to run out of space on this test, you are writing too much! The graders are not looking for long answers; they are looking for quality answers.)

Your Essay Score

Your essay (Language Arts, Writing Test Part II) is scored on a 1-point through 4-point scale. Two professional, trained readers will evaluate your answer, and each of them will assign a point value of 1 (worst) through 4 (best); the two scores are then averaged. If the two readers assign scores that differ by more than one point, a chief reader will be called in to read your essay and make the final decision regarding your score.

The scores are holistic scores, which means that your essay is judged as a whole without assigning point values to the specific characteristics that the graders are looking for.

Essay readers look for the following:

- Well-focused main points
- Clear organization
- Specific development of ideas
- Good sentence structure, punctuation, grammar, word choice, and spelling

The most important thing to know about this essay is that *there is no correct answer*! The readers are looking at the essay as an example of your ability to write a clear, concise piece. *Do not waste time* by trying to figure out what the test writers would prefer to read.

The GED graders use something called a *rubric* when assigning scores to essays. Basically, a rubric is a checklist of characteristics that the grader is supposed to look for when reading your essay. If your essay is more like the one described in the rubric as being a 4 than a 3, the grader will assign your essay a 4. The rubric that the graders use is public information at this point. It is posted on the GED website and in the official publications. They are not keeping the grading system a secret.

Because everyone knows what is expected, and there is virtually no chance that the grader will know the person who wrote a given essay, the system is reasonably fair. The following is a general overview of the scoring rubric:

- **Level 4**—The essay is *effective*. It has a focused main idea and is logical and well organized. There are good transitions and very little, or no, irrelevant information. There is a solid introduction and conclusion that are consistent with each other and with the idea presented. While there may be a few errors, they are minor and infrequent. Control of the conventions of Edited American English is nearly perfect. Vocabulary is effective, appropriate, and varied. The reader follows and understands the expression of ideas in the essay.

- **Level 3**—The essay is *adequate*. It has a focused main idea and is logical and well organized. Development of ideas may be uneven. Conventions of Edited American English are generally correct; any errors do not interfere with comprehension.
- **Level 2**—The essay is *marginal*. It addresses the prompt, but may lack detail or stray from the main idea. Organization may be limited to listing or repetition. Word choice is generally narrow, and some words may be used incorrectly. Control of Edited American English is inconsistent. All these factors interfere with the reader's comprehension of the ideas in the essay.
- **Level 1**—The essay is *inadequate*. It lacks a main idea, although it may address the prompt. There is little or no organization and possibly some irrelevant information. Word choice is limited, and some words are used incorrectly. Control of Edited American English is poor. The reader has difficult following the ideas in the essay.

Note that neatness is not specifically mentioned. It may have an impact on the graders, though, as they assign a score to your essay. Make it easy on your grader to interpret subtleties in your writing in your favor. Remember that they have probably read hundreds of these essays before, so don't make it any harder on them to figure out your handwriting. There is nothing in the rules that prevents you from printing rather than writing in cursive. So, if your printing will be easier for graders and admissions officials to read, then by all means, print. Furthermore, you must write the GED essay in pen, so avoid scribbling out a lot of words.

Interpreting Your Score

Suffice it to say that a score of 1 or a 2 usually indicates to graders and evaluators that the person who wrote the essay either did not put forth a reasonable effort or is probably lacking even basic writing skills. A 3 or 4 score means that the grader sees solid basic writing skills.

Keep in mind that the scores that are assigned by the graders are based on the essay only. The graders do not get to see your Part I scores. They just assign a point value to the essay and move on to the next one. They are not making comments on your worth as a human being or even your intelligence or ability. They are just giving feedback regarding how the essay stacks up to the rubric.

GED will report your Language Arts, Writing Test score as a statistical combination of your scores on Parts I and II. Part II, the essay, makes up about 40% of this combination, although this is subject to change because of statistical norming, the process of making sure each GED can compare as closely as possible to other GEDs. Like the other subject tests, the combined score is between 200 and 800.

Skills Measured

This part of the GED is designed to measure your writing skills. The graders will reward you with more points if you stay focused on your main idea throughout your essay and back up your position by giving examples and information that are specific. You will certainly do well if you have a clear, logical structure and if your language is correct and free of errors in grammar or vocabulary. Don't take any vocabulary risks when writing this essay. If you are not sure what a word means, don't use it. It should go without saying, but remember that you should not fill your essay with vernacular, slang, jargon, or profanity.

There is a big overlap between Part I and Part II of the Language Arts, Writing Test. If you can recognize proper English and point out common errors on the multiple-choice portion, you should be able to avoid making those same errors on the essay. Refer to Chapter 7, "Overview of English Usage," Chapter 8, "Grammar and Sentence Structure," Chapter 9, "Effective Writing," and Chapter 10, "Writing Mechanics," for a review of the proper usage of Edited American English.

The Writing Process

After completing Part I of the Writing Test, you are likely to be somewhat tired. Try to focus on the fact that you are almost finished, and do what you can to keep your focus for the 45 minutes of writing time. Both parts of the Language Arts, Writing Test must be passed together, or you will need to retake both parts. A passing score on the essay is 2 or better. If you score below 2, your score will be reported as two asterisks, indicating you have not passed the GED essay.

You will be given some scratch paper for this part of the GED. In the section "Step 3: Plan Your Essay" later in the chapter we'll discuss some specific ideas for the best way to use it. Be certain that you do use it. This is not the time to just jump in and start writing a stream-of-consciousness, shoot-from-the-hip answer off the top of your head. You might not have time to do a full first and second draft of this essay. However, you should make use of the time that is given to you to be sure that you plan what you are going to say before you actually start writing your final answer.

On the GED Language Arts, Writing Test Part II, you will have two pages of lined answer space on which you are to confine your essay. It may not sound like a lot of space, but the students who write the most and complain about not having enough room to finish are usually spending too much time on irrelevant discussion or have needless repetition in their answers. You may use an ink pen only, which the testing center supplies. No pencils are allowed.

Steps to Writing Well

There are concrete steps that are likely to result in the best essay possible in such a short period of time. The steps are laid out so that you can perform them one at a time. This is not the time for "multitasking." If you read the prompt and then try to write your answer out from the beginning to the end on the lined pages, you will certainly be doing several tasks at once. You create the logical structure of your essay at the same time as you search your memory for useful vocabulary and relevant examples, all the while trying to apply the rules of grammar, punctuation, and spelling correctly. In short, those students who try to write without planning are setting themselves up for a score that is less than their potential because they try to do too many things simultaneously. Follow these steps to write an effective essay:

1. Read the prompt.
2. Think.
3. Plan your essay.
4. Write your essay on the answer pages.

A more detailed discussion of each step follows.

Step 1: Read the Prompt

It's okay to read it over more than once to be certain that you understand what you are reading. Use your scratch paper to write some initial thoughts you might have on the topic. The stimulus is short, so reading carefully will not take up much of your time; however, it may save you from making a mistake in responding to the prompt.

You must know what the task is before you begin. Rushing through this step can cost valuable points and make some of your hard work worthless.

One or two minutes will probably be sufficient time to read the prompt carefully.

Step 2: Think

If the topic is something that you have thought about or discussed in the past, you might already have something to write about. If not, take a short time to formulate your evidence. That is what these essays are really all about: supporting what you say. That is why there is really no correct or incorrect essay. The truth is that anything can be supported with evidence. The test writers are careful to choose topics that are very broad and can be addressed successfully by all test takers. Remember that one of the criteria of the grading rubric is how clearly you present your views. This is not the time to be overly diplomatic. Take a side and support it.

This thinking process should not take very long, a few minutes at most.

Step 3: Plan Your Essay

Your essay should start out with a clear statement of your opinion on the issue. From the beginning of your essay, there should be no doubt in the reader's mind about what your overall view is. You should use the scratch paper that is provided to outline the structure of your essay.

There is an old saying about effective essays: "Tell them what you are going to tell them. Tell them. Then, tell them what you have told them." In other words, you should have a clear introduction, a body, and a conclusion that echoes the introduction. You may choose to do a traditional five-paragraph essay, but it is possible to produce a very effective essay with more paragraphs or fewer.

Your outline does not have to include complete sentences. It does have to include the ideas that you will put into your final draft. You need to be sure that you have a clear picture of where you are going and how you will get there before you start to write on the answer pages.

After compiling a list of thoughts on the topic, many test takers use a cluster diagram, which is a visual representation of how details are used to support a main idea. Figure 11.1 shows an example of a cluster diagram used to plan an essay about technology.

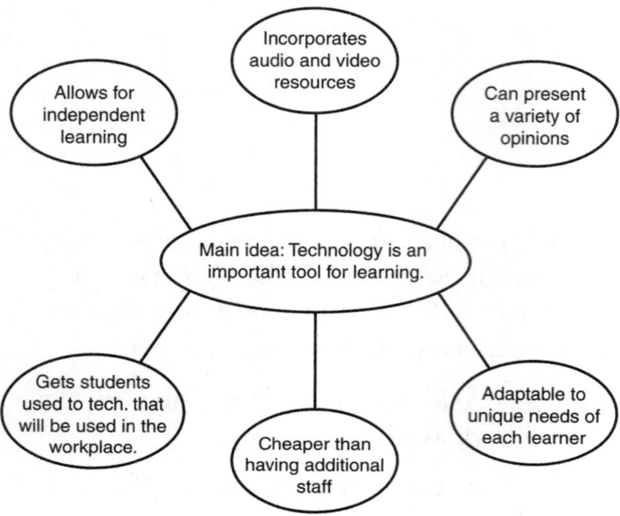

FIGURE 11.1 A cluster diagram.

In a cluster diagram, supporting details are linked to the central idea. If you plan your specific evidence, each item would appear as a bubble attached to the statements that surround the main idea. This task is sometimes called *webbing* because the result is something that resembles a web with lines radiating from the center.

Each bubble represents a distinct idea that could stand alone in a paragraph. Think about which bubble contains your strongest reasoning, or the idea that you can most easily write about. By prioritizing your reasoning and examples, you are better prepared to leave out some examples if you run short on time.

EXAM PREP Study TIP

The planning stage is the most important stage. Even if you spend more than 15 minutes on this stage, you will probably still be able to finish on time and your essay will certainly be better than if you had simply started writing your thoughts with no planning.

On test day, you will hear some of the other test-takers around you scratching furiously with their pens from the beginning of the 45-minute period. Sometimes that sound can make you feel like you are getting behind. You are not. Forty-five minutes is a long time to write two to four pages on a one-paragraph prompt.

Step 4: Write Your Essay on the Answer Pages

Be sure to make your views clear and support them with evidence. Apply the characteristics of effective writing covered in Chapter 9 and avoid the common mistakes mentioned in that chapter.

Remember that the completeness of your essay is important. Before beginning a new example or argument, consider whether you have at least 5 to 10 minutes to write your conclusion and review your essay for major errors.

Reasons to Write

The point of writing is to convey information to a reader for entertainment, persuasion, instruction, or some other purpose. Imagine all the different kinds of writers: novelists, reporters, essayists, philosophers, and so on. Each writer has a specific purpose and an intended audience. A writer must seriously consider whether the piece of writing is supposed to entertain, convince, teach, and so on. For example, articles that appear in scholarly journals are written for other scholars to read. They are highly technical and include vocabulary that untrained individuals would not understand. By speaking to the author of a scholarly article, a reporter could decipher exactly why the information in the article might have implications for a much more general audience. The reporter could then restate the information in the article in a plainer, more concise form that is accessible to the general public. This is an instance of preparing information differently according to the intended audience.

For the GED, you should assume you are addressing a very general audience. This means you should not assume the reader is more or less intelligent or educated than you. Similarly, you should not assume the reader would understand certain terms and concepts you think are not widely known across American English-speaking cultures. For example, do not include a sentence like "I enjoy warm sopapillas" without explaining what a *sopapilla* is (a Latin American deep-fried pastry).

Revision and Editing

You will probably have little time to read over your essay, so do not expect to be able to catch each of your mistakes. Errors in mechanics (see Chapter 10) should be fixed, but not at the expense of correcting faults of logical reasoning or gaps in support for your opinions. Remember that grading on the GED essay is holistic, meaning the readers take your essay as a whole and do not deduct from your score for each relatively minor mistake. If your essay fails on a conceptual level, though, your score will suffer. Take care of your logic and evidence errors first, and then change spelling, punctuation, and grammar. Do this neatly, with a minimum of scratch-outs. To eliminate something that you have written, draw a single line through it. Do not make a big blue or black patch over each word.

Example Essays

The following is a sample essay prompt and examples of essays representing each level of the scoring rubric:

Is technology important as a teaching tool?

> In your essay, identify whether you think technology is important as a teaching tool. Explain how students do or do not benefit from it. Use your personal observations, experience, and knowledge to support your essay.

The following sections contain example essays at each of the four scoring levels as well as analysis of why each scored at that level.

Example Essay, Score 1

Of course we should have computers in classrooms. Computers are everywhere now. Kid might play games sometimes or whatever but so what? Kids will always find a way to waste time. Sometimes, I read magazines, in class, anyway, but I still learned. Everyone knows that computers are everywhere now and you can't really get a job without knowing how to work one. I don't think that we should go without computers just because they pay teachers too much or waste money on other things like cheerleading outfits and that kinds of stuff. Other schools have computers and its not fair if everyone don't have them just because they are rich!!

This essay scores a 1 because it demonstrates very little understanding of the task. The author assumes that computers and technology are the same thing and fails to consider that classrooms can have technology without having computers. There are several distracting grammatical errors, and the discussion is focused on irrelevant personal details. There are some interesting points raised, such as equality of opportunity and budget priorities, but they are not developed at all. Overall, this essay is poor.

Example Essay, Score 2

I think that technology would help to get students to use computers more for research and to send e-mails to teachers. Information is everywhere on the Internet now. I used a web sight to write a report for work and my boss liked it. Bad students might use technology for cheating but the teachers can catch them right away if they use the technology too. If I am going to use computers and the Internet all the time in college anyway, we may as well get started now so that we now how to do it right and get good grades in college so we can get good jobs later in life. Isn't that the point of school anyway? So we can get ready for our jobs? I think so and so do my parents and I'm sure that they agree that we should have internet computers in class. If we don't, then what are we going to do? Just work out of books like my grandma did? And do work on the board? I don't think that is the best way to learn about how to survive in the modern world. And, that is what the schools should do for us all!

This essay scores a 2 because it shows some skill in responding to the prompt. There is a clear point of view, and it is supported by examples. This essay does consider counter arguments. However, it includes irrelevant information and some grammar and punctuation issues. The essay does a fairly good job of responding to counter arguments and has some structure. However, the essay leaves most of its potential undeveloped, and the conclusion does not effectively respond to the prompt or tie in to the author's main point. There is also a good deal of pronoun ambiguity. This is an example of a low average essay.

Example Essay, Score 3

I believe that bringing technology in the classroom would be in the best interests of the students and the teachers also. Teachers would find ways to use computers and the Internet to help students in many ways.

First, teachers can use the Web to show students web sites to help teach important subjects that are not in our books yet. A lot of information that is newer can only be found on the web. For example, there are web sites that show pictures of Mars from NASA that are so new that they aren't in any of our books. They are interesting and can get students excited to learn more. If a classroom didn't have Internet access, they might not get to see the pictures at all.

Second, technology can save steps in doing research for papers and assignments. Instead of trying to find books in the library, students can search the Web and find great resources to support our thesis statements. In addition, students could use information databases to search for evidence much more quickly than walking up and down the rows of shelves in the library and trying to find books that aren't even there sometimes anyway.

Finally, e-mail can be a great way to ask questions even after class. Teachers can answer e-mail questions whenever they get a chance and maybe even take a little extra time to look up some answers for their students. For example, if a student asks to learn about Mars in an e-mail, a teacher can find details and maybe some links and put them in the answer to the student.

Therefore, as shown, it is clear that schools should have technology in the classrooms so that teachers can teach students better.

This essay scores a 3. It uses a simple, straightforward structure and examples to support its points. There are few technical errors, and the vocabulary is varied and used appropriately. The introduction and conclusion echo each other, and there is little or no irrelevant information in the passage. The author is not excessively self-referential as some of the previous authors were. Overall, this is an example of a good, solid, well-constructed essay in the high average range.

Example Essay, Score 4

As schools consider the question of bringing technology into the classroom, it seems that the best choice would be in favor of computers, the Internet, and other valuable technological tools. After considering both sides of the issue, it should be clear that technology is more of a positive than a negative. It is important for students to have the most up to date tools as they pursue their education.

Everyone should agree that computer use is only likely to increase in the future. Students will need to have computer skills in order to compete in college and in the job market later. While it may be true that there are some issues to consider, there are several good reasons to provide computers and Internet access to classrooms.

For instance, educators can access a wide variety of useful and current information at their fingertips, such as fresh images from outer space to help explain planets and galaxies to students. Students are sure to respond better to beautiful photos from the orbiting Hubble telescope than to the tired, old models that are found in most school science classrooms.

Even though students may find ways to abuse Internet connections, it seems that teachers and staff should be able to control things like cheating and chatting or surfing during class time. It is true that there are sites that sell term papers to students, the teachers can access the same sites and should not be fooled unless they are not on the ball. As for chatting and surfing, the computers can be turned off when they aren't being used just like cell phones are now.

E-mail can be important also. Students and teachers can exchange e-mail messages on weekends or during holidays. Teachers can send e-mails out to an entire class reminding them of quizzes or exams, or giving links to important web sites that can help students to understand subjects.

Finally, I think that it comes down to a simple matter of staying up with the times. In earlier generations, students used chalkboards and shared books that were only updated every few years. As society progressed, we began to add chemistry labs and biology dissections along with slide and movie projectors and televisions with educational video tapes. It seems to me that the next obvious step is to get up with the times and get technology in the classroom where it belongs.

This essay scores a 4. While not perfect, it is nearly error-free and well structured. The author's points are clearly stated and then backed up with relevant examples. The paragraphs are each built around a subtopic that adds support to the author's response to the prompt. The essay reveals a depth of thought and creativity in raising potential arguments and dealing with them effectively. The vocabulary choices are appropriate and varied. This is a well-above-average essay.

What's Next?

The next chapter includes a set of Language Arts, Writing multiple-choice questions and an essay prompt. Use what you learned in Part IV to attack these questions with confidence.

12

CHAPTER TWELVE

Language Arts, Writing Practice Questions and Answer Explanations

This chapter includes 25 simulated GED Writing Test I questions, followed by explanations for each question. Allow approximately 35 to 40 minutes to complete this section. Fill in your answers on the answer sheet provided on page xx. This chapter also includes a practice essay topic.

Do not worry about your score at this point. These practice questions should help you to become more familiar with the types of questions you will encounter on your actual GED test.

Use the answer sheet on the following page to mark your answers. Then compare your answers to the answers and explanations at the end of this chapter. Be sure to read through the explanations thoroughly. Identify and review topics with which you've consistently struggled.

Please note that this chapter does not follow the precise format of the GED.

Answer Sheet

1. ① ② ③ ④ ⑤
2. ① ② ③ ④ ⑤
3. ① ② ③ ④ ⑤
4. ① ② ③ ④ ⑤
5. ① ② ③ ④ ⑤
6. ① ② ③ ④ ⑤
7. ① ② ③ ④ ⑤
8. ① ② ③ ④ ⑤
9. ① ② ③ ④ ⑤
10. ① ② ③ ④ ⑤
11. ① ② ③ ④ ⑤
12. ① ② ③ ④ ⑤
13. ① ② ③ ④ ⑤
14. ① ② ③ ④ ⑤
15. ① ② ③ ④ ⑤
16. ① ② ③ ④ ⑤
17. ① ② ③ ④ ⑤
18. ① ② ③ ④ ⑤
19. ① ② ③ ④ ⑤
20. ① ② ③ ④ ⑤
21. ① ② ③ ④ ⑤
22. ① ② ③ ④ ⑤
23. ① ② ③ ④ ⑤
24. ① ② ③ ④ ⑤
25. ① ② ③ ④ ⑤

Practice Questions

Directions: Choose the one best answer to each question.

Questions 1 through 10 refer to the following letter of complaint.

Breezy Suites, Inc.
4589 Ocean Blvd.
Palacios, CA 22476

To Whom It May Concern:

(A)

(1) Since I was staying at your hotel last week, I was dismayed to find my room in a state of disarray each day until late afternoon. (2) And also, whenever I approached one of your employees to ask when my room would be cleaned, I was met with anger and rudeness.

(B)

(3) I had been spending a lot of time researching the best place to stay during my visit to Palacios. (4) Your website indicated that your facility was outstanding in every way. (5) I even went so far as to calling your front desk, and the receptionist seemed very friendly. (6) After talking to her, I felt strongly that you're hotel would be a fine place for me to stay for five days.

(C)

(7) I arrived at your hotel. (8) There were many people waiting to register. (9) Not only there is a new trainee at the front desk, but also she was totally unsupervised. (10) It seemed to me that there should have been at least two employees on duty, since it was after 5:00 p.m. (11) Having a new person behind the desk alone at such a busy time did not seem to be a proper procedure for a hotel of your size. (12) I probably stood in line for about 30 minutes way too much time for a weary traveler. (13) To top it off, it occurred that my room key did not work reliably.

(14) I am requesting that at least one day of my hotel charge be refunded to me. (15) I am sending you a copy of my receipt.

Sincerely,

Susan Austin

Susan Austin

1. Sentence 1: Since I was staying at your hotel last week, I was dismayed to find my room in a state of disarray each day until late afternoon.

   The most effective revision of Sentence 1 would begin with which group of words?

   (1) Staying at your hotel last week, I was dismayed

   (2) I was dismayed, my room in a state of disarray

   (3) Your hotel, I was dismayed, finding my room

   (4) I had stayed at your hotel, since I was dismayed

   (5) Having stayed at your hotel last week, until late afternoon

2. Sentence 2: And also, whenever I approached one of your employees to ask when my room would be cleaned, I was met with anger and rudeness.

   Which correction should be made to Sentence 2?

   (1) Change approached to has approached.

   (2) Remove the comma after cleaned.

   (3) Remove And also.

   (4) Change I was to I were.

   (5) Change approached to had been approached.

3. Sentence 3: I had been spending a lot of time researching the best place to stay during my visit to Palacios.

   Which is the best way to write the underlined portion of this sentence? If the original is the best way, choose option 1.

   (1) had been spending

   (2) has spent

   (3) had spent

   (4) have spent

   (5) having been spending

4. Sentence 5: I even went so far as to calling your front desk, and the receptionist seemed very friendly.

   Which is the best way to write the underlined portion of this sentence? If the original is the best way, choose option 1.

(1) calling your front desk

(2) call your front desk

(3) called your front desk

(4) your front desk and calling

(5) your front desk called

5. Sentence 6: After talking to her, I felt strongly that you're hotel would be a fine place for me to stay for five days.

   Which correction should be made to sentence 6?

   (1) Remove the comma after her.

   (2) Replace you're with your.

   (3) Replace strongly with strong.

   (4) Insert a comma after stay.

   (5) Insert a comma after hotel.

6. Sentences 7 and 8: I arrived at your hotel. There were many people waiting to register.

   Which is the most effective combination of sentences 7 and 8?

   (1) I had arrived at your hotel, so there were many people waiting to register.

   (2) There were many people waiting to register after I arrived at the hotel.

   (3) At the hotel, there were many people waiting when I arrived.

   (4) At the hotel, where I arrived, there were many people waiting to register.

   (5) When I arrived at your hotel, there were many people waiting to register.

7. Sentence 9: Not only there is a new trainee at the front desk, but also she was totally unsupervised.

   Which is the best way to write the underlined portion of this sentence? If the original is the best way, choose option 1.

   (1) Not only there is

   (2) Only there is

   (3) There was

   (4) Not only was there

   (5) There was not only

8. Sentence 11: Having a new person alone behind the desk at such a busy time did not seem to be a proper procedure for a hotel of your size.

   Which revision should be made to the placement of sentence 11?

   (1) Remove sentence 11.

   (2) Move sentence 11 to follow sentence 8.

   (3) Move sentence 11 to follow sentence 12.

   (4) Begin the paragraph with sentence 11.

   (5) Move sentence 11 to the end of the paragraph.

9. Sentence 12: I probably stood in line for about <u>30 minutes way too</u> much time for a weary traveler.

   Which is the best way to write the underlined portion of this sentence? If the original is the best way, choose option 1.

   (1) 30 minutes way too

   (2) 30 minutes, and way too

   (3) 30 minutes, way too

   (4) 30 minutes, way too,

   (5) 30 minutes way too,

10. Sentence 13: To top it off, it occurred that my room key did not work reliably.

    Which correction should be made to sentence 13?

    (1) Remove the comma after <u>off</u>.

    (2) Replace <u>occurred</u> with <u>occurs</u>.

    (3) Insert a comma after <u>work</u>.

    (4) Remove <u>it occurred that</u>.

    (5) No correction is necessary.

<u>Questions 11 through 18</u> refer to the following letter to a customer.

Hamilton Land Management Associates, Inc.

Ms. Marlene Matter
1145 Greenlawn Drive
White Bear Lake, MN 55110

Dear Ms. Matter,

(A)

(1) Thank you for your interest in Private Landowner Forestry. (2) You are joining thousands of landowners interested in improving their woodlands. (3) There is a wealth of information available from our office that will assist you in making important decisions regarding your land. (4) We hope you will utilize our services. (5) Also many of the services are available on our website.

(B)

(6) As you indicated in your letter, you are interested in preserving your forested land and also in improving its ability to provide natural habitat for wildlife. (7) This includes cataloging the types of trees currently present, including their relative age and health. (8) Our expert advisors will first need assessing the present condition of your land. (9) In some cases, our advisors recommend harvesting either individual trees or stands of trees in order to improve the overall health of the forest. (10) These recommendations can only be made after careful assessment and consideration of your property. (11) As well as your short and long-term goals.

(C)

(12) There are many things to consider in determining specific goals for your land. (13) That help with all of the concerns and issues that inevitably arise, our office provides informational workshops free to our clients. (14) Please take the time to peruse the enclosed materials and choose one or two workshops to start with.

(D)

(15) We look forward to meeting you and learn more about your forest. (16) Please do not hesitate to contact me personally with any further questions or concerns.

Sincerely,

John Blade

John Blade
Director

11. Sentence 2: You are joining thousands of landowners interested in improving their woodlands.

    Which correction should be made to sentence 2?

    (1) Insert a comma after landowners.

    (2) Replace their with there.

    (3) Remove in after interested.

    (4) Insert a comma after interested.

    (5) No correction is necessary.

12. Sentences 4 and 5: We hope you will utilize our services. Also many of the services are available on our website.

    Which is the best way to write the underlined portion of these sentences? If the original is the best way, choose option 1.

    (1) utilize our services. And also many of the resources

    (2) utilize our services, also many of the services

    (3) utilizing our services, many of which

    (4) utilize our services, many of which

    (5) utilize our services and also many of the services

13. Sentence 7: This includes cataloging the types of trees currently present, including their relative age and health.

    Which revision should be made to the placement of sentence 7?

    (1) Move sentence 7 to the beginning of paragraph B.

    (2) Move sentence 7 to follow sentence 9.

    (3) Move sentence 7 to follow sentence 8.

    (4) Move sentence 7 to the end of paragraph A.

    (5) Move sentence 7 to the end of paragraph B.

14. Sentence 8: Our expert advisors will first need assessing the present condition of your land.

    Which correction should be made to sentence 8?

    (1) Replace will first need with should first need.

    (2) Change assessing to to assess.

    (3) Replace need with needing.

    (4) Change assessing to assessed.

    (5) Replace will first need with first needed.

15. Sentence 9: In some cases, our advisors recommend, harvesting either individual trees or stands of trees in order to improve the overall health of the forest.

    Which correction should be made to sentence 9?

    (1) Change recommend to recommended.

    (2) Remove the comma after recommend.

    (3) Replace either with neither.

    (4) Insert a comma after trees.

    (5) Replace stands with stance.

16. Sentences 10 and 11: These recommendations can only be made after careful assessment and consideration of your property. As well as your short and long-term goals.

    Which is the best way to write the underlined portion of these sentences? If the original is the best way, choose option 1.

    (1) your property. As well as

    (2) your property; as well as

    (3) your property and as well as

    (4) your property but

    (5) your property as well as

17. Sentence 13: That help with all of the concerns and issues that inevitably arise, our office provides informational workshops free to our clients.

    The most effective revision of sentence 13 would begin with which group of words?

    (1) In helping with all

    (2) In order to be helpful

    (3) Our office provides

    (4) Helping with all

    (5) All of the concerns and issues

18. Sentence 15: We look forward to meeting you and learn more about your forest.

    Which correction should be made to sentence 15?

    (1) Replace meeting with meet.
    (2) Replace learn with learning.
    (3) Insert a comma after you.
    (4) Change look forward to looking forward.
    (5) No correction is necessary.

Questions 19–25 refer to the following notice.

Embroidery Sewing Machines

(A)

(1) Anyone who has sewn clothes over the past 40 years have seen the enormous impact technology has had on today's sewing machines. (2) Most modern sewing machines contain computer chips and keypads, and many of today's seamstresses rely on the Internet for their patterns and designs.

(B)

(3) Embroidery machines are particular exciting. (4) Once a design is entered into the machine, sewing is automatic by re-creating even the most complicated designs quickly and accurately. (5) For example, a floral pattern can easily be stitched onto the neckline of a sweater, or a seasonal graphic can be added to a jacket. (6) Another use for the embroidery machine is to sew a name or monogram onto a garment or accessory, such as a duffle bag. (7) The possibilities are virtually endless.

(C)

(8) As the machines themselves have improved and upgraded, so too have the fabrics and threads that are available. (9) Walking into any fabric store will leave the shopper feeling both elated and confused with so many choices. (10) Todays threads come in a vast array of colors and materials, ranging from rayons to metallics. (11) Consideration also has to be given to the correct needle, presser foot and embroidery hoop size whenever embarking on a new embroidery project. (12) Technology has complicated sewing as it has improved it. (13) Learning to use these new machines can be a daunting experience. (14) Just as in learning how to use a computer for the first time, computerized sewing machines can have a rather lengthy learning curve. (15) Most reputable sewing machine dealers realize that purchasers of these new machines may need help in learning how to use them and will offer free courses to get them started. (16) Before long, the seamstress will be covering every piece of clothing, towels, and tote bags she owns with colorful designs and fancy letters.

19. Sentence 1: Anyone who has sewn clothes over the past 40 years have seen the enormous impact technology has had on today's sewing machines.

    Which correction should be made to sentence 1?

    (1) Replace has with have.

    (2) Place a comma after years.

    (3) Replace have with has.

    (4) Replace today's with todays.

    (5) No correction is necessary.

20. Sentence 4: Embroidery machines are particular exciting.

    Which correction should be made to sentence 4?

    (1) Replace particular with particularly.

    (2) Change exciting to excited.

    (3) Delete the word are.

    (4) Change machines to machine.

    (5) Change particular to particulars.

21. Sentence 4: Once a design is entered into the machine, sewing is automatic by re-creating even the most complicated designs quickly and accurately.

    Which is the best way to write the underlined portion of this sentence? If the original is the best way, choose option 1.

    (1) automatic by re-creating

    (2) automatic, re-create

    (3) automatic, re-creating

    (4) automatic, re-creates

    (5) automatic and re-creating

22. Sentence 8: As the machines themselves have improved and upgraded, so too have the fabrics and threads that are available.

    Which is the best way to write the underlined portion of the sentence? If the original is the best way, choose option 1.

    (1) have improved

    (2) has improved

    (3) improved

    (4) have been improving

    (5) have been improved

23. Sentence 10: Todays threads come in a vast array of colors and materials, ranging from rayons to metallics.

    Which correction should be made to sentence 12?

    (1) Change Todays to Today's.

    (2) Remove the comma after materials.

    (3) Change ranging to ranges.

    (4) Replace from with to.

    (5) Insert a comma after ranging.

24. Sentences 12 and 13: Technology has complicated sewing as it has improved it. Learning to use these new machines can be a daunting experience.

    The most effective combination of sentences 12 and 13 would include which group of words?

    (1) learning sewing has been complicated

    (2) learning sewing, complicated

    (3) improved it, so learning

    (4) these new machines, technology

    (5) learning complicated sewing

25. Which revision would improve the effectiveness of the document?

    Begin a new paragraph with

    (1) Sentence 6

    (2) Sentence 10

    (3) Sentence 11

    (4) Sentence 12

    (5) Sentence 16

Essay Topic

The following is a sample essay topic for you to practice the essay portion of the Language Arts, Writing exam. Write your essay on the lined pages that follow the topic.

Topic

If you could make one important change in your life within the next year, what would it be?

In your essay, identify the change you would make and explain the reasons for your choice. Use your personal observations, experience, and knowledge to support your essay.

Answers and Explanations

1. **The best answer is (1).** It is clear, succinct, and has correct word order. The original sentence and answer choice 4 incorrectly use "since"; there is no cause-effect relationship between choosing a certain hotel and having a bad experience at that hotel. The other answer choices have awkward word order.

2. **The best answer is (3).** This sentence elaborates on the problem presented in the preceding sentence. The phrase "And also" is unnecessary.

3. **The best answer is (3).** The researching took place at a time prior to the writer's bad experience at the hotel and is finished. The past perfect ("had" + past participle) is the appropriate tense.

4. **The best answer is (2).** The phrase "go so far as" must be followed by a verb in the infinitive form ("to" + simple verb). The "to" is given in the sentence, so answer choice 2, which begins with a simple verb, is the correct answer choice.

5. **The best answer is (2).** This question tests your ability to recognize common homonyms. Here, the possessive determiner "your" is appropriate immediately preceding a noun ("hotel").

6. **The best answer is (5).** Using "when" is the most effective way to link these two clauses, and answer choice 5 uses "when" in the most natural way.

7. **The best answer is (4).** Beginning a sentence with negation requires some kind of inversion: subject-auxiliary (Never <u>had I</u> laughed so hard as when Joe fell off his chair.), subject-"do" (Not only <u>did I</u> finish dinner, but I ate dessert too.), "there"-"be" (Never were there fish in this pond before the flood.). Answer choice 4 is best because it correctly applies this inversion rule and uses the correlative conjunction "not only…but also."

8. **The best answer is (1).** Sentence 10 adequately states the same idea, so sentence 11 can be eliminated.

9. **The best answer is (3).** The phrase beginning with "way too" modifies "30 minutes"; therefore, it should be set off from the sentence by a comma that precedes it. No other commas should be used. In the case of answer choice (2), the conjunction "and" is not properly used.

10. **The best answer is (4).** Remember that simpler is better in conveying meaning in writing. The sentence as written is wordy and awkward. Eliminating "it occurred that" results in no change of meaning and makes the sentence clear.

11. **The best answer is (5).** The sentence is complete and grammatically correct as it is written. Answer choices 1 and 4 would insert commas. Remember to read very critically because incorrectly adding or removing commas is a common mistake test takers make.

12. **The best answer is (4).** These clauses can be combined because the final noun ("services") from the first sentence is the subject noun in the following sentence. This is an appropriate occasion to use the relative pronoun "which." Answer

choice 4 correctly sets the relative clause apart from the main clause with a comma and the bare verb "utilize" matches with "will" to form the simple future tense.

13. **The best answer is (3).** The pronoun "This" requires an antecedent. Placing it after sentence 8 means "This" refers to the assessment of the land, which makes sense.

14. **The best answer is (2).** The verb "need" takes a verb in the infinitive, not a gerund. There is no problem with the tense of the verb "need," because the assessment had not taken place yet at the time of writing the letter.

15. **The best answer is (2).** This usage of "recommend" requires a phrase beginning with a gerund to follow it. As it is a constituent (that is, a direct object) of the verb, no comma must divide it.

16. **The best answer is (5).** The phrase "as well as" serves as a conjunction and requires no punctuation before it.

17. **The best answer is (3).** This sentence is composed of two clauses that are not correctly linked. The verb "help" refers to "informational workshops." A corrected sentence would begin "Our office provides free to all of our clients informational workshops that help…"

18. **The best answer is (2).** This question relies on your ability to evaluate a sentence for parallel structure. The verbs "learn" and "meeting" must be in the same form. Answer choice (2) is correct because the expression "look forward" takes the "-ing" form of the verb.

19. **The best answer is (3).** The indefinite subject pronoun "anyone" takes verbs in singular form.

20. **The best answer is (1).** The word "particular" should modify the adjective "exciting," so use the adverb "particularly" instead.

21. **The best answer is (3).** The phrase beginning with "re-creating" modifies "sewing is automatic" by giving a more detailed description. Using the gerund and setting the phrase apart with a comma are necessary. The preposition "by" is awkward and unnecessary.

22. **The best answer is (5).** This question tests your ability to determine whether a sentence has parallel structure. In this sentence, "have" is a clue that a present perfect tense should be the correct answer choice. Remember that within a sentence, the second part to a parallel construction may contain just an auxiliary without the main verb, for example: *I've visited more states than you have [visited].*

23. **The best answer is (1).** "Todays" is missing an apostrophe to make it possessive. The phrase "today's threads" means "the threads of today."

24. **The best answer is (3).** These two sentences represent a cause-effect relationship, so the subordination conjunction "so" is appropriate.

25. **The best answer is (4).** Sentence 12 introduces the concept that the subsequent sentences detail. Furthermore, paragraphs can be tied together with good transition sentences. Sentence 11 would close paragraph C well and lead the reader into the new "paragraph D."

Essay

Because grading the essay is subjective, we've chosen not to include any "graded" essays here. Your best bet is to have someone you trust, such as your personal tutor, read your essays and give you an honest critique. Make the scoring rubric mentioned in Chapter 11, "The GED Essay," available to whoever grades your essays. If you plan on grading your own essays, review the grading criteria and be as honest as possible regarding the structure, development, organization, technique, and appropriateness of your writing. Focus on your weak areas and continue to practice to improve your writing skills.

What's Next?

The next chapter includes a list of Language Arts, Writing terms with definitions. Reviewing this chapter will help you better understand Edited American English (EAE).

CHAPTER THIRTEEN

13

Language Arts, Writing Terms

The terms included here are terms used in the book and on official GED practice tests. You most likely will not be tested directly on these terms but should use them as a reference for the topics covered in this book.

NOTE

Because reading and writing are inherently interconnected, some terms may appear in Chapter 20, "Language Arts, Reading Terms," instead of in this chapter, or vice versa.

A–B

adjective Part of speech. Modifies a noun or noun phrase by limiting, qualifying, or specifying: a *meager* wage, the *red* car, ten *tired* babies.

adverb Part of speech. Modifies a verb, adjective, or another adverb. Many adverbs are formed by adding the "-ly" suffix to adjectives, although there are many exceptions: walk *slowly*, laughing *heartily*, sleep *well*, drive *fast*.

agreement In grammar, the property of language that some elements must have a certain form to match other elements. In English, subject and verb must agree in person and number. The same is true for pronoun and antecedent (what the pronoun refers to). *Incorrect*: Each dad *are* playing with *their* son. *Correct*: Each dad *is* playing with *his* son.

bias Preference or prejudice that inhibits fair judgment.

C

clause A sentence or part of a sentence containing a subject and a predicate. A clause is *dependent* if it cannot stand alone as a separate sentence; a clause is *independent* if it can stand alone.

conclusion A proposition stated at the end of an essay that is supported by the evidence given in the essay.

conjunction Part of speech. Connects words, phrases, clauses, and sentences. The most common conjunctions in English are *and* and *or*, but words such as *but* and *because* are conjunctions, too.

coordination Linking two structurally equal elements in a sentence using a coordinating conjunction, usually *and* or *or*: the lions *and* tigers, vanilla *or* chocolate.

D–L

direct object The object that receives the direct action of the verb, such as "the pastry" in "Jordan dunked the pastry in his coffee."

fragment A string of words that is missing one or more elements necessary to be a complete sentence.

gerund The form of a verb taking the "-ing" suffix and that bears no tense information. Gerunds can stand as nouns or be used with an auxiliary verb to form continuous tenses.

grammar The study of how words and parts of words combine to form sentences.

indirect object The object that is the recipient of the action of the verb, such as "me" in "Sing me a song." Indirect objects often take or imply the preposition "to": "Sing a song to me."

inference Conclusion based on evidence.

M–O

main idea The topic of an essay or a paragraph.

mechanics Formal elements of writing (in English: spelling, punctuation, and capitalization).

modification The application of an adjective or adjective phrase to a noun or noun phrase.

noun Part of speech. Names a person, place, thing, quality, or action. Nouns can be subjects or objects of verbs and prepositions or can stand alone as appositives: *Sue* met ten *people* in the *boardroom*, including *Jane*, *president* of the *company*.

number In English, the indication of being singular or plural. Nouns, pronouns, and (to a lesser extent) verbs are marked for number.

object In grammar, a noun or noun phrase that is either the goal of the action of the verb or the goal of a prepositional phrase. (See also *direct object* and *indirect object*.)

P–R

paragraph A unit of prose that is composed of sentences that address a single coherent topic.

parallel structure *or* **parallelism** The use of identical structure in corresponding phrases or parallel verbs. For example: I like *swimming* and *running*. I like *to swim* and *to run*.

parenthetical An explanatory statement that is set off from the sentence by parentheses.

part of speech One of the traditional classifications of words according to their use in sentences.

person The indication of someone or something's role in the discourse. First person refers to the speaker, second person refers to who is being addressed, and third person is anything or anyone else. Verbs and pronouns must agree in person with subject and antecedent, respectively.

preposition Part of speech. Defines the relationship between a noun or noun phrase and a verb, adjective, or other noun or noun phrase: I sailed *under* the bridge. Climb hand *over* hand. You should be watchful *in* dark alleys.

pronoun Part of speech. One from the discrete set of words that can represent a noun or noun phrase (its antecedent) and that must agree with it in person and number.

restate Repeat in a different manner.

run-on Improper combination or two or more independent clauses that should be separate sentences.

S

sentence The basic unit of language that conveys a complete thought.

structure Organization of a piece of writing with respect to clarity and precision of meaning.

subordination Placement of a clause in a position where it depends on another clause: It was raining, *so I opened my umbrella*. Here, the word *so* is called a subordinating conjunction. The clause *I opened my umbrella* depends on the clause *It was raining*.

summary Reduction of information to its main points.

synonymous Equal or nearly equal in meaning: *glowing/radiant*, *assault/attack*, *cry/weep*.

synopsis See *summary*.

T–Z

tense Place in time as it relates to a verb: past, present, or future. More broadly, the term *tense* describes one of the many verb forms in English that expresses both position in time and duration.

verb Part of speech. In English, expresses action, existence, or state of being: I *play* baseball. Lincoln *was* an important president. Evening sunshine *fades* as winter approaches.

voice In grammar, the property of verb constructions that indicates the relationship between subject and verb. A sentence has active voice if the subject is the agent (who or what is performing the action): *Monkeys eat bananas*. Passive voice occurs when the agent is not the subject: *Bananas are eaten by monkeys*. Passive voice sentences can usually be reworded to have active voice. Passive voice is often used when the agent is unknown or unimportant in the sentence: *The contestants were hit in the face with cream pies*. (Who threw the cream pies is unknown or unimportant.)

PART V
Language Arts, Reading

This part of the book explains what the GED Language Arts, Reading Test involves and the basic critical reading skills you will need to maximize your score. The Reading Test contains multiple-choice questions about short reading passages.

Part V includes the following chapters:

Chapter 14 About the Language Arts, Reading Test

Chapter 15 Prose Fiction

Chapter 16 Poetry

Chapter 17 Drama

Chapter 18 Prose Nonfiction

Chapter 19 Language Arts, Reading Practice Questions and Answer Explanations

Chapter 20 Language Arts, Reading Terms

14

CHAPTER FOURTEEN

About the Language Arts, Reading Test

The GED Language Arts, Reading Test consists of 40 multiple-choice questions that you will be given 65 minutes to complete. The questions assess your ability to read and analyze various short passages. These may be whole works or excerpts from larger works.

Format

The test includes seven short passages divided this way:

- Two prose nonfiction (25% of questions)
    - One general nonfiction passage
    - One commentary on a visual medium
- Three prose fiction (45% of questions)
    - One passage written before 1920
    - One passage written between 1920 and 1960
    - One passage written after 1960
- One poetry (15% of questions)
- One drama (15% of questions)

EXAM ALERT

Each passage begins with a "purpose question" printed in all capital letters. These are not titles. They are intended to focus your reading and may help you to grasp the meaning of the passages.

Some questions will reference certain parts of the passage by their line numbers. For these, use the line numbers along the left side of the passage. Every fifth line is indicated, so find the number nearest the one you want and count up or down.

Between four and eight multiple-choice questions follow each passage and test your ability to do the following:

- Interpret the passage as a whole.
- Apply something from the passage to new information or a new situation.
- Analyze the style and structure of the passage.

You will need certain critical thinking skills to do well on the test:

- **Comprehension**—Could you explain what you just read to someone else? (20% of questions)
- **Application**—Can you use what you read in new situations? (15% of questions)
- **Analysis**—Can you trace cause/effect relationships and draw conclusions? Do you notice elements of style and how the passage is put together? (30–35% of questions)
- **Synthesis**—Can you analyze tone, point of view, style, and the author's purpose? Can you find connections between what you read and elements of your prior knowledge? (30–35% of questions)

These critical thinking skills come from the Cognitive Domain of Bloom's Taxonomy of Educational Objectives, which is explained in detail in Chapter 4.

Scores

If you choose to answer all the questions on the Reading Test, you will have about eight or nine minutes to work on each of the seven passages and still have enough time to mark the answers on your answer sheet. We have determined from Official GED Practice Tests that if you get approximately 29 to 34 of the 40 questions correct, you end up with a scaled Reading Score of about 500, which is the national average score for graduating high school students. (There is variation in scaled scores from one exam to the next.) A 500 on the Reading Test means that your reading score is well within the passing range, which for most jurisdictions in the United States is 410 and above. Remember that all your GED test scores must average 450 and that a few jurisdictions will have stricter score requirements. Inquire about the requirements in your jurisdiction. (Refer to Chapter 1, "Understanding the GED," for a list of state, provincial, and territorial agencies).

Of course, we recommend that you strive to do your best, and we hope that all readers of this book score well into the above-average range on the GED. However, it pays to be realistic about what is possible for you on test day. If, after a reasonable amount of practice and study, you are still able to tackle only six of the seven passages comfortably within the 65 minutes you are given, you are not in very bad shape. If you can get nearly all of those 32 to 36 questions correct, and pick up a few correct answers by guessing on the remaining 10, you could still realistically hope to end up with an above-average score on the Reading Test.

If you are closer to the lower end of the passing range on the Reading Test and find that you are able to really understand only five passages and their accompanying questions in the time allowed, you are still likely to get credit for a few more correct responses by guessing on the remaining 8 to 16 questions. In fact, because there are five answer choices for each question, you should predict that you would get about 20% correct when guessing at random. This means that guessing on 15 questions should yield about three correct answers. If you manage to answer correctly only 20 of the 25 questions that go with the five passages that you work on carefully, you would still have a scaled score hovering around the passing mark of 410. Nevertheless, you want to be confident about your test performance, so use this book to practice diligently until you can make it through as many of the seven passages as possible.

NOTE

You must receive an average score of at least 450 on the GED. Therefore, if you score a 410 on one or two of the five tests, be sure your scores on the remaining tests are sufficiently high enough to bring your average up to at least 450.

Practice and Testing Strategies

Most students have distinct preferences for certain types of passages. Conversely, there is probably at least one type of passage that always seems to account for the bulk of the questions that you miss on practice Reading Tests. Let your practice testing help you to decide which passages to take on first, so you aren't scrambling at the end of the 65 minutes on a passage you might otherwise do well on.

Remember to always fill in every answer "bubble" on your answer sheet; there is no extra penalty for guessing incorrectly, as there is on some other tests.

Although vocabulary is not tested directly on the GED Language Arts, Reading Test, there is certainly an advantage to knowing what the words mean as you try to decipher a passage. We have included a general vocabulary list in Appendix C that includes pre-college–level words. Even if none of the words on the list shows up on your exam, you should at least get an idea of the type of word that is likely to be seen and the level of difficulty that you can expect to find on your test. Chapter 20 contains a list of specific literary terms that can help you as you prepare for the GED Language Arts, Reading Test.

What's Next?

The chapters that follow include information about each of the passage types in the GED Language Arts, Reading Test. You will learn how to approach each of the passages and accompanying questions with confidence.

CHAPTER FIFTEEN

Prose Fiction

Prose is ordinary writing without meter (the rhythmic quality important to many forms of poetry). Prose fiction, then, includes a great variety of written works: novels, short stories, folk tales, fables, myths, and so on. The fiction passage you will see on the GED are excerpts from novels or short stories. Novels and short stories use imaginary elements that interact to mirror something the reader understands from real life.

Fiction may use certain facts and realistic situations in addition to imaginary elements. For example, in preparing his novel *The Red Badge of Courage*, author Stephen Crane interviewed many U.S. Civil War veterans. The result is a story about a fictional soldier set in very realistic wartime situations. In fact, although the great battle of the book is never named in the text, many historians believe it closely mimics the real Battle of Chancellorsville. Readers often feel closely tied to characters by the end of stories, which is one of the pleasures of reading fiction.

The Elements of Fiction

The basic elements of fiction include setting, plot, and characterization. The manner in which these elements are used is called style, which includes diction, tone, and use of imagery. Point of view describes from whose perspective the story is told. Every work of fiction has at least one theme, which is the overarching message the author is trying to convey.

Table 15.1 on the next page provides information regarding the elements of fiction.

TABLE 15.1 The Elements of Fiction

Basic Element	Subelement	What It Means	Brief Examples
setting	time	when the action takes place	1941, today, yesterday, the not-so-distant future, 65 million years ago, New Year's Eve, Bill's birthday last year
	place	where the action takes place	Chesapeake Bay, a classroom, the moon, Sherwood Forest, the ocean deep, Omaha Beach
	atmosphere (mood)	the physical and emotive qualities of the place	bright, uplifting, gloomy, eerie, rainy, hot, smoky, windy, freezing, silent, awkward
plot		the action	a boy matures into adulthood; a baseball team wins the state championship; a woman cares for her dying husband; a sheriff tries to take control of a frontier town but fails; two children come to love a dog in spite of its bad behavior
characterization		who is involved in the action and how the author develops and presents characters to the reader	"I," Bob, the neighborhood kids, the Johnson High School cheerleading team, King Henry VIII, the Martian ambassador
theme		the lesson(s) the author wants to convey	cheating is wrong; marriage is difficult; war is a necessary evil; the bond of family is stronger than any other; asking too many questions can get you into trouble
point of view		the perspective from which the story is told	first person (the main character narrates); third person, limited (disembodied narrator relates one character's experience); third person, omniscient (disembodied narrator knows and sees all, even things no character can see)
style	diction	word choice	*aroma* (pleasant) v. *odor* (unpleasant); *slice* (controlled) v. *hack* (violent); *police officer* (formal) v. *cop* (informal)

(continues)

TABLE 15.1 *Continued*

Basic Element	Subelement	What It Means	Brief Examples
	tone	the author's attitude	sarcastic, pleading, drab, dire, light-hearted, sinister, bitter, humorous, ironic
	imagery	images used to appeal to the reader's senses	steaming-hot buttered biscuits, endless fields of pungent yellow flowers, the sharp click-clack of train cars rolling across the bridge

The setting in fiction is the time when an action occurs, the place where it occurs, and the atmosphere (also called mood) under which it occurs. Plot can evolve during more than one period of time and at several locations. The atmosphere, which can change during the course of a story, includes physical properties and the weather of a place, as well as the emotions a place stirs up in the characters.

Setting Exercise

Authors may state their stories' settings directly, but some settings must be inferred from clues in the text. For the following groups of sentences, identify the three parts of the setting: time, place, and atmosphere.

1. "I write my stories in the dingy one-bedroom apartment I keep in Brooklyn. My office window overlooks a once fly-ridden dumpster, but since it is winter now, the dumpster is hidden behind huge piles of dirty snow."	time	
	place	
	atmos.	
2. "The cold sea is crashing over the breakwater, but the last of the ships has made it back safely with her catch—a bountiful one at that. I suppose all the hard-working men will be rabblerousing in the tavern tonight."	time	
	place	
	atmos.	
3. "John knew the summer had arrived in Phillipsburg when he could fully submerge his index finger in a stripe of tar on the road. He couldn't wait to gather his friends and find the spray of a fire hydrant to play under."	time	
	place	
	atmos.	

Answers:

(Yours may vary slightly because interpretation rests with the reader.)

1. winter/narrator's one-bedroom apartment in Brooklyn/dirty, miserable, cold
2. now (end of the work day)/harbor of a fishing community/chilly yet uplifting
3. summer/outdoors in Phillipsburg/excited, playful

The action and events that occur in a story make up the plot. Figure 15.1 shows the rising and falling action in a plot and what the divisions of plot are called.

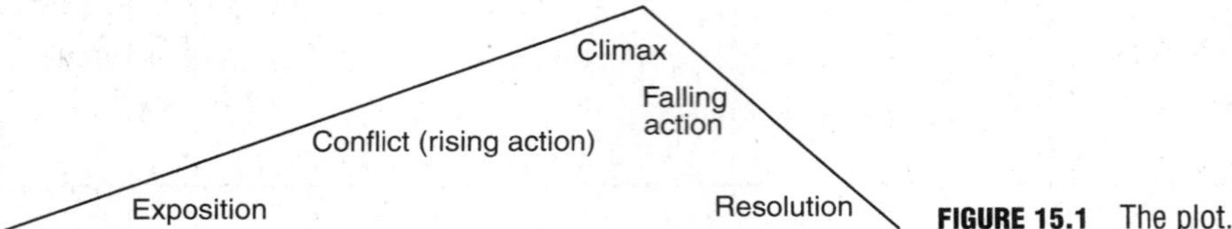

FIGURE 15.1 The plot.

Exposition is the noun form of the verb "expose." Background information that initiates the plot and introduces setting and main characters is called the exposition.

Conflict (or "rising action") is the basis of action in a story. In fiction, characters must overcome one or more kinds of opposition. Generally, conflict falls into one of four patterns:

- **human v. self**—Inner dilemmas that characters suffer, often involving a difficult decision

  Examples: reconciling a past misdeed, living with depression, managing the stress of responsibilities

- **human v. human**—Struggles between characters

  Examples: The bully steals kids' lunch money; the king is oppressing poor farmers; a hockey team works hard to beat the crosstown rival.

- **human v. society**—Struggles between characters and the rules of their communities and their cultures' social conventions

  Examples: A black man fights for a job under segregation; a reporter risks his life to interview people in a highly secretive society.

- **human v. nature**—Struggles between characters and forces beyond their control, including natural phenomena (weather, natural disasters, wilderness, animals), one or more gods, and other intangible forces (evil, magic spells).

  Examples: A ship and her crew battle a raging sea; heavy snowstorms cause a plane crash; a woman fights against the curse the gods put on her after her many crimes; two lost hikers are stalked by a bear.

Climax is the height of the action in a plot. Imagine a sports story. The climax would be the moment a player shoots the game-winning basket at the final buzzer or the wide receiver comes down with the "Hail Mary" pass in the end zone. In war stories, the climax is usually a culminating battle or a moment of great self-sacrifice. In many plots, the climax involves the death of an important character or some other significant upheaval. In mystery stories, the climax is the point where the riddle is solved.

Falling action refers to the part of the plot following the climax where any "loose ends" created in the action of the plot are resolved.

Resolution usually comes at the very end of a work of fiction. All plot lines are concluded and the theme of the entire work is revealed, if it was not before.

The basic pattern of plot given in this chapter is just that—a basic pattern. Authors continually develop new approaches to the art of writing fiction, and many novels and short stories do not strictly adhere to this pattern. For example, some stories leave the action unresolved at the end. In any case, you can observe the general rising and falling of action in nearly every plot.

Plot Exercise

Read the following sentences and number them 1 thorough 8 according to their logical order in a plot. Think about rising and falling action.

A.	Three days before her audition, Marianne woke to coughing and a bad case of bronchitis.	
B.	The judges marveled at her keyboard skills and decided to listen again to a recording of Marianne's singing from a few months before.	
C.	Marianne was a budding opera student.	
D.	A teacher at the conservatory suggested Marianne audition on piano, which for Marianne was not as strong as her singing.	
E.	Marianne was heartbroken.	
F.	She worked on her voice exercises every day for a year before her audition at the local conservatory.	
G.	Soon you may see her on some concert hall stage!	
H.	Marianne was accepted to the conservatory based on her piano, but she will begin opera lessons, too, after her voice recovers.	

Answers:

A. 3, B. 6, C. 1 D. 5 E. 4 F. 2 G. 8 H. 7

Analyzing Characters, Themes, and Points of View

Characters are the imaginary people in a novel or short story. Characters might even be plants, animals, and objects that the author personifies—that is, portrays with human characteristics. A good example of this kind of personification is in *Charlotte's Web*, by E. B. White, in which a spider, pig, and other farm animals interact and speak to each other. *Characterization* describes how an author makes the fictional people in a work believable. Readers learn about characters through the following:

- Actions taken by the character
- Speech of the character
- Emotions and internal thoughts of the character
- Opinions on the character given by other characters

The author's purpose for writing or the lesson(s) the author wants to convey to the reader is called *theme*. All the elements of fiction serve to present one or more themes, or central ideas, in a work. A theme may be a life lesson, commentary on a social issue, or a new perspective on what it means to be human. Good fiction requires readers to draw their own conclusions about theme from the elements of the story.

Fiction is told from a certain *point of view*, which corresponds in part to the grammatical feature of *person* (see Chapter 7, "Overview of English Usage"). All novels and short stories are narrated in some way, sometimes by a main character, but most often by a third party. When a main character tells the story (use of the pronoun "I" is the biggest clue), a work of fiction is said to have first-person narration. If someone else narrates the story, it has third-person narration. (You do not need to know about the exceptionally rare second-person narration.) There are two subtypes of third-person narration:

- **Third-person limited**—Narrator captures the experience of one character and is not privy to the inner thoughts of other characters. (Imagine that the character is being followed by a camera that records the story for the reader.)

  "Lily, the caretaker's daughter, did housemaid's work for them. Though their life was modest, they believed in eating well; the best of everything: diamond-bone sirloins, three-shilling tea and the best bottled stout. But Lily seldom made a mistake in the orders, so that she got on well with her three mistresses. They were fussy, that was all. But the only thing they would not stand was back answers.

  Of course, they had good reason to be fussy on such a night. And then it was long after ten o'clock and yet there was no sign of Gabriel and his wife."

  —James Joyce, excepted from *Dubliners*. (London: Grant Richards Ltd., 1914.)

- **Third-person omniscient**—Narrator is all knowing, exposes private thoughts of all characters.

  "The ladies of Longbourn soon waited on those of Netherfield. The visit was soon returned in due form. Miss Bennet's pleasing manners grew on the goodwill of Mrs. Hurst and Miss Bingley; and though the mother was found to be intolerable, and the younger sisters not worth speaking to, a wish of being better acquainted with them was expressed towards the two eldest. By Jane, this attention was received with the greatest pleasure, but Elizabeth still saw superciliousness in their treatment of everybody, hardly excepting even her sister, and could not like them; though their kindness to Jane, such as it was, had a value as arising in all probability from the influence of their brother's admiration."

  —Jane Austen, excerpted from *Pride and Prejudice*. (London: Richard Bentley and Son, 1881.)

Prose Style

Authors use language in a particular *style* to build fiction from the basic elements that you read about in the "The Elements of Fiction" section. Style comprises diction, tone, and use of imagery. Authors generally maintain a recognizable style throughout their writing careers, and many authors become famous for it.

Diction describes the author's choice of words. One way of enriching a character is to reflect the character's dialect in writing. This includes using regional vocabulary and verb constructions, as well as representing pronunciations in spelling. Though challenging at first, reading a different dialect can be enjoyable because it vividly establishes how the author intended the character to speak and helps to identify the character's background.

Prose Style Exercise

Consider the following passage from *The Adventures of Huckleberry Finn* by Mark Twain (New York: Harper and Brothers, 1912). Circle any words and expressions that you would not use in your own dialect of English, and then propose where and when you think the narrator lives.

> "Well three or four months run along and it was well into the winter now. I had been to school most all the time and could spell and read and write just a little and could say the multiplication table up to six times seven is thirty-five and I don't reckon I could ever get any further than that if I was to live forever. I don't take no stock in mathematics anyway.
>
> At first I hated the school but by and by I got so I could stand it. Whenever I got uncommon tired I played hookey and the hiding I got next day done me good and cheered me up. So the longer I went to school the easier it got to be."

Answer:

The narrator (Huckleberry Finn) is from rural Missouri of the 19th century. Use of dialect was essential to this work of Mark Twain. Consider this explanatory note the author included in the front of the book:

> *In this book a number of dialects are used, to wit: the Missouri negro dialect; the extremest form of the backwoods Southwestern dialect; the ordinary "Pike County" dialect; and four modified varieties of this last. The shadings have not been done in a haphazard fashion, or by guesswork; but painstakingly, and with the trustworthy guidance and support of personal familiarity with these several forms of speech.*
>
> *I make this explanation for the reason that without it many readers would suppose that all these characters were trying to talk alike and not succeeding.*
>
> *The Author.*

Writers carefully choose which words to use because beyond their strict definitions, words carry unspoken meanings, or connotations. Differences in connotation can be in the following:

- **Strength or degree**—*cute* v. *pretty*, *hot* v. *sweltering*
- **Judgment of quality or prestige**—*lotion* v. *moisturizer*, *Lakeview High School* v. *Lakeview Academy*
- **Political, social, cultural, or historical**—*Indian* v. *Native American*, *crippled* v. *disabled*

In some cases, words and phrases may be euphemisms, which means the words are chosen instead of more literal terms in order not to offend or disturb the reader. English is rich in euphemisms for the profane, which are terms for sexual ("sleep together") and excretory ("go to the bathroom") things. Also prevalent are euphemisms for death ("passed away") and states of the human body ("visually impaired"). In the public sphere, doublespeak is common, which is essentially a usage of euphemisms. Many people prefer the phrase "death camp" over the euphemistic "concentration camp" that came to English directly translated from German. Similarly, in wartime, the military and the media sometimes report that soldiers "receive friendly fire"; they are not "attacked by their own side." Today's public figures must choose their level of "political correctness" carefully. They do not want to upset anyone with the words they choose, on one hand by being overly euphemistic, or on the other hand by using terms offensive to certain groups.

Another element of word choice is the use of "figures of speech," which are phrases not meant to be taken literally. You've already read about one kind of figure of speech, the euphemism. You hear many other kinds of figures of speech in your daily life. They offer vivid, original detail. In writing, they can keep readers from becoming bored. Similes, metaphors, and personification are common figures of speech:

- Similes draw comparisons between two unlike things, usually using the words *like*, *than*, or *as*. For example:

  His unwavering stare ran through me like a cold needle.

  That boxer is as tough as nails.

- Metaphors imply that one thing is something else, thereby drawing a comparison between the two. Metaphors do not use *like*, *than*, or *as*. For example:

  "All the world's a stage, / And all the men and women merely players / They have their exits and their entrances;" —William Shakespeare, excerpted from *As You Like It* (New York: Henry Holt and Co., 1911)

- Personification imparts human characteristics or behaviors upon animals or objects. For example:

  "The yellow fog that rubs its back upon the window-panes, / The yellow smoke that rubs its muzzle on the window-panes, / Licked its tongue into the corners of the evening, / Lingered upon the pools that stand in drains, / Let fall upon its back the soot that falls from chimneys, / Slipped by the terrace, made a sudden leap, / And seeing that it was a soft October night, / Curled once about the house, and fell asleep." Excerpted from "The Love Song of J. Alfred Prufrock" by T.S. Eliot (from *Prufrock and Other Observations*. London: The Egoist Ltd., 1917)

More information on figures of speech appears in Chapter 16, "Poetry."

Tone refers to the attitude of the author toward the subject of the book, as evidenced in diction, characters (especially dialog between characters), sentence structure, and even punctuation. When analyzing tone, ask yourself: How does the author feel about the subject matter? What words or details reveal how the author feels?

Author's Tone Exercise

Consider the following passage from *A Modest Proposal* by Jonathan Swift (from *Prose Writing of Swift. Chosen and Arranged by Walter Lewin*. London: Walter Scott Ltd., 1886). It caused some uproar in Ireland in 1729 because many people failed to recognize the author's tone in the short work. Circle any words and expressions that reveal the author's tone, and then describe the tone in a few words. Note that the author's original spelling, which varies from that of today's English, has been preserved.

> "It is a melancholy object to those, who walk through this great town, or travel in the country, when they see the streets, the roads and cabbin-doors crowded with beggars of the female sex, followed by three, four, or six children, all in rags, and importuning every passenger for an alms. These mothers instead of being able to work for their honest livelihood, are forced to employ all their time in stroling to beg sustenance for their helpless infants who, as they grow up, either turn thieves for want of work, or leave their dear native country, to fight for the Pretender in Spain, or sell themselves to the Barbadoes.
>
> I think it is agreed by all parties, that this prodigious number of children in the arms, or on the backs, or at the heels of their mothers, and frequently of their fathers, is in the present deplorable state of the kingdom, a very great additional grievance; and therefore whoever could find out a fair, cheap and easy method of making these children sound and useful members of the common-wealth, would deserve so well of the publick, as to have his statue set up for a preserver of the nation.
>
> But my intention is very far from being confined to provide only for the children of professed beggars: it is of a much greater extent, and shall take in the whole number of infants at a certain age, who are born of parents in effect as little able to support them, as those who demand our charity in the streets.
>
> As to my own part, having turned my thoughts for many years, upon this important subject, and maturely weighed the several schemes of our projectors, I have always found them grossly mistaken in their computation. It is true, a child just dropt from its dam, may be supported by her milk, for a solar year, with little other nourishment: at most not above the value of two shillings, which the mother may certainly get, or the value in scraps, by her lawful occupation of begging; and it is exactly at one year old that I propose to provide for them in such a manner, as, instead of being a charge upon their parents, or the parish, or wanting food and raiment for the rest of their lives, they shall, on the contrary, contribute to the feeding, and partly to the cloathing of many thousands."

Answer:

The author uses a very sarcastic, tongue-in-cheek tone. He certainly does not intend what he writes (a proposal for harvesting babies) to be taken seriously.

The following are some examples of words and phrases that reveal the author's tone in the preceding exercise:

1. "...prodigious number of children...a very great additional grievance..."
2. "...cheap and easy method of making these children sound and useful members of the common-wealth..."
3. "...have his statue set up for a preserver of the nation..."
4. "...at most not above the value of two shillings..."
5. "...exactly at one year old...instead of being a charge upon their parents...they shall, on the contrary, contribute to the feeding..."

Imagery is the use of vivid language that appeals to any of the five senses: sight, hearing, taste, touch, and smell. Imagery enhances how the reader pictures people, places, and things in fiction. This usage of language is vitally important to poetry. You can read more about interpreting imagery in Chapter 16, "Poetry."

What's Next?

Chapter 16, "Poetry," provides information and exercises to help you understand the poetry that you will encounter on the GED.

CHAPTER SIXTEEN

Poetry

Poetry is highly expressive language—carefully selected words arranged in an artful manner to evoke certain ideas and emotions. For ages, humans have used poetry to stimulate thought, mourn the dead, rejoice in victory, and express the spectrum of human emotion.

On the GED Language Arts, Reading Test, you will see one short poem that you must read and interpret to answer questions about its theme.

Take these poetic epitaphs as examples. An *epitaph* is an inscription on a grave marker. As you read silently, pay close attention to the sound and rhythm of the words, in addition to their meaning.

A once-common epitaph in the United States:

> Come blooming youths, as you pass by
> And on these lines do cast an eye
> As you are now, so once was I;
> As I am now, so must you be;
> Prepare for death and follow me.

Did you notice the rhyme in this poem? What is the author saying about death? What is the tone of the poem?

An epitaph for an Old West gunslinger, buried in Silver City, Nevada:

> Here lies a man named Zeke
> Second-fastest draw in Cripple Creek.

How is this epitaph different from the previous one? Did this one make you smile or laugh?

Poetry can be simple, like the epitaphs here, or very complex. The goal of the poet is to create meaning through the best combination of words. Sometimes, rich themes can be conveyed in very few words. For this reason, you should read poetry very carefully. Do not hesitate to read a poem (or parts of it) several times, until you grasp the true sense of the words. To use a cliché (don't put it in your GED essay!), "read between the lines."

Forms of Poetry

Poems range in length from just a few words or sounds to thousands of lines, such as the *Odyssey*, by Greek poet Homer. In fact, that particular work was originally an oral poem meant to be read to audiences in a specific rhythm. For the GED, you will see only complete poems, so their length will be limited.

Whereas prose is made up of sentences that form paragraphs, most poetry contains lines that form stanzas. Like a new paragraph, a new stanza often indicates a change in idea within a poem. If you've ever sung a song in school, a band, or church, you've seen lines and stanzas. In fact, many songs and hymns began as poetry before they were set to music.

Traditionally, each line of a poem begins with a capital latter, and the last line ends with a period. Within a poem, the full variety of punctuation may be used. Take a moment to pause at commas, semicolons, dashes, and so on. Many poets use punctuation to dictate rhythm in their work.

Different forms of poetry have specific names and conventional formats. Following are some common ones you may have heard of. *Quatrains* and *couplets* refer to groups of rhyming lines. You will read about rhyme in the next section.

- **Haiku**—Composed of three lines, the first containing five syllables, the second containing seven syllables, and the third containing five syllables. No rhyme. Often about nature or a season.
- **Sonnet**—Composed of 14 lines using a rhyme scheme. English style: three quatrains and one couplet. Expresses a single idea.
- **Ode**—Lyric poem of elaborate form and meter. Exuberant emotion. Sometimes meant to be sung.
- **Limerick**—Composed of five lines. Lines 1, 2, and 5 rhyme. Lines 3 and 4 form a couplet. Humorous poem.
- **Epic**—Book-length poem about a heroic or mythological person.

Naturally, because poetry is a creation of language, poets may stray as much as they like from traditional formats.

Hearing Poetry

One characteristic of poetry is meter, or rhythm. The way poetry is read aloud figures crucially into how an audience will interpret it. In addition, some poems use rhyme to evoke certain feelings or draw attention to an idea. The most common type of rhyme is *end rhyme*, repetition of the last sound of a line. Consider the rhyme and meter of this limerick:

> There was an Old Lady whose folly,
> Induced her to sit in a holly;
> Whereon by a thorn,
> Her dress being torn,
> She quickly became melancholy.
> —"58." By Edward Lear, from *A Book of Nonsense*, © 1846

Read the limerick aloud to yourself, emphasizing the metrical pattern of limericks. Here is the poem again, this time with the stressed syllables underlined. Remember that the stress pattern of a word in everyday speech may not correspond to its stress pattern in a particular poem!

There was an Old Lady whose folly,
Induced her to sit in a holly;
Whereon by a thorn,
Her dress being torn,
She quickly became melancholy.

Notice how the poem has a rhyme scheme. For this limerick, the scheme can be described as A-A-B-B-A. The A lines end with the sound "oly" and the B lines end with the sound "orn." The rhyme in this poem is true end rhyme—the sounds are the same.

Groups of rhyming lines are named according to the number of lines: couplets have two, triplets have three, quatrains have four, and so on.

In addition to end rhyme, poems may use *slant rhyme*, also called *near rhyme*. Sometimes a word may be the right one, although it doesn't perfectly fit into the rhyme scheme. For example, lines ending with "phone" and "Rome" could be said to have slant rhyme because the final sounds are very similar. Generally, slant rhyme does not negatively affect the overall impact of the poem.

Another element of the sound of poetry is called *alliteration*, which is repetition of a sound in consecutive words. Alliterative lines and phrases are an aid to memory; therefore, advertisers use them frequently in their slogans. Nursery rhymes and tongue twisters are rich in alliteration, for example: *Peter Piper picked a peck of pickled peppers.*

Onomatopoeia is the use of words that imitate sounds. Children learn animal sounds very early: *moo*, *quack*, *oink*, and so on. Onomatopoeia also includes sound-imitating words such as *clang*, *boom*, *whiz*, *crash*, and the like.

Figurative Language

The figures of speech of similes, metaphors, and personification are introduced in Chapter 15, "Prose Fiction." Consider the following examples in poetry.

Love is compared to a red rose in one simile, and to a melody in a second simile:

O my Love's like a red, red rose,
That's newly sprung in June:
O my Love's like the melody,
That's sweetly play'd in tune.
—Excerpted from "A Red, Red Rose" by Robert Burns, © 1794

Life and love are compared with hosts of a gathering in this metaphor:

What delightful hosts are they—
Life and Love!
Lingeringly I turn away,
This late hour, yet glad enough
They have not withheld from me
Their high hospitality.
So, with face lit with delight
And all gratitude, I stay
Yet to press their hands and say,
"Thanks.—So fine a time! Good night."
—"The Parting Guest" by James Whitcomb Riley, © 1907

Autumn is personified in this excerpt:

Who hath not seen thee oft amid thy store?
Sometimes whoever seeks abroad may find
Thee sitting careless on a granary floor,
Thy hair soft-lifted by the winnowing wind;
Or on a half-reap'd furrow sound asleep,
Drows'd with the fume of poppies, while thy hook
Spares the next swath and all its twined flowers:
And sometimes like a gleaner thou dost keep
Steady thy laden head across a brook;
Or by a cyder-press, with patient look,
Thou watchest the last oozings hours by hours.
—Excerpted from "To Autumn" by John Keats, © 1820

Interpreting Imagery, Symbolism, and Theme

A poet may enrich his work by appealing to the reader's five senses. Poetry that seems to stimulate smell, taste, touch, sight, and hearing is very effective at conveying emotions and ideas.

Imagery Exercise

The following excerpt from a poem is rich with imagery. Read it, and then circle the words or phrases that appeal to any of the five senses. Imagine yourself seeing, hearing, touching, tasting, or smelling what the poem describes. Pay attention to your "mental picture" as you read.

Far from my dearest Friend, 'tis mine to rove
Through bare grey dell, high wood, and pastoral cove;
Where Derwent rests, and listens to the roar
That stuns the tremulous cliffs of high Lodore;
Where peace to Grasmere's lonely island leads,
To willowy hedge-rows, and to emerald meads;
Leads to her bridge, rude church, and cottaged grounds,
Her rocky sheepwalks, and her woodland bounds;
Where, undisturbed by winds, Winander sleeps
'Mid clustering isles, and holly-sprinkled steeps;
Where twilight glens endear my Esthwaite's shore,
And memory of departed pleasures, more.

—Excerpted from "An Evening Walk" by William Wordsworth, © 1793

Answers

Examples of imagery: bare grey dell, high wood, pastoral cove, roar, tremulous cliffs, willowy hedge-rows, emerald meads, cottaged grounds, rocky sheepwalks, undisturbed by winds, clustering isles, holly-sprinkled steeps, twilight glens

Symbolism is the use of ideas, people, or objects to represent a concrete thing or an abstraction. Examples of abstractions are love, hate, evil, God, heaven, hell, depression, addiction, liberty, justice, happiness, purity, youth—anything intangible and complex on which people have different points of view.

Symbolism Exercise

The following poem is rich with symbolism. Read it carefully a few times, and then answer the questions that follow.

O rose, thou art sick!
The invisible worm,
That flies in the night,
In the howling storm,

Has found out thy bed
Of crimson joy,
And his dark secret love
Does thy life destroy.

—"The Sick Rose" by William Blake, © 1794

1. What are three objects or abstractions that a rose might symbolize? ____________________
2. How is the worm portrayed? (Think about mood.) ____________________
3. The entire poem is a symbol for some event or action. What is your interpretation of the theme of the poem? ____________________

Answers

1. A rose might symbolize youth, beauty, new love, enduring love, purity, or virginity.
2. The worm is portrayed as evil and harmful to the rose. The poet uses the imagery of *night* and *the howling storm* to paint the worm as evil. The last two lines of the poem reinforce this notion.
3. There are many possible interpretations of the poem. Some people see it as a symbol of the hazards of falling in love too young. Some see it as a warning to young girls about the ill intentions of men. Many scholars who know the social and political leanings of the poet believe the poem is a statement about religion. They believe Blake is asserting the ungodliness of priests and warning young women not to allow themselves to be corrupted by priests' teachings.

Theme is the ultimate, unifying idea of a poem. You will need to identify theme in prose and poetry on the GED. Pay particularly close attention to the mood the poem creates.

Mood

Poets choose words carefully to create a certain mood. Like prose, poetry can be serious, funny, sad, or reflective of any other human emotion.

Mood Exercise

The two poems that follow were written in reaction to World War I. Read them carefully, assess the mood of each, and then answer the questions that follow.

"Anthem for Doomed Youth"

by Wilfred Owen, © 1917

What passing-bells for these who die as cattle?
Only the monstrous anger of the guns.
Only the stuttering rifles' rapid rattle
Can patter out their hasty orisons.*
No mockeries now for them; no prayers nor bells;
Nor any voice of mourning save the choirs,-
The shrill, demented choirs of wailing shells;
And bugles calling for them from sad shires.

What candles may be held to speed them all?
Not in the hands of boys, but in their eyes
Shall shine the holy glimmers of goodbyes.
The pallor of girls' brows shall be their pall;
Their flowers the tenderness of patient minds,
And each slow dusk a drawing-down of blinds.

* prayers

"In Flanders Fields"

by John McCrae, © 1919

In Flanders fields the poppies blow
Between the crosses, row on row,

That mark our place; and in the sky
The larks, still bravely singing, fly
Scarce heard amid the guns below.

We are the Dead. Short days ago
We lived, felt dawn, saw sunset glow,
Loved and were loved, and now we lie
In Flanders fields.

Take up our quarrel with the foe:
To you from failing hands we throw
The torch; be yours to hold it high.
If ye break faith with us who die
We shall not sleep, though poppies grow
In Flanders fields.

1. What imagery does the Owen poem use to establish its mood? ______________________
2. What is the mood of the Owen poem? ______________________
3. What is the central symbol in the McCrae poem? ______________________
4. What is your interpretation of the symbolism in the third stanza of the McCrae poem? ______________________
5. How are the moods of these two poems different? ______________________

Answers

1. Examples of violent or sad imagery: die as cattle, monstrous anger of the guns, stuttering rifles' rapid rattle, shrill, demented choirs of wailing shells, holy glimmers of goodbyes, pallor of girls' brows, (funeral) flowers, slow dusk, drawing-down of blinds.
2. The Owen poem portrays World War I as a complete horror. The poem is shocking and violent.
3. Poppies are the central symbol of the McCrae poem. They represent the soldiers who died on the battlefield where the poppies grow.
4. The torch represents liberty or righteousness. In the third stanza, the dead soldiers pass responsibility for winning the war to the living soldiers and warn that their deaths cannot be reconciled unless the living soldiers maintain that responsibility.
5. The Owen poem portrays the violence and death of World War I, and so does the McCrae poem, though not nearly as strongly or vividly. Whereas the Owen poem is horrific, the McCrae poem is sad for the dead and honors them. The McCrae poem is also hopeful for the future, a sentiment not expressed in the Owen poem.

What's Next?

Chapter 17, "Drama," provides information and exercises to help you understand the dramatic passages that you will encounter on the GED.

17

CHAPTER SEVENTEEN

Drama

Drama is literature performed by actors, whether on stage, in films, on television, or (to a lesser extent in this modern age) on radio. The skills required for reading and interpreting drama are the same as those required for reading other types of fiction.

On the GED Language Arts, Reading Test, you will see one excerpt from a play that you must read and interpret to answer questions about its characters, plot, and theme.

The basic work of drama is the play, which is written as dialogue with directions for the actors' performances. Producing a play usually involves many people: the actors, financers, stage directors, set designers, costume designers, and so on. In the time before mass media, when most people could not read, plays were among the limited exposure to literature many people had. In English playwright William Shakespeare's time, for example, every person had the right to attend the theater, if attendance could be afforded. Richer people would crowd the upper-level seats, and poorer people would pack the area of ground in front of the stage. People were passionate about the theater and were occasionally rowdy when a play did not meet their expectations.

Today in the United States and Canada, live theater has been replaced by television and movies as the preferred forms of drama. These modern media do not represent a radical change, though. Scripts written for television and movies evolved from the centuries-old art of playwriting.

Dialogue and Stage Directions

When actors study for a play, they "learn their lines," meaning they memorize what they will say and when and how they will say it. In print, each line of speech begins with the name of the character speaking. Look for punctuation that indicates pauses, interruptions, and periods of silence.

Sometimes there are stage directions between speakers, within a line, or after a line, that call for the actor(s) to perform an action or deliver the line in a particular way. Longer stage directions usher characters on or off stage or provide for some action to take place when characters are not speaking. You can recognize stage directions by their parentheses ( ), brackets [ ], or italic type.

Stage Direction Exercise

The following excerpt from a play uses stage directions. Read the excerpt carefully a few times, and then answer the questions that follow.

COUNTY ATTORNEY: *(rubbing his hands)* This feels good. Come up to the fire, ladies.

MRS. PETERS: (*after taking a step forward*) I'm not—cold.

SHERIFF: *(unbuttoning his overcoat and stepping away from the stove as if to mark the beginning of official business)* Now, Mr. Hale, before we move things about, you explain to Mr. Henderson just what you saw when you came here yesterday morning.

—Susan Glaspell, excerpted from *Trifles*, © 1916

1. Why is the County Attorney rubbing his hands? ______________________
2. What might explain the apparent discrepancy between Mrs. Peters' action in the stage direction and her line? ______________________
3. How do you think the action in the Sheriff's stage direction would affect the other people in the scene? ______________________

Answers

1. The County Attorney rubs his hands over a fire to warm them.
2. To "step forward" seems to mean to step toward the fire, which conflicts with Mrs. Peters' statement that she" not cold. Either "step forward" means step away from the fire, or Mrs. Peters is not telling the truth. Her hesitation, as indicated by the dash, may show she is lying about not being cold, or perhaps shivering.
3. The action of taking off his overcoat and stepping away from the stove (presumably toward the group or perhaps a desk) would most likely cause the other people in the room to pay closer attention to the Sheriff.

Dramatic Structure

The elements of fiction explained in Chapter 15, "Prose Fiction," are present in works of drama, too. The main character, whose conflicts propel the action in the play, is called the *protagonist*. You can review in Chapter 15 the four categories of conflict and the basic structure of plot.

A play can consist of any number of acts. Acts are divided into scenes, which are units where the dialogue and unfolding plot are, usually, confined to a single place and time. The time between scenes and acts allows the audience to reflect on what they have just watched and heard. The time between acts and scenes also allows actors to change costumes and for necessary changes to be made to the stage. Shakespeare is credited with formalizing the pattern of drama that we still use today.

Classical theater used the prologue in the absence of stage decorations. One actor, often playing the role of a narrator, would come onstage before the others to deliver details about the play's setting or any important background information. The epilogue was also common in classical theater. An actor would deliver a solo speech at the end of a play to help the audience understand the story it just witnessed. Many modern plays include neither of these speeches.

Analyzing Characters

When watching a play, you can learn about characters through what they say, their mannerisms, tone of voice, and costume. When reading a play, you must rely on printed lines and stage directions. Plays generally describe in the opening page before the dialogue the overall personality and physical attributes of the characters. Some plays specifically indicate what the character is wearing. Stage directions within the dialogue reveal characters' movements and gestures. As you read, ask yourself what motivates the characters to act in a certain way or say a certain thing. Use these kinds of details to help understand the characters in plays you read.

Analyzing Characters Exercise

Read the following excerpt from a play, and then answer the questions that follow about the characters.

[Lieutenant Richard (Dick) Coleman is a handsome, finely built man of about thirty-two. He is a West Pointer, is a good oarsman, a crack shot, and a good fellow all around. No finicking about him, no nerves. Just a sane, healthy, fine fellow.]

DICK: Hello! Many happy returns, Phil. *(Shakes hands)* Where's your Aunt Georgiana! *(Silence)* Is she out?

PHIL: No, she's under the table!

CHRISTOPHER AND TOOTS: *(Delighted)* She's under the table! She's under the table!

DICK: *(Laughing)* What!

PHIL: Hide and seek.

[Dick looks under the table; he and Georgiana laugh.]

DICK: Good morning, are you at home?

GEORGIANA: *(Very embarrassed)* Oh, mercy! Do go away so I can get out!

DICK: *(Tremendously amused)* Come on out!

GEORGIANA: No! I can't with you there. *(Laughing)* Please leave the room for just one minute!

DICK: Not if I know it! Come on out!

GEORGIANA: Not for worlds! Go away, please! *(Dick shakes his head "No")* Then I shall never come out.

DICK: Ah, but that's hardly fair, because I want to talk to you comfortably.

GEORGIANA: Well, then, come on under!

DICK: Is there room?

GEORGIANA: A cable car conductor who knew his business could seat four more people in here.

DICK: Still—I think I'm more comfortable up here.

GEORGIANA: Selfish! Go on away! *(Dick shakes his head)* Children, if you love your auntie, go for Mr. Dick with all your might and main and push him into the hall.

[The children shout and rush toward Dick; they catch hold of him.]

THE CHILDREN: Go away!

DICK: *(With mock ferocity)* The first child I get hold of I'll *spank*!

[The children laugh and shout and run away from him to behind the table.]

—Clyde Fitch, excerpted from *Her Own Way* © 1907, London: Macmillan & Co., Ltd.

1. What do the stage directions and Dick's interaction with the children say about his personality? ____________________
2. What does Georgiana's refusal to come out from under the table say about her personality? ____________________
3. How old do the children seem? ____________________

Answers

1. Dick is a good man with a playful side and a sense of humor.
2. Although Georgiana is playful, she shows a modest or bashful side of her personality when she refuses to come out from under the table. Perhaps her hair or clothes are mussed, or maybe she can't easily come out without assuming some kind of unladylike pose.
3. The children speak in full sentences and are wildly amused by the game of hide-and-seek with Georgiana. They are probably elementary-school age.

What's Next?

Chapter 18, "Prose Nonfiction," provides information and exercises to help you understand the nonfiction passages that you will encounter on the GED.

CHAPTER EIGHTEEN

Prose Nonfiction

Any literature based on fact or opinion is called *nonfiction*. By definition, nonfiction does not present imaginary information as fact, in the way fiction does.

On the GED Language Arts, Reading Test, you will see two short nonfiction passages that you must read and interpret to answer a total of 10 multiple-choice questions. One passage will be a commentary on a visual medium (for example, television, movies, visual arts), and the other passage will be from one of the other categories described in the next section.

The best way to improve your skill at reading and interpreting nonfiction is to expose yourself to it. Find a newspaper you like and read the articles, editorials, and letters to the editor. Find a magazine on a subject that interests you and read it. Go online and read and listen to the speeches of current and former political and civic leaders. Consider becoming a pen pal with a friend or family member. This will also help the quality of your writing, the speed at which you write, and even your penmanship. As you read nonfiction, have a critical eye for the facts. Ask yourself whether what you are reading sounds like fact or opinion. Consider whether something you write could be interpreted another way by a reader.

Forms of Nonfiction

You are exposed to a variety of forms of nonfiction every day. Following are the most common forms of nonfiction that you might see on your GED:

- Literary nonfiction, including
    - Essay—Written to present a point of view on a topic
    - Biography—Written about someone's life
    - Autobiography—Written about the author's own life
- Journalism, including
    - Articles—Written to inform or entertain
    - Editorials—Written to persuade and based on fact
- Artistic commentary, such as reviews of plays, movies, television shows, works of art, exhibitions, and so on.
- Speech, such as President Reagan's 1986 *Challenger* disaster speech and Martin Luther King, Jr.'s "I have a dream" speech

- Practical documents, including
    - Explanations of rights, responsibilities, or procedures for employers and employees (for example, safety policies, job descriptions, disciplinary actions)
    - Government publications (for example, income-tax return rules)
    - Documents exchanged in a business relationship (for example, contracts, agreements, corporate policies)
- Correspondence, such as letters and email exchanged between people and/or businesses

The Author's Purpose and Tone

A primary goal of a reader of nonfiction is to determine the purpose that the author had for writing something. A writer of nonfiction might simply want to document something for posterity. Other times, the author tries to analyze a subject or give commentary on it. Nonfiction can also inform or entertain.

Keep in mind that you cannot write on your GED test booklet.

As you read, you might want to identify clue words that reveal something about the author's purpose and tone and whether statements are fact or opinion.

The following are some words that might help to identify the author's opinion:

- may, might
- should, could, ought, need
- think, feel, believe, suppose, seem
- probably, most likely, possibly, usually
- good, bad, pretty, ugly, easy, difficult, boring, exciting (Look for any subjective judgments like these.)
- always, never, everyone, no one (Read about the traps of these "100% words" in Chapter 9, "Effective Writing.")

Complete the following exercise to test your understanding of fact versus opinion.

Fact Versus Opinion Exercise

Read each of the following sentences and answer whether it is a fact or an opinion. If it is an opinion, rewrite it as a fact, adding any elements to the sentence that you need.

Example: Bobby should do his homework before dinner. *(Opinion) Bobby's mother wants him to do his homework before dinner.*

1. Sears Tower in Chicago is no longer the tallest building in the world. ______________________
2. Professional athletes are probably overpaid. ______________________
3. Senior citizens should be vaccinated against the flu each winter. ______________________
4. It rained for more than two hours yesterday. ______________________
5. Neon signs are usually a distraction for drivers. ______________________

Answers

1. (Fact)
2. (Opinion) Possible Correction: Some people think that professional athletes are overpaid.
3. (Opinion) Possible Correction: The Health Department recommends that senior citizens be vaccinated against the flu each winter.
4. (Fact)
5. (Opinion) Possible Correction: Some people believe that neon signs are a distraction for drivers.

Cause and Effect

When one element affects another, the two elements are said to have a cause-effect relationship. For example, because running makes you thirsty, running is the cause of the thirst.

Writers often signal cause-and-effect relationships with the following words and phrases:

- To introduce an example

  For example, if…then…

  For instance, if…then…

  To illustrate, when…then…

- To introduce cause or effect

  Therefore,…

  As a result,…

  Because…

  Since…

  Accordingly,…

Complete the following exercise to test your ability to relate cause and effect.

Cause and Effect Exercise

Read the following passage and answer the questions that follow. Indicate whether the question asks for a cause or an effect.

In the spring of 1999, a university student—also an avid hunter—stalked the woods of Louisiana's Pearl River Wildlife Management Area. Turkey license in hand, he had no expectation of discovering a far rarer bird, one that had been declared extinct in 1994. The student's report of seeing a pair of ivory-billed woodpeckers would lead to an exhaustive search for the lost species in the vast 35,000-acre wilderness.

Extensive logging and unregulated hunting in the 1800s decimated the population of the ivory-billed woodpecker in its native habitat of the Southeastern United States. By the 1920s, the species had been given up as extinct. By 1938, however, around 20 ivory-billed woodpeckers were known to exist in an isolated tract of old-growth forest in Louisiana. Despite pleas from four state governments and the National Audubon Society, logging began in the forest, and by 1944, the last known ivory-billed woodpecker was gone from the ruined habitat. The only evidence of the species' survival before its rediscovery at the end of the century was an unconfirmed recording of its distinctive call made in Texas in 1967.

New hope of finding an ivory-billed woodpecker rose from the sighting of 1999. In 2002, biologists from Louisiana State University spent nearly a month in the Pearl River Wildlife Management Area searching for the bird. They made a sound recording originally believed to be the distinctive double rap sound of the elusive bird but later determined it was likely the echoes from a gunshot. Evidence of active woodpeckers was found, though, in markings and large cavities in tree trunks. In the end, existence of the ivory-billed woodpecker could not be proven.

1. Why was the university student in the Wildlife Management Area in the spring of 1999?
2. What was the impact of 19th-century logging on the ivory-billed woodpecker?
3. In 1938, how were 20 ivory-billed woodpeckers able to survive?

Answers

1. He was hunting turkey. (cause)
2. Logging ruined the woodpecker's habitat, decimating their population. (effect)
3. An isolated portion of the forest had not yet been logged. (cause)

Comparing and Contrasting

Effective analysis of an idea requires comparing and contrasting. *Comparing* refers to examining similarities, whereas *contrasting* refers to examining differences.

Complete the following exercise to test your understanding of comparing and contrasting.

Comparing and Contrasting Exercise

Read the two paragraphs, compare and contrast them, and then answer the questions that follow.

The three days of the Battle of Gettysburg, Pennsylvania, constitute the bloodiest fight of the Civil War—50,000 combatants fell dead or wounded or disappeared. Gettysburg is often cited as the last crucial battle of the war before the Confederate surrender. In the intervening two years, the Confederate Army would never again attempt such a grand offensive in the North. On the last day of battle, Union forces anticipated and put down what is now known as Pickett's Charge, the final assault ordered by General Robert E. Lee, leaving Confederate forces in tatters.

Nine times as many Americans fell in the farmlands near Antietam Creek, Maryland, in the fall of 1862 than fell on the beaches of Normandy on D-Day, the so-called "longest day" of World War II. The bloodiest single day of war in the nation's history came when General Robert E. Lee's Confederate Army undertook its first engagement on Northern soil. According to the Antietam National Battlefield, when the fighting had subsided, more than 23,000 soldiers lay dead or wounded, more than all the dead or wounded Americans in the Revolutionary War, War of 1812, Mexican War, and Spanish-American War combined.

1. How is the tone regarding casualty rates similar between the two paragraphs? ______

2. How do the paragraphs differ with regard to the outcome of the battles? ______

Answers

1. Each paragraph emphasizes the human cost of the particular battle. In fact, the first sentence in each paragraph and the mention of approximations of casualties in each battle make a clear appeal to the reader's sense of shock at the loss of so many soldiers. Both paragraphs have an objective tone that is colored by a sense of horror.

2. The first paragraph indicates that the Battle of Gettysburg left "Confederate forces in tatters," whereas the second paragraph describes the overall devastation to both sides of the Battle of Antietam without indicating a victor.

Inference

Sometimes details are left for the reader to figure out by *inference*. Police officers often rely on their ability to infer because details about complicated situations can be hazy or missing. For example, an office light left on in a business at night might not be suspicious by itself, but additional clues—such as an open garage door, a broken gate, or a vehicle parked outside—might lead the officer to *infer* that a burglary is in progress.

Successful nonfiction guides the reader to the author's theme and purpose for writing without explicitly stating what the reader should feel or believe.

Complete the following exercise to test your understanding of inference.

Inference Exercise

Read the paragraph, and then answer the questions that follow.

> A few blocks south of the apartment I'm renting, Joe's Lunch Bucket serves up classic sandwiches. The owner runs the place, so he stays open as long as he has customers, usually until some time after midnight. His space is at the end of an alley. If you sit on the last stool by the window, you can see the big public fountain in the adjacent square. There are usually swarms of children and teenagers milling around the area; no one really enforces the curfew, especially in the summer when the nights turn warm and families stroll around the shops and public spaces downtown.

1. What can you infer from the paragraph about the speaker's attitude toward Joe's Lunch Bucket? ______________________

2. Why do you think the author mentions that Joe's Lunch Bucket is located at the end of an alley? ______________________

Answers

1. The paragraph includes pleasant details about the restaurant and its surroundings that reveal the author's fondness for the place.
2. The author probably mentions the out-of-the-way location of Joe's to reinforce its homey appeal. The speaker may value its obscurity in the neighborhood. Cities often have so-called "best-kept secrets," which can be excellent restaurants that survive on regular customers and word of mouth alone.

Summarizing

A good test of whether you understand what you have just read is attempting to summarize it for yourself or another person. A *summary* is a short piece that paraphrases the information in a longer work. It includes all important conclusions but leaves out insignificant or unnecessary details.

Complete the following exercise to test your understanding of summarizing.

Summarizing Exercise

Read this paragraph, and then read how one person summarized it:

> If you ever travel to Europe, you will likely want to visit the monuments and museums of Paris, one of the most beautiful cities in the world. You will immerse yourself in art, architecture, and the history of Western civilization. The cultural treasures of France's capital are awe inspiring, but what amazes most about visiting Paris is the ease by which you can tour the city using the extensive network of the subway, what the French call the *Métropolitain*, or simply the Metro.

Summary: The speaker believes tourists should tour the cultural attractions of Paris by its Metro.

In this summary, "cultural attractions" takes the place of "monuments and museums" and "art, architecture, and the history of Western civilization." The summary also restates the paragraph in the third person ("The speaker believes…"), taking the tone of a general statement. Explanatory details are eliminated as well.

Read each of the following paragraphs, evaluate their overall meaning, and then summarize each one in one or two sentences.

1. I appreciate the arguments in favor of television, video games, and other electronic entertainment. They are dynamic and, for the most part, engaging. There's indeed something for everyone. I also believe, however, that these new forms of entertainment have taken time away from "unplugged" fun. A good hands-on hobby should be an important part of any childhood. Instead of simple storybooks, toddlers have interactive learning computers that read for them. When children aren't watching satellite television, they have console games to entertain themselves. It seems to me that more and more of the joys of childhood are being lost to the allure of the video screen.

   ____

   ____

   ____

2. The Strait of Mackinac between Lakes Huron and Michigan divides Michigan's Upper and Lower Peninsulas. Native Americans in the former wilderness territory knew how to paddle between several islands to make their way across. Settlers in the 18th and 19th centuries crossed the Mackinac Strait by ferry. Ferries would soon prove costly in both lives and money. By the 1880s, Mackinac Island, which had become a popular summer tourist retreat, abandoned as unfeasible year-round ferry service after numerous failed attempts. By this decade, too, the Michigan Legislature began discussing the idea of a bridge to span the Mackinac Strait, having seen the success of the newly built Brooklyn Bridge. Many hurdles, though, stood in the way of the Mackinac Bridge, which was not completed until 1957.

   ____

   ____

   ____

Example Summaries

1. The speaker believes that, although fun, video entertainment is keeping children from the joys of simpler, "unplugged" entertainment.
2. Historically, the water route between Michigan's peninsulas was navigated by canoe and later by ferry. The Mackinac Bridge was proposed to span the strait after ferry service failed in the 1880s; however, it was not completed until 1957.

What's Next?

The next chapter includes simulated GED Language Arts, Reading Test practice questions with answers and explanations. Attempt all the questions, referring to the previous chapters as necessary.

19

CHAPTER NINETEEN

Language Arts, Reading Practice Questions and Answer Explanations

This chapter includes 20 simulated Language Arts, Reading questions in multiple-choice format. Carefully read the directions and answer the questions. Allow yourself 30 to 35 minutes to complete these practice questions.

The practice questions are followed by answers and detailed explanations. Read the explanations for the answers, and review the previous chapters in Part V, "Language Arts, Reading," as needed.

Use the answer sheet on the following page to mark your answers. Then compare your answers to the answers and explanations at the end of this chapter. Be sure to read through the explanations thoroughly. Identify and review topics you've consistently struggled with.

Please note that this chapter does not follow the precise format of the GED.

Answer Sheet

1. ① ② ③ ④ ⑤
2. ① ② ③ ④ ⑤
3. ① ② ③ ④ ⑤
4. ① ② ③ ④ ⑤
5. ① ② ③ ④ ⑤
6. ① ② ③ ④ ⑤
7. ① ② ③ ④ ⑤
8. ① ② ③ ④ ⑤
9. ① ② ③ ④ ⑤
10. ① ② ③ ④ ⑤
11. ① ② ③ ④ ⑤
12. ① ② ③ ④ ⑤
13. ① ② ③ ④ ⑤
14. ① ② ③ ④ ⑤
15. ① ② ③ ④ ⑤
16. ① ② ③ ④ ⑤
17. ① ② ③ ④ ⑤
18. ① ② ③ ④ ⑤
19. ① ② ③ ④ ⑤
20. ① ② ③ ④ ⑤
21. ① ② ③ ④ ⑤
22. ① ② ③ ④ ⑤
23. ① ② ③ ④ ⑤
24. ① ② ③ ④ ⑤
25. ① ② ③ ④ ⑤

Practice Questions

Directions: Choose the one best answer to each question.

Questions 1 through 5 refer to the following excerpt from a novel.

HOW DOES THE NARRATOR REACT TO THE ISLAND?

The appearance of the island when I came on deck next morning was altogether changed. Although the breeze had now utterly ceased, we had made a great deal of way during the night and were now lying becalmed about half a mile to the south-east of the low eastern coast. Grey-coloured woods covered a large part of the surface. This even tint was indeed broken up by streaks of yellow sand-break in the lower lands, and by many tall trees of the pine family, out-topping the others—some singly, some in clumps; but the general colouring was uniform and sad. The hills ran up clear above the vegetation in spires of naked rock. All were strangely shaped, and the Spy-glass, which was by three or four hundred feet the tallest on the island, was likewise the strangest in configuration, running up sheer from almost every side and then suddenly cut off at the top like a pedestal to put a statue on.

The *Hispaniola* was rolling scuppers under in the ocean swell. The booms were tearing at the blocks, the rudder was banging to and fro, and the whole ship creaking, groaning, and jumping like a manufactory. I had to cling tight to the backstay, and the world turned giddily before my eyes, for though I was a good enough sailor when there was way on, this standing still and being rolled about like a bottle was a thing I never learned to stand without a qualm or so, above all in the morning, on an empty stomach.

Perhaps it was this—perhaps it was the look of the island, with its grey, melancholy woods, and wild stone spires, and the surf that we could both see and hear foaming and thundering on the steep beach—at least, although the sun shone bright and hot, and the shore birds were fishing and crying all around us, and you would have thought anyone would have been glad to get to land after being so long at sea, my heart sank, as the saying is, into my boots; and from the first look onward, I hated the very thought of Treasure Island.

We had a dreary morning's work before us, for there was no sign of any wind, and the boats had to be got out and manned, and the ship warped three or four miles round the corner of the island and up the narrow passage to the haven behind Skeleton Island. I volunteered for one of the boats, where I had, of course, no business. The heat was sweltering, and the men grumbled fiercely over their work. Anderson was in command of my boat, and instead of keeping the crew in order, he grumbled as loud as the worst.

"Well," he said with an oath, "it's not forever."

I thought this was a very bad sign, for up to that day the men had gone briskly and willingly about their business; but the very sight of the island had relaxed the cords of discipline.

Robert Louis Stevenson, excerpted from *Treasure Island*, © 1883

1. When the narrator says that "instead of keeping the crew in order" Anderson "grumbled as loud as the worst" (line 30), he is implying which of the following?

   (1) Anderson was inexperienced in leading crew members.

   (2) Anderson was usually a very difficult boss.

   (3) As commander of the boat, Anderson had a responsibility to set an example for his crew.

   (4) Anderson was usually cheerful and talkative.

   (5) Anderson was unusually sensitive to heat.

2. On the basis of the narrator's reaction to the island revealed in this excerpt, how would the narrator most likely act if he were captain of the ship?

   He would probably

   (1) force his crew to dock at the island

   (2) ignore the island

   (3) ignore his crew's response to the island

   (4) refuse to dock at the island

   (5) circle the island looking for inhabitants

3. When the narrator says, "[T]his standing still and being rolled about like a bottle was a thing I never learned to stand without a qualm or so" (lines 16-17), what is he suggesting about himself?

   The narrator is

   (1) an excellent sailor with years of experience

   (2) inexperienced at sea but eager to prove himself to the other sailors

   (3) always more comfortable on land than on sea

   (4) easily seasick when the ship sways

   (5) never sick

4. The narrator would probably identify which one of the following traits as *not* essential to being a good sailor?

   (1) good work ethic

   (2) ability to cook

   (3) physical strength

   (4) obedience to orders

   (5) resistance to seasickness

5. Which of the following phrases is closest in meaning to the phrase "cords of discipline" in line 33?
   (1) sea ropes
   (2) good humor
   (3) self-restraint
   (4) camaraderie
   (5) chain of command

Questions 6 through 11 refer to the following poem.

HOW DOES THE SPEAKER DIFFER FROM OTHERS?

Alone

From childhood's hour I have not been
As others were; I have not seen
As others saw; I could not bring
My passions from a common spring.
From the same source I have not taken
My sorrow; I could not awaken
My heart to joy at the same tone;
And all I loved, I loved alone.
Then—in my childhood, in the dawn
Of a most stormy life—was drawn
From every depth of good and ill
The mystery which binds me still:
From the torrent, or the fountain,
From the red cliff of the mountain,
From the sun that round me rolled
In its autumn tint of gold,
From the lightning in the sky
As it passed me flying by,
From the thunder and the storm,
And the cloud that took the form
(When the rest of Heaven was blue)
Of a demon in my view.

"Alone" by Edgar Allan Poe, © 1830.

6. What might the speaker mean when he says, "From childhood's hour I have not been/As others were; I have not seen/As others saw" in lines 1–3?

   The speaker

   (1) has bad vision

   (2) was forbidden to play with other children

   (3) was afraid of other children

   (4) dislikes crowds

   (5) has always felt he was different from other people

7. What does the speaker imply about his life when he writes "in my childhood, in the dawn/Of a most stormy life" in lines 9–10?

   His life has been

   (1) inspiring to others

   (2) full of happiness

   (3) full of anxiety

   (4) difficult from the beginning

   (5) successful

8. How might the speaker react if he observed a group of people laughing at a clown?

   The speaker might

   (1) stand apart from the crowd but enjoy the clown

   (2) ignore the clown in order to avoid the crowd

   (3) pretend to enjoy the show with the others

   (4) run from the clown in fear

   (5) see a sinister side to the clown not seen by the others

9. What is the main effect of the lines "And the cloud that took the form/(when the rest of Heaven was blue)/Of a demon in my view" (lines 20–22)?

   (1) to emphasize the speaker's melancholy nature

   (2) to indicate that clouds sometimes represent danger

   (3) to reinforce that the speaker is afraid of storms

   (4) to link the weather to the speaker's need to be alone

   (5) to clarify his views on meteorology

10. Edgar Allen Poe, the author of the poem, is known for his grim and sometimes morbid stories, such as "The Tell-Tale Heart," in which a man commits the perfect murder yet is driven by paranoia to confess his crime. What evidence of Poe's interest in horror can be found in this poem?

    (1) repetitive structure

    (2) dark imagery

    (3) social commentary

    (4) verse form

    (5) insistence on being alone

Questions 12 through 15 refer to the following business document.

HOW MUST AN EMPLOYEE HANDLE TELEPHONE CALLS?

North Washington Pediatrics
Employee Handbook

Telephone Procedures

The success of our medical practice depends on efficient handling of telephone calls and accurate recording of messages. While most calls are very simple to deal with, great care must be taken with calls involving matters of scheduling, billing, and patient health. The following telephone procedures should be followed by all staff in the office.

1. **Answering.**
    a. Pick up the receiver and select the line that is ringing. (Volume should be low, so watch for the flashing red light.)
    b. Say "North Washington Pediatrics, [your first name] speaking. How may I help you?"
2. **Responding.**
    a. Transfer all calls regarding urgent medical situations, especially hospital admissions, to the first available doctor.
    b. When patients are waiting for a doctor in the office, that doctor is to receive no non-emergency calls. Take written messages.
    c. Determine the purpose of the call. If you can quickly help the caller without transferring the call, do so.
    d. Ask unsolicited callers to remove the office's phone number from their calling list.
    e. Take messages from vendor representatives for review by the doctors.

3. **Record keeping.**
    a. Keep pens and message pads by every phone.
    b. Record messages for doctors with any details the caller gives you (those regarding patient status especially).
    c. When applicable, ask these questions, then forward the call to the doctor along with your message.
        i. When did the child first become sick?
        ii. What has the child eaten and drunk in the last two days?
        iii. What are the child's symptoms? His/her temperature, color, mood?
    d. Enter all notes (except those unrelated to the practice) in the practice-management database on the reception-desk computer.
4. **Personal calls.**
    a. Feel free to use the break-room phone on your breaks or at lunch, but remember that the office walls are thin.
    b. Cellular phone calls must be taken outdoors.
    c. Reception-area phones must not be used for personal calls.

Employees who fail to follow these procedures will first be reminded of the procedures. Upon a second infraction, employees will be subjected to disciplinary action as defined in this handbook.

This is a composite of several similar documents.

11. Why must employees "keep pens and message pads by every phone" (line 21)?

    The practice will

    (1) create clutter
    (2) indicate a professional atmosphere
    (3) allow staff to work more effectively
    (4) improve the quality of messages
    (5) let management know when to order new supplies

12. Who is responsible for entering patient information into the office database?

    (1) the parent of the sick child
    (2) the office supervisor
    (3) the office doctors
    (4) the office staff
    (5) the office nurses

13. What is the meaning of "unsolicited" (line 17)?
    (1) not asked for
    (2) unpopular
    (3) requested
    (4) unpopular
    (5) voluntary

14. When would a person need to read this document?
    (1) when applying for a job at North Washington Pediatrics
    (2) after becoming a pediatric nurse
    (3) after retiring from North Washington Pediatrics
    (4) before being considered for promotion to a supervisor position
    (5) before beginning work as a staff member at North Washington Pediatrics

15. Calls from which of the following people would be transferred to a doctor even if patients were waiting?
    (1) the guardian of an infant who experienced convulsions after a fall
    (2) a vendor with a new drug to sell
    (3) the parent of a child who has the flu
    (4) a friend of the doctor calling to confirm dinner plans
    (5) a vendor selling office furniture

Questions 16 through 20 refer to the following excerpt from a play.

WHAT IS THE DISAGREEMENT BETWEEN JAMES AND HIS FATHER?

[James Moynihan has finished tea; Anne Hourican is at the back, seated on the settle knitting, and watching James. James Moynihan is about twenty-eight. He has a good forehead, but his face is indeterminate. He has been working in the fields, and is dressed in trousers, shirt, and heavy boots. Anne Hourican is a pretty, dark-haired girl of about nineteen.]

[James Moynihan rises.]

ANNE: And so you can't stay any longer, James?

JAMES: *(With a certain solemnity)* No, Anne. I told my father I'd be back while there was light, and I'm going back. *(He goes to the rack, takes his coat, and puts it on him)* Come over to our house to-night, Anne. I'll be watching the girls coming in, and thinking on yourself; there's none of them your match for grace and favour. My father wanted me to see a girl in Arvach. She has three hundred pounds, besides what the priest, her uncle, will leave her. “Father,” says I, “listen to me now. Haven’t I always worked for you like a steady, useful boy?” “You have,” says he. “Did I ever ask you for anything unreasonable?” says I. “No,” says he. “Well then,” says I, “don’t ask me to do unreasonable things. I’m fond of Anne Hourican, and not another girl will I marry. What’s money, after all?” says I, “there’s gold on the whin-bushes if you only knew it.” And he had to leave it at that.

ANNE: You always bring people around.

JAMES: The quiet, reasonable way is the way that people like.

ANNE: Still, with all, I’m shy of going into your house.

JAMES: Don’t doubt but there’ll be a welcome before you; come round with Maire.

[Anne rises, and comes to him. She has graceful, bird-like movements.]

ANNE: *(putting her hands on James’ shoulders)* Maybe we won’t have a chance of seeing each other after all.

[James Moynihan kisses her reverently.]

JAMES: Sit down now, Anne, because there’s something I want to show you. Do you ever see “The Shamrock”?

ANNE: Very seldom.

[James and Anne go to the settle; they sit down.]

JAMES: There be good pieces in it sometimes. There’s a poem of mine in it this week.

ANNE: Of yours, James? Printed, do you mean?

JAMES: Ay, printed. *(He takes a paper out of his pocket, and opens it)* It’s a poem to yourself, though your name doesn’t come into it. *(Gives paper)* Let no one see it, Anne, at least not for the present. And now, good-bye.

[Goes to the door. Anne continues reading the verse eagerly. At the door James turns and recites:]

When lights are failing, and skies are paling,
  And leaves are sailing a-down the air,
O, it’s then that love lifts my heart above
  My roving thoughts and my petty care;
And though the gloom be like the tomb,
  Where there’s no room for my love and me,
O, still I’ll find you, and still I’ll bind you,
  My wild sweet rose of Aughnalee!

That’s the first stanza. Good-bye.

[James goes out. Anne continues reading, then she leaves the paper down with a sigh.]

Padraic Colum, excerpted from *The Fiddler’s House*, Dublin: Maunsel, © 1907.

16. Which of the following best explains why James's father wants him to marry the girl from Arvach?

    (1) The girl from Arvach has more money than Anne Hourican.
    (2) James's father is from Arvach.
    (3) The girl from Arvach is prettier than Anne Hourican.
    (4) James has expressed an interest in moving to Arvach.
    (5) James is known to be irresponsible and unable to make up his mind.

17. What can the reader conclude about the girl from her statements in this excerpt?

    She

    (1) falls in love easily
    (2) feels sorry for James
    (3) is shy around strangers
    (4) dislikes James's father
    (5) is not convinced James will be able to marry her

18. Which of the following best describes James Moynihan and Anne Hourican?

    (1) employee and customer
    (2) close friends
    (3) brother and sister
    (4) boyfriend and girlfriend
    (5) neighbors

19. In this excerpt, how does the author use James's poem in "The Shamrock"?

    To express

    (1) James's desire to be a professional writer
    (2) James's romantic feelings for Anne
    (3) Anne's love of poetry
    (4) the importance of literature in their small community
    (5) the author's sympathy for Irish writers

20. When James Moynihan tells Anne, "I told my father I'd be back while there was light, and I'm going back" (line 8), what does it indicate about him?

    He is

    (1) expecting someone at home
    (2) afraid of his father
    (3) unused to walking home in the dark
    (4) eager to leave Anne's company
    (5) a man who keeps his word

Answers and Explanations

This section contains the answers and explanations.

Prose Fiction

1. **The best answer is (3).** The question is an analysis question because it asks the reader to infer Anderson's responsibilities as commander of the boat. Anderson, the narrator implies, should model good work habits instead of grumbling about the assignment.
2. **The best answer is (4).** The question is a comprehension question because the passage clearly states the narrator's strong reluctance to land at Treasure Island. It can be inferred that, were the narrator in command of the boat, he would choose to sail past the island.
3. **The best answer is (4).** This comprehension question is primarily about context and vocabulary. The ship is at rest, but still bobbing on the waves. The unusual motion causes the narrator to feel queasy, or seasick.
4. **The best answer is (2).** The narrator never directly states the qualities of a good sailor. Instead, the reader must gather clues, often relying on what the characters fail to do as much as what they do. This makes it an application question. In this passage, sailors inappropriately grumble about orders, complain about hard work, and nearly get seasick. The only trait not mentioned is the ability to cook.
5. **The best answer is (3).** This comprehension question is another vocabulary item. The narrator describes the sailors as having been strong and willing workers, but that their behavior changed when they saw the island. They no longer willingly obey orders; they grumble at their tasks. They are no longer disciplined in their work. In other words, they lack self-restraint.

Poetry

6. **The best answer is (5).** This comprehension question gets at the heart of the poem "Alone." The speaker analyzes why he has always felt separate, even

different, from other people. The answer, he says, is that he has always experienced life differently, even as a child.

7. **The best answer is (4).** Another comprehension question that emphasizes that the speaker is aware that he has had a difficult life from earliest childhood. The imagery reiterates that his life has been "stormy," not peaceful, from its "dawn," or very beginning. The storm becomes a motif, or recurring image, of trouble in the poem.

8. **The best answer is (5).** This is an application question. The reader must predict the speaker's response to a situation not mentioned in the poem itself. The speaker directly states that he does not experience events as other people do. Therefore, the reader can infer that he would not join the group and laugh at the clown. Further, the speaker has a tendency to look on the dark and troubling side of things. If he is likely to see a "demon" in the form of a cloud (lines 20–22), he is most likely to see a dark, or sinister, side of a clown.

9. **The best answer is (1).** Like the preceding and subsequent questions, this analysis question asks the reader to analyze the speaker's mindset. The title of the poem tells the reader that the speaker is "alone." Its verses clarify how and why the speaker feels this solitude. In this case, the speaker explains he takes a neutral, even innocent, image, such as a cloud, and habitually turns it into something malevolent. This is an act of extreme melancholy, or depression.

10. **The best answer is (2).** In this synthesis question, the reader is told that the poet, Edgar Allan Poe, has a strong interest in the macabre. This interest can be found in this poem through its imagery. Poe links his habitual solitude not to a love of nature or learning, like Romantic or Neoclassical poets, but rather to mystery, storms, and a tendency to see the strange and evil in things.

Prose Nonfiction

11. **The best answer is (3).** This analysis question expects the reader to understand the reason for keeping pens and pads by the telephone. The passage explains to the reader the importance of accurate and effective phone communication in the office. Having the necessary tools always close at hand will facilitate both accuracy and efficiency.

12. **The best answer is (4).** The passage directly states that it is the responsibility of the staff to enter all notes into the office database. Therefore, this is a comprehension question.

13. **The best answer is (1).** The vocabulary word in this comprehension question can be inferred from the context. Unsolicited calls, or "cold calls," usually refer to business contacts not initiated, or asked for, by the company.

14. **The best answer is (5).** This is an analysis question. The document explains the details of a job as a staff member at North Washington Pediatrics. Only staff members would need to be familiar with all the details and only after having accepted the job.

15. **The best answer is (1).** This is a synthesis question. The document directs staff members to take written messages for non-emergency calls or, if possible, to assist the caller without transferring the call. Only answer choice 1 has a clear emergency (the child with convulsions), and it can be inferred that no staff member would be expected to make a diagnosis over the telephone. A doctor would clearly expect to field the call even if there were patients waiting.

Drama

16. **The best answer is (1).** This comprehension question asks the reader to understand the motivations of James's father. James mentions the girl and says she has "300 pounds"—a form of Irish currency—in addition to an expected inheritance from her uncle. James answers his father that he prefers Anne Hourican and that money doesn't matter. This implies that Anne is not as rich as the girl from Arvach.

17. **The best answer is (5).** This synthesis question asks the reader to draw conclusions about Anne. We know that Anne and James have discussed marriage because he tells her about his conversation with his father. Anne, however, still expresses doubts about their future at different points in the passage. She claims to be shy of going to his house and worries that they won't have a chance to be together ("a chance of seeing each other") after all. Her final sigh is also ambiguous. In all, the reader should conclude that Anne is not convinced that James will marry her.

18. **The best answer is (4).** This comprehension question asks the reader to recognize the relationship between James and Anne. The discussion of marriage, the "reverent" kiss, and James's love poem to Anne in "The Shamrock" all indicate that the relationship is warmer than that of close friends, and that they are indeed boyfriend and girlfriend.

19. **The best answer is (2).** This is a comprehension question. As noted above, James's poem allows him to tell Anne how he feels about her. Unlike his father, who thinks a marriage is about money, James has romantic feelings toward Anne, and he expresses them in "The Shamrock."

20. **The best answer is (5).** This is an analysis question. James clearly enjoys Anne's company and invites her to visit him that evening. That raises the question of why he chooses to leave her then. He gives the reader the answer: he told his father he would do something—leave while it was still light—and that is what he does. This implies that he is a man who keeps his word. There is no indication in the passage that he is afraid of his father or of walking in the dark.

What's Next?

Chapter 20 includes a list of Language Arts, Reading terms with definitions. Reviewing this chapter will help you approach the Reading section on your GED with confidence.

CHAPTER TWENTY 20

Language Arts, Reading Terms

The terms included here are terms used in the book and on Official GED Practice Tests.

A

adjective Part of speech: modifies a noun or noun phrase by limiting, qualifying, or specifying: "a *meager* wage, the *red* car, ten *tired* babies."

adverb Part of speech: modifies a verb, an adjective, or another adverb. Many adverbs are formed by adding the "ly" suffix to adjectives, although there are many exceptions: walk *slowly*, laughing *heartily*, sleep *well*, drive *fast*.

aesthetic Appealing to the senses because of perceived beauty.

agreement In grammar, the property of language that some elements must have a certain form to match other elements. In English, subject and verb must agree in person and number. The same is true for pronoun and antecedent (what the pronoun refers to). *Incorrect*: Each dad *are* playing with *their* son. *Correct*: Each dad *is* playing with *his* son.

alliteration Literary device of repeating sounds (consonants or vowels) at the beginning of words in a phrase or clause: *P*eter *P*iper *p*icked a *p*eck of *p*ickled *p*eppers.

allusion Indirect reference to something without directly mentioning it.

analogy Comparison of similarities between two or more things.

article Words that mark or specify nouns. In English, the definite article is *the*, and the indefinite articles are *a* and *an*.

autobiography Story about a person written by that person.

B

bias Preference or prejudice that inhibits fair judgment.

biography Story about a person's life.

brochure Small pamphlet or booklet, often distributed as advertising.

C

character Person portrayed in a literary or other artistic work.

climax Height of the action in the plot.

commentary Written or spoken interpretation of something.

conclusion Proposition stated at the end of an essay that is supported by the evidence given in the essay.

conflict Adversity faced by characters that propels the action in the plot. The forms of conflict are human v. nature, human v. human, human v. himself.

conjunction Part of speech: connects words, phrases, clauses, and sentences. The most common conjunctions in English are *and* and *or*, but words like *but* and *because* are conjunctions, too.

context Text or spoken words that surround a word or passage and help determine meaning; circumstances that surround an event.

coordination Linking two structurally equal elements in a sentence using a coordinating conjunction, usually *and* or *or*: the lions *and* tigers, vanilla *or* chocolate.

correspondence Communication, especially in writing, between individuals and/or organizations.

critique Review of, or commentary on, a creative work; criticize.

D

dialogue Speech; drama is primarily written as dialogue.

document Written or printed paper that serves as a record and as evidence.

drama In literature: a work that is intended for stage performance.

E

epic Extended poem in elevated language that narrates the trials and adventures of a classic or mythical hero.

essay Short work of literature that addresses a single topic and usually presents the opinions of the writer.

exclamation Excited utterance: *Aw, shucks! Wow!*

F

fact Something considered true (contrast with *opinion*).

fiction Of the imagination.

figurative language Creative use of words and phrases that does not use their literal meaning.

figure of speech Expression of figurative language.

fragment String of words that is missing one or more elements necessary to be a complete sentence.

G–J

grammar Study of how words and parts of words combine to form sentences.

headline Title of a newspaper article, usually in large type.

imagery Use of vivid and figurative language in literature and art to evoke images.

inference Conclusion based on evidence.

inversion In grammar: the reversal of the standard position of two elements. Some elements can always be inverted in a sentence, but doing so often makes reading more difficult: My car broke down, so *to school I walked.*

irony Use of words to express a meaning that is the opposite of the real meaning; similar to and often confused with *sarcasm*, which means: words used to insult or scorn.

journalism Gathering information and preparing news stories for media outlets such as newspapers, magazines, and television.

K–L

letter One of the characters of the alphabet; piece of written correspondence.

M

main idea Topic of an essay or a paragraph.

mechanics Formal elements of writing (in English: spelling, punctuation, and capitalization).

metaphor Use of a word to designate something else, thereby making a comparison: John is a *gorilla*; he should play football.

meter Rhythm in poetry.

modification Application of an adjective or adjective phrase to a noun or noun phrase.

mood In literature: the general feeling or atmosphere created by a piece of writing.

moral Lesson taught by a story or fable.

myth In literature, a traditional, usually ancient story involving gods or heroes of a particular society that outlines aspects of that society's history and culture.

N

narrative Writing that recounts a series of actions and events.

narrator Someone who tells a story.

nonfiction Factual writing.

noun Part of speech: names a person, place, thing, quality, or action. Nouns can be subjects or objects of verbs and prepositions or can stand alone as appositives: "*Sue* met ten *people* in the *boardroom*, including *Jane*, *president* of the *company*."

novel Long work of prose fiction.

number In English, the indication of being singular or plural. Nouns, pronouns, and to a lesser extent verbs are marked for number.

O

ode Long lyric poem composed of stanzas.

onomatopoeia Written representation of sounds: *oink*, *moo*, *buzz*.

opinion Belief held with confidence, but which is not fully supported by proof (contrast with *fact*).

P

paradox Statement that seems contradictory but is actually true.

paragraph Unit of prose that is composed of sentences that address a single coherent topic.

parallel structure *or* **parallelism** Use of identical structure in corresponding phrases or clauses: I like *swimming* and *running*. I like *to swim* and *to run*.

parenthetical Explanatory statement that is set off by parentheses or commas.

parody Creative work that imitates the style of a person or another work for comic effect or ridicule.

part of speech One of the traditional classifications of words according to their use in sentences.

person Indication of someone or something's role in the discourse. First person refers to the speaker ("I"), second person refers to who is being addressed ("you"), and third person is anything or anyone else ("them"). Verbs and pronouns must agree in person with subject and antecedent, respectively.

personification Use of human traits with nonhuman elements in literature.

persuasion Act of trying to change opinion through argument and reasoning.

play Written work of drama or such a work performed onstage.

plot Sequence of events in a literary work.

poetry Literature in metrical form (contrast with *prose*).

point of view Attitude or outlook of an author, narrator, or character in literature.

preposition Part of speech: defines the relationship between a noun or noun phrase and a verb, adjective, or other noun or noun phrase: "I sailed *under* the bridge." "Climb hand *over* hand." "You should be watchful *in* dark alleys."

pronoun One of the limited set of words that can represent a noun or noun phrase (its antecedent) and must agree with it in person and number. For example, "I" is the first-person singular subject pronoun and "them" is the third-person plural object pronoun.

prose Ordinary speech or writing without meter (contrast with *poetry*).

protagonist The main character of a story or tale.

Q–R

restatement Repeat in a new form.

review (verb) Examine in order to criticize or correct; (noun) essay or article that critiques a creative work.

rhythm In poetry: pattern of sounds and syllable stress.

run-on Improper combination or two or more independent clauses that should be separate sentences.

S

scan Examine a text quickly for specific elements.

sentence Basic unit of language that conveys a complete thought.

setting Time and place where a narrative or drama takes place.

short story Prose narrative, usually much shorter than a novel.

skim Study a text as quickly as possible while still comprehending the meaning of it.

stage directions Notes within a work of drama that call for certain actions, expressions, entries, and exits on the part of actors.

structure Organization of a piece of writing with respect to clarity and precision of meaning.

style Sum of distinctive features of an author or artist's creative expression.

subordination Placement of a clause in a position where it depends on another clause: It was raining, *so I opened my umbrella*. Here, the word *so* is called a subordinating conjunction. The clause *I opened my umbrella* depends on the clause *It was raining*.

summary Reduction of information to its main points.

synonymous Equal or nearly equal in meaning: *glowing/radiant*, *assault/attack*, *cry/weep*.

synopsis (see *summary*).

T

tense Place in time as it relates to a verb: past, present, or future. More broadly, one of the many verb forms in English that expresses both position in time and duration.

theme Recurring idea or general topic, either apparent or hidden, within a creative work.

tone Manner of expression in speech or writing, reflective of the author or the narrator's emotions or opinions.

U–Z

verb Part of speech: in English, expresses action, existence, or state of being: I *play* baseball. Lincoln *was* an important president. Evening sunshine *fades* as winter approaches.

voice Literature: the specific qualities of an author's writing, strongly tied to word choice and structure; grammar: the property of verb constructions that indicates the relationship between subject and verb. A sentence has active voice if the subject is the agent (who or what is performing the action): *Monkeys eat bananas*. Passive voice occurs when the agent is not the subject: *Bananas are eaten by monkeys*. Passive-voice sentences can ordinarily be reworded to have active voice. Passive voice is often used when the agent is not known or not important in the sentence: *The contestants were hit in the face with cream pies.* (Who threw the cream pies is unknown or unimportant.) In general, writing in active voice is more appropriate.

PART VI
Social Studies

This part of the book explains what the GED Social Studies Test involves and the basic critical-thinking skills you will need to be successful. The Social Studies test contains multiple-choice questions that refer to written and graphical information.

Part VI includes the following chapters:

Chapter 21 About the Social Studies Test

Chapter 22 History of the World

Chapter 23 History of the United States

Chapter 24 Civics and Government

Chapter 25 Economics

Chapter 26 Geography

Chapter 27 Social Studies Practice Questions and Answer Explanations

Chapter 28 Social Studies Terms

21

CHAPTER TWENTY-ONE

About the Social Studies Test

The GED Social Studies Test consists of 50 multiple-choice questions that you will be given 70 minutes to complete. You will have to draw on prior knowledge of history, civics and government, economics, and geography; however, you will not have to recall facts. To succeed on the Social Studies Test, you will need to think critically and understand how to interpret visual representations of information such as charts, graphs, maps, photos, diagrams, advertisements, editorial cartoons, and public documents.

Format and Content

The Social Studies Test includes the following:

- Questions based on short reading passages (about 40% of the test)
- Questions based on visuals (about 40% of the test)
- Questions based on combinations of reading passages and visuals (about 20% of the test)

Content areas covered include the following:

- U.S. History (25%)
- World History (15%)
- Civics and Government (25%)
- Economics (20%)
- Geography (15%)

Many concepts in social studies reach across several of these categories, as do the questions on the GED Social Studies Test. For example, a discussion of the U.S. Civil War could involve history, geography, government, and economics.

Documents of particular importance to the GED Social Studies Test are the Declaration of Independence, the U.S. Constitution, the Bill of Rights, and excerpts from landmark Supreme Court cases.

Creators of the GED Social Studies Test define 10 themes present in the content:

- Culture
- Time, continuity, and change

- People, place, and environments
- Individual development and identity
- Individuals, groups, and institutions
- Power, authority, and governance
- Production, distribution, and consumption
- Science, technology, and society
- Global connections
- Civic ideals and practice

For the GED Social Studies Test, the skill of analysis is essential. This comes from the GED's adaptation of Bloom's Taxonomy of Educational Objectives, which is explained in more detail in Chapter 4, "The Cognitive Domain of Bloom's Taxonomy."

Creators of the GED Social Studies Test assess the following thinking skills:

- Analyzing ideas (30%)
- Applying ideas (30%)
- Evaluating ideas (20%)
- Understanding ideas (20%)

What's Next?

The chapters that follow include specific information on the content areas tested on the GED Social Studies Test. You should refer to these chapters as necessary during your practice.

CHAPTER TWENTY-TWO

History of the World

World history is the record of the human race from ancient times to the present day. Civilization emerged millennia ago, and the state of humanity today is the result of constant social, political, economic, industrial, agricultural, and religious evolution that has occurred over so long a time. Studying our ancient human ancestors reveals much about our modern condition.

Of course, it would be impossible to include every detail about humanity's past in this book. The text we have included for your GED preparation should be considered a broad overview. Most of the information is written with a focus on European history. This is intentional because the GED is designed around a general American high school curriculum. Past events, philosophies, arts, and literatures of Europe molded the general Western culture that influences every part of your life. People raised in America or who have spent some time living here are influenced by the legacy of Western history. How we think, how we dress, how we raise children, what we eat, the stories and music we like, how we run our government—many of these things and more have evolved from elements of Europe's past. Some relevant information about Eastern history has been included, but if you desire to read more, by all means, browse the Internet and your local library for interesting sources. If you have an art or historical museum near you, pay it a visit; you will surely find something you will enjoy observing and thinking about. Receiving the lessons of world history can help you put modern situations in sharper perspective, as well as strengthen arguments in your conversations and writing.

Prehistory

The time period before any known written account of human activity is called *prehistory*. Because there are no written records to analyze, evidence of ancient human behavior must be found in the remnants of their lives—cave drawings, fossilized skeletal remains, and artifacts such as cut stone and primitive tools, weapons, and pottery. Archaeologists search for, unearth, and, together with other anthropologists, analyze these ancient remains to glean some perspective on the earliest human cultures.

The Stone Age

Anthropologists label the period beginning around 200,000 years ago as the Old Stone Age, or the Paleolithic period—the time of the emergence of *Homo sapiens* (meaning "knowing man" in Latin) and the earliest instances of human culture. The Old Stone Age is so called because of the variety of stone implements from the time period that have been uncovered—knives, spears, hatchets, arrowheads, and bowls, among other kinds. Artifacts became increasingly refined and elaborate over time. Human language emerged in the Paleolithic. People adorned their bodies for the first time. Burial of the dead began, suggesting early humans may have supposed some relationship between illness and decaying cadavers. Old Stone Age humans gathered in groups and had leaders but not yet governments and laws. They were hunter-gatherers and nomadic, meaning they followed herds of animals on which they depended for food. By the end of the Paleolithic, humans had spread over all the continents except Antarctica.

The Mesolithic period, or Middle Stone Age, saw increased social and technological development in humans, as evidenced by more complex artifacts—meticulously hewn fishing tackle, chopping tools, bows, and canoes. As the glaciers of the last ice age retreated north around 10,000 years ago, humans profited from warmer climates. The Mesolithic period ended with the development of agriculture. Through farming, humans could leave their nomadic lifestyle and establish communities. The end of the Middle Stone Age marks the emergence of human civilization.

Early Civilizations

In a broad sense, *civilization* refers to groups of humans who settle and organize to obtain their food from agriculture, the systematic raising of plants and animals. Being able to settle in fixed communities led to division of labor, by which each human took on a specific role of providing a good (such as plants, animals, textiles, tools, and pottery) or service (such as primitive medical care, woodcutting, and bricklaying) to the other community members. People began trading extensively. Evidence from the first civilizations shows that spiritual beliefs emerged within communities to help explain the world around them.

The earliest known farmers were the Sumerians of around 9500 B.C., who settled in Mesopotamia (modern-day southeastern Iraq). By 6000 B.C., farming had begun in Egypt and a millennium later in China.

Egypt

Ancient Egypt is considered one of the most advanced of the early civilizations. It sprang up in the fertile Nile River valley of northeast Africa around 3500 B.C. and is generally thought to have ended in 51 B.C., when the Roman Empire annexed Egypt as a province. Today, some magnificent ancient Egyptian monuments and statuary remain. Modern tourists flock to the Egyptian desert to ponder the Sphinx, the Pyramids at Giza, and many other remnants of the civilization. Apart from such massive construction, artifacts from tombs (such as mummies, jewelry, and pottery), especially those containing Egyptian writing (such as stone tablets and wall inscriptions), have continually fascinated scholars and laypeople alike. Egyptians used a complex system of picture-character writing called *hieroglyphics*. For ages, scholars struggled to decipher the meaning of the writing they discovered. Modern Egyptology (the study of ancient Egypt) is made possible by the work of a French scholar named Jean Champollion, who, in 1822, succeeded in translating the Rosetta Stone, a large fragment of a slab of black granite on which two hieroglyphic scripts and one ancient Greek script are engraved. By comparing the hieroglyphics to the better-understood ancient Greek, Champollion devised a way to translate ancient Egyptian writing, a task anthropologists and other scholars had struggled to perform previously. Reading ancient Egyptian writing allowed and continues to allow researchers to fill in the gaps of our knowledge of ancient Egypt.

Ancient Egyptians were very religious people. They believed strongly in the afterlife. Prominent members of the society, such as rulers, religious figures, and the wealthy, underwent the process of *mummification* upon their death. Mummies were encased in decorated coffins and entombed with all manner of precious articles. The acts of preserving the body and sealing it away with luxury goods and spiritual paraphernalia were meant to ensure a person's status into the realm of the dead.

Egypt was ruled by a succession of leaders called *pharaohs*, who believed themselves to be godlike. They ruled with a heavy hand and acted as tax collectors. Because ancient Egypt had no currency, tax was paid in goods and services. In addition to a portion of goods that a person had to levy to the state, each year one member from each household had to provide several weeks of unpaid labor to the state. People could avoid the "labor tax" by paying others to work in their place, a common practice among the wealthy. This modern understanding of Egyptian labor practices disputes the older notion that creations such as the pyramids could not have been built without a massive slave labor force.

Although laborers were paid, Egyptian society was socially divided to a great degree. The social stratification can be represented as a pyramid, with workers in the lower tiers being more numerous and supporting the tiers above, as shown in Figure 22.1.

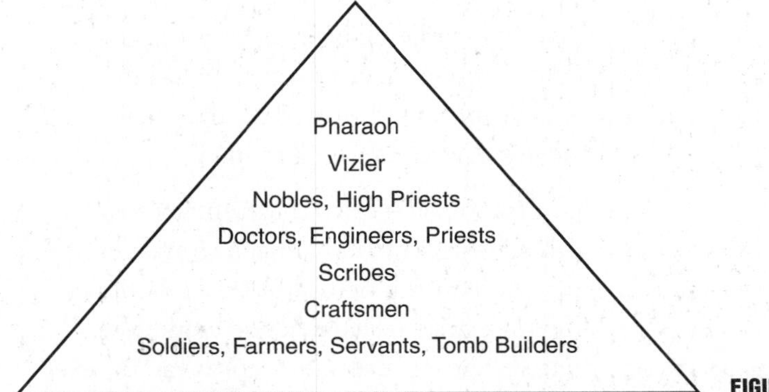

FIGURE 22.1 Ancient Egyptian society.

Scribes made up the lowest social class of those whose members could read and write. Only scribes were able to ascend to work as doctors, building engineers, and priests.

Many early civilizations arose along the eastern coastline of the Mediterranean Sea between Europe and Africa. Archaeologist James Henry Breasted is credited with coining the term "Fertile Crescent" to describe this region, which has an impressive record of human activity due in large part to the plentiful irrigation provided by the Nile, Jordan, Tigris, and Euphrates rivers. As civilizations in the Fertile Crescent expanded, trade among them increased, and competition for land and natural resources sometimes led to violence. Contact between societies—whether positive or negative—brought cultural and technological exchange. Some civilizations flourished, absorbing smaller cultural groups and creating vast empires.

Ancient Greece and Rome

The two most important civilizations to the history of the West—and crucial to world development in general—were ancient Greece and Rome. Many historians consider the Greek Empire to be the foundational culture of the West. The Roman Empire took much of the knowledge and culture of the Greeks and spread it throughout Europe.

Like the Egyptians, members of Greek society promoted the development of what are broadly known as *liberal studies* today: art, music, literature, theater, philosophy, architecture, and the sciences. The so-called Golden Age of Greece (500 B.C. to 300 B.C.) was characterized by great philosophers and teachers such as Socrates, Aristotle, Plato, and Pythagoras. Greek philosophers laid the foundation for Western culture. For the first time, the value of an individual in society was seen to be linked to learning and physical health.

The Greeks conceived the Olympic games in the eighth century B.C. Although the original motivation for the games is disputed, historians generally agree that the ancient Olympics represented a revolutionary sporting event. In a sense, the games were intercultural; athletes from all the various Greek city-states were welcome to compete. Competition was strong; to compete, athletes had to be young, fit, and swear before a statue of Zeus (the ruler of the gods) that they had been training for at least 10 months. Initially, the Olympics consisted of only a footrace but later expanded to include boxing, *pankration* (similar to today's mixed marital arts), wrestling, chariot racing, and three field events: long jump, discus throw, and javelin throw. Ancient Greece held 292 Olympic games, one every four years. Today's Olympics are inspired by the ancient Greek version, but were revived only a little over a century ago, in 1896.

Gradually, the Romans dominated the Greeks. From the Greeks, the Romans took knowledge of science, architecture, and the arts. Culturally, the Romans continued the tradition of using an elaborate system of gods to explain the natural world around them. Both ancient Greece and Rome used mythology to explain what science could not. Rome even adapted some Greek gods into their system as Greek territory was annexed to the Empire. Greek and Roman myths continue to be relevant today because of their elaborate plots and timeless themes. Table 22.1 includes information on important ancient Greek and Roman gods and goddesses.

TABLE 22.1 Ancient Greek and Roman Gods and Goddesses

Greek Name	Roman Name	Major Mythological Role
Aphrodite	Venus	Goddess of beauty, sexuality, and love
Apollo	Apollo	God of the sun, light, and music
Ares	Mars	God of war
Artemis	Diana	Goddess of hunting and the moon
Athena	Minerva	Goddess of arts, crafts, and wisdom
Cronus	Saturn	God of agriculture
Demeter	Ceres	Goddess of grain
Dionysus	Bacchus	God of wine and vegetation
Eros	Cupid	God of love
Gaea	Terra	Mother Earth
Hephaestus	Vulcan	God of fire
Hera	Juno	Goddess of marriage and childbirth; Queen of the gods
Hermes	Mercury	Messenger of the gods
Hades	Pluto	God of the underworld
Poseidon	Neptune	God of the sea and earthquakes
Uranus	Caelus	God of the sky
Zeus	Jupiter	God of thunder; King of the gods

Astronomers often name celestial bodies (planets, moons, asteroids, and so on) after classical gods like these. Can you name the only planet in our solar system that isn't named (in English) after one? You're correct if you said "Earth." For speakers of the Romance languages (such as Spanish, Italian, and French), which descended from Latin (the language of ancient Rome), our home planet is named after a Roman god, Terra.

Departing from the Greek tradition, Rome was strongly committed to military conquest. At its height around 117 A.D., Rome controlled much of the Middle East, North Africa, most of continental Europe, and all of England. The people of all these regions assimilated portions of Roman culture, knowledge, and language. Roman armies were the most capable of the age. They developed combat skills and tactics that persist today. Gladiator fighting and war reenactments became fixtures of Roman entertainment.

Rome was an important early republic. Society was divided between the People and the Senate. Wealth and social status determined whether a citizen of Rome was worthy of voting in the Senate, which held significant executive powers. Any citizen not in the Senate was considered part of the People. Two assemblies and one council of the People made laws in Rome. Although the Senate had no lawmaking powers, it still had considerable clout. The Senate had the authority to wage war, appropriate public funds for projects, install officials in public lands and outlying provinces, and call for a dictator in case of emergency.

In the first century B.C., the Roman republic became the Roman Empire. As an empire, Rome continued its expansion of power in Europe, the Middle East, and North Africa.

Roman society is credited with great technological achievements, including construction of long roads and aqueducts throughout the vast provinces of the Empire. Roman roads were so thick and solid that many of them remain in use today; the same is true for some aqueducts. The discovery of cement made durable construction possible on such a great scale. Moving people, goods, services, and water to and from distant lands made central control of the Roman Empire possible.

Although the rights of people changed over the course of the ancient Roman civilization, residents of the Roman Empire could be divided roughly into four classes:

- Slaves were considered property of their owners. They had few rights and could be sold or brutalized on the whim of the owners. Interestingly, a Roman slave could be granted citizenship when freed by the owner.
- Natives of lands conquered by the Roman Empire and other people from affiliated states could receive a kind of second-class citizenship having limited rights.
- Roman citizens enjoyed all the benefits of Roman society to the extent that their economic class allowed. After citizenship was recognized, very little could allow the state to strip it. Here is a partial list of rights granted the citizen:
    - Right to vote
    - Right to enter into contracts
    - Right to marry
    - Right to hold public office
    - Right to sue in the courts
    - Right to appeal court rulings
    - Right to defend oneself in court
    - Protection against torture
    - Protection against execution, except when convicted of treason
- Women's status varied greatly over time in Rome. Eventually, female citizens would have many of the same rights as male citizens; however, women were never permitted to vote or stand for public office. In addition, women generally remained under the control of the eldest man of the household.

Besides advances in art, science, construction, government, and warfare, the Roman legacy includes the calendar the world uses today. Emperor Julius Caesar introduced a new calendar system in 46 B.C. to correlate the days and months more closely to the natural passing of seasons. The Julian calendar uses 12 months with different numbers of days. Every fourth year, a "leap day" is added to account for the fact that the earth year is not evenly divisible by the 24-hour day.

The Roman Empire was divided into the Western and Eastern Roman Empires in the fourth century. Although the reasons for the ultimate fall of the Western Empire are continually debated, most historians agree that some combination of attacks from native peoples, combined with overall political turmoil and reduced tax revenue, led to the breakup of the Empire. Scholars generally mark the date as 476 A.D. The Eastern Empire lasted until about 610 A.D., when its emperor made sweeping reforms to government and changed the language of administration from Latin to Greek. Soon, control of the government would fall into the hands of the Greeks.

The Emergence of Religion

At the height of Roman expansion in Europe, Africa, and the Middle East, the mysticism and spirituality of the Egyptians, Greeks, and Romans was based in a polytheistic (multiple-god) system. The tribes of Israel practiced Judaism, a monotheistic (single-god) faith.

Judaism is founded on writings and traditions, not on the central authority of a person or a group of people. Followers of Judaism believe that God revealed his laws and commandments to the Jewish people in the form of the Torah, sometimes called the "Five Books of Moses." (This same text would become important to Christianity later.) Today, about 14 million people practice some form of Judaism.

From the Jewish tradition sprang Christianity. Christians believe that Jesus of Nazareth is Christ, the Messiah, the son of God. Jesus was born in the Palestinian town of Bethlehem. According to the Bible, the sacred text of Christianity, some people were attracted to Jesus' teachings and believed that he was the only son of God. Having amassed a great following, Jesus was seen as a threat to Rome by certain elements of the Roman state. He was eventually crucified (executed on a cross). Christians believe that Jesus' execution was his ultimate gesture of atoning human sins. According to the Bible, Jesus' body disappeared, and he ascended into heaven to rejoin God, his father. The new Christian religion that Jesus spawned was spread by his disciples (devoted followers).

Because Rome was the center of Western civilization at the time, the center of the Christian church was established there. Continuing through today, the Pope at the Vatican (an independent city-state within Rome) oversees the doctrine of the Roman Catholic Church throughout the world. In the early centuries of the church, Christianity was spread throughout Europe in many ways, both peaceful and violent.

Beginning in 1095 A.D., European royalty organized sieges, called the Crusades, on the Holy Land (modern-day Israel and Palestine). Christian soldiers were sent to fight the enemies of the Roman Catholic Church, who, in the Middle East, were Muslims, followers of the religion of Islam. The Crusades were fought to take back control of the Holy Land from Muslims and reconnect the two sects of Christianity (Roman Catholicism and Eastern Orthodoxy) that had been fractured since the end of the Roman Empire.

The prophet Mohammed founded Islam in 612 A.D. Muslims believe that God's word for humanity was given to Mohammed through the angel Gabriel and earlier prophets, including Adam, Noah, Abraham, Moses, and Jesus. The sacred text of Islam is called the Qu'ran (sometimes written "Koran"). About 1.4 billion people practice Islam today.

Hinduism is another of the world's most-followed religions. It is considered the oldest of the major religions, having evidence of roots going back to 3000 B.C. Hinduism does not have a well-defined, uniform set of characteristics. Many people prefer to think of it as having both spiritual and cultural implications. Unlike many spiritual practices, Hinduism has no one founder. There are many sects, rituals, and philosophies held across the broad spectrum of Hinduism. Today, about 1 billion people practice some form of it. The majority of modern Hindus follow the Vendanta philosophy, which is monotheistic. These Hindus believe in a single supreme cosmic spirit, Brahman, who is worshipped in different forms.

Buddhism evolved from the teachings of Buddha, who lived on the Indian subcontinent from about 566 B.C. to about 460 B.C. Buddha's teachings were spread throughout east Asia over the millennia following his death. The goal of Buddhists is to achieve Nirvana, the end of worldly suffering. Buddhists train to purify their minds by adhering to the Four Noble Truths, which explain suffering, the cause of suffering, the cessation of suffering, and the Noble Eightfold Path: right view, right intention, right speech, right action, right livelihood, right effort, right mindfulness, and right concentration. Today, most estimates of the number of Buddhists worldwide range from 230 to 500 million, although much larger figures have been cited.

Confucius was a Chinese philosopher of the same time period as Buddha. Confucian teachings emphasize high morality and social harmony. Confucianism is an intellectual pursuit, a philosophy; it is not a religion by definition. Today in China, Confucianism is practiced along with other religions, such as Buddhism, Taoism (China's indigenous religion), and traditional folk belief systems.

China

Separated from the early civilizations in the West, China had been flourishing for centuries. Philosophers Confucius and Lao Tzu, the founder of Taoism, lived during China's classical age. Although political disorder was significant, these Chinese people enjoyed written laws, a currency-based economy, and iron tools that made agriculture and building trades easier and more efficient. China was unified under the Ch'in Dynasty (221 B.C.–206 B.C.) of Emperor Shin Huang-ti. The feudal system (powerful landowners and poor tenant farmers) was replaced by a system of strong hierarchical central government. The country was divided into provinces, and the emperor appointed leaders to each one to carry out the emperor's wishes throughout the kingdom. Roads and canals were built to connect and provision the provinces. The Great Wall was constructed mostly during the Ch'in Dynasty, as a defense against invading nomadic tribes. Written Chinese language was standardized.

The Han Dynasty (202 B.C.–220 A.D.) succeeded the Ch'in Dynasty and was characterized by sustained national unity with less severe leadership. Under the Han emperors, Confucian thought was emphasized. Imperial soldiers repelled invaders in the north and west. China entered a period of heightened cultural development; an encyclopedia and a dictionary were produced, as well as fine porcelain pottery.

European Middle Ages

The period between the end of the Roman Empire and the beginning of the Renaissance is called the Middle Ages. When the Western Roman Empire fell in 476 A.D., the power void in western Europe was quickly filled by local leaders, chiefs, and kings. Europe operated under the feudal system, by which wealthy landowners granted land to vassals in exchange for military service. Peasants worked as tenant farmers and other laborers in villages established on the feudal lands. The landowners, called lords, were directly responsible for supplying tax revenue to their king. The central belief underpinning feudalism is that conflict may be mitigated when citizens have prescribed roles in the society. Knights, who were trusted with the protection of the kingdom, were bound by a code of religious and personal virtue called chivalry, which forbade them to exploit the helpless peasants.

Magna Carta is the most significant political document to arise from the Middle Ages. In the early thirteenth century, England was suffering from Viking invasions, as well as from conflict with the Roman Catholic Church. In an attempt to settle the debate over the roles of church and state, King John ordered wealthy English landowners to pay steep taxes to the church. When these barons resisted, King John was forced to agree to their proposed Magna Carta, a proclamation of citizen's rights and a decree limiting the powers of the monarchy. The document extended to every person: lords, peasants, and even the king. Under Magna Carta, the monarchy had to obey the laws of England. Magna Carta is popularly known to English citizens as the origin of constitutionalism in their country.

In 911, a group of Vikings was permitted to settle in northern France, under the pretext that they would protect France from future Viking sieges. These Viking settlers became known as Normans, and their region as Normandy. The plan worked, and the Normans settled permanently in the region, converting to Christianity and assuming the local language. Viking additions to the local language resulted in a unique Norman language. As Normandy succeeded in repelling Viking attacks, England suffered much worse. In 991, the Anglo-Saxon English king agreed to marry the daughter of the Duke of Normandy to solidify a military alliance against the invaders. Viking attacks became so bad in England that the Anglo-Saxon kings fled to Normandy in 1013 and did not return to England until 1042. In 1066, the Anglo-Saxon king died heirless, creating a vacuum of power in England. Three nobles with competing interests in England vied for the throne. Eventually, the Norman known as William the Conqueror defeated his rivals and took control of England. The most significant impact of the Norman Conquest was the displacement of Anglo-Saxon language by the Latin-based Anglo-Norman language. Modern English developed for centuries in the context of Anglo-Norman. As a result, about one fifth of English vocabulary comes from Latin through early French. In addition, the Norman Conquest of England brought tension to French-English relations, an effect that would last for centuries.

Economic rivalries between France and England led to the Hundred Years' War, a conflict ultimately sparked by English kings' claims to the French throne. The war was actually a group of wars with intermittent peace, the whole series lasting about 120 years. Such a protracted fight took its toll on French citizens, whose villages were being pillaged by advanced English armies. Fatigue, famine, and taxes spurred a revolt of French peasants against their king. Out of the despair rose Joan of Arc, a French peasant girl who claimed to hear voices from God telling her to lead the fight against the English invasion. After making a surprising prediction about a military reversal near Orleans, Joan's fame spread throughout French nobility. At her request, she was dispatched to the siege of Orleans as part of a relief mission in April 1429. She wore the gear of a knight, which she gathered from donations. Contrary to the cautious tactics of the regular military leadership, Joan inspired French soldiers to make repeated fierce attacks on English fortresses, which were successful overall. The men of the military were inspired by her heroic leadership and religious fervor. Joan led many French victories, but she was eventually captured by the English in May 1430. A year later, following a politically motivated trial, Joan was burned at the stake (a form of execution reserved for heretics). She was 19 years old. Joan of Arc remains an important heroic figure in France and was made a saint of the Roman Catholic Church in 1920.

The Hundred Years' War began on the eve of Europe's worst-ever epidemic. The feudal system of medieval times was crucially dependent on agriculture. Occasional interruptions to the food supply weakened the general state of health in Europe, so suffering from infectious diseases was a routine part of life. In the mid-fourteenth century, however, Black Death swept across Europe and simultaneously in India and China. Between one and two thirds of all Europe's people perished from the disease also called bubonic plague. Worldwide death tolls are estimated at about 75 million people. Today, scientists know that the plague is caused by a specific bacterial infection of the lymph nodes and that it is spread by fleas. Poor sanitation in the Middle Ages meant fleas could freely commingle with humans, having been brought in on the bodies of rats and other rodents. The plague spread quickly—within just a few years, whole farms and villages were entirely decimated. Western Europe fell into deeper economic collapse. It would take more than 120 years before the European population would begin increasing again.

The Renaissance and the Enlightenment

The trying times of the Middle Ages soon gave way to a more politically and socially stable Europe at the outset of the fifteenth century. Nobility and wealthy merchants were again able to preoccupy themselves with cultural pursuits such as music, literature, and the arts. The period known as the Renaissance began. Although people have a hard time pinpointing exactly when it began, historians agree that the movement originated in Florence, Italy. The term "Renaissance" comes to English from French, meaning "rebirth," which describes the reinvigorated interest in the knowledge of the classical civilizations of Greece and Rome. Wealthy people became patrons of the arts, commissioning great paintings and sculptures from French and Italian artists. Michelangelo was a celebrated Renaissance painter and sculptor famous today for his statue of David and his frescoes on the ceiling of the Sistine Chapel in Rome. The powerful Medici family in Florence commissioned many of his works. The Renaissance was also a period of great technological advancement. The most famous thinker of the age was Leonardo da Vinci. Universally considered a creative genius, da Vinci was what people would call a "Renaissance man" today. He was gifted in a variety of intellectual pursuits: architecture, anatomy, engineering, geometry, mathematics, music, painting, sculpture, and science in general. His art includes the world-famous *Mona Lisa* and the drawing called *Vitruvian Man*, which is a study of the proportions of the human body. Both are pictured in Figure 22.2. Da Vinci spent the last three years of his life under the patronage of King Francis I of France, living in a house on the grounds of the royal estate. The Renaissance was a time when many great writers, artists, and inventors thrived.

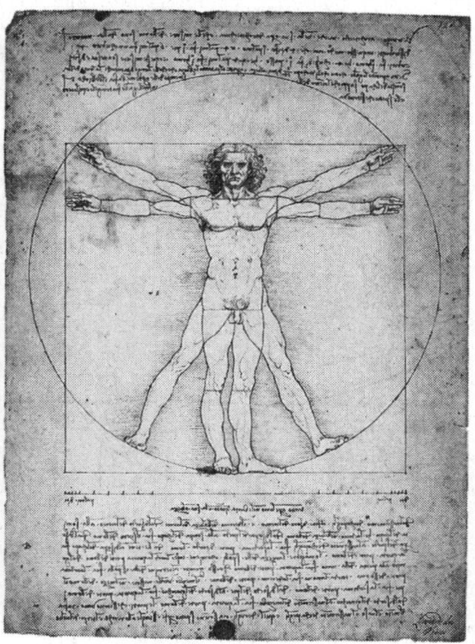

FIGURE 22.2 *Mona Lisa* (c. 1503) and *Vitruvian Man* (c. 1492), by Leonardo da Vinci. Source: The Louvre, France and Galleria dell' Academia, Venice, Italy.

The way Europeans recorded information was radically changed upon the invention of the movable-type printing press in 1447 by German engraver Johannes Gutenberg. His first production was a Bible, the most important book in European life. Previously, only the super-wealthy could afford a Bible; each had to be handwritten by a monk, a process that would take months. Gutenberg was able to significantly reduce the cost of producing books. With time, books became inexpensive enough that anyone could own them. Gutenberg's press started a revolution of knowledge and literacy.

The period beginning in the fifteenth century and continuing into the early seventeenth century is known as the Age of Discovery. Europeans set out on sea voyages to discover new lands, resources, and water routes. The most famous explorer of the New World was Christopher Columbus. Commissioned by the Spanish monarchy to find a faster route to east Asia, Columbus believed he could save time by heading directly west instead of heading south to sail around the perilous Cape of Good Hope of southern Africa. Columbus trusted that the Earth was round, but he had no idea that North and South America existed and would block his passage to China. When Columbus landed in the Caribbean in 1492, he thought he had reached the East Indies of Asia. He is generally considered the first European discoverer of America, although the Icelandic explorer Leif Eriksson had landed in present-day Canada nearly 500 years earlier. Some people dispute the notion that Columbus discovered anything, because humans had migrated to the Americas from Asia beginning about 12,000 years ago. It is significant, nevertheless, that explorers like Columbus introduced new lands to Europe.

Table 22.2 lists some notable New World explorers.

TABLE 22.2 Notable New World Explorers

Years	Explorer	Sponsor Country	Area Explored
1000	Leif Eriksson	Iceland	Greenland and Newfoundland
1492–1504	Christopher Columbus	Spain	The Caribbean, the Atlantic coast of Central America and northern South America
1500	Pedro Alvares Cabral	Portugal	Brazil
1519–1521	Ferdinand Magellan	Spain	Attempted circumnavigation of the globe: sailed around South America to the Philippines (where he died); his crew continued south around Africa and north back to Spain
1534–1542	Jacques Cartier	France	Quebec and the St. Lawrence River
1608–1616	Samuel de Champlain	France	Quebec, the St. Lawrence River, the Great Lakes
1768–1799	James Cook	Great Britain	Around South America to Tahiti and other South Pacific islands, New Zealand, Australia, the Hawaiian Islands, the coast of California north to Alaska

The intellectual and cultural rebirth of Europe had religious implications in addition to creative, economic, and political ones. A blow to the power of the Roman Catholic Church came in 1517, when a German monk named Martin Luther famously nailed his list of complaints to the door of the Castle Church in Wittenberg, Germany. The Christian faith became divided between Catholics and Protestants in a movement called the Protestant Reformation. As a result, noble landowners were freed from the mandatory payment of taxes to Rome, and the Catholic Church saw its land holdings shrink.

The English King Henry VIII had problems with the Catholic Church, too. He wanted a divorce from his wife, Catherine of Aragon, because she had not produced a son in more than 18 years of marriage. The Pope refused the divorce. Undeterred, Henry VIII seized control of the Catholic Church in England in 1529. Subsequent legislation gave him official power over it.

In the 1500s, Spain and its leaders remained strongly allied to the Catholic Church. Seeing the spread of Protestantism increasing, Spanish King Philip II launched military campaigns in an attempt to reassert the power of the Catholic Church in Europe.

Troops were dispatched to the Netherlands to enforce Catholic theology because foreign preachers were helping the Dutch move toward Protestant beliefs. The Dutch repelled the Spanish in 1581 with the help of English forces, who saw themselves as a potential target of Spanish aggression. In 1588, the Spanish Armada (group of ships) assembled in the English Channel for a naval battle with England. English victories in a few skirmishes sent the Armada scrambling back toward Spain. This, and the fact that the Spanish had not adequately prepared for the adverse sea and weather conditions, meant that Spain lost thousands of men and more than half its fleet. England did not lose a single ship.

The seventeenth and eighteenth centuries were the Ages of Reason and Enlightenment in Europe. Scholars understood reason to be the means for human beings to obtain the truth about the universe. Philosophers and scientists began asking questions about the true nature of things. Scientific experimentation advanced rapidly. Astronomer Nicolaus Copernicus proposed in 1543 that the planets orbited the sun, as shown in Figure 22.3. The prevailing view in Europe at the time was that the Earth was the stationary center of the universe. In 1676, scientist Anton van Leeuwenhoek built a microscope and observed single-celled organisms for the first time. At the time, members of the established science community doubted his credibility because single-celled organisms were entirely unknown to exist. Van Leeuwenhoek discovered bacteria, blood flow in capillaries, sperm cells, and muscle fibers. As a devout Protestant, he marveled at what he saw through his microscope and he considered it evidence of the greatness of God's creation in things both large and small. Overall, though, emerging science like this was making Europeans ask questions about the origin and meaning of life.

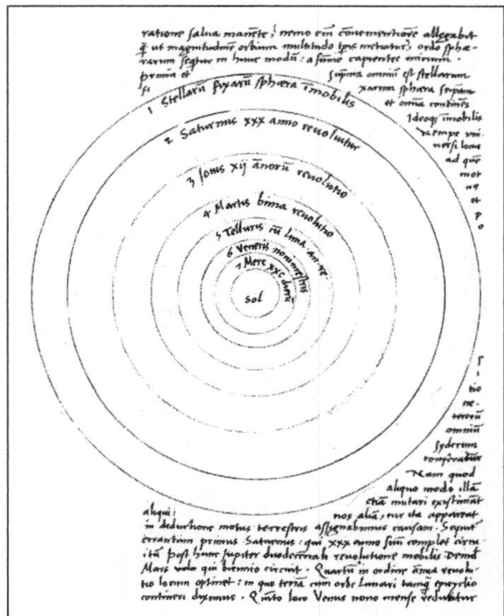

FIGURE 22.3 Copernicus proposed that the planets revolved around the sun. Source: *On the Revolutions of the Heavenly Spheres* (1543), Nicolaus Copernicus.

Enlightenment thinkers believed knowledge was the solution to every question or social ill. Each person was by nature good and was endowed with reason. Sound reason and scientific inquiry were seen as the means to acquire knowledge, and knowledge as the vehicle for improvement of self and society. Old ways of life were being increasingly questioned.

The French Revolution

In 1789, French society erupted in revolution. In the eyes of the revolutionaries, the old regime of kings had worn out its usefulness. Europe and America watched as France rejected absolutism in favor of a system where the many citizens constituted the political force. The slogan of the French Revolution was "Liberty! Equality! Fraternity! Or Death!"

King Louis XVI had nearly depleted the royal treasury by 1789. Most French citizens were poor and resented the aristocracy. The tax system was far from equitable. Sensing the agitation of his subjects, the king ordered the Estates-General into session in May 1789 for the first time since 1614. In the previous meeting, the representative assembly of the people had been divided into the Three Estates, each one having an equal number of representatives. The First Estate was the clergy, the Second Estate the nobility, and the Third Estate all the other citizens of France. The Three Estates would vote on matters of taxation, so the Third Estate objected to what it saw as clear domination of the assembly by the First and Second Estates. In response, a proposal was made to double the delegates of the Third Estate, from 300 to 600. The king's finance chief agreed. Eventually, the larger, reinvigorated Third Estate voted in favor of declaring themselves the National Assembly (see Figure 22.4). Subsequent actions by the Assembly limited powers of the crown and the Catholic Church. In the so-called Tennis Court Oath, the National Assembly assembled in secret in a tennis building to resolve not to separate until a constitution was drafted for France. Sensing revolution, some members of the clergy and the nobility joined the cause. Louis XVI was sensing the end of his reign, so he dispatched soldiers to his royal residence at Versailles and onto the streets of Paris.

FIGURE 22.4 The National Assembly vowed not to disband until a constitution was drafted for France. Source: *The Oath of the Tennis Court*, Jacques-Louis David, 1791, National Museum of the Chateau of Versailles, France.

On July 14, 1789, a group of revolutionaries stormed the Bastille royal prison in what was seen as an act of defiance. The group killed the prison administrator and several of his guards. At the time, fewer than 10 prisoners were in the fortress; many people believe that the mob was mostly interested in stealing some weapons and ammunition. Nevertheless, popular portrayal of the act framed it as a manifestation of revolt against the oppressive state. By the end of that month, the Great Fear began; peasants stormed the country chateaux of wealthy nobility, seizing and burning business records and deeds to property. The revolution would continue to build. As a first step toward a constitution, on August 26, 1789, the National Assembly issued the Declaration of the Rights of Man and Citizen, inspired by the U.S. Declaration of Independence. The first article declares: "Men are born and remain free and equal in rights. Social distinctions can be founded only on the common utility." The revolution stood for giving people equal rights in a system where every person is rewarded according to his or her contributions to society.

The French Revolution was bloody and turbulent. Many regimes took hold in the years following the outbreak of violence. The National Assembly established a constitution in 1791. In that same year, Louis XVI and the queen Marie Antoinette were discovered attempting to flee the country to modern-day Belgium. They were placed under house arrest by the Assembly. The National Assembly's successor, the Legislative Assembly, failed in less than a year. It was then replaced by the National Convention, which ruled from September 1792 to October 1795. It was during this period, in 1792, that the Convention tried the king, convicted him, and in 1793, executed him at the guillotine. The queen was guillotined later that year. From 1793 to 1794, France suffered The Terror, a violent campaign of intimidation and execution characterized by widespread paranoia that foreign monarchies or domestic promonarchy groups would mount a counterrevolution. Besides the king and queen, the Revolutionary Tribunal sentenced thousands to be beheaded. Political opponents and nobility were executed, but other people were executed as well, such as writers, petty criminals, and intellectuals—some without much cause.

The final regime of the revolution was called the Directory. It ruled until 1799, when the young General Napoleon Bonaparte overthrew it and installed the Consulate in its place. Napoleon drafted a new constitution that appointed him First Consul, the ruler of France (see Figure 22.5). In general, the people respected Napoleon for his skillful military victories over British and Austrian forces. Napoleon was victorious in Syria and Egypt and brought many antiquities back to France with him. In May 1804, the Consulate voted to make Napoleon the emperor of France.

One of Napoleon's first acts as emperor was to issue his code of laws. The Napoleonic Code was intended to be a clear outline of civil law for all of France. Previously, laws and legal procedures varied in different places in the country. The code forbade secret and ex post facto (applied after the fact) laws, encouraged judges to make reasonable interpretations of the law, established property and trading rights, and provided rules for marriage and divorce.

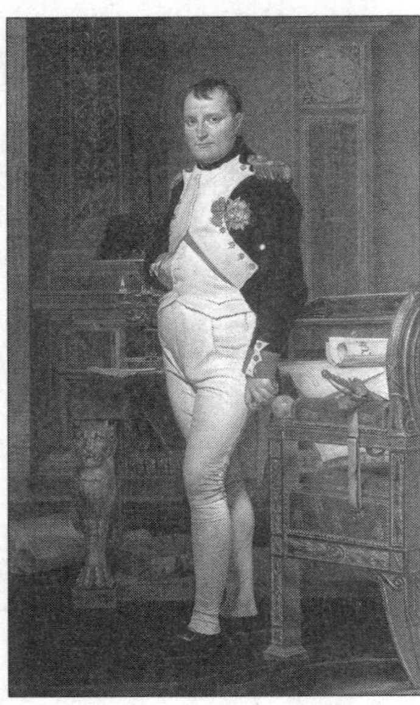

FIGURE 22.5 Napoleon is portrayed next to his writing desk, on which his civil code is resting. Source: *Napoleon in His Study*, Jacques-Louis David, 1812, National Gallery of Art, Washington, D.C.

Napoleon, as shown again in Figure 22.6, aspired to conquer the many monarchies of France. His armies engaged the British to the north and south and the Austrians, Prussians, and Russians to the east. Napoleon had many victories, and France's empire grew significantly. Eventually, though, Napoleon's forces dwindled and stood vastly outstretched and outnumbered. Forces allied against Napoleon occupied Paris, and all sides signed a treaty, which called for Napoleon's exile to the island of Elba. Napoleon was a persistent man, however, and eventually escaped back to France, where he succeeded in raising a small army. He reigned for one hundred days until the army, outmatched and suffering in the winter weather, fell in the Battle of Waterloo. Napoleon was captured attempting to flee to the United States by boat. He formally surrendered to British forces, who exiled the fallen leader to the island of St. Helena, where he died in 1821.

FIGURE 22.6 Napoleon wanted to be seen as a capable and powerful civil and military leader. Source: *Napoleon Crossing the Alps*, Jacques-Louis David, 1801, Kunsthistorisches Museum, Vienna, Austria.

The Caribbean and Central America

Revolution in France in 1789 and in the United States in 1776 began a movement toward colonial independence and social equality throughout the New World.

The first New World revolution after the United States' revolution was in Haiti. Slaves had been pressing the colonial authorities to take up a similar declaration of human rights as the United States and France had. Eventually, in 1790, a group of about 350 slaves rose up against the colonial powers of France and Spain. The revolution spread rapidly. By 1794, the French National Assembly had outlawed slavery in France and in all its territories. The armies of slaves stopped their fight against the French to ally with them against Spanish and British forces. Having repelled France's enemies, the Haitian fighters were betrayed when Napoleon sent a fresh contingent of troops to the island to quell any resistance. Fighting between France and the slaves resumed, and the slaves eventually won. Haiti declared independence in 1804.

In 1821, a congress of Central American *criollos* (people born in the Americas of two Spanish parents) declared independence from Spain. In 1823, the nation of the United Provinces of Central America was formed from Guatemala, El Salvador, Honduras, Nicaragua, and Puerto Rico. It was intended to be a federal republic modeled after the United States of America. This new union dissolved quickly, though, because of conflict between the government and factions allied with Roman Catholic clergy, and because of difficulties establishing infrastructure, especially a canal to connect the Pacific Ocean to the Caribbean Sea—a measure that would have generated much money for the region.

Several more attempts were made in the eighteenth century to unite the nations of Central America. None succeeded. Costa Rica established a successful democracy in 1889, but the other countries of the region would have to wait until the twentieth century to find an acceptable, stable government.

The Industrial Revolution

Advancements in machine technology and mechanization spurred the Industrial Revolution of nineteenth-century Europe and the United States. Whereas consumer products previously had been made on a small scale by individual craftsmen, many products could now be produced faster and more cheaply in large factories. The Industrial Revolution changed Europe and America from predominantly farming societies to ones with greater manufacturing capacity. As large production facilities were built in cities, people began settling around them in hopes of finding work. During the Industrial Revolution, a new working class was created as people who lived in rural areas abandoned their farms to take up life in the more crowded, bustling cities. People believed in the rising middle class's ability to overcome through hard work the history of cultural domination by exclusive privileged classes.

New jobs and opportunities to turn a profit arose in the areas of mining, metals, chemicals, textiles, and end-production fabrication. Telegraph wires and rail lines were moving people, materials, and ideas faster and more cheaply than ever. The steam engine conceived by James Watt is generally considered the most important invention of the early Industrial Revolution. Engines allowed for automation and powered machine tools. The assembly line was developed to improve worker efficiency. No longer would a worker be assigned to construct an entire product. Instead, the worker would be trained to perform one task over and over on the line. Output increased sharply.

Inventions such as electric light led to an expanded work day, and in the pursuit of profits, many early industrial barons made their fortunes from overworking and underpaying their employees, as well as taking shortcuts on safety. Child labor was an early concern. The first law regulating it was the Factory Act of 1833 in England, which forbade children under nine years old from working and forbade any children to work at night or for more than 12 hours per day. As history progressed, more safety rules were implemented in Europe and the United States to protect children and adult workers alike.

Hazardous working conditions were nothing new to the labor force that arose during the Industrial Revolution. People had always been at risk during work. Consolidation of employees into factories, however, made organizing unions much easier. Early industrial workers saw that if they banded together, they could make more effective demands of their employers by threatening a total work stoppage—skilled workers were hard to replace on short notice. Labor unions have always been controversial from a social and economic perspective. Questions always arise about the extent of power that unions should have and what measures they should be allowed to take to steer the course of company management. In some industrial nations today, labor unions are strongly restricted or forbidden outright; however, today most nations have some form of organized labor.

The Industrial Revolution brought about the era of capitalism, the economic system by which an open public market determines the price of goods and services. German philosopher Karl Marx disagreed with the capitalist system because of the working conditions he observed in industrialized nations and the ways he predicted the working classes would be economically exploited by capitalism. Marx felt capitalism made the poor poorer and the rich richer. He proposed his ideas in the *Das Kapital* (which includes the *Communist Manifesto*), the philosophy of which appealed to a great number of people. Among them was Vladimir Lenin, who brought Communism to Russia. (See "The Bolshevik Revolution and Communism" later in this chapter.)

New World Powers and World War I

In 1815, after the defeat of Napoleonic France, ambassadors from Europe's major powers convened the Congress of Vienna to redraw the lines of Europe. Results of the Congress included the enlargement of Russia and Prussia; creation of a German Confederation under the control of Prussia and Austria; division of Poland by Russia, Prussia, and Austria; annexation of northern Italy by Austria; and the break-up of the rest of Italy. The Hapsburgs of Austria sat on many European thrones, and many cultural groups saw their rule as an example of the aristocratic dominance the French revolution had rejected.

The nineteenth century was fueled by democratic and nationalistic fervor, and many revolts against imperial rulers took place around the world. Beginning with the Haitian Revolution, the practice of slavery around the world began to wane. Britain banned the trade of slaves in its Empire by 1807, and in 1833, the United Kingdom had outlawed slavery altogether. Soon after, Russia, the United States, and Brazil abolished slavery.

Many people feared a royal backlash against the new middle class the Industrial Revolution had established. Advances in electricity, metal alloys (especially steel), and petroleum products enabled the United States, Japan, and Germany to become significant world powers along with Great Britain.

After imperial France stopped its European conquests, the United Kingdom emerged as the first global superpower. At its height of influence in the middle to late 1800s, the United Kingdom controlled one third of the land on earth and one quarter of its population. British possessions included Canada, India, Australia, New Zealand, several countries in Central and South America and Africa, and islands across all the world's oceans. As the United Kingdom grew, the Spanish, Portuguese, and Ottoman (based in present-day Istanbul, Turkey) empires began to crumble.

Nationalism strained multiethnic empires in the nineteenth century. Negotiations between Russia and Austria over control of the Balkan provinces fueled resentment in Serbia, which had aspirations of one day ruling the region itself. During an official visit to the Serb capital of Sarajevo on June 28, 1914, the heir to the Austrian throne, Archduke Franz Ferdinand, and his wife were assassinated by Serb nationalists. Initially, much of Europe sympathized with Austria, which resolved to end any uncertainty over whether the state of Serbia should form part of the empire. Austria sent a letter to Serb leaders that has come to be called the July Ultimatum. In it, Austria demanded a total purge of military or government leaders having any hostility toward Austria and the capture and prosecution of Franz Ferdinand's assassins. With the promise of military support from Russia, Serbia only conditionally accepted the terms of the ultimatum and mobilized its troops. Austria declared war on Serbia on July 28, 1914. Two days later, Russia and Austria were mobilizing their full armies. The next day, Austrian ally Germany called for Russia to stop mustering troops within 12 hours. That time passed, and Germany declared war on Russia. Austria had planned to engage enemies to the east, and Germany had ideas of bringing the fight to France. On August 3, Germany declared war against France and entered Belgium on the march to the northeastern border. France, Germany, and Britain had previously agreed to respect Belgian neutrality in Europe. By invading it, Germany had violated this accord. Though initially neutral on the crises in continental Europe, Britain declared war on Germany on August 4.

World War I had begun. Fighting was concentrated on the Western Front, the Eastern Front, and at sea. The Western Front saw continual, nightmarish fighting. Soldiers were concentrated in trenches on either side of swathes of barren earth called "no man's land." Military technology had been vastly improved in the preceding decades; however, few tactics had been developed to counter the new, deadlier equipment. Soldiers had miserable experiences in the trenches. Barbed wire, artillery shells, tanks, and machine guns limited infantry advances. Germany began using poison gas in 1915. Neither side of the fight gained much ground along the Western Front, although casualties were massive. The British Army suffered the bloodiest single day in its history at the Battle of the Somme, losing about 57,000 soldiers.

The Eastern Front saw a series of advances and retreats while the Western Front was stalemated. Initially, Russia saw some success from its attacks on Austrian and German territory. Russian industry and leadership turned out to be inadequate to the task of supporting the army, and by the spring of 1915, the Central Powers of Germany and Austria had forced Russia back and completely out of Poland, which it had previously occupied.

At sea, Germany had a small fleet of small ships scattered around the world hunting Allied merchant ships. Britain, the world's foremost naval power, dispatched its fleet to find and destroy the German threat. In December 1914, British ships destroyed a German fleet of six vessels in the Battle of the Falkland Islands off the coast of Chile. Germany was defeated by British forces again at the Battle of Jutland in the North Sea off the coast of Denmark. From that point forward, Germany's surface fleet was largely confined to port.

Germany's submarine service kept up the fight, however. *U-boats*, as German submarines are called, threatened the crucial shipping lanes between Britain and North America. In violation of British and American honor code, U-boats regularly sank merchant ships without allowing the crew to escape. Germany eventually agreed to take mercy on civilian sailors. The promise was short lived, though, and in 1915, German Kaiser Wilhelm II declared a policy of unrestricted naval warfare. Not shortly after, a German U-boat sunk the RMS *Lusitania*, pictured in Figure 22.7, a long passenger liner carrying British and American citizens, among others. Germany had suspected it of running ammunition and military supplies across the Atlantic Ocean, a suspicion that was later confirmed. Nevertheless, Britain and the United States saw the act as a civilian massacre. The United States stayed out of the war until three more ship sinkings and a formal offer from Berlin to Mexico to be allies against the United States changed the opinion of President Woodrow Wilson and the U.S. Congress. America declared war on Germany on April 6, 1917. The United States declared war on Austria the following December. By the summer of 1918, American soldiers were arriving in Europe at the rate of 10,000 per day.

FIGURE 22.7 The RMS *Lusitania*, en route from New York, was torpedoed and sunk by a German submarine on May 7, 1915, just eight miles from her destination in Ireland. Nearly 1,200 passengers died, fomenting American anger toward Germany's policy of unrestricted naval warfare. Source: Department of Defense.

Allied victory in World War I came by late 1918. More than 16,000,000 soldiers had fallen dead or went missing, and more than 21,000,000 soldiers were wounded. Formal peace was established between Germany and the Allies in 1919 by the Treaty of Versailles, which placed strong military and economic restrictions on Germany. Adolf Hitler, a young army officer at the time, resented the way the treaty placed all the blame for the war on Germany and forced his country to pay reparations to other afflicted nations. His sense of humiliation is often cited as a cause of his ultimate rise to dictatorship and the ultranationalist actions he led beginning nearly 20 years later, which prompted World War II.

The Bolshevik Revolution and Communism

As fighting raged in Europe, political turmoil was growing in Russia. Citizens were becoming increasingly resentful of the czarist government. ("Czar" is the Russian term for emperor; "Czarina" is empress.) In February 1917, a popular uprising caused Czar Nicolas II to abdicate (give up power) in a nearly bloodless transfer of power. Various reformist leaders and organizations banded together to form a provisional government. The new authority decided to continue involvement in World War I, an unpopular choice among many. When fighting did not meet expectations, public discord created an opportunity for Vladimir Lenin and his supporters to take power. In October 1917, Lenin and the Bolsheviks staged a revolution of their own.

In the October Revolution, also called the Bolshevik Revolution, the Bolshevik faction of the Marxist Russian Social-Democratic Labor Party seized power in Russia. This particular group had strong socialist and internationalist opinions. The leader of the revolution was Vladimir Lenin, a devoted believer of the communist teachings of Karl Marx. Lenin founded the Communist International, an organization dedicated to fighting "by all available means, including armed force, for the overthrow of the international bourgeoisie [upper middle class] and for the creation of an international Soviet republic as a transition stage to the complete abolition of the State." The Bolsheviks envisaged a classless society and created the Soviet Union. Lenin used violence against dissenters. Shortly after taking power, former czar Nicolas II and his family (including the legendary Grand Duchess Anastasia) were executed. For a long time, the Bolshevik regime denied that the family had been put to death, causing many rumors to circulate about what their fate had actually been.

In March 1918, the Bolsheviks signed the Treaty of Brest-Litovsk with Germany, ending the war between them and causing Russia to lose much territory in Europe. Lenin dissolved the Russian army. When Lenin died in 1924, another Bolshevik, Josef Stalin, was prepared to succeed him. Under Lenin, Stalin had ascended to the upper tier of leaders in the Russian Communist Party. Stalin knew Lenin's successor would need to appear to the people as very loyal to Lenin. Stalin worked hard to appear as a common man to the people. He stressed the industrialization of Russia so the country could catch up to the economic level of western Europe and America. Stalin pushed for collectivization of land and its produce. Eventually, Stalin took the title of General Secretary of the Central Committee of the Communist Party of the Soviet Union, a position he kept until his death in 1953. Stalin maintained absolute control over Russia in a totalitarian state.

World War II

Adolf Hitler's message of national pride and economic recovery appealed to the German masses discouraged by the outcome of World War I. Their country was in social and financial chaos, and the charismatic National Socialist (Nazi) leader inspired hope for rebuilding the nation. Hitler's rhetoric placed blame for the devastation of World War I and the overall state of Germany on minority groups, especially Jews. The Nazi Party under Hitler used intimidation to create a state of general suspicion within the population. People feared being accused of dissension, possibly being arrested and sent away to a concentration camp, and then perhaps killed. The program of forced internment and execution of Jews and other minority groups was called the Holocaust, which claimed the lives of millions of Europeans.

Germany signed a peace treaty with the Soviet Union in 1939, just a week before Germany invaded Poland. Fulfilling terms in the treaty, the Soviet Union soon invaded Poland from the east. The country would fall within the month. The Soviet Union proceeded to attack Finland and the Baltic countries. By the summer of 1941, German forces had swept through Denmark, Norway, the Netherlands, Luxembourg, Belgium, and most of France. Surprising the Soviet Union, Germany launched a massive invasion of their territory.

Italy and Japan allied with Germany in World War II, forming what was called the Axis. Each Axis country had designs on territorial expansion. In summer 1941, British Prime Minister Winston Churchill and U.S. President Franklin D. Roosevelt met to discuss the war; they issued the Atlantic Charter, which took a stand against these expansionist powers. The two leaders also agreed that Germany was the most urgent threat. Later that year, on December 7, Japan launched a devastating surprise aerial bombardment on the Pearl Harbor Naval Base in Hawaii. The next day, the United States declared war on Japan. Within three days, Germany and Italy had declared war on the United States in return.

In the Pacific, Japan was engaged in heavy fighting with China when the United States entered the Pacific theater of World War II, following the attack on Pearl Harbor. Allied surface and submarine vessels engaged the Japanese throughout the Pacific Ocean and its islands. Hard battles at Tarawa, Okinawa, and Iwo Jima caused significant casualties on both sides, but Japan eventually retreated. The Allies were hesitant to initiate a land invasion of Japan, deciding instead to bombard industrial sites within cities. After one bombing of Tokyo, more than 100,000 people died in a massive fire. Japan continued to fight as a total naval blockade cut off trade, and bombardments ruined the food supply and industrial capacity. In August 1945, the United States dropped atomic bombs on Hiroshima and Nagasaki (see Figure 22.8); more than 200,000 people died as a direct result of the nuclear attack. Total Japanese deaths from all U.S. bombing that month totaled more than 1,000,000. Japan surrendered on August 15, 1945.

FIGURE 22.8 The nuclear bombs dropped on Hiroshima and Nagasaki (pictured) convinced Japan to agree to peace terms with the Allies. Source: National Archives, Department of Defense, United States Army.

The Allies—the United States, Britain, Canada, and others—defeated Germany in a long series of battles pushing Nazi forces back to their homeland. U.S. involvement began in July 1942 when aircraft units were deployed to Britain to support the bombardment of German forces. The air offensive shifted to aerial support of ground troops beginning June 6, 1944. On that date, U.S., British, and Canadian forces mounted the single largest sea-borne invasion in history, which had been in planning for more than a year. Figure 22.9 shows a picture from the invasion. Nearly 3,000,000 Allied troops crossed the English Channel from England to German-occupied France or were dropped in by parachute behind German coastal defenses. The day was won by the Allies, but nearly 53,000 soldiers died. German losses are difficult to ascertain but were probably even greater.

FIGURE 22.9 The Allies forced Nazis out of occupied France, beginning with the invasion of Normandy on D-Day, June 6, 1944. Source: National Archives, Department of Defense, United States Coast Guard.

The aftermath of World War II left the Soviet Union in control of much of Eastern Europe. Germany and France, among other nations, were left to rebuild destroyed cities and economies. The period after World War II was America's golden age as a global superpower. The United States stood with other Western countries in support of democracy and capitalism and against the government of the Soviet Union. The two sides remained in a state of military standoff for decades until the breakup of the Soviet Union in 1991. This period is known as the Cold War. People on both sides of the conflict lived with the fear that an attack—especially a nuclear one—might occur.

The World After Global War

After World War II, countries involved in the war sought peace from fringe political beliefs and acts of violence. Industrial nations focused on science and technology to answer questions about the universe and make life more comfortable and satisfactory. Televisions, radios, and telephones were used in nearly every home. People demanded the exchange of information.

Development of electronics led to the latest generation of machines. Starting in the 1950s, the United States and the Soviet Union were rivals in the space race. Both countries wanted to be the first to achieve feats high in earth's atmosphere and beyond. In 1957, the Soviets launched Sputnik I, the first earth-orbiting satellite. The American space agency NASA landed astronauts on the moon in 1969. Electronics made these missions possible. Circuits and microprocessors can make calculations precisely and accurately much more quickly than the human mind can. Today, information is interconnected in a massive computer network called the Internet, which was originally developed for the U.S. Department of Defense. In many other ways, too, modern people can access plentiful information resources more quickly than ever.

The spread of technology and communication tools have led to a "shrinking" of the world in both a social and an economic sense. One modern viewpoint holds that all humans have a shared responsibility for the future of the planet and the well being of its human population. In this age of instant news, the world's problems cannot be hidden as easily as they once were. In an economic sense, the world is shrinking because no longer must all work on a project take place in a single location. With electronic communication and data exchange, many jobs can be as easily performed in one country as another. In addition to Europe and the Americas, Asia now plays a significant role in the global service industries. This increase in interconnectedness of the world economy is called globalization.

As they always have in the past, the world's civilizations will continue to evolve and adapt to changing circumstances. As you read about history, think about the ways humans have and have not learned from the lessons of the past in making important decisions.

What's Next?

Chapter 23, "History of the United States," includes a discussion of significant events in the history of the United States. Refer to the chapters in Part VI if you struggle with the Social Studies sections as you work through the practice tests in this book.

CHAPTER TWENTY-THREE

History of the United States

This chapter reviews the history of the United States of America, from before European settlement of North America to the present. Knowing U.S. history helps people take full advantage of being an American citizen. It lets us learn from others' past triumphs and mistakes and shows us how we arrived at where we are today. History makes clear why the future impacts of today's decisions are important to weigh carefully.

Native Peoples

Since long before explorers such as Leif Ericson or Christopher Columbus made landfall in the New World, diverse tribes of people have called the Americas home. The most widely held theory is that the first people to settle in the modern-day United States were nomadic tribes that followed large game herds across the Bering Land Bridge about 17,000 years ago. During the ice ages of the Pleistocene, sea level around Alaska had dropped as much as 60 meters, exposing the shallow seafloor between Siberia and Alaska. As the ice ages subsided, the land bridge flooded again and human tribes were prevented passage. Humans had migrated from Alaska to the southern tip of South America and east to the Atlantic by about 10,000 years ago.

Over the millennia, North American nomadic people spread out and diversified into hundreds of distinct cultures. Some tribes maintained their nomadic lifestyle, but many settled into organized villages and farmed their food. Societies ranged in size and expanse from very small to quite large and complex, such as the Iroquois Nation, a group of tribes in present-day New York and southeast Canada that was organized under a constitution as early as the eleventh or twelfth century.

Arrival of Europeans beginning in the fifteenth century had a devastating effect on indigenous populations. Although interactions were often peaceful and profitable for both sides, enslavement, disease, war, and displacement ravaged indigenous societies. Europeans brought smallpox, chicken pox, measles, and other diseases to which native people had no immunity. Competition over land and resources led to numerous conflicts, large and small, between natives and settlers. By the nineteenth century, most indigenous Americans had been moved from their lands, and many began life in Indian reservations established by the federal government. Continuing to today, federally recognized Indian tribes have a great degree of autonomy from the United States in matters of law, business, and natural resource use, as prescribed in the many treaties signed between tribes and the federal government. After World War I, members of Indian tribes were granted U.S. citizenship under the Indian Citizenship Act of 1924.

Colonization

Successful voyages to and from North America by early explorers (see "The Renaissance" in Chapter 22, "History of the World") led the wealthy monarchies in Europe to dispatch colonists to the New World. Still more came of their own free will, seeing an opportunity for a new, freer life in the vast new territories. Spain was growing ever wealthier as it profited from land claims in Central and South America. France held lands in modern-day Canada. The English settled along what is now the U.S. Atlantic coast. The famous Pilgrim colony at Plymouth (Massachusetts), settled in 1620, became the second successful British colony in North America. The Pilgrims' survival of the first year in the new land was facilitated by a group of local indigenous people who instructed the settlers on how to farm native crops and hunt local game. The Pilgrims and the Wampanoag tribe that helped them celebrated the Pilgrims' first harvest feast in 1621. Personal accounts reveal that on the feast day, the harvest had been collected and a party of Pilgrim and Wampanoag men had returned from the hunt with enough fowl for a week. The Pilgrims celebrated their plenty and gave thanks to God for their opportunities in the New World. In the United States today, we mark the anniversary of the Pilgrims' first harvest feast as Thanksgiving.

Settling in the New World was not without its challenges, however. Early colonists like the Pilgrims faced a perilous life of unstable local government, internal conflict such as sedition, scarcity of money, harsh weather, disease, and often uncertain interactions with indigenous people. English settlers chose to brave the new existence in North America for the chance to own some land, have a trade, and practice their religion freely. The English throne supported the colonies because it aspired to increase its land holdings, and it drew tax revenue from the activities there.

The Thirteen Original Colonies

English territory in the New World filled with colonists, who began to push westward over the Appalachian Mountains into the territory claimed by France, which dominated Canada. Between 1754 and 1763, France and its indigenous allies fought Britain and its indigenous allies for control of the land that both empires claimed between the Appalachians and the Mississippi River. Britain won the war, and the resulting Treaty of Paris of 1763 ceded Canada and all of France's southern territories east of the Mississippi River to Britain. Florida, which had been claimed by Spain, was given over to the British in exchange for France giving Spain all the western territories of North America that it claimed. The lands from modern-day Maine south to Georgia became known as the thirteen colonies. King George III appointed councils and governors to oversee the colonies and collect taxes.

Slavery

Beginning in the seventeenth century, British colonists became used to the practice of indentured servitude in the colonies: a person would receive passage to the New World in exchange for a period of years of unpaid labor, after which they would receive clothing, tools, provisions, and perhaps some land. In practice, indentured servitude made people accustomed to using violence to compel others to work. Many servants did not survive their unpaid labor period; however, many people successfully completed their period of indentured servitude and began independent lives in America.

Indentured servants became scarce during a period of good economic times in mid-seventeenth-century England. African slaves were first brought to the British colony in Carolina in 1670, and soon slavery was a widespread labor practice in the southern colonies. Northern colonists bought slaves, too, who worked predominantly as artisans, workshop assistants, dock workers, and domestic servants. Southern slaves were mostly assigned agricultural work. Colonies began establishing so-called slave codes, which substantiated forced labor under the law.

Triangular trade describes the trade among Europe, Africa, and the Americas during the eighteenth century. New World crops such as sugar, tobacco, and cotton were exported to Europe. Europe traded manufactured goods, textiles, and New World products with Africa, which supplied the Americas with slaves. Although the British outlawed the trade of slaves within its empire in 1807, the practice of forced labor would continue in the colonies (which became the United States) until the end of the U.S. Civil War in the mid-nineteenth century.

The American Revolution

Following the French and Indian War, which lasted from 1754 to 1763, England needed to repay its debts accrued from financing the army and navy. The king believed that because the colonists were the first beneficiaries of the British victory, they should pay for the war effort. It 1765, the British Parliament and the king passed the Stamp Act, which required all legal documents bear a new government seal issued for a fee. Two years later, the Townshend Acts placed a tax on common imports such as paper, paint, glass, lead, and tea. In 1768, colonists rioted in the thirteen colonies, shouting the slogan attributed to Boston lawyer James Otis: "No taxation without representation!" The Tea Act of 1773 made an exception to the tea tax for the British East India Company, allowing the British firm to import its tea more cheaply, thereby undercutting smaller merchants' prices. Soon, boycotts of tea sprang up throughout the colonies, and on December 16 of that year, about 150 men, organized by Samuel Adams and dressed as Mohawks, stormed three cargo ships in Boston Harbor and dumped 342 crates of tea into the water. The king and the British parliament reacted to the grand protest by imposing a series of laws known as the Intolerable Acts. Under these four new laws, the king attempted to strengthen his command over the colonies.

The First Continental Congress of representatives from all thirteen colonies was convened in September 1774. The Congress demanded the repeal of the Intolerable

Acts and wanted status equal to that of other British citizens. The king and parliament did not accept this proposition, and armed conflicts soon began between colonists and British forces, most famously involving the minutemen at Lexington and Concord, Massachusetts, in April 1775. In January 1776, Thomas Paine published his pamphlet *Common Sense*, which denounced British rule and invigorated the colonists' desire for independence. In June 1776, a committee of the Second Continental Congress was formed to draft a formal resolution rejecting British rule. Inspired by Paine's work, committee member Thomas Jefferson drafted the Declaration of Independence, listing all the colonies' grievances against the king and British rule, and the Second Continental Congress approved it on July 4, 1776. The Revolutionary War officially began.

Take the time to read the Declaration of Independence, reprinted here. It reveals many of the principles on which the U.S. government is based:

> IN CONGRESS, July 4, 1776.
>
> ---
>
> The unanimous Declaration of the thirteen united States of America,
>
> When in the Course of human events, it becomes necessary for one people to dissolve the political bands which have connected them with another, and to assume among the powers of the earth, the separate and equal station to which the Laws of Nature and of Nature's God entitle them, a decent respect to the opinions of mankind requires that they should declare the causes which impel them to the separation.
>
> We hold these truths to be self-evident, that all men are created equal, that they are endowed by their Creator with certain unalienable Rights, that among these are Life, Liberty and the pursuit of Happiness.—That to secure these rights, Governments are instituted among Men, deriving their just powers from the consent of the governed, —That whenever any Form of Government becomes destructive of these ends, it is the Right of the People to alter or to abolish it, and to institute new Government, laying its foundation on such principles and organizing its powers in such form, as to them shall seem most likely to effect their Safety and Happiness. Prudence, indeed, will dictate that Governments long established should not be changed for light and transient causes; and accordingly all experience hath shewn, that mankind are more disposed to suffer, while evils are sufferable, than to right themselves by abolishing the forms to which they are accustomed. But when a long train of abuses and usurpations, pursuing invariably the same Object evinces a design to reduce them under absolute Despotism, it is their right, it is their duty, to throw off such Government, and to provide new Guards for their future security. —Such has been the patient sufferance of these Colonies; and such is now the necessity which constrains them to alter their former Systems of Government. The history of the present King of Great Britain is a history of repeated injuries and usurpations, all having in direct object the establishment of an absolute Tyranny over these States. To prove this, let Facts be submitted to a candid world.
>
> He has refused his Assent to Laws, the most wholesome and necessary for the public good.

He has forbidden his Governors to pass Laws of immediate and pressing importance, unless suspended in their operation till his Assent should be obtained; and when so suspended, he has utterly neglected to attend to them.

He has refused to pass other Laws for the accommodation of large districts of people, unless those people would relinquish the right of Representation in the Legislature, a right inestimable to them and formidable to tyrants only.

He has called together legislative bodies at places unusual, uncomfortable, and distant from the depository of their public Records, for the sole purpose of fatiguing them into compliance with his measures.

He has dissolved Representative Houses repeatedly, for opposing with manly firmness his invasions on the rights of the people.

He has refused for a long time, after such dissolutions, to cause others to be elected; whereby the Legislative powers, incapable of Annihilation, have returned to the People at large for their exercise; the State remaining in the mean time exposed to all the dangers of invasion from without, and convulsions within.

He has endeavoured to prevent the population of these States; for that purpose obstructing the Laws for Naturalization of Foreigners; refusing to pass others to encourage their migrations hither, and raising the conditions of new Appropriations of Lands.

He has obstructed the Administration of Justice, by refusing his Assent to Laws for establishing Judiciary powers.

He has made Judges dependent on his Will alone, for the tenure of their offices, and the amount and payment of their salaries.

He has erected a multitude of New Offices, and sent hither swarms of Officers to harrass our people, and eat out their substance.

He has kept among us, in times of peace, Standing Armies without the Consent of our legislatures.

He has affected to render the Military independent of and superior to the Civil power.

He has combined with others to subject us to a jurisdiction foreign to our constitution, and unacknowledged by our laws; giving his Assent to their Acts of pretended Legislation:

For Quartering large bodies of armed troops among us:

For protecting them, by a mock Trial, from punishment for any Murders which they should commit on the Inhabitants of these States:

For cutting off our Trade with all parts of the world:

For imposing Taxes on us without our Consent:

For depriving us in many cases, of the benefits of Trial by Jury:

For transporting us beyond Seas to be tried for pretended offences

For abolishing the free System of English Laws in a neighbouring Province, establishing therein an Arbitrary government, and enlarging its Boundaries so as to render it at once an example and fit instrument for introducing the same absolute rule into these Colonies:

For taking away our Charters, abolishing our most valuable Laws, and altering fundamentally the Forms of our Governments:

For suspending our own Legislatures, and declaring themselves invested with power to legislate for us in all cases whatsoever.

He has abdicated Government here, by declaring us out of his Protection and waging War against us.

He has plundered our seas, ravaged our Coasts, burnt our towns, and destroyed the lives of our people.

He is at this time transporting large Armies of foreign Mercenaries to compleat the works of death, desolation and tyranny, already begun with circumstances of Cruelty & perfidy scarcely paralleled in the most barbarous ages, and totally unworthy the Head of a civilized nation.

He has constrained our fellow Citizens taken Captive on the high Seas to bear Arms against their Country, to become the executioners of their friends and Brethren, or to fall themselves by their Hands.

He has excited domestic insurrections amongst us, and has endeavoured to bring on the inhabitants of our frontiers, the merciless Indian Savages, whose known rule of warfare, is an undistinguished destruction of all ages, sexes and conditions.

In every stage of these Oppressions We have Petitioned for Redress in the most humble terms: Our repeated Petitions have been answered only by repeated injury. A Prince whose character is thus marked by every act which may define a Tyrant, is unfit to be the ruler of a free people.

Nor have We been wanting in attentions to our Brittish brethren. We have warned them from time to time of attempts by their legislature to extend an unwarrantable jurisdiction over us. We have reminded them of the circumstances of our emigration and settlement here. We have appealed to their native justice and magnanimity, and we have conjured them by the ties of our common kindred to disavow these usurpations, which, would inevitably interrupt our connections and correspondence. They too have been deaf to the voice of justice and of consanguinity. We must, therefore, acquiesce in the necessity, which denounces our Separation, and hold them, as we hold the rest of mankind, Enemies in War, in Peace Friends.

We, therefore, the Representatives of the united States of America, in General Congress, Assembled, appealing to the Supreme Judge of the world for the rectitude of our intentions, do, in the Name, and by Authority of the good People of these Colonies, solemnly publish and declare, That these United Colonies are, and of Right ought to be Free and Independent States; that they are Absolved from all Allegiance to the British Crown, and that all political connection between them and the State of Great Britain, is and ought to be totally dissolved; and that as Free and Independent States, they have full Power to levy War, conclude Peace, contract Alliances, establish Commerce, and to do all other Acts and Things which

> Independent States may of right do. And for the support of this Declaration, with a firm reliance on the protection of divine Providence, we mutually pledge to each other our Lives, our Fortunes and our sacred Honor.

The Revolutionary War

The Revolutionary War was a long, bloody conflict between Britain and the Continental Army. Throughout the war, the British used its superior navy to capture coastal cities and fortifications, but the interior of the continent was more difficult for them to manage. American uniformed and plain-clothed fighters used guerilla-style tactics—waiting in ambush and hiding effectively—to counter the larger British Army, which predominantly used traditional linear formations. General George Washington commanded the Continental Army and rose to fame during the war. The American defeat of the British Army at the Battle of Saratoga in 1777 emboldened the French king to dispatch his navy to the aid of the colonists. A major French sea victory in Chesapeake Bay in September 1781, and the subsequent joint siege of Yorktown, caused British General Lord Cornwallis to surrender his forces to the Continental Army. The 1783 Treaty of Paris formally ended the war, marking Britain's recognition of the independence of the colonies.

The First American Government

The United States of America were first incorporated in 1781 under the Articles of Confederation, a document that was carefully prepared not to infringe on the individual liberties of the colonies. Congress was sanctioned under the Articles, but it lacked the enforcement power needed to be an effective instrument for war, manager of the economy, negotiator in trade disputes, and tax collector. The Articles of Confederation were eventually replaced by the Constitution, which took effect in 1789, and which continues to govern the Union today (see "The U.S. Government" in Chapter 24, "Civics and Government"). The Preamble to the U.S. Constitution, reprinted here, explains the motivation behind it:

> "We the People of the United States, in Order to form a more perfect Union, establish Justice, insure domestic Tranquility, provide for the common defense, promote the general Welfare, and secure the Blessings of Liberty to ourselves and our Posterity, do ordain and establish this Constitution for the United States of America."

The Constitution was designed as a careful compromise between the Federalists, led by Alexander Hamilton, who believed in a central government with authority over the states, and the Anti-federalists, led by Thomas Jefferson, who feared a central power would eventually tread on the rights of the individual states. Read more about the U.S. federal system in Chapter 24.

Westward Expansion

Around the turn of the nineteenth century, the United States increased its territory. Beyond the original colonies, Vermont, Kentucky, Tennessee, and Ohio joined the Union. In 1803, President Thomas Jefferson bought the Louisiana Territory from cash-strapped Napoleonic France (see "The French Revolution" in Chapter 22) for $15 million, effectively doubling the size of the United States. Jefferson called on Captain Meriwether Lewis and Second Lieutenant William Clark of the army, along with a corps of men, to trek from Missouri to the Pacific Ocean, mapping the land and water and cataloging plants and animals along the way. Their successful voyage focused attention on the West and established a legacy of continued exploration of the new territory by the army. People in the East traveled the long trails west with the promise of new opportunities in the unsettled lands. The Conestoga wagon was the main freight carrier on the voyage west in the nineteenth century. Pulled by a team of horses, mules, or oxen, the wagon could travel about 15 miles per day.

Congress declared war on Great Britain in 1812 in part because of British interference with American transatlantic trade; a blockade was in force and some American sailors were being forced to join the British navy. Britain had also supported indigenous revolts in the West. Finally, Britain had refused to give up some of its Western forts promised to the United States in the Treaty of Paris of 1783. Fighting took place on land and at sea. Both sides had their share of victories. British forces landed at Washington, D.C., and burned the federal government buildings, including the President's House, to the ground. President James Madison and First Lady Dolly Madison were forced to flee the city. In another famous event, lawyer and amateur poet Francis Scott Key composed his poem known as "The Star-Spangled Banner" about the American defense of Fort McHenry in Maryland. The war reached a stalemate in 1814, and the United States and Great Britain agreed to peace terms preserving the pre-war boundaries between the United States and British Canada.

In a defining moment of U.S. foreign policy, President James Monroe expressed in 1823 that the long-standing powers in Europe should no longer establish colonies in the Americas and should not interfere in the affairs of the United States. This opinion is known as the Monroe Doctrine.

In 1830, Congress passed the Indian Removal Act, which empowered the president to make treaties with indigenous tribes that would exchange their lands in the eastern United States for lands west of the Mississippi River. President Andrew Jackson is remembered as taking a hard line with regard to native societies. Treaties he signed with tribes led to their hesitant and often forced migration to the West. President Martin Van Buren enforced a treaty made with a group of prominent Cherokees by marching their tribe toward Oklahoma along what has come to be called the Trail of Tears. Nearly 4,000 people died along the way, mostly from disease.

Texas was annexed by the United States in 1845. Mexico had claimed the territory and would not accept the annexation. The Mexican-American War broke out in 1846. U.S.

soldiers and volunteers defeated Mexican forces, which were poorly led and supplied. The 1848 Treaty of Guadalupe Hidalgo gave California, New Mexico, and adjacent areas to the United States.

The Civil War and President Lincoln

The addition of new states and territories to the Union raised many questions about the role of the federal government in deciding state issues, notably slavery. The Missouri Compromise of 1820 had forbidden slavery in any new northern states, but the Kansas-Nebraska Act of 1854 permitted the citizens of the new Nebraska territory (north of the line dividing north and south) to decide on the question of slavery for themselves. This effectively nullified the Missouri Compromise.

The northern states were increasing in population and industrial output faster than the southern states. By this time in U.S. history, northern and southern people were developing increasingly different cultural identities, too. The nation became divided between the North, which largely opposed slavery, and the South, whose plantation economy depended on slaves. After the election of Abraham Lincoln to the presidency, eleven southern states seceded from the Union in 1860 and 1861. They formed a new nation, the Confederate States of America. The Civil War began when a Confederate general ordered his subordinates to open fire on the Union's Fort Sumter, which was located in Confederate territory.

Initially, the Union tried to end the war with as little bloodshed as possible. A blockade of southern shipping ports prevented the export of cotton, the main cash crop, causing widespread economic collapse in the South. Nevertheless, Southern resistance increased.

Confederate forces made their first invasion of Northern territory in the fall of 1862. The Battle of Antietam in Maryland remains the bloodiest single day of war in U.S. history. In the aftermath of the battle, President Lincoln issued the Emancipation Proclamation, an executive order freeing all slaves in Confederate states. After the Proclamation, Union soldiers freed slaves as they encountered them throughout the South. The following is an excerpt from President Lincoln's Emancipation Proclamation:

> "That on the first day of January in the year of our Lord, one thousand eight hundred and sixty-three, all persons held as slaves within any State, or designated part of a State, the people whereof shall then be in rebellion against the United States shall be then, thenceforward, and forever free; and the executive government of the United States, including the military and naval authority thereof, will recognize and maintain the freedom of such persons, and will do no act or acts to repress such persons, or any of them, in any efforts they may make for their actual freedom."

The "high water mark" of the Confederacy is considered to be on the battlefield at Gettysburg, Pennsylvania. After the Union victory there in 1863, Confederate troops under General Robert E. Lee were forced to move south. In the West, the Union navy had captured the port of New Orleans on the Mississippi River delta, and the army under General Ulysses S. Grant controlled the Mississippi River. The Confederacy was thus split in two. The Battle of Gettysburg lasted three days and remains the bloodiest battle with the most casualties in U.S. military history.

Four and a half months following the Battle of Gettysburg, President Lincoln issued his most famous speech, which espoused the ideas of equality and freedom established by the Declaration of Independence. Lincoln's Gettysburg Address is short and was delivered before a crowd of about 15,000 people gathered to inaugurate the new soldiers' cemetery created on the battlegrounds:

> "Four score and seven years ago our fathers brought forth on this continent a new nation, conceived in liberty, and dedicated to the proposition that all men are created equal. Now we are engaged in a great civil war, testing whether that nation, or any nation so conceived and so dedicated, can long endure. We are met on a great battlefield of that war. We have come to dedicate a portion of that field as a final resting-place for those who here gave their lives that this nation might live. It is altogether fitting and proper that we should do this. But, in a larger sense, we cannot dedicate…we cannot consecrate…we cannot hallow…this ground. The brave men, living and dead, who struggled here, have consecrated it far above our poor power to add or detract. The world will little note nor long remember what we say here, but it can never forget what they did here. It is for us, the living, rather, to be dedicated here to the unfinished work which they who fought here have thus far so nobly advanced. It is rather for us to be here dedicated to the great task remaining before us…that from these honored dead we take increased devotion to that cause for which they gave the last full measure of devotion; that we here highly resolve that these dead shall not have died in vain; that this nation, under God, shall have a new birth of freedom; and that government of the people, by the people, for the people, shall not perish from the earth."

By 1864, Confederate forces were overwhelmed by the Union, which had a better-supplied army and superior financial and industrial infrastructure. In the summer, more battles raged in Virginia between Grant's and Lee's forces. Union General William Tecumseh Sherman marched his troops through Georgia, capturing Atlanta and the port of Savannah, destroying crops, livestock, and civilian infrastructure in a scorched-earth campaign to break the Confederate capacity to make war. In 1865, Lee surrendered to Grant; the Confederacy collapsed, and slaves were freed. The Civil War cost the United States more than 970,000 casualties—more than 3% of the national population.

The period known as Reconstruction started at the end of the Civil War. Major issues needing attention were the return of the southern states into the Union and how to integrate former slaves into the legal, economic, and social systems of the United States. Reconstruction was fraught with controversy and violence. Only days after General Lee's surrender, a Confederate radical named John Wilkes Booth assassinated President Lincoln in an attempt to bring chaos to the Union long enough to allow the Confederacy to resurrect itself. Booth's act did not accomplish his goal, but rather angered Northern political leaders, causing them to support harsh punishment of the South.

Historians generally believe that Reconstruction was a failure because it left white people in the South in a position of control of black people by denying them civil rights and economic opportunities.

From Noninterventionism to Imperialism

The United States was founded on the principle of *noninterventionism*, also called *isolationism*. The idea that the United States should remain politically uninvolved with foreign countries was brought to the public's attention by Thomas Paine in his 1776 pamphlet *Common Sense*. President George Washington is generally credited with starting the American tradition of noninterventionism. The following is from his farewell address on September 19, 1796:

> "The great rule of conduct for us, in regard to foreign nations, is in extending our commercial relations, to have with them as little political connection as possible. Europe has a set of primary interests, which to us have none, or a very remote relation. Hence she must be engaged in frequent controversies the causes of which are essentially foreign to our concerns. Hence, therefore, it must be unwise in us to implicate ourselves, by artificial ties, in the ordinary vicissitudes (ups and downs) of her politics, or the ordinary combinations and collisions of her friendships or enmities."

The United States departed from its isolationist tradition in 1867, when it purchased the Alaskan Territory from Russia. Secretary of State William Henry Seward had always had expansionist views and lobbied strongly for the purchase in Congress. Somewhat grudgingly, the Senate ratified the treaty with Russia, and the whole Congress approved the $7.2 million (equivalent to about $1.6 billion today) for the purchase. Initially, acquiring Alaska for such a large amount of money was unpopular with the general public, who called the decision "Seward's Folly." Most people understood Alaska to be a nearly uninhabited, remote, frigid land. Seward responded to the criticism by delivering a speech in which he described in detail all the desirable features of the territory's land, water, flora, fauna, and mineral resources. The value of Alaska was eventually well understood in the United States; however, by entering into a land purchase agreement with a foreign power, the United States had departed from its pattern of noninterventionism.

By the end of the nineteenth century, the United States had become trading partners with nations around the world. American ships sailing the Pacific established business on islands that provided a strategic stopping point. The United States already laid claim to various uninhabited islands in the South Pacific, but eventually extended its reach onto inhabited islands. Hawaii's monarchy was overthrown in 1893 by some of its citizens and resident American businessmen. At the request of the new authority, Hawaii was annexed by the United States in 1898.

In the summer of 1898, the United States joined Cuban rebels in fighting the colonial power of Spain after being provoked by an explosion off the coast of Cuba, which sank the USS *Maine*, a battleship dispatched to ensure the safety of Americans on the embattled Caribbean island. More than 260 sailors died. Many people believed Spain was responsible for the attack, although evidence of the cause of the explosion was scarce and unreliable. Nevertheless, the United States declared war against Spain and four months later achieved victory. The Treaty of Paris of 1898 was signed to end the Spanish-American War. The United States acquired the Philippines, Guam, and Puerto Rico from Spain at a cost of $20 million ($4.5 billion today).

Incorporating territories in other parts of the world signaled a shift in American foreign policy from noninterventionism toward imperialism.

Industrialization and Immigration

The period starting after the Civil War and continuing into the twentieth century was marked by fast industrial development in the United States, particularly in the North. Population also swelled in the postwar period. The United States was increasingly becoming one of the world's great economic and political powers. The abundance of land and natural resources allowed for cheap energy, fast transportation, and great amounts of capital for establishing new industries and expanding existing ones.

The railroad was an important innovation in America, allowing ready access to areas of the country previously undeveloped. Technologies such as telegraph and telephone systems allowed industrialists to conduct business over long distances. The shareholder corporation emerged in the late nineteenth century as a means to finance large-scale industrial projects. Corporations took control of competing companies to create monopolies. (Rules for business administration were not as comprehensive as they are today.) The federal government also bolstered domestic industry by placing high tariffs on imported goods. The end of the nineteenth century saw the first American class of super-rich industrialists. Figure 23.1 depicts a scene symbolic of the late nineteenth-century industrialization.

FIGURE 23.1 Indigenous people look down from the top of the hill on one of the first trains to travel the first transcontinental rail line.

New immigrants to the United States provided booming industry with a plentiful supply of cheap labor. Between 1840 and 1920, about 37 million people moved to the

United States to find work, farm some land, or escape hardships such as the Irish Potato Famine. During this period, most immigrants came from countries in Europe. Use of the metaphor "melting pot" was popularized around 1908 to describe the way American culture is a fusion of many world cultures brought to the United States.

Ellis Island in New York City received more than 12 million immigrants to the United States. Prior to being admitted, each person was interviewed by government officials and screened by doctors for contagious diseases and other medical conditions.

The United States and World War I

The United States entered World War I in 1917, after Germany had declared a campaign of unrestricted naval warfare and after the revelation that Germany was inviting Mexico to join it in war against the United States. Fresh American troops were crucial in supporting the Allied victory over Germany's final great offensive of the war. While the European Allies imposed strict penalties on Germany under the Treaty of Versailles, the U.S. Senate would not ratify the treaty. Instead, the United States signed separate, less strict treaties with the Central Powers: Germany, Austria-Hungary, the Ottoman Empire, and Bulgaria. Nevertheless, the Treaty of Versailles brought severe economic decline to Germany and is seen as an impetus for Adolf Hitler's rise to power, and by extension, World War II.

Back in the United States, the "dry" (anti-alcohol) movement had existed since the mid-1800s, but anti-German sentiment during World War I strengthened it. (Germany is famous for its beer.) The Eighteenth Amendment to the Constitution was approved in 1920 to ban the manufacture, sale, and transport of alcohol. Prohibition lasted until 1933, when the Twenty-First Amendment overturned the Eighteenth. Among the problems associated with Prohibition was the ascent of organized crime groups in large cities. "Rum runners" smuggled alcohol, and in the process corrupted law-enforcement officers, judges, and other official figures by offering them bribes in exchange for turning a blind eye or providing protection.

Women and the Right to Vote

The 1920 ratification of the Nineteenth Amendment to the Constitution gave all women the right to vote in the United States. Previously, some state laws permitted the female vote, but the amendment to the Constitution effectively mandated women's suffrage throughout the country. The amendment was the culmination of decades of female struggle to become fully franchised in the political system. Numerous women's suffrage organizations staged regular protests and rallied support among the public and politicians.

> The Nineteenth Amendment
>
> ---
>
> The right of citizens in the United States to vote shall not be denied or abridged by the United States or by any State on account of sex.
>
> Congress shall have power to enforce this article by appropriate legislation.

The Great Depression

The United States enjoyed a period of industrial prosperity in the 1920s, although agricultural production and worker wages fell. Industrial profits were underpinned by increased debt, and the ultimate effect was the stock market crash of 1929. Heavy personal investment had taken place prior to the crash. Many people borrowed money from banks to purchase stock shares. On October 24, after a lengthy period of steady increase, the stock market average went down. Panic set in among investors, and nearly 13 million shares were traded as people tried to sell off their holdings before they became worthless. Over the next few days, millions more shares changed hands. Lending banks found themselves deep in debt, and many entered bankruptcy. Businesses lost customers and closed, causing widespread unemployment. The Great Depression set in, and its effects reverberated around the world.

Unable to sustain their previous lifestyle, many people lost their homes to foreclosure. Homelessness increased. Many manufacturers of high-end goods failed as the public began economizing every aspect of their lives. Most people affected by the Depression endured it through prudent spending. For example, there was an emphasis on reusing household items and minimizing food waste.

The Dust Bowl was the area of the Plains states devastated by drought during the 1930s. Poor soil conservation techniques left the land with little or no topsoil in which farm crops could root. Many farms failed, and many farmers left their lands for jobs in Midwest industry or on successful California farms. For much of the country, economic misfortune was exacerbated by agricultural decline. Figure 23.2 shows a dust storm, which likely resulted from inadequate soil conservation measures.

FIGURE 23.2 The Dust Bowl: Drought and soil erosion led to massive dust storms like this one in Texas.

It was during the Depression that the Hollywood movie industry flourished. New sound films were created that portrayed carefree and often humorous characters and plots that offered burdened Americans moments of escape. Movies featuring Shirley Temple, the Three Stooges, and the Marx Brothers, among others, allowed weary audiences to forget their troubles and feel hope for the future.

The New Deal

President Franklin D. Roosevelt, shown in Figure 23.3, promoted a series of government programs called the New Deal to help the United States and its citizens during the Great Depression.

FIGURE 23.3 Franklin D. Roosevelt is remembered as the New Deal president.

Under the terms of the New Deal, many "alphabet agencies" were established to help three causes, which the president called the "3 R's": direct relief, economic recovery, and financial reform. New Deal programs involved significant government spending, yet FDR made efforts to balance the federal budget. Although historians debate whether the New Deal ended the Great Depression, they generally agree that it had the effect of limiting economic decay. Table 23.1 outlines some notable New Deal programs.

TABLE 23.1 Important New Deal Legislation and Programs

Name	Acronym	Purpose
Civilian Conservation Corps	CCC	Provide unskilled work to young men in rural areas
Tennessee Valley Authority	TVA	Build and maintain dams to generate hydroelectric power in the impoverished area comprising most of Tennessee
Agricultural Adjustment Act	AAA	Boost farm prices by limiting total production
National Recovery Act	NRA	Empower the president to establish codes for fair business practices, wages, and prices
Public Works Administration	PWA	Build large public works projects (for example, Grand Coulee Dam) using private contractors
Federal Deposit Insurance Corporation	FDIC	Insure bank deposits to restore public confidence in banks

(continues)

TABLE 23.1 Continued

Name	Acronym	Purpose
Securities and Exchange Commission	SEC	Establish standards for buying and selling stock
Civil Works Administration	CWA	Provide temporary jobs to millions of unemployed people
Social Security Act	SSA	Provide financial aid to the elderly and disabled; funded by employee and employer contributions
Works Progress Administration	WPA	Provide construction jobs for men; sewing jobs for women; and art projects for artists, musicians, writers, and so on; and remains a striking example of New Deal spending.
National Labor Relations Act	NLRA	Establish National Labor Relations Board to oversee employer-employee relations; favored labor unions
Fair Labor Standards Act	FLSA	Establish a maximum 40-hour work week and a minimum wage

The Grand Coulee dam (see Figure 23.4) on the Columbia River irrigates and generates electricity for the Pacific Northwest. Its construction was made possible in part by the Public Works Administration, and the dam's reservoir was named Franklin Delano Roosevelt Lake, in honor of the New Deal president.

FIGURE 23.4 The Grand Coulee dam.

The Home Front During World War II

Although World War II (1939 to 1945) was decided in Europe and the Pacific Ocean, it had major effects on the United States homeland. (Read more about World War II in Chapter 22, "World History.") During World War II, the United States was characterized by the massive increase in industrial activity required to support the war effort. In fact, war spending doubled the national gross domestic product, helping to alleviate the lingering Great Depression. Patriotic fervor allowed businesses to overlook burdensome new taxes and workers to put in long hours manufacturing important goods for the armed forces, which required supplies as fast as the country could produce them. Many industries converted for the war. For example, automobile factories stopped making new passenger cars in order to produce military trucks and tanks. Jobs were plentiful, as about 12 million young men were called away from theirs to fight in the war. Many women assumed factory jobs once held by men. The federal government told the people that industrial workers at home were as critical to the war as the soldiers overseas.

The federal War Production Coordinating Committee commissioned posters (like the one in Figure 23.5 depicting "Rosie the Riveter") to encourage people, especially women, to help the war effort by working in manufacturing.

FIGURE 23.5 "Rosie the Riveter." [We Can Do It!, J. Howard Miller, 1943]

Americans became accustomed to having commodities rationed, which the military greatly needed. Most notably, civilians were limited to how much gasoline, clothing, leather goods, and certain food products they could buy. The federal government issued coupons in equal numbers to every American, regardless of age, to spend on rationed products. Drivers were limited to three gallons of gasoline per week. Restaurant patrons, in addition to paying for their meal in cash, had to spend food coupons. Although some illegal manufacturing and trading of coupons existed, American society generally accepted the rationing with patriotic and egalitarian spirit.

Year-round daylight savings time was established during World War II as a measure to conserve energy resources. The rationale is that by shifting the period of daylight to match the work day more closely, the country would need less electric light. The government performed blackout drills in major cities to train citizens to live for a period of time in the dark should a blackout become necessary as a countermeasure to aerial bombardment.

When soldiers returned from war, the United States experienced a "baby boom." Reunited couples settled into homes and started families. Young soldiers' wives received free medical care during pregnancy and childbirth. The generation of Americans born between the end of World War II (around 1945) and about 1960 are called baby boomers.

The Korean War

The United States and the Soviet Union occupied the Korean Peninsula, which Japan had controlled for 35 years, following the Japanese defeat in World War II. The United States occupied the southern half of the peninsula and the Soviet Union the northern half.

As the tension of the cold war between the United States and the Soviet Union increased, each side believed the other would try to obtain control over the entire peninsula. In 1950, South Korea elected a democratic government and North Korea came under the control of a communist government. Each government considered itself the true government of all Korea. Military forces on both sides gathered at the border. The Korean War began when North Korea launched a massive attack on the South. U.S. President Harry S. Truman then committed troops to defend South Korea. Forces from other Western nations joined the Americans in South Korea under the flag of the United Nations. North Korea was backed by the Soviet Union and eventually China, two communist states. The Soviet Union provided the North Koreans with the bulk of their war material.

Some people refer to the Korean War as the Korean Conflict because UN military activities are generally considered police actions and not wars. In addition, Congress never declared war on North Korea.

The fighting devastated the civilian population in Korea. About 2.5 million Koreans died during the war, which lasted until 1953. About 54,000 U.S. soldiers died, along with many more from the coalition nations.

The Korean War ended with a truce agreement, not a peace treaty. Under the terms of the truce, Korea would remain divided between the communist North and the democratic South, just as it remains today. A demilitarized zone about four kilometers wide spans the peninsula around the 38th parallel north and serves as the de facto international border. Today, Korea remains in a state of military tension along the line, making it the last stand-off of the cold war between communist and capitalist nations. Most recently, North Korea has heightened the tension by conducting ballistic missile tests, which the United States has interpreted as a sign that the communist state is seeking nuclear weapons technology.

The Eisenhower Years

Dwight D. Eisenhower earned the respect of the American people when he served as Supreme Commander of Allied forces in Europe during World War II (see Figure 23.6).

One of his duties was planning and carrying out the unprecedented invasion of Nazi-occupied France on D-Day (see "World War II" in Chapter 22). Eisenhower returned from Europe a hero to the American people, who called for him to declare his candidacy in the 1952 presidential election. Eisenhower campaigned on a platform of reforming the U.S. policy toward communism established by outgoing President Truman. It was Eisenhower, after winning the election, who worked to end the Korean War.

FIGURE 23.6 General Eisenhower giving orders to American paratroopers in England prior to their deployment behind German lines in France on D-Day.

Eisenhower was president in the age of McCarthyism, a vigorous anticommunist movement named after it chief proponent, Senator Joseph McCarthy of Wisconsin. Many people feared that a complex communist conspiracy was threatening the United States. During this scare, many people of all walks of life, but especially educators, writers, and celebrities, were accused of being communists or communist sympathizers. Government and private groups, most famously the House Un-American Activities Committee, pursued aggressive investigations and interviews of suspected individuals. Thousands of people had their careers and reputations ruined by the public accusations; most claims were later proven unfounded.

The 1950s saw great technological advancements in the United States, especially in the area of space exploration. The launch of the satellite Sputnik I by the Soviet Union in 1957 drew the United States into the "space race" (see "The World After Global War" in Chapter 22).

President Eisenhower approved of the Supreme Court's decision in the case of *Brown v. Board of Education of Topeka, Kansas.* The Court held unanimously that the "separate but equal" doctrine that governed racial segregation of schools was unconstitutional. The racially divided South largely objected to the ruling, which meant that black and white students could enroll in schools together. In one famous act of defiance in 1957, Arkansas Governor Orval Faubus dispatched National Guard soldiers to the all-white Little Rock Central High School to prevent nine black students from entering. This act sparked a showdown between Faubus and President Eisenhower, who negotiated the removal of the troops stationed at the school. Nine days later, the same students attempted to enter the school, again without success. An angry mob had gathered at the school, and police struggled to manage it. The next day, Eisenhower dispatched army soldiers to Little Rock to protect the students and see that federal court orders to allow them to enter the school were carried out. Over the next year, the students endured physical and verbal abuse. The symbolic impact of their persistence fueled the emerging Civil Rights Movement.

President John F. Kennedy

President John F. Kennedy, pictured in Figure 23.7, was and remains unique among U.S. presidents. At age 43, he became the youngest man elected to the office of president (Theodore Roosevelt became president at age 42, following the assassination of President William McKinley). In addition, Kennedy remains the only Catholic president in U.S. history. He was a celebrated World War II veteran and was admired for his engaging personality and glamorous life, having grown up in the prominent Irish-American Kennedy family of Massachusetts.

FIGURE 23.7 John F. Kennedy, the youngest man ever elected president, was assassinated during his third year in office.

President Kennedy was an engaging public figure who garnered respect for the presidency and represented a new era in American social and political life. His most famous speech called on Americans to help their country thrive and deliver the message of freedom to the rest of the world. The following is an excerpt from that inaugural address on January 20, 1961:

> "In the long history of the world, only a few generations have been granted the role of defending freedom in its hour of maximum danger. I do not shrink from this responsibility—I welcome it. I do not believe that any of us would exchange

> places with any other people or any other generation. The energy, the faith, the devotion which we bring to this endeavor will light our country and all who serve it. And the glow from that fire can truly light the world.
>
> And so, my fellow Americans, ask not what your country can do for you; ask what you can do for your country.
>
> My fellow citizens of the world, ask not what America will do for you, but what together we can do for the freedom of man.
>
> Finally, whether you are citizens of America or citizens of the world, ask of us here the same high standards of strength and sacrifice which we ask of you. With a good conscience our only sure reward, with history the final judge of our deeds, let us go forth to lead the land we love, asking His blessing and His help, but knowing that here on earth God's work must truly be our own."

During the Kennedy administration, the U.S. space program became an icon of the adventurous American spirit. Astronaut Alan Shepard Jr. became the first American in space after completing a 15-minute suborbital flight in 1961. Nine months later, during a 5-hour space flight, astronaut John Glenn became the first American to orbit the Earth.

The space race between the United States and the Soviet Union was a less-sinister rivalry of the cold war, compared to the stand off that emerged in 1961. The Cuban Missile Crisis, as it is called, was a period when pro-Soviet Cuba began positioning nuclear missiles on the island, which lies only 90 miles from the tip of Florida. In response, President Kennedy ordered a naval blockade of Cuba to prevent any Soviet vessel from reaching the island. Kennedy demanded that Soviet Premier Nikita Khrushchev immediately organize the dismantlement of the missiles. Not wishing to turn the cold war any "hotter," Khrushchev agreed to have the missile battery removed.

President Kennedy was an advocate for individual rights and democracy in the world. He continued the policy of assuring civil rights to black Americans begun by Eisenhower, although the marches, protests, and dynamic leaders of the Civil Rights Movement secured full franchise for America's black minority. Baptist Reverend Dr. Martin Luther King Jr. was the most prominent of the civil rights leaders of the 1950s and '60s. His many speeches and rallies, culminating with a historic march on Washington, D.C., furthered the cause of civil rights for minorities in the United States. In 1968, a segregationist named James Earl Ray shot and killed King. Neither King nor President Kennedy lived to see the goals of the Civil Rights Movement come to fruition.

President Kennedy was shot and killed while riding in an open car during a Dallas, Texas, parade on November 22, 1963. The official investigation of the assassination determined that Lee Harvey Oswald, a Marxist and an ex-military rifleman, perpetrated the killing. Oswald waited by a sixth-floor window of the Texas School Book Depository, located along the president's parade route. As the president's car passed, Oswald fired three shots, striking the president twice, killing him.

By the rule of presidential succession established in the Constitution, Vice-President Lyndon B. Johnson was sworn in as president after learning that President Kennedy had died. Many of Kennedy's proposals died with him, but President Johnson stayed the course on Kennedy's promised civil rights reform. The Civil Rights Act of 1964 was Johnson's most important achievement as president. The act forbade discrimination on the basis of race, color, sex, national origin, or religion in public facilities, government institutions, employment, and all other federally funded or regulated activities.

The Vietnam War

Many people consider the Vietnam War and the Korean War similar in that both were rooted in the ideological conflict at the heart of the cold war. Although the Soviet Union and the United States had reservations about fighting a large-scale war (likely involving nuclear weapons) against one another directly, tensions still led to armed conflict in other countries where the United States saw Soviet communism spreading.

The Vietnam War was fought between democratic South Vietnam with its allies, predominantly the United States, and communist North Vietnam with its allies. The United States never declared war on North Vietnam, but the total human cost of the fighting makes many people hesitant to label the conflict a "police action," a moniker more often given to the Korean War.

After World War II, Vietnam fought for independence from its colonial power, France. Vietnamese communists, supported by better-equipped Chinese troops, made repeated attacks against French positions in the north of the country. France suffered heavy losses, and the conflict became increasingly unpopular among French citizens. The United States began supporting France politically and financially against the communist forces. In 1954, the Geneva Accords were signed to create a provisional divide between North Vietnam, controlled by communists, and South Vietnam, still controlled by the Vietnamese emperor. After a year, the emperor's prime minister deposed him and subsequently refused to enter into the countrywide elections with the North as called for in the Geneva Accords. Violence broke out anew when Northern forces invaded the South.

U.S. military personnel were involved in supporting South Vietnam beginning in 1959, but not in great numbers until 1965, during the administration of President Johnson. The Vietnam War would ultimately be his undoing.

By 1968, more than 500,000 American soldiers were fighting in Vietnam. Beginning in 1969, the Selective Service System conducted a draft lottery to select young men for the army. Supporters of U.S. involvement in Vietnam insisted the fight was necessary to limit the spread of communism in the world. Opponents viewed the conflict as an internal struggle in which the United States had no need to participate. The disagreement over Vietnam strongly divided the country and led to years of public debate and demonstration.

The Vietnam War created the impassioned antiwar movement of the 1960s and 1970s. Protests erupted in cities and on college campuses throughout the country. Many young men fled the United States to Canada to avoid the draft. Although in a climate of strong political discord, President Johnson continued his pursuit of military victory in Vietnam, but eventually felt the costs of fighting were overcoming the good that came from it. President Johnson did not seek reelection in 1968, leaving the office of the presidency open for new leadership.

The Nixon Years

The Vietnam War continued under President Richard Nixon, who was elected to replace President Johnson. The United States sustained its heavy bombing of enemy territory, but surrender never came. Nixon did, however, gradually draw American forces out of Vietnam, which was arranged under the 1973 Paris Peace Accords, for which National Security Adviser Henry Kissinger was awarded the Nobel Peace Prize. Under the accords, the United States would remove its personnel in Vietnam, and both sides of the conflict would release their prisoners. American soldiers returned home to a mixed welcome; some people appreciated their sacrifice, whereas others condemned them for participating in the war. After Nixon left office, in Vietnam, the communist North continued its offensive against the South, eventually seizing control of it. In 1976, North Vietnam declared the two sides united, forming the Socialist Republic of Vietnam.

President Nixon, pictured in Figure 23.8, worked to ease cold-war tension during and after the American involvement in Vietnam. He was instrumental in negotiations with the Soviet Union over the stockpiling of nuclear weapons. The first Strategic Arms Limitation Talks, or SALT I, refers to the years of dialog between the two cold-war superpowers that ended in the 1972 agreement to freeze the number of nuclear weapons at its present level. Nixon also improved relations with the communist People's Republic of China. In 1960, China had broken its allegiance with the Soviet Union, and in 1972, Nixon made a diplomatic visit to the People's Republic, the first president to do so. The American focus on the cold war shifted toward the Soviet state, an effect that gave the United States a clearer advantage in the conflict.

FIGURE 23.8 Nixon was the first U.S. president to visit communist China.

In spite of his accomplishments, one great scandal dominates Nixon's legacy. In June 1972, during Nixon's reelection campaign, a group of men was discovered burglarizing the headquarters of the Democratic National Committee, Nixon's opposition in the election. Investigations revealed that the burglars intended to place wiretaps inside the offices and photograph confidential documents to help Nixon win the election. The investigation took a long time to develop, during which Nixon won his reelection. Eventually, though, Nixon was implicated in the scandal, when witness testimony revealed that Oval Office conversations were regularly audiotaped. The tapes were subpoenaed by the Senate Watergate Committee and proved Nixon knew about the crime and discussed covering it up. Seeing impeachment ahead of him, Nixon resigned the presidency—the first and only to do so.

The Last Decades of the Twentieth Century and the Start of the Twenty-First Century

In this section we'll discuss some significant decisions made by U.S. presidents since 1972.

President Ford

Nixon's vice president, Gerald Ford, took over the presidency after the resignation. In fact, Ford was the only president never to be elected as either president or vice president. By the rules of succession, the House Minority Leader Ford became Nixon's vice president when Nixon's first vice president resigned in 1973 over charges of tax evasion and money laundering. President Ford's administration oversaw the final removal of Americans from Vietnam, but Ford had difficulties accomplishing many of his own plans. Competing with a majority-Democratic Congress, many of Ford's vetoes were overridden. In the 1976 election, he was narrowly defeated by Democratic candidate Jimmy Carter.

President Carter

President Jimmy Carter served from 1977 to 1981. His major domestic initiatives included consolidating many government agencies into the new cabinet-level Department of Energy, enacting strong environmental legislation, and strengthening Social Security. In foreign affairs, President Carter facilitated peace talks between Israel and Egypt, returned the Panama Canal zone to Panama, and established full diplomatic relationship with the People's Republic of China. Further arms control negotiations resulted in the SALT II Treaty with the Soviet Union. Carter's presidency was not without conflict, however. Student supporters of the regime in Iran seized control of the U.S. Embassy in Tehran and held 66 Americans hostage for 444 days. Months into the crisis, President Carter ordered a secret rescue attempt, which failed, taking the lives of eight soldiers. Many historians see this disaster as a primary reason for Carter's inability to gain reelection. They were finally released the day Carter left office. At the end of 1979, the Soviet Union invaded Afghanistan, and President Carter decided the United States would boycott the 1980 Summer Olympics in Moscow.

President Reagan

Ronald Reagan, a Republican, defeated Jimmy Carter in the next election and served two terms, from 1981 to 1989. At age 69, he was the oldest person ever elected to the office. Before entering politics, President Reagan was a well-liked screen actor. He was charismatic and delivered many memorable speeches.

Reagan's economic and foreign policies are generally considered the foundation of the modern "conservative" movement. He was committed to democratic capitalism and the defeat of communism. His arms negotiations with the Soviet Union are often credited with hastening the fall of that country's government. British Prime Minister Margaret Thatcher, a close friend and ally, once said, "Ronald Reagan won the cold war without firing a shot."

The major scandal that befell President Reagan was called the Iran-Contra Affair, which refers to the sale of arms to Iran (a sworn enemy), the proceeds from which went to fund the Contras, a paramilitary, anticommunist group in Nicaragua.

President Bush (the Elder)

Republican George H. W. Bush succeeded Ronald Reagan and served from 1989 to 1993. From the outset, foreign policy dominated the Bush presidency. During his term in office, communism collapsed in the former Soviet countries of Eastern Europe. American troops were dispatched to Panama in 1989 to overthrow the military dictator, General Manuel Noriega. He was brought to the United States, tried, and convicted in 1992 on several drug-trafficking-related charges. He was sentenced to 40 years in federal prison, later reduced to 30.

The major armed conflict during the elder Bush's administration was the Persian Gulf War. The United States led a United Nations coalition invasion of Iraq after it had invaded its oil-rich neighbor Kuwait. A devastating series of air attacks brought the U.N. swift victory. By a decision often questioned today, Bush allowed the Iraqi dictator, Saddam Hussein, to remain in power, a situation that Bush's son, George W. Bush, would revisit during his own presidency, beginning in 2001.

President Clinton

Democrat Bill Clinton defeated George Bush and independent candidate Ross Perot in the 1992 presidential election. Clinton's domestic initiatives included the North American Free Trade Act (NAFTA), a treaty with Mexico and Canada that was designed to make cross-border trade cheaper and more efficient. Much of the foreign policy focus during Clinton's administration was on the ethno-political conflict in the region of southeastern Europe known as the Balkans. The nation of Bosnia and Herzegovina seceded from Yugoslavia in 1992, sparking an internal civil war. Bosnians of Serbian descent disapproved of the split, and Muslim Bosnians and Bosnians of Croatian descent favored it. The Bosnian Serbs, supported by the country of Serbia, were a stronger force. President Clinton initially sought strong action against the Serbs, but receiving little support from European countries, he opted instead to negotiate a general cease-fire and new organization of the besieged country. Negotiations between the parties were held in Dayton, Ohio, and the result was the Dayton Accords, under which Bosnia and Herzegovina would remain an independent nation, but with two separate entities tied by a central government.

Tensions in the Balkans arose again during the Clinton years when Serb forces from the Federal Republic of Yugoslavia (now the nations of Serbia and Montengro) took up positions in the southern province of Kosovo, a significant majority of whose residents were Muslims and ethnic Albanians that desired independence. Accounts of ethnic cleansing and other atrocities compelled the United States and European allies to take military action against the Serb forces after a peace settlement failed. Air strikes destroyed many critical Serbian targets. In June 1999, a peace plan was prepared and air strikes stopped after the Serb surrender.

The scandal that rocked President Clinton's reputation came when it was revealed that he lied to a federal grand jury about accusations of his marital infidelity. Clinton became only the second president in history to be impeached by Congress. Charges of perjury and obstruction of justice were passed by the House of Representatives, but did not receive the two-thirds majority vote in the Senate, as required by the Constitution. Clinton served out the rest of his term.

President Bush (the Younger)

Republican George W. Bush, son of President George H. W. Bush, took office in January 2001. His presidency began in relative calm domestically, until on September 11, 2001, Islamic extremists crashed airliners into both towers of the World Trade Center in New York City, which caused them to collapse, and the Pentagon in Washington, D.C. A fourth airliner crashed in rural Pennsylvania after passengers intervened, preventing the plane from reaching the hijackers' intended target, which may have been the U.S. Capitol building, according to one terrorism suspect's statements. Nearly 3,000 people died in the "9/11" attacks. The devastation at the World Trade Center towers is pictured in Figure 23.9.

FIGURE 23.9 Burning jet fuel from the crashed airliners weakened the steel supports of the World Trade Center towers until they became deformed and began buckling. The towers collapsed, killing the people who remained inside, along with many police officers and firefighters helping to evacuate the buildings.

Intelligence reports indicated that a Saudi Arabian named Osama bin Laden, who had previously arranged bombings of U.S. embassies in Africa, had orchestrated the terrorist acts. In response, President Bush, with the approval of most of the world and military support from many countries, ordered the U.S. invasion of Afghanistan and unseated the extremist Taliban regime, which had supported and harbored bin Laden and his Islamic paramilitary group, called Al-Qaeda.

President Bush declared the fight against terrorist violence the "War on Terror." As part of this war, Bush ordered the invasion of Iraq, whose leader, Saddam Hussein, was purported to be developing weapons of mass destruction; that claim has been widely disputed. As of 2007, the U.S. military and some allied forces occupy Iraq, and Saddam Hussein was tried, convicted, and hanged for war crimes he allegedly committed against some of his citizens in the past. Many people believe that religious fundamentalism and liberal democracy will take sides in the great ideological struggle of the twenty-first century.

What's Next?

Chapter 24 includes a discussion of civics and government, defining and describing different forms of government and the role of the citizen.

CHAPTER TWENTY-FOUR

Civics and Government

The study of the duties and privileges of citizens is called *civics*. Knowing how the government works is an important facet of life, especially in a *representative system*, where elected officials steer the course of a city, a state, or a nation. Government brings order to society by imposing a certain framework for public life. In many countries, including the United States, Canada, and Mexico, the power is vested in the people in a system broadly called a *democracy*. Many countries have democracies, each with its unique policies and institutions. Other countries have different systems of government.

Forms of Government

Governments can have many forms determined by how power is granted and shared within them. Table 24.1 provides a basic overview of the theoretical forms of government.

TABLE 24.1 Basic Forms of Government

Oligarchy	Autocracy	Democracy	Monarchy
Power held by very few people. Citizens do not elect their leaders.	One person dominates and controls all aspects of public life. Sometimes called "dictatorship." Citizens do not elect their leader.	Power derives from the consent of the people. True democracy allows citizens to decide directly. Representative democracy allows citizens to elect a body of representatives (legislature, congress, parliament, and so on).	One royal family passes power from generation to generation. In absolute monarchy, the royal family holds complete power. In parliamentary monarchy, government is operated as a democracy with a parliament; the royal family has limited powers.

The U.S. Government

The Constitution was established in 1789 as the basis of the U.S. government. The Constitution represents the supreme law of the country, the standard against which any potential law is measured. Amendments have been made to the Constitution since 1789, but the original language that establishes government has remained largely unchanged.

The U.S. government is founded on the principles of *federalism*, as outlined in the Constitution. The powers of authority are balanced between the states and the central (federal) government in Washington, D.C. The Constitution defines the duties and privileges of the three branches of the federal government: the *legislative branch* (the law-making Congress of the Senate and House of Representatives), the *executive branch* (the president, who enforces the laws), and the *judicial branch* (the courts, which interpret laws). The concept behind the three-branched system is separation of powers, or checks and balances, which means that no part of government has authority to dominate the entire government. The federal democracy of the United States relies on both effective communication among the different branches of government and active participation by citizens.

The Legislative Branch: Congress

Article One of the Constitution establishes the *legislative* branch of government. The legislature, called the Congress, is composed of the Senate and the House of Representatives. The two houses share power, and any potential law (called a *bill*) must be approved by each house.

Seats in the House of Representatives are allocated according to population. More populated states have more representatives, and each one represents a district within the state having roughly the same amount of people as any other district. The total number of representatives is fixed at 435, with several states having only one and California, the nation's most populated state, currently having 53. The Senate balances this system of allocation by assigning exactly two Senate seats to each state. For example, whereas Alaska currently has only one representative and California has 53, both states have just two senators each.

Representatives are elected by their constituents—people from their district—and serve for a period of two years. Today, senators are similarly elected, and serve for six years, although the Constitution originally called for senators to be elected by state legislatures. Unlike some government positions, such as the presidency, for example, members of Congress may serve an unlimited number of terms. (The longest-serving senator is Robert Byrd of West Virginia, who took office in 1959.)

Article One states the following:

A representative must be at least 25 years old, a citizen of the United States for at least 7 years, and a resident, at the time of election, of the state he or she will represent.

A senator must be at least 30 years old, a citizen of the United State for at least 9 years, and a resident, at the time of election, of the state he or she will represent.

Although the Constitution grants some flexibility in the role of the Congress to meet unforeseeable needs, Article One of the Constitution clearly establishes specific powers held by Congress:

- Impose taxes
- Borrow money
- Regulate commerce among the individual states and foreign countries
- Make new laws
- Amend (change) existing laws
- Mint money
- Declare war
- Maintain the armed forces
- Admit new states to the Union
- Senate-specific powers:
    - Ratify treaties
    - Approve presidential appointments
- House-specific powers:
    - Impeach the president
    - Introduce a tax bill

The Executive Branch: the President and Vice President

Article Two of the Constitution establishes the *executive* branch of government: the offices of the president and vice president. The president serves four-year terms, and federal law mandates a maximum of two terms. If the president dies or cannot execute his or her duties, the vice president becomes president.

According to Article Two, the president must be at least 35 years old, a natural-born U.S. citizen, and a resident of the United States for at least 14 years. The Twelfth Amendment to the Constitution mandates that vice presidents meet these same requirements.

Article Two grants the president the following powers:

- Serve as commander-in-chief of the armed forces
- Grant pardons for violations of federal law

- Appoint justices to the Supreme Court, judges to other federal courts, and foreign ambassadors, all pending approval by the Senate
- Appoint certain executive officers
- Veto bills approved by Congress

In addition to the official duties, the president acts as the symbolic leader of the United States, engaging with other world leaders and steering many elements of foreign and domestic policy.

Besides being first in the line of presidential succession, the vice president serves as the president of the Senate, and may break tie votes in that legislative body.

The president appoints officers to the Cabinet, whose role is to advise and assist the president. The number of cabinet-level departments has varied throughout U.S. history. There are currently 15 of them:

- Department of Agriculture
- Department of Commerce
- Department of Defense
- Department of Education
- Department of Energy
- Department of Health and Human Services
- Department of Homeland Security
- Department of Housing and Urban Development
- Department of Interior
- Department of Justice
- Department of Labor
- Department of State
- Department of Transportation
- Department of Treasury
- Department of Veterans Affairs

The Attorney General heads the Justice Department. The heads of the remaining cabinet departments are given the title "Secretary."

The Judicial Branch: the Supreme Court and Lower Federal Courts

Article Three of the Constitution establishes the *judicial* branch; specifically, the Supreme Court of the United States and lower courts established under the authority of Congress. The highest court in the country, the Supreme Court is responsible for ensuring that laws passed by Congress and the state legislatures, actions of the executive branch, and decisions made by lower courts conform to the standards of the Constitution. A government action is said to be unconstitutional if the Supreme Court finds that it violates some part of the Constitution.

The Supreme Court has nine justices, who the president appoints for a lifetime term. Seats are vacated when justices resign, retire, die, or are impeached and then convicted. The president also appoints lower federal judges to the 11 circuit courts, which are also known as Federal Appeals Courts, and approximately 90 district courts.

As a general rule, the president appoints justices and judges whose legal and philosophical beliefs align with the president's own. In addition, because approval of appointments by the Senate is required, appointees tend to have extensive prior legal or judicial experience. The Constitution, however, does not require any specific qualifications of potential justices and judges.

Each of the 50 states has its own separate, independent court system. Most of these state court systems are similar in structure to the federal court system, and handle cases based on state law.

The Supreme Court has the power to rule on the following:

- Conflicts and legal cases involving two or more states
- Cases between a state and residents of a different state
- Cases between citizens of one state and those of another state
- Conflicts over patents and copyrights

A ruling requires a majority vote among the justices. Majority rulings of the Supreme Court are given in court opinions; justices who voted against a ruling may offer dissenting opinions, which explain each justice's reasoning.

Many Supreme Court cases arise because of the question of states' or individuals' rights versus the rights of the federal government. The Supreme Court has a major responsibility to interpret many of the finer points of the separation of powers in the United States. Table 24.2 outlines some monumental Supreme Court cases.

TABLE 24.2 Monumental Supreme Court Cases

Case Name	Ruling
Marbury v. Madison (1803)	The Supreme Court has the power to strike down acts of Congress it finds unconstitutional.
Dred Scott v. Sandford (1857)	Blacks cannot be U.S. citizens. (This decision was voided by the Thirteenth and Fourteenth Amendments to the Constitution.)
Plessy v. Ferguson (1896)	Segregated facilities for blacks and whites are legal under the "separate but equal" doctrine. (This decision was voided by the Brown v. Board of Education decision.)
Brown v. Board of Education of Topeka, Kansas (1954)	Racially segregated schools violate the Equal Protection Clause of the Fourteenth Amendment.
Mapp v. Ohio (1961)	Evidence gathered pursuant to an "unreasonable search and seizure" may not be used in criminal prosecution of a suspect.
Gideon v. Wainwright (1963)	State courts must provide an attorney to suspects who desire an attorney but cannot afford to hire one.
Miranda v. Arizona (1966)	Suspects must be informed of their rights to counsel and against self-incrimination before being questioned by police.
Roe v. Wade (1973)	Restrictions on most early term abortions are unconstitutional.

Checks and Balances and the Legislative Process

The writers of the Constitution lived under British colonial power and observed how the executive control of the colonies was detrimental to American society. The Founding Fathers knew that power in the new country needed to be carefully distributed and balanced. The U.S. Constitution explicitly defines the roles of the different branches of government so that no single branch can dominate any other. This is the concept of *separation of powers*, often called *checks and balances.*

The most basic separation of powers lies in the legislative process, by which laws are made. Following is an outline of the legislative process:

1. A bill is introduced in the House or Senate and assigned to the appropriate committee.
2. The committee debates the bill, makes changes to it, and sends it back to the main body.
3. The main body debates the bill, and possibly changes it.
4. The body votes on the bill.
    a. If passed, the bill is sent to the other house of Congress.
    b. If voted down, the bill dies.
5. The second house follows the same procedure as the original house.
6. If passed, the bill normally goes to a joint committee for final changes and approval.

7. The president considers the bill.
    a. The president signs the bill, making it law.
    b. The president vetoes the bill, sending it back to Congress.
8. Congress decides whether to pursue the bill any further.
    a. A two-thirds vote in both houses overrides the president's veto.
    b. Without a two-thirds vote in both houses, the bill dies.

Outside the basic system outlined in the Constitution, Congress determines its own rules for debating and voting on bills. Many bills stall in the middle of the legislative process because of lack of support. Nevertheless, changes in the makeup of the Congress or the needs of the country can result in a previously failed bill being reintroduced by a legislator in a similar or significantly altered form. For example, in May 1911, Representative Frank Mondell of Wyoming proposed a bill to fund an iron stairway from the foot to the summit of the newly established Devil's Tower National Monument, a site he wanted to develop as a tourist attraction. The bill was sent to the House Committee on Appropriations, where it died, apparently very unpopular with committee members. Undaunted, Mondell reintroduced the bill two years later in the new House. The new version died in committee, too. Mondell remained committed to his legislation, though, and in 1915 and 1917, he proposed two new bills for road construction "and for other purposes." These bills, too, were defeated. Mondell never succeeded in securing funding for his stairway through Congress, although through steadfast pressure placed on the Secretary of the Interior and the director of the National Park Service, funds for improvements to the Devil's Tower site were eventually allocated.

Although the legislative process is long and complicated, it is designed to ensure that many different points of view are debated. This is fundamental to the notion of checks and balances in the U.S. Congress.

Normally, the House and Senate conduct their business separately. However, a joint session of Congress convenes in the chamber of the House for the president's annual State of the Union speech and other special circumstances.

Constitutional Amendments

In the history of the United States, there have been only 27 amendments made to the Constitution. The first ten were approved in 1791 and are collectively known as the Bill of Rights. These amendments represent the basic personal freedoms guaranteed by the Constitution. Amendments to the Constitution are very rare because each amendment must be approved by three fourths of state legislatures. Table 24.3 outlines the Bill of Rights.

TABLE 24.3 The Bill of Rights: The First Ten Amendments to the Constitution

Amendment	Subject
1st	Freedom of religion, speech, press, petition, and assembly
2nd	Right to keep and bear arms
3rd	Housing of soldiers in private homes is not allowed during wartime
4th	Search and seizure
5th	Due process of law; double jeopardy protection; compensation for government taking of private property; right not to be compelled to testify against oneself
6th	Right to a speedy criminal trial; trial by jury; representation by counsel
7th	Right to trial by jury in civil cases
8th	Excessive bail and fines; cruel and unusual punishment
9th	People retain rights not specifically included in the Constitution
10th	States and citizens hold the powers not granted to the federal government by the Constitution

The Electoral System

In the United States, the president is not directly elected by winning a majority of the popular vote (the total vote of all voting citizens). Instead, the president is elected by the body of delegates called the Electoral College, which the framers of the Constitution established as a check on citizen's power in electing the chief executive. The original idea behind the Electoral College was that a group of people knowledgeable about politics and government should have the final determination about the next president, as a protection against the election being swayed by uninformed voters. When voters cast ballots for a presidential candidate, they are actually voting for a certain elector appointed to a district in their state by the candidate's political party. Ordinarily, an elector from a certain political party would cast his or her vote for the party's candidate; however, as it has occurred in rare cases, an elector may choose to cast the vote for a competing candidate. (There are penalties for this in 24 states.) Being a "faithless elector" has never changed the ultimate result of a presidential election, though. The winner of the presidential election is the candidate who receives a majority of electoral votes. If no candidate receives a majority, the House of Representatives votes to decide the president.

States have as many electors as representatives and senators combined. The important aspect of the Electoral College is that in most states, the winner of the popular vote within the state is granted all the state's electoral votes. Consider this example. If a state has 14 electoral votes, one candidate will win all 14 votes. That candidate may have received 75% of votes cast, but still takes all 14 electoral votes, not a number of votes equivalent to 75% of 14. Most recently, only two states have used any kind of proportional system for granting electoral votes based on the popular vote.

Some people have called for abolishment of the Electoral College system, citing a variety of reasons why it negatively affects the election system. In 1824, 1876, 1888, and 2000, the man elected president won without a plurality (the most, though not a majority) of popular votes. The Electoral College creates so-called swing states, whose large number of electors and past close election results cause candidates to focus on them more than smaller states or those with apparently predictable voting patterns.

Supporters of the Electoral College view it as a good way to require a more widespread popular mandate—one that does not derive just from highly populated areas. The Electoral College preserves a part of the federal model conceived in the beginnings of the country. Some people worry about a slide toward tyranny when the states give up their individual powers to the federal government.

The Role of the Citizen

In the United States a citizen has the fundamental right to vote in elections (although some states restrict this right for felons, and the federal government restricts voting rights for naturalized citizens) and to be protected by the federal government when overseas. All U.S. citizens are permitted to live anywhere in the United States without any immigration requirements. Citizens enjoy the rights, privileges, freedoms, and services granted to them by the Constitution, federal law, and the laws of the state in which they work and/or reside. The responsibilities of a U.S. citizen include obeying the laws of the state and the federal government, performing jury service when called upon by the court, and paying taxes.

Today, citizenship may be earned by any one of the following:

- Being born in the United States or born to two U.S. citizens overseas.
- Being born to one U.S. citizen if that citizen parent was a citizen at the time of his/her birth, lived at least five years in the U.S., and lived at least two of those five years after turning age 14.
- Naturalization, which is the process of becoming a U.S. citizen as an adult. Requirements include the following:
    - Being at least 18 years old
    - Having legal permanent resident status for five years prior to application
    - Being present in the United States for at least 30 months out of the last 60, and not overseas for more than 6 months at a time during that span
    - Being a "person of good moral character"
    - Passing a test on U.S. history and government
    - Having a working knowledge of English
    - Upon approval for citizenship, taking the Oath of Allegiance:

I hereby declare, on oath, that I absolutely and entirely renounce and abjure all allegiance and fidelity to any foreign prince, potentate, state or sovereignty, of whom or which I have heretofore been a subject or citizen; that I will support and defend the Constitution and laws of the United States of America against all enemies, foreign and domestic; that I will

> *bear true faith and allegiance to the same; that I will bear arms on behalf of the United States when required by the law; that I will perform noncombatant service in the armed forces of the United States when required by the law; that I will perform work of national importance under civilian direction when required by the law; and that I take this obligation freely without any mental reservation or purpose of evasion; so help me God.*

U.S. Citizenship and Immigration Services has released sample questions from its citizenship exam. One reads: "What is the most important right granted to United States citizens?" Answer: "The right to vote." Many people come to the United States for economic opportunity and to have the freedom to choose their leaders based on their own free will. It is the concept of free elections on which American democracy is based.

In special cases, the normal five-year waiting period before naturalization may be shortened. This is true of non-citizen spouses, who are required to wait only three years. Other groups, such as non-citizen military personnel, have their own special naturalization rules and procedures.

State and Local Government

In addition to the federal government, states and municipalities (such as townships and cities) also have established governments.

States

Article Four of the U.S. Constitution establishes the roles of state government, the structure of which largely mirrors that of the federal government. The state legislative body is called by different names across the 50 states: simply "the legislature," the "state legislature," the "General Assembly," the "General Court," or the "Legislative Assembly." These all perform the same function as the federal Congress—passing laws. All the states have a similar two-house legislature, with the exception of Nebraska, which has a *unicameral* (single-house) legislature. The chief executive of a state is called the governor, who holds veto power and is the chief advocate for the state within the Union. States also have their own hierarchical court systems, with the state supreme courts holding powers of judicial review of legislation and decisions of lower courts. The great proportion of court activities most citizens will encounter happen within the state systems.

Like the federal government, each state is founded on basic principles outlined in a charter or constitution. Like the U.S. Constitution, the state constitutions outline the rights and duties of the various offices within their scope. The U.S. Constitution checks the power of the state constitutions in the Supremacy Clause (Article VI, Paragraph 2), which states that the U.S. Constitution is the "supreme law of the land," which cannot be overruled by any law on the federal or state level.

States are responsible for most of the civil and criminal law relevant to everyday life. State government regulates business charters, contracts, sales tax, and marriage, among many other issues. States are also responsible for managing their land and water resources, as well as sanctioning community government.

Municipalities

Typically, states are further divided in two tiers: *counties* ("parishes" in Louisiana and "boroughs" in Alaska) and *municipalities*. Counties may tax residents and businesses, organize development plans, maintain the roads, and establish school districts, among doing other functions. Municipalities (villages, towns, cities, and so on) also tax residents and businesses, and generally provide police and fire protection and some utility services (for instance, water and sewer). Both counties and municipalities have a board or council that may enact ordinances and local laws that are not already state laws, or that serve to strengthen existing state laws. For example, state law may have a general penalty for disturbing the peace, but a local ordinance may specify exactly what disturbing the peace is (for example, loud music after 10 p.m. or a dog that barks for more than a minute at a time) and impose a fine for the civil infraction.

Municipal government in the United States can take one of three general forms:

- **Mayor-council**—Power is shared between an executive (the mayor) and a legislative body (the city/town/village council).
- **Weak-mayor**—The council manages the budget and appoints municipal government officials. Common in small towns.
- **Strong-mayor**—The mayor appoints and replaces city officials without consent of the council and prepares and administers the city budget.
- **Council-manager**—The mayor holds only ceremonial duties or acts as a member of the council. The council hires a city manager to supervise government operations and carry out council mandates. The city manager reports specifically to the council. Used by the majority of U.S. cities with populations greater than 12,000.
- **Commission**—Citizens elect commissioners to specific roles within the municipal government: education, fire and police, water and sewer, parks, roads, and so on. As a group, the commissioners act as the legislative body of the municipality.
- **Town meeting**—Practiced in many New England communities. Generally, residents of a community gather once per year to vote on budgets, laws, special projects, and so on.

Municipalities receive most of their revenue from local taxes and fees, but also receive money from the state and federal levels. To undertake larger projects, depending on state and local laws, councils may vote to issue bonds or increase taxes, or the question may be included on a public-election ballot.

What's Next?

Chapter 25, "Economics," includes a discussion on economics and the role of government in establishing economic policy. Refer to the chapters in Part VI if you struggle with the Social Studies sections as you work through the practice tests in this book.

CHAPTER TWENTY-FIVE

Economics

Whether managing your personal budget or that of a large enterprise, a basic understanding of economics is crucial for being an effective consumer in the marketplace. *Economics* is the study of how people use resources to create goods and services to meet the many wants and needs of consumers. Careful decisions must be made to ensure that resources are used efficiently.

Elements of Production

Although many economic systems exist, each must respond to three fundamental questions:

- What goods and services should be produced to meet the needs and wants of consumers?
- How and by whom should they be produced?
- Who should receive the goods and services and how should they be delivered to these consumers?

These questions must be answered in view of what resources, and in what quantity, are available to the society. Basic resources are the elements of production, as shown in Table 25.1.

TABLE 25.1 Basic Elements of Production

Elements	Definition	Examples
Natural resources	Raw materials taken from the Earth	Water, iron ore, trees, soil
Capital	Production equipment and money invested in production of a good or delivery of a service	Factories, printing presses, delivery trucks
Labor	People, their time, and their effort used to produce a good or provide a service	Assembly line work, running a cash register, serving tables in a restaurant

Demand for natural resources, capital, and labor exceed the supply of them in most cases. Economics is concerned with making the best decisions about how to use them and how much to use. Economists understand that many resources are strictly limited on earth, such as coal, petroleum, clean air, and clean water. A sound economic system allows for growth of society without jeopardizing the economic and ecological sustainability of future generations of people.

Supply and Demand

Open markets, like those in the United States, are controlled by the natural forces of supply and demand. *Supply* is the amount of a good or service available at all different prices. *Demand* is how much of a good or service consumers are willing to buy at all different prices. When determining price, producers and retailers each analyze the most efficient price for a good, which accounts for production cost plus a profit. If a firm cannot earn enough of a profit on a good or service at any price, it will not be produced. Conversely, if consumers do not demand a good or service at any price, it will not be produced. Producers seek the highest possible price, whereas consumers seek the lowest possible price. These opposing forces lead to a natural equilibrium price, which fluctuates over time.

In general, the more profit a good or service generates, the more that good or service will be produced. A good contemporary example of this phenomenon involves "energy drinks." In the past, only one major brand of energy drink existed. As the popularity of the drink increased, so did demand. At around $2 per can, this particular energy drink generated significant profit for its producer. In response, other firms began producing their own energy drinks for sale. Each company sought its own share of the energy drink market.

When supply of a good or service increases, it may eventually exceed consumer demand. Consumers will not buy the product as fast as it is produced, creating surplus. As a result, prices fall. Firms with more efficient production remain in the marketplace, but some are forced out if they cannot make enough profit to sustain themselves.

Consider the simulated supply-and-demand curves for energy drinks in a particular market in Figure 25.1.

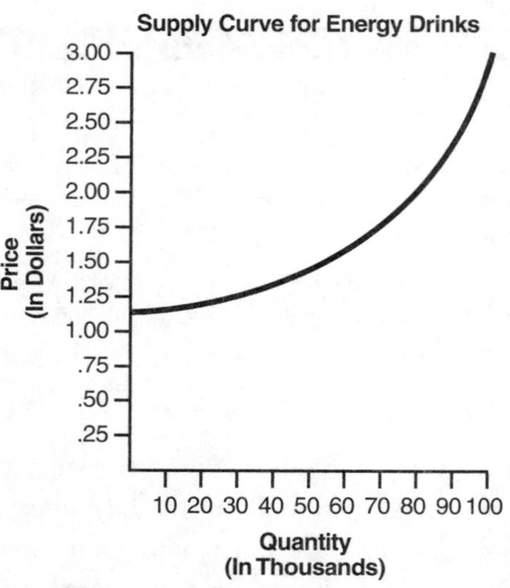

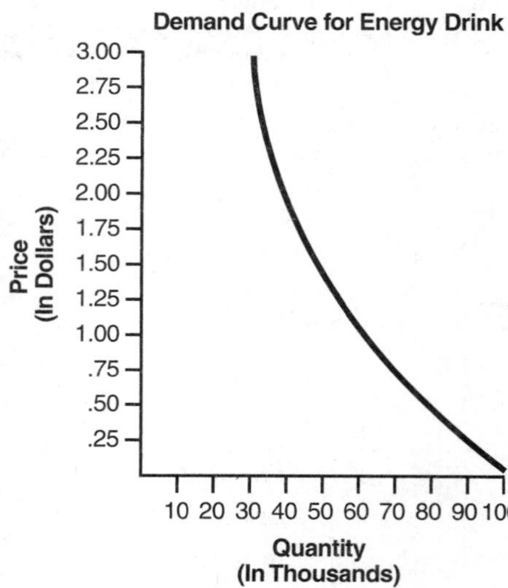

FIGURE 25.1 Supply and demand curves.

The supply curve shows that as price increases, the quantity supplied increases. Also, the changing slope of the curve shows that quantity supplied increases more rapidly with increased price at the low end and more slowly with increased price at the high end. This graph shows that producers cannot supply any quantity of energy drinks at a price less than about $1.12. How many energy drinks will producers supply if the price of one is $1.75? You are right if you said about 70,000. What if the price decreased to $1.25? The quantity supplied would decrease to about 30,000.

The demand curve shows that the number of energy drinks demanded by consumers in the market demand increases as price decreases. How many drinks do consumers demand when each is priced at $1.75? According to the graph, consumers would demand about 40,000 energy drinks if the price of each was $1.75.

Equilibrium

Equilibrium price is represented by the point of intersection of supply and demand curves of a particular good or service—when quantity supplied equals quantity demanded. The equilibrium price is the natural market price.

If the actual price of a good or service is greater than the equilibrium, the quantity demanded decreases, creating a surplus. Price begins to fall. If the price is less than the equilibrium, the quantity demanded increases, causing a shortage of the good or service. Price then increases.

Equilibrium price of the energy drinks from the previous sections can be found by plotting the supply and demand curves on one set of axes, as shown in Figure 25.2.

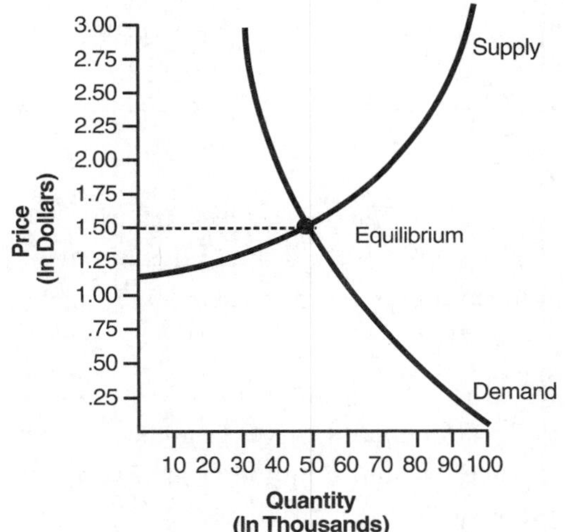

FIGURE 25.2 Equilibrium price.

At what price does the quantity supplied equal the quantity demanded? The point of intersection of the two curves shows the equilibrium price as $1.50. At the equilibrium price, total welfare is maximized, meaning the sum of producer profit and consumer benefit is as high as it can be for this particular pair of curves.

Complete the following exercise to test your understanding of supply and demand.

Supply and Demand Exercise

Using the supply-and-demand graph for energy drinks in Figure 25.1 and information you read about market forces, answer the following questions:

1. How much would the quantity demanded change from the equilibrium if producers supplied energy drinks at a price of $2.00?
   a. Quantity demanded would decrease by about 10,000.
   b. Quantity demanded would decrease by about 20,000.
   c. Quantity demanded would decrease by about 50,000.
   d. Quantity demanded would increase by about 20,000.
   e. No quantity would be demanded at a price of $2.00.
2. What would happen to the quantity supplied if the quantity demanded suddenly increased to 80,000?
   a. There would be a surplus of energy drinks and price would fall.
   b. There would be a surplus of energy drinks and price would increase.
   c. There would be a shortage of energy drinks and price would fall.
   d. There would be a shortage of energy drinks and price would increase.
   e. There would be a shortage of energy drinks and the price would remain the same.

Answers

1. (b) In the absence of other economic factors, increased price reduces quantity demanded. Find the point on the demand curve at $2.00, and then calculate the difference between that point and the equilibrium point on the horizontal (quantity) axis: 50,000 – approx. 30,000 = approx. 20,000.
2. (d) In the absence of other economic factors, increased quantity demanded causes increased price. Find the points of the supply and demand curves at 80,000 energy drinks. The supply curve indicates that producers would supply that many drinks at a price of about $2.25, an increase from the equilibrium price of $1.50.

Growth

A major goal of an economic system—and a standard by which governments are judged—is *economic growth*, overall increase in production capacity. In "boom" times, economic growth peaks and consumers are more able to afford goods and services. In "recession" times, economic growth slows and consumers spend less. Ideally, an economic system limits the extent to which economic growth fluctuates. You may notice an economic boom in your community if new homes are built and new businesses opened. Lots of "help wanted" signs usually indicate business is good. In contrast, recessions are marked by increased "for sale" signs on homes and empty storefronts, as well as job cuts.

A good example of a period of economic prosperity in America was the late Industrial Revolution, when natural resources, capital, and labor were cheap and plentiful. The deepest recession in U.S. history was the Great Depression, when jobs were few, wages low, and expendable income scarce. Read about these two time periods in Chapter 23, "History of the United States."

Inflation and Monetary Policy

When too much money is available and production cannot satisfy demand, economies enter a period of inflation. In the United States, the Federal Reserve controls inflation by adjusting the federal funds rate, the percentage banks pay the Federal Reserve to take out overnight loans from other banks. This is necessary because banks are bound by law to maintain typically 10% of their outstanding liabilities in reserve. Banks with excess reserves lend funds to banks needing greater reserves. Decreasing the federal funds rate promotes economic growth because firms and individuals can more cheaply borrow money to buy or build. Decreasing the federal funds rate has the effect of increasing inflation, however.

Increasing the federal funds rate has the effect of curbing inflation, but may ultimately lead to deflation characterized by lowered business profits and wages. The Federal Reserve adjusts the federal funds rate and other interest rates to balance economic growth.

Measuring Growth

Many statistical instruments exist for assessing complex economic conditions. You have probably heard various figures on the news or read them in newspapers or online. Among the most commonly cited measures of economic health are stock market indexes, new home sales or construction, gross domestic product, unemployment percentages, and the Consumer Price Index.

Gross Domestic Product (GDP) is the sum of the values of all goods and services produced within a nation's borders during one year. *Gross National Product* (GNP) is the GDP plus profit earned by a nation's capital invested in other countries. For example, GNP would include Ford Motor Company's sales of cars in Europe, but GDP would not. Both these measures of economic income and output may be calculated per capita (per person) by dividing total GDP by population to give a sense of average individual wealth in a country. Figure 25.3 shows the recent top 10 countries by gross domestic product per capita.

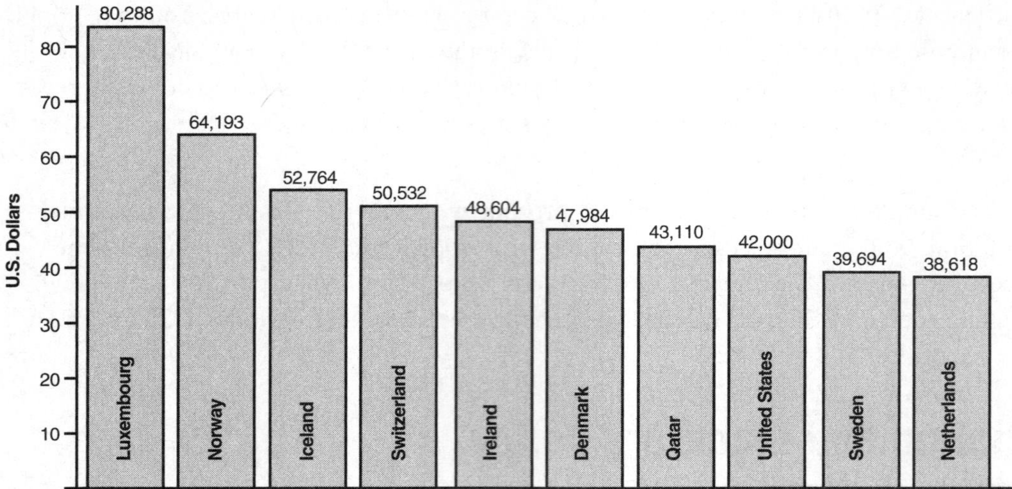

FIGURE 25.3 Top 10 countries by GDP per capita. (Source: International Monetary Fund, World Economic Outlook Database, September 2006 http://www.imf.org/external/pubs/ft/weo/2006/02)

Unemployment data also gives a good indication of the health of an economy. Think about your spending habits or those of any adult during the years displayed on the graph in Figure 25.4. Did spending increases and decreases correspond to downward and upward trends in unemployment?

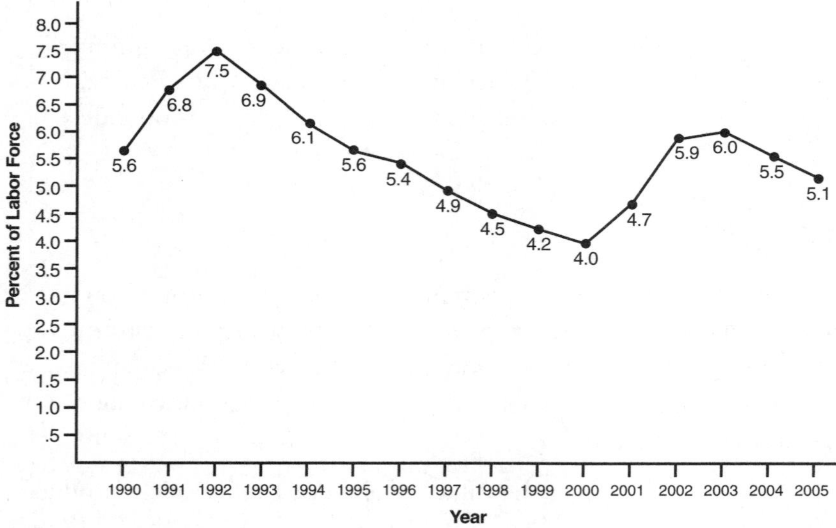

FIGURE 25.4 U.S. unemployment percentage of civilians age 16 and over, annual average. (Source: U.S. Department of Labor, Bureau of Labor Statistics)

The Role of the Government

Types of political systems and types of economics systems are inextricably linked. This explains the phrase, "People vote with their pocketbooks." In essence, people's economic success directly affects their happiness and well-being—just what government is expected to provide. Many of the hot-button topics discussed by political leaders are directly related to the state of the economy: trade, income tax, sales tax, pollution control, health care, unemployment, wages, energy costs; the list is practically unlimited.

Three basic economic systems are in place in the world today:

- Capitalism
- Socialism
- Communism

A discussion of each follows.

Capitalism

Capitalism is founded on the principle that people should make their own decisions as to how to spend their income. Government intervention in the allocation of goods and services is limited. Production, distribution, and price are determined by the natural action of an open market. (Note: economists prefer this term to "free market" because there are always some rules and limitations in every market.) Government regulates the open market only to ensure that the general welfare of society is protected; examples include health, safety, and fairness rules.

The United States is one government that practices a strong form of capitalism, which is tied to the fundamental belief in personal freedom. Some examples of American capitalism are the private health-care system and the personal responsibility for paying for college. Can you think of other things you choose to spend your money on that might be provided by the government in other countries?

Other economic systems consider the collective well-being of society over individual freedom to spend as one pleases.

Socialism

Socialist countries use a greater mix of public (government-run) and private enterprises to meet the needs and wants of consumers. To accomplish this, taxes are generally higher in these countries. France is one country that tempers capitalism with many socialist aspects. For example, the main over-the-air television channels are owned by the government. Other enterprises, such as Airbus, an aerospace manufacturer, and Air France, the major airline, are quasi-governmental, meaning the government has significant, but not total, control over the businesses. In France and many other countries, in exchange for higher taxes, health care is provided at nearly no out-of-pocket cost to the consumer, as is college tuition for those who qualify. The goal of socialist economies is to provide equal opportunity to all, although some personal choice in how money is spent is sacrificed.

Communism

The origin of the word *communism* is "commune," a society that works together for the benefit of the common good. A fundamental belief of communism is that private property leads to division between rich and poor and, therefore, should be eliminated. Under a communist economic system, the government owns all property and regulates all production, deciding what is produced and how much. Distribution of goods and services is strictly regulated in view of supporting the common good of all people. The People's Republic of China and the former Soviet Union are examples of communist societies.

In practice, however, pure communism has been shown to fail. People naturally desire greater amounts and better quality of goods and services. Attempts at pure communism inevitably lead to rampant corruption: extortion, bribery of public officials, black markets, and so on. Communism today is tempered with some socialist and capitalist elements.

The same is true with all economic systems. Each incorporates some elements of the others. For example, in the United States, children must attend school, which is provided through tax revenue by the government. Employees and employers must fund Social Security to be paid out upon each person's retirement. Production of some agricultural products (such as corn) and industrial commodities (such as steel) are subsidized (partially funded to reduce price) by the government.

Read about the political history of communist government in Chapter 22, "History of the World," and Chapter 23, "History of the United States."

Money

Ancient people used direct exchange of goods and services before the invention of currency. A money system creates a medium of exchange that can be converted into anything a person or firm chooses to spend it on. Bills, coins, and electronic records of bank deposits make up a country's money supply. The term *currency* refers to the type of money specific to a country or, more generally, physical bills and coins. A few currencies are shared among nations; the Euro, used in the European Union countries, and the CFA franc, used in 12 formerly French-ruled African countries, are two examples. In the United States, the dollar is supplied by the Federal Reserve. Once tied to the value of gold, the dollar is now backed by faith that the government will continue to receive revenue through taxes and other means, and that the economy will continue to supply the goods and services that people need.

Fiscal Policy

The President of the United States prepares a draft budget each year and submits it to Congress, which debates whether the proposed programs are needed, and if so, where funds will be appropriated to pay for them. The vast majority of government activity is paid for by taxes assessed to businesses and consumers. The government mainly spends tax revenue on public projects (such as highways), institutions (such as schools and courts), and defense (supporting the military and other national security operations). How government spends money and how much tax they assess fluctuate under varying economic and political circumstances. Politicians are hesitant to propose tax increases, however, because doing so is generally unpopular.

The major concern regarding contemporary fiscal policy is how the United States will pay off its massive public debt owed to domestic and foreign creditors. This must be accomplished through some combination of reduced government spending, increased taxation, and debt cancellation (simply not paying), although policy makers and economists disagree on how urgently debt must be reduced.

Finally, if fiscal policy can be used as a means of controlling inflation in combination with monetary policy.

The Consumer

Workers in the United States earn a certain amount of money, some of which is withheld by state, federal, and, in some cases, local government as tax. Adults also have to account for their annual income and submit income tax paperwork to the federal government and, with few exceptions, their state. The money left over is personal income. Some people's earnings are predictable, such as an annual salary or fixed hourly wages from a steady job. Other people rely predominantly or completely on work performance; for example, many real estate agents are paid a percentage of the transactions they complete. In either case, a sound understanding of personal finances is critical to the well-being of every American and any family he or she may need to support. Preparing a budget is a sound way to plan the spending and saving of money.

The U.S. Bureau of Labor Statistics collects data about how American households spend their money. The Consumer Expenditure Survey from 2004 is shown in Table 25.2. How does your household compare to this data?

TABLE 25.2 Consumer Expenditure Survey, 2004 (Source: U.S. Department of Labor, Bureau of Labor Statistics: http://www.bls.gov/cex)

	Income Class, Before Taxes				
	Lowest 20%	**Second 20%**	**Third 20%**	**Fourth 20%**	**Highest 20%**
Average income	$9,168	$24,102	$41,614	$65,100	$132,158
Average annual expenditures	$17,837	$27,410	$36,980	$50,974	$83,710
Expenditure Item					
Food at home	$2,044	$2,659	$3,209	$3,836	$4,984
Food away from home	$923	$1,480	$2,169	$2,926	$4,669
Alcoholic beverages	$194	$264	$408	$554	$876
Housing	$6,760	$9,505	$12,144	$15,741	$25,424
Clothing and related services	$837	$1,058	$1,477	$2,052	$3,654
Transportation	$2,629	$5,005	$6,827	$9,954	$14,580
Health care	$1,421	$2,139	$2,529	$2,969	$3,810
Entertainment	$764	$1,377	$1,728	$2,735	$4,484
Personal care products and services	$271	$400	$507	$641	$1,086
Reading	$55	$82	$112	$145	$256
Education	$641	$314	$396	$811	$2,363

(continues)

TABLE 25.2 *Continued*

	Income Class, Before Taxes				
	Lowest 20%	**Second 20%**	**Third 20%**	**Fourth 20%**	**Highest 20%**
Tobacco products and smoking supplies	$214	$287	$340	$327	$272
Miscellaneous	$312	$482	$646	$766	$1,243
Cash contributions (child support, supporting a student away from home, donations of any kind)	$343	$790	$1,106	$1,422	$3,376
Personal insurance and pensions	$429	$1,568	$3,379	$6,095	$12,632

As shown in the consumer expenditures table, in 2004, on average, households in the lower 40% income range spent more than they earned. Consumer debt is a major issue in American society today. With credit cards and car, home, and student loans, many people are spending a significant portion of their adulthood paying creditors. Some people struggle for years to make even partial payments. The main consequence is that interest builds on the principal, and people could end up paying many times more that what they originally owed by the time they are debt free. Many people remain in poverty because of debt, and some have to resort to filing bankruptcy. When people declare themselves bankrupt, a federal bankruptcy court seizes their personal assets, such as money and wholly owned property, and redistributes them to creditors. A small amount of money is reserved in certain categories (clothing, food, housing) to allow bankrupt people to resume life in the workplace.

A solid understanding of economics is essential for making sound decisions about employment, investment, and purchasing goods and services in the open market. As you learn about economic conditions in the United States, think critically about their causes and potential effects.

What's Next?

Chapter 26, "Geography," includes a discussion of the geography topics covered on the exam. Refer to the chapters in Part VI if you struggle with the Social Studies sections as you work through the practice tests in this book.

26

CHAPTER TWENTY-SIX

Geography

Geography is the study of the variations in the features of the surface of the Earth, especially with regard to topography (the shape of the land), soil, vegetation, bodies of water, climate, and human factors such as land use, population distribution, and political divisions. Study of the physical and chemical composition of the Earth, its history, and the forces that act on it is called *geology*, which is reviewed in Chapter 31, "Earth and Space Science." Geography differs from geology in the way that it focuses on human interaction with the Earth.

The Earth

The Earth is the third planet from the sun and is unique for its moderate temperatures, oxygen-rich atmosphere, and abundance of water—three crucial properties that support life. The Earth has a diameter of about 7,900 miles and a circumference of about 24,800 miles.

The surface of the Earth is composed of bodies of water and areas of land. Water makes up about 70% of the surface of the Earth and is concentrated in saltwater oceans. The remainder is land taking a variety of forms: deserts, plains, mountains, forests, and so on. The Earth's land is traditionally divided into seven continents:

- Africa
- Antarctica
- Asia
- Australia
- Europe
- North America
- South America

Earth's salt water lies in a single, massive, and interconnected basin, which is divided geographically into five oceans:

- Atlantic
- Pacific
- Indian
- Arctic
- Southern

Many smaller bodies of salt water also exist, such as the Mediterranean Sea and the South China Sea. Fresh water makes up lakes, ponds, streams, and rivers on the Earth's surface.

Knowing Earth's "extremes" gives a good sense of the scale and diversity of the planet. Consider the following examples:

- The northernmost point of permanent land is on Kaffeklubben Island, north of Greenland in the Arctic Circle. The southernmost point of permanent land is the South Pole in Antarctica.
- The highest point on Earth is the summit of Mt. Everest in Nepal at 29,035 feet above sea level. The lowest point on land is along the shore of the Dead Sea in the Middle East at 1,371 feet below sea level. The deepest point in the ocean is the Challenger Deep near the Mariana Islands in the Pacific Ocean. A probe recently measured its depth at 35,797 feet below sea level.
- The highest roads on Earth (about 18,300 feet above sea level) are in the Himalayan Mountains that make up the borders of Tibet, India, China, and Nepal.
- The point farthest inland from any ocean lies in China about 1,645 miles from the nearest coastline.
- The hottest inhabited place is Dallol, Ethiopia, with an average temperature of about 93° Fahrenheit. Eureka, Canada, is the coldest inhabited place, with an average temperature of about –3.5° Fahrenheit.

Although it appears small against the backdrop of several other planets, the Sun, and the greater universe, the Earth remains a vast, mysterious place in many respects.

Humans occupy most areas of the Earth and have a great effect on its land, water, and atmospheric condition. Consider the following facts:

- Human population exceeds 6.5 billion worldwide.
- Median age is about 27 years.
- About 20 babies are born per 1,000 people per year.
- Slightly fewer than 9 out of every 1,000 people die every year.
- Average life expectancy worldwide is about 65 years.
- On average, 2.59 children are born to each woman.
- Christianity is the most widely practiced religion.
- Mandarin Chinese is the most widely spoken language.
- About 82% of people age 15 or over are literate. Over two-thirds of the world's illiterate people are concentrated in only 8 countries: India, China, Bangladesh, Pakistan, Nigeria, Ethiopia, Indonesia, and Egypt.
- The U.S. government recognizes 272 "nations, dependent areas, and other entities." The United Nations has 192 member states.

Measuring the Earth

The art and science of mapmaking is called *cartography*. Maps exist for a variety of purposes—the most common ones are described in Chapter 5, "Interpreting Graphical Information." This section will review how geographers measure the surface of the Earth, especially by using imaginary lines.

Experts from many countries meet to decide on standards and definitions in any scientific field. In astronomy, experts must decide what constitutes a planet, for example. In the case of measurement, standards must be adopted. A meter in the United States needs to be a meter in every other part of the world so that data is not misunderstood. Geography needs its own standards.

Latitude and Longitude

Because the Earth is roughly spherical and continuously rotates, there are no natural "sides" of the earth. What determines east and west is a human construct and has, in fact, varied over time. The modern *prime meridian* was agreed upon in 1884 and provides the base line of 0° longitude. All points on Earth are measured a certain number of degrees (up to 180) east or west of the prime meridian, which passes through England, France, Spain, five African countries, and Antarctica. Perpendicular to the prime meridian is the *equator*, the imaginary circle around the Earth equidistant from the poles. The equator marks 0° latitude, and all points on Earth are between 90° north and 90° south latitude. Halves of the Earth to one side of either the prime meridian or the equator are called *hemispheres*. The United States lies in the Western and Northern Hemispheres. Each point on the surface of the earth has unique geographic coordinates described by its *latitude* and *longitude*. Both are measured in degrees, divided into 60 minutes (labeled with a single quotation mark) each, then 60 seconds (double quotation mark) each minute. For example, the Statue of Liberty in New York Harbor is located at 40° 41' 21" north latitude, 74° 2' 40" west longitude.

The imaginary circles north and south of the equator and parallel to it are called *latitude lines*, or simply parallels. The lines east and west of the prime meridian and parallel to it are called *longitude lines*, or simply meridians. On maps, it is common to see the two sets of imaginary lines create a grid over the surface of the Earth as shown in Figure 26.1.

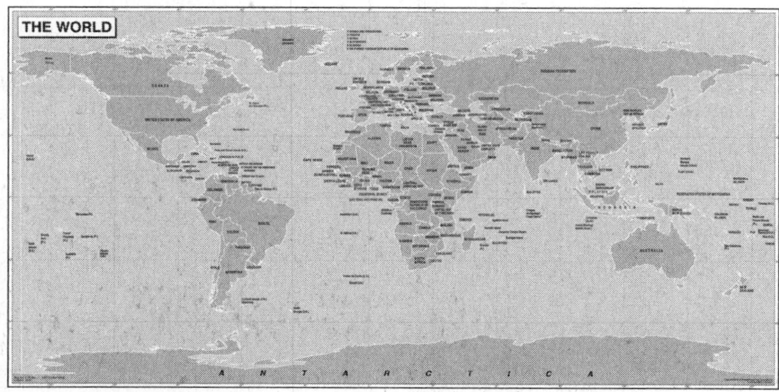

FIGURE 26.1 Map of the world showing major parallels and meridians. (Source: "Political Map of the World, April 2006," CIA World Factbook 2006)

Time Zones

Because of the rotation of the Earth, day and night come and go at different times in different places. Time zones were established to create a more standard day regardless of location on Earth. For example, a person in London, England, wakes at 8 a.m. to go to work by 9 a.m. in the same way a person in New York City wakes at 8 a.m. to go to work by 9 a.m. These two events take place at the same time in each person's time zone, but their days are actually offset by five hours. This is the phenomenon that leads to jet lag, the symptoms of having one's biological sleep rhythms upset by fast longitudinal movement across the Earth. Imagine an eight-hour flight from Frankfurt, Germany, to New York City, traveling against the west-to-east rotation of the Earth. You leave Frankfurt at 8 p.m. and cross six time zones over eight hours to arrive in New York. Local time is just 10 p.m., but your body feels that it is still on Frankfurt time: 4 a.m. the next day!

Complete the following exercise to test your understanding of time zones.

Time Zone Exercise

Look at the map in the figure below and answer the following questions.

U.S. Time Zones *(Source: The National Atlas of the United States of America, U.S. Geological Survey)*

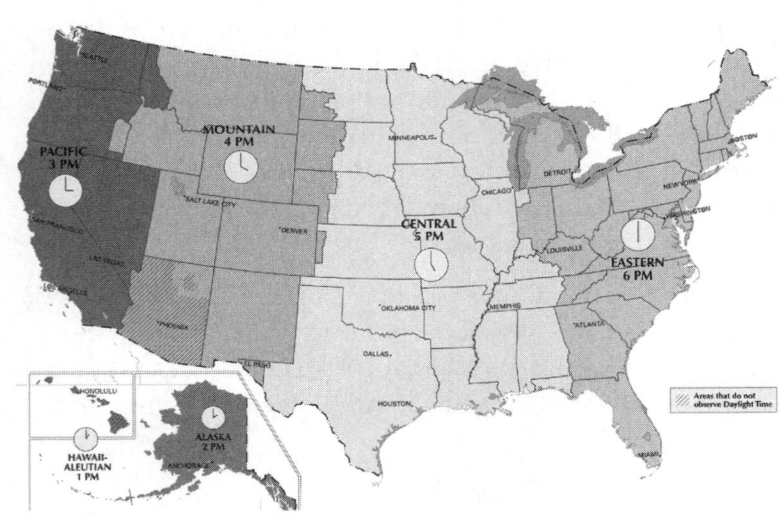

1. When is the latest you could call from Boston to a business in San Francisco that closes at 5 p.m. Pacific Standard Time?
   A. 2 p.m. Eastern Standard Time
   B. 5 p.m. Eastern Standard Time
   C. 7 p.m. Eastern Standard Time
   D. 8 p.m. Eastern Standard Time
   E. 9 p.m. Eastern Standard Time
2. Time zone boundaries are much straighter in the world's oceans. Why do you think they are not very straight in the United States?

   ____

Answers:

1. D. The map indicates that there is a three-hour difference between Eastern Standard Time and Pacific Standard Time, so the work day begins and ends in San Francisco three hours later than in Boston.
2. Time zones are created for human convenience. In the United States, they vary due to population density; boundaries of cities, counties, and states; natural boundaries (such as rivers); and nearby business centers. For example, an area of Northeast Indiana is in the Central Time zone because many people commute to Chicago for work.

Physical Geography

Regions of the Earth can be defined by their physical characteristics in addition to their spatial characteristics. A basic characteristic of land is *elevation*, the height above standard sea level. Topographical maps use contour lines to indicate areas of the same elevation. Densely grouped *contour lines* indicate steep changes in elevation, whereas increased spacing indicates more gradual slope. Contour lines are labeled (sometimes all of them, but normally just every fourth or fifth) for elevation above sea level. Reading contour lines can tell you whether a landform is a hill, a mountain, a plateau, a valley, or some other type.

Complete the following exercise to test your understanding of contour lines.

Contour Lines Exercise

Look at the contour lines in the figures below and answer the following questions.

Map #1

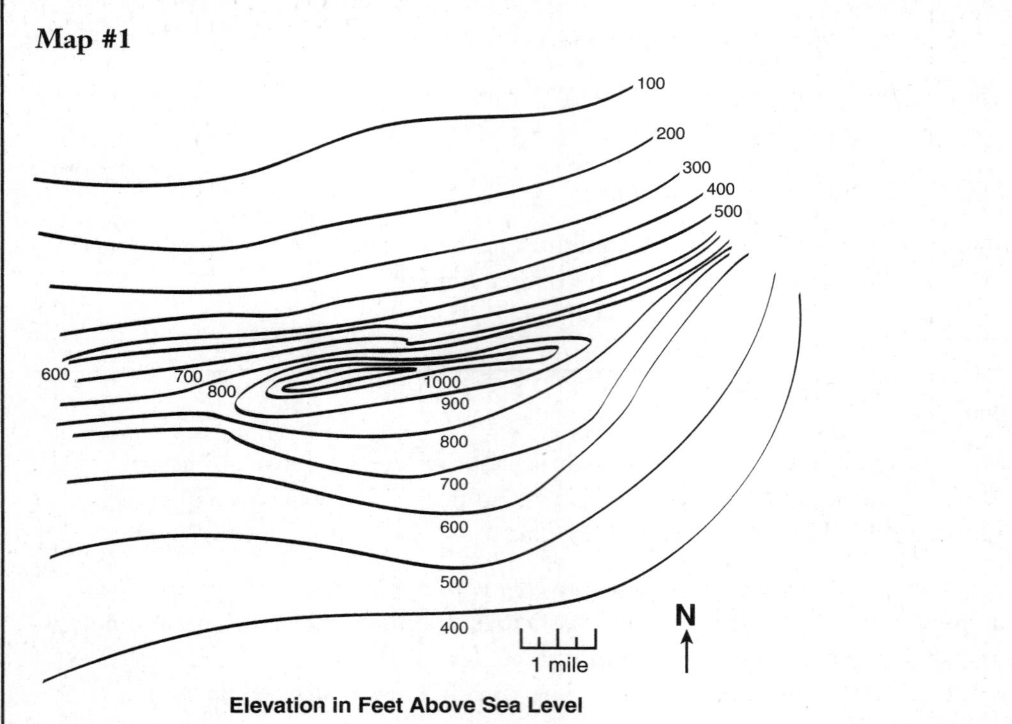

Map #2

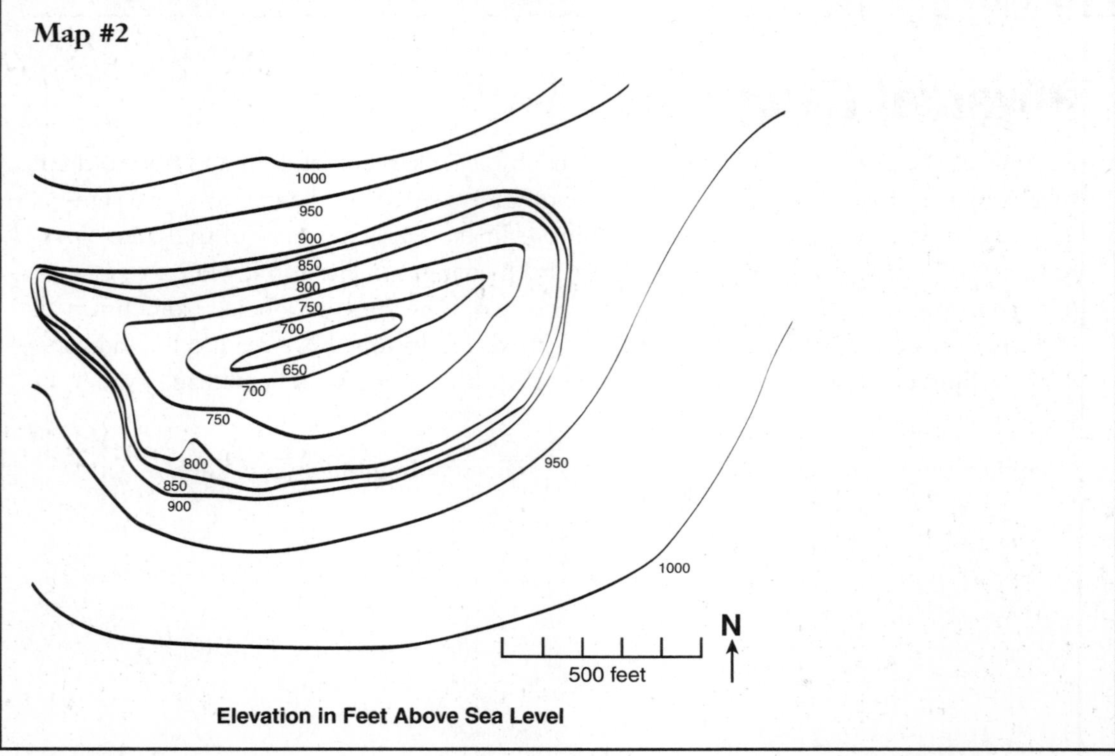

1. How would you describe the elevation change as you move from north to south across the map #1?
   A. The land is level at first, then slopes downward, and then slopes upward.
   B. The land slopes steeply downward at first and then steeply upward.
   C. The land slopes gradually upward at first, then steeply upward to a peak, and then gradually downward.
   D. The land slopes steeply upward at first, then slowly upward to a peak, and then steeply downward.
   E. The land slopes slowly upward and downward several times.
2. How would you describe the landform in map #2?
   A. Mountain
   B. Plateau
   C. Plain
   D. Canyon
   E. Hill

Answers:

1. C. As you move from north to south, the contour lines show elevation increasing from 100 to 1,100 feet (in the narrow innermost contour ring). The lines become increasingly closer together, indicating the elevation change occurs increasingly quickly as you walk. Starting south from the peak, the slope down is more gradual, as indicated by more evenly spaced lines.
2. D. The lines at 900, 850, and 800 feet are very close together. According to the scale, the 100-foot elevation drop occurs over less than 100 feet in some places, indicating a very steep slope downward. Among the answer choices, this map seems to represent a canyon best.

Climate

The physical characteristics of the Earth affect the weather patterns of any particular place. *Climate* describes the typical, predictable weather phenomena in a defined geographical location. Different land types are characterized by certain climate types.

Deserts are dry, sandy areas with little vegetation because they experience high heat and only limited rainfall. Plains areas are mainly flat, treeless expanses that allow air masses to move quickly across them, often bringing high heat in the summer and bitter cold in the winter. The high elevation of mountains greatly affects their climate and climates of adjacent areas. As moist air passes up the side of a mountain, it cools. Cooler air has decreased capacity for retaining water vapor. Eventually, the air reaches the temperature called the *dew point*, when water begins precipitating. The precipitation may be rain or snow, depending on the elevation and air temperature. Low pressures and temperatures allow some tall mountains to remain snow-capped year-round. The *leeward* (facing away from the wind) side of the mountain may experience a rain shadow. Precipitation on the upward slope and peak of the mountain leaves the air dry as it descends the opposite slope. For this reason, many deserts are found on the leeward side of tall mountain ranges.

Demographics

Ancient people settled in areas with favorable weather and adequate food resources. Today, people settle in a particular place for a variety of reasons, whether practical, impractical, or outside their control. Demographics are statistical data about human populations and their distribution in the world.

Most of the world's population is settled in temperate climate zones without hot and cold extremes. In addition, people tend to settle where movement is easy and land is suitable for construction and agriculture. In general, humans prefer to build on even ground, so mountain villages, for example, exist mainly in the spaces between mountains where soil is deeper and more level.

People change homes for many reasons. As in the Industrial Revolution, some people move from rural areas to the city to find work. Some people move to find a better life in a new place. After having children, a city couple might decide to raise their family in a suburb where the pace of life is less hectic and the schools are better and safer. People might move to a particular neighborhood to be with people of similar lifestyle or ethnicity. A writer might want to live among other writers, or a Chinese man might want to live in a community with other Chinese people, Chinese markets, and where Chinese is widely spoken.

Populations migrate for unfortunate reasons, too. Desertification of lands once able to support crops has forced some people in Africa to abandon their villages and move closer to a water source. Wars in every region of the world cause some people to abandon their homes and move away, sometimes becoming refugees. Violence can erupt when one ethnic group feels entitled to an area of land occupied by another ethnic group. Populations can move in small proportions or in large waves, depending on the circumstances. The ultimate concern over population shifts is whether the newly settled land can support the increase in human activity.

Overpopulation is a problem being addressed today that will only intensify in the coming years. The total population of the Earth is increasing at a rate of over 1% per year. The United Nations reports that world population could approach 9 billion by the year 2050. As with any organism, the environment is limited in how many people it can support with clean water, clean air, and good food supplies. Some people believe the human population will eventually reach the carrying capacity of the Earth, a point where population stabilizes because any additional population growth would lead to negative effects such as rampant starvation and disease. Others believe human technology and innovation will overcome the challenges of overpopulation, just as they have extended life span and improved overall health. In any case, making prudent decisions about population growth and resource use and consumption will only become more crucial in the future.

Figure 26.2 shows just how quickly the world's population is growing.

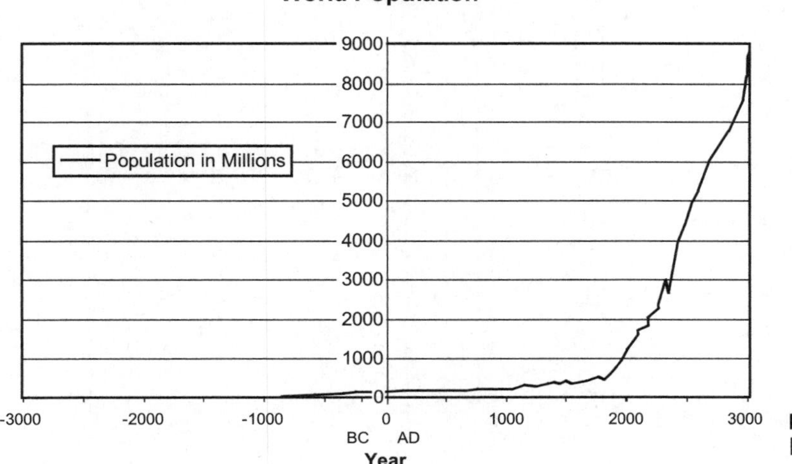

FIGURE 26.2 World population.

What's Next?

Chapter 27 includes simulated GED Social Studies Test practice questions with answers and explanations. Attempt all the questions, referring back to the previous chapters as necessary.

27

CHAPTER TWENTY-SEVEN

Social Studies Practice Questions and Answer Explanations

This chapter includes 25 simulated Social Studies questions in multiple choice format. Carefully read the directions and answer the questions. Allow yourself 35 minutes to complete these practice questions.

Use the answer sheet on the following page to mark your answers. Then compare your answers to the answers and explanations at the end of this chapter. Be sure to read through the explanations thoroughly. Identify and review topics you've consistently struggled with.

Please note that this chapter does not follow the precise format of the GED.

Answer Sheet

1. ① ② ③ ④ ⑤
2. ① ② ③ ④ ⑤
3. ① ② ③ ④ ⑤
4. ① ② ③ ④ ⑤
5. ① ② ③ ④ ⑤
6. ① ② ③ ④ ⑤
7. ① ② ③ ④ ⑤
8. ① ② ③ ④ ⑤
9. ① ② ③ ④ ⑤
10. ① ② ③ ④ ⑤
11. ① ② ③ ④ ⑤
12. ① ② ③ ④ ⑤
13. ① ② ③ ④ ⑤
14. ① ② ③ ④ ⑤
15. ① ② ③ ④ ⑤
16. ① ② ③ ④ ⑤
17. ① ② ③ ④ ⑤
18. ① ② ③ ④ ⑤
19. ① ② ③ ④ ⑤
20. ① ② ③ ④ ⑤
21. ① ② ③ ④ ⑤
22. ① ② ③ ④ ⑤
23. ① ② ③ ④ ⑤
24. ① ② ③ ④ ⑤
25. ① ② ③ ④ ⑤

Practice Questions

Directions: Choose the one best answer to each question.

Questions 1 and 2 refer to the following map.

2000 Electoral Vote [Source: National Atlas of the United States of America (nationalatlas.gov)]

1. According to the figure, which of the following can be assumed about the geographic distribution of Democratic voters in the 2000 presidential election?

   Democratic voters

   (1) outnumbered Republican voters in the central United States.

   (2) outnumbered Republican voters on the eastern and western coasts of the United States.

   (3) in the central United States are unlikely to vote in presidential elections.

   (4) are found mostly in the southern United States.

   (5) rarely live in the central United States.

2. According to the figure, which one of the following is false?

   (1) A presidential candidate can win the highest number of popular votes but still lose the election.

   (2) No candidate in the 2000 presidential election won an absolute majority of the popular vote.

   (3) Each state has an equal number of electoral votes.

   (4) The United States has primarily a two-party political system.

   (5) The electoral voting system is part of the United States Constitution.

Question 3 refers to the following information.

The Immigration Act of 1924 is a U.S. federal law that originally limited the number of immigrants who could be admitted from any country to 2% of the number of people from that country living in the United States, as reported in the 1890 Census.

Between 1890 and 1924, immigration to the United States shifted dramatically from northern European countries to southern and eastern European countries.

3. Based on this information, what was the chief effect of the 1924 Immigration Act?

   (1) Immigration to the United States was restricted primarily to northern Europeans.

   (2) Italian workers were forced to learn English before moving to the United States.

   (3) Southern European immigrants were welcomed in American cities.

   (4) Large cities such as New York City quickly established communities of southern and eastern Europeans.

   (5) Northern Europeans preferred to immigrate to the United States over neighboring Canada.

Question 4 refers to the following information.

The Chinese Exclusion Act of 1882 was a U.S. federal law that excluded all Chinese laborers from immigrating to the United States for 10 years. The act was the first immigration law passed in the United States targeted at a specific ethnic group.

Other young, developing nations also had racially restrictive immigration policies against the Chinese.

4. Based on this information, which of the following countries most likely did NOT have anti-Chinese immigration policies in the late-nineteenth and early-twentieth centuries?

   (1) The United States

   (2) Australia

   (3) Canada

   (4) New Zealand

   (5) France

5. Supply and demand are economic principles that attempt to describe the forces that determine prices in the marketplace. According to supply and demand, prices go up when demand is high, and prices go down when demand is low. Sherry wants to buy a new model of a popular car. According to the theory of supply and demand, when would she get the best price?

    (1) At the beginning of the year, when the new models become available for sale

    (2) At the end of the year, when the next year's models become available for sale

    (3) When interest rates are low

    (4) When most other people are shopping for new cars

    (5) When she has enough money saved to pay for her purchase all at once

Questions 6 and 7 refer to the following cartoon.

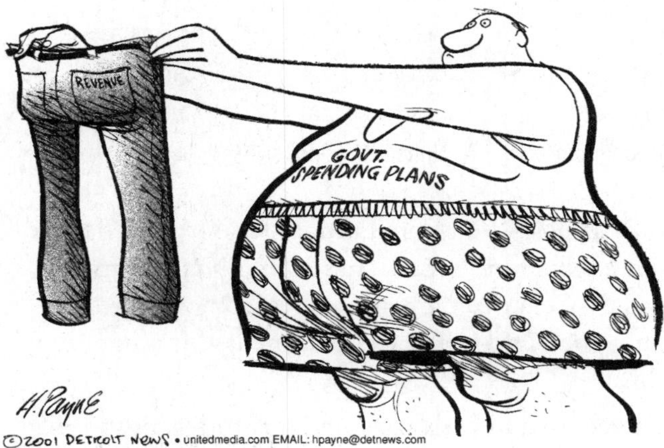

Editorial cartoon (Henry Payne: © Detroit News/Dist. By United Feature Syndicate, Inc.).

6. In the preceding cartoon, what is the cartoonist implying about government spending?

    (1) Government spending is limited by government income from taxes.

    (2) The government spends money on necessary but expensive projects.

    (3) The government is fiscally responsible.

    (4) Politicians are usually overweight.

    (5) The government spends much more money than it receives.

7. Based on the cartoon, would the cartoonist most likely agree with a tax increase?
   (1) Yes, because tax revenues are clearly not enough to meet expenses.
   (2) Yes, because the government is ethically obligated to pay its bills.
   (3) No, because government spending is excessive.
   (4) No, because the government receives enough money to pay for its activities already.
   (5) No, because governments should not fund social programs.

Questions 8 through 11 refer to the following table and information.

Top Five Countries of Birth of the Foreign-Born Population of the United States

	1960	1970	1980	1990
1	Italy	Italy	Mexico	Mexico
2	Germany	Germany	Germany	Philippines
3	Canada	Canada	Canada	Canada
4	Poland	Mexico	Italy	Cuba
5	United Kingdom	United Kingdom	United Kingdom	Germany

Modern immigration, also known as post-1965 immigration, has forever changed American society. In 1965, amendments to the Immigration and Nationality Act, more commonly known as the Hart-Cellar Act, greatly increased non-European immigration. In the 40 years since the Hart-Cellar Act became law, immigration has continued to increase steadily.

Compared with those of the nineteenth and early twentieth centuries, post-1965 immigrants to the United States are distinctly diverse. These new immigrants settle in different areas, come from a variety of countries, and have different socioeconomic backgrounds. In fact, unlike the Ellis Island immigrants, modern immigrants hail principally from non-European nations. Modern immigration will have a significant impact on the size and design of America's population. Since the 1960s, new immigrants represented over a third of America's total growth. Although all ethnic groups are contributing to America's growth, Asian and Latin American immigrant populations continue to grow larger and faster than all the others. The size of immigrant groups of Asian and Latin American origin has tripled or quadrupled over the last 30 years.

8. Which statement best summarizes the ideas in the passage?

    (1) Modern immigration resembles the immigration of the nineteenth and twentieth centuries.

    (2) Immigration from Asian and Latin American countries has been declining since the end of the nineteenth century.

    (3) Immigrants come from a greater variety of countries today than they did in past centuries.

    (4) The U.S. population does not reflect a significant number of immigrants.

    (5) The U.S. economy depends on a steady stream of immigrants.

9. According to the information presented, how did immigration change in 1965?

    The Hart-Cellar Act

    (1) eased the process of immigrating to the United States from a European country.

    (2) made it difficult for a person of any nationality to immigrate to the United States.

    (3) contributed to an increase in immigration from a greater variety of countries.

    (4) limited immigration based on total U.S. population growth.

    (5) was repealed to make immigration easier for anyone who wanted to live in the United States.

10. According to the information presented, what would most likely explain a decline in immigration from Asian and Latin American countries to the United States beginning in the twenty-first century?

    (1) Immigration from European countries would have increased, reducing the number of immigrants allowed to come from other countries.

    (2) The U.S. population would have declined overall.

    (3) The United States would have established unrestricted immigration under the law.

    (4) New restrictions to immigration would have been established under the law.

    (5) The United States would no longer have work opportunities for new immigrants.

11. Which conclusion about immigration to the United States can be verified by using only the table as a source of information?

 (1) The United States is home to more people born in European countries than in other countries.

 (2) One result of immigration is the integration of foreign customs into the American culture.

 (3) Immigration from European countries will probably not increase in the future.

 (4) Immigrants to the United States come from many countries around the world.

 (5) Immigration is crucial to economic growth in the United States.

Questions 12 through 15 refer to the following information.

The far-famed Donner Party are, in a peculiar sense, pioneer martyrs of California. Before the discovery of gold, before the highway across the continent was fairly marked out, while untold dangers lurked by the wayside and unnumbered foes awaited the emigrants, the Donner Party started for California. In 1846, comparatively few had dared attempt to cross the almost unexplored plains. Hence it is that a certain grandeur, a certain heroism seems to cling about the men and women composing this party, even from the day they began their perilous journey.

The states along the Mississippi were but sparsely settled in 1846, yet the fame of the fruitfulness, the healthfulness, and the almost tropical beauty of the land bordering the Pacific tempted the members of the Donner Party to leave their homes. Early in April, the original party set out from Springfield, Illinois, and by May reached Independence, Missouri. Here, the party was increased by additional members, and the train comprised about one hundred persons.

In later years the road was broadly and deeply marked, and good camping grounds were distinctly indicated. But in 1846 the way was through almost trackless valleys waving with grass, along rivers where few paths were visible, and over mountains and plains where little more than the westward course of the sun guided the travelers.

Adapted from *History of the Donner Party, a tragedy of the Sierra*, by C. F. McGlashan, originally published in 1880.

12. In this passage, why is the "far-famed" Donner Party referred to as "martyrs"?
    (1) The members of the party suffered religious persecution in their home states.
    (2) The Donner Party was a famous religious cult.
    (3) Most of the members died on their way to California.
    (4) The Donner Party engaged in religious war with the local Native American tribes.
    (5) Only brave people attempted to travel to the west coast in the mid-nineteenth century.

13. Based on the passage, why were the members of the Donner Party moving west?

    The Donner Party members were
    (1) seeking gold.
    (2) seeking employment on the transcontinental railway.
    (3) tempted by the wonderful reputation of California.
    (4) tired of Midwestern winters.
    (5) acting on the advice of friends.

14. Based on the passage, why was travel particularly difficult in 1846?
    (1) One hundred persons in a wagon train were too many for comfortable travel.
    (2) One hundred persons in a wagon train were not enough for safe travel.
    (3) The road westward was rutted and heavily marked by earlier travelers.
    (4) The route did not match the careful descriptions of earlier travelers.
    (5) The route was new and not well marked.

15. When the author writes, "In 1846, comparatively few had dared attempt to cross the almost unexplored plains," what is he assuming about the "few" people?
    (1) Few Native Americans lived on the plains.
    (2) Harsh winters made the plains uninhabitable.
    (3) The Mississippi River was a natural barrier that slowed migration westward.
    (4) They do not include native inhabitants of the plains.
    (5) They did not succeed in crossing the plains.

Questions 16 through 18 refer to the following graph and information.

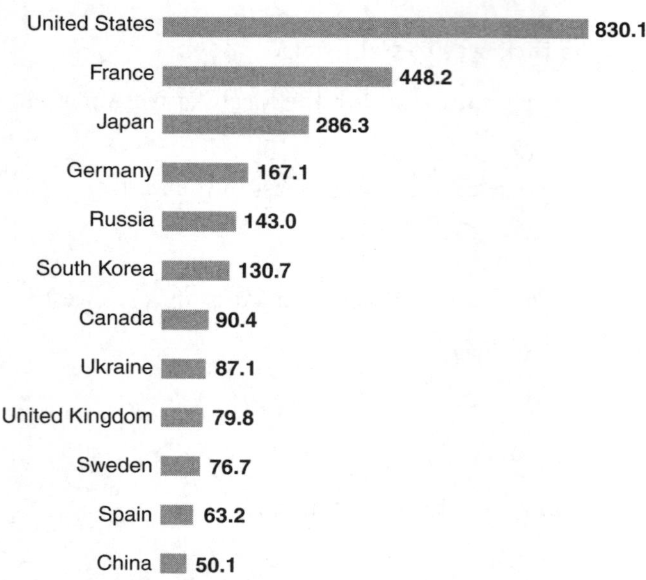

Source: *BP Statistical Review of World Energy, June 2006*

Nuclear energy is praised by some for its low levels of atmospheric pollution when compared with energy generated from the burning of fossil fuels. Nevertheless, nuclear energy generation poses other risks, many of which are not yet fully understood. The nuclear fission that takes place in reactors releases an enormous amount of energy, but in the process, hazardous radioactive compounds are created. These wastes are put into containers to be stored indefinitely above ground or underground. Little is known about the long-term impact of nuclear waste storage on the health of soil and water and, therefore, on the health of humans and other living beings.

16. What does the graph suggest about nuclear energy consumption?

    (1) Generating nuclear energy pollutes less than generating most other forms of energy.

    (2) Nuclear energy technology is well established in many of the world's most industrialized nations.

    (3) Countries that generate nuclear energy are not as concerned about environmental quality as countries that do not.

    (4) Nuclear energy is very expensive compared to other forms of energy.

    (5) The amount of nuclear energy consumption by a country is directly related to population size.

17. Which government policy to reduce the patterns shown in the graph would likely be most acceptable to private consumers and energy generating companies in industrialized countries?

    (1) Taxing nuclear energy producers based on how much they pollute
    (2) Prohibiting the generation of nuclear energy
    (3) Balancing investment between nuclear technology and emerging low-pollution energy technologies
    (4) Switching from heavy industry to agricultural production
    (5) Providing increased security to nuclear waste storage sites

18. Which resource might countries with low levels of nuclear energy consumption use to avoid the nuclear energy consumption trends shown in the graph without drastically hurting their economic growth or environmental quality?

    (1) Solar energy
    (2) Coal fields
    (3) Oil deposits
    (4) Natural gas wells
    (5) Forests

Questions 19 refers to the following map.

Selected eastern U.S. and Canadian cities settled by early French explorers and colonists.

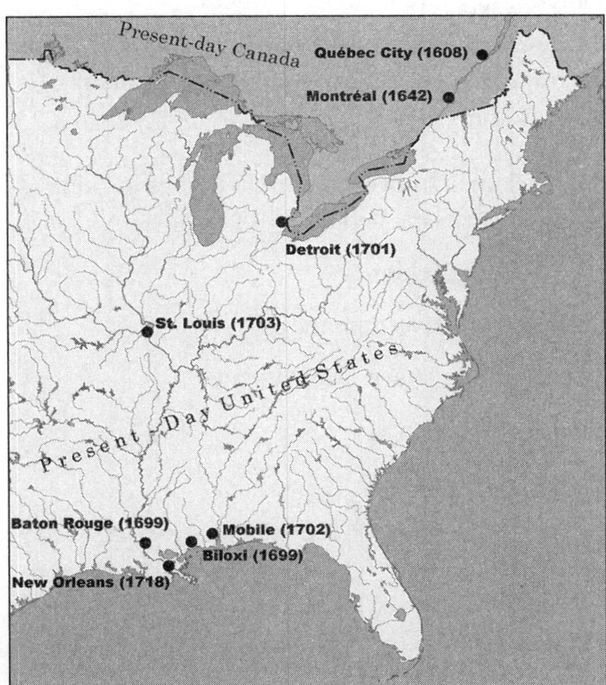

19. What conclusion about early French settlements in the present-day United States and Canada is confirmed by clear evidence in the map?

    (1) The French were not concerned with expansion into the West.

    (2) French explorers first arrived in the south and then moved north through the present-day United States into present-day Canada.

    (3) Early French settlers chose settlement sites along major waterways.

    (4) Early French settlers found sustaining coastal settlements difficult.

    (5) Most French settlers supported themselves through the fur trade.

Questions 20 through 23 refer to the following information.

In his work, *Philosophy and Opinions*, Marcus Garvey wrote, "Where is the black man's government? Where is his king and his kingdom? Where is his president, his country and his ambassador, his army, his navy, his men of big affairs?" Garvey was a writer, orator, businessman, entrepreneur, political candidate, and philosopher. The questions he posed clearly enumerated his goals and dreams for the Black-Nationalist movement.

Garvey had many bold ideas for African Americans. He admired and supported the legendary "Back to Africa" movement known as Black Nationalism. Black Nationalism was a revitalized interest in African American emigration to Liberia. Liberia had been established as a colony for African Americans as early as 1822. Garvey supported the return to Africa in part because he believed that the races could never mix and live together in harmony. Garvey despised integration and believed African Americans should own their own businesses, have their own churches, and live in their own countries, separate from other races.

Garvey's life was a notable one. His views never wavered even when he was harshly criticized. Today, the United Negro Improvement Association promotes many of the same values Garvey preached back in the 1920s.

20. When Garvey writes, "Where is the black man's government? Where is his king and his kingdom?" what is he implying about black people?

    (1) Black people are best governed by monarchies.

    (2) Black people have never had their own government.

    (3) Black people need to be in charge of their own governments.

    (4) Black people are best governed by theocracies.

    (5) Black people can find equality only in Africa.

21. When Garvey's United Negro Improvement Association started the Black Nationalism movement, what was its main purpose?

    (1) Economic and political independence for black people
    (2) Westernization of Liberia
    (3) Freeing Liberia from European control
    (4) Colonizing Africa by former slaves
    (5) Starting a new religious movement

22. Compare Marcus Garvey's view of race relations to Martin Luther King Jr.'s.

    (1) Garvey's view was the same as King's. They both believed blacks and whites should live and work together.
    (2) Garvey's view was the same as King's. They both believed blacks should be governed by whites.
    (3) Garvey's view was different from King's because Garvey believed blacks should govern over whites.
    (4) Garvey's view was different from King's. Garvey believed blacks and whites should live independently of each other, whereas King believed the races should live and work together.
    (5) Garvey's view was different from King's because King believed whites should govern over blacks.

23. Based on the passage, would Garvey have approved of integration of whites and blacks in public schools?

    (1) Yes, because people of different races need to know one another to accept one another.
    (2) Yes, because racially separate schools can never offer the same quality of education.
    (3) No, because integration often requires students to spend long hours in commute.
    (4) No, because integration doesn't stop segregation within a school.
    (5) No, because for black children to have a proper education, they must be educated separately from white children.

Questions 24 and 25 refer to the following graph and information:

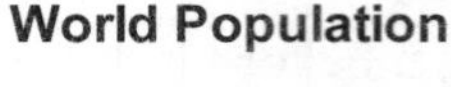

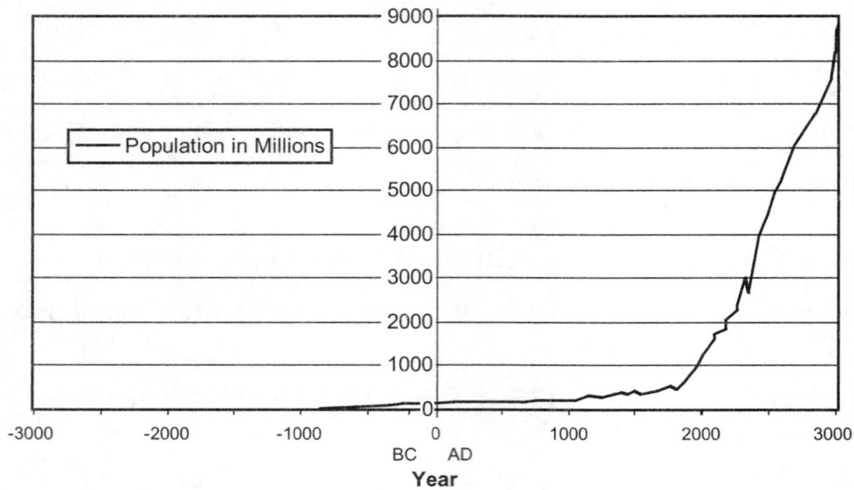

The world population is the total number of humans alive on the planet at a given time. In 2006, the world population was estimated at 6.5 billion. This figure continues to grow at unprecedented rates.

Still, the future population growth of the world is difficult to predict. Birth rates are declining slightly on average but vary greatly between developed countries and developing countries. Death rates can also change because of disease, wars and catastrophes, or advances in medicine.

24. Based on the graph, what is the anticipated world population for the year 2100?

    (1) Approximately 1,000 million people

    (2) Approximately 4,000 million people

    (3) Approximately 2,000 million people

    (4) Approximately 9,000 million people

    (5) Impossible to determine based on the information provided

25. Which of the following, if true, best accounts for the sudden increase in world population?

    (1) The development of effective birth control

    (2) Dramatic improvements in public health

    (3) An increase in the rate of childhood mortality

    (4) The development and use of weapons of mass destruction

    (5) A change in the average age of women at marriage

Answers and Explanations

1. **The best answer is (2).** In the Electoral College system, nearly every state's electoral votes go to the party with the most popular votes in that state. According to the map, the Democratic candidate won the states of Washington, Oregon, and California on the West Coast and most of the New England states on the East Coast. Therefore, only answer choice (2) is supported by the map.

2. **The best answer is (3).** The map is titled "2000 Electoral Vote" and shows that the number of electoral votes varies from state to state. California had the greatest number of electoral votes in that election (54) and Washington, D.C., had the fewest (2).

3. **The best answer is (1).** The Immigration Act of 1924 tried to revert U.S. immigration to pre-1890 geographic sources. According to the passage, those sources were predominantly northern European countries. Post-1890 immigration, mainly from southern and eastern Europe, was restricted under the act.

4. **The best answer is (5).** The United States, Australia, Canada, and New Zealand were all young, developing countries at the turn of the nineteenth century. Each has a legacy of British colonial rule. Among the answer choices, only France could be considered a mature country by the nineteenth century.

5. **The best answer is (2).** Theoretically, demand for a new car model goes down when the next year's model comes out, because more buyers will want the newer model. Therefore, according to supply and demand, the price of the car Sherry wants should go down after the next model debuts.

6. **The best answer is (5).** According to the cartoon, government spending (represented by the very large man) clearly exceeds revenues (represented by the tiny pants).

7. **The best answer is (3).** The obesity of the man called "Govt. spending plans" implies that government spending is overweight. The cartoonist most likely believes that trimming back planned spending is preferable to raising taxes.

8. **The best answer is (3).** The passage focuses on one piece of immigration law that was responsible (at least in part) for the diversification of immigration to the United States. Specifically, the passage states that the sources of immigrants have shifted from Europe to other parts of the world, such as Asia and Latin America.

9. **The best answer is (3).** The table shows that four of the top five countries of birth for foreign-born U.S. residents in 1960 were European countries. The passage states that the Hart-Cellar Act was passed in 1965 (between 1960 and 1970). According to the table, beginning with 1970, people born in different parts of the world began to be increasingly represented in the U.S. population. Mexico appears in the top five countries of birth in 1960. It becomes number 1 in 1980. By 1990, the Philippines and Cuba take over spots in the top five.

10. **The best answer is (4).** The passage focuses on the important effects of legislation on the distribution of immigrants' original nationalities. Because immigration from Asian and Latin American countries has increased significantly, in part because of the Hart-Cellar Act, it makes the most sense that a new and different change in the law could restrict immigration.

11. **The best answer is (4).** Only this answer choice is supported by the table, which includes only information about the birth countries of foreign-born residents of the United States. The top five countries are given for each census year, so you can assume other countries below the top five are not given.

12. **The best answer is (3).** A martyr is a person who dies for his or her cause. In the passage, the Donner Party are called "pioneer martyrs of California," indicating that their risky journey west resulted in deaths.

13. **The best answer is (3).** The first sentence of the second paragraph lists the virtues of California ("the land bordering the Pacific") that inspired the Donner Party to leave their homes. The key word "fame" mirrors the word "reputation" from answer choice (3).

14. **The best answer is (5).** Paragraph 3 states that early travel across the plains was difficult because the paths were not well marked.

15. **The best answer is (4).** This question tests the reader's understanding of the author's assumptions. Although the plains had, in fact, been populated for a long time by native tribes, the author has limited the exploration of the plains to that done by people of European descent.

16. **The best answer is (2).** The countries in the graph compose many of the world's most developed (or "industrialized") nations. The graph does not included data on pollution, cost, or population, so the other answer choices may be eliminated.

17. **The best answer is (3).** The graph shows that nuclear energy consumption is generally directly related to economic development. The paragraph states that nuclear energy produces wastes with many unknown future implications. To reduce the trends shown in the graph—that is, to limit nuclear energy consumption as development increases—the most acceptable option would be to begin investing in new ("emerging") low-pollution energy technologies.

18. **The best answer is (1).** This question is asking which answer choice would provide additional sources of energy without contributing to a drastic increase in pollution. Answer choices (2), (3), and (4) are fossil fuel sources, which are significant pollution sources. Answer choice (5), "forests," could be an energy source (wood for burning) but would pollute also. Only answer choice (1) is a clear low-pollution source.

19. **The best answer is (3).** The map does not have many of the markings to which you may be accustomed to seeing on a U.S. map. In fact, only land and water are clearly indicated. (Two shades differentiate the United States and Canada.) Showing only water features emphasizes that all the cities are located along major waterways. The two Canadian cities are located along the St. Lawrence River,

which empties into the Atlantic Ocean. Detroit is located on the Great Lakes system. St. Louis, Baton Rouge, and New Orleans lie along the Mississippi River. Mobile and Biloxi are on the coast of the Gulf of Mexico.

20. **The best answer is (3).** While Garvey may have approved of any or all of the choices, only answer choice (3) is supported by the quotation. The passage emphasizes Garvey's support for Black Nationalism, which means he supported separate and independent institutions by and for black people.

21. **The best answer is (1).** The last line of paragraph 2 describes Garvey's dream for blacks. Separate business, churches, and countries imply economic and political independence.

22. **The best answer is (4).** Dr. Martin Luther King Jr. was a noted integrationist who believed that all people should be able to live together in harmony regardless of the color of their skin. This is the primary message of his famous "I Have a Dream" speech. Garvey would have disagreed with King's message. Note that answer choice (3) is wrong because Garvey did not want to establish blacks in political power over whites; he wanted the races to be completely separate.

23. **The best answer is (5).** Again, Garvey's main message was segregation for the benefit of blacks. Only answer choice (5) offers a positive view of segregation for the benefit of all children.

24. **The best answer is (4).** This question asks the reader to read the graph. Find the approximate point 2100 on the horizontal axis. This is about where the horizontal axis ends. The value of the line is about 9,000 million people at that point.

25. **The best answer is (2).** The passage implies that death rates can slow because of advances in medicine, which would include improvements in public health. Answer choices (1), (3), and (4) would most likely decrease, or at least slow the increase, in world population. The effect of answer choice (5) on population growth is undefined.

What's Next?

Chapter 28, "Social Studies Terms," includes a list of social studies terms that might appear on your GED Social Studies Test. These terms have also likely been used throughout the chapters in Part VI.

CHAPTER TWENTY-EIGHT

28 Social Studies Terms

The terms included here are terms used in the book and on Official GED Practice Tests.

A

abolitionist (adj.) Relating to the elimination of slavery; (n.) someone with abolitionist beliefs.

alien (adj.) Foreign; (n.) foreign citizen residing in another country.

Allies Group of nations (primarily Great Britain and its commonwealth nations, France, and the United States) that fought against the Axis in World War II.

ally Helpful friend or associate, as in diplomacy.

amendment Change to a former document, specifically a constitution of an organization or country. The United States Constitution has 27 amendments, the first 10 of which are known as the Bill of Rights.

anarchy The absence of the rule or authority of law.

ancestry Deceased members of cultural or family lineage considered as a group.

apartheid Formal policy of discrimination in South Africa that once withheld from black people many rights and privileges afforded to white people.

appeal Challenge an opinion or ruling, especially in a higher court.

apprenticeship Period of on-the-job training under a more experienced worker.

aquifer Underground layer of porous material that yields water for wells and natural springs.

aristocratic Having the qualities of the elite ruling class.

Axis Group of nations (primarily Germany, Italy, and Japan) that fought against the Allies in World War II.

B

baby boom Period of a rise in birthrate in the United States following World War II, having long-term economic effects.

Bachelor's degree Credential earned from a college or university following about four years of study in a particular field.

bar graph Graph using rectangular bars, usually vertical, whose lengths are proportional to quantities.

bill Draft of a law for approval by a legislature.

Bill of Rights In the United States, the first 10 constitutional amendments, which were enacted in 1791 and which guarantee certain rights and privileges of citizens.

bloc Group of nations in special alliance.

Bolshevik Revolution 1917 Marxist communist revolution in Russia led by Vladimir Lenin.

boycott (v.) Abstain from using, buying, or otherwise engaging in business as an expression of protest; (n.) act of boycotting.

budget Sum of money allocated for a specific purpose.

bureaucrat Official in government (a term usually used in an insulting manner).

C

capital (n.) Money used for investment or to create wealth; headquarters of a government or the city in which it is located; (adj.) involving death or calling for the death penalty.

capitalism Economic system founded on the principle that people should make their own decisions on how to spend their income.

Capitol Building in Washington, D.C., where the U.S. Congress meets.

checks and balances Principle behind the three-branch U.S. government model: ability of each part of government to oversee and limit the powers of other parts of government.

child labor Employment of people younger than the acceptable working age, often leading to exploitation, underpayment, and injury.

circle graph *or* **pie chart** Circular graph with radii dividing the circle into sections that are proportional in angle and area to quantities.

civics Social science of municipal affairs and the rights and duties of citizens.

civil rights Rights guaranteed to a person by virtue of citizenship: in the United States, especially the freedoms and privileges contained in the Thirteenth and Fourteenth Amendments to the Constitution, and other federal laws, the denial of which to certain minority groups spurred the Civil Rights Movement of the 1950s and 1960s.

civil war Conflict between parties within a nation; (capitalized) the U.S. Civil War, 1861–65, fought between Southern states—the Confederacy—and the federal army—the Union.

civilian Person not in the service of the military or police.

civilization Advanced state of human society, marked by progress in art and science and the establishment of social and political institutions.

climate Characteristic weather conditions of a particular place.

cold war State of political and military tension between nations that does not escalate into armed conflict; the cold war between the United States and the Soviet Union that emerged after World War II and ended with the breakup of the Soviet Union in 1991.

colony Settlement established in a distant land by immigrants who maintain strong ties to the parent country.

communism Political and economic system marked by common ownership of property and the organization of labor for the benefit of all citizens.

compatriot Someone from one's own country; colleague.

Confederacy Group of 11 Southern states that seceded from the United States between 1860 and 1861 and that fought the federal government in the Civil War.

conquistador Spanish for "conqueror": one of the Spanish conquerors of Mexico and Peru in the sixteenth century.

conservative Tending to oppose change, especially with regard to social values.

constituency Group of citizens who have the power to elect an official; an electoral district.

constitution Document that establishes a government and fundamental law; (capitalized) the U.S. Constitution, prepared in 1787, ratified in 1789, and amended many times since.

consumer Buyer of goods and services in an economic system.

corporation Business entity with distinct rights and responsibilities separate from those of its owners, managers, and employees.

crude oil Unrefined petroleum.

currency Any money in paper or metal form; the money particular to a country, for example the U.S. dollar or the Japanese yen.

D

Declaration of Independence Proclamation of the Congress of the Thirteen United States of America on July 4, 1776, that asserted the states' independence from Great Britain.

demand In economics, the amount of a good or service that people are willing to buy at a given price.

democracy Political system marked by governance by the people or by elected representatives.

demographics Characteristics of human populations and population distribution.

dictatorship Government in which power is held by a single individual who controls nearly all aspects of public life.

discrimination Unjust treatment based on class or category.

drought Period of little or no rainfall.

draft Process of selecting civilians for military service.

due process of law Legal concept that provides for a person's rights when action is brought against the person by the government: in the United States, the Fifth and Fourteenth Amendments to the Constitution state that no person shall be deprived of "life, liberty, or property, without due process of law."

durable goods In economics, goods that are not depleted with use, such as a household appliance or a car.

dynasty Succession of rulers from the same family.

E

economics Science dealing with the production, distribution, and consumption of goods and services.

efficiency Action or production with minimum waste of time, money, effort, and so on.

electoral college Body of electors chosen by popular vote in each U.S. state to elect the President and Vice President.

electorate Collective people of a nation who posses the right to vote.

elevation Geographic feature of height, usually measured in feet or meters above sea level.

Emancipation Proclamation Order issued by U.S. President Abraham Lincoln on January 1, 1863, that called for the freedom of all slaves in the Confederate states.

emigration The act of leaving one country and traveling to live in another.

empire Expansive territory, often including many nations, that is controlled by a single government or ruler.

environment Physical, chemical, and biological factors that affect the survivability of organisms.

equator Parallel equidistant from the poles that establishes 0° latitude.

estimate (n.) Approximate calculation; (v.) make an estimate.

ethnicity Cultural and racial association.

executive branch In the United States, the arm of government led by the president, whose duties and powers are established by Article II of the Constitution.

expatriate (v.) Banish; move from one's native land; (n.) one who lives in a foreign country.

F

federal deficit Amount of money spent by the federal government in excess of its revenue.

federal government In the United States, the central government that comprises the legislature, the executive, and the judiciary, who make and administer federal law, deal in foreign affairs, maintain the armed forces, and regulate trade among the states.

fjord Long, narrow, deep inlet lined by steep slopes, common in Norway.

free trade Exchange of goods and services with little or no government regulation or taxation.

G

geography Study of the earth and its surface features, including human population patterns.

government Body with the authority and power to make and enforce laws.

H

Hispaniola Island divided between Haiti in the western third and the Dominican Republic in the eastern two-thirds on which Christopher Columbus established the first Spanish colony in the New World in 1493.

humidity Measure of moisture in the air.

I

iceberg Massive body of ice afloat at sea that broke away from a glacier.

ideological Relating to the fundamental ideas of an individual or group.

impeach Charge a public official with improper or illegal conduct.

inalienable Impossible to take away.

inauguration Formal initiation or induction, as of the president.

indentured servant Person bonded to work for a specific period of time in exchange for job training or travel expenses, as to the New World.

indigenous Native to or naturally existing in a certain area.

Industrial Revolution Period of shift from home-based manufacturing to large-scale factory production due to advances in machine technology that occurred first in England in the eighteenth century, and then later in the United States.

institution Establishment; pillar of society, for example, the institution of marriage.

interest In economics, the percentage of principal paid to lenders, or the percentage of savings paid to bank account holders.

internment Confinement during wartime against one's will.

internship Work, often unpaid, of a student or recent graduate in a certain professional field.

J–K

judicial branch In the United States, the arm of government led by the Supreme Court, whose duties and powers are established by Article III of the Constitution.

justice Fairness under the law; judge of the U.S. Supreme Court.

Korean War Conflict between North Korea, supported by China, and South Korea, supported by United Nations forces consisting mainly of U.S. military personnel.

L

labor Work; workers considered as a group.

labor union Organization of workers formed to negotiate wages and workplace conditions with management.

latitude Measure, in degrees, of position on the earth north or south of the equator.

legislative branch In the United States, the arm of government led by the Congress composed of the House of Representatives and the Senate, whose duties and powers are established by Article I of the Constitution.

legislature Official lawmaking body within a government.

liberal Favoring reform and tolerant of other people's beliefs and values.

line graph Graph using one or more lines connecting data points to show change in quantities.

logic System of reasoning.

longitude Measure, in degrees, of position on the earth east or west of the prime meridian.

M–O

market In economics, a place or institution where goods and services are offered for sale.

media (plural of "medium") Means of mass communication, such as television, radio, newspapers, or magazines.

meridian Any imaginary circle around the earth, used to determine longitude, that passes through both poles and is perpendicular to parallels.

minuteman Armed man pledged to fight British forces at a moment's notice immediately before and during the American Revolution.

monarchy Government in which power is held by royalty. In an absolute monarchy, the royal family has complete power. In a parliamentary monarchy, government is run as a democracy and the royal family has limited powers.

oligarchy Government in which very few people hold power and citizens do not elect their leaders.

P

parallel Any imaginary circle around the earth, used to determine latitude, that is parallel to the equator and perpendicular to meridians. (see also *parallel* in Chapter 49, "Mathematics Terms")

parliament Official legislative body in a parliamentary system that is led by the prime minister, for example, in Canada or Great Britain.

political cartoon *or* **editorial cartoon** Drawing, usually in one pane, distributed in magazines and newspapers that uses humor to comment on a current event or other issue in society or government.

political map Map that emphasizes political features, such as names and boundaries of cities, counties, states, and countries.

political party Group organized to promote a common agenda and support candidates for public office.

politics Art and science of governing.

precipitation Water in the air that has condensed and falls to the ground as rain, snow, sleet, or hail.

prime meridian Meridian passing through Greenwich, England, that has established the worldwide standard of 0° longitude since 1884.

prime minister Chief executive in a parliamentary democracy.

province Subdivision of a nation, as in Canada or China, similar to a state.

Q–R

quota In trade, the amount of a good that may be imported.

racism Discrimination or prejudice based on skin color or cultural origin.

recycling Processing used or waste materials to make new products.

region Specific area of land, usually unified by common geographic, environmental, cultural, or political features.

Renaissance (usually capitalized) Period of European history from the fourteenth to the mid-seventeenth centuries characterized by a revival of art, science, and literature that led to the modern age.

repeal (v.) Rescind; remove from the law; (n.) act of repealing.

republic Political system in which the power lies with the people who elect representatives and not a supreme ruler.

revolution Uprising, sometimes violent, of people against their government or ruler.

Revolutionary War Conflict between Great Britain and its 13 American colonies from 1775 to 1783 that resulted in American independence.

S

sanction (n.) Permission, especially from authority or derived from public opinion; penalty or economic restriction imposed by one or more nations against another nation to persuade it to comply with international law; (v.) provide sanction; impose a sanction.

scale Printed on a map, the ratio of map size to actual size on earth or the ratio of linear distance on the map to linear distance on earth.

separation of powers (see *checks and balances*)

smallpox Highly infectious viral disease that causes high fever, muscle aches, and blisters all over the body, and is often fatal. European settlers and African slaves, who were immune to the disease, unknowingly brought it to the New World, causing a fatal epidemic among the indigenous people. Today, because of widespread vaccination, the disease is considered eradicated.

socialism Political and economic system in which a mix of government-run and private enterprises meet the wants and needs of citizens.

sound (see also *sound* in Chapter 34, "Science Terms") Long, wide ocean inlet; for example, Puget Sound in northwestern Washington state.

stock market Place where shares of publicly traded companies are bought and sold.

strike Work stoppage by employees to protest wages, working conditions, and so on.

subtropical Near the tropical areas of the world; extremely humid and hot climate.

suffrage The right to vote.

supply In economics, the amount of a good or service available for purchase at a given price.

T

table Orderly arrangement of data in rectangular form.

tariff Tax on imported or exported goods.

tax Fee assessed by the government on people or organizations to support the activity of government.

timeline Linear representation of events arranged chronologically.

topsoil Uppermost layer of earth in which plants take root.

trade deficit Value of imported goods in excess of exported goods.

treason Betrayal of loyalty, especially to a nation.

tree line Elevation above which trees do not grow; northern or southern latitude beyond which trees do not grow.

tropical Near the equator; having a frost-free climate with high temperatures that can support year-round vegetation.

tundra Treeless area between the tree line and polar ice that supports low-growing vegetation and small shrubs.

tyranny Absolute power exercised by an oppressive ruler.

U–Z

union (see *labor union*)

vaccination Introduction, usually by injection, of a disease-causing microorganism, which has been rendered harmless, to cause the body to develop immunity to the microorganism.

value Monetary worth; principle or moral belief.

vegetation Plant life.

veto (n.) Executive power to strike down bills that have been passed by the legislature; (v.) exercise veto power on (a bill). In the United States, if the President vetoes a bill, the legislature may override the veto with a two-thirds majority vote.

Vietnam War Military conflict from 1954 to 1975 between communist North Vietnam, supported by China and the Soviet Union, and South Vietnam, supported by the United States.

warrant Authority granted by a judge, in light of evidence, to a police officer for search and seizure of property or the arrest of a person.

World War I Conflict in Europe from 1914 to 1918 in which Great Britain, France, Russia, Belgium, Italy, Japan, and the United States defeated Germany, Austria-Hungary, and the Ottoman Empire.

World War II Deadliest conflict in history, from 1939 to 1945, in which the Allies defeated Germany and Italy in Europe and Japan in the Pacific Ocean.

PART VII
Science

This part of the book explains what the GED Science Test involves and the basic critical-thinking skills you need to maximize your score. The Science Test contains multiple-choice questions about written and graphical information.

Part VII includes the following chapters:

Chapter 29 About the Science Test

Chapter 30 Life Science

Chapter 31 Earth and Space Science

Chapter 32 Physical Science

Chapter 33 Science Practice Questions and Answer Explanations

Chapter 34 Science Terms

CHAPTER TWENTY-NINE

About the Science Test

The GED Science Test consists of 50 multiple-choice questions that you must complete in 80 minutes. You will have to draw on some of your existing knowledge of life science, earth and space science, and physical science (chemistry and physics); however, you will not have to recall facts. To succeed on the Science Test, you will need to distinguish facts from hypotheses, apply information to new situations, analyze relationships between ideas, and synthesize information from different sources.

Format and Content

The test is based on the National Science Education Standards, Scientific Understanding Strands, as follows:

- Life science (about 45% of the test)
- Earth and space science (about 20% of the test)
- Physical science: chemistry and physics (about 35% of the test)

Most questions (about 75%) stand alone in the test, but some (about 25%) are arranged in groups and address a single reading passage or graphic. Overall, questions on the test are divided nearly equally between those that cover reading material and those that are based on visual representations of information.

Creators of the GED Science Test define six themes present in the content (the most prevalent listed first):

- Fundamental understandings (about 60% of the test)
- Science in personal and social perspectives
- Unifying concepts and processes
- Science as inquiry
- Science and technology
- History and nature of science

Many concepts on the Science Test are interdisciplinary and may reach across several of these themes and/or the concepts on other GED subject tests. For example, caring for a sick tree involves applying biology (plant nutrition, for example), using technology (cutting limbs with a chainsaw, for example), and mathematics (such as measuring limbs to determine how they will fall).

What's Next?

The chapters that follow include specific information on the content areas tested on the GED Science Test. You should refer to these chapters as necessary during your practice.

CHAPTER THIRTY

Life Science

Life is defined as the set of processes necessary for organisms to survive in the environment. An *organism* can be single celled or composed of many cells. There are certain properties that all life shares:

- **Organization**—Composed of one or more cells.
- **Metabolism**—Converts nonliving and living material into energy used for body functions.
- **Excretion of waste**—Releases unneeded nutrient material, including byproducts of metabolism, into the environment.
- **Growth**—Increases in size in all its parts; populations tend to increase in number and expand.
- **Homeostasis**—Regulates the body to maintain a normal state within the changing environment (for example, muscles shiver to produce heat when the body is sufficiently cold).
- **Response to stimuli**—Reacts to internal or external change; often expressed by motion (for example, a Venus flytrap closes around a fly when the fly touches the trigger hairs).
- **Reproduction**—Creates new life, whether sexually (involving males and females) or asexually (on the organism's own).
- **Adaptation**—Changes in response to the environment over a period of time, and as determined by heredity (genetics).

Biology is the science of life and living things. A basic knowledge of biology is useful for maintaining personal health and assessing the condition of the people, plants, and other organisms important to you. The GED will test your ability to read short science passages and answer questions about them. Becoming more familiar with life science will help you read and respond to questions faster and more accurately.

The Cell

The basic unit of life is the *cell.* Cells are typically about 10 micrometers (1/100,000 of a meter) across, and each of them takes in nutrients, converts them into energy, performs specialized functions, and reproduces periodically. The smallest organisms have only one cell, but others can be composed of an abundance of them. The human body is estimated to have about 100 trillion. English inventor and scientist Robert Hooke first described cells in his 1665 book *Micrographia*. He discovered plant cells on a thin slice of cork he placed under his microscope. He used the term "cells" because he thought what he saw resembled cells in a monastery. The first observations of single-celled organisms—bacteria and protozoa—were made by Anton van Leeuwenhoek in 1676. Hooke, as a member of England's Royal Society, was asked to confirm Leeuwenhoek's findings. He did, and the notion of the cell gained widespread acceptance in the scientific community.

In plants and animals, cells differentiate to perform all the various functions the organism needs for survival. (Humans have muscle cells, skin cells, liver cells, and so on.) Cells can be divided between plant and animal cells to illustrate the basic features of each. Plant cells are distinguished from animal cells by the present of chloroplasts, used in photosynthesis, and rigid cell walls. Figure 30.1 shows the structure of an animal cell.

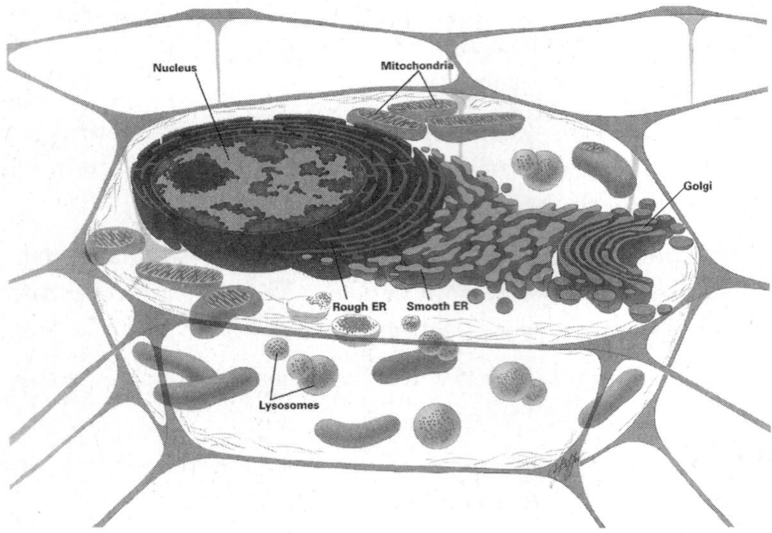

FIGURE 30.1 An animal cell, emphasizing the various important organelles. (Source: U.S. Department of Health and Human Services, National Institutes of Health, NIH Publication No. 05-1051, Revised September 2005.)

The various structures and organelles of the cell are enclosed in the semipermeable cell membrane. In plant cells, the cell wall surrounds the cell membrane. Both animal and plant cells have an inner membrane-enclosed body called the *nucleus*, which contains the organism's genetic material, including DNA. Outside the nucleus in the cell, the various *organelles* have specialized functions. The most notable ones are given in Table 30.1.

TABLE 30.1 Important Cell Organelles

Cell Organelles	Function
Mitochondria	Produce energy needed for cell functions (movement, division, contraction, and so on) by combining sugars and oxygen to create adenosine triphosphate (ATP), the "energy currency" of cells.
Lysosomes	Contain digestive enzymes; digest food molecules, old organelles, viruses, and bacteria captured in the cell.
Smooth endoplasmic reticulum (ER)	Network of tiny tubes connected to the membrane of the nucleus and having varying functions depending on cell type within the organism.

TABLE 30.1 *Continued*

Cell Organelles	Function
Rough endoplasmic reticulum (ER)	Collects and distributes proteins synthesized by the ribosomes.
Golgi apparatus	Creates lysosomes; modifies and "repackages" proteins and lipids (fats).
Chloroplast (plant cells only)	Contains chlorophyll, which gives plants their green color and generates energy through photosynthesis.

Organelles exist in *cytoplasm*, a jelly-like material that fills cells. It helps the cell maintain its shape and also stores many chemicals vital to cellular processes.

Molecules pass into and out of the cell through the cell membrane through either active transport, which involves chemical energy, or passive transport, which does not involve chemical energy. One example of active transport common to all cells is the concept of the sodium-potassium pump, by which energy stored in the form of the chemical ATP regulates internal proportions of sodium and potassium, crucial for maintaining the electrical and physical properties of the cell. The predominant form of passive transport is called *osmosis*, by which cells diffuse water across their membranes as controlled by the concentration of salts on both sides of the membrane. This explains why humans cannot be hydrated by salt water. The high concentration of salt would draw water from inside cells into the salt and water solution, dehydrating the body. Various mechanisms of active and passive transport move water and nutrients into the cell and waste products out of it.

Cells reproduce in a process called *mitosis*. When a cell prepares to reproduce, it first duplicates its genetic material. The cell then enters a process of division into two genetically identical daughter cells. The basic stages of mitosis are described and illustrated in Table 30.2.

TABLE 30.2 Stages of Mitosis

Stage	Diagram	Description
Prophase		The genetic material in the cell nucleus begins condensing into chromosomes, each a pair of sister chromatids. Centromeres (appearing above the nucleus) coordinate the separation of genetic material in later stages of mitosis. They begin to push outward in opposite directions.
Metaphase		The chromosomes line up equidistant from the centers of the centromeres. The pairs of sister chromatids become visible.

(continues)

TABLE 30.2 *Continued*

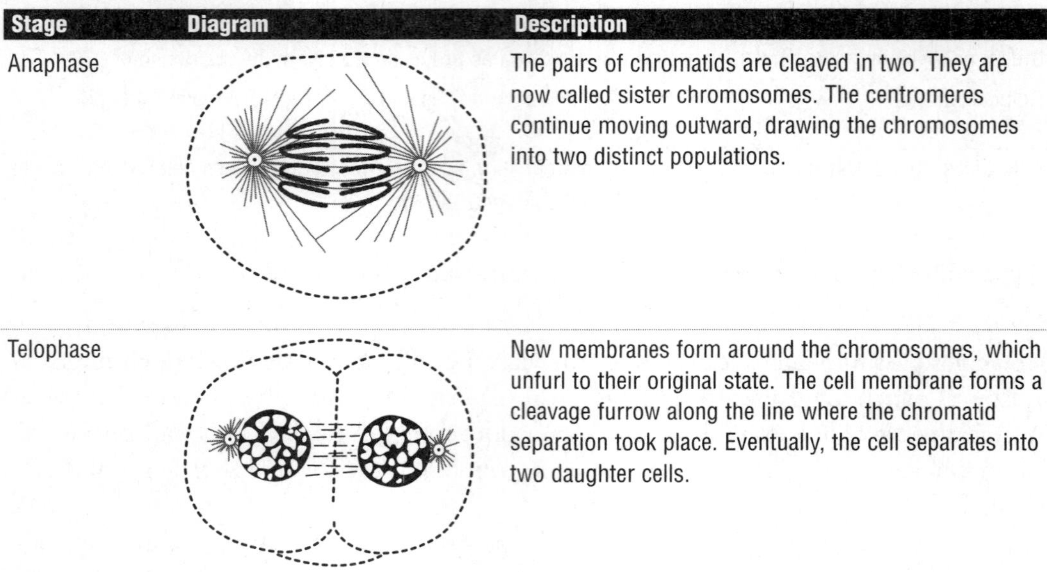

Stage	Diagram	Description
Anaphase		The pairs of chromatids are cleaved in two. They are now called sister chromosomes. The centromeres continue moving outward, drawing the chromosomes into two distinct populations.
Telophase		New membranes form around the chromosomes, which unfurl to their original state. The cell membrane forms a cleavage furrow along the line where the chromatid separation took place. Eventually, the cell separates into two daughter cells.

In sexual reproduction, a male *gamete* (sex cell), called a *spermatozoon*, penetrates the cell membrane of a female gamete, an *ovum* (egg), fertilizing it. In humans, the spermatozoon and ovum each contribute a single set of 23 chromosomes to the zygote (fertilized ovum). The process by which sex cells are created is called *meiosis*, as shown in Figure 30.2.

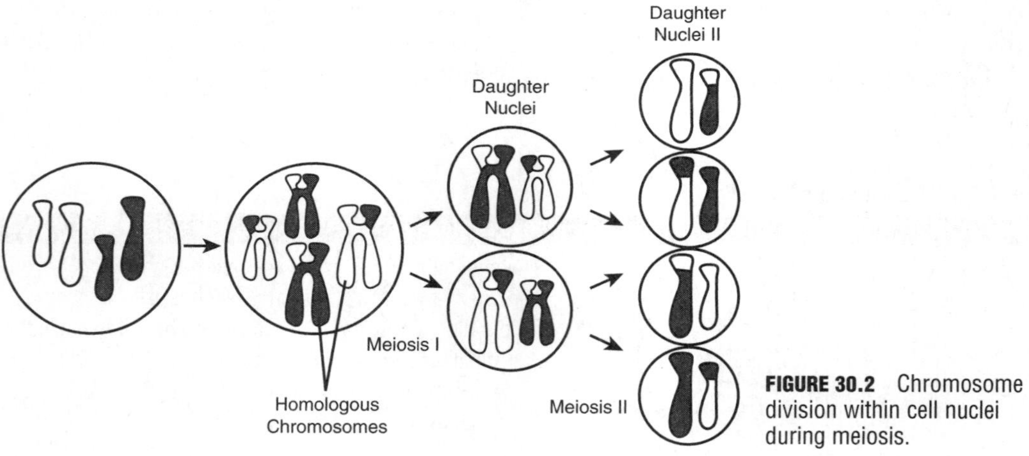

FIGURE 30.2 Chromosome division within cell nuclei during meiosis.

In human meiosis, a precursor cell replicates its double complement of 46 chromosomes. In meiosis I, this cell then divides into two daughter cells, called diploid cells, each containing a replicated set of half the chromosomes. In meiosis II, the two daughter cells divide to become four haploid cells, each containing a single set of 23 chromosomes. During meiosis, the chromosomes undergo a process of genetic recombination, by which specific portions of DNA are shuffled between chromosomes, thereby creating genetic variation in the offspring. This is the fundamental process that assures no two humans (except in the case of identical twins) share the same genetic code.

Genetics and DNA

In the previous section, the notions of genetics and DNA were introduced. You probably have a general understanding about why these two concepts are important. At some point in your life, someone has probably said to you something like, "You look like your father" or "You've got your mother's eyes." Have you ever considered how that happened? You already read about how chromosomes are duplicated in mitosis and meiosis. In this section, you'll see how crucial the genetic code is to the characteristics and survivability of a human or any other organism.

Genes are segments of the DNA strand that each code for a specific trait. Generally, a human receives two sets of genes, one from each parent. The manner in which the pairs interact determines which traits of the mother and father will be expressed in their child. The notion of heredity applies to all other organisms, too.

The pioneer of the field of genetics was nineteenth-century Austrian monk Gregor Mendel, who studied the variation in pea plants. He proposed that the color of the plants' flowers (white or pink) was determined by some natural law. The *allele* (gene variation) for purple color is dominant, and the allele for white color is recessive.

In a simple dominance relationship like this one, the *dominant allele* is always expressed if it is present. The *recessive allele* is expressed only if it is paired with another recessive allele. The proportion of purple to white flowers in a generation of offspring can be predicted using *Punnett squares*. The dominant allele is always capitalized, while the recessive allele is lowercase. The squares illustrate the probabilities of offspring receiving a certain pair of alleles:

1. Neither parent carries the recessive (white) allele.

Parent plant #2 (PP) \ Parent plant #1 (PP)	P	P
P	PP	PP
P	PP	PP

100% of offspring have purple flowers. None carry the recessive allele.

2. One parent carries one recessive allele.

Parent plant #2 (PP) \ Parent plant #1 (Pp)	P	p
P	PP	Pp
P	PP	Pp

100% of offspring have purple flowers. 50% carry exactly one recessive allele.

3. One parent has two recessive alleles.

Parent plant #2 (PP) \ Parent plant #1 (pp)	p	p
P	Pp	Pp
P	Pp	Pp

100% of offspring have purple flowers. 100% carry exactly one recessive allele.

4. Both parents have one recessive allele each.

Parent plant #2 (Pp) \ Parent plant #1 (Pp)	P	p
P	PP	Pp
p	Pp	pp

75% of offspring have purple flowers; 25% have white flowers. 25% are "purebred" white; 25% are "purebred" purple; 50% carry one of each allele.

5. One parent has two recessive alleles, and the other parent has one recessive allele.

Parent plant #2 (Pp) \ Parent plant #1 (pp)	p	p
P	Pp	Pp
p	pp	pp

50% of offspring have purple flowers; 50% have white flowers. 50% are "purebred" white; 50% carry one of each allele.

6. Both parents have two recessive alleles each.

Parent plant #2 (pp) \ Parent plant #1 (pp)	p	p
p	pp	pp
p	pp	pp

100% of offspring have white flowers. None carry the dominant gene.

Genes are expressed in organisms many other ways, and in ways science has not yet revealed. When mistakes occur in an organism's genetic composition, they are called *mutations*. Mutations are natural and are the genetic basis of the theory of evolution; however, many mutations have negative consequences for an organism's health. In humans, conditions such as Down syndrome and certain cancers are passed on to children through the genetic code inherited from the parents.

Advanced research in genetics has allowed humans to begin experimenting with cloning. The issue was brought to the forefront when scientists in Scotland announced they had successfully cloned a mammal from an adult cell for the first time. Their sheep, named Dolly, was created through a process called *somatic cell nuclear transfer*, by which an ovum's nucleus is removed and replaced by an adult cell containing the full complement of genetic material. Since Dolly, many more animals have been successfully cloned.

Researchers believe this kind of genetic experimentation has great potential benefits, including new ways to treat human health problems. Opponents are concerned about the moral and ethical questions posed by cloning. Many people think it reaches too far in changing the natural processes of life. Some see cloning as another step down a slippery slope of genetically engineering Earth's plants and animals. Even more controversial than cloning in general is the cloning of humans. In the first years of the twenty-first century, many of the world's powerful nations developed laws banning human cloning and human cloning research in most circumstances. In 2005, the United Nations General Assembly issued a resolution calling upon member states "to prohibit all forms of human cloning inasmuch as they are incompatible with human dignity and the protection of human life." Scientists and lawmakers in the United States will be faced with deciding the appropriateness of cloning research long into the future.

Organ Systems

A newly formed zygote has the potential to become an embryo, and the embryo a new human. Fertilization typically occurs in the fallopian tubes. The embryo travels from the fallopian tubes down to the uterus, where it implants itself into the uterine lining. Throughout this process, the zygote is continuously dividing through mitosis. The inner layer of cells will become the *embryo*, and the outer layer of cells will become the *placenta*. The placenta supplies the embryo with the nutrients and oxygen that the group of cells needs. Over time, differentiation occurs, which is the process of cells changing forms to perform all the specialized functions of the body.

Nervous System

The *nervous system* controls everything that occurs in the body. It is made up of nerves, which emit electrical signals throughout the body, stimulating muscles to work and reporting information back and forth from the brain. For example, nerves transmit pain messages from your skin to your brain when you burn yourself.

The nervous system is split into two divisions, the *central nervous system* and the *peripheral nervous system*. The central nervous system is composed of the brain and the spinal cord, whereas the peripheral nervous system is composed of the nerves outside of the brain and the spinal cord. The brain is the central processing center of the body. It is composed of three main parts:

- The cerebrum
- The cerebellum
- The brain stem

The *cerebrum* is composed of the right and left hemispheres, as well as four lobes: frontal, parietal, occipital, and temporal. The *cerebellum* helps control balance and coordinated movement. The *brain stem* connects the brain to the spinal cord, as well as controls unconscious functions such as breathing. The spinal cord carries information from the brain to its 31 different segments, directing the information to different levels of the body. Damage to the spinal cord can produce a wide range of problems. Minor damage could result in loss of sensation in certain parts of the body. More severe injury could lead to paraplegia (loss of function in both legs) or complete paralysis. Many of the functions of the nervous system and brain have not been completely discovered, and many processes remain a mystery that current research is attempting to solve.

Respiratory System

The *respiratory system* controls the body's oxygen intake and carbon dioxide release. The lungs are the primary organs of the respiratory system. Air flows through the respiratory system in the following order: nose/mouth → pharynx (upper throat) → larynx (lower throat) → trachea ("windpipe") → bronchi (major airway tracts of the lungs) → alveoli (sites in the lungs where gas molecules enter and exit the bloodstream). Inhalation is an active process in which energy is required, and exhalation is a passive process in which no energy is required. When air is inhaled, oxygen is exchanged for carbon dioxide in the lungs. Oxygen is the gas on which animals, including humans, rely for sustaining all the body's functions. Carbon dioxide is produced in the body as an end product of cellular respiration and can be toxic if it is present in high levels.

The respiratory system and the circulatory system work together to oxygenate the body. Oxygen and carbon dioxide are both carried by hemoglobin, a compound that resides in red blood cells. Hemoglobin carries oxygen from the lungs to the tissues, where it releases the oxygen in exchange for carbon dioxide. The hemoglobin then carries the carbon dioxide to the lungs, where it passes back through the respiratory system to be exhaled. The deoxygenated blood carrying carbon dioxide first reaches the right side of the heart, which pumps this blood to the lungs. After the exchange of carbon dioxide for oxygen, the newly oxygenated blood travels to the left side of the heart and is then shipped off to the rest of the body. Diseases of the respiratory system include asthma, edema, and bronchitis. The condition of asthma is due to environmental allergens or bodily stress and is characterized by constriction of the airways of the respiratory tract, limiting the air that enters the lungs. Edema occurs when there is fluid buildup in the lungs, causing a disruption in respiratory flow. Bronchitis is inflammation of the bronchioles (subdivision of the bronchi), which causes a persistent cough, and is very common among smokers. All these respiratory diseases can block oxygen intake and ultimately cause death.

Circulatory System

The *circulatory system* provides the body with continuous flow of blood containing oxygen and nutrients. The heart and the blood vessels make up the circulatory system. The two main types of blood vessels are arteries and veins. Arteries usually carry blood away from the heart toward the tissues, whereas veins carry blood away from the tissues toward the heart. Mammals have a closed circulatory system and a four-chambered heart. The heart consists of a right and left side, and each side can be further divided into an atrium and a ventricle. The circulatory system and respiratory system work together to oxygenate blood. The veins carry the deoxygenated blood toward the heart from the tissues, and arteries carry oxygenated blood toward the tissues. The flow of blood in the heart is as follows: veins → right atrium → right ventricle → lungs → left atrium → left ventricle → arteries. After the blood leaves the lungs, it is again oxygenated. Capillaries connect veins and arteries. Capillaries and tissues interact with each other to exchange such substances as nutrients and hormones. A capillary bed supplies blood flow and nutrients to a specific organ. Diseases of the circulatory system are referred to as cardiovascular diseases, meaning that they involve the heart and the blood vessels. These include heart disease, arterial disease, and blockage of flow to areas of the body (ischemia). These could ultimately lead to congestive heart failure or myocardial infarction (heart attack).

Digestive and Excretory Systems

The *digestive system* breaks down all the substances that are ingested by the body. Enzymes break down food when it enters through the mouth and throughout the digestive tract. Food travels through the digestive tract in the following order: oral cavity → pharynx → esophagus → stomach → small intestine → large intestine → colon → rectum → anus. As food travels down the digestive tract, different enzymes and substances are constantly working on breaking down and digesting the food to absorb all the nutrients. All substances are broken down into their smallest units, such as proteins into amino acids and fats into lipids. This process is necessary to allow passage of nutrients into cells. The accessory organs of the digestive tract that produce enzymes and other digestive substances are the liver, the pancreas, and the gallbladder. The appendix branches off of the large intestine but has no known function. The appendix can become inflamed and painful, called appendicitis, and must be removed. Food that cannot be digested travels through the intestines and empties out through the anus. Problems of the digestive and *excretory* systems range from simple "heartburn" (pain associated with upward flow of stomach acid) to colon cancer. An important preventive measure against digestive problems is a healthy diet.

The *urinary system* excretes wastes in the form of urine. The kidneys remove wastes and excess water from the blood through filtering. The urine formed leaves the kidneys, travels down to the urinary bladder, and exits the body through the urethra. A common problem that can occur in the urinary system is the presence of kidney stones. Kidney stones are solid crystals of minerals that can be very painful. If they are small enough in size, they can pass through the urethra and out of the body unnoticed.

Skeletal and Muscular Systems

The *skeletal system* of the body provides physical support, protection of organs, and assistance with movement. Some animals have an external skeleton called an *exoskeleton*. Mammals have an internal skeleton, called an *endoskeleton*, which is made up of bones and supported by cartilage. Bones also produce blood cells. The different types of bones are long bones, short bones, flat bones, and irregular bones. *Cartilage* supports the skeleton by aiding in joints and acting as additions on bone. Ears are made out of cartilage, for example. Bones are connected to other bones by ligaments, which are made from connective tissue. Ligaments are slightly elastic. Muscle is connected to bone through tendons, which are also made from connective tissue and are very similar to ligaments. (One notable tendon is the Achilles tendon connecting the heel to the calf. The tendon is so-named because the invincible Achilles of Greek mythology was killed only when he was shot with an arrow in this vulnerable spot at the back of the foot.) The most frequent problems that occur with bones are bone fractures. Arthritis is also common among the elderly, a disorder characterized by inflamed or damaged joints, causing sensations of pain and stiffness.

The *muscular system* works together with the skeletal system to allow for motion. Muscles provide force by contracting and relaxing. There are three types of muscle:

- Smooth muscle
- Cardiac muscle
- Skeletal muscle

Smooth muscle and *cardiac muscle* are "involuntary" muscles; they remain active without conscious instruction. Smooth muscle assists in unconscious activities such as digestion. Cardiac muscle is present only in the heart and allows for the beating of the heart. *Skeletal muscle* is "voluntary" muscle that allows for movement and is activated by conscious thought. This type of muscle would allow for running or lifting. Problems associated with muscle usually occur when muscles weaken. *Atrophy* is the decrease in muscle mass.

Endocrine System

The *endocrine system* regulates many of the body's functions through the release of hormones. These functions include *metabolism* (converting food to energy), growth, reproduction, and sexual development. Hormones are made in many locations in the body, but the two main organs that produce the most hormones are the hypothalamus in the brain and the reproductive organs (ovaries in females and testes in males). Other areas that produce hormones are the pancreas, the parathyroid glands, the pineal body, the pituitary gland, the thymus gland, and the thyroid gland. Hormones are released into the bloodstream by the glands that produce them. Most hormones control what occurs in our body by rhythmic secretions. Testosterone aids in the formation of sperm, as well as sexual development of the male body. Estrogen helps control the menstrual cycle and sexual development in females. Hormones such as acetylcholine control our digestive system and other slow-acting functions. Epinephrine and norepinephrine aid in the "fight or flight" system, a short-term stress response, with functions such as constricting the eyes in the presence of a bright light or giving a short burst of incredible strength in life-or-death situations. Other common hormones include insulin and growth hormone.

Many diseases are associated with endocrine problems. One example is diabetes, which is characterized by high levels of blood sugar and may be caused by insulin deficiency inhibiting the uptake of sugar into cells. Osteoporosis is a disease occurring mainly in women that causes a decrease in bone density, often because of estrogen deficiency.

Energy and Living Things

All organisms use sugars to create energy within their cells. Energy is necessary for motion, internal functioning, and growth. Animals eat plants, animals, and other living and nonliving things to nourish their bodies. Plants create the sugars they need by converting carbon dioxide and water using sunlight in a process called photosynthesis. The green pigment chlorophyll captures solar energy and uses it to split water (H_2O) into its component hydrogen and oxygen. The oxygen is released into the atmosphere, and the hydrogen bonds with carbon dioxide (CO_2) molecules to form sugars in the plant.

Plant and animal cells use the form of sugar called glucose. Mitochondria in each cell take in glucose molecules and convert them to ATP for use in many processes within the cell. Energy left unused by the cell is released as heat.

Classification of Organisms

The modern system of classifying organisms was developed by Swedish botanist, zoologist, and medical doctor Carolus Linnaeus in 1735. Linnaeus spent years studying the commonalities and differences among populations of plants and animals, and he assigned each species a long name indicating its relationship to other species. Today, the modern system of scientific classification uses many levels to distinguish species, and every species is known by its Latin-language binomial classification. Latin is used because it is a dead language, meaning it is not subject to regional and temporal variation. Humans, for example, are the species *Homo sapiens* and sunflowers are the species *Helianthus annuus*. By convention, the first part (the genus) of the binomial name is capitalized, and the second part (the species) is lowercase.

Genus and species are the last two levels of the standard six-kingdom system of scientific classification of organisms. Table 30.3 shows this system for six species, one under each kingdom. In the last column, the various levels to which the human being belongs are explained. Note that advances in evolutionary biology will continue to lead to new ways of classifying species. This six-kingdom approach, oulined next, is still widely taught because it emphasizes important characteristics of organisms' cells.

1. Eubacteria
2. Archaebacteria

   The two types of prokaryotes: organisms whose cellular genetic material is not contained within the nucleus. The classification is made based on modern genetic research that reveals that the evolution of these two groups diverged substantially enough and a long enough time ago to support the distinction being made. They are all unicellular, although some may aggregate and behave as one organism in some ways.

3. Protista

   Animal-, plant-, and fungus-like organisms that are generally unicellular or multicellular without advanced tissues.

4. Fungi

   Digests food externally and absorbs component nutrients into its cells; the primary decomposers of dead material in most land ecosystems

5. Plantae

   Cell walls; obtain energy from photosynthesis

6. Animalia

   Genetic material contained in membrane-bound cell nuclei; generally multicellular; consumption and internal digestion of food; no cell walls

TABLE 30.3 Classification of Organisms

Kingdom	Eubacteria	Archaebacteria	Protista	Fungi	Plantae	Animalia
Example organism	Bacterium *E. Coli*	Salt-water-dwelling archaean *Halobacterium volcanii*	*Amoeba proteus*	Yellow morel mushroom	Sugar maple	Human
Phylum	Proteobacteria	Euryarchaeota	Amoebozoa	Ascomycota	Magnoliophyta	Chordata (the vertebrates)
Class	Gamma proteobacteria	Halobacteria	Tubulinea	Pezizomycetes	Magnoliopsida	Mammalia (warm-blooded, mothers nurse offspring, live birth, hair or fur)

TABLE 30.3 *Continued*

Kingdom	Eubacteria	Archaebacteria	Protista	Fungi	Plantae	Animalia
Order	Entero-bacteriales	Halobacteriales	Tubulinida	Pezizales	Saoin-dales	Primates (lemurs, monkeys, and apes)
Family	Entero-bacteraceae	Halobacteriaceae	Amoebidae	Morchellaceae	Aceraceae	Hominidae (humans, chim-panzees, gorillas, and orangutans)
Genus	*Escherichia*	*Halobacterium*	*Amoeba*	*Monchella*	*Acer*	Homo (humans and human ancestors)
Species	*coli*	*volcanii*	*proteus*	*esculenta*	*sacch-arum*	*sapiens* (our species)

Evolution

The theory of evolution describes how species adapt and change in response to environmental factors. It was first proposed by English geologist and naturalist Charles Darwin in his 1859 book titled *On the Origin of Species by Means of Natural Selection, or The Preservation of Favoured Races in the Struggle for Life*. The book was the culmination of Darwin's observations made aboard the HMS *Beagle* on his famous voyage to South America, the Galapagos Islands, and beyond, including the years he spent afterward formulating his theories. In the book, Darwin proposed that populations of organisms change over time by means of natural selection. Individual organisms that are weaker or less suited to survive die out, and the stronger, better adapted individuals live to reproduce. The theory of evolution holds that by this process, every species on Earth descended from a common primordial organism.

As you read earlier in the chapter, organisms inherit characteristics of their parents genetically, and the copying of genetic material involves variation called mutation. Mutations can be beneficial or detrimental to an organism. Through natural selection, positive mutations persist in the population, and negative ones die off. Darwin provided abundant evidence of beneficial mutations in *The Origin of Species* and in his preliminary work called *The Voyage of the Beagle*.

The theory of evolution remains controversial in some parts of the world because certain people believe its explanations defy religious teachings. In the United States, the major objection to evolution comes from certain Christian groups who believe in creationism, a belief that God created humans and the other creatures of the Earth and that they have remained unchanged throughout time. Some people have reconciled evolution and the explanations given for life by their religion by considering that their god designed the natural processes of the universe, including biological evolution.

Ecology

Ecosystems are combinations of biological and physical factors that act as self-contained environments. All organisms in an ecosystem depend on one another for survival in some way. The basic roles of organisms in an ecosystem are as producers, consumers, and decomposers.

In general, green plants constitute the producers in an ecosystem. Chemical components from the air and soil and energy provided by the sun create input into the system. The first order of consumers eats plants, deriving energy from them. The second order of consumers kills and eats living animals for energy. The third order eats the remains of animals partially eaten by second-order consumers. For example, on the African savannah, antelopes feed on grasses, lions feed on antelopes, and vultures eat the antelope carcass after the lion has left it. After consumers feed, or when they die, decomposers such as bacteria and fungi consume the carcasses, returning their component molecules to the soil. The cycle is completed when plants use these nutrients.

Ecologists monitor the health of delicate ecosystems. Change in just one population of organisms or one inorganic factor (climate, soil quality, water quality, for example) can have significant lasting effect. For example, the U.S. Forest Service had maintained a policy of total wildfire suppression for decades. In the 1960s, many scientists began discrediting the policy because they noticed that some tree species that use fire to reproduce had not been reproducing. Eliminating fire, which the organisms of the forests had evolved with over time, also led to a buildup of fuel on the forest floor. Many of the fiercest wildfires in the United States today are difficult to control because of the amount of wood available to burn because of so many years of human intervention in the ecosystem.

In the United States, the federal government is responsible for regulating applications of scientific research in the areas of medicine and the environment. Table 30.4 describes some federal agencies responsible for human and environmental health.

TABLE 30.4 U.S. Federal Agencies for Human and Environmental Health

Agency	Full Name of Agency	Description
BLM	Bureau of Land Management	Sustains the health, diversity, and productivity of the public lands (about one eighth of the country).
CDC	Centers for Disease Control and Prevention	Protects public health and safety; works to prevent and control infectious diseases, injuries, environmental health threats, and so on.
EPA	Environmental Protection Agency	Develops and enforces regulations to promote a healthy environment.
FDA	Food and Drug Administration	Regulates foods, cosmetics, drugs, medical devices, and biological products like proteins and blood.
FWS	Fish and Wildlife Service	Works to conserve, protect, and enhance fish, other wildlife, and plants and their habitats.
NIH	National Institutes of Health	Serves as the primary federal biomedical research agency.

TABLE 30.4 *Continued*

Agency	Full Name of Agency	Description
USDA	United States Department of Agriculture	Promotes agriculture, protects natural resources, and assures food safety.
USFS	United States Forest Service	Administers the nation's forests by regulating their use and the measures taken to ensure their health.
USGS	United States Geological Survey	Provides information on the structure of the Earth to minimize loss of life and property from natural disasters and to manage ecosystem components such as water, organisms, and other natural resources.

What's Next?

Chapter 31, "Earth and Space Science," introduces earth and space science, emphasizing astronomy (study of space objects), geology (study of the composition of the Earth), meteorology (study of atmospheric phenomena), and paleontology (study of ancient life through fossils).

31

CHAPTER THIRTY-ONE

Earth and Space Science

Earth science is concerned with the physical and chemical properties of Earth, as well as the planet's origin in the universe. *Space science* refers to the study of stars, planets, and other bodies in space, and the origin of the universe itself. The two fields are grouped for the GED because both involve the study of minerals and their component elements, as well as physics on a vast scale over an extremely long period of time. Together, earth and space science include various disciplines such as astronomy (study of space objects), geology (study of the composition of the Earth), meteorology (study of atmospheric phenomena), and paleontology (study of ancient life through fossils).

The Universe

Humans have long questioned the place of the Earth in the universe. Before astronomy proved otherwise, many people believed that the Earth was the center of the universe, around which all things revolved. Centuries of observation and research show, however, that the Sun, the Earth, and the rest of the solar system are just a few parts of an unimaginably large space filled with other stars, planets, and free-floating celestial bodies. The origin and significance of the Earth is not purely a scientific question, though, because for centuries many cultural and religious beliefs have held how the Earth, the Sun, and other stars and planets have come into being. The science of the origin of the universe is not completely resolved either.

The *big bang theory* is the most popular explanation of the origin of the universe. According to its proponents, about 14 billion years ago, all the matter in the universe exploded from a central point and began moving outward in all directions. Evidence from cosmic radiation and the observed expansion of the universe support the big bang theory. Whether the universe's expansion will continue indefinitely is uncertain. One hypothesis is that the universe will continue to limitlessly broaden. Another view is that the universe contains enough mass to begin gravitating back together, eventually slowing and stopping the expansion. The increasingly large pieces of matter would continue gravitating toward other large pieces. The ultimate result could be a repeat of the big bang, where all the matter would explode again from a concentrated point.

Observation

The universe is so vast that scientists cannot know the current state of deep space. On Earth, the scale of observations is very small. Think about driving a car. If you see brake lights ahead of you, even if the car is only a short distance away, you almost always have time to apply your own brakes. The red brake light is emitted from the car, travels to your eye, and gets interpreted by the brain, which sends an electrical impulse to your leg to press down on the brake pedal. The travel of radiation occurs at the speed of light, which on Earth seems inconceivably fast. Over a span of the universe, however, the speed of light limits how current the "information" is that arrives from distant objects. When you look at the Sun, the light radiation that enters your eye began traveling about eight minutes earlier. Similarly, humans cannot know what is happening currently with deep-space objects. The most distant objects in the universe are so far away that their radiation observed on Earth originated many billions of years ago. The nearest star system to our sun is Alpha Centauri, which is more than four light years away, meaning that the Earth will not observe for more than four years what is happening there right now. Because deep-space observation is so time delayed, it is likely that many of the objects we observe now no longer exist, and many new objects exist that we cannot yet observe.

Stars and Galaxies

The gravitation among gases in the universe following the big bang led to the formation of *stars*. As gases coalesce, pressure increases, and the collisions between particles produce heat. Stars develop when gas temperature is sufficient to sustain nuclear fusion. A star spends about 90% of its life fusing pairs of hydrogen atoms to make helium. Stars of various sizes burn continuously from hundreds of thousands of years to billions of years. When all the hydrogen in a star is exhausted, fusion ends, and the layers of gases that remain are compacted because of gravitation. Eventually, heavier elements are fused, and a massive release of energy blows the remaining gases away from the star in an event called a supernova. The gases that are expelled form clouds of gas and dust called *nebulae* (singular: nebula). What remains of the star may be a dwarf star, or in the case of more massive collapses, a super-dense and dark neutron star. The most massive collapses may form black holes, which are the remnants of the stars' strong gravitation. *Black holes* are theorized to be points in the universe with such strong gravitation that nothing, not even light, can escape from them.

Galaxies are formations of stars and interstellar dust and gas that orbit a common center of gravity. Typically, they contain between about 10 million and 1 trillion stars and have diameters between several thousand and several hundred thousand light years. (Note: *light year* is a measure of distance—how far light travels in an Earth year—not time.) Galaxies are normally separated from one another by millions of light years. The arrangement of stars into galaxies is one example of how the universe is both immense and highly organized space.

Our galaxy, the Milky Way, is a barred spiral galaxy composed of at least 100 billion stars. On very dark, clear nights, you may be able to see a slightly cloudy band in the sky; this is an arm of the spiral galaxy and is what inspired the name Milky Way. Other galaxy shapes include elliptical, spiral, and irregular. NASA's Hubble Space Telescope (see Figure 31.1) has taken awe-inspiring photographs of numerous galaxies.

FIGURE 31.1 The Hubble Space Telescope. Source: NASA, STScI

The Solar System

Our sun is one of the billions of stars in the Milky Way and the center of our *solar system*. The sun is a star of average size and age, about 865,000 miles in diameter (109 Earth diameters) and 4.6 billion years old. The solar system is composed of the inner four planets—Mercury, Venus, Earth, and Mars—which are small and solid, the outer planets—Jupiter, Saturn, Uranus, and Neptune—which are large and gaseous, and the outer dwarf planets—a very new category of solar system objects. As of 2006, Pluto, formerly a planet, is considered a dwarf planet, as is the (former) large asteroid Ceres and the scattered disc object Eris. The International Astronomical Union determines the status of celestial bodies and will consider in the future whether other objects in the solar system belong in the dwarf-planet category. Besides the Sun, planets, and dwarf planets, the solar system is home to planetary satellites (moons) and thousands of asteroids, meteoroids, comets, and bits of space dust. Table 31.1 includes information about some of the celestial bodies that make up our solar system.

Table 31.1 The Planets and Dwarf Planets in Order from the Sun

Category	Name	Diameter (in Earth diameters)	Mass (in Earth masses)	Orbital period (Earth years)	Day (in Earth days; negative means opposite rotation)	Moons	Rings	Atmosphere
Planets—terrestrial	Mercury	0.39	0.06	0.24	58.64	0	No	None
	Venus	0.95	0.82	0.62	–243.02	0	No	96% carbon dioxide; 4% nitrogen; suspended sulfuric acid droplets
	Earth	12,745 km	5.9742×10^{24} kg	1 year ≈ 365.25 days	1 day ≈ 24 hours	1	No	78% nitrogen; 21% oxygen; other trace gases; suspended water vapor
	Mars	0.53	0.11	1.88	1.03	2	No	95% carbon dioxide; 3% nitrogen; trace gases
Dwarf planet—terrestrial	Ceres	0.08	0.0002	4.60	0.38	None	No	None
Planets—gas giant	Jupiter	11.21	317.8	11.86	0.41	63	Yes	86% hydrogen; 14% helium
	Saturn	9.41	95.2	29.46	0.43	56	Yes	93% hydrogen; 5% helium
	Uranus	3.98	14.6	84.01	–0.72	27	Yes	83% hydrogen; 15% helium
	Neptune	3.81	17.2	164.8	0.67	13	Yes	80% hydrogen; 19% helium
Dwarf planet—ice dwarf	Pluto	0.18	0.0022	248.09	–6.39	3	No	None
	Eris	0.19	0.0025	557 (est.)	0.3 (est.)	1	No	None

The following are descriptions of the celestial bodies in Table 31.1:

- **Mercury**—Smallest of the terrestrial (rocky) planets, only slightly larger than Earth's moon. Close, fast orbit of the sun. Very hot surface temperatures.
- **Venus**—Similar in size and composition to Earth. Densest atmosphere of the terrestrial planets. Air pressure is 90 times that of Earth. Extremely hot surface temperatures.
- **Earth**—Largest of the terrestrial planets. The only planet capable of supporting life.
- **Mars**—The "Red Planet." Similar rotation and seasonal cycles as Earth. Relatively thin atmosphere. Cold surface temperatures.
- **Ceres**—Formerly considered an asteroid. Located in the asteroid belt between Mars and Jupiter. Very spherical compared to other asteroid belt objects. Many times smaller than Earth's moon.
- **Jupiter**—2.5 times more massive than all other planets combined. Normally the fourth-brightest object in the sky. Radiates more heat than it receives from the sun. The Great Red Spot characteristic of Jupiter is considered a permanent storm on the planet's surface.
- **Saturn**—The only planet less dense than water. Bulges slightly at its equator. Best known for its rings composed of ice crystals, rocks, and dust.
- **Uranus**—The first planet discovered in modern times, with help from a telescope. Teal color caused by absorption of red light by methane in its atmosphere. Axis tilted 98 degrees toward the sun.
- **Neptune**—Similar to Uranus in size, mass, and composition. Blue color caused by methane in its atmosphere. Strongest winds among the planets.
- **Pluto**—Many details unknown; no close visits by probes. Less than 20% the mass of Earth's moon. Composed of rock and ice. Orbits on a different plane from all the planets.
- **Eris**—Discovered in 2005. The most distant solar system object from the sun. Slightly larger than Pluto. Extremely long orbital period; currently at the farthest point from the sun along its orbit.

Humans have forever been fascinated by the cosmos. During the space age, technology was developed that allowed people to construct machines for making observations of distant planets and other celestial phenomena. The first probes and satellites orbited Earth. The former Soviet Union had the first successful impactor probe mission to the Moon in 1959. In the 1960s, detailed study was made of the Sun and Moon. In the 1970s, the Soviet Union succeeded in attaining photos of the surface of Venus. Probe landings on Mars first succeeded in the decade, too. By the end of the 1970s and into the 1980s, NASA's Voyager probes 1 and 2 began sending back data, including photos, of the gas giants Jupiter, Saturn, and Neptune. In 1990, the Hubble Space Telescope was sent into orbit. It continues to provide valuable deep-space images that enhance human understanding of astrophysics.

In the 1990s, NASA developed a new generation of Mars exploration probes that were designed to maximize cost efficiency. The 1996–1997 Mars Pathfinder mission succeeded in deploying a robotic vehicle for analyzing soil and rocks. The 2001 Mars Odyssey mission sent a probe to orbit Mars and search for evidence of water on the surface of the planet. As of 2006, the mission continues, and researchers hope data collected from it will help answer the question of whether life once existed, or could still exist, on Mars. The Mars Exploration Rover mission began in 2003. Two separate rovers, Spirit and Opportunity, landed on Mars in January 2004 and began taking remarkable photos and surface measurements. Evidence from compounds in the rocky soil indicated that Mars once had seas of salty water. NASA plans to continue funding the mission through late 2007.

As of 2007, NASA has several notable probe missions underway. The Messenger mission will begin orbit and observation of Mercury in 2011. In 2015, the New Horizons probe will reach Pluto and begin making observations. In the following five years, it may be able to send data back to Earth about objects in the deepest reaches of the solar system.

Earth

Earth is the only celestial body known to support life. Like the plants and animals it supports, Earth is a complex set of structures and systems in delicate balance. Humans study the physical earth to learn more about its past, help predict its future, and solve the problems of conservation and environmental quality.

Atmosphere

The mass of air retained by Earth's gravity is called the *atmosphere*. It protects life on Earth by absorbing damaging ultraviolet radiation from the sun and moderating temperature changes between night and day. There is no abrupt end to the atmosphere; it becomes gradually thinner farther into space. Astronauts in "space" are still within the Earth's atmosphere.

Study of the atmosphere and weather is called *meteorology*. Through observations of the interaction of solar radiation (light and heat from the sun), air, and water, meteorologists make predications about such weather phenomena as wind, air temperature, and precipitation.

Meteorologists follow warm and cold air masses as they move around the Earth. In the continental United States, cold, dry air normally originates from the northern portions of central Canada. Warm, moist air masses usually form over the Gulf of Mexico. The Pacific Northwest is most affected by the cool, moist air that arrives from the Pacific Ocean. In the Southwest, warm, dry air dominates.

Storms occur when unstable cold air meets warm air. Because warm air is less dense than cold air, warm air rises above the cold air mass. Moisture in the warm air then quickly condenses into fluffy cumulus clouds. If enough moisture condenses, the clouds may become darker cumulonimbus clouds that can release a torrent of precipitation very quickly. Strong storms may also be accompanied by electrostatic discharge called lightning, which creates thunder by superheating air fast enough to cause it to expand with a series of sonic booms.

Warm air masses are associated with steady winds and different types of cloud formations. Cirrus clouds are very high, wispy clouds. Stratus clouds are low lying and can appear nearly formless, obscuring the blue sky. Stratus clouds can be various shades of gray (the darkest being called nimbostratus clouds) and can bring drizzle, mist, and fog, especially in summer months.

The line along which two different air masses collide is called a *front*. Turbulence associated with a front can vary considerably. Strong fronts generally cause precipitation of some of the moisture in the air. Warm fronts are where a warm air mass advances as a cold air mass retreats. Cold fronts are the opposite phenomenon. At stationary fronts, the two opposing air masses do not move and often bring a period of light, sustained precipitation.

In the continental United States, spring is associated with increased advances of warm, moist air, causing frequent rain showers. Tornadoes are another consequence of the push of warm, moist air against retreating cold air. Strong upward movement of warm, moist air is affected by the rotation of the Earth, initiating tight counterclockwise spiraling of air having destructive effects. Reintroduction of cold air masses from the north by the end of the summer season bring increased thunderstorms. In the oceans, the end of the summer is associated with the formation of hurricanes. Reduced solar radiation in the Northern Hemisphere allows ocean water to cool. These cool water currents meet the warm, low-pressure air and water currents near the equator and sometimes begin circulating. Fueled by warm ocean waters, hurricanes build in strength and move with the large-scale winds. In the Atlantic Ocean, hurricanes move toward the Caribbean Sea and the United States because of the trade winds. Hurricanes usually dissipate when they enter an area of cooler water or after they make landfall. Hurricanes such as Andrew in 1992, Georges in 1998, and Katrina in 2005 demonstrate the destructive power of tropical storms.

Hydrosphere

The accumulation of water on and below the Earth's surface is called the *hydrosphere*. Most of the world's water is contained in the oceans, and the rest is found in lakes, rivers, streams, and underground aquifers. The circulation of water between the ground and the atmosphere is called the water cycle.

Lakes and oceans are fed water from rivers, the Earth's surface, and groundwater discharge. Solar radiation evaporates some of the accumulated water into the atmosphere, where it moves with air currents back over land. When moist air cools, precipitation occurs, recharging surface sources and groundwater. The cycle perpetuates.

Oceans cover more than 70% of the Earth's surface, earning our planet the nickname "the Blue Planet." Oceans contain water with a high amount of dissolved salts. Saltwater is not suitable for human drinking, but because evaporation of ocean water leaves the salts behind, the supply of fresh water for human, plant, and animal consumption is continuously recharged. Although fresh water is plentiful, people must remain aware of chemical pollution introduced into the water supply. This reality has led some experts to dispute whether water is truly a renewable resource.

Biosphere

The totality of life on earth is called the *biosphere*. Preserving the quality of the physical elements of the environment is important for the future vitality of the biosphere. The atmosphere, hydrosphere, and biosphere are inseparably linked. When people discuss the "environment," they are usually referring to the interrelationship of these three facets of the Earth.

The Earth is the only planet in the universe known to support life. The predominant theory about the origin of life places its genesis between 3.5 and 3.9 billion years ago, when the first simple cells emerged as a result of complex electrochemical reactions. The atmosphere became rich with oxygen when early plants spread across the surface of the earth, converting carbon dioxide into oxygen.

Paleontologists search ancient rock layers for fossil evidence of ancient life forms. The fossil record provides rich evidence of the changes the Earth has undergone over its billions of years of existence. When animals die, their bones, entire bodies, or impressions (like footprints) may become covered in layers of sediment, as occurs at the bottoms of lake and streams. Pressure associated with accumulation of sediment eventually turns loose material into rock. Fossils are created when the impressions or spaces left by decayed animal parts fill with mineral-rich water. The minerals are left behind and harden along with the rock. These mineral fossils can be very detailed, highlighting the textures of extinct creatures. Plant fossils also exist showing the definition of individual cells.

The fossil record helps humans understand what caused massive extinction events in the past. The dinosaurs are the most famous example. These ancient reptiles dominated the Earth for millions of years. From time to time, paleontologists uncover fossils of a previously unknown species of dinosaur. The prevailing theory of why dinosaurs seem to have suddenly gone extinct was first proposed in the 1970s. Scientists examining layers of rock observed a thin layer of iridium-rich clay deposited all over the world about 65 million years ago. The iridium is believed to have been deposited in the K-T Event, when a 6-mile-wide asteroid collided with the Earth on the Yucatan Peninsula in present-day Mexico. Global firestorms and dust clouds thick enough to block the sun are blamed for wiping out between 50 and 80% of all plant and animal species on Earth, including all the flightless dinosaurs.

Lithosphere

The *lithosphere* is the outer layer of the Earth known as the crust. The lithosphere is composed of many adjacent tectonic plates, the gradual movement of which explains the orientation of the continents as we known them today as well as the existence of earthquakes, ocean trenches, and mountains.

Plate Tectonics

On the extremely slow geological timescale, the layer of the earth below the lithosphere flows like a liquid. The lithosphere, which is broken into many pieces called plates, essentially floats on top of it. These plates move in relation to one another at one of three types of plate boundaries: convergent, divergent, and transform. Motion occurs at the rate of about an inch per year, although this varies.

Millions of years ago, the Earth's continents fit together rather snugly as one supercontinent called Pangaea. The movement of the various tectonic plates separated the continents to their present positions. Movement of these plates continues, and its effects can be observed and measured. This process is known as *continental drift*.

Plates diverge predominantly on the ocean floor, where currents of partially molten rock rise to the surface and push the adjacent plates outward. This is called a *divergent plate boundary*. Where two opposing plates meet, one plate is forced under the other, where it eventually melts. The results could be the formation of volcanoes from the upwelling of magma or the pushing up of land to create mountains. The Cascade Mountains of the Pacific Northwest were created at a convergent boundary between the North American Plate and the Juan de Fuca Plate. When this subduction occurs at sea, volcanoes may accumulate and appear on the surface as islands. The Aleutian Islands were created this way, at the northern convergent boundary between the Pacific Plate and the North American Plate.

Earthquakes occur at *transform boundaries*. The San Andreas Fault is the rift between the Pacific Plate and the North American Plate located in California. These two plates slide against each other in opposite directions. Fluid slippage has no destructive effect, but if motion is impeded, energy may build up and eventually release all at once, sending strong vibrations through the Earth's crust. The strength of these vibrations is measured on the Richter magnitude scale. Earthquakes measuring 4.5 or greater are considered strong enough to be detected on seismographs (vibration-measuring equipment) around the world. The Indian Ocean earthquake that created the devastating tsunami of December 2004 is estimated to have had a magnitude between 9.1 and 9.3. Experts believe the energy released by the earthquake was equivalent to an explosion of about 100 billion tons of TNT. Most earthquakes, however, are not nearly as strong or as devastating as that one was. In fact, measurable earthquakes occur many times every day, and the vast majority of them go unnoticed by people.

Figure 31.2 shows worldwide earthquake data from 1963 to 1998.

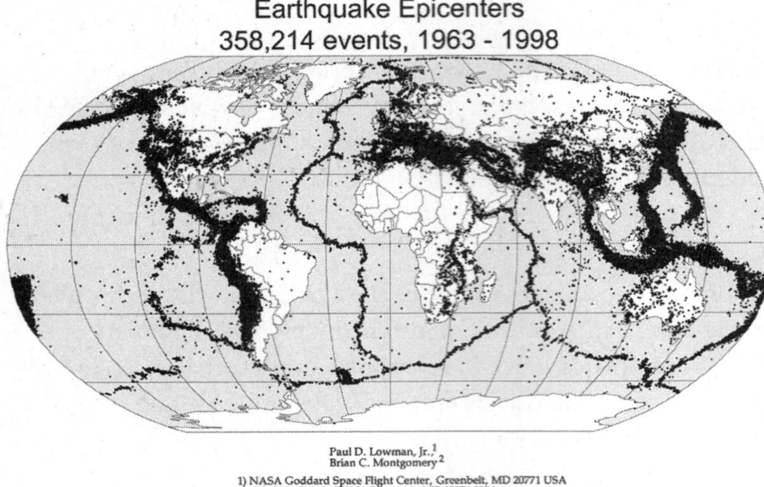

FIGURE 31.2 Earthquake data. Source: NASA

Rocks

Rocks are the hardened combinations of various minerals found in the Earth. They are described according to their composition and origins. *Igneous rocks* form when magma is released onto the earth's surface as lava cools and hardens. *Sedimentary rocks* form when minerals, sediments, and weathered pieces of rock settle and become compacted together over time. In general, the deeper the sedimentary rock, the older it is. *Metamorphic rock* forms when other types of rock are physically altered by high pressure and temperature within the earth's crust.

Rocks are formed from one or more minerals occurring in the Earth. *Minerals* are carbon-less compounds having a unique composition and structure. Most of the Earth's crust is made up of minerals formed from combinations of the elements oxygen and silicon. Some minerals are vital for human, plant, and animal health, and some are useful for creating metals or ceramics.

Soil

The uppermost layer of the Earth's crust is known as the *pedosphere*, or soil layer. Soil is the combination of minerals, decomposing organic matter, and living things that provides a medium in which plants and fungi may grow and certain animals live. Soil health is crucial to the health of the biosphere and the human food supply.

Erosion is a significant problem affecting the soil layer. The weathering of rock by wind, water, and gravity does not replenish soil mineral stocks fast enough to prevent the net degradation of soil because of sedimentation. When wind and water pass over a bare parcel of land, they pick up bits of soil and carry it away, eventually depositing it in a lake, stream, or ocean. Within moving streams and rivers, sediments are carried away from the bed and banks and deposited elsewhere downstream. In the case of large rivers, sediments settle when the water moves slowest, at the point where the river meets the lake or sea. Sometimes a delta is created, where the river breaks up into many smaller rivulets that snake their way through the thick sediment deposits. Although soil is enriched at this point downstream, farmers upstream are left with only thin layers of topsoil in which to grow their crops. Erosion, combined with poor nutrient management of the soil, can spell disaster for agriculture. (Read about the U.S. Dust Bowl in Chapter 22, "History of the United States.") Farmers today are wiser about soil, and they limit erosion. An example of the sustainability measures they take is planting rows of trees, called windbreaks, which reduce the amount of bare soil exposed to wind.

What's Next?

Chapter 32, "Physical Science," includes an introduction to physical science, focusing primarily on chemistry and physics.

CHAPTER THIRTY-TWO

Physical Science

Physical science refers to the study of the nonliving natural world. It generally encompasses the structure and properties of matter, energy, motion, and forces. This chapter will focus primarily on chemistry and physics.

Chemistry

The universe is made of *matter*—any substance that takes up space and has mass. *Chemistry* is the science of matter, its structure, and behavior. There are four states of matter: solid, liquid, gas, and plasma (highly ionized gas that makes up stars and is present throughout space). The basic unit of matter is the *atom*, and the basic unit of one particular substance is called an *element*. A basic understanding of chemistry in based on these two concepts.

The Atom

Chemistry describes how substances are built and how they behave on a submicroscopic level. The atom is the basic unit of matter that has all the properties of a particular element. Elements cannot be broken down into simpler substances. Less than 100 elements are known to exist in nature; however, chemists are able to create many other elements synthetically in laboratories. Individual atoms combine chemically with other atoms of the same or different elements to form molecules. Molecules are the smallest unit of a particular compound.

Fifth-century Greek scholar Democritus coined the term *atomos*, meaning "indivisible." He is attributed with articulating for the first time that the "stuff" of the universe is composed of a limited set of elements that organize themselves in different proportions and arrangements to create different things. Democritus's hypothesis was eventually reexamined beginning in the Renaissance. By the early nineteenth century, English chemist John Dalton had postulated what is called atomic theory, the main point of which holds that atoms cannot be created, destroyed, nor divided into smaller particles in a chemical process; chemical reactions change only the way atoms are grouped together. Although later chemists and physicists discovered how to isolate subatomic particles within the atom, Dalton's realizations marked a revolutionary change in human understanding of chemistry.

Later in the nineteenth century, Russian chemist Dmitri Mendeleev proposed his periodic table of the elements, in which elements are organized according to atomic number and, for the first time, by the "periodic" trends that appear in the series. Elements are defined by the number of protons they have in the nucleus, called the atomic number. Neutrons—particles with no charge—also exist in the nucleus, and their numbers may vary. The sum of protons and neutrons in an atom is called the atomic weight. The different types of an element as determined by the number of neutrons are called isotopes. On the modern periodic table, the atomic weight given is usually the proportional average of all the different isotopes known to exist. The nucleus is surrounded by a certain number of negatively charged particles called electrons. Their mass is so slight that it is not considered in calculating atomic weight. Figure 32.1 is a diagram of a simple helium atom.

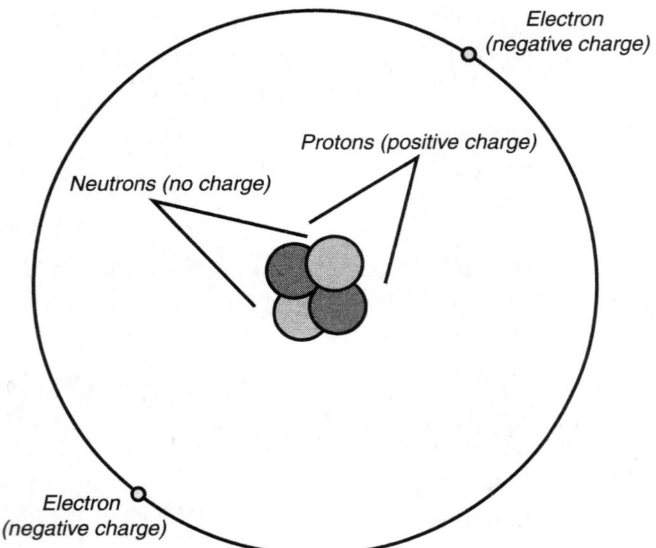

FIGURE 32.1 A helium atom, atomic number 2, atomic weight 4.

The Periodic Table

The modern *periodic table* arranges elements by their atomic and physical properties. The elements are arranged in rows from left to right in ascending order by atomic number. Columns group elements based on their electron orbital configuration, which determines certain physical properties of the element. Physical properties include color, sheen, density, odor, boiling point, flash point (temperature at which a substance gives off vapor that can be ignited), hardness, malleability (ability to be made thinner by pounding), and solubility (ability to dissolve in liquid). Figure 32.2 illustrates the periodic table.

IUPAC*Periodic Table of the Elements

Key: atomic number / **Symbol** / name / standard atomic weight

1	2	3	4	5	6	7	8	9	10	11	12	13	14	15	16	17	18
1 H																	2 He
3 Li	4 Be											5 B	6 C	7 N	8 O	9 F	10 Ne
11 Na	12 Mg											13 Al	14 Si	15 P	16 S	17 Cl	18 Ar
19 K	20 Ca	21 Sc	22 Ti	23 V	24 Cr	25 Mn	26 Fe	27 Co	28 Ni	29 Cu	30 Zn	31 Ga	32 Ge	33 As	34 Se	35 Br	36 Kr
37 Rb	38 Sr	39 Y	40 Zr	41 Nb	42 Mo	43 Tc	44 Ru	45 Rh	46 Pd	47 Ag	48 Cd	49 In	50 Sn	51 Sb	52 Te	53 I	54 Xe
55 Cs	56 Ba	57-71 lanthanoids	72 Hf	73 Ta	74 W	75 Re	76 Os	77 Ir	78 Pt	79 Au	80 Hg	81 Tl	82 Pb	83 Bi	84 Po	85 At	86 Rn
87 Fr	88 Ra	89-103 actinoids	104 Rf	105 Db	106 Sg	107 Bh	108 Hs	109 Mt	110 Ds	111 Rg							

57 La	58 Ce	59 Pr	60 Nd	61 Pm	62 Sm	63 Eu	64 Gd	65 Tb	66 Dy	67 Ho	68 Er	69 Tm	70 Yb	71 Lu
89 Ac	90 Th	91 Pa	92 U	93 Np	94 Pu	95 Am	96 Cm	97 Bk	98 Cf	99 Es	100 Fm	101 Md	102 No	103 Lr

*The International Union of Pure and Applied Chemistry is the world's foremost standardization ordanization for chemical science.

FIGURE 32.2 The periodic table.

Based on an element's chemical bonding properties, three categories exist:

- **Metals**—Shiny, ductile (able to be deformed without breaking), malleable. High densities and melting points. Conduct heat and electricity well.
- **Metalloids**—Share properties of metals and nonmetals.
- **Nonmetals**—Dull, not very ductile. Less dense than metals. Low melting points and conductivity.

To find these three groups on the periodic table, first find the metalloids, which lie along a diagonal line:

- Boron (5)
- Silicon (14)
- Germanium (32)
- Arsenic (33)
- Antimony (51)
- Tellurium (52)
- Astatine (85)

The metals lie to the left of the metalloids, and the nonmetals lie to the right. The only special case is hydrogen (1), which behaves like a nonmetal in most situations.

Within columns of the periodic table, it generally occurs that as the atomic number increases, the shared properties of the group manifest to a greater degree. For example, consider the elements of the first column of the period table (excluding hydrogen), called the alkali metals. One property of the alkali metals is that they react vigorously in water, and these reactions become increasingly vigorous for each element down the column. For this reason, pure alkali metals must be kept submerged in oil, away from moisture. Placing a tiny amount of lithium in a dish of water causes the lithium to release enough heat to begin dancing around in the water and to burn skin. Performing the same procedure with a tiny piece of cesium requires much more care. Upon hitting the water, the cesium explodes, releasing so much energy so quickly that it shatters the glass container holding the water.

Chemical Reactions

A *chemical reaction* changes two or more substances into a different substance or group of substances. Chemical reactions are represented by a system of notation. The reactants are shown to combine using the plus sign. The product of the reaction is preceded by a right-pointing arrow, as shown next:

$$Na + Cl \rightarrow NaCl$$

This reaction shows that one atom of sodium (Na) reacts with one atom of chlorine (Cl) to produce sodium chloride (NaCl), commonly called table salt.

Chemical equations must be balanced, meaning they obey the Law of Conservation of Matter. The Law of Conservation of Matter states that matter cannot be created or destroyed. In chemical equations, this means that every atom in the reactants must be present among the products.

In chemical equations, ratios of reactants and products are written using coefficients, and numbers of atoms within a molecule are written as subscripts to elements' symbols, as shown next:

$$2H_2 + O_2 \rightarrow 2H_2O + \text{heat}$$

In this combustion equation, two molecules of two atoms of hydrogen combine with one molecule of two atoms of oxygen to produce two water molecules (H_2O) and heat. This particular reaction is commonly used in rocket engines. Heat is given as a product in this reaction because chemical equations must also be balanced for energy. The First Law of Thermodynamics holds that energy may be transferred from one body to another and converted into various forms, but it may never be created or destroyed. In chemistry, reactions that need heat energy are called endothermic, and those that give off heat energy are called exothermic.

Chemical Versus Physical Change

A *chemical change* occurs when atoms and molecules rearrange their configuration to form one or more new substances. A *physical change* occurs when the form or other characteristics of a substance change, but the chemical structure does not. For example, water (H_2O) can be ice, liquid, or vapor. This kind of physical change is called *phase change*.

Compounds, Mixtures, and Solutions

Two or more elements combined in a chemical reaction are called a *compound*. Ordinarily, compounds have different properties from any of their component atoms. Compounds can be broken down and reconfigured in chemical reactions.

Mixtures are composed of different elements or compounds that retain their unique properties. For example, baking powder is commonly a chemical mixture of sodium bicarbonate (baking soda—$NaHCO_3$) and two acid salts, potassium bitartrate (cream of tartar—$KC_4H_5O_6$) and calcium aluminum phosphate ($CaAl_3[PO_4]_2[OH]_5$). The water in batter or dough activates a reaction among the compounds in the baking power, creating carbon dioxide (CO_2) gas, which causes the baked good to rise.

Solutions are homogeneous mixtures, most often meaning solids, liquids, or gases, that are evenly dissolved in a liquid. A dissolved substance is called a solute and the liquid in which it is dissolved is called a solvent. Solutions are often aqueous, meaning water is the solvent. Salted water for boiling pasta is a good example of an aqueous solution.

Chemical Bonding

Atoms that are bound together chemically are said to share a *chemical bond*, which results from the transfer or sharing of electrons. *Ionic bonds* form from electron transfer, as in the sodium chloride (table salt) molecule, which is created when an electron from a sodium atom is transferred to a chlorine atom, as shown in Figure 32.3.

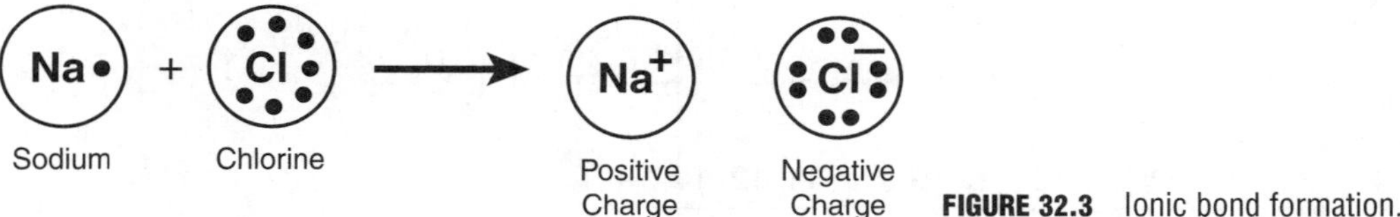

FIGURE 32.3 Ionic bond formation.

The reactants sodium and chlorine begin as electrically neutral atoms, meaning they have no charge. When the sodium atom loses its electron to the chlorine atom, the atoms have opposite charge, and so they attract one another. The electrons pictured in this reaction are those of the outer electron shell. Electrons are arranged in these specific orbitals around the atom.

Sharing of electrons between atoms forms *covalent bonds*. Covalent compounds are generally liquids and gases at standard temperature and pressure and have low conductivity and solubility.

Why two chlorine atoms form a covalent bond can be explained by the *octet rule*, which states that atoms tend to bond in such a way that they have eight electrons in their outer electron shell, as shown in Figure 32.4.

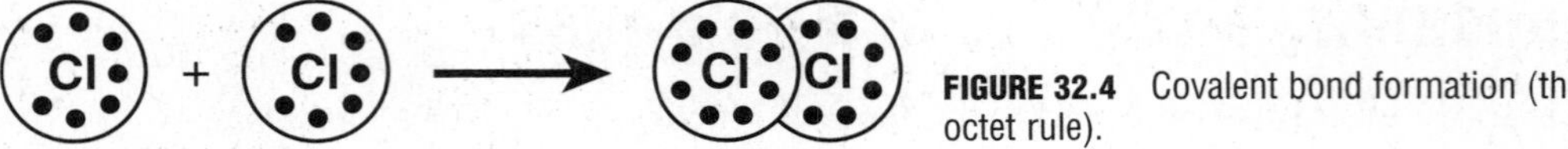

FIGURE 32.4 Covalent bond formation (the octet rule).

Acids and Bases

Many chemical compounds are classified as acids or bases according to their ionization properties when dissolved in water. *Ions* are electrically charged atoms. *Acids* are covalent compounds that produce positively charged hydrogen ions (H^+) in solution. Acids are characterized by sour taste, stinging or burning of the skin, corrosive action on metals, and good electrical conductivity. People use many different acids in daily life. Salad dressing is composed of oil and an acid. Vinegar's main component is acetic acid. Citrus fruit is rich in citric acid. Vitamin C is ascorbic acid. Car batteries use a sulfuric-acid reaction to generate electricity.

Bases are compounds that produce negatively charged hydroxide ions (OH^-) in solution. Bases are characterized by bitter taste, slimy or slippery feel to the touch, and corrosion of organic material. Common bases include ammonia (NH^3) and lye (NaOH), which is sodium hydroxide, an important chemical in soaps, drain-opening liquids, preparation of certain kinds of food, and many other things.

The relative strength of acids and bases are measured on the pH scale, which ranges from 0 to 14. Pure water has a pH value of 7, which is neutral. Acids have pH values below 7, and bases have pH values above 7. Figure 32.5 has some approximate pH values.

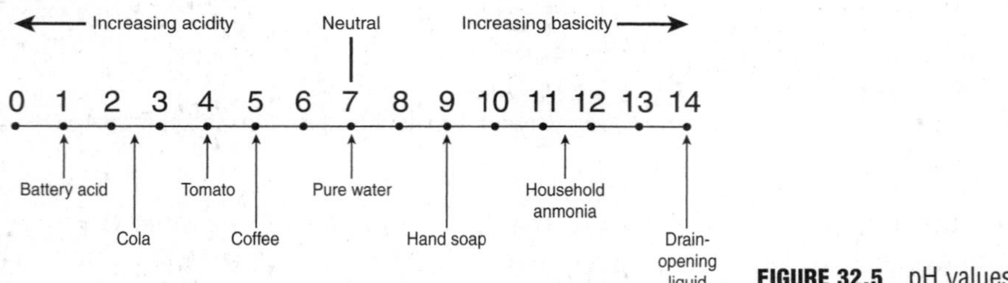

FIGURE 32.5 pH values.

Acids and bases react with each other to produce salts. The free hydrogen and hydroxide ions form water molecules, and the remaining ions form an electrically neutral ionic compound. You can observe acid-base reactions and the formation of salts by combining acetic acid (vinegar) and calcium bicarbonate (baking soda). As with any chemical reaction, be careful with what reactants you combine. Combining certain household chemicals can produce toxic gases or even explosive reactions. Consult expert information before attempting any chemical experimentation of your own!

The Chemistry of Pollution

The introduction of non-native chemicals into the environment can have many negative consequences. Chemicals that enter streams, lakes, and oceans can affect pH values of the water. Many species of fish and amphibians are noticeably harmed by acidification of their habitat. For example, fish eggs do not hatch below about a pH value of 5. In addition, frogs are considered an environmental indicator species because they quickly respond to changes in their environment. Their skin absorbs chemicals in the water quickly, so frogs are among the first organisms to appear deformed or sick as pollution increases.

Pollutants such as sulfur dioxide and nitrogen oxides are emitted into the atmosphere from industrial sources and some natural phenomena like wildfires and volcanic eruptions. These pollutants are further oxidized high in the atmosphere in a variety of chemical reactions with water, oxygen, and other chemicals. The result is a mildly acid solution of nitric and sulfuric acids. The acid falls to earth as liquid precipitation or in combination with dust and smoke particles. Acid rain, as it is called, pollutes surface water and soil. It also corrodes certain building materials. Many of the world's great outdoor statues, monuments, and fountains are made of limestone, sandstone, marble, or granite—all of which corrode because of acid rain. To see for yourself, visit a cemetery near you to see how the old grave markers have become rough and pitted, perhaps even illegible, from years of repeated mild acid washes.

Physics

Whereas chemistry is the study of the construction, composition, and properties of matter, *physics* deals with the behavior of matter and the forces that cause it. At the source of all physical phenomena is energy, which is the capacity for matter to do work. Physics can explain why a curveball works, why the planets orbit the sun, and how your heart pumps blood throughout your body. These are all inquiries into mechanics, the branch of physics that deals with forces acting on bodies of matter.

Mechanics

Formal investigation into mechanics began in ancient Greece, where scholars such as Aristotle examined the way objects (for example, stones) behaved when they were thrown through the air. Aristotle theorized that heavier objects fell to Earth faster than lighter bodies. He was later proven incorrect when Galileo observed that similarly shaped objects of different weights fell to Earth at the same rate. Science could not yet explain, however, exactly what forces were at play. English physicist and mathematician Isaac Newton revolutionized mechanics with publication of his treatise *Principia Mathematica* in 1687. In this three-volume work, Newton describes universal gravitation and the three laws of motion.

Universal Gravitation

- Every object exerts an attractive force on every other object in the universe that is proportional to the masses of the objects and the distance between them.
- *Mass* is the amount of matter contained in an object.

- Gravitation has constant acceleration.
- The planets remain in orbit because of the gravitation between them and the sun.

Newton's First Law: Inertia

- An object remains in motion or at rest unless acted upon by a force.
- *Inertia* is an object's resistance to changing its motion. For example, when you are driving and slam on the brakes, your body continues moving forward and presses against the seat belt.
- Friction is an important force that resists objects' motion. For example, without friction between a hockey puck, an ice surface, and the air, the puck could theoretically slide forever.

Newton's Second Law: Applied Forces

- The rate of change of momentum of an object is directly proportional to a force acting on it, and the direction of the change of momentum occurs in the direction of the force.
- *Momentum* is an object's tendency to continue to move in the same direction.
- Newton's second law applies to the game of tug-of-war and shows how so much energy can be used without much motion. For some time, the teams may match each other's pulling force, which is in opposite directions, and so neither team moves. Only when the force becomes unbalanced in one direction do the teams and the rope move.

Newton's Third Law: Equal and Opposite Reaction

- To every force applied there is an equal force applied in the opposite direction.
- In billiards, you can strike the cue ball into the 8-ball, causing the cue ball to stop and the 8-ball to move forward. The equal and opposite force applied by the 8-ball stops the cue ball.

Work occurs when a force moves an object it is acting on. Work can be calculated when you know the mass of the object moved and the distance it moved. For motion in the same direction as the direction of the applied force, work can be expressed as

Work = Force × Distance

Common units for work are the foot-pound (ft. lb.) in the U.S. system and the joule (J) in the metric system. The *joule* is roughly equivalent to the minimum amount of energy required to lift a one-kilogram object up 10 centimeters.

Power is the rate at which work is performed. It is measured in foot-pounds per second, horsepower, or watts (W). *Watts* are most commonly used in relation to electricity, where they represent the joules of work performed in one second. On your electrical bill, you are charged by the kilowatt-hour, which is equal to 1,000 watts of power supplied for one hour.

Energy

The concept of energy in physics derives from an object's capacity to perform work. Energy is classified as either *kinetic* or *potential.*

- Kinetic energy is the energy present in an object in motion.
- Potential energy is stored energy available for use by an object.

For example, taking aim with a slingshot, you pause as you hold the sling back. The stretched rubber has great potential energy that is released as kinetic energy as soon as you let go.

As it does in chemistry, the Law of Conservation of Energy applies in physics. Energy cannot be created nor destroyed; it can only move between objects and change form. For example, some people have solar cells on their homes. Light energy is converted to electrical energy in the solar cells, which is transferred through wires to a circuit-breaker panel, where the energy is sent to various circuits around the house. In the living room, devices such as the stereo and the television convert electrical energy into light energy and the mechanical energy that creates sound. No energy transfer is 100% efficient, however. Generally, energy transfers are associated with a loss of heat, which can be from simply rubbing your hands together or, on a larger scale, like moving hot water through pipes in a building. Electrical energy also has this property of dissipating slightly over long distances.

Simple Machines

A *machine* transmits or alters forces to help people accomplish tasks. A simple machine is one that requires only a single force to work.

The traditional simple machines are

- The inclined plane
- The wheel and axle
- The lever
- The pulley
- The wedge
- The screw

These machines operate by applying a small force over a long distance.

The *inclined plane* is a surface set at an angle that allows an object to overcome a large resistance by applying a relatively small force over a long distance. Mountain roads that switch back and forth as you drive them operate on the principle of the inclined plane. The shortest distance down or up the mountain would be impossible to drive because the forces acting against your car as you go up and with your car as you go down would be too great.

The *wheel and axle* involves a cylinder around which a cord or rope is wrapped. The distance of the rotation is greater than the distance the rope is pulled, so the force necessary to apply is less than the force needed to overcome. Doorknobs are an example of the wheel and axle. The distance you have to turn the knob is greater than the distance the latch moves, but the work required to move it is spread over the longer distance. (Note that the wheels and axles of automobiles and the like are not examples of the simple machine wheel and axle.)

A *lever* can help you lift a heavy object by spreading the required work over a longer distance. A lever consists of a rigid surface set on a fulcrum (pivot point). The heavy object is placed on the end closer to the fulcrum, and the force to lift it is applied to the other end of the surface. Figure 32.6 shows an example of a lever.

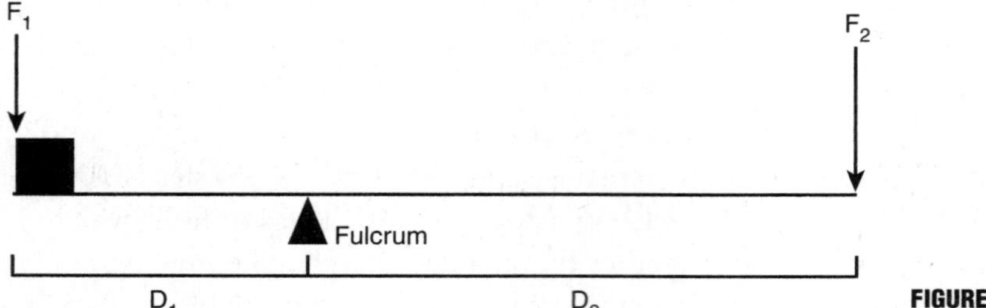

FIGURE 32.6 A lever.

A lever of this type is balanced when the following equation is true.

$F_1D_2 = F_2D_2$

F = downward force due to gravity

D = distance between the object and the fulcrum (the pivot point of the lever)

Pulleys are grooved wheels for rigging ropes or cables to reduce the force required to lift a load. Sailboats use pulleys to raise, lower, and maneuver the heavy, cumbersome sails.

Wedges are double-inclined planes used to separate two objects (or one object into two) by converting force applied to the wide end into force perpendicular to the inclined surfaces. Axes are wedges because they use the force of the swing to push the material on both sides of the blade outward.

Screws convert a rotational force to a linear force, and vice versa, by using a spiraling inclined plane. Screws for wood, for example, would be impossible to push into the material by hand, but by spreading the work out over a longer rotational distance, a person can slowly move a screw into the wood.

Heat

Heat is a form of energy resulting from the motion of molecules. Heat can be created by nuclear reactions (for example, the fusion that takes place in stars), chemical reactions (such as burning), electromagnetic dissipation (as in hair dryers), and mechanical dissipation (for example, the friction from rubbing two sticks together). A substance's phase of matter can be changed by changing its temperature.

Physics defines four states of matter:

- *Solids* contain molecules in direct contact with one another having limited movement. Solids hold their shape.
- *Liquids* are composed of freely moving molecules held together by attractive forces. Liquids are fluid and form to the shape of their container.
- *Gases* are substances whose molecules move freely and randomly. Increasing temperature increases the kinetic energy (motion) of the molecules and decreases density and pressure.
- *Plasma* is a highly ionized gas found in stars. It is the least important phase of matter to know for the GED.

Temperature is a measure of the heat in a substance. Each degree of temperature represents change in the heat of a substance per unit mass. The most common temperature scales are the Celsius (metric) and Fahrenheit (U.S.) scales. The Celsius scale was set to the sea-level freezing and boiling points of water. There are many conflicting views of how the Fahrenheit scale was defined. One degree of temperature on the Celsius represents a greater change in temperature than one degree Fahrenheit represents. For this reason, converting between the two scales is not something most people can do mentally. It is best to memorize some important temperature values in both scales, if you don't already know them. These are shown in Table 32.1. Figure 32.7 compares the two temperature scales.

TABLE 32.1 Important Temperatures

Scale	Equilibrium Point of the Two Scales	Freezing Point of Water at Sea Level	Boiling Point of Water at Sea Level
Celsius	–40° C	0° C	100° C
Fahrenheit	–40° F	32° F	212° F

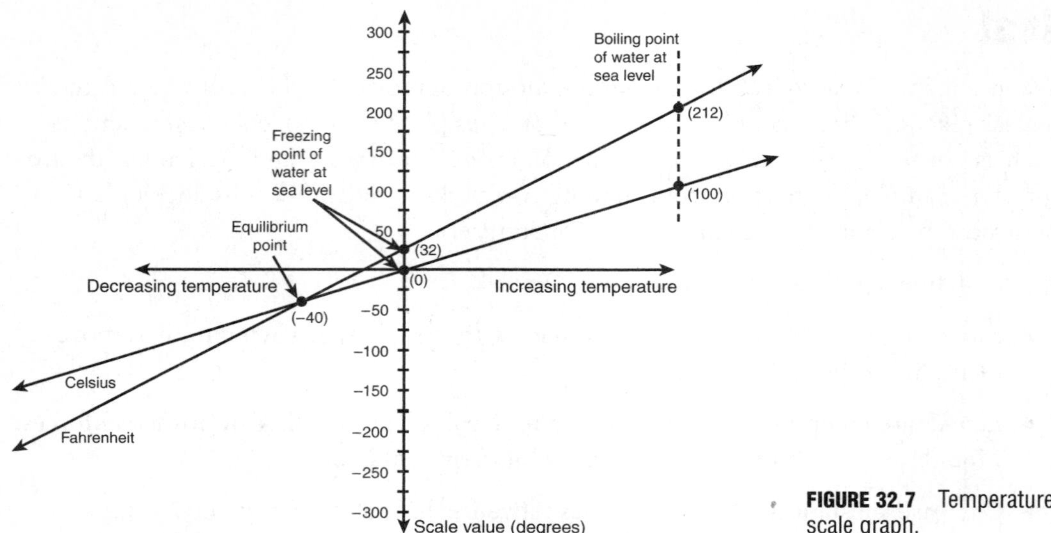

FIGURE 32.7 Temperature scale graph.

Simple thermometers measure temperature using the predictable expansion and contraction of certain fluids, such as mercury or alcohol, when they are exposed to a substance of a higher or lower temperature. Although temperature is the measure of heat contained in a substance, the actual output of heat is commonly measured in BTUs (British Thermal Units, as used with barbecue grills and furnaces, for example) or calories. One BTU is the amount of heat that raises one pound of water one degree Fahrenheit. One calorie is the amount of heat that raises one gram of water one degree Celsius. (Note that the term "calorie" found on food labels refers to "kilocalorie," exactly 1,000 calories, or the amount of heat that raises one kilogram [2.2 pounds] of water one degree Celsius.)

Heat transfer occurs in three ways:

- *Conduction* is heat transfer by vibration of molecules in direct contact with one another.

  Examples: Electric stoves, touching ice.

- *Convection* is heat transfer through currents in fluids (that is, liquids and gases).

  Examples: Cumulonimbus ("thunderhead") clouds, the rise of hot water and the descent of cool water in a pot on a stove, the sea/land breeze effect (see Figure 32.8).

- *Radiation* is heat transfer through waves.

  Examples: sun heating your skin through a window, electric heaters

The next time you are by a sea, ocean, or large lake, take notice of the sea breeze and land breeze. They are opposite convection currents in the air. Sea breeze occurs during the day, and land breeze occurs at night. The different heat properties of the water and the land cause the reversal of air circulation. Figure 32.8 is a diagram of sea and land breezes.

With sea breeze, during the day, the sun heats the water and the land at the same rate; however, as Figure 32.8 shows, (1) land radiates a greater amount of heat into the atmosphere than the water does. (2) The air above the land heats, expands, and thus creates an area of lower air pressure. (3) The air rises and gradually cools. The difference in pressures over land are greater than (4 and 5) those over the water, so to return to equilibrium pressure (6 and 7), the two regions of high-pressure air move horizontally toward the adjacent area of low pressure. The steady wind moving from the water to the land is called a sea breeze.

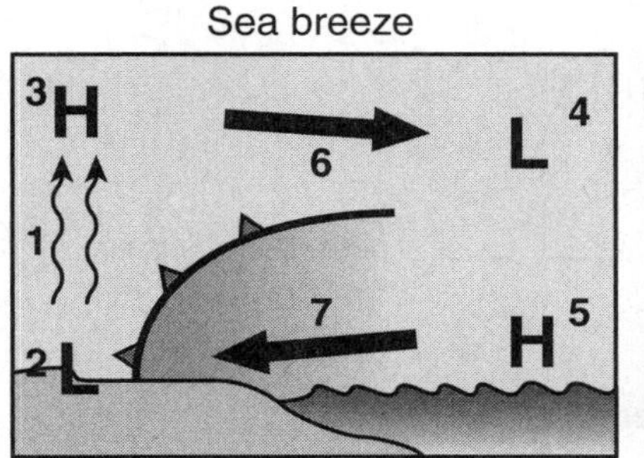

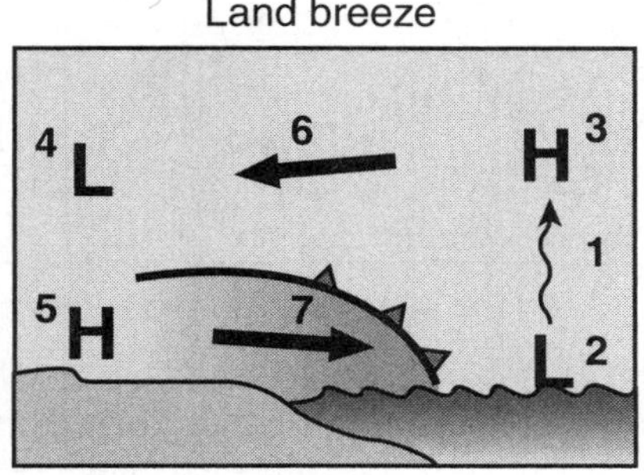

FIGURE 32.8 Examples of convection currents in the environment.

With land breeze, at night, the sun no longer heats the land and water as significantly, so eventually the temperature of the land drops below that of the water. In a similar manner as the sea breeze, the less dense, warmer air over the water rises and then cools. The high-pressure air above the land and water moves toward the adjacent low-pressure area. Land breeze is the resulting steady wind moving from the land to the water.

Waves

Thermal radiation, as introduced in the previous section, is heat behaving as a wave. In fact, many natural phenomena occur in waves. A *wave* is an oscillating disturbance in space. Some waves require a medium (for example, air or water) in which to travel, whereas other types of waves can move through the vacuum of space. Liquid, sound, electromagnetic radiation, and seismic vibrations travel in waves. Waves are most often associated with a transfer of energy. Waves have two forms, *longitudinal* and *transverse*.

- Longitudinal wave particles move in the same direction as the wave.

  Examples: Sound waves, "compression" waves caused by earthquakes.

- Transverse wave particles move in a perpendicular direction to the direction of the wave.

  Examples: Ripples in water, vibration of a guitar string, "shear" waves caused by earthquakes, as shown in Figure 32.9.

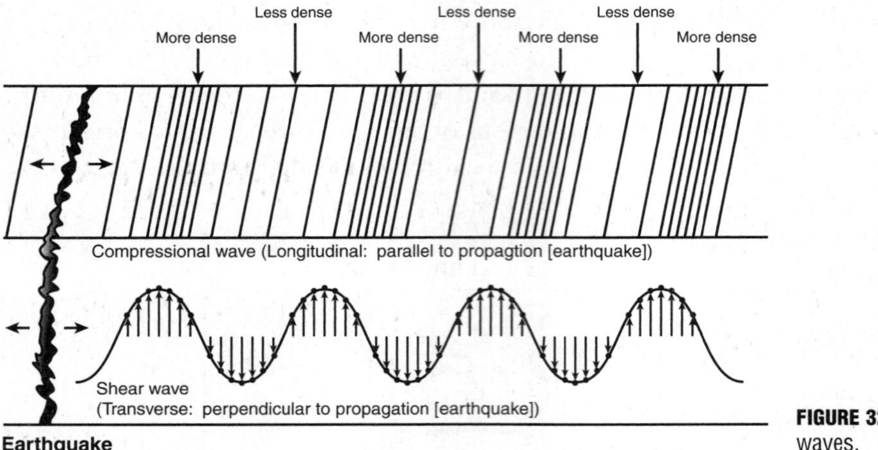

FIGURE 32.9 Seismic waves.

Earthquakes produce one longitudinal and one transverse "body" wave.

Figure 32.10 illustrates the properties of a wave.

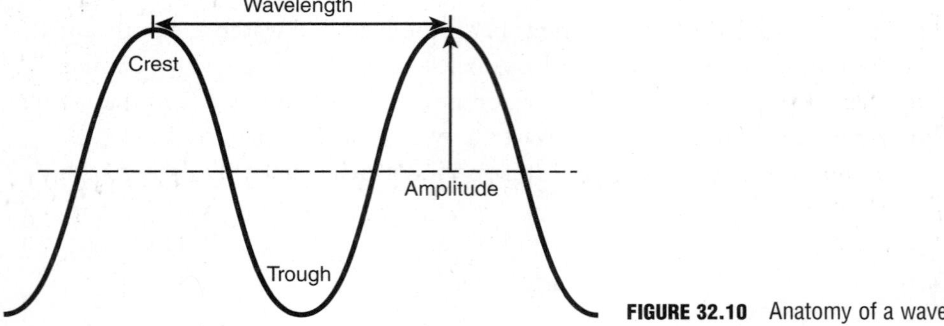

FIGURE 32.10 Anatomy of a wave.

The highest points of a wave are called *crests*, and the lowest points are called *troughs*.

Waves can be defined by their amplitude, wavelength, and frequency:

- *Amplitude* is the height of the wave, from the center line to a crest or trough.
- *Wavelength* is the length of one complete cycle of the wave, from a crest to the next crest or from a trough to the next trough.
- *Frequency* is the measure of how many cycles the wave completes per unit of time. Wave frequency is commonly measured in Hertz (Hz), which is defined as cycles per second.

  For example, the A key above the middle C key on a piano is tuned to 440 Hz, which is known as "concert pitch."
- Human hearing is limited to the pitch range of 20 to 20,000 Hz, although the upper limit decreases with a person's age. Sound with pitch above this range is called *ultrasound*. Sound with pitch below the range is called *infrasound*.

Amplitude of sound waves is commonly measured in decibels (dB), which correspond to loudness, as shown in Figure 32.11.

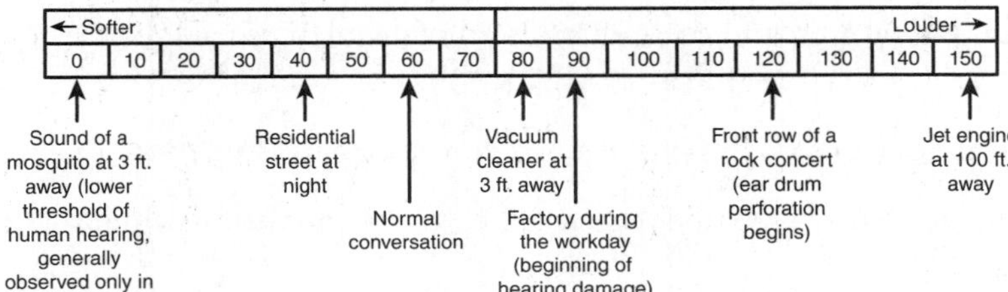

FIGURE 32.11 Loudness examples (dB).

Sound waves are compressional waves, meaning they are created by the mechanical compression of their medium of travel. Sound can travel through gases, liquids, and solids, but cannot travel in a vacuum. To illustrate this compression of the medium, think about a stereo speaker. By converting electrical energy to mechanical energy, a speaker can create sound. Vibration of the (normally round and black) driver component of the speaker compresses the molecules of air outside it, propagating sound waves.

A sound source can affect this compression of the air by being in motion. Sound waves moving in the direction of travel of the source will be more compressed than those traveling in the opposite direction. Imagine standing outside at a train station. A train approaches while blowing its whistle. If the train continues moving through the station, you'll hear the whistle's pitch peak the moment the train passes you, and then drop significantly as the train moves away. This is an example of the Doppler effect. Police use the Doppler effect to measure driving speeds using a radar device. Meteorologists use it in weather radar to track storms. Astronomers study the Doppler effect in light from stars and galaxies to determine how fast they are moving toward or away from Earth.

Electromagnetic Radiation

Self-propagating waves having electrical and magnetic properties are called *electromagnetic radiation*. Characteristics of these waves are associated with frequency. The electromagnetic spectrum, as shown in Figure 32.12, is a graphical representation of electromagnetic radiation across the wide range of its frequencies. The section representing light visible to the human eye is small compared to the whole spectrum.

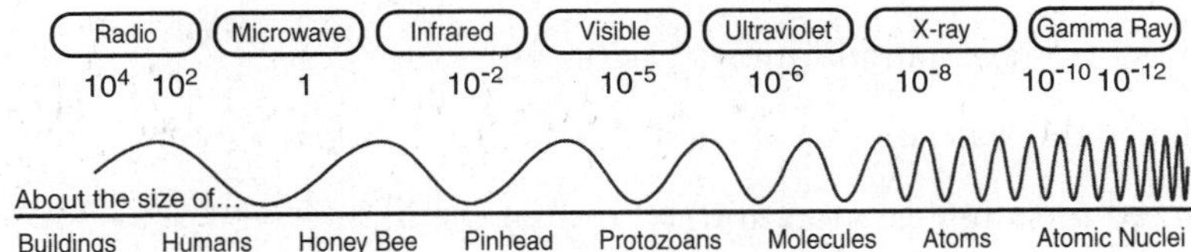

FIGURE 32.12 The electromagnetic spectrum.

Within the visible spectrum, color is determined by wavelength. To remember the order of visible light wavelengths from longest to shortest, recall the order of colors in the rainbow: red, orange, yellow, green, blue, indigo, violet. Notice how electromagnetic radiation "below" red is called *infra*red and the radiation "above violet" is called *ultra*violet.

Humans have found innovative uses for all the types of electromagnetic radiation:

- **Radio waves**—Radio and television transmissions, heart rate monitors, cellular phones.
- **Microwaves**—Reheating food, wireless Internet connections, radar.
- **Infrared waves**—Detected by night vision goggles; used to measure temperatures remotely (as from satellites), send signals for electronics from remote controls.
- **Visible waves**—Light the human eye can see.
- **Ultraviolet waves**—Responsible for skin tanning and damage; used to analyze minerals, kill germs, disinfect water, attract insects.
- **X-rays**—Medical imaging, inspecting cargo and luggage; astronomers study x-ray emissions from deep space objects.
- **Gamma rays**—Used to kill bacteria and cancer cells; modern machines use gamma rays to scan cargo containers in ports.

In physics, *wave-particle duality* holds that light behaves in some ways like a wave and in other ways like particles. The first comprehensive theory of light was developed by seventeenth-century Dutch physicist Christiaan Huygens. He proposed that light existed as a wave. Huygens's theories became overshadowed by those of the already well-established scientist Isaac Newton, who thought light consisted of tiny particles. He was able to explain the phenomenon of reflection using his theories. By the nineteenth century, some scientists had provided new evidence for Huygens's wave theory of light. The scientific debate of wave versus particle behavior thrived. By the early twentieth century, Albert Einstein theorized that light contained tiny quantities of energy with particulate characteristics. He called these particulate quantities *photons*. Einstein was awarded the 1921 Nobel Prize in Physics for research of the photoelectric effect. He provided evidence of the photon by showing that light energy absorbed by certain metals caused electrons to be emitted from the metal.

The three basic dimensions of light are the following:

- Intensity (measured as the wave's amplitude) = brightness
- Frequency (measured as the wavelength) = color
- Polarization (also called the angle of vibration) = "tilt" of the light wave

Light reflected off of shiny, transparent materials becomes partly or totally polarized. Filters, like those on good sunglasses, remove light polarized at one angle—vertically, in the case of sunglasses. This allows drivers to see through glare on the road and anglers to see fish below the surface of the water.

Electricity and Magnetism

Electricity is the flow of loose electrons. *Magnetic forces* arise from the motion of an electric charge. The term "electromagnetism" is commonly used in physics because these two phenomena occur simultaneously. A changing magnetic field produces an electric field (as in electric generators and transformers). Conversely, a changing electric field generates a magnetic field.

The points of attractive and repulsive force at the ends of a magnet are called *poles*. Magnets have at least two poles, called north (positive) and south (negative) since the time of the earliest compasses, which operate by magnetism. Opposite poles attract each other, and similar poles repel each other. The space around a magnet is called its *magnetic field*. The magnets of daily life are called permanent magnets and can be composed of only certain metallic elements and alloys. Permanent magnets have easily observable attraction and repulsion at the poles, as shown in Figure 32.13.

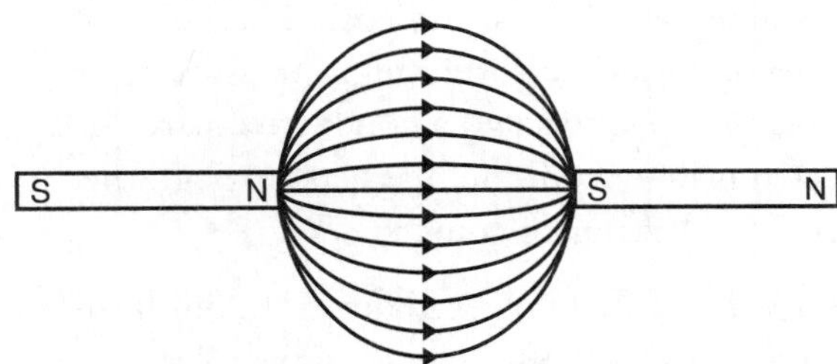

Opposite poles of magnets (N-S) attract each other.

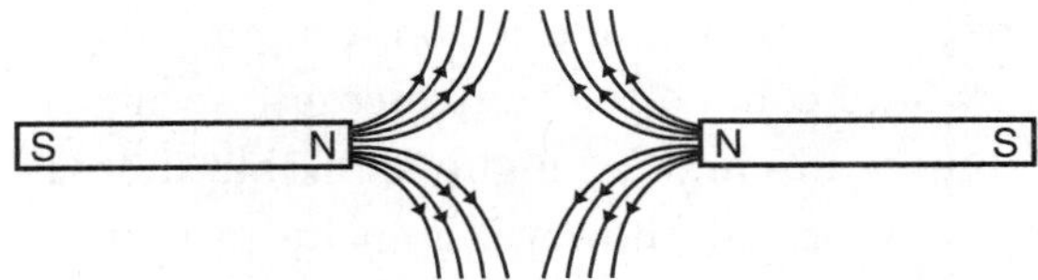

Like poles of magnets (N-N or S-S) repel each other.

FIGURE 32.13 Properties of a permanent magnet.

Before a substance becomes magnetized, its various molecules are unordered so that their attractive forces cancel out each other. A substance becomes magnetized when the molecules arrange themselves parallel to the lines of force, with the north poles facing one way and the south poles facing the opposite way. In permanent magnets, these forces are too weak to rearrange themselves after they have lined up this way.

Static electricity is an electric charge that does not move between conductors. It is caused by friction between two objects with opposing charges. For example, rubbing a balloon on a wool sweater causes the balloon to become negatively charged. The balloon can then be held against the wall, which lacks an excess of positive or negative charge, by magnetic forces of attraction. The human body experiences little shocks from static electricity when the built-up charge exits through a finger, for example, in contact with a conductor having opposite charge (such as a metal doorknob).

The flow of electricity occurs in materials classified as *conductors*. Conductivity is a property of substances important in chemistry in addition to physics. Metals, acids, mineral oxide solutions, and hot gases are all good conductors. Some materials are called insulators because they almost completely resist any electrical charge. For example, copper wires can be coated in rubber and certain plastics to prevent any electrical charge from leaving the wire.

Electric currents pass through conductive material to power many of the modern conveniences humans enjoy today. Electricity demanded by civilization is supplied by power generation companies, which (in most cases) use electromagnetism to convert mechanical energy to electrical energy. Most of the world's power comes from burning fossil fuels, which include substances like gasoline, natural gas, and coal. The heat released from fossil fuel combustion is used to boil water, creating high-pressure steam, which propels a turbine. The turbine contains two magnets and a conductive wire coil. When the turbine is spun by the steam, electrons flow from the magnets through the wire and onto the widespread "electrical grid" for serving customers.

Nuclear power uses the same turbine system as fossil-fuel power generation, but heats the water by a controlled nuclear fission reaction instead. Nuclear reactions release great amounts of energy, although the drawbacks of using them include environmental risks from "meltdown" (uncontrolled reaction) and having to dispose of spent nuclear fuel.

Solar power generation does not involve mechanical energy. Solar cells are arranged in photovoltaic arrays facing the sun. Photons from the sun excite electrons on pure silicon wafers in the solar cells, and the electrons flow onto conductive wires. Because solar power involves very little pollution, many communities find it a highly desirable alternative to fossil fuel or nuclear options. The cost of solar cells, however, remains prohibitively high in many cases.

Besides solar power, wind power is an increasingly viable "alternative energy" source. Wind power generation is possible only in areas where winds are plentiful. Historically, many cultures have harnessed wind power to draw water with a pump or to turn a millstone for grinding grain. In modern systems, a wind turbine resembling an airplane propeller mounted on a pole turns an electrical generator when forced by wind. As with solar power, wind power is very "clean" environmentally, but costly by comparison to most other sources of electricity.

Hydroelectric power generation is possible in areas of moving water. Dams built across rivers, for example, use moving water to turn turbines inside them. Limitations of hydroelectric power include suitability of water sources, as well as possible negative impacts to animal species that need to move up and down the river. After they are established, hydroelectric operations can also affect the navigability of rivers. In general, hydroelectric power is cost competitive and environmentally sustainable.

What's Next?

The next chapters in this section include GED Science practice questions and answers (Chapter 33), as well as a glossary of scientific terms (Chapter 34). Review the glossary and attempt to answer all the practice questions, using your critical thinking skills and knowledge of science. Refer to Chapters 30 through 32 as necessary.

CHAPTER THIRTY-THREE

Science Practice Questions and Answer Explanations

This chapter includes 25 simulated Science questions in multiple-choice format. Carefully read the directions and answer the questions. Allow yourself 40 minutes to complete these practice questions.

The practice questions are followed by answers and detailed explanations. Read the explanations for the questions that you missed, and review the previous chapters in Part VII as needed.

Use the answer sheet on the following page to mark your answers. Then compare your answers to the answers and explanations at the end of this chapter. Be sure to read through the explanations thoroughly. Identify and review topics you've consistently struggled with.

Please note that this chapter does not follow the precise format of the GED.

Answer Sheet

1. ① ② ③ ④ ⑤
2. ① ② ③ ④ ⑤
3. ① ② ③ ④ ⑤
4. ① ② ③ ④ ⑤
5. ① ② ③ ④ ⑤
6. ① ② ③ ④ ⑤
7. ① ② ③ ④ ⑤
8. ① ② ③ ④ ⑤
9. ① ② ③ ④ ⑤
10. ① ② ③ ④ ⑤
11. ① ② ③ ④ ⑤
12. ① ② ③ ④ ⑤
13. ① ② ③ ④ ⑤
14. ① ② ③ ④ ⑤
15. ① ② ③ ④ ⑤
16. ① ② ③ ④ ⑤
17. ① ② ③ ④ ⑤
18. ① ② ③ ④ ⑤
19. ① ② ③ ④ ⑤
20. ① ② ③ ④ ⑤
21. ① ② ③ ④ ⑤
22. ① ② ③ ④ ⑤
23. ① ② ③ ④ ⑤
24. ① ② ③ ④ ⑤
25. ① ② ③ ④ ⑤

Practice Questions

Directions: Choose the one best answer to each question.

1. Energy from sunlight allows photosynthesis to occur in plants. Oxygen is a product of photosynthesis. The energy transfer that occurs in this process is

    (1) radiation to thermal

    (2) radiation to chemical

    (3) radiation to electrical

    (4) chemical to radiation

    (5) electrical to thermal

Question 2 refers to the following information.

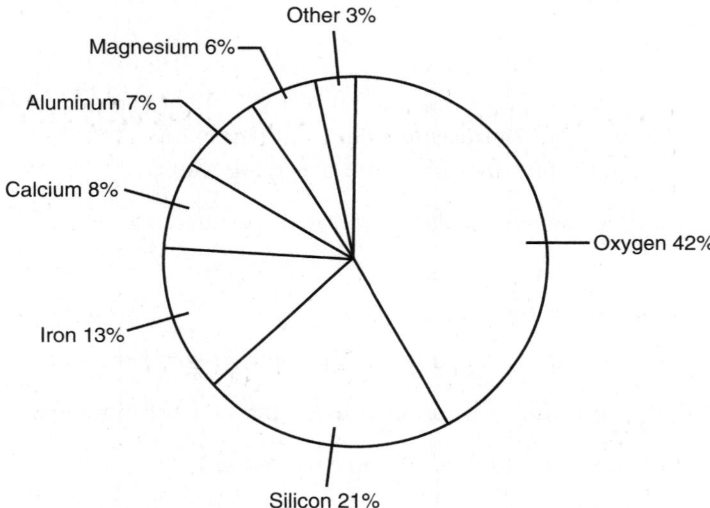

2. Lunar soil is principally composed of which of the following elements?

    (1) oxygen and iron

    (2) iron, calcium, and magnesium

    (3) silicon, iron, and magnesium

    (4) oxygen and silicon

    (5) aluminum, silicon, and iron

Question 3 refers to the following information.

Urea, a waste product of urine, is composed of four elements: oxygen, carbon, nitrogen, and hydrogen. There are twice as many hydrogen atoms than nitrogen atoms in a urea molecule. The structural formula of this organic compound is as follows:

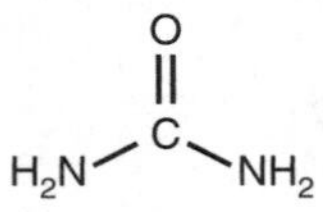

$$H_2N-\overset{\displaystyle O \atop \displaystyle \|}{C}-NH_2$$

3. Of the following compounds, which molecular formula best represents urea?

    (1) N_2H_4CO

    (2) $N_2H_4C_2O_2$

    (3) NH_4

    (4) NHCO

    (5) NHC

4. In 2004, a tsunami devastated parts of southeastern Asia. Tsunamis can occur when the sea floor temporarily elevates, displacing the overlying water.

    Which of the following would be the best explanation for the occurrence of a tsunami?

    (1) Heavy rainfall caused a huge wave.

    (2) A hurricane of massive scale approached land, developing a giant wave.

    (3) An earthquake resulted from the collision of oceanic plates, creating a wave.

    (4) The lunar changing of the tides resulted in a massive wave.

    (5) A strong wind created an enormous wave.

5. In most parts of the world, it is dark during the night and light during the day. What is the best explanation for this?

    (1) The Earth rotates on its own axis.

    (2) The Earth revolves around the sun.

    (3) Other planets are blocking the sun from Earth during the night.

    (4) The sun shines only during the day.

    (5) The Earth's tilt relative to its orbit changes throughout the day.

Questions 6 through 9 refer to the following information.

One way to classify the regions of the Earth is by biomes. Biomes are organized by their flora and fauna, as well as their altitude, terrain, latitude, and natural environment. Biomes are classified as either terrestrial or aquatic. Listed next are different types of biomes:

(1) **tundra**—An area that has low temperatures and short growing seasons, with a mostly treeless terrain that includes many grasses, lichens, and mosses.

(2) **grassland**—An area that has moderate temperatures and is composed of a continuous stretch of grass.

(3) **taiga**—An area consisting primarily of coniferous forests; this is the largest terrestrial biome and also a major source of oxygen.

(4) **tropical rain forest**—An area that includes a great variety of flora and fauna; characterized by humid temperatures and high annual rainfall.

(5) **desert**—An area that is very dry with extreme temperatures, composed primarily of sand and rock; receives very little annual rainfall.

Each of the following questions refers to one of the terms given above. In each question, select the best answer for the given statement. A specific term may be used once, more than once, or not at all.

6. Ranchers need open land to graze and pasture their cattle.

   This statement best corresponds to which of the following biomes?

   (1) tundra

   (2) grassland

   (3) taiga

   (4) tropical rain forest

   (5) desert

7. Antarctica has extremely cold temperatures and rocky areas with nearly 700 algae species.

   This statement best corresponds to which of the following biomes?

   (1) tundra

   (2) grassland

   (3) taiga

   (4) tropical rain forest

   (5) desert

8. These areas are known for their diversity in both plants and animals.

   This statement best corresponds to which of the following biomes?

   (1) tundra
   (2) grassland
   (3) taiga
   (4) tropical rain forest
   (5) desert

9. The deforestation of this biome would have the most detrimental consequences for the Earth's atmosphere.

   This statement best corresponds to which of the following biomes?

   (1) tundra
   (2) grassland
   (3) taiga
   (4) tropical rain forests
   (5) desert

10. Scientists use Punnett Squares to predict the probability of traits being passed on through inheritance. A Punnett Square gives all the possible genotypes of one particular mating.

Punnett Square

	E	e
E	EE	Ee
e	Ee	ee

E = hanging earlobes
e = attached earlobes

E = hanging earlobes
e = attached earlobes

The gene for hanging earlobes is dominant, while the gene for attached earlobes is recessive. For the Punnett Square shown, what is the probability of inheriting the gene for attached earlobes without expressing the trait?

(1) 100%
(2) 75 %
(3) 50%
(4) 25%
(5) 0%

Question 11 refers to the following information.

$6CO_2 + 6H_2O + \text{light energy} \rightarrow C_6H_{12}O_6 + 6O_2$

Humans inhale O_2 and exhale CO_2. Oxygen and carbon dioxide are both used in photosynthesis, which is one of the most important biochemical processes on Earth.

11. Which of the following are products of photosynthesis?

    (1) CO_2 and light energy

    (2) $C_6H_{12}O_6$ and O_2

    (3) $C_6H_{12}O_6$ only

    (4) O_2 only

    (5) CO_2, light energy, O_2, and $C_6H_{12}O_6$

12. An empty box is placed at the top of a ramp. After it is in place, the box does not move. Which of the following best explains why the box does not slide down the ramp?

    (1) The ramp is too steep.

    (2) The force of gravity is greater than the force of friction.

    (3) The force of friction is greater than the force of gravity.

    (4) The force of friction is weakened by the Earth's gravity.

    (5) The force of gravity is equal to the force of friction.

13. As part of a laboratory experiment, four students each measured the length of the same mouse four times. They recorded 16 slightly different lengths. All the work was done carefully and correctly. Their goal was to be as accurate as possible and keep experimental error to a minimum.

    Which of the following is the best method to report the length of the mouse?

    (1) Discard the longest of the lengths recorded.

    (2) Average all the recorded lengths.

    (3) Average only the longest and the shortest lengths.

    (4) Ask another student to measure the mouse.

    (5) Report only the first measurement.

Questions 14 and 15 refer to the following table.

Milk Chocolate Chip Cookies

Serving Size	1 cookie (70 g)
Nutritional facts	**Amount per serving**
Calories	300
Calories from fat	140
Total fat	15g
Saturated Fat	10g
Total carbohydrates	40g
Dietary Fiber	<1g
Cholesterol	45mg
Sodium	200mg
Sugars	20g
Protein	5g
	% of Daily Value
Vitamin A	8%
Calcium	3%
Vitamin C	0%
Iron	5%

14. How would you describe the nutritional value of a milk chocolate chip cookie based on the information presented in the table?

    (1) This is a snack high in nutritional value.

    (2) By observing the fat content and calories, this is not a healthy snack.

    (3) By observing the fiber and protein values, this is a healthy snack.

    (4) The % Daily Values indicate that this snack is well balanced.

    (5) This is a snack low in calories and sodium.

15. The recommended daily caloric intake for an average person is about 2,000 calories. One cookie makes up what percent of the recommended daily caloric intake of an average person?

    (1) 7%

    (2) 15%

    (3) 20%

    (4) 30%

    (5) 45%

Question 16 refers to the following information.

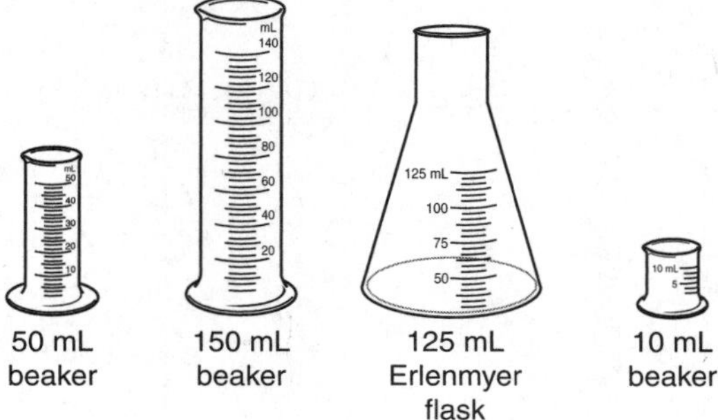

16. Using the laboratory equipment shown, which method would be the fastest way to measure out 350 mL of a liquid substance?

    (1) a + 2b

    (2) 2a +2c

    (3) a + b + c

    (4) 2b + 5d

    (5) 3c

Question 17 refers to the following information and graph.

Elements that are naturally abundant have existed on Earth for many billions of years. Radioactive elements that take a very long time to decay are said to have a very long half-life. Half-life is the time it takes for half of an amount of substance to decay. The most abundant form of uranium, uranium-238, has a half-life of 4.5 billion years. Because its half-life is so long, the amount of uranium-238 on Earth does not fluctuate substantially.

The graph below represents the radioactive decay of uranium-238.

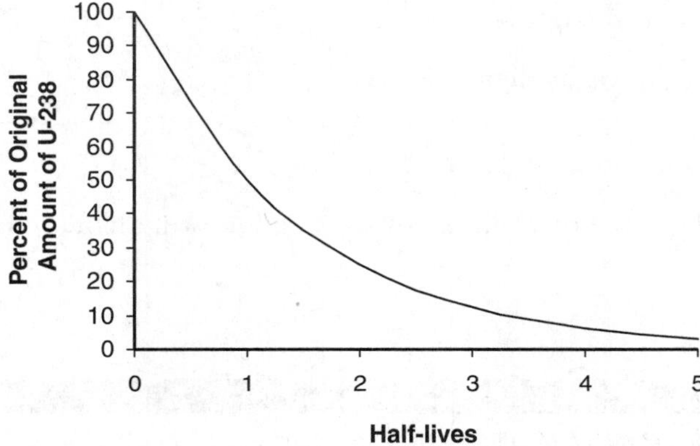

17. Approximately how much time must pass for only 25% of an original amount of uranium-238 to remain?

    (1) 2 billion years

    (2) 4 billion years

    (3) 7 billion years

    (4) 9 billion years

    (5) 20 billion years

Question 18 refers to the following table.

The Electromagnetic Spectrum

	Approximate Wavelength in Centimeters
Radio waves	10^4
Microwaves	1
Infrared waves	10^{-2}
Visible light	10^{-5}
Ultraviolet light	10^{-6}
X-Rays	10^{-8}
Gamma Rays	10^{-12}

18. Both bees and humans have three types of cones in their eyes to detect different wavelengths of light. Unlike humans, however, bees can detect ultraviolet light. Which of the following is the best reason for why bees can detect ultraviolet light and humans cannot?

    (1) Bees can detect waves with longer wavelengths than can humans.

    (2) Humans can detect a higher frequency of light than bees.

    (3) Bees can detect waves with shorter wavelengths than can humans.

    (4) Humans do not need night vision, but bees do.

    (5) Ultraviolet rays are part of the visible light spectrum.

Question 19 refers to the following information and table.

Some people believe that plant remedies provide healing power. The following table shows some uses for certain plants.

Selected Medicinal Herbs

Herb	Use
Aloe Vera	Applied to skin for healing and soothing of cuts, burns, and rashes
Echinacea	Capable of boosting the body's immune system; used to fight infections such as colds
Lemon Balm	When crushed and applied to skin, acts as mosquito repellent
Ginkgo Biloba	Used primarily to boost memory; also used to treat fatigue and asthma, among other ailments
Green Tea	Ingested to prevent and treat cancers; also used to protect skin from sun

19. Athlete's foot is a fungal infection that occurs primarily on the foot, but can occur all over the body. Its symptoms include scaling, dryness, and itching of the skin, as well as blisters, and inflammation. According to the table, which of the following plants would be the best remedy for athlete's foot?

    (1) Aloe Vera

    (2) Echinacea

    (3) Lemon Balm

    (4) Ginkgo Biloba

    (5) Green Tea

20. Meiosis is important in sexual reproduction among eukaryotes (primarily multicellular organisms). In this process, a cell containing two chromosomes divides into two cells that contain only one chromosome each. Three cells undergoing meiosis will yield cells containing a total of how many chromosomes?

    (1) 2

    (2) 3

    (3) 6

    (4) 9

    (5) 12

<u>Question 21</u> refers to the following information.

Smog is the name given to thick clouds of air pollutants that can be a major problem in urban areas such as London, Los Angeles, and Mexico City. This pollution is often caused by emissions of highly reactive chemicals, produced in part by human activity, into the atmosphere. Environmental causes can also be a factor in the creation of smog. Smog can lead to breathing problems and, if present in high levels, smog can be toxic to humans.

21. Which of the following choices would not be a source of smog?

    (1) sulfur dioxide particles released by volcanoes

    (2) the burning of coal, which releases smoke that mixes with pollution present in the air

    (3) forest fires releasing huge billows of dust particles and smoke into the atmosphere

    (4) fireworks producing smoke and chemicals

    (5) evaporation of water into rain clouds

Question 22 refers to the following information and graph.

Pollen bears the male reproductive cells of plants. Dust containing pollen can aggravate allergies in humans. The actual concentrations of three categories of pollen in a sample of local air were measured over two months.

The graph below shows the concentrations of birch, poplar/aspen, and spruce pollen measured during May and June.

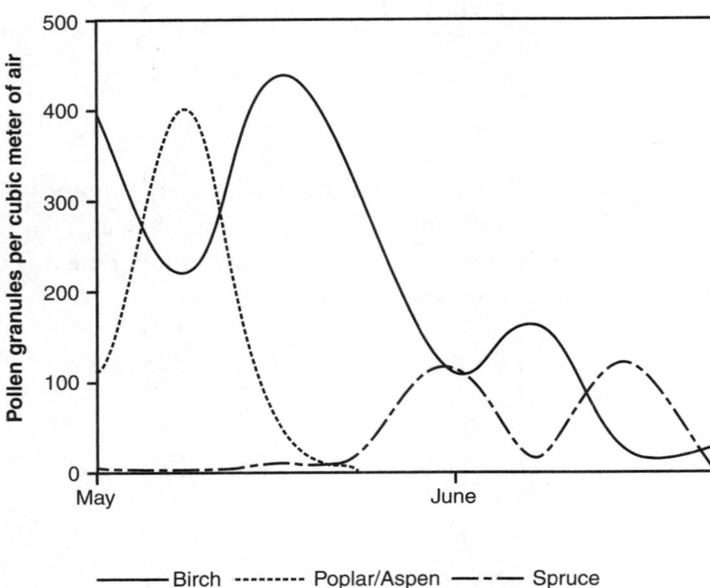

22. Approximately how many granules of birch pollen per cubic meter of air, on average, were present during May?

    (1) 450

    (2) 300

    (3) 150

    (4) 100

    (5) 50

<u>Question 23</u> refers to the following information and graph.

The pH scale measures how acidic or basic a substance is on a scale of 0 to 14. Lower numbers indicate increasing acidity, and higher numbers indicate increasing basicity. The ideal pH of swimming pool water is near 7.5. The pH of pool water has tremendous impact on the effectiveness of chlorine in keeping swimming pools sanitary.

The effectiveness of chlorine at different pH levels is shown below as a percentage of potential effectiveness.

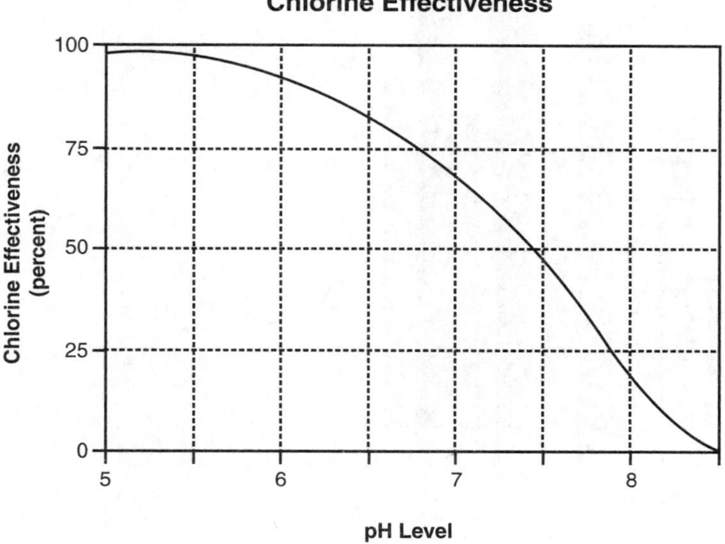

23. At approximately what pH level does the effectiveness of chlorine in a swimming pool fall below 75%?

    (1) below 5.0

    (2) between 6.5 and 7.0

    (3) between 7.0 and 7.5

    (4) between 7.5 and 8.0

    (5) above 8.0

Question 24 refers to the following information and graph.

Studies have shown that acid rain damages the skin pigmentation in certain species of salamanders. This results in an inability to change color and be protected from predators. Increased predation accounts for a decrease in the percentage of salamanders that survive to adulthood.

The following graph shows the percentage of salamanders that survive to adulthood.

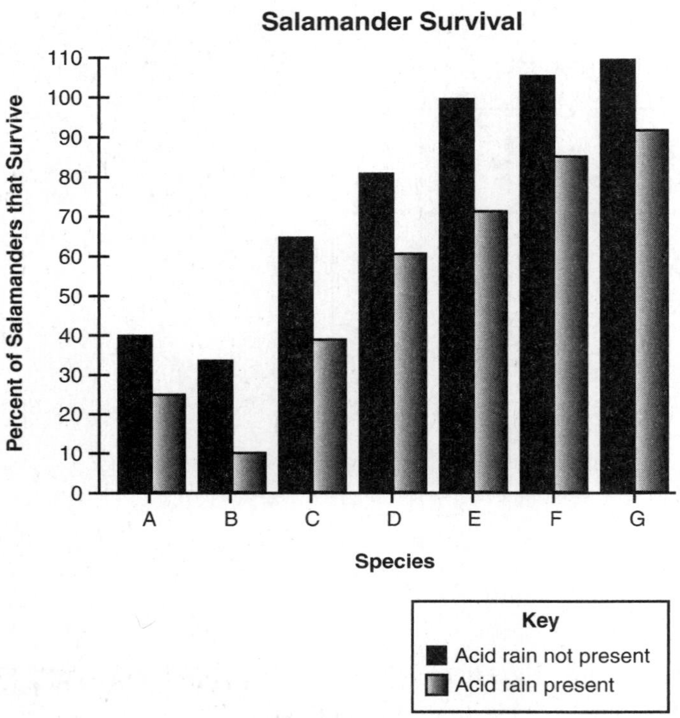

24. Which species had the fewest number of salamanders survive to adulthood?

    (1) Species A

    (2) Species B

    (3) Species F

    (4) Species G

    (5) Species D

25. The figure below shows predicted levels of acid rain over time in four geographic regions.

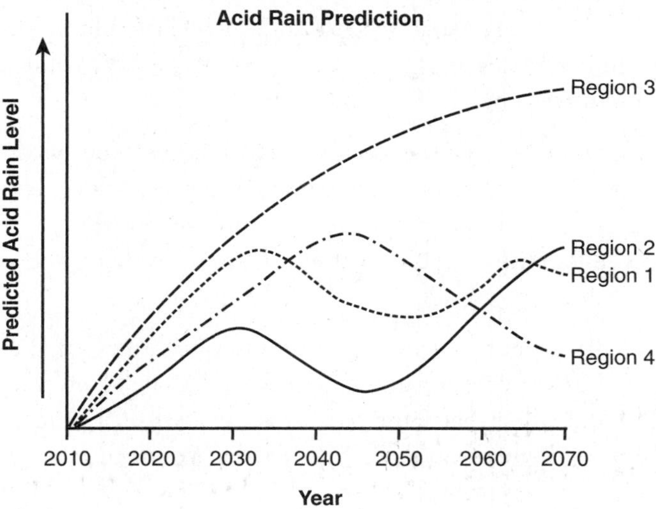

For which of the following regions is an increase in acid rain level NOT predicted for the time period 2050 to 2060?

(1) Region 1 only

(2) Region 2 and Region 3

(3) Region 3 only

(4) Region 4 only

(5) An increase in acid rain level is predicted for all regions.

Answers and Explanations

1. **The best answer is (2).** Radiation energy is also known as "light energy" and is the energy derived from sunlight. Photosynthesis is a chemical process during which chlorophyll in plants converts energy from the sun into usable energy in the form of sugars.

2. **The best answer is (4).** According to the figure, lunar soil is composed mainly of oxygen (42%), so you can eliminate any answer choice that does not include oxygen. This process of elimination leaves answer choices (1) and (4). Because the figure shows that lunar soil contains more silicon (21%) than iron (13%), answer choice (4) is correct.

3. **The best answer is (1).** According to the information, there are twice as many hydrogen atoms as nitrogen atoms in urea. Therefore, you can eliminate answer choices (4) and (5) because they indicate that there is one nitrogen atom and one hydrogen atom. Likewise, you can eliminate answer choice (3), which includes one nitrogen atom and four hydrogen atoms. The figure shows one oxygen atom and one carbon atom, which makes answer choice (1) correct.

4. **The best answer is (3).** The given information explains that tsunamis occur when the seafloor is temporarily elevated. The earth's surface, including the seafloor, is made up of tectonic plates, which can collide or separate, causing earthquakes. Answer choice (3) is best because it is the only one that addresses movement of the seafloor.

5. **The best answer is (1).** The Earth rotates, or turns, on its axis once every 24 hours as it revolves around the sun. When a certain part of the Earth is facing the sun, it will experience daylight, and when that same part is facing away from the sun, it will experience nighttime. The rotation of the Earth on its axis accounts for the shift between day and night.

6. **The best answer is (2).** A grassland is described as "a continuous stretch of grass." A grassland would best suit ranchers who need open space on which to graze their cattle.

7. **The best answer is (1).** A tundra is described as containing "many grasses, lichens, and mosses." Because Antarctica has rocky areas with nearly 700 algae species, it is likely a tundra.

8. **The best answer is (4).** A tropical rain forest is described as including "a great variety of flora and fauna." This suggests that a tropical rain forest is very diverse.

9. **The best answer is (3).** A taiga is described as "an area consisting primarily of coniferous forests; this is the largest terrestrial biome and also a major source of oxygen." Therefore, deforestation of these important biomes would likely result in detrimental consequences for the Earth and its occupants.

10. **The best answer is (3).** The Punnett Square shown characterizes the recessive gene as "e" and the dominant gene as "E." Only offspring that inherit both of the recessive genes from the parents will express the recessive trait. In other words, offspring characterized as "ee" will express the recessive trait. Therefore, 25% of the offspring will have attached earlobes (the recessive trait) and 75% of the offspring will have hanging earlobes (the dominant trait). However, 25% of the offspring with hanging earlobes receive two dominant genes, characterized as "EE." The remaining 50% inherit one recessive gene and one dominant gene, characterized as "Ee." This means that 50% of the offspring will inherit the recessive gene but will not express it.

11. **The best answer is (2).** During photosynthesis, oxygen and sugar are produced. The information to the right of the arrow indicates the products of the chemical process of photosynthesis.

12. **The best answer is (3).** Friction is the force resisting the motion of the box. Gravity is the force that would move the box down the ramp. If the friction between the box and the ramp overcomes the force of gravity, the box does not move.

13. **The best answer is (2).** Because each of the measurements is slightly different, the best method of reporting the length of the mouse is to take the average of all 16 measurements. This will provide the researchers with the most accurate estimate of the length of the mouse.

14. **The best answer is (2).** According to the nutritional information presented in the table, milk chocolate chip cookies are high in both calories and fat; therefore, they would not be a healthy snack.

15. **The best answer is (2).** To solve this problem, set up a proportion:

    calories in one cookie (300) to total daily calories (2,000) = unknown % (call it x%) to 100%

    This is equivalent to

    $$\frac{300}{2{,}000} = \frac{x}{100}$$

    Now, cross-multiply and solve for x, as follows:

    $$2{,}000x = 30{,}000$$

    $$x = \frac{30{,}000}{2{,}000} = 15$$

16. **The best answer is (1).** One way to eliminate answer choices is to count the number of steps involved in each. Answer choice (1) involves 3 steps; answer choice (2) involves 4 steps, so it can be eliminated; answer choice (3) involves 3 steps; answer choice (4) involves 7 steps, so it can be eliminated; and answer choice (5) involves 3 steps. Next, look at the remaining 3-step answer choices—(1), (3), and (5)—and determine which one results in 350 mL, as follows:

    Answer choice (1): 50 + 2(150) = 50 + 300 = 350. This is the correct answer.

    Answer choice (3): 50 + 150 + 125 = 325, which is incorrect.

    Answer choice (5): 3(125) = 375, which is incorrect.

17. **The best answer is (4).** The first step in answering this question is to locate 25% on the vertical (y) axis of the graph. Then follow along to the right to see where 25% intersects the curved line. Finally, follow down to see how many half-lives this intersection represents (on the horizontal, or x axis). It takes 2 half-lives to reduce the amount of U-238 to 25%. You are given that one half-life of U-238 is 4.5 billion years, so it would take $2 \times 4.5 = 9$ billion years.

18. **The best answer is (3).** Because the table lists wavelength in centimeters, and the question asks about different wavelengths, you can disregard any answer choice that does not refer to wavelengths. Frequency, night vision, and the visible light

spectrum are not relevant to the question asked. Therefore, based on the process of elimination, answer choice (3) must be correct. You also know that answer choice (3) is correct because ultraviolet light has a shorter wavelength (10^{-6}) than visible light (10^{-5}).

19. **The best answer is (1).** According to the table, aloe vera relieves cuts, burns, and rashes. It would be the best treatment for athlete's foot, whose symptoms include itching, blisters, and dryness.

20. **The best answer is (3).** Each of the three original cells contains two chromosomes. During meiosis, each of the three original cells divides into two cells, resulting in a total of six cells. Each of these six new cells contains one chromosome, which means that there are a total of six chromosomes at the end of meiosis.

21. **The best answer is (5).** According to the information, smog is a pollutant that results from certain chemical emissions, often brought on by human activity. The word smog comes from combining the words smoke and fog. The evaporation of water into rain clouds is a natural process that does not cause smog, so it is the correct answer.

22. **The best answer is (2).** To answer this question, first locate the solid line on the graph (according to the key, the solid line corresponds to birch pollen). The solid line fluctuates during May, indicating a range in the number of pollen granules from about 450 granules per m^3 at the highest point to about 100 granules per m^3 at the lowest point. You can roughly approximate the middle value of the curve by calculating the average: $(450 + 100) \div 2$, or $550 \div 2$, or 275 granules per m^3. This approximation is closest to 300.

23. **The best answer is (2).** To answer this question, follow the curved line on the graph until it intersects the dashed line that corresponds to 75% on the vertical (y) axis. This point of intersection is between 6.5 and 7 on the pH level scale (horizontal or x-axis).

24. **The best answer is (2).** According to the graph, Species B has the shortest bars whether or not acid rain was present. These bars correspond to the percent of salamanders surviving to adulthood on the vertical, or y-axis. Shorter bars mean a lower percent, which means that fewer Species B salamanders survived to adulthood.

25. **The best answer is (4).** According to the graph, Regions 1, 2, and 3 show an increase in predicted acid rain level from 2050 to 2060 (notice the upward slopes of the lines). Only Region 4 shows a decreasing trend over this time period.

What's Next?

Chapter 34, "Science Terms," includes a list of science terms that might appear on your GED Science Test. These terms have also likely been used throughout the chapters in Part VII.

34

CHAPTER THIRTY-FOUR

Science Terms

The terms included here are terms used in the book and on Official GED Practice Tests.

A

acceleration Rate of change of velocity.

acidity Having a pH less than 7 (contrast with alkalinity, which is having a pH greater than 7).

adaptation Genetic or behavioral change that improves an organism's survivability in its environment.

aerobic Involving the consumption of oxygen by the body.

aerosol Solid or liquid particles suspended in gas.

alkalinity Having a pH greater than 7 (contrast with acidity, which is having a pH less than 7).

altitude Elevation above a level of reference, usually given in feet above sea level.

amino acids Organic compounds that link together to form proteins.

anatomical Related to the structure of an organism.

anthropology Study of human origins, behavior, culture, and civilization.

antibiotic Drug that fights bacteria in the body.

antibody Protein produced by white blood cells for combating a specific microorganism in the body.

aqueduct Channel or pipe that primarily uses gravity to distribute water from a reservoir.

asphalt Soft, black material used in roofing and roadway paving.

asteroid Small celestial bodies that revolve around the sun, concentrated in the asteroid belt between the inner planets and the outer planets.

atmosphere Gas mixture surrounding a planet (earth's atmosphere contains nitrogen, oxygen, other trace gases, and water vapor).

atom Smallest unit of an element.

B

bacteria (pl. of "bacterium") Single-celled microorganisms without distinct nuclei.

basalt Solidified lava; a dense, dark gray, fine-grained igneous rock.

biology Science of life.

biomass Total mass of all the living matter within a given area.

biosynthesis Production of a chemical compound within the body.

boiling point Temperature a liquid must be to change states from liquid to gas.

brood Group of animal offspring, especially birds.

buoyant Tending to float.

by-product Something (often undesirable, like exhaust gases) created in the production of something else.

C

capacity Maximum amount that an object or area can hold; mental ability.

capillary Very slim tube; one of a network of extremely small blood vessels.

catalyst Agent that causes or speeds up a chemical reaction.

celestial Relating to the sky.

cell Smallest unit of an organism that can function independently and is surrounded by the cell membrane.

Celsius Temperature scale that measures the boiling point of water at 100° and its freezing point at 0°.

chemistry Science of matter and its interactions.

chlorophyll Green pigment produced in response to sunlight during photosynthesis.

cholesterol Soft, waxy compound produced in the body and found in the food we eat; important for cell membranes but has adverse effects on heart health when accumulated in excess.

combustion Burning, the chemical change of oxidation that produces light and heat.

comet Celestial body having an elongated, curved tail of dust and ice crystals that is seen only in the part of its orbit that is relatively close to the sun.

compost Organic material, such as food waste and grass clippings, that is broken down by worms, insects, fungi, and microorganisms to create a nutrient-rich soil additive.

compound Chemical combination of atoms of two or more elements that cannot be physically separated.

condensation Change of water vapor to liquid water by cooling.

continent One of the major land masses on earth: Africa, Antarctica, Asia, Australia, Europe, North America, or South America.

continental shelf Relatively shallow seafloor that surrounds a continent.

control group In experimentation, subjects that do not undergo the experiment in order to be compared to subjects who do undergo the experiment.

core Center of the earth, probably consisting of iron and nickel, with a liquid outer layer and a solid inner layer.

crust Upper layer of the earth consisting of rock and soil.

D

density Ratio of mass to volume.

diagram Chart or drawing that demonstrates how something works or the relationship among different things.

DNA Deoxyribonucleic acid, the basis for genetics that is contained in every cell nucleus of an organism.

E

earth and space science Study of the properties of the earth as a planet, the solar system, and the universe.

ecology Science of the relationships between organisms and their environments.

ecosystem Basic ecological unit, consisting of all the living things in a certain area and the nonliving elements with which they interact.

egg Ovum, the female reproductive cell having a half set of chromosomes that must fuse with a male reproductive cell to complete the set of chromosomes in a process called fertilization.

elastic Able to stretch and then return to its original shape.

electron Negatively charged subatomic particle.

element Unique type of matter distinguished by the number of protons (the atomic number) in the nucleus of the atom; for example, hydrogen (1), carbon (6), xenon (54).

emulsion State in which one liquid is suspended in another because the liquids will not dissolve in one another.

energy Ability of matter to do work.

eon The longest division of geologic time.

equilibrium State of balance.

erosion Wearing away, as of a hillside or rock formation, by outside forces such as wind or water.

evaporation Change from liquid to vapor form, usually by heating.

evolution Change in organisms due to adaptation and natural selection.

experiment Procedure for testing a hypothesis.

extinct No longer in existence.

F

Fahrenheit Temperature scale that measures the boiling point of water at 212° and its freezing point at 32°.

fat Semisolid organic compound rich in energy that is found throughout animal tissue and in seeds, nuts, and fruits.

fermentation Chemical process of breaking down an organic substance into simpler substances, such as the change of sugar to alcohol by yeast.

fetus Unborn young of an animal whose body resembles that of the adult.

force In physics, directional quantity that causes acceleration of an object.

fossil Remnant of an ancient organism preserved in the earth's crust.

fossil fuel Petroleum, coal, natural gas, and so on that are produced from the abundant remnants of ancient plant material within the earth's crust.

freezing Passage of a liquid to a solid due to loss of heat.

frequency How often something occurs; number of complete cycles per unit time, as with radio waves.

friction Force that resists motion of two objects in contact.

G

gas Neither solid nor liquid: a fluid (as air) that is not independent in shape or volume but tends to expand.

gene Specific portion of DNA that determines one or more characteristics in an organism.

genetics Branch of biology that deals with heredity, the inheritance of characteristics from one generation of a species to the next.

geology Study of the physical properties of Earth.

glacier Huge mass of ice formed from heavy, sustained snowfall that slowly flows over land.

gravity Force of attraction between two bodies of mass.

greenhouse effect Phenomenon of solar heat retention by so-called greenhouse gases in the atmosphere.

groundwater Water beneath the earth's surface that accumulates in aquifers and emerges many years later in artificial wells and natural springs.

gypsum A yellowish-white mineral used to make plaster.

H

hydraulic Operated by fluid pressure.

hydrocarbon Organic compound, such as methane or octane, found in fossil fuels.

I–J

igneous rock Hardened masses of minerals formed by the cooling and solidification of lava.

immerse Completely submerge.

incinerate To set fire to and burn until reduced to ashes.

inclined plane Simple machine of a surface set at an angle to the horizontal; for example, a screw or a wheelchair ramp.

infrared Light energy having a wavelength below the visible range that is experienced as heat.

inner planets Planets in the solar system closest to the sun: Mercury, Venus, Earth, and Mars.

isotope One of any atoms with identical atomic numbers and differing electrical charges.

joint Point of motion, such as an elbow or knee, between two or more bones.

K–L

laser Concentrated, highly directional beam of light, commonly used for pointing, surgical procedures, and cutting in manufacturing.

lever Simple machine using a rigid surface pivoting on a fixed point for lifting one end when the other end is pushed down.

life cycle Series of changes in an organism over the course of its life.

life science Broad category of science comprising biology, anthropology, medicine, and ecology.

ligament Tissue that connects bones to other bones or internal organs (contrast with *tendon*).

light Electromagnetic radiation that is perceived as different colors by the eye.

lipid Organic compound, such as fat, oil, or wax, that cannot be dissolved in water.

liquid Neither solid nor gas; a substance that takes the shape of its container.

lithosphere Outer part of the earth that includes the crust and upper mantle.

M

mammal Animal with a backbone and hair or fur that gives live birth and nurses young with milk from the mother.

mantle Layer of the earth between the core and the crust, containing rock and constituting about 70% of the earth's volume.

map Representation, usually on paper, of all or some of the surface of the earth.

marine Relating to the sea.

melting point Temperature at which a solid becomes a liquid.

metamorphic rock Hardened masses of minerals formed in conditions of great heat and pressure deep within the earth.

meteorology Study of weather and atmospheric phenomena.

microorganism Microscopic or very small living thing.

mitosis Process of cell division.

molecule Basic unit of a chemical, composed of two or more atoms.

molten Turned to liquid because of heat.

momentum Measure of motion equal to the product of an object's mass and velocity.

mutation Change in a gene.

N

natural resource Material gathered from the earth that has economic value.

natural selection Evolutionary process theorized by Charles Darwin, in which organisms well suited to their environment thrive and reproduce while poorly suited organisms tend to die off.

neural Relating to the nervous system.

neurological Relating to neurology, the study of the nervous system.

neutron Uncharged subatomic particle found in the nuclei of atoms.

nucleus (pl. "nuclei") In biology: core of a cell containing genetic material, such as DNA; in chemistry: center of an atom composed of protons and neutrons.

O

ore Mineral or combination of minerals from which valuable metal can be extracted.

organic Derived from living organisms.

organism Living thing: one of the plants, animals, fungi, bacteria, algae, or protozoa (animal-like single-celled organisms).

osmosis Passage of a fluid through a semipermeable membrane, as water through the cell membrane.

osteoporosis Disease causing brittle bones that are easily broken, occurring primarily in women following menopause.

outer planets Planets in the solar system farthest from the sun: Jupiter, Saturn, Uranus, Neptune, and (traditionally) Pluto.

oxidation Chemical combination of a substance with oxygen.

ozone Poisonous substance composed of molecules of three oxygen atoms found in a layer in the atmosphere crucial for protecting the earth from intense ultraviolet radiation from the sun.

P

paleontology Study of ancient life forms through fossils.

percolate Pass slowly through a porous substance.

pH Scale that measures how acidic or alkaline (basic) a substance is on a scale of 0 to 14. Lower numbers indicate increasing acidity, and higher numbers indicate increasing basicity.

phenomenon An event or circumstance that is significant or extraordinary.

photosynthesis The process by which plants turn carbon dioxide and water into energy with the aid of sunlight.

physics Study of interactions of matter and energy.

pigmentation Coloration.

pitch Characteristic of sound determined by its frequency.

pivot Turn against a fixed point (see also *lever*).

placenta Afterbirth; blood-filled organ that develops in female mammals during pregnancy that provides nourishment to the fetus through the umbilical cord and which is expelled following childbirth.

pollution Process or substance responsible for harmful contamination of air, land, or water.

primordial Happening first or very early.

protein Compound that consists of amino acids and plays various structural, mechanical, and nutritional roles within organisms.

Q–R

radiate Emit energy or light that extends from a single source.

renewable resource Natural material gathered from the earth that can be replenished in a relatively short period of time, for example, water or wood.

reservoir Artificial pond or lake, as behind a dam, used to retain water for public supply.

resonate Produce vibrations.

revolve To turn about a fixed point; for example, "The earth revolves around the sun." (see also *rotate*)

rift Split or a break, as in rock formations.

rotate To turn on an axis; for example, "The Earth rotates once each day." (see also *revolve*)

S

scientific method Standard procedure for scientific investigation: observe a phenomenon, form a hypothesis, design and perform an experiment, evaluate the results, and then form a conclusion.

sediment Solid materials that sink to the bottom of a liquid.

sedimentary rock Hardened masses of minerals formed from the deposition of particles over time, usually occurring under water.

seedling Young plant grown from seed.

solar system Group of planets and other celestial bodies and the sun around which they orbit.

solid Neither gas nor liquid; a substance of the same or coherent texture that holds its shape.

solute Dissolved substance.

solution Mixture of two or more substances.

sound Vibrations in air, a liquid, and so on that stimulate the auditory nerves and produce the sensation of hearing. (see also *sound* in Social Studies Terms)

species Particular type of organism.

spleen Vascular, ductless organ that is located in the left abdominal region close to the stomach and which performs important blood-cleaning and storage activities.

sprain Painful stretching or cutting of a ligament.

stratosphere Layer of the atmosphere between the troposphere and mesosphere, 10 to 30 kilometers above the earth.

synchronized Occurring at the same time and at the same rate.

synthesis Combining separate elements to form a whole.

T

tendon Tissue that connects muscles to bones (contrast with *ligament*).

terrestrial Relating to dry land as opposed to water; relating to the earth as opposed to other planets.

territorial Trait of an animal exhibiting behavior protective of its habitat .

toxin Poison.

translucent Allowing light to pass through, but clouded or frosted in such a way that objects on the other side are not clearly visible (often confused with "transparent," which means "clear").

U–Z

ultraviolet Relating to invisible rays of light with wavelengths above the visible spectrum but below x-rays and gamma rays.

uterus Womb; hollow muscular organ in female mammals in which a fetus develops during pregnancy.

vaporize Change into a cloud of diffused matter.

velocity Speed of motion.

virus Submicroscopic parasite that causes infection.

viscosity Fluid's resistance to flow.

voltage Measure of the energy of an electric current.

water cycle Phenomenon of water movement through continuous evaporation, condensation, and precipitation.

wavelength Distance between repeating peaks, or crests, of a wave.

work In physics, transfer of energy from one system to another.

zygote Cell formed from the fusion of the male and female reproductive cells that undergoes cell division to become a fetus.

PART VIII
Mathematics

This part of the book explains what the GED Mathematics Test involves and the basic mathematics skills you will need to succeed on this test. For about half of the questions you may use a calculator, and for the other half you may not. Most of the questions are in multiple-choice format, but there are some questions in two alternate free-response formats.

Part VIII includes the following chapters:

Chapter 35 About the Mathematics Test

Chapter 36 Number Relationships

Chapter 37 Basic Operations

Chapter 38 Symbols and Figuring

Chapter 39 Decimals

Chapter 40 Fractions

Chapter 41 Statistics

Chapter 42 Percentages

Chapter 43 Probability

Chapter 44 Data Analysis

Chapter 45 Measurement

Chapter 46 Algebra

Chapter 47 Geometry

Chapter 48 Mathematics Practice Questions and Answer Explanations

Chapter 49 Mathematics Terms

CHAPTER THIRTY-FIVE

About the Mathematics Test

The GED Mathematics Test consists of 50 questions that you will be given 90 minutes to complete. The test is divided into two parts, each having its own test booklet. On Part I, you may use a calculator, which the testing center provides. (Information about this calculator is found in Appendix B, "Calculator Directions.") On Part II, you may not use a calculator.

Questions cover the areas of math important in everyday life and in the workplace. Information on the test is given in words, diagrams, charts, graphs, and pictures. Your ability to do arithmetic, algebra, and geometry problems will be tested. Besides being able to recall particular mathematical operations, you must apply your problem-solving skills.

Generally, the mathematics question-answering process involves the following:

- Grasping precisely what the question is asking
- Identifying information you need to solve the problem
- Choosing the appropriate mathematical operation
- Computing the answer
- Checking the answer, first for overall reasonableness, and second, if necessary, for figuring errors

Most questions are in multiple-choice format, like the rest of the GED. Some questions, though, have an alternative format. On these questions, no answer choices are provided. You may have to enter a whole number, a decimal, or a fraction on a grid. Some questions require you to fill in a bubble on a coordinate grid that represents a point defined by an ordered pair.

Content areas covered include the following, each representing about an equal portion of the test:

- *Algebra, Functions, and Patterns*—Expressions and functions applied to data from words, tables, charts, and graphs
- *Data, Statistics, and Probability*—Measures of central tendency applied to data from words, tables, charts, and graphs
- *Measurement and Geometry*—Perpendicularity, parallelism, congruence, similarity, length, perimeter, area, volume, angle measure, capacity, weight, mass
- *Number Sense and Operations*—Whole numbers, integers, fractions, decimals, percents, exponents, scientific notation, ratios, proportions, and square roots

Creators of the GED Mathematics Test identify the general mathematics skills tested:

- Following mathematical procedures (15–25% of the test)
- Understanding concepts (25–35% of the test)
- Applying problem-solving skills (about 50% of the test)

As previously stated, a calculator provided by the testing center may be used on Part I of the GED Mathematics Test. The other resources available to you are a standard list of formulas found in the test booklets and scratch paper provided by the testing center. Use all these resources to maximize your score on the Mathematics Test.

What's Next?

The chapters that follow include information about each of the content areas and question types on the GED Mathematics Test. You will learn how to approach the questions with confidence.

CHAPTER THIRTY-SIX

Number Relationships

Like nearly all the math you will learn or have learned in your lifetime, GED math is based in the domain of real numbers. *Real numbers* is a technical term that describes all the numbers that may be expressed on a number line. This includes all the negative numbers, zero, and all the positive numbers.

Place Value

Place value refers to the value of digits within a number relative to their position. Starting from the decimal point and moving left, the values of the digits are ones, tens, hundreds, and so on. Starting from the decimal point and moving right, the values are tenths, hundredths, thousandths, and so on. Review more about this in Chapter 39, "Decimals."

The Number Line

All real numbers correspond to points on the number line, as shown in Figure 36.1.

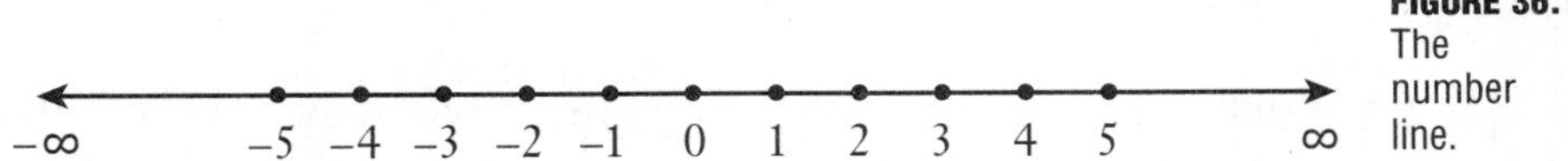

FIGURE 36.1 The number line.

All real numbers except zero are either positive or negative. On a number line, such as that shown in Figure 36.1, numbers that correspond to points to the right of zero are positive, and numbers that correspond to points to the left of zero are negative.

NOTE

The symbol ∞ represents infinity and indicates that the numbers continue to increase in value indefinitely as you move to the right along the number line, and they decrease in value indefinitely as you move to the left along the number line.

For any two numbers on the number line, the number to the left is always less than the number to the right.

Treating Positive and Negative Numbers

If you consider the number line, numbers represent distance from zero. Thus, –7 and 7 are both 7 units from zero, although in opposite directions. Adding them together equals zero. The concept of "distance from zero" is called *absolute value*, which is represented by enclosing a quantity in vertical bars. Absolute value can be defined as the numerical value of a real number without regard to its sign. This means that the absolute value of 10, $|10|$, is the same as the absolute value of –10, $|-10|$, in that they both equal 10. Think of it as the distance from –10 to 0 on the number line and the distance from 0 to 10 on the number line. Both distances equal 10 units.

Essentially, absolute value means "make negative numbers positive." See the following example:

$$|10 - 12| = |-2| = 2$$

The absolute value of 10 – 12 is the absolute value of –2, which is 2. This is true because –2 is 2 units to the left of 0 on the number line.

Just as with absolute value, it is crucial to treat the presence and absence of negative signs carefully. Subtracting a number and adding its negative are equivalent operations.

Example: $25 - 7 = 25 + -7$

Conversely, subtracting a negative number is like adding its negative (the negative of a negative number is positive).

Example: $25 - (-7) = 25 + 7$

Multiplication and division involving negative numbers can result in sign change. If you multiply two numbers with the same sign, the product, or result, is positive. If you multiply two numbers with different signs, the product is negative. The same is true of division.

Examples:

Multiplication:

$-2 \times -1 = 2$

$-2 \times -1 \times -1 = -2$

$-2 \times -1 \times -1 \times -1 = 2$

$-2 \times -1 \times -1 \times -1 \times -1 = -2$

Division:

$-2 \div -1 = 2$

$2 \div -1 = -2$

$-2 \div -1 = 2$

$-2 \div 1 = -2$

This shows that repeated multiplication by a negative number causes repeated sign changes. Notice how an even number of multiplications by a negative number yields a positive number, whereas an odd number of multiplications by a negative number yields a negative number.

NOTE

Any number or quantity multiplied by zero equals zero. Division by zero is undefined in the domain of real numbers. If you try to divide a number by 0 on a calculator, you will receive an error message.

Practice Questions

Test your knowledge of number relationships on the following questions.

1. Which number is greater, –50 or 35?
2. Which number is less, 2 or –1?
3. How many units is the number 14 away from 0 on the number line?
4. Where is the number –35 in relation to the number –37 on the number line?
5. What is the distance between 17 and –24 on the number line?
6. What is the distance between –105 and 16 on the number line?
7. $| -14 | = ?$
8. $21 - (-7) = ?$
9. $8 + -8 = ?$
10. $-5 \times -1 \times -1 \times -1 = ?$

Answers and Explanations

1. **The correct answer is 35.** Positive numbers are greater than negative numbers.
2. **The correct answer is –1.** Negative numbers are less than positive numbers.
3. **The correct answer is 14.** A number represents how many units more (in the case of positive numbers) or less (in the case of negative numbers) a quantity is than zero.
4. **The correct answer is "two units to the right."** Numbers decrease going left and increase going right. Remember that –35 is greater than –37.
5. **The correct answer is 41.** Imagine moving 24 units to the right of –24 to reach 0, and then moving 17 more units to the right of 0 to reach 17. $24 + 17 = 41$.
6. **The correct answer is 121.** Imagine moving 105 units to the right of –105 to reach 0, and then moving 16 more units to the right of 0 to reach 16. $105 + 16 = 121$.
7. **The correct answer is 14.** The absolute value of a negative number is its positive.
8. **The correct answer is 28.** Subtracting a negative number is equivalent to adding the number's positive. $21 + 7 = 28$

9. **The correct answer is 0.** Adding a negative number is equivalent to subtracting the number's positive. 8 – 8 = 0

10. **The correct answer is 5.** Remember that repeatedly multiplying a number by a negative number causes the result to switch back and forth between negative and positive. In this case, you start with a negative number, –5. Multiplying by –1 doesn't change the numeral 5, but does result in a sign change. Two more multiplications by –1 result in two more sign changes. The final result is the positive number 5.

What's Next?

Chapter 37, "Basic Operations," includes an introduction to basic mathematical operations, as well as some practice questions.

37

CHAPTER THIRTY-SEVEN

Basic Operations

Arithmetic is the simplest and most elementary branch of mathematics. It is difficult to imagine a day when you wouldn't have to perform some basic arithmetic. Imagine sitting at a restaurant with some friends. When the bill comes, you find the prices of the items you ordered and use addition to find their sum. You can subtract that sum from the total on the bill to find what the other people owe. Finally, you use multiplication to compute the server's tip based on a rate such as 15%. When you calculate how much tip to leave, you can divide that amount by the number of people at the table to find how much each person should contribute. A scenario like this shows that simple mathematical skills are crucial in life. Practicing arithmetic will help you quickly perform some operations mentally, saving you time on the GED.

Addition and Subtraction

Addition is the combination of two numbers into a single number. This operation is indicated by the plus sign (+). Addition is commutative (orders that numbers are written in can be reversed) and associative (grouping by parentheses can be changed), so the order in which numbers are added does not matter. The result of addition is called the *sum*.

Example:

$10 + 16 = 16 + 10 = 26$

Subtraction, indicated by the minus sign (–), yields the *difference* between two numbers. It is essentially the opposite of addition. Unlike addition, however, subtraction is neither commutative nor associative—order matters.

Example:

$10 - 16 = -6$

$16 - 10 = 6$

Multiplication and Division

Multiplication essentially represents repeated addition of one number. On the GED, this operation is indicated by the multiplication sign (×). In addition, multiplication is implied when terms are written next to each other with only an intervening parenthesis or with no symbol at all. Two numbers being multiplied are called *factors*, and the result of multiplication is called the *product*.

Example:

$3 \times a = 3a = 3(a)$

The repeated addition represented by this multiplication is $a + a + a$.

Because multiplication is like repeated addition, it is commutative and associative like addition. Multiplication is also distributive over addition and subtraction, which means that multiplication of a quantity by a number represents the sum of the products of that number and each term of the quantity.

Example:

$2(a - 6b + 4c) = 2a - 12b + 8c$

$2a - (2 \times 6)b + (2 \times 4)c =$

To distribute multiplication by 2 over this quantity, multiply each of the terms within the quantity by 2, paying close attention to positive and negative signs.

Division is the opposite of multiplication, meaning that division by some number x is equivalent to multiplication by $1/x$. Division is indicated by the division sign (÷) or the fraction bar. The result of the operation is called the *quotient*. In fractions, the quotient is the numerator (top number) divided by the denominator (bottom number).

Example:

$\frac{12x}{3} = 4x$

Problem-Solving Strategies

Most of the calculations are fairly simple and will not require the use of a calculator. If you do use your calculator, be sure that you have a good idea of what your answer should look like ahead of time. If the answer you get from your calculator is not at least in the ballpark that you expected, try again. The following are problem-solving strategies for basic operations.

Multistep Problems

If the problem requires three steps to reach a solution and you completed only two of the steps, it is likely that the answer you arrived at will be one of the choices. However, it will not be the correct choice! Don't quit early—reason your way through the problem so that it makes sense. Keep in mind, though, that these questions have been designed to take an average of 1–8 minutes each to complete. They do not involve intensive calculations.

Word Problems

Simple arithmetic on the GED is often obscured by the wording of the problems. Sometimes, numbers that are not necessary for the calculation are inserted to lead you astray. The most effective way of maintaining accuracy in math word problems is to translate the sentences directly into mathematical symbols as you read.

Example:

A pharmacy buys aspirin from the manufacturer for $3.00 per bottle and resells it to customers for $8.00 per bottle. The pharmacy has a sale that offers "Take 25% off the retail price of aspirin." What is the sale price of a bottle of aspirin?

First, read the problem and restate what it is asking in simpler terms: "How much is aspirin during this sale?" If you did not notice at first, this simple restatement should reveal that the wholesale price of $3.00 given in the problem is irrelevant.

Second, assign variables to data and formulate an equation:

p (retail price) = 8

s (sale price) = $p - .25p = .75p$

Now solve for s:

$s = .75 \times 8$

$s = 6$

Therefore, the sale price of a bottle of aspirin is $6.00.

Extra or Missing Information

Remember that you can mark up your scratch paper as much as you want, so take advantage of that right to minimize your computational errors. Likewise, if you make mental calculations, write them down quickly and clearly on scratch paper.

Using Sketches and Diagrams

Visualizing the problem can help you understand the mathematical operations required to answer it. This strategy should not take a lot of time, yet it can prevent careless errors. Your sketches can be quick and even a little messy. Sometimes the test gives you a figure, but many times you have to make your own.

Examples of drawings that can quickly and effectively be made during testing are geometric figures (such as rectangles and triangles), points on a coordinate plane, number lines, and data arranged in tables.

Especially with geometrical figures, as soon as you calculate a missing value, write it on your scratch paper. You also might want to redraw some figures there, so that you can insert measurements and so on.

Practice Questions

Test your knowledge of basic operations on the following questions.

1. 300 – 215 = ?
2. –31 – 28 = ?
3. 16 + 97 = ?
4. –7 × –20 = ?
5. $4a$ × –4 = ?
6. 120 ÷ 3 × 2 = ?
7. 48 ÷ 16 = ?
8. Ryan, John, Kyle, and Jeremy are in a relay race. Ryan runs the first leg in 11 seconds, John runs the second leg in 10 seconds, Kyle runs the third leg in 9 seconds, and Jeremy runs the last leg in 13 seconds. If they finished in second place, behind the first-place team by 3 seconds, how long, in seconds, did it take the first-place team to complete the race?
9. Aaron and Amanda are moving boxes to their new house. Aaron's truck can carry 14 boxes, and Amanda's car can carry 5 boxes. After three trips each, there are 7 boxes remaining to be moved. How many total boxes do Aaron and Amanda have?
10. Jessica is a teacher and wants to provide her 25 students with a healthy snack. She decides to pick apples for them at the local orchard. The orchard is 4 acres in area, and there are 15 trees per acre. If Jessica collects 5 apples from each tree, how many apples would she be able to give to each of her students?

Answers and Explanations

1. **The correct answer is 85.** This is the difference between 300 and 215. In other words, 300 – 215 = 85.
2. **The correct answer is –59.** This is the difference between –38 and 21. In other words, –38 – 21 = –59. Pay close attention to the negative sign because without it, subtraction from a negative number would seem to make the result greater, not less.
3. **The correct answer is 113.** This is the sum of 16 and 97. In other words, 16 + 97 = 113.
4. **The correct answer is 140.** This is the product of –7 and –20. Remember that multiplying two negative numbers results in a positive number.
5. **The correct answer is –16*a*.** Multiplying a positive quantity by a negative number results in a negative quantity.

6. **The correct answer is 80.** Perform the calculations from left to right: 120 divided by 3 equals 40, and 40 times 2 equals 80.
7. **The correct answer is 3.** This is the quotient of 48 and 16, meaning that 16 can be divided exactly 3 times into 48.
8. **The correct answer is 40.** First, add all the individual times together to get the team's total time:

   $11 + 10 + 9 + 13 = 43$

   Because the first-place team was 3 seconds faster, the first team's total time was 3 seconds less than 43 seconds.

   $43 - 3 = 40$
9. **The correct answer is 64.** First, calculate the total number of boxes the two people have already moved during the three trips:

   Aaron can move 14 boxes per trip: $14 \times 3 = 42$

   Amanda can move 5 boxes per trip: $5 \times 3 = 15$

   Therefore, the sum of 42 and 15 equals the total number of boxes moved so far, 57.

   If 7 boxes remain, the total number of boxes Aaron and Amanda have equals the number already moved plus 7:

   $57 + 7 = 64$
10. **The correct answer is 12.** Begin by calculating the total number of apples Jessica picks:

    There are 15 trees per acre in a 4-acre orchard:

    $15 \times 4 = 60$ total trees

    Jessica collects 5 apples from each tree:

    $5 \times 60 = 300$ total apples

    There are 25 students in the class, and the apples will be divided equally among them:

    $300 \div 25 = 12$ apples per student

What's Next?

Chapter 38, "Symbols and Figuring," includes an introduction to mathematical symbols and figuring, as well as some practice questions. You should become comfortable in recognizing and using the math notation covered in Chapter 38.

38

CHAPTER THIRTY-EIGHT

Symbols and Figuring

Chapter 37 reviews the basic arithmetic operations of addition and subtraction, multiplication and division, and their symbols (+, –, ×, ÷ or fraction bar). This chapter will add exponents, square roots, and parentheses to the inventory of math notation you should be comfortable using on the GED.

Exponents and Square Roots

Exponents are the superscript numbers indicating *powers* of a *base* number. Powers in mathematics represent repeated multiplications of a base number by itself. For example, 2^3 ("two to the third power") represents $2 \times 2 \times 2$, which equals 8. The power of two is called the *square*. For example, 3^2 ("three squared") represents 3×3, which equals 9. The following are explanations of the treatment of exponents:

1. $a^m \times a^n = a^{(m+n)}$

   When you multiply the same base number raised to any power, add the exponents. For example: $3^2 \times 3^4 = 3^6$. Likewise, $3^6 = 3^2 \times 3^4$; $3^6 = 3^1 \times 3^5$; and $3^6 = 3^3 \times 3^3$.

2. $(a^m)^n = a^{mn}$

   When you raise an exponential expression to a power, multiply the exponent and power. For example: $(3^2)^4 = 3^8$. Likewise, $3^8 = (3^4)^2$; $3^8 = (3^1)^8$; $3^8 = (3^8)^1$, and so on.

3. $(ab)^m = a^m \times b^m$

   When you multiply two different base numbers and raise the product to a power, the product is equivalent to raising each number to the power and multiplying the exponential expressions. For example: $(3 \times 2)^2 = 3^2 \times 2^2$, which equals 9×4, or 36.

4. $\left[\frac{a}{b}\right]^m = \frac{a^m}{b^m}$

   When you divide two different base numbers and raise the quotient to a power, the result is equivalent to the quotient of the base numbers, each raised to the power. For example: $\left(\frac{2}{3}\right)^2 = \frac{2^2}{3^2}$, or $\frac{4}{9}$.

5. $a^0 = 1$, when $a \neq 0$

   When you raise any number except 0 to the power of 0, the result is always 1. For example: $10^0 = 1$; $(-952)^0 = 1$, and so on.

6. $a^{-m} = \frac{1}{a^m}$, when $a \neq 0$

   When you raise a number to a negative power, the result is equivalent to the inverse (1 over the number) raised to the power made positive. For example: $3^{-2} = \frac{1}{3^2} = 1/9$.

Raising a negative number to an even-numbered power yields a positive result. For example, $(-2)^2 = 4$ and $(-2)^4 = 16$.

The square root of a number *n* is written as $\sqrt{n}$, which represents the nonnegative value *a* that fulfills the expression $a^2 = n$. For example, "the square root of 5" is expressed as $\sqrt{5}$, and $(\sqrt{5})^2 = 5$. Square roots inevitably arise when dealing with right triangles and the Pythagorean Relationship (see Chapter 47, "Geometry") on the GED, so make sure you are comfortable with them.

Parentheses

Mathematical expressions can be written with parentheses to indicate the order in which operations should be performed. Expressions within parentheses are called *quantities*. Mathematical operations in quantities are performed first, before any operations between quantities.

Errors are common in dealing with distribution of signs (positive or negative) over quantities. Remember that subtraction of a negative number is like addition of that number's positive.

Example:

$2 - (10a + 6b - 2.5c + 65 - 8)$

First, perform the operations within the parentheses. Here the terms with variables are simplified, but subtraction of 8 from 65 is possible.

$2 - (10a + 6b - 2.5c + 57)$

Second, distribute the minus sign over the quantity.

$2 - 10a - 6b - (-2.5c) - 57$

Change subtraction of the negative to addition of the positive, and then perform the subtraction of 57 from 2.

$-10a - 6b + 2.5c - 55$

Order of Operations

Following is a description of the correct order in which to perform mathematical operations. The acronym PEMDAS stands for Parentheses, Exponents, Multiplication/Division, Addition/Subtraction. It should help you to remember to do operations in the correct order, as follows:

1. P—Do the operations within the *parentheses*, if there are any.
2. E—Do the *exponents*, if there are any.
3. M/D—Do the *multiplication* and *division*, in order from left to right.
4. A/S—Do the *addition* and *subtraction*, in order from left to right.

Using Formulas

Formulas are simplified equations that allow you to substitute some value or values for variables to compute some result. The formulas you should know for the GED are reviewed throughout the math chapters and are summarized in Appendix D, "Mathematics Formulas."

EXAM PREP StudyTIP

The official GED formula sheet is printed in the test booklet for each part of the GED Mathematics Test.

Practice Questions

Test your knowledge of exponents, parentheses, and the order of operations on the following questions. Do not use a calculator on 1 through 7. Use a calculator on 8 through 10 if you need to; however, they are good practice of "mental math."

1. $33^{12} \times 33^5 = ?$ (Simplify only to a number with an exponent.)
2. $5^4 \times 12^4 = ?$ (Simplify only to a number with an exponent.)
3. $(19^5)^3 = ?$ (Simplify only to a number with an exponent.)
4. $\left(\frac{1}{21}\right)^{-6} = ?$ (Simplify only to a number with an exponent.)
5. $4^{-2} = ?$ (Simplify completely.)
6. $(-5)^3 = ?$ (Simplify completely.)
7. $2 - (6x + 18 + 4y - 39z) = ?$
8. $3(4+12) - 2 \times 3^2 = ?$
9. $(26 - 32)^2 \times (5^2 - 23) \div 4 = ?$
10. $4(2^3 - 35 \div 7)^2 + 5(61 + 11 \times 8) = ?$

Answers and Explanations

1. **The correct answer is 33^{17}.** When you multiply the same base number raised to any power, add the exponents.
2. **The correct answer is 60^4.** When you multiply two numbers or expressions with identical powers, multiply the base numbers.
3. **The correct answer is 19^{15}.** When you raise an expression with an exponent to another power, multiply the two exponents.

4. **The correct answer is 21^6.** When you raise a number to a negative power, the result is equivalent to the inverse (1 over the number) raised to the same power made positive. To find the inverse of a fraction, flip the numerator and denominator.

5. **The correct answer is $\frac{1}{16}$.** When you raise a number to a negative power, the result is equivalent to 1 over the number raised to the same positive power.

6. **The correct answer is –125.** Recall how sign change occurs with every multiplication of a number by a negative number. Therefore, a negative number raised to an odd power results in a negative answer.

7. **The correct answer is $-6x - 4y + 39z - 16$.** Distribute the subtraction sign preceding the parentheses through the quantity inside of parentheses:

   $2 - 6x - 18 - 4y - (-39z)$

   Change subtraction of the negative to addition of the positive:

   $2 - 6x - 18 - 4y + 39z$

   Reorder the terms by grouping and ordering the variables and then place constants at the end:

   $-6x - 4y + 39z + 2 - 18$

   Perform the subtraction of 18 from 2.

   $-6x - 4y + 39z - 16$

8. **The correct answer is 30.** Use the proper order of operations to obtain the answer. Begin by performing the operation in parentheses:

   $3(4 + 12) - 2 \times 3^2$

   $3(16) - 2 \times 3^2$

   Simplify the number with the exponent:

   $3(16) - 2 \times 9$

   Perform the multiplications:

   $48 - 18$

   Perform the subtraction:

   30

9. **The correct answer is 18.** Use the proper order of operations to obtain the answer. Begin by performing the operations in parentheses, starting with the exponent and then performing the subtraction:

   $(26 - 32)^2 \times (5^2 - 23) \div 4$

   $(26 - 32)^2 \times (25 - 23) \div 4$ [Exponent within parentheses first.]

   $(-6)^2 \times 2 \div 4$ [Subtraction within quantities second.]

Simplify the number with the exponent (remember that a negative times a negative yields a positive):

$36 \times 2 \div 4$

Perform the multiplication and division as written, left to right:

$72 \div 4$

18

10. **The correct answer is 781.** Use the proper order of operations to obtain the answer. Begin by performing the operations in parentheses following the order of operations:

$4(2^3 - 35 \div 7)^2 + 5(61 + 11 \times 8)$

$4(8 - 35 \div 7)^2 + 5(61 + 11 \times 8)$ [Exponent within parentheses first.]

$4(8 - 5)^2 + 5(61 + 88)$ [Multiplication and division within parentheses second.]

$4(3)^2 + 5(149)$ [Addition and subtraction within parentheses last.]

Now that the quantities in parentheses are simplified, simplify the whole expression following the order of operations:

$4(3)^2 + 5(149)$

$4(9) + 5(149)$ [Exponent first.]

$36 + 745$ [Multiplication second.]

781 [Addition last.]

What's Next?

Chapter 39, "Decimals," includes an introduction to decimals and estimation, as well as some practice questions.

39

CHAPTER THIRTY-NINE

Decimals

The modern number system is called the decimal, or base 10, system. This probably originated because humans normally have a total of 10 digits on their hands. The decimal system is a positional number system, meaning the digits 0, 1, 2, 3, 4, 5, 6, 7, 8, and 9 are set in different positions (for example, units or ones, tens, hundreds, thousands) to indicate a certain multiplier of 10. Each place to the left is 10 times greater than the previous place. Conversely, each place to the right is 10 times less than the previous place. A decimal point marks the space between the single unit's place and the tenth's place.

Decimals Defined

A number can be thought of as the sum of the values of each digit times its multiplier.

Example:

$107.986 = (1 \times 100) + (0 \times 10) + (7 \times 1) + (9 \times \frac{1}{10}) + (8 \times \frac{1}{100}) + (6 \times \frac{1}{1000})$

Multiplying a number by 10 can be thought of as simply moving the decimal point one place to the right. If the number is an integer (no decimal point), add a zero to the end each time you multiply by 10.

Examples:

$26.82 \times 10 = 268.2$

$15 \times 10 = 150$

Conversely, division by 10 can be thought of as moving the decimal point one place to the left.

Examples:

$26.82 \div 10 = 2.682$

$15 \div 10 = 1.5$

Comparing Decimals

A number can contain any combination and number of digits, but the location of the decimal point is the crucial feature to determine how great or small a value is. In fact, the ratio between two numbers remains constant when the decimal point is shifted an equal number of places left or right in each. For example, to gather a rough idea of how many times greater one number is than another, it might be helpful to shift decimal places in the numbers:

How many times greater is 350 than 0.0001?

To solve this, shift the decimal places in each number until 0.0001 equals 1. This means you shift both decimal points right four places. Therefore, 350 is 3,500,000 times greater than 0.0001.

Rounding

Digits to the right of the decimal point may repeat infinitely, as in the decimal equivalent of $\frac{1}{3}$, 0.3333333... or $\frac{1}{7}$, 0.142857142857.... Other numbers may be irrational, meaning the digits continue infinitely but do not repeat, as in the decimal equivalent of $\sqrt{2}$, 1.414213.... The number pi (π) crucial to geometry is an irrational number, so an estimated value of it can be used.

When digits at the end of a number are cut off, the number is said to be *truncated*. In many cases, though, rounding is a better means of ending lengthy (or infinitely long) decimals.

When you round a number, you round it to a certain decimal place. Consider the example of pi:

$\pi = 3.14159...$

In most math figuring, pi rounded to the hundredths place is suitably precise. To round pi to the hundredths place, compare the digit in the hundredths place to the digit in the place immediately to the right (the thousandths place). If the thousandths digit is 5 or greater, round the number up by adding 1 to the hundredths digit and truncating the rest of the digits to the right. If the thousandths digit is 4 or less, round the number down by leaving the hundredths digit the same and truncating the rest of the digits to the right. Therefore, pi rounded to the hundredths place is 3.14.

See the following additional examples of rounding:

39.9 rounded to the nearest whole number = 40.

$4.25 rounded to the nearest dollar = $4.00

8.18965 rounded to the nearest tenth = 8.2

Scientific Notation

Scientists and engineers often deal with very large and very small numbers. Instead of dealing with many zeros, they can use scientific notation to express numbers. Scientific notation represents a number with many digits, as to a number between 1 and 10 times a power of 10.

Example: $0.0000256 = 2.56 \times 10^{-5}$

This very small number is easier to manipulate when expressed in scientific notation.

To form scientific notation, shift the decimal point right or left to create a number between 1 and 10. Multiply this number by 10 raised to the power of how many places you shifted the decimal point. If you shifted it right, make the power negative. If you shifted the decimal point left, make the power positive.

Here are some examples of very large or very small numbers expressed in scientific notation. Note how the number of digits indicates how precise the value is. (Many large or small measurements from nature are only estimations.)

92.95×10^{6} mi: Average distance from Earth to the sun.

1.41×10^{18} km^3: Volume of the sun.

2.99×10^{-23} g: Mass of a water molecule.

7×10^{-6} m: Typical human red blood cell size.

Addition and Subtraction of Decimals

When adding and subtracting decimals, be sure to line up the decimal points.

For example: $\begin{array}{r} 36.78 \\ +113.219 \\ \hline 149.999 \end{array}$ $\quad$ $\begin{array}{r} 78.90 \\ -23.42 \\ \hline 55.48 \end{array}$

To add, begin with the rightmost column and record each column's sum moving left. If a sum is 10 or greater, record the unit's digit, "carry" the 1 to the next column, and include it in that next sum.

To subtract, begin with the rightmost column and record the difference between the top digit and the bottom digit. If the bottom digit is greater than the top digit, "borrow" 10 from the column to the left. For example, in the hundredths column of the preceding subtraction example, 2 is greater than 0, so borrow 10 from the tenths column. Change the 0 hundredths to 10, and the 9 tenths you "borrowed" from to 8, and continue the subtraction.

Multiplying and Dividing Decimals

When multiplying decimals, it is not necessary to line up the decimal points. Simply multiply the numbers, and then count the total number of places to the right of the decimal points in the decimals being multiplied to determine placement of the decimal point in the product.

For example: $173.248 \times .35 = ?$

Set up the numbers one above the other:

```
  173.248
×     .35
```

Begin with the rightmost digit of the bottom number. Multiply that digit by each digit of the top number, moving right to left. If a product is 10 or greater, record the units digit, "carry" the other digits to the next column, and then *add* (not multiply!) them to the next product. After you finish with the rightmost digit, repeat this procedure with the next digit to the left, recording the products below the first set of products and beginning in the next column to the left. Continue until you've multiplied every digit on the bottom with every digit on the top. Your work will look like this:

```
  173.248
×     .35
   866240
  519744
```

Now, add those two numbers, keeping in mind that the alignment of the columns is crucial. (You may want to write a 0 in decimal places left empty by the left shift.)

```
   866240
+5197440
  6063680
```

Remember that the placement of the decimal point depends on how many decimal places right of the decimal point are in the numbers you multiplied. The number 173.248 has 3 such places and .35 has 2 such places. The sum is 5, so count 5 decimals places from the right of the product and insert the decimal point.

60.63680

This number can be further simplified by eliminating the final zero: 60.6368

When dividing decimals, first move the decimal point in the divisor to the right until the divisor becomes an integer. Then move the decimal point in the dividend the same number of places.

> For example: 58.345 ÷ 3.21 = 5834.5 ÷ 321 (The decimal point was moved two places to the right.)

Now set up the problem using the long division bracket:

$321\overline{)5834.5} = ?$

To divide, work left to right. Begin by considering the entire divisor (321) and leftmost digit of the dividend (5). Ask yourself, "How many times can 321 be divided *completely* into 5?" Clearly, the answer is 0, so move on.

Next, consider the divisor and the left two digits of the dividend (58). The divisor 321 cannot divide even once into 58, so move on.

Next, consider the divisor and the left three digits of the dividend (583). The divisor 321 can divide once into 583, so mark a 1 above the tens place of the dividend.

```
        1
321 )5834.5
```

Multiply 1 by 321 and write the product, 321, below 583. Calculate the difference, and then bring down the next digit to the right in the dividend.

```
        1
321 )5834.5
     -321↓
      2624
```

Next, determine how many times 321 can divide into 2624. To do this mentally, use the guess-and-check method. Approximate a number, check the result, and change your guess accordingly. For example, you may guess 10, resulting in $321 \times 10 = 3210$, so you need to guess lower. Try 9: you can see you need to guess even lower without performing the complete multiplication because $300 \times 9 = 2700$, which still exceeds 2624. Try 8—multiply 8 by 321 mentally this way: $8 \times 300 = 2400$, $8 \times 20 = 160$, and $8 \times 1 = 8$. Now add them up: $2400 + 160 + 8 = 2568$. This number confirms that 321 divides 8 times into 2624. Fill in 8 above the bracket in the units place. Write the product of 8 and 321 below 2624 and subtract as you did before.

Repeat this procedure for as many decimal places as you want to obtain. If you run out of digits to bring down, bring down some zeros. Remember that 1930 = 1930.00. Here, the result is computed to the thousandths place.

```
        18.176
321 )5834.5
     -321↓
      2624
     -2568↓
        565
       -321↓
        2440
       -2247↓
         1930
```

NOTE

If your remainder is zero, you have computed the precise answer and can stop.

Estimation

You probably estimate a lot of values in a given day because making precise calculations is not always necessary. For example, with so many prices in stores ending with 95 or 99 cents, it is reasonable to round the prices up to the next dollar if you were keeping track of many different prices, or if you wanted to know how much a certain quantity of some product would cost in total.

Consider this situation:

> Fresh chicken is sold for \$1.95 per pound. How much would 8 pounds cost?

Instead of first finding the precise answer, make an estimate. Consider that the chicken costs exactly \$2.00 per pound. The total cost estimate, therefore, is \$2.00 × 8 = \$16.00. The precise total cost is \$1.95 × 8 = \$15.60. The estimate of \$16.00 is probably close enough for your purposes.

EXAM PREP Study TIP

The GED will also use words such as "approximately" and "nearest" to indicate that you should estimate.

On the GED, estimate problems to determine a good "ballpark" figure for your answer. Answer choices that appear way off can then be eliminated. Use rounding to create numbers that are easier in math operations.

Practice Questions

Practice manipulating decimals with these problems. Do not use a calculator.

1. Without writing out calculations, solve the expression 56,251.34 ÷ 100.
2. How many times greater than .001 is 1.2369?
3. Round 23.72063 to the nearest thousandth.
4. Write the decimal 2,543.112 in scientific notation.
5. Write the number 5.78×10^{-4} in decimal form.
6. 56.324 + 198.4 = ?
7. 1,067.83 – 253.5 = ?
8. 0.3 × 2.4 = ?
9. 182.5 ÷ 3.5 = ? (Round your answer to the nearest tenth.)
10. Dennis is buying shirts at the local department store. He wants to purchase four shirts costing \$23.05 each. Approximately how much should Dennis expect to pay?

Answers and Explanations

1. **The correct answer is 562.5134.** Dividing by 10 equates to moving the decimal point one place to the left, so dividing by 100 equates to moving the decimal point two places to the left.
2. **The correct answer is 1,236.9.** Shift both decimal points three places to the right to get the values 1 and 1,236.9.
3. **The correct answer is 23.721.** The digit in the thousandths place is 0. The digit to the right, 6, is between 5 and 9, so you must round the 0 thousandths up to 1.
4. **The correct answer is 2.543112×10^3.** Moving the decimal point three places to the left means 10^3 must be used.
5. **The correct answer is .000578.** The power of –4 on the 10 means you must move the decimal point left 4 places.

6. **The correct answer is 254.724.** Remember to line up the decimal points before adding or subtracting. It might help to add zeroes, as shown next, before you do the addition.

$$\begin{array}{r} 56.324 \\ +198.400 \\ \hline 254.724 \end{array}$$

   Remember that you must "carry" a 1 from the units column to the tens column, and then again from the tens column to the hundreds column.

7. **The correct answer is 814.33.** Remember to line up the decimal points before adding or subtracting. It might help to add zero, as shown next, before you do the subtraction.

$$\begin{array}{r} 1{,}067.83 \\ -253.50 \\ \hline 814.33 \end{array}$$

   Remember that you must "borrow" 1 from the thousands place of the top number in order to add 10 to the hundreds place of the top number.

8. **The correct answer is 0.72.** The simplest way to approach this problem without a calculator is to convert the numbers to whole numbers, perform the multiplication, and then shift the decimal point afterward.

   Shift the decimal point one place to the right in 0.3 to yield 3.

   Shift the decimal point one place to the right in 2.4 to yield 24.

   $3 \times 24 = 72$

   Shift the decimal point in the product back the number times you shifted the decimal point in the products.

   $72 \rightarrow .72$

9. **The correct answer is 52.1.** To solve this problem without a calculator, first simplify $182.5 \div 3.5$ to $1825 \div 35$, and then perform the following steps:

$$\begin{array}{r} 52.14 \\ 35\overline{)1825} \\ -175 \\ \hline 75 \\ -70 \\ \hline 50 \\ -35 \\ \hline 150 \\ -140 \\ \hline 10 \end{array}$$

   Because the problem asks you to round to the nearest tenth, look at the hundredths digit. Because the hundredths digit 4 is between 0 and 4, you round down to the nearest tenth. This means you truncate (cut off) the number after the tenths place: 52.1. Remember to always go an extra decimal place beyond what the question asks so you can round properly. For example, if the calculation were 52.16, the answer would be 52.2, but you might not have gotten that if you stopped calculating at 52.1.

10. **The correct answer is approximately $92.00.** The word "approximately" signifies an estimation problem. $23.05 is very close to $23.00, which is a whole number easier to work with. Multiply $23.00 by 4 to obtain a good approximation.

    You could also use $25 as an estimate because it is even easier to work with. Because $25 > 23$ and $25 \times 4 = 100$, you can guess that the answer would be a little less than 100. Most of the GED questions involving approximation are multiple choice questions, and this rough estimation will likely be accurate enough to lead you to the correct answer.

What's Next?

Chapter 40, "Fractions," includes an introduction to fractions, as well as some practice questions.

CHAPTER FORTY

Fractions

Fractions are expressions of division. Conceptually, fractions represent parts of a whole. For example, the fraction $\frac{5}{8}$ ("five eighths") means 5 of 8 equal pieces of the whole. This chapter reviews how to manipulate fractions using mathematical operations. Directions on how to use the calculator fraction key are found in Appendix B, "Calculator Directions."

Fractions Defined

There are several types of fractions as determined by the numerator (top number) and denominator (bottom number).

- Proper fractions have smaller numerators than denominators (for example, $\frac{1}{2}$, $\frac{7}{9}$, $\frac{110}{341}$).
- Improper fractions have numerators the same as or greater than their denominators ($\frac{5}{5}$, $\frac{8}{3}$, $\frac{22}{7}$).
- Mixed numbers combine a whole number and a proper fraction. All improper fractions can be expressed as mixed numbers, and vice versa ($\frac{3}{2} = 1\frac{1}{2}$, $\frac{19}{5} = 3\frac{4}{5}$, $\frac{16}{7} = 2\frac{2}{7}$).

Equivalent Fractions

Two fractions are equivalent to each other when their numerators and denominators have the same ratio, meaning that if you multiply or divide both the numerator and denominator by the same value, the resultant fraction will be equivalent. Consider the following example:

Original Fraction: $\frac{1}{2}$

Multiply top and bottom by 2: $\frac{2}{4}$

Multiply top and bottom by 150: $\frac{150}{300}$

Reducing a fraction means putting the fraction into its simplest terms. If no integer can be divided into both numerator and denominator, a fraction is simplified. Consider the following example:

Original Fraction: $\frac{7}{21}$ is not simplified.

Divide top and bottom by 7.

$\frac{1}{3}$ is simplified.

Fractions and Decimals

All fractions correspond to a decimal value, and all decimals (with the exception of a few irrational numbers) have equivalent fractions. Consider the following example:

Original decimal: $0.34 = \frac{34}{100}$

Divide top and bottom by 2 to simplify: $\frac{17}{50}$

You will likely encounter some problems on the GED in which you will have to use decimals and fractions at the same time. To do this effectively, you must convert all decimals to fractions or all fractions to decimals. Remember, however, that you may enter both improper fractions and mixed numbers into the official GED calculator.

Mixed Numbers and Improper Fractions

To make a mixed number from an improper fraction, first write how many times the denominator can divide evenly into the numerator, and then express the remainder as a proper fraction beside it. Consider the following example:

$\frac{22}{7}$ is an improper fraction.

$3 \times 7 = 21$, so the remainder is $22 - 21 = 1$ of the original 22 sevenths.

Therefore, $\frac{22}{7} = 3\ \frac{1}{7}$

Convert mixed numbers into fractions by multiplying the whole number by the denominator and adding that product to the numerator. Consider the following example:

Original Fraction: $3\ \frac{1}{7}$

$3 \times 7 = 21$

$21 + 1 = 22$

Therefore, $3\ \frac{1}{7} = \frac{22}{7}$

Comparing Fractions

When comparing one fraction to another, use these general facts to help your analysis.

A fraction increases as its numerator increases, and vice versa.

Example: $\frac{1}{2} < \frac{2}{2} < \frac{3}{2} < \frac{4}{2} < \frac{5}{2} \ldots$

A fraction decreases as its denominator increases, and vice versa.

Example: $\frac{1}{2} > \frac{1}{3} > \frac{1}{4} > \frac{1}{5} > \frac{1}{6} \ldots$

To compare two fractions having dissimilar numerators and denominators, a common denominator can be used.

Example: Which fraction is larger, $\frac{4}{7}$ or $\frac{11}{21}$? Multiplying both the numerator and the denominator of $\frac{4}{7}$ by 3 yields $\frac{12}{21}$. Now the two fractions can be compared. $\frac{12}{21} > \frac{11}{21}$. Therefore, $\frac{4}{7} > \frac{11}{21}$.

Remember that you can also compare fractions by converting them to decimals.

Operations with Fractions

Fractions are easier to work with if they are not part of a mixed number. To avoid confusion, you might want to convert mixed numbers to proper or improper fractions before carrying out mathematical operations on them.

Addition and Subtraction of Fractions

Addition and subtraction of fractions requires that the fractions have a common denominator. When they don't, you must express one or both fractions in different terms. Adding and subtracting fractions with common denominators involves performing the following operations with the numerators:

Addition of fractions: $\frac{a}{z} + \frac{b}{z} = \frac{a+b}{z}$

Subtraction of fractions: $\frac{a}{z} - \frac{b}{z} = \frac{a-b}{z}$

Note: z must be the same for both fractions. If it is not, you must convert one or both so that they are the same before you add or subtract.

Example: $\frac{5}{8} + \frac{1}{8}$

These fractions have a common denominator (8). Add the numerators, and then reduce the fraction.

$$\frac{5+1}{8} = \frac{6}{8} = \frac{3}{4}$$

Example: $\frac{2}{3} - \frac{1}{4}$

To perform this subtraction, you must find a common denominator, which is a number that is a multiple of both 3 and 4. The simplest way to find a common multiple is to multiply the two denominators of the problem together; in this case $3 \times 4 = 12$. Now, to change the fractions so that they both have this common denominator, multiply each fraction's numerator and denominator by the other fraction's denominator:

$$(\frac{2}{3} \times \frac{4}{4}) - (\frac{1}{4} \times \frac{3}{3}) = \frac{8}{12} - \frac{3}{12}$$

Subtract the numerators, and then reduce the fraction:

$$\frac{8-3}{12} = \frac{5}{12}$$

Note that this fraction is already reduced.

Multiplication and Division of Fractions

No common denominator is necessary for multiplication and division of fractions. You may choose to reduce fractions, however, before multiplying or dividing them, to make reducing the result easier later.

To multiply two fractions, multiply numerator by numerator and denominator by denominator.

Example:

$$\frac{5}{9} \times \frac{1}{4}$$
$$= \frac{5 \times 1}{9 \times 4}$$
$$= \frac{5}{36}$$

Note that this fraction is already reduced.

$$\frac{7}{16} \times \frac{2}{3}$$
$$= \frac{7 \times 2}{16 \times 3}$$
$$= \frac{14}{48}$$

Reduce the fraction to its simplest form:

$$\frac{7}{24}$$

Because division is the opposite operation from multiplication, division can be expressed as multiplication by the inverse of the divisor (what you are dividing by). The inverse is known as the *reciprocal*, which is a fraction that is "flipped." Consider the following example:

$$\frac{3}{4} \div \frac{5}{6}$$
$$= \frac{3}{4} \times \frac{6}{5} \text{ (this is the } \frac{5}{6} \text{ flipped)}$$
$$= \frac{3 \times 6}{4 \times 5}$$
$$= \frac{18}{20}$$

Reduce the fraction to its simplest form:

$$\frac{9}{10}$$

As seen in this process, dividing a fraction by an integer is equivalent to multiplying the denominator by the integer:

$$\frac{1}{8} \div 7 \text{ (remember that 7 is the same as } \frac{7}{1}\text{)}$$
$$= \frac{1}{8} \times \frac{1}{7}$$
$$= \frac{1 \times 1}{8 \times 7}$$
$$= \frac{1}{56}$$

Word Problems with Fractions

In speaking and writing, fractions are usually expressed in the form *fraction* + "of" + *whole unit*.

Example:

I bought $\frac{3}{4}$ of a pound of ham.

The car needs about $\frac{1}{2}$ of a tank of gas.

Big John ate $\frac{5}{8}$ of that pie.

Suppose that these whole units—"pound of ham," "tank of gas," and "that pie"—have some proportional values assigned to them:

Ham costs $4.75 per pound.

It costs me $30 to fill the car's empty tank with gas.

The whole pie has 300 grams of fat.

Now you can use multiplication to calculate some new information:

$$\frac{3}{4} \times \$4.75$$
$$= \frac{3 \times \$4.75}{4}$$
$$= \frac{\$14.25}{4}$$
$$= \$3.5625 \approx \$3.56 \text{ (Round down.)}$$

I spent $3.56 on ham.

$$\frac{1}{2} \times \$30$$
$$= \frac{1 \times \$30}{2}$$
$$= \frac{\$30}{2}$$
$$= \$15$$

The car needs $15 of gas.

$$\frac{5}{8} \times 300$$
$$= \frac{5 \times 300}{8}$$
$$= \frac{1500}{8}$$
$$= 187.5$$

Big John ate 187.5 grams of fat.

Practice Questions

Some questions involving fractions might not have any answer choices provided. Instead, you are required to write and "bubble in" your answer. Write it first, and then bubble it in, being sure to bubble in the fraction bar.

1. Write the improper fraction $\frac{78}{15}$ as a mixed number.
2. Convert the decimal .23 to a fraction.
3. Place these fractions in order from least to greatest: $\frac{4}{15}$, $\frac{1}{3}$, $\frac{3}{10}$
4. $\frac{5}{12} + 3\frac{2}{3} = ?$ (Write the answer as a mixed number.)
5. $8\frac{4}{7} - \frac{13}{14} = ?$ (Write the answer as a mixed number.)
6. $\frac{2}{9} \times \frac{3}{4} = ?$ (Simplify if necessary.)
7. $\frac{2}{5} \div \frac{7}{9} = ?$ (Simplify if necessary.)
8. A farmer purchases 6,250 pounds of fertilizer but only uses $\frac{3}{4}$ of it. How much fertilizer, in pounds, does the farmer have left?
9. Cory and Liz share an order of hot wings. Cory eats 15 wings and Liz eats the remaining 10. If the cost of the hot wings is $8.50, how much money should Cory have to pay?
10. Bob and Ishmael are bricklayers working together. If in one day Bob lays 96 bricks and Ishmael lays $\frac{5}{8}$ as many, how many total bricks did they lay together that day?

Answers and Explanations

1. **The correct answer is 5 $\frac{1}{5}$.** 15 divides evenly 5 times into 78. Therefore, 5 becomes the whole number in the mixed number. The remainder of the division is 3. Set that as the numerator over the denominator 15 in the fraction part of the mixed number. The fraction $\frac{3}{15}$ reduces to $\frac{1}{5}$.
2. **The correct answer is $\frac{23}{100}$.** Recognize that 23 is a prime number; therefore, fractions with 23 as the numerator cannot be simplified. To create a fraction from any decimal, shift the decimal point to the right until you have a whole number; then place that number over a denominator that is 1 with the decimal point shifted to the right the same number of places.
3. **The correct answer is $\frac{4}{15} < \frac{3}{10} < \frac{1}{3}$.** The lowest common denominator is 30.

   Change all the fractions so they all have 30 as the denominator. $\frac{4}{15} = \frac{8}{30}$, $\frac{3}{10} = \frac{9}{30}$, and $\frac{1}{3} = \frac{10}{30}$.

4. **The correct answer is 4 $\frac{1}{12}$.** First, convert the mixed number to an improper fraction, as follows:

   $3\frac{2}{3} = \frac{9}{3} + \frac{2}{3} = \frac{11}{3}$

   The least common denominator of $\frac{5}{12}$ and $\frac{11}{3}$ is 12 because $3 \times 4 = 12$. Convert $\frac{11}{3}$ to twelfths, as follows:

   $\frac{11}{3} \times \frac{4}{4} = \frac{44}{12}$.

   Now, add the fractions:

   $\frac{5}{12} + \frac{44}{12} = \frac{49}{12}$.

   Convert this improper fraction to a mixed number:

   $49 \div 12 = 4$, remainder 1. Therefore, the correct answer is 4 $\frac{1}{12}$.

5. **The correct answer is 7 $\frac{9}{14}$.** The least common denominator of $\frac{4}{7}$ and $\frac{13}{14}$ is 14.

   Convert $\frac{4}{7}$ to fourteenths:

   $\frac{4}{7} \times \frac{2}{2} = \frac{8}{14}$

   $\frac{8}{14} - \frac{13}{14} = -\frac{5}{14}$

   Add $-\frac{5}{14}$ to the whole number 8 (turn it into a subtraction operation to make it clearer).

   $8 - \frac{5}{14} = 7\frac{9}{14}$

   Check your math by making sure the numerators 9 and 5 sum 14 because $\frac{14}{14} = 1$.

6. **The correct answer is $\frac{1}{6}$.** To multiply fractions, multiply numerators and denominators.

   $\frac{2}{9} \times \frac{3}{4} = \frac{6}{36}$

   Simplify by dividing the numerator and denominator by their greatest common factor of 6.

   $\frac{6}{36} \div \frac{6}{6} = \frac{1}{6}$

7. **The correct answer is $\frac{18}{35}$.** Division of a fraction by another fraction is the same as multiplication of the dividend fraction by the inverse (also called reciprocal) of the divisor fraction. Therefore:

   $\frac{2}{5} \div \frac{7}{9} = \frac{2}{5} \times \frac{9}{7}$

   Multiply numerators and denominators.

   $\frac{12 \times 9}{5 \times 7} = \frac{18}{35}$

   Because 18 and 35 do not have a common factor besides 1, the fraction is simplified.

8. **The correct answer is 1,562.5.** There are two ways to solve this problem. One way is to calculate the amount of fertilizer the farmer used, $6{,}250 \times \frac{3}{4}$, and then subtract that value from the initial number of pounds, 6,250.

   $6{,}250 \times \frac{3}{4} - 6{,}250 = 1{,}562.5$

   The other way is to figure out what fraction of the fertilizer remains by subtracting $\frac{3}{4}$ from 1. Using this method, it can be determined that $\frac{1}{4}$ of the fertilizer remains. Multiply the initial amount by $\frac{1}{4}$.

   $6{,}250 \times \frac{1}{4} = 1{,}562.5$

9. **The correct answer is $5.10.** To determine the fraction of wings eaten by Cory, first find the total number of wings.

   $15 + 10 = 25$

   Because Cory ate 15, he had $\frac{15}{25}$ of the total. Simplify the fraction to $\frac{3}{5}$. Now multiply $\frac{3}{5}$ by the cost, $8.50. When dealing with a fraction and a decimal, one must be converted in order to multiply. Because a monetary amount is wanted in the answer, it would be best to convert $\frac{3}{5}$ to decimal form.

   $\frac{3}{5} = \frac{6}{10} = 0.6$

   Multiply .6 by $8.50 to find Cory's fair share of the cost of the wings.

   $0.6 \times \$8.50 = \$5.10$

10. **The correct answer is 156.** To find out how many bricks Ishmael lays, multiply $\frac{5}{8}$ and 96.

    $\frac{5}{8} \times 96 = \frac{480}{8} = 60$

    Remember that you multiply the values in the numerators and the values in the denominators.

    Next, add the number of bricks Ishmael lays to the number Bob lays. $60 + 96 = 156$

What's Next?

Chapter 41, "Statistics," includes an introduction to statistics, or organized data, as well as some practice questions.

CHAPTER FORTY-ONE

Statistics

Organized data are called *statistics*. If you like sports, you probably know a whole range of different types of "stats." At work, you may know facts and figures about your company and the industry it's in. The main purpose of statistics is to provide a means to analyze similar types of information through comparison.

For the GED, you need certain statistics skills, including being able to calculate ratios, rates, and proportions. These concepts are reviewed in this chapter. In subsequent chapters you can review percentages, probabilities, and data analysis using measures of central tendency.

Ratio

A *ratio* is the relation between two quantities, sometimes expressed as one divided by the other. For example, if there are three blue cars and five red cars, the ratio of blue cars to red cars is 3/5, or 3:5, both pronounced "3 to 5."

To determine from a ratio what fraction of the whole each quantity represents, add up all the quantities and make it the denominator of each fraction.

> Example:
>
> If the ratio of blue cars to red cars is 3:5, the ratio of blue cars to all cars is 3 to 8, which can be written as 3/8 or 3:8. The red cars make up 5/8 of the cars.

Rate

If a ratio compares two quantities with different units that cannot be converted to a common unit, the ratio is called a *rate*.

Rates often use the word "per" to establish the ratio. For example, the residential speed limit is 25 miles per hour. A car traveling at that speed would move 25 miles in 1 hour. To use rates in mathematics, write them in the form of a fraction. Often these will be improper fractions.

> Example:
>
> "2 miles per half hour" = 2 miles/(1/2) hour = 4 miles/1 hour
>
> "6 pounds per gallon" = 6 pounds/1 gallon
>
> "3 games for $5" = 3 games/$5

Proportion

A *proportion* indicates that one ratio is equal to another ratio. Rates become useful when set in proportion to another fraction. Consider this example:

> A ferry can travel 100 miles in two hours. How many minutes would the ferry take to make a 27-mile journey?

First, to set up a proportion, you must have equal units between numerators and denominators. This means hours must be converted to minutes.

> 100 miles/2 hours = 100 miles/120 minutes

Now you can set the ratios equal to each other.

> 100 miles/120 minutes = 27 miles/ m minutes

Because you want to find how many minutes the ferry would take to travel 27 miles, represent the unknown number of minutes as a variable such as m.

To begin to solve this equation for m, cross-multiply the ratios: Multiply a top value by the other ratio's bottom value, and a bottom value by the other ratio's top value, and then set these products equal to each other, as shown next.

Cross-multiply:

$$\frac{100 \text{ miles}}{120 \text{ minutes}} \times \frac{27 \text{ miles}}{m \text{ minutes}}$$

$100 \times m = 27 \times 120$

$100m = 3240$

$m = 32.4$

Therefore, the ferry would take 32.4 minutes to travel 27 miles.

Practice Questions

Test your knowledge of ratios, rates, and proportions in the following questions. Use a calculator only for questions 5–10.

1. A local hardware store carries 12 hammers and 18 rubber mallets. What is the ratio of rubber mallets to hammers?
2. If the ratio of box turtles to snapping turtles in an aquarium is 2/5, what fraction of the turtles are snapping turtles?
3. In a classroom, the fraction of people taking notes is 14/17. What is the ratio of people not taking notes to people taking notes?

4. Lee wins a pie-eating contest by finishing 6 pies in 4 minutes. What was his pie-eating rate in pies per minute?
5. If Rochelle drives 312 miles in 4 hours at constant speed, how fast did she travel in miles per minute?
6. A racecar travels at 184 miles per hour. How many laps around a 2-mile track would the racecar complete in 2.5 hours?
7. In a bag of blue and red marbles, there are a total of 120 red marbles. If the ratio of blue marbles to red marbles is 7:5, how many blue marbles are in the bag?
8. A toy factory can produce 35 toys every 2 minutes. How long, in minutes, would it take to produce 3,010 toys?
9. Joan can type 189 words in 3 minutes. How many words could she type in 20 seconds?
10. In a city election between two candidates for mayor, the ratio of votes for candidate A to votes for candidate B is exactly 6/5. If 39,116 people voted in the election, how many votes did candidate A receive?

Answers and Explanations

1. **The correct answer is 3:2.** The ratio of hammers to rubber mallets is 18:12, which should be reduced. The greatest common factor of 18 and 12 is 6: $6 \times 3 = 18$ and $6 \times 2 = 12$. Therefore, the ratio of hammers to rubber mallets is 3:2.
2. **The correct answer is 5/7.** The fraction 2/5 means that there are 2 box turtles for every 5 snapping turtles. Therefore, in every 7 turtles, there are 5 snapping turtles.
3. **The correct answer is 3:14.** The fraction 14/17 means that for every 17 people in the class, 14 of them are taking notes. This means that $17 - 14 = 3$ people are not taking notes. So the ratio of people taking notes to people not taking notes is 3:14.
4. **The correct answer is 1.5.** Set up the proportion, assigning a variable to the number of pies per minute, and solve for the variable.

   Cross-multiply:

   $$\frac{p \text{ pies}}{1 \text{ min}} \times \frac{6 \text{ pies}}{4 \text{ min}}$$

   $6 \times 1 = 4p$

   $6 = 4p$

   $\frac{6}{4} = p$

   $1.5 = p$

5. **The correct answer is 1.3.** Begin by converting 4 hours into minutes:

   4 hr × 60 min/1 hr = 240 min

   Set up the proportion, assigning a variable to the number of miles per minute, and solve for the variable.

   Cross-multiply:

   $$\frac{m \text{ miles}}{1 \text{ minute}} \times \frac{312 \text{ miles}}{240 \text{ minutes}}$$

   $312 \times 1 = 240m$

   $\frac{312}{240} = m$

   $1.3 = m$

6. **The correct answer is 230.** Calculate the distance the race car travels, in miles, in 2.5 hours, and then convert those miles to laps:

   $2.5 \text{ hr} \times \frac{184 \text{ miles}}{1 \text{ hr}} = 460 \text{ miles}$

   Convert miles to laps:

   $\frac{1 \text{ lap}}{2 \text{ miles}} \times 460 \text{ miles} = 230 \text{ laps}$

7. **The correct answer is 168.** Set up a proportion and solve for the variable.

   Cross-multiply:

   $$\frac{7 \text{ blue}}{5 \text{ red}} \times \frac{n \text{ blue}}{120 \text{ red}}$$

   $5n = 7 \times 120$

   $5n = 840$

   $n = \frac{840}{5}$

   $n = 168$

8. **The correct answer is 172.** Set up a proportion and solve for the variable.

   Cross-multiply:

   $$\frac{35 \text{ toys}}{2 \text{ minutes}} \times \frac{3{,}010 \text{ toys}}{n \text{ minutes}}$$

   $35n = 2 \times 3{,}010$

   $35n = 6{,}020$

   $n = \frac{6020}{35}$

   $n = 172$

9. **The correct answer is 21.** Begin by converting 3 minutes into seconds, and then set up a proportion and solve for the variable:

$$3 \text{ minutes} \times \frac{60 \text{ seconds}}{1 \text{ minute}} = 180 \text{ seconds}$$

Cross-multiply:

$$\frac{189 \text{ words}}{180 \text{ seconds}} \times \frac{w \text{ words}}{20 \text{ seconds}}$$

$$180w = 189 \times 20$$

$$180w = 3{,}780$$

$$w = \frac{3780}{180}$$

$$w = 21$$

10. **The correct answer is 21,336.** The ratio 6/5 means that for every 6 votes for candidate A, there are 5 votes for candidate B. Therefore, in every 6 + 5 = 11 votes, 6 votes are for candidate A.

Set up a proportion and solve:

Cross-multiply:

$$\frac{6 \text{ “A” votes}}{11 \text{ total votes}} \times \frac{a \text{ “A” votes}}{39{,}116 \text{ total votes}}$$

$$11a = 6 \times 39116$$

$$11a = 234{,}696$$

$$a = \frac{234{,}696}{11}$$

$$a = 21{,}336$$

What's Next?

Chapter 42, “Percentages,” includes an introduction to percentages, as well as some practice questions.

CHAPTER FORTY-TWO

Percentages

As a consumer, you encounter percentages all the time. They are represented using the percent sign (%). If you finance a car or a home, you pay back your creditor the principal plus a certain percentage of interest. Items on sale in a store may have a discount based on a certain percentage reduction of the price. Percentages are used because they are practical for use in mathematics.

Percent Defined

Percent means "out of 100." For example, if 30% of your pay goes to taxes, 30 dollars of every 100 dollars you make goes to taxes, or 30 cents of every dollar. As with any fraction, you can imagine the whole unit being broken into a number of pieces corresponding to the denominator. In the case of percent, the number of pieces is 100.

Percents greater than 100 indicate more than the whole. For example, "crime levels are 300% of what they were last year" means that three times more crime has occurred this year than occurred last year.

In applying percentages in mathematics, you first need to change percents to their equivalent decimals or ratios.

Equivalent Percents, Ratios, and Decimals

Because percent means "out of 100," ratios equivalent to percents are easy to determine. Simply make the percent value the top value and 100 the bottom value, and then reduce the ratio as necessary.

Example: $70\% = \frac{70}{100} = \frac{7}{10}$

To convert a percent to a decimal, divide it by 100. With decimals, this means you shift the decimal point two places to the left.

Example: 5% = .05

If a percent is a fraction or mixed number, convert it first to a decimal, and then shift the decimal point two places to the left.

Example: $(\frac{1}{2})\% = .5\% = .005$

Example $(33\ \frac{1}{3})\% = 33.333...\% = .333...$

Solving Percentage Problems

Percent problems on the GED will ask you to find the part of the whole, the whole, or a percentage part of the whole. For example, if Sue spent 25% of her $500 holiday bonus on dinner:

- 25% represents the percent part
- $500 is the whole
- 25% of $500, or $125, is the part

You must read problems carefully to make sure you understand which of these three values the question is looking for. Read the answer choices, if they are given, to get an idea of what result you are looking for.

In any case, you should identify the missing value and set up a proportion to solve for it:

$$\frac{\text{part}}{\text{whole}} \times \frac{\text{part}}{100 \text{ (the whole)}}$$

The preceding example of Sue's holiday bonus would be represented like this:

$$\frac{d}{\$500} = \frac{25}{100}$$

Cross-multiply (see Chapter 41), and then solve for the unknown value *d*.

$$\frac{d}{\$500} \times \frac{25}{100}$$

$100d = 500 \times 25$

$100d = 12{,}500$

$d = 125$

Consider another example: If 45% of x is 120, what is x?

Here the unknown value x is the whole. Set up the proportion accordingly and solve using cross-multiplication.

$$\frac{120}{x} \times \frac{45}{100}$$

$45x = 120 \times 100$

$45x = 12{,}000$

$x = 266.666\ldots = 266\frac{2}{3}$

Interest Calculations

Interest is the percentage of a sum of money paid to a creditor. If you deposit money in a savings account, the bank pays you interest as a percentage of your account balance. If you take out a loan, you pay the bank interest as a certain percentage of the principal you borrow.

The interest you pay on a loan is an example of *simple interest*. This is the type of interest calculation you will need to know for the GED. It is expressed as *principal* × *interest rate* × *time*.

The most common way to express interest is as a percentage of principal per year. Thus, the formula would be *principal* × *annual interest rate* × *the number of years*. This means that if the time is less than one year, you must convert the time into year units.

> Example: How much interest does Claudia earn after one year on $1,300 deposited in a savings account that pays 3.5% per year?

Convert the percentage to a decimal, set up the interest formula, and then solve.

> $1,300 × .035 × 1 = $45.50

The bank pays Claudia $45.50 interest after one year. To find how much money Claudia has in the savings account after one year, add the interest to the principal:

> $1,300 + $45.50 = $1,345.50

You might see an interest problem in which the time is given in days. In this case, first convert days to years by dividing the days by 365 (the standard number of days in a year).

> Example: Frank borrows $20,000 at 5% annual interest to finance the purchase of new furniture in his restaurant. If Frank repays the loan in 100 days, how much interest will he have paid?
>
> $20,000 × 0.05 × 100/365 = $273.98 (Round up.)
>
> Frank pays $273.98 in interest to the bank after 100 days. I

Practice Questions

Test your knowledge of percentages in the following questions. Use a calculator as necessary.

1. Convert the decimal .045 into a percentage.
2. Convert 186.3% into a decimal.
3. Convert $42\frac{2}{5}$ % into a decimal.
4. What is 35% of 120?
5. 345 is what percentage of 250?

6. 96 is 75% of what number?
7. A family has a gross income of $4,500 per month. If $1,350 goes to taxes, $1,200 goes to rent, and $375 goes to food, what percentage of their gross income is left for other expenses?
8. Nathaniel places $3,500 in an account that pays an annual interest rate of 4%. How much interest does he accumulate after 1 year?
9. A certain type of loan charges interest at a rate of 5% per month. If John accepts this loan and borrows $4,200, how much money, in dollars, would he owe in one year if he did not make any repayments during that time?
10. Jessica financed one year of college with $7,800 in student loans. After graduation 4 years later, her loan balance is $8,548.80. If she made no payments toward the loan during college, what was the annual interest rate she was charged for the loan?

Answers and Explanations

1. **The correct answer is 4.5%.** To convert decimals to percents, shift the decimal point two places to the right.
2. **The correct answer is 1.863.** To convert percents to decimals, shift the decimal point two places to the left.
3. **The correct answer is 0.424.** First convert the mixed number $42\frac{2}{5}$ into a decimal.

   $42\frac{2}{5} = 42.4$

   Shift the decimal point two places to the left.

   $42.4\% = 0.424$

4. **The correct answer is 42.** Set up a proportion, as follows.

   Cross-multiply:

   $\frac{\text{(part) } x}{\text{(whole) } 120} \times \frac{35}{100}$

   $120 \times 35 = 100x$

   $4{,}200 = 100x$

   $42 = x$

5. **The correct answer is 138%.** Set up a percent proportion, cross-multiply, and solve for the variable.

   Cross-multiply:

   $$\frac{\text{(part) } 345}{\text{(whole) } 250} \times \frac{x}{100}$$

   $250x = 345 \times 100$

   $250x = 34{,}500$

   $x = 138$

6. **The correct answer is 128.** Set up the proportion, cross-multiply, and solve for the variable.

   Cross-multiply:

   $$\frac{\text{(part) } 96}{\text{(whole) } x} \times \frac{75}{100}$$

   $75x = 96 \times 100$

   $75x = 9{,}600$

   $x = 128$

7. **The correct answer is 35%.** First subtract all the expenses from the gross income.

   $4{,}500 - 1{,}350 - 1{,}200 - 375 = 1{,}575$

   Next, set up the proportion, cross-multiply, and solve for the variable.

   Cross-multiply:

   $$\frac{\text{(part) } 1{,}575}{\text{(whole) } 4500} \times \frac{x}{100}$$

   $4500x = 1{,}575 \times 100$

   $4500x = 157{,}500$

   $x = 35$

8. **The correct answer is $140.** Remember that the formula for simple interest is principal × interest rate × time = interest. In this problem, the principal is the amount $3,500, the interest rate is 4% per year, and the time is 1 year.

   $3{,}500 \times 0.04 \times 1 = 140$

   Be careful to read whether interest problems want the interest earned or the sum of the interest earned and the principal!

9. **The correct answer is $6,720.** Calculate the total interest first. Remember to convert 1 year to 12 months because the interest is calculated monthly.

   $4{,}200 \times 0.05 \times 12 = 2{,}520$

   Add the interest and the principal to determine how much John owes after one year without making payments.

   $4{,}200 + 2{,}520 = 6{,}720$

10. **The correct answer is 2.4%.** First determine the total interest after the 4-year period by finding the difference between the initial and final loan balances.

    $8,548.80 – $7,800 = $748.80

    This value is the interest accrued over 4 years. Divide this value by 4 to calculate the interest accrued over 1 year.

    $748.8 \div 4 = 187.2$

    Finally, set up another proportion to calculate the annual interest rate.

    Cross-multiply:

    $$\frac{\text{(part) } \$187.20}{\text{(whole) } \$7{,}800} \times \frac{x}{100}$$

    $7800x = 187.2 \times 100$
    $7800x = 18{,}720$
    $x = 2.4$

What's Next?

Chapter 43, "Probability," includes an introduction to probability, or the likelihood that something will occur or be true, as well as some practice questions.

CHAPTER FORTY-THREE

Probability

Probability is the likelihood that something will occur or be true. For example, at the beginning of a football game, the referee tosses a coin to determine which team will kick off first. This method is fair because a coin has equal probability of landing heads-up as it does of landing tails-up. Probability has important implications in statistics and in the business world. Casinos maintain carefully weighted probabilities on all their games to ensure that they will not pay out more money than they take in. Climate forecasters use past data to make predictions on the probability of phenomena such as hurricanes and tornados.

In probability, a favorable outcome is the occurrence you are observing. Probability is the ratio of favorable outcomes to possible outcomes. Consider the example of a six-sided die:

> A standard die has an equal probability of landing on any of its six sides. What is the probability that you will roll a 1 or a 5 on your first roll of the die?
>
> There are 2 favorable outcomes: rolling a 1 or a 5.
>
> There are 6 possible outcomes: rolling 1, 2, 3, 4, 5, or 6.
>
> Therefore, the probability that you will roll a 1 or a 5 with one roll of the die is
>
> $\frac{2}{6} = \frac{1}{3}$

If you want to know the percentage of times you will have a favorable outcome, convert this ratio into a decimal and multiply by 100, as follows:

> $\frac{1}{3} = 0.3333...$
>
> $0.3333... \times 100 = 33.3333...\% = 33\frac{1}{3}\%.$

A slightly more complicated example involves Table 43.1.

TABLE 43.1 Mrs. Peterson's Fifth Grade Class

	Bring lunch	Buy lunch
Boys	12	21
Girls	17	15

Table 43.1 shows how many students in Mrs. Peterson's fifth grade class bring their own lunch and how many buy it. What is the probability that one student, chosen at random, buys lunch?

Because you need to choose from among all the students, calculate the total number of students, which represents the number of possible outcomes in the probability ratio.

Total students = 12 + 21 + 17 + 15 = 65

Now calculate the number of favorable outcomes (the number of students who buy lunch):

Lunch buyers = 21 + 15 = 36

Divide the number of favorable outcomes by the number of possible outcomes:

36/65 ≈ 55.4% (rounded up)

The probability that one student, chosen at random, buys lunch is about 55.4%.

The Significance of 0 and 1 in Probability

A probability of 0 or 0% means that the favorable outcome will not occur. A probability of 1 or 100% means that the favorable outcome is certain to occur. This derives from the fact that probabilities are calculated using positive proper fractions. If during your figuring of a problem you calculate a negative probability or a probability greater than 1, you should check your work for mistakes.

Dependent Probability

Dependent probability describes the situation where the probability of one outcome depends on the previous outcome. Consider this example of a cooler with various drinks inside:

> A cooler contains 3 cans of cola, 3 cartons of orange juice, and 6 bottles of water. What is the probability that you will choose a can of cola if you choose one drink from the cooler at random?
>
> First, add the number of possible outcomes: 3 + 3 + 6 = 12
>
> Next, divide the number of favorable outcomes (3 cans of cola) by the number of possible outcomes: $\frac{3}{12} = \frac{1}{4} = .25 = 25\%$
>
> The probability of choosing a can of cola at random is $\frac{1}{4}$, or 25%.

Suppose you succeeded in choosing a can of cola and then removed it from the cooler. What is the probability that the next person to choose a drink chooses a carton of orange juice?

> First, recognize that the cooler now has one fewer can of cola, and then add the number of possible outcomes: 2 + 3 + 6 = 11
>
> Next, divide the number of favorable outcomes (3 cartons of orange juice) by the number of possible outcomes: 3/11 = .273 = 27.3%
>
> The probability of choosing a carton of orange juice at random is approximately 27.3%.

With probability problems, be sure you consider whether a chosen item is removed or replaced after each round of choosing.

Practice Questions

Test your knowledge of probability in the following questions. Use a calculator as necessary.

1. Inside a bag are 12 red, 3 purple, 6 blue, and 21 green marbles. If one marble is pulled out randomly, what is the probability, rounded to the nearest tenth of a percent, that it is a red marble?
2. There are 60 students in a high school English class. If one student is randomly selected, the probability of him or her being left-handed is 5%. How many students in the class are likely to be right handed?
3. A city is holding elections for seats on the board of trustees. In polling residents, it was determined that the probability of an eligible voter voting is 78%. If 11,895 people voted, how many eligible voters likely did not vote?
4. Inside a child's toy chest are 10 trucks, 25 blocks, 4 army men, 3 balls, and 6 stuffed animals. If one toy is pulled out at random, what is the probability that it is either a stuffed animal or a truck? (Show your answer as a mixed number percentage.)
5. Thomas wants a yellow gumball from a gumball machine. The machine contains a total of 120 gumballs. There are 32 red, 23 blue, 29 green, 17 white, and 19 purple. What is the probability that Thomas will have a favorable outcome?
6. Use data from problem 5. After buying two gumballs, one white and one red, Thomas decides he wants a blue gumball. What is the probability, rounded to the nearest tenth of a percent, that he will get a blue gumball on his next try?
7. Marissa is in class preparing for a spelling bee. Each student writes his or her name on a piece of paper and puts it into a box. The teacher will randomly draw names to determine the order for the spelling bee. If the classroom is composed of 32 students, and 4 have already been drawn, what is the probability, rounded to the nearest hundredth of a percent, that Marissa will be next?
8. At a factory, every eighth product is inspected for defects. What is the probability that a customer who will buy the product will buy one that was inspected?
9. What is the probability of rolling two different numbers with exactly two rolls of a standard die? (Show your answer as a mixed number percentage.)
10. Some members of the astronomy club are chosen at random to work various functions at the annual New Year's Eve stargazing party. Two telescope operators, one cook, and one emcee are chosen from among the club's 28 members. What is the probability, rounded to the nearest tenth of a percent, that a club member will not have to work at the party?

Answers and Explanations

1. **The correct answer is 28.6%.** First, add the total number of marbles ("possible outcomes").

   $12 + 3 + 6 + 21 = 42$

   The total number of marbles is 42. The number of red marbles ("favorable outcomes") is 12.

   $12/42 = 0.2857$

   Convert the decimal to a percent and round to the nearest tenth.

   $0.2857 \approx 28.6\%$

2. **The correct answer is 57 students.** The best way to solve this problem involves first setting up a proportion to find the number of left-handed students.

   Cross-multiply:

   $$\frac{x \text{ left-handed students (part)}}{60 \text{ total students (whole)}} \times \frac{5 \text{ (percent part)}}{100 \text{ (percent whole)}}$$

   $100x = 60 \times 5$
   $100x = 300$
   $x = 3$

   Subtract the left-handed students from the total students to determine the right-handed students.

   $60 - 3 = 57$

   Therefore, 57 students are right handed.

3. **The correct answer is 3,355.** To figure out how many people did not vote, the total number of residents is needed. To calculate the total number of residents, set up a proportion and solve.

   Cross-multiply:

   $$\frac{11{,}895 \text{ eligible voters who voted (part)}}{x \text{ total eligible voters}} \times \frac{78 \text{ (percent part)}}{100 \text{ (percent whole)}}$$

   $78x = 11{,}895 \times 100$
   $78x = 1{,}189{,}500$
   $x = 15{,}250$

   From the proportion, it can be determined there are a total of 15,250 eligible voters. Subtract the number of people who voted from the total number of eligible voters.

   $15{,}250 - 11{,}895 = 3{,}355$

4. **The correct answer is $33\frac{1}{3}$%.** Add all the quantities of toys (possible outcomes).

   $10 + 25 + 4 + 3 + 6 = 48$

   Next, add up the number of trucks and stuffed animals.

   $10 + 6 = 16$

   Divide the favorable outcomes (16) by the possible outcomes (48), and then convert the decimal result to a percent.

   $\frac{16}{48} = \frac{1}{3} = .3333... = 33\frac{1}{3}\%$

5. **The correct answer is 0%.** There are a total of 120 gumballs, and none of them are yellow. Therefore, there is no chance for Thomas to have his favorable outcome.

6. **The correct answer is 19.5%.** Two gumballs were removed, making the total 118. Because neither of the gumballs removed were blue, 23 blue ones still remain.

   Divide favorable outcomes (23) by possible outcomes (118).

   $23 \div 118 = 0.1949...$

   Convert the decimal to a percent rounded to the nearest tenth.

   $0.1949... \approx 19.5\%$

7. **The correct answer is 3.57%.** Because 4 students have already been chosen, this means that 4 fewer students could be picked next.

   $32 - 4 = 28$

   This is the number of possible outcomes for the fifth pick. Marissa represents one of those possible outcomes. Divide this single favorable outcome by the number of possible outcomes.

   $1 \div 28 = 0.03571$

   Convert the decimal to a percent and round to the nearest hundredth.

   $0.03571 \approx 3.57\%$

8. **The correct answer is 12.5%.** If every eighth product is inspected, then $\frac{1}{8}$ of all products are inspected. Simply convert 1/8 to a decimal, and then to a percent.

   $\frac{1}{8} = .125 = 12.5\%$

9. **The correct answer is $83\frac{1}{3}$%.** A standard die has 6 sides, therefore 6 possible outcomes. You can roll any number on your first roll, so your probability of that favorable outcome is 100%. On your second roll, your probability of rolling a number other than the one you first rolled is $\frac{5}{6}$. Convert $\frac{5}{6}$ to a decimal, and then to a percent.

   $\frac{5}{6} = 0.8333...\text{(repeating)} = 83.333...\%$

   Because 0.333... is equivalent to the fraction $\frac{1}{3}$, the mixed number of 83.333... is $83\frac{1}{3}$.

10. **The correct answer is 85.7%.** Begin by adding the number of workers needed:

    $2 + 1 + 1 = 4$

    Because 4 of the 28 members will be working, 24 of them will not be working. Not working is the "favorable outcome."

    $24 \div 28 = 0.85714...$

    Convert the decimal to a percent rounded to the nearest tenth.

    $0.85714... \approx 85.7\%$

What's Next?

Chapter 44, "Data Anaysis," includes an introduction to data analysis, as well as some practice questions.

CHAPTER FORTY-FOUR

Data Analysis

The GED tests your ability to understand and draw conclusions from sets of data. Many times, the Mathematics Test asks you to reduce a set of values to a more manageable single value (such as the mean or median). You will also see sets of data expressed in charts, table, and graphs. These visuals help you to recognize the center, range, and any patterns in the data.

Mean and Median

The page of formulas included in the GED Mathematics Test booklets includes descriptions of the two measures of central tendency important to understand for the test. These measures represent two ways of looking at the center of a set of data. The more commonly used measure is called the mean, otherwise known as the average. The second measure used on the GED is the median.

To calculate the *mean*, or *average*, of a set of data, add the items in the set, and then divide that sum by the number of items in the set. For example, to find the average age of the five starters on a basketball team, add their ages, and then divide by five:

Johnson: 23

Smith: 17

Mohammed: 25

Tomasello: 19

Van Cline: 22

$(23 + 17 + 25 + 19 + 22) \div 5 = 106 \div 5 = 21.2$

The mean age of the five starters on the basketball team is 21.2 years

Median is the middle value of a set of data. To calculate median, you must first arrange items in the set in increasing or decreasing order. If the set has an odd number of items, the median is the number exactly in the middle. If the set has an even number of items, the median is the average of the two middle values. For example, consider the test scores from two different classes—one with an odd number of students and one with an even number of students.

Class A (9 students): 78, 76, 94, 92, 88, 78, 88, 98, 99

To find the median, begin by arranging the data in order, and then find the middle number, as shown next:

76 78 78 88 88 92 94 98 99
↑ (under the fifth value, 88)

Because the set has 9 items, the middle item is the fifth item from the left and the right. The median test score for Class A is 88.

Class B (10 students): 69, 70, 66, 98, 98, 79, 83, 84, 80, 92

To find the median of a set with an even number of elements, begin by arranging the data in order, and then calculate the average of the two middle values, as shown next:

66 69 70 79 80 83 84 92 98 98
↑ ↑ (under 80 and 83)

Because the set has 10 items, the middle item is the average of the fifth item from the left and the fifth item from the right:

$(80 + 83) \div 2 = 81.5$

The median test score for Class B is 81.5.

Charts and Tables

When you examine charts and tables, pay close attention to the following aspects of them:

- The title (what is the chart or table showing?)
- Headings (what data is shown?)
- Format of the data (are they fractions, decimals, or percentages?)
- Labels and units of the data (do the number represent people, inches, milliliters, money?)

A specific type of chart is called a *table*. Tables arrange data in horizontal rows and vertical columns. This type of representation of data is particularly useful when making a comparison between two types of information.

For example, a multiplication table shows the product of each one of a set of numbers by each one of another set of numbers, as displayed in Table 44.1.

TABLE 44.1 Multiplication Table

	1	2	3	4	5	6	7	8	9	10	11	12
1	1	2	3	4	5	6	7	8	9	10	11	12
2	2	4	6	8	10	12	14	16	18	20	22	24
3	3	6	9	12	15	18	21	24	27	30	33	36
4	4	8	12	16	20	24	28	32	36	40	44	48
5	5	10	15	20	25	30	35	40	45	50	55	60
6	6	12	18	24	30	36	42	48	54	60	66	72
7	7	14	21	28	35	42	49	56	63	70	77	84
8	8	16	24	32	40	48	56	64	72	80	88	96
9	9	18	27	36	45	54	63	72	81	90	99	108
10	10	20	30	40	50	60	70	80	90	100	110	120
11	11	22	33	44	55	66	77	88	99	110	121	132
12	12	24	36	48	60	72	84	96	108	120	132	144

Graphs

As described in Chapter 5, "Interpreting Graphical Information," many types of graphs are included on the GED. These include bar graphs, line graphs, and circle graphs (also called pie charts).

The GED will ask you to interpolate and extrapolate data from graphs. Interpolation is the process of estimating a value between values given in a graph.

In general, patterns in data tend to persist. For example, if bars in a graph increase steadily, you may assume that the data would continue to increase beyond the domain of the graph. In addition, if the graph reveals some kind of cycle, you may assume that the cycle would persist beyond the domain of the graph.

On line graphs, the horizontal and vertical axes have tick marks that correspond to increasing values. The axes are named and units are defined for the values given along the axes. As is the case in Geometry, the horizontal and vertical axes are often called the x-axis and the y-axis, respectively. Normally, the origin (point of intersection of the axes) represents zero on both axes.

Horizontal and vertical values are said to have a positive correlation when the vertical values increase as the horizontal values increase. For example, consider the line graph representing a road trip shown next.

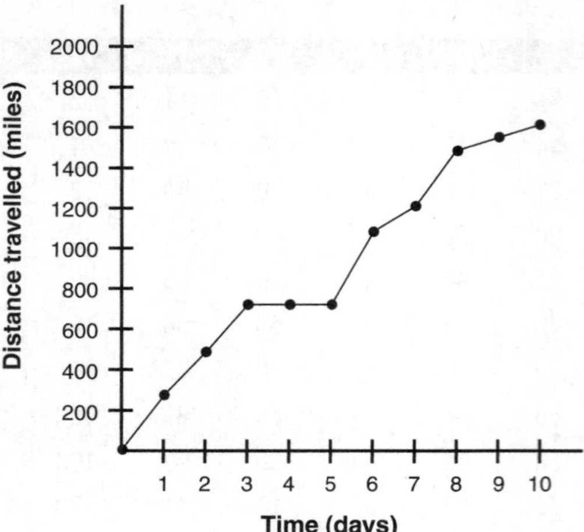

There is a positive correlation between the distance traveled and the time spent on the trip.

Conversely, horizontal and vertical values are said to have a negative correlation when the vertical values decrease as horizontal values increase. For example, consider the line graph below, which represents the effects of mercury on trout in a test pond.

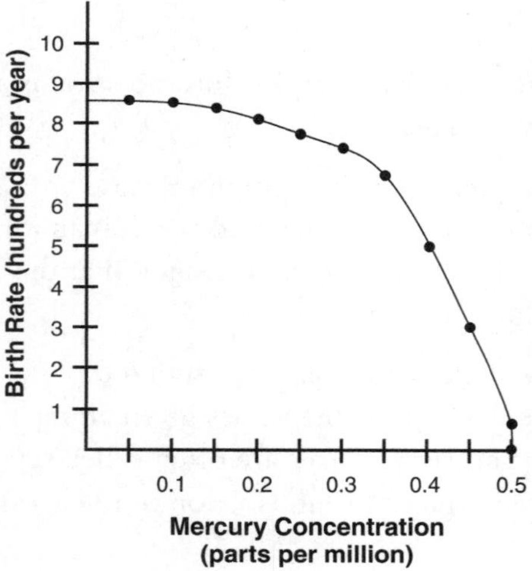

There is a negative correlation between the concentration of mercury in the water and the birth rate of rainbow trout.

Practice Questions

Test your knowledge of data analysis in the following questions. Use a calculator as necessary.

1. Calculate the mean of this data set: {17, 2, 54, 1, 34, 34, 92, 6}
2. Calculate the mean of this data set: {102, 321, 100, 540, 96, 191}

3. Calculate the mean of this data set: {1/3, 2/3, 3/4, 5/12, 1/12, 1/3, 1/4}
4. Calculate the median of this data set: {86, 745, 23, 73, 578, 256, 65}
5. Calculate the median of this data set: {20, 923, 83, 495, 93, 423}
6. Calculate the median of this data set: {2/5, 3/4, 3/10, 7/20, 4/5, 1/2, 1/5}
7. The table below shows yesterday's ice cream sales at a small sandwich shop. Vanilla and chocolate ice cream are sold in cups or cones.

Yesterday's Ice Cream Sales at a Small Sandwich Shop

	Vanilla	Chocolate	TOTAL
Cup	14		
Cone			54
TOTAL	31		82

How many cups of chocolate ice cream did the sandwich shop sell yesterday?

8. The table below shows last year's enrollment in Chef Davis' two cooking classes.

Last Year's Enrollment in Chef Davis' Two Cooking Classes

	Jan	Feb	Mar	Apr	May	Jun	Jul	Aug	Sep	Oct	Nov	Dec
Selecting and Preparing Meats	14	17	18	17	15	13	18	19	19	20	17	14
Basic Bread-baking	7	11	12	13	15	9	12	11	15	13	12	10

Which course experienced the greatest drop in enrollment from one month to the next? When did that occur?

9. Some travelers spent two days camping and fishing in the wilderness. During what days of their trip did they likely do these activities? Use the graph below to answer this question.

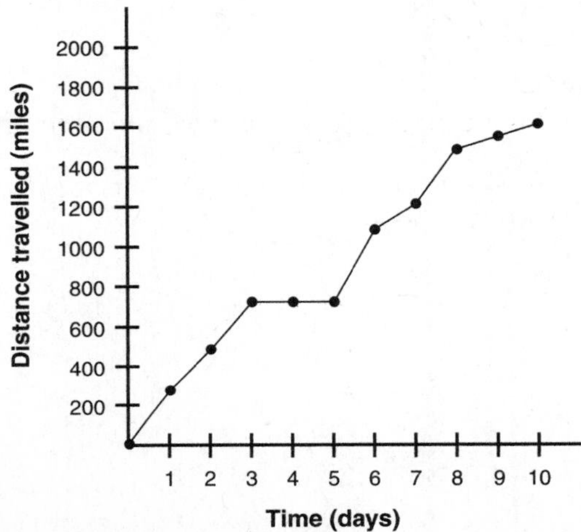

10. Which action would have the greatest effect on increasing rainbow trout birth rates in Test Pond A? Use the graph below to answer this question.

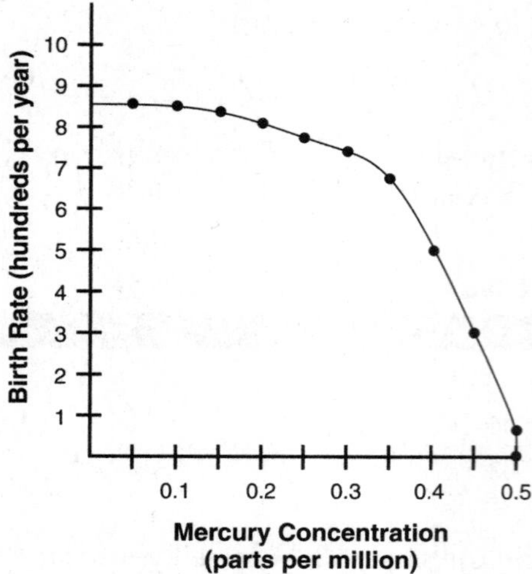

1. Increase mercury concentration in the water from 0 to 0.1 parts per million.
2. Increase mercury concentration in the water from 0.4 to 0.5 parts per million.
3. Decrease mercury concentration in the water from 0.3 to 0.2 parts per million.
4. Decrease mercury concentration in the water from 0.4 to 0.3 parts per million.
5. Decrease mercury concentration in the water from 0.5 to 0.4 parts per million.

Answers and Explanations

1. **The correct answer is 30.** To find the mean, compute the sum, and then divide it by the number of items in the set.

   17 + 2 + 54 + 1 + 34 + 34 + 92 + 6 = 240

   240 ÷ 8 = 30

2. **The correct answer is 225.** To find the mean, compute the sum, and then divide it by the number of items in the set.

   102 + 321 + 100 + 540 + 96 + 191 = 1,350

   1,350 ÷ 6 = 225

3. **The correct answer is $\frac{17}{42}$.** To find the mean, compute the sum, and then divide it by the number of items in the set. The best way to add these fractions is to convert them to fractions with a common denominator.

   The least common denominator of 3, 4, and 12 is 12.

   {1/3, 2/3, 3/4, 5/12, 1/12, 1/3, 1/4} = {4/12, 8/12, 9/12, 5/12, 1/12, 4/12, 3/12}

   4/12 + 8/12 + 9/12 + 5/12 + 1/12 + 4/12 + 3/12 = 34/12

   $\frac{34}{12} \div 7 = \frac{34}{12} \times \frac{1}{7}$

   $\frac{34}{12} \times \frac{1}{7} = \frac{34}{84}$, which reduces to $\frac{17}{42}$.

4. **The correct answer is 86.** To find the median, arrange the set in numerical order, and then determine the middle value. Because this set has seven elements (an odd number), there will be only one middle value.

   {86, 745, 23, 73, 578, 256, 65} = {23, 65, 73, 86, 256, 578, 745}

   The middle value of the ordered set is 86.

5. **The correct answer is 258.** To find the median, arrange the set in numerical order, and then determine the middle value. Because this set has six elements (an even number), there are two middle values. The median of the set is the mean of those two middle values.

   {20, 923, 83, 495, 93, 423} = {20, 83, 93, 423, 495, 923}

   The middle values of the ordered set are 93 and 423. Calculate the mean.

   93 + 423 = 516

   516 ÷ 2 = 258

6. **The correct answer is 2/5.** To find the median, arrange the set in numerical order, and then determine the middle value. Since this set has seven elements (an odd number), there will be only one middle value. The best way to compare these fractions numerically is to convert them to fractions with a common denominator.

   The least common denominator of 2, 4, 5, 10, and 20 is 20.

   {2/5, 3/4, 3/10, 7/20, 4/5, 1/2, 1/5}= {8/20, 15/20, 6/20, 7/20, 16/20, 10/20, 4/20}

   Now place the fractions in order.

   {8/20, 15/20, 6/20, 7/20, 16/20, 10/20, 4/20} = {4/20, 6/20, 7/20, 8/20, 10/20, 15/20, 16/20}

   The middle value of the ordered set is 8/20. Reduce the fraction.

   8/20 = 2/5

7. **The correct answer is 14.**

   To determine the number of cups of chocolate ice cream, you must determine the value of, minimally, one other piece of data missing from the table.

   The lower-right corner cell represents the *grand* total of ice cream sales, whether vanilla or chocolate, cup or cone. The cell immediately above it represents the total *cone* sales, whether vanilla or chocolate. Therefore, the next cell above represents the total *cup* sales, whether vanilla or chocolate. Find this value by subtracting the *cone* total from the *grand* total.

   82 – 54 = 28

   Fill this value into the table, as shown here.

	Vanilla	Chocolate	TOTAL
Cup	14		28
Cone			54
TOTAL	31		82

   Because you are given the number of vanilla cups sold (14), and you now have the total number or cups sold, you can determine the number of chocolate cups sold.

   28 – 14 = 14

	Vanilla	Chocolate	TOTAL
Cup	14	14	28
Cone			54
TOTAL	31		82

8. **The correct answer is "Basic Bread-baking" from May to June.** This question tests your ability to select only the relevant data from a table containing many units of data. The question asks you to find the class that experienced the greatest one-month drop in enrollment. Enrollment in the Basic Bread-baking class dropped from 15 to 9, a difference of 6 students, between May and June. No class between any two months of last year experienced as sharp a decline in enrollment.

9. **The correct answer is "the fourth and fifth days."** The graph is titled "Distance Traveled on a Road Trip." The horizontal axis shows time in days. Each unit on the axis represents one day. The vertical axis shows the total distance traveled.

   If the travelers are camping and fishing over two days, then they are not likely traveling many miles, if any at all. (Note how the vertical axis has 200 miles between tick marks.)

   If time elapses and no travel takes place, then the graph is horizontal. The only horizontal section of the graph spans two days, the fourth and fifth, as called for in the question.

10. **The correct answer is (5).** The graph shows a negative correlation between mercury concentrations in the water and the birth rate of rainbow trout. In addition, the slope of the graph decreases from left to right, indicating that each additional unit of mercury in the water has an increased negative effect on the rainbow trout birth rates. Therefore, positive effect on rainbow trout birth rates is greater when higher mercury concentrations are reduced.

    Observe this fact on the graph. Measure the difference between the top and bottom values of certain sections of the graph. The change in birth rate is 500 fish per year between 0.4 and 0.5ppm of mercury. Between 0.3 and 0.4ppm of mercury, the change in birth rate is about 250 fish per year. As you move right to left, the positive effect of mercury concentration reduction becomes less.

What's Next?

Chapter 45, "Measurement," includes an introduction to basic measurement and units of measurement, as well as some practice questions.

CHAPTER FORTY-FIVE

Measurement

Measurement is the means of assigning values from the number system to things in the physical world. Having standard units of measurement is important because so much depends on the accurate description of real-world objects, phenomena, and situations. For example, when surveyors measure land, they must be able to accurately and precisely report the data they gather to engineers, architects, geologists, and so on. For this reason, all these various professions rely on a standard set of measurement units that is recognized and understood universally. If understanding the survey data required a lot of guessing, estimation, and conversion, then the risk of building unsound roads and buildings would probably increase. Measurements are indispensable in daily life, too. You probably have your height, weight, pants size, shoe size, and so on memorized. You probably have a good sense of the distances represented by a foot, an inch, and a mile.

The basic, essential measurements describe the following:

- Length
- Weight (or mass)
- Volume
- Time

Other units are called *derived* units because they combine units from the basic categories, for example:

- Velocity = Length (or distance) / Time
- Density = Mass / Volume
- Momentum = Mass × Velocity = Mass × (Distance / Time)

It is important to be familiar with derived units, but the GED will provide this information for you on your test.

U.S. Customary Units

The units of measurement commonly used in the United States originated in England over many centuries. Although many of these units are recognized in many of the former British Commonwealth nations, the United States is the only country to continue using them so extensively. Nearly every other country in the world has adopted the metric system as its standard measurement system. Metric units are described in the next section.

On the GED, you will probably see both measurement systems used. You should know how to use each one, but you do not need to know how to convert between systems. You will need to know how to convert within one system: for example, between feet and inches.

The basic U.S. customary units, their abbreviations, and some important conversion factors are the following:

- Length:
    - 1 mile (mi) = 5,280 feet (ft)
    - 3 feet = 1 yard (yd)
    - 1 foot = 12 inches (in)
- Weight:
    - 1 ton (T) = 2,000 pounds (lb)
    - 1 pound = 16 ounces (oz)
- Volume:
    - 1 gallon (gal) = 128 ounces (oz) = 16 cups (c) = 8 pints (pt) = 4 quarts (qt)
    - 1 quart = 32 ounces = 4 cups = 2 pints
    - 1 pint = 16 ounces = 2 cups
    - 1 cup = 8 ounces
- Time:
    - 1 year (yr) = 365 days ≈ 52 weeks
    - 1 week = 7 days
    - 1 day = 24 hours (hr)
    - 1 hour = 60 minutes (min)
    - 1 minute = 60 seconds (sec)

Of course, units of time are universal.

The Metric System

The metric system is used in other countries besides the United States and internationally in the scientific and academic community. The main advantage of the metric system is that all its units are based on powers of the number 10 (see also Chapter 39, "Decimals"). This allows for simple conversion between units.

The basic metric units, their abbreviations, and approximate conversions to U.S. units, in order to give you perspective (you need not memorize them):

- Length: meter (m), ≈ 39 inches.
- Weight: gram (g), ≈ 3/100 of an ounce.
- Volume: liter (L), ≈ 33.8 ounces.
- The metric system uses the same time units as the U.S. system.

The metric system uses prefixes to derive other units based on the powers of 10, which correspond to place value in the decimal system (think shifting the decimal point):

nano- (n) = 1/1,000,000,000 [one billionth] = 10^{-9}
micro- (μ) = 1/1,000,000 [one millionth] = 10^{-6}
milli- (m) = 1/1,000 [one thousandth] = 10^{-3}
centi- (c) = 1/100 [one hundredth] = 10^{-2}
deci- (d) = 1/10 [one tenth] = 10^{-1}

BASE UNIT = 1 = 10^0
deca (da) = 10 [ten] = 10^1
hecto- (h) = 100 [hundred] = 10^2
kilo- (k) = 1,000 [thousand] = 10^3
mega- (M) = 1,000,000 [million] = 10^6
giga- (G) = 1,000,000,000 [billion] = 10^9

We suggest that you memorize the prefixes milli-, centi-, and kilo-.

Examples of derived metric units:

1 kilogram (kg) = 1,000 grams (g)
1 megameter (Mm) = 1,000 kilometers (km)
52 grams = .052 kg
104,500 nanometers (nm) = 104.5 micrometers (μm)
1,500 milliliters (mL) = 1.5 liters (L)

Unit Conversion

When working with different measurement units, you often have to make conversions between units. You can convert a smaller unit to a larger one (for example, feet to miles) or a larger unit to a smaller one (for example, liters to milliliters).

To convert units, you need to know the appropriate conversion factor. These are simply ratios (fractions) set up using equivalency values like those given in the previous two sections of this chapter. For example, because there are 16 ounces in a pound, the conversion factor of ounces to pounds is 1/16. Conversely, the conversion factor from pounds to ounces is 16/1, or simply 16.

To convert units, use the appropriate conversion factor in a proportion.

Example:

How many feet is 94 inches?

There are 12 inches in a foot. Therefore, the conversion factor of inches to feet is 12/1. Set up a proportion, cross multiply, and solve as follows.

Cross-multiply:

$$\frac{94 \text{ in}}{x \text{ ft}} \times \frac{12 \text{ in}}{1 \text{ ft}}$$

$12x = 94 \times 1$

$12x = 94$

$x = 7.8333\ldots \approx 7.8$

Therefore, 94 inches is equivalent to about 7.8 feet.

The first step you should take to check your unit conversions is to see whether the change in value is reasonable. Remember that converting from smaller units to larger units means the numerical value of the measurement decreases. Conversely, converting from larger units to smaller units means the numerical value increases.

In the metric system, because units are based on powers of 10, you can simplify conversions by shifting the decimal point the number of places corresponding to the difference in the power of 10 between the unit you are converting from and the unit you are converting to.

Example:

How many grams is 0.005 kilograms?

There are 1,000 grams in a kilogram. The number 1,000 is the number 1 after the decimal point is shifted 3 places to the right (thus adding 3 zeros). This means 1,000 = 10^3. Because gram is the base unit, the power of ten is 0. The difference between kilograms and grams, therefore, is 3 – 0 = 3 decimal places. Shift the decimal point three places to the right to convert kilograms to grams.

Shift decimal point 3 times:

0.0.0.5. kilograms = 5 grams

Money

The GED includes many questions involving units of money. In the United States, Canada, and some other countries, this means the dollar. Dollars are divided into 100 cents. In mathematics, you can treat dollar values like any other decimal.

You can expect to see questions that ask you to calculate the total cost of a quantity purchased based on the unit price. You can also expect to be asked to find the unit cost based on a total cost for a certain number of items. Remember that total cost (c) equals the cost per item (rate = r) times the number of items (n):

$c = nr$

Like any equation in algebra, if you know all the values of the variables but one, you can solve for the missing value.

Example:

How much does one pound of bananas cost if 12 pounds cost $6?

First, set up the equation: $\$6 = 12r$

Solve for r, the cost per pound of bananas:

$6/12 = r$

$0.5 = r$

Bananas cost $0.50, half a dollar or 50 cents, per pound.

Example:

Sheets of plywood cost $11.50 each. How much would 45 of them cost?

First, set up the equation: $c = 45(11.50)$

Solve for c, the total cost of the plywood:

$c = 517.5$

The total cost of 45 sheets of plywood is $517.50

Another common math problem involving money is subtraction of total cost from an amount tendered to calculate change owed to a customer.

Example:

Bob bought a hamburger for $1.25, French fries for $1.00, and a milkshake for $2.50. He gave the cashier a $20 bill. How much change was Bob owed?

First, add all the prices, and then subtract the sum from the amount tendered:

$20 - (1.25 + 1.00 + 2.50) = 20 - 4.75 = 15.25$

Bob is owed $15.25 change.

Time

Money values can be treated as regular decimals, but care must be taken to convert time units properly. In the English-speaking world, time of day is represented using a colon between the hour of the day and the minute of the hour. In addition, English speakers use a 12-hour clock during the 24-hour day. Midnight until noon are the a.m. hours, and noon until the following midnight are the p.m. hours. For example, 3 a.m. comes 12 hours before 3 p.m.

To use times of day in mathematics, you must remember that there are 60 minutes in an hour (not 100). Therefore, convert hours and minutes to hours using the 1/60 conversion factor for minutes to hours.

Example:

Susan punched in at work at 7:45 a.m. She punched out at 1:30 p.m. How many hours did she work that day?

First, convert hours and minutes to just hours:

7:45 a.m. = 7 hours + 45/60 hours = 7 hours + $\frac{3}{4}$ hours = 7.75 hours

1:30 p.m. (remember to add 12 to p.m. hours to account for the 12-hour clock) = 12 hours + 1 hour + 30/60 hours = 13 hours + $\frac{1}{2}$ hours = 13.5 hours.

Next, subtract the converted punch-in time from the converted punch-out time:

13.5 hours – 7.75 hours = 5.75 hours

Susan worked 5.75 hours.

Finally, if called for in the problem, you can convert the portion to the right of the decimal point back to minutes:

Set up a proportion, cross multiply, and solve as follows.

Cross-multiply:

$$\frac{.75\text{ hr}}{x\text{ min}} \times \frac{1\text{ hr}}{60\text{ min}}$$

$1x = 60 \times .75$

$x = 45$ minutes

Don't forget about the hours part! Susan worked 5 hours plus 45 minutes.

Understanding Scale

Maps, blueprints, diagrams, and so on are drawn to scale, meaning the dimensions within them are proportional to what they represent in the real world. For example, if a map is in 1:1,000 scale, you know that one inch on the map corresponds to 1,000 inches in the real world. Notice that scales don't require units. In the previous example, one centimeter would correspond to 1,000 centimeters, 1 millimeter would correspond to 1,000 millimeters, and so on. Many times, however, the GED includes a scale with units. For example: 1 inch = 8 miles. In this case, the problem would require you to make the same sort of conversion.

Example:

Pedro is building a 1:50 scale model of a 49-foot fighter jet. How long, in feet, will his finished model be?

To solve this problem, set up a proportion with the real-world measurement and the conversion factor of 1/50, cross multiply, and solve.

Cross-multiply:

$$\frac{\text{(model) } x \text{ ft}}{\text{(real thing) } 49 \text{ ft}} \times \frac{1}{50}$$

$50x = 49 \times 1$

$x = .98$

Pedro's model will be 0.98 feet long.

Practice Questions

Test your knowledge of measurement in the following questions. As you work through them, identify which conversion factors you need to review, and look them up in the chapter as necessary.

1. Convert 72 inches to feet.
2. Convert 112 ounces to quarts.
3. Ben's Gourmet Catering plans to bake two desserts for a wedding. One recipe calls for 1,500 g of flour, and another recipe calls for 3.5 kg of flour. How much flour, in kilograms, does the company need to bake the two desserts?
4. A 0.75 L can of blue paint contains 10 mL of pigment. What percent of the volume of the paint does the pigment make up?
5. Laura bought 6 pounds of apples and paid with a $20.00 bill. She received $8.00 change. How many dollars did Laura pay for each pound of apples?
6. Randall wants to buy 4 concert tickets. Each ticket costs $45 and has an additional $5 service fee. How many dollars does Randall need to buy the tickets?
7. Miguel can assemble computers at a rate of 4 per hour. He is paid $20 for each computer he assembles. How many dollars will Miguel earn after a workweek of 30 hours?
8. Martha sleeps from 10 p.m. to 7:30 a.m. every night. How many hours does she sleep at night in 1 week?
9. Roger started work at 7:45 a.m. and left for lunch at 12:30 p.m. He returned from lunch at 1:15 p.m. and stayed at work until 6:45 p.m. How long, in hours and minutes, did Roger work?

10. A 1:50,000 scale map shows a large area of hiking trails. If your planned hiking route is 15 inches long on the map, how far, rounded to the nearest tenth of a mile, would you actually hike?

Answers and Explanations

1. **The correct answer is 6 feet.** There are 12 inches in a foot. Divide inches by 12 to convert to feet. $72 \div 12 = 6$

2. **The correct answer is 3.5 quarts.** There are 32 ounces in a quart. Divide ounces by 32 to convert to quarts. $112 \div 32 = 3.5$

3. **The correct answer is 5 kg.** The question calls for an answer in kilograms. You must convert 1,500 g. to kilograms. There are 1,000 g. in 1 kg. Divide grams by 1,000 to convert to kilograms. $1{,}500 \div 1{,}000 = 1.5$. Add the converted measurement to the second measurement, already in kilograms. $1.5 + 3.5 = 5$

4. **The correct answer is $1\frac{1}{3}$%.** Calculate the fractional part of the volume of the paint that is made up of pigment. You must divide the volume of the pigment by the total volume of the paint. Before you can do that, however, you must make the units match. The best way is to convert liters to milliliters. There are 1,000 milliliters in a liter.

   $0.75 \times 1{,}000 = 750$

   Now divide the pigment volume by the total volume.

   $10 \div 750 = 0.01333\ldots$

   Multiply by 100 to convert to percent. Express the repeating decimal .33333… as a fraction in a mixed number.

   $0.013333\ldots \times 100 = 1.33333\ldots\% = 1\frac{1}{3}\%$

5. **The correct answer is \$2.** Begin by calculating the total cost of all 6 pounds of apples. Subtract the change Laura received from the amount she handed to the cashier.

   $\$20 - \$8 = \$12$

   The total cost of the apples was \$12. Because you know that Laura bought 6 pounds of apples, the cost of each pound of apples can be calculated.

   $\$12 \div 6 = \$2$

6. **The correct answer is \$200.** One concert ticket has two costs (\$45 and \$5). Find the total cost.

   $\$45 + \$5 = \$50$

   Randall wants 4 tickets, so multiply the number by the total cost of 1 ticket.

   $4 \times \$50 = \$200$

7. **The correct answer is $2,400.** Multiply the number of computers Miguel can assemble in an hour by the number of hours in the workweek.

   $4 \times 30 = 120$

   Miguel can assemble 120 computers in one 30-hour work week. He is paid $20 per computer, so multiply this rate by the week's quantity of computers to calculate Miguel's earnings for the week.

   $120 \times \$20 = \$2{,}400$

8. **The correct answer is 66.5 hours.** Recall that on the 12-hour clock, 10 p.m. is actually 10 + 12, or 22 hours into the day. The time 7:30 a.m. the next morning is actually 7.5 + 12 + 12, or 31.5 hours after the start of the day. Subtract these values to calculate the nightly hours of sleep: 31.5 – 22 = 9.5. Multiply the nightly hours of sleep by 7 to calculate the weekly hours of sleep.

   $9.5 \times 7 = 66.5$

9. **The correct answer is 10 hours 15 minutes.** There are several approaches to adding and subtracting time. You can convert the minutes part to a decimal part (by dividing minutes by 60), or you can simply count the hours and minutes, perhaps imagining the hands of a clock. Secondly, in situations such as in this problem, where a span of time has a piece missing in the middle (for example, taking a lunch break), you can either (1) calculate the total span of time and then subtract the missing piece or (2) calculate the time on both sides of the missing piece separately, and then add them together.

   7:45 a.m. to 6:45 p.m. is a span of 11 hours. Lunch from 12:30 to 1:15 lasted 45 minutes, or $\frac{3}{4}$ of an hour. Subtract $\frac{3}{4}$ from 11 to equal 10 $\frac{1}{4}$ hours, or 10 hours 15 minutes.

   7:45 a.m. to 12:30 p.m. is a span of 4 hours 45 minutes. 1:15 to 6:45 is a span of 5 hours 30 minutes. Add the two values: 4 hours 45 minutes + 5 hours 30 minutes = 10 hours 15 minutes.

10. **The correct answer is 11.8 miles.** Because the map has 1:50,000 scale, every length unit on the map corresponds to 50,000 of that length unit in the real world. Therefore, 15 inches on the map is 50,000 times as much on the ground.

    $15 \times 50{,}000 = 750{,}000$

    Convert 750,000 inches to miles by converting the inches to feet and then the feet to miles:

    12 inches in a foot: $750{,}000 \div 12 = 62{,}500$ feet

    5,280 feet in a mile: $62{,}500 \div 5{,}280 = 11.837\ldots$ miles

    Round to the nearest tenth of a mile: 11.8 miles

What's Next?

Chapter 46, "Algebra," includes an introduction to algebra, as well as some practice questions.

46

CHAPTER FORTY-SIX

Algebra

The GED tests your understanding of basic algebra, which is the branch of mathematics that uses expressions formed with constants, variables, and the operation symbols explained in Chapter 37, "Basic Operations," and Chapter 38, "Symbols and Figuring."

Algebraic Expression

The basic unit of statements in algebra is the expression, which may contain numbers, variables, and operations. There is no equality or inequality relationship indicated in algebraic expressions.

Examples of expressions:

- 2
- $2x$
- $2x + 3$
- $2x^2 - 3y$
- $\sqrt{2x^2 + 3y}$

Equations

An equation is a statement that two expressions are equal. In an equation, two expressions are separated by the equal sign (=), indicating that they have equivalent value. Generally, an equation contains one or more variables. Algebra is the system you use to simplify equations and solve them for individual variables.

Examples of equations:

- $x = 4$
- $6c = 2e$
- $r = 12t + n$
- $(x + 10)^2 + 6y + 2 = y^2$
- $\frac{(x + y)^2}{10 + x} = 2$

Common Word Problems

A limitless number of real-life situations (and, therefore, GED word problems) can be represented using algebraic equations. Consider a simple example:

> At the library, you must buy a photocopy card to make copies. The card costs 50 cents and copies cost 10 cents each. How much will it cost you, in dollars, to make copies the first time, if you want to make 27 copies?

First, represent the two quantities as variables:

number of copies = n

total cost = t

Next, set up the equation.

$t = 0.50 + 0.10n$

This equation shows that the total cost is equal to 50 cents (0.5 dollars) plus 10 cents (0.10 dollars) times the number of copies. This would be the total cost equation for anyone making copies for the first time in the library.

Replace n with its value, in this case:

$t = 0.50 + 0.10 \times 27$

Use arithmetic, following the order of operations, to solve for t.

$t = 3.20$

Therefore, it will cost you $3.20 to make 27 copies for the first time.

In this example, all the work was performed on one side of the equation. Mathematical operations can be applied to both sides of an equation, too. Consider this example:

> A shirt in a clothing store is marked $20. A sign above it says "Sale. Originally $32." What is the percentage discount currently offered on this shirt?

The sale price is the original price minus the discounted portion of the original price:

Let d be the discount rate.

$20 = 32 - 32d$

This equation shows that the sale price of $20 is equal to the original price of $32 minus the percentage of $32 that is discounted.

The first step in solving for d is to perform operations to both sides of the equation to isolate the variable d. When performing addition, subtraction, multiplication, division, or when applying exponents or square roots to a function, you must do what you do to one side of the equation to the other side.

The first step in this problem is to move constants to one side. Subtract 32 from both sides of the equation.

$$\begin{array}{rcl} 20 & = & 32 - 32d \\ -32 & & -32 \\ \hline -12 & = & -32d \end{array}$$

To leave d by itself, divide both sides by –32.

$$-12/-32 = -32d/-32$$

$$0.375 = d$$

Therefore, 0.375 represents the discount rate. Multiply by 100 to convert it to a percentage.

The discount offered on the shirt is 37.5%.

Simplifying Algebraic Expressions

When you simplify algebraic expressions, you perform all the operations you can within them. The first task of simplification is to reduce an expression to the fewest number of terms. A term is a unit within an expression that cannot be combined with other terms. A term may be a number, a variable, or a variable multiplied or divided by a number. Terms are combined in an equation using addition and subtraction.

Examples of terms in an expression:

$6x^2y^2$	+	$3x$	−	$\frac{y}{2}$	+	1
Term		Term		Term		Term

When manipulating algebraic expressions, you may combine only *like terms*, which have the same variable(s) raised to the same power(s). (Remember that no exponent on a variable indicates a power of 1.)

Examples of pairs of like terms:

x	$5x$
b^2	$\frac{b^2}{2}$
$4yz$	$9yz$
$2x^3y$	$8x^3y$

To combine like terms, add or subtract (as indicated) the coefficients (the numbers being multiplied by the variables).

$$2x^3y + 8x^3y = (2 + 8)x^3y = 10x^3y$$

Remember that if you reorder terms in an expression, you must be careful to keep their signs:

$$6x + 7x + 10xy - 2xy - 2x$$

$$= 7x + 6x - 2x + 10xy - 2xy$$

$$= 11x + 8xy$$

When simplifying algebraic equations, use the following steps:

1. Combine like terms on each side of the equation.
2. Isolate the variable by "undoing" operations in *reverse* of the order of operations (see the PEMDAS method in the "Order of Operations" section of Chapter 38). You may think of this process as "stripping" operations from the target variable.

Example of solving an equation:

$4x + 13 - 2x = 5x - 20$

Combine like terms. In this case subtract the $2x$ from the $4x$ on the left side:

$2x + 13 = 5x - 20$

"Undo" addition and subtraction (in this case, we add 20 to both sides, which cancels out the –20 on the right, and we subtract $2x$ from both sides, which cancels out the $2x$ on the left):

$$\begin{array}{rcl} 2x + 13 & = & 5x - 20 \\ -2x + 20 & & -2x + 20 \\ \hline 33 & = & 3x \end{array}$$

"Undo" multiplication (divide both sides by 3):

$$\begin{array}{rcl} 33 & = & 3x \\ \div 3 & & \div 3 \\ \hline 11 & = & x \end{array}$$

Patterns

You might be asked to recognize patterns within a series of numbers. These patterns can be represented by algebraic equations.

Example: What is the next number in the series {... 10, 17, 24, 31 ...}?

Begin by analyzing what is happening from one number in the series to the next. On the GED, this will be an operation of addition, subtraction, multiplication, or division. In this case, a number in the series is 7 greater than the previous number:

$10 + 7 = 17$

$17 + 7 = 24$

$24 + 7 = 31$

Therefore, the next number is $31 + 7 = 38$.

A simple equation for this pattern uses the variable x for a value in the series and the variable n for the position of x in the series.

$x_{n+1} = x_n + 7$

This equation shows that the *next* x equals *this* x plus 7.

Example: What number comes immediately before the first number in the series {... 16, 32, 64, 128 ...}?

$16 \times 2 = 32$

$32 \times 2 = 64$

$64 \times 2 = 128$

$x_{n+1} = 2x_n$

Set x_{n+1} equal to 16 and solve for x_n:

$16 = 2x_n$

$8 = x_n$

The number that comes before 16 in the series is 8.

Inequalities

Inequalities state a relationship between two expressions that are not equal in some way. There are four such relationships, each having a unique inequality symbol:

- Greater than (>)
- Greater than or equal to (≥)
- Less than (<)
- Less than or equal to (≤)

EXAM PREP Study TIP

To help you remember which way the inequality symbols point, think of them as an animal's jaws that would rather bite down on a bigger piece of food than a smaller piece. For example, 2 fish > 1 fish.

Inequalities involving one variable do not have single solutions. In fact, they have an infinite number of solutions that can be expressed as inequalities. To simplify an algebraic inequality, follow the same steps as you would with simplifying an algebraic equation, with one special rule added:

1. Combine like terms.
2. Isolate the variable by "undoing" operations in *reverse* of the order of operations. You may think of this process as "stripping" operations from the target variable.
3. Change the direction of the inequality sign when you multiply or divide by a negative number.

Here is an example of how the symbol change arises:

$10 > 4$

By the rules of algebra, you may multiply both sides by any number:

$10(-3) < 4(-3)$

The sign needs to be changed. The proof is visible when you simplify the inequality:

$-30 < -12$

No such symbol change occurs when multiplying and dividing by positive numbers. Think of multiplying and dividing by negative numbers as involving reflection across zero on the number line (negative to positive or positive to negative).

Example of solving an equality:

$$2x + 3 > 3x$$

Isolate the x-terms:

$$\begin{array}{rcl} 2x + 3 & > & 3x \\ -2x & & -2x \\ \hline 3 & > & x \end{array}$$

By convention, write simple inequalities with the variable first:

$$x < 3$$

This means that the solution set of x for the inequality $2x + 3 > 3x$ includes all the numbers less than 3.

The inequality $x < 3$ can be shown on the number line as shown in Figure 46.1.

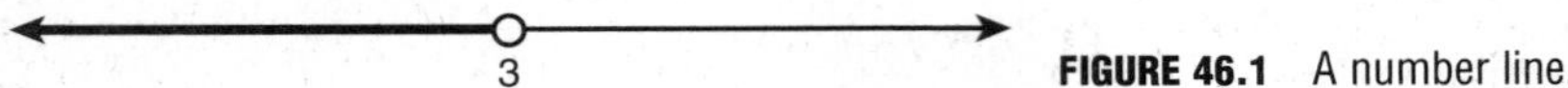

FIGURE 46.1 A number line.

The hollow point at 3 indicates that the set of numbers includes every number approaching 3, such as 2.999, but not 3 itself.

Number line representations of "greater than or equal to" and "less than or equal to" inequalities use a solid point to indicate that the set includes the number that defines it.

The number line of $x \leq 3$ is shown in Figure 46.2.

FIGURE 46.2 A number line representing $x \leq 3$.

The Coordinate Plane

You might have already noticed from the science and social studies material in this book that the GED emphasizes skills in analyzing visual representations of data. Line and bar graphs, for example, use a vertical and a horizontal axis to plot the relationships of two types of data. In mathematics, the rectangular coordinate plane (sometimes called the standard coordinate plane or the Cartesian coordinate plane after mathematician René Descartes) is used to plot equations written in two variables. By convention, the horizontal axis is called the x-axis and the vertical axis is called the y-axis. Values of x and y are determined by their distance along each axis starting from the origin, the point of intersection of the two axes, as shown in Figure 46.3. Every point in the coordinate plane has one x value and one y value. These can be expressed as an ordered pair in the form (x,y). The first term always refers to the x value and the second term always refers to the y value.

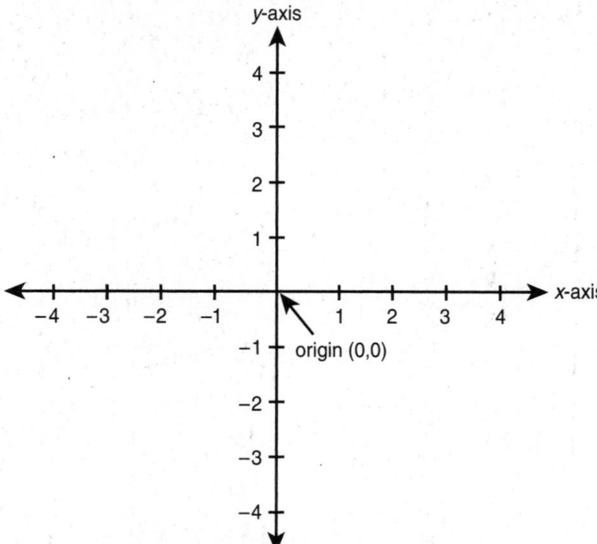

FIGURE 46.3 The coordinate plane.

To plot a point in the coordinate plane, start at the origin and count out the *x* value of the ordered pair, to the right if it is positive and to the left if it is negative. Next, count out the *y* value of the ordered pair, up if it is positive and down if it is negative.

The example in Figure 46.4 plots the point (3,–4) in the coordinate plane.

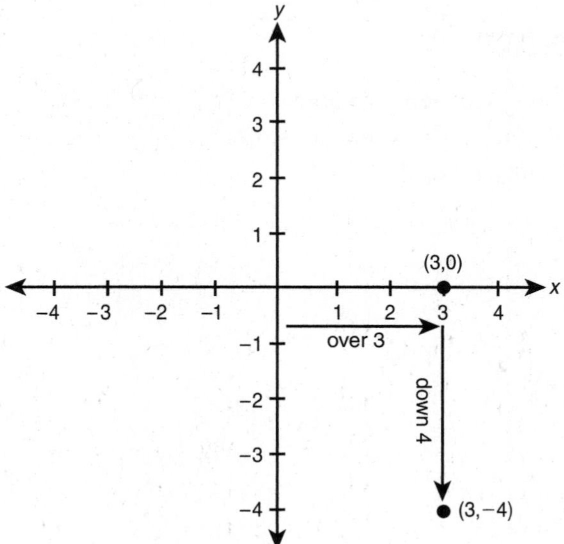

FIGURE 46.4 Point (3,–4) in the coordinate plane.

The coordinate plane has four quadrants bounded by the two perpendicular axes. Whether the *x* and *y* values are positive or negative depends on the quadrant in which the point is located. Figure 46.5 (on the next page) shows the quadrants and their roman numeral designations.

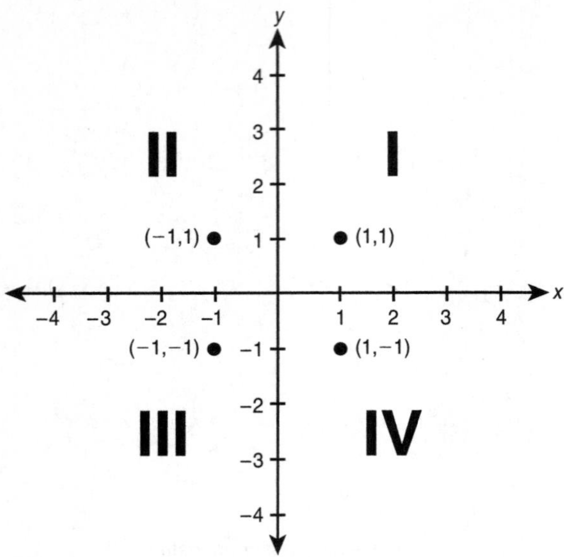

FIGURE 46.5 Coordinate plane quadrants.

First quadrant ("I"): (positive x, positive y)
Second quadrant ("II"): (negative x, positive y)
Third quadrant ("III"): (negative x, negative y)
Fourth quadrant ("IV"): (positive x, negative y)

Distance Between Two Points

There are two ways of calculating the distance between two points on the coordinate plane. First, if the two points have an equal x or y value, you can simply subtract the values that are different. Consider the following example.

Find the distance between the points on the coordinate plane shown below:

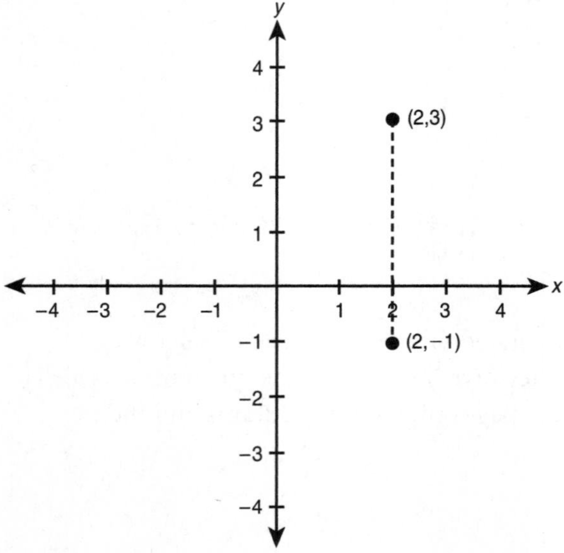

Because the *x* values of the points are equal, to calculate the distance between the points, simply subtract the larger *y* value from the smaller *y* value:

$3 - -1 = 3 + 1 = 4$

When two points share neither their *x* nor *y* values, you will need to use a formula for the distance between two points. This formula will be included on the GED Mathematics Test formulas page in the test booklet. Although you don't need to memorize the distance formula, you should become familiar with when to use it.

The distance formula derives from the Pythagorean Relationship, which defines the proportions between the sides and hypotenuse of right triangles. Review this important concept in Chapter 47, "Geometry."

The distance formula:

$$d = \sqrt{(x_2 - x_1)^2 + (y_2 - y_1)^2}$$

In the formula, (x_1, y_1) is the ordered pair of one point, and (x_2, y_2) is the ordered pair of the other point. It doesn't matter which order you choose.

Consider the coordinate plane in Figure 46.6 showing the points (–1,–2) and (2,3). The dotted segments show how the quantities $(x_2 - x_1)$ and $(y_2 - y_1)$ in the distance formula represent the lengths of legs of an imaginary right triangle.

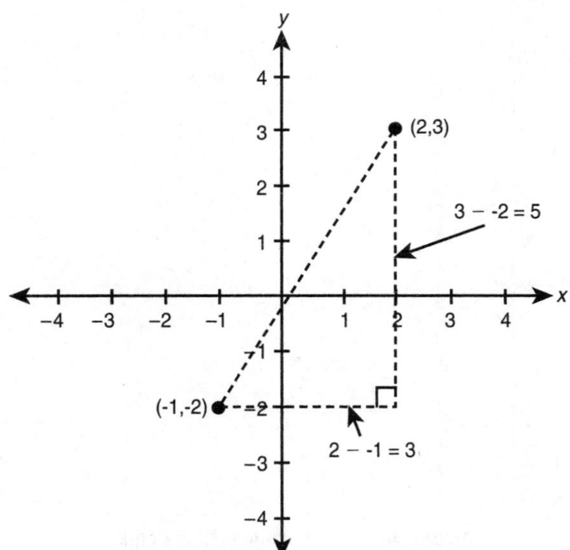

FIGURE 46.6 The relationship of distance between points and right triangles.

To use the distance formula for these two points, replace the variables with the appropriate numerical values, and then simplify the expression.

$$d = \sqrt{(x_2 - x_1)^2 + (y_2 - y_1)^2}$$

$$d = \sqrt{(2 - -1)^2 + (3 - -2)^2}$$

$$d = \sqrt{3^2 + 5^2}$$

$$d = \sqrt{9 + 25}$$

$$d = \sqrt{34}$$

$$d = 5.83\ldots$$

The distance between the points (–1,–2) and (2,3) is 5.83.

Linear Equations

The graph of a linear equation is a straight line. Linear equations are written in y in terms of the first power of x.

Figure 46.7 is the graph of the simplest linear equation: $y = x$

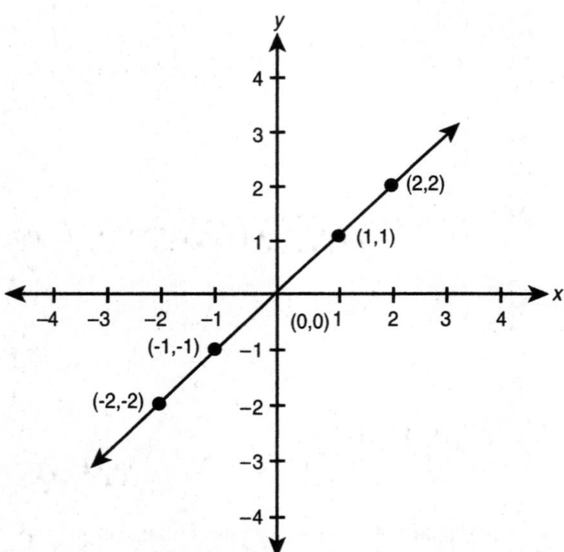

FIGURE 46.7 The simplest linear equation.

The line passes through every point whose y value equals its x value.

The general form (called the slope-intercept form) of the linear equation is $y = mx + b$, where y and x are the variables, m represents the slope of the line, and b represents the y-intercept (the y value at which the line crosses the y-axis).

Slope of a Line

When a line is straight, it means that every change in x value has a proportional change in y value. This concept is known as slope of the line.

Calculate slope by dividing the change in y-coordinates by the change in x-coordinates between two points on a line. The formula for slope is

$$m = \frac{(y_2 - y_1)}{(x_2 - x_1)}$$

For example, the slope of a line that contains the points (3, 6) and (2, 5) is equivalent to

$$\frac{(6 - 5)}{(3 - 2)}$$

Positive slope means that the graph of the line trends up and to the right. Negative slope means that the graph of the line trends down and to the right. Horizontal lines have slope 0 because the y values do not change. Vertical lines have an undefined slope (Remember the slope formula and that division by zero is undefined.)

Two lines are parallel if and only if they have the same slope. For example, the two lines with equations $y = 3x + 3$ and $y = 3x - 1$ have the same slope of 3, but have different y-intercepts, as shown in Figure 46.8.

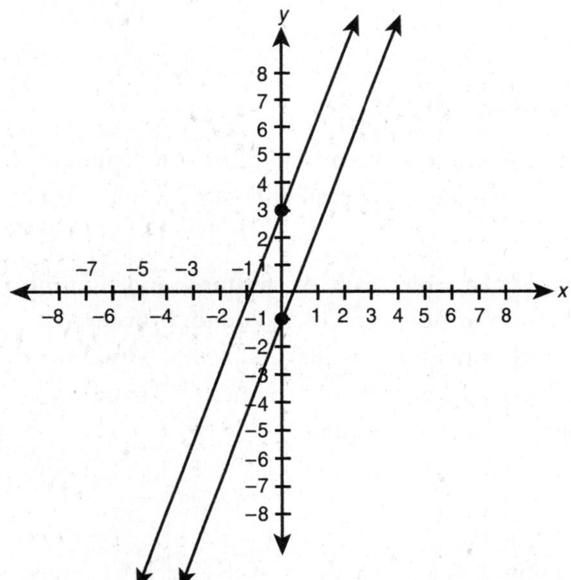

FIGURE 46.8 Parallel lines showing different *y*-intercepts.

Special GED Coordinate Grid Problems

On the GED Mathematics Test, you will be asked to complete some questions in a special alternate coordinate grid format. Your answer sheet will show a coordinate plane for these questions. You must fill in the one circle corresponding to the point that the question is asking you to identify.

Coordinate Grid Example #1

The graph of a circle is shown on the grid below.

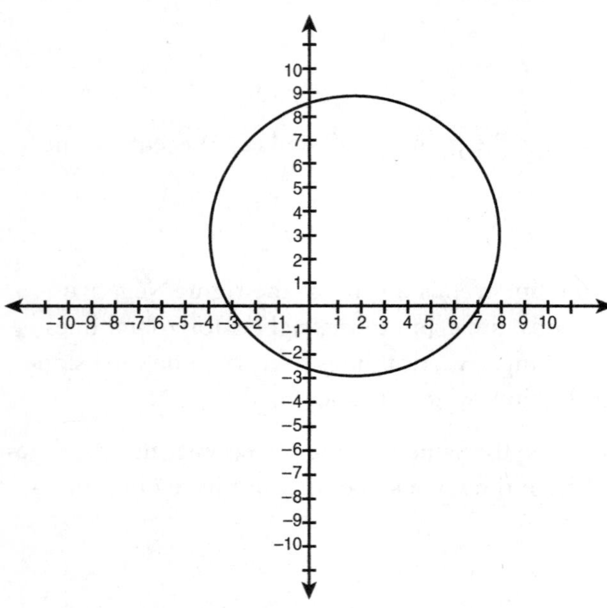

What point is the location of the center of the circle?

To solve this problem, recognize that a circle's center is the midpoint of any diameter. The two diameters you know from the graph are the horizontal and vertical ones. You can use either one to find the circle's center.

To find the circle's center from the horizontal diameter, mark the leftmost and rightmost points on the circle. Count left or right then up or down to determine their ordered pairs. The leftmost point is (–4,3) and the rightmost point is (8,3). Halfway between these points is the center of the circle. You already know that the y value is 3, and to determine the x value, calculate the average of the two x values:

$$\frac{-4+8}{2} = \frac{4}{2} = 2$$

Therefore, the center of the circle is the point (2, 3). The x value of the circle's center can also be found by simply counting the whole way across the circle, and then counting halfway back.

Coordinate Grid Example #2

Three vertices of rectangle ABCD are shown on the next graph.

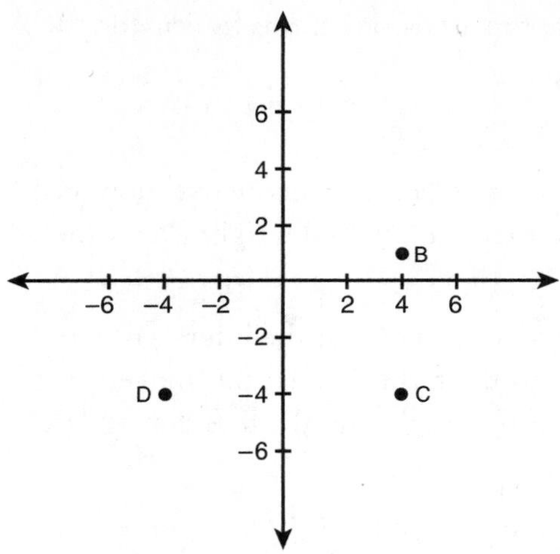

What is the location of point A, the fourth vertex of the rectangle?

To solve this problem, recognize that a rectangle has two pairs of equal sides and four right angles. (Review geometric figures in Chapter 47.) Point A should be the same distance from point D as point B is from point C. Point B is 4 units up from point C, so point A is 4 units up from point D, at (–4, 1).

Coordinate Grid Example #3

Parts of the graphs of the linear functions $y_1 = \left(-\frac{1}{3}\right)x + \frac{1}{3}$ and $y_2 = x - 1$ are shown on the coordinate plane grid below.

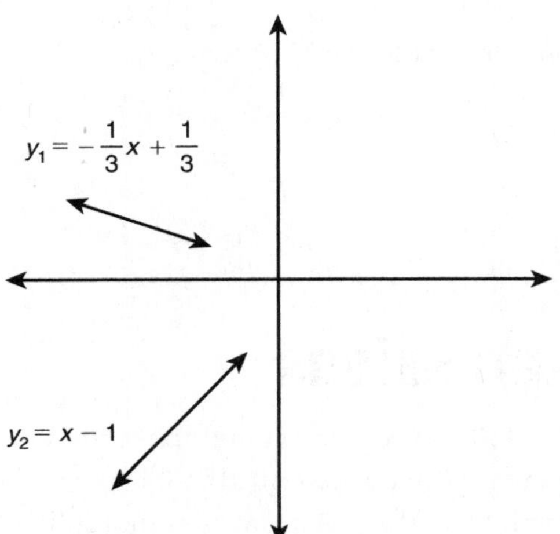

What is the point that is common to the graphs of both functions?

In this problem, you are given the equations of the functions. With this information, you have two choices of how to proceed.

1. Extend the lines using the slope value from the equation.
   a. The slope of the top line is $-\frac{1}{3}$. Start from a point at the intersection of two grid lines. Count 1 unit down and then 3 units to the right. Mark the point and extend the line through it.
   b. The slope of the bottom line is 1. Start from a point at the intersection of two grid lines. Count 1 up then 1 unit to the right. Repeat this movement until you have crossed the path of the top line. Extend the line through the new points.
   c. Determine where the two functions intersect. On the GED, the ordered pair will contain whole numbers.
   d. The point of intersection is (1,0).
2. Set the expressions in terms of x equal to one another. This will give the y-coordinate of the intersection point. After finding the y-coordinate, substitute the value for y in either of the two functions and solve for x. This is the x-coordinate of the intersection point. Here are the equations:

   $\left(-\frac{1}{3}\right)x + \frac{1}{3} = x - 1$

   $\frac{4}{3} = \left(\frac{4}{3}\right)x$

   $1 = x$

   Substitute for x in either equation (the second one is easier):

   $-y = 1 - 1$

   $y = 0$

   Therefore, the point of intersection is (1,0).

Multiplying Algebraic Expressions

When multiplying algebraic expressions, be sure to follow the rules of multiplication described in Chapter 37 and the rules of multiplying exponents described in Chapter 38. Also, remember that because multiplication is distributive, if some quantity is multiplied by a number, the number must be distributed over each term of the quantity.

Example:

$2x(3x - 7) = 6x^2 - 14x$

$2x(3x) - 2x(7) = 6x^2 - 14x$

Use the FOIL method to multiply a two-term quantity by another two-term quantity. FOIL stands for "first times first (F), outside times outside (O), inside times inside (I), last times last (L)," and describes the order in which you should carry out the distributive multiplication, as shown in the example in Figure 46.9. The resulting products of multiplication are then added.

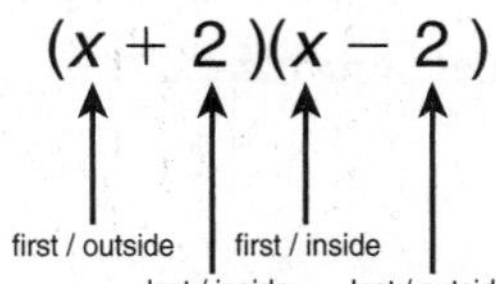

FIGURE 46.9 The FOIL method.

1. First times first: $x \times x = x^2$
2. Outside times outside: $x \times -2 = -2x$
3. Inside times inside: $2 \times x = 2x$
4. Last times last: $-2 \times 2 = -4$
5. Add the products:

   $x^2 + -2x + 2x + -4$

   $= x^2 - 2x + 2x - 4$

   $= x^2 - 4$

Factoring

When manipulating algebraic expressions and equations, you sometimes have to factor them. Factoring is the process of separating numbers that have been multiplied.

The use of the term *factor* first arose in the review of fractions in Chapter 40, "Fractions." When adding or subtracting fractions, they must have a common denominator. If you are adding two fractions, the least common denominator is the smallest number that has both fractions' denominators as factors—that is, whole numbers that can be multiplied by other whole numbers to equal the common denominator. Consider the following examples.

Example:

1. $\frac{1}{3} + \frac{1}{4} = ?$

Begin by determining a number that 3 and 4 can divide into evenly. The first (and least) number is 12. Use conversion factors equivalent to 1 to convert these fractions to twelfths.

$$\left(\frac{1}{3} \times \frac{4}{4}\right) + \left(\frac{1}{4} \times \frac{3}{3}\right)$$

$$= \frac{4}{12} + \frac{3}{12}$$

$$= \frac{7}{12}$$

Factoring skills are also useful for simplifying some algebraic expressions and equations. Think of factoring expressions as finding common factors and then "pulling them out."

2. $2x + 14 = 2y$

This equation is not simplified. The terms on the left side of the equal sign have a common factor of 2, so you can "pull out" a 2 from each one.

$$2(x + 7) = 2(y)$$

Notice that this is a good factored form because you can now easily divide each side of the equation by 2 to further simplify it.

$$x + 7 = y$$

When factoring, you can pull out variables in addition to constants. Look at this example of an expression written with three variables.

Example:

3. $5x^3 + 5x^2 - 7y^2 + 2y$

To factor an expression with multiple terms, it is helpful to arrange the terms in conventional order as they are here: arrange terms according to the variables they contain and then from highest power to lowest power.

Consider the x terms separately from the y terms. Because 10 and 5 have a common factor of 5, you can pull out 5 from them. In addition, you can pull out x^2.

$$5x^2(x + 1) - 7y^2 + 2y$$

Now factor the y terms.

$$5x^2(x + 1) - y(7y - 2)$$

Did you notice the sign change before the 2? Remember that a negative times a negative equals a positive. When factoring, you create quantities that weren't present before. Because multiplication is distributive, you must make sure your signs are changed as appropriate. To avoid confusion, you can change the order of terms before factoring.

Original: $5x^2(x + 1) - 7y^2 + 2y$

Reordered: $5x^2(x + 1) + 2y - 7y^2$

Now no sign changes need to be made.

$$5x^2(x + 1) + y(2 - 7y)$$

If you ever have doubts about the accuracy of your factoring, all you need to do is expand the factored form back to the unfactored form and check the results.

Consider also that it might be faster for you to use the process of elimination with the answer choices. Apply each answer choice to the equation to find the correct answer.

You can factor an expression in the form $x^2 + bx + c$ (where b and c are constants) by reversing the FOIL method of multiplication. To perform this factoring task, begin by determining which two factors have a product equal to the constant c and a sum equal to the constant b. These factors may be both positive, both negative, or one positive and one negative. Consider the following examples of the reverse FOIL process of factoring.

1. $x^2 + 5x + 6$

What two factors of 6 add up to 5? The answer is 2 and 3. (Note that if there were no whole numbers that satisfied this test, you could conclude that the expression cannot be simplified by the reverse FOIL process.)

Make the factors terms in two binomials with x.

$(x + 2)(x + 3)$

Check your work by expanding the factored form.

$(x + 2)(x + 3) = x^2 + 5x + 6$

2. $x^2 - 9x + 14$

What two factors of 14 add up to –9? The answer is –7 and –2.

$(x - 7)(x - 2)$

Check your work by expanding the factored form.

$(x - 7)(x - 2) = x^2 + 9x + 14$

3. $x^2 - 2x - 8$

What two factors of 8 add up to –2? The answer is 2 and –4.

$(x + 2)(x - 4)$

Check your work by expanding the factored form.

$(x + 2)(x - 4) = x^2 - 2x - 8$

4. $x^2 + 8 + 16$

What two factors of 16 add up to 8? The answer is 4 and 4.

$(x + 4)(x + 4)$

When the two factors are the same, this factored form can be further simplified.

$(x + 4)^2$

Check your work by expanding the factored form.

$(x + 4)^2 = (x + 4)(x + 4)$

$(x + 4)(x + 4) = x^2 + 8 + 16$

Practice Questions

1. Solve for x: $3x + 14 = 26$
2. Solve for x: $25 = x - 13$
3. Rob and Jenna run a business checking on dogs whose owners are away. Rob and Jenna charge $10 for every visit they make, plus $10 per hour for any time they spend with the dog(s). How much would Rob and Jenna charge if they made one visit to a dog that lasted 45 minutes?
4. An orange grower expects to lose 14% of her crop to various environmental factors such as wind, insects, and disease. She estimates that her trees will produce 2,900 pounds of oranges this season. How much of that quantity of oranges, in pounds, will the grower be able to harvest?
5. The line between which of these pairs of points has the greatest slope?
   (1) (3, 15) and (5, 19)
   (2) (–4, –11) and (6, 19)
   (3) (8, 2) and (–4, –1)
   (4) (18, 0) and (–12, –5)
   (5) (7, 3) and (0, –4)
6. Three vertices of a rectangle have the coordinates (3,7); (8,7); and (8, 2) on the coordinate plane. What are the coordinates of the fourth vertex of the rectangle?
7. Expand: $(x + 2)(x - 4)$
8. Expand: $2y(y + 8)^2$
9. Factor: $6x^3 + 21x + 18y^2 + 27y + 4$
10. Factor: $2y^3 + 4y^2 + 2y$

Answers and Explanations

1. **The correct answer is 4.**

   $3x + 14 = 26$

   Subtract 14 from both sides.

   $3x = 12$

   Divide both sides by 3.

   $x = 4$

2. **The correct answer is 38.**

   $25 = x - 13$

   Add 13 to both sides.

   $38 = x$

3. **The correct answer is 17.50.** The visit lasts for 45 minutes, or $\frac{3}{4}$ of an hour. The charge for each visit can be expressed by the equation:

   $C = 10 + 10h$

   Substitute $\frac{3}{4}$ for h and solve.

   $C = 10 + 10(\frac{3}{4})$

   $C = 10 + 7.5$

   $C = \$17.50$

4. **The correct answer is 2,494.** The grower will lose 14% of what the trees will produce. Therefore, the grower can harvest 100 – 14 = 86% of what the trees will produce. Calculate 86% of 2,900 pounds, as shown next:

   $2{,}900 \times 0.86 = 2{,}494$

5. **The correct answer is (2).** To solve this problem, you must use the formula for the slope of a line between two points (x_1, y_1) and (x_2, y_2):

   $$\frac{(y_2 - y_1)}{(x_2 - x_1)}$$

Now work through the answer choices:

(1) $\dfrac{(19 - 15)}{(5 - 3)} = \dfrac{4}{2} = 2$

(2) $\dfrac{(19 + 11)}{(6 + 4)} = \dfrac{30}{10} = 3$

(3) $\dfrac{(-1 - 2)}{(-4 - 8)} = \dfrac{-3}{-12} = \dfrac{1}{4}$

(4) $\dfrac{(-5 - 0)}{(-12 - 18)} = \dfrac{-5}{-30} = \dfrac{1}{6}$

(5) $\dfrac{(-4 - 3)}{(0 - 7)} = \dfrac{-7}{-7} = 1$

Answer choice (2) has the greatest slope, 3.

6. **The correct answer is (3,2).** Notice how the points (3,7) and (8,7) have the same *y* value and thus lie on a horizontal line (one of the sides of the rectangle). The point (8,7) has the same *x* value as the point (8,2) and thus the two lie on a vertical line (another side of the rectangle). The fourth vertex must share the *x* value of (3,7) and the *y* value of (8,2), thus the fourth vertex is located at (3,2). The rectangle looks like this:

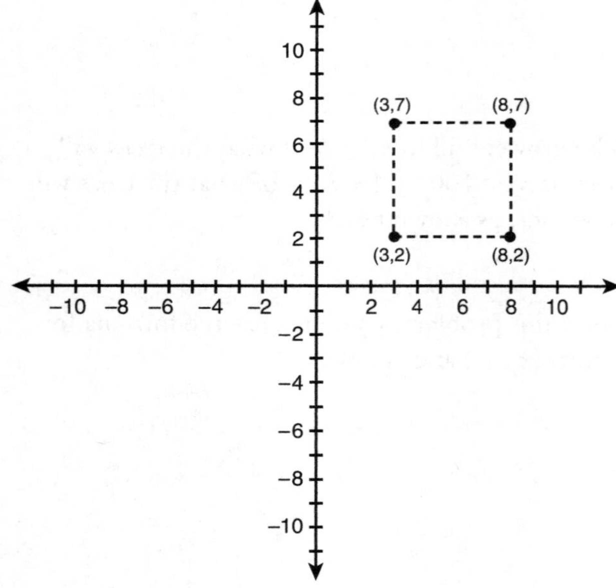

7. **The correct answer is $x^2 - 2x - 8$.** Use the FOIL method to multiply a two-term quantity by another two-term quantity.

   $(x + 2)(x - 4)$

   First times first: $x \times x = x^2$

   Outside times outside: $x \times -4 = -4x$

   Inside times Inside: $2 \times x = 2x$

   Outside times outside: $2 \times -4 = -8$

   Add the terms. Change adding negatives to subtracting positives.

   $x^2 - 4x + 2x - 8$

   Combine like terms.

   $x^2 - 2x - 8$

8. **The correct answer is $2y^3 + 32y^2 + 128y$.** According to the order of operations, you must deal with exponents first. Expand the squared quantity following the FOIL process as in practice question #7.

   $2y(y + 8)^2 = 2y(y^2 + 16y + 64)$

   Now distribute the $2y$ through the quantity.

   $2y \times y^2 + 2y \times 16y + 2y \times 64 = 2y^3 + 32y^2 + 128y$

9. **The correct answer is $3x(2x^2 + 7) + 9y(2y + 3) + 4$.** To factor this long polynomial, treat the x terms and y terms separately. You may find it helpful to enclose the terms in parentheses, paying strict attention to any negative signs.

   $(6x^3 + 21x) + (18y^2 + 27y) + 4$

   Pull out $3x$ from the first quantity.

   $3x(2x^2 + 7) + (18y^2 + 27y) + 4$

   Pull out $9y$ from the second quantity.

   $3x(2x^2 + 7) + 9y(2y + 3) + 4$

10. **The correct answer is $2y(y + 1)^2$.** Begin by pulling out $2y$ from all the terms:

    $2y(y^2 + 2y + 1)$

    The numbers 1 and 1 are two factors of 1 that add up to 2. You can factor the trinomial further:

    $2y(y^2 + 1)^2$

What's Next?

Chapter 47, "Geometry," includes an introduction to geometric concepts, as well as some practice questions.

CHAPTER FORTY-SEVEN

Geometry

The GED Mathematics Test includes questions that require geometry skills. You need to understand the basic concepts of parallel and perpendicular lines, triangles, rectangles and other polygons, circles, area, perimeter, volume, and angle measure in degrees.

A General Inventory of Geometric Concepts

This section introduces the various elements of basic geometry on which you might be tested on your GED Mathematics Test. A solid comprehension of geometry pays dividends in real life, too, whether you're estimating the quantity of paint you'll need to paint a room or working with 2-D or 3-D figures in a computer class.

Points and Lines

The concept of the point is first reviewed in Chapter 46, "Algebra." A point is a location in space that has no volume, area, or length. It is represented by a dot and is sometimes designated by a letter and labeled by its coordinate pair (when it appears on the standard coordinate plane, as in Figure 47.1).

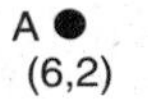

A ●
(6,2)

FIGURE 47.1 A point in the coordinate plane.

A line segment is defined by two points and includes those two points and every point in between, as shown in Figure 47.2.

FIGURE 47.2 A line segment.

As the name suggests, a line segment is a portion of a line. A line is an infinitely long, perfectly straight set of points, as shown in Figure 47.3. Two points are sufficient to define a line. The line extending through two points includes those two points, all the points in between, and all the points extending straight out from the points, continuing to infinity.

FIGURE 47.3 A line.

Angles

An angle is formed when two lines or line segments intersect one another. Angle measure describes the difference in the slope of the lines. In geometry, angles are measured in degrees. The angle of a full circle measures 360°, so a straight line measures 180°. When two intersecting lines or line segments create 90° angles, they are said to be perpendicular to one another. Lines with equal slope cannot intersect each other at a point, so they cannot create angles. Such lines are described as being parallel to one another.

A 90° angle is called a right angle. Right angles are indicated by a small square set in the angle (this is shown in Figure 47.4). Angles with measures less than 90° are called acute, and angles with measures greater than 90° are called obtuse.

Quadrilaterals

A quadrilateral is a four-sided figure. The measures of all the interior angles of a quadrilateral add up to 360°.

Trapezoids are quadrilaterals with one pair of parallel sides, as shown in Figure 47.4.

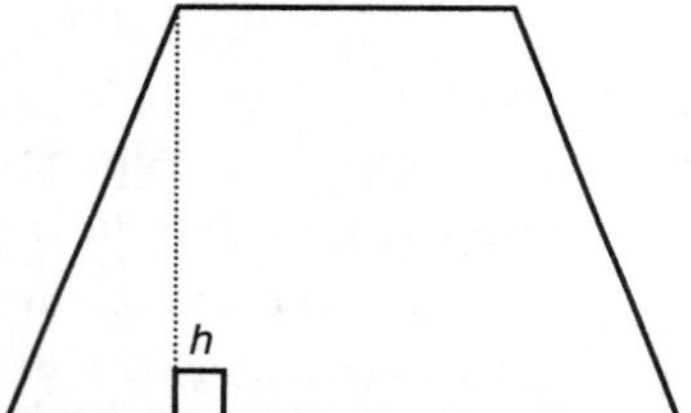

FIGURE 47.4 A trapezoid.

A trapezoid's height is defined as the distance between the parallel bases.

Parallelograms are special quadrilaterals having two pairs of equal sides and two pairs of equal angles, as shown in Figure 47.5.

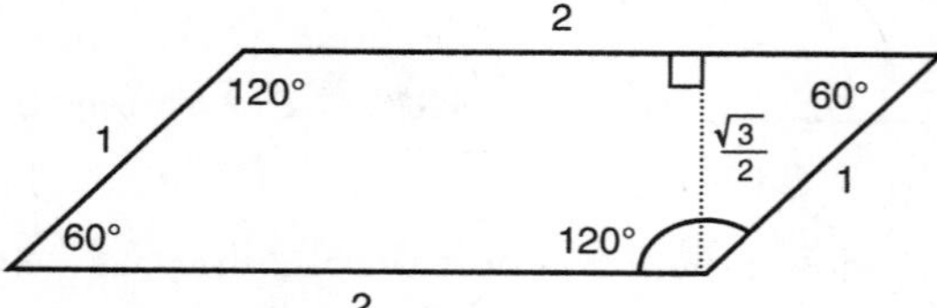

FIGURE 47.5 A parallelogram.

A parallelogram's height is defined as the distance between the base and its opposite side.

A rectangle (shown in Figure 47.6) is a special type of parallelogram: all angles measure 90°. Remember that a 90° angle is indicated by the small square in the corner.

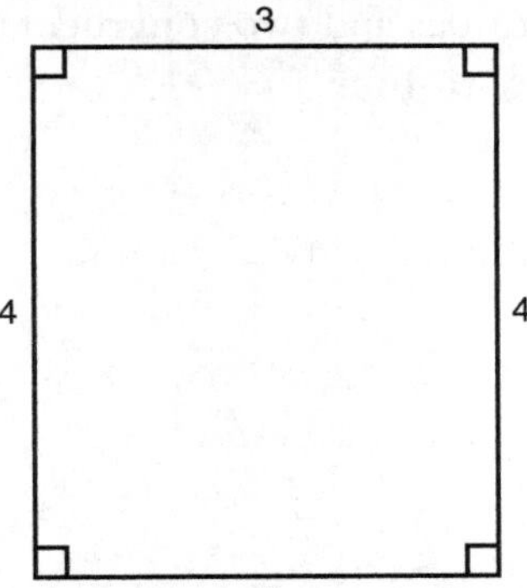

FIGURE 47.6 A rectangle.

A square (shown in Figure 47.7) is a special rectangle that has four congruent (identical) sides.

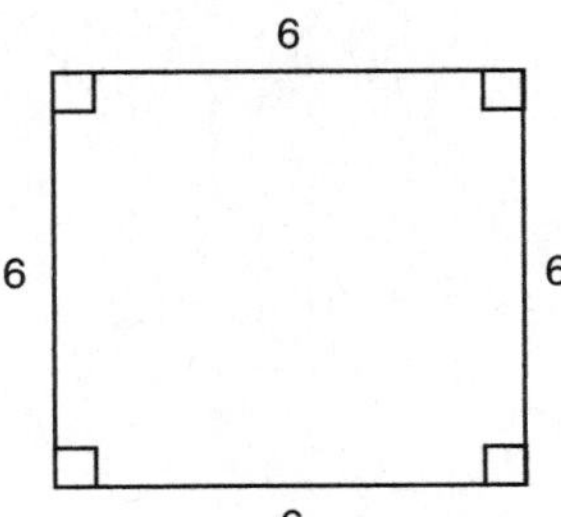

FIGURE 47.7 A square.

Triangles

A triangle is a three-sided figure. The measures of all the interior angles of a triangle add up to 180°. Triangles can take a variety of shapes, but several important special types are covered here.

Equilateral triangles (shown in Figure 47.8) have congruent sides and angles (so each angle measures 180° ÷ 3 = 60°).

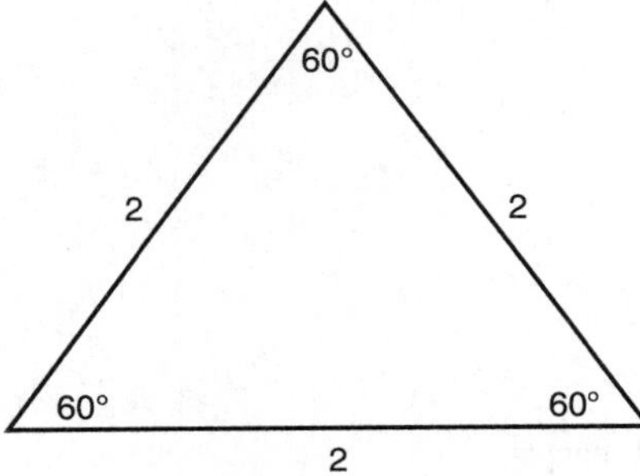

FIGURE 47.8 An equilateral triangle.

An isosceles triangle (shown in Figure 47.9) has two congruent sides and two congruent angles. Bisecting the third angle creates two right triangles back-to-back.

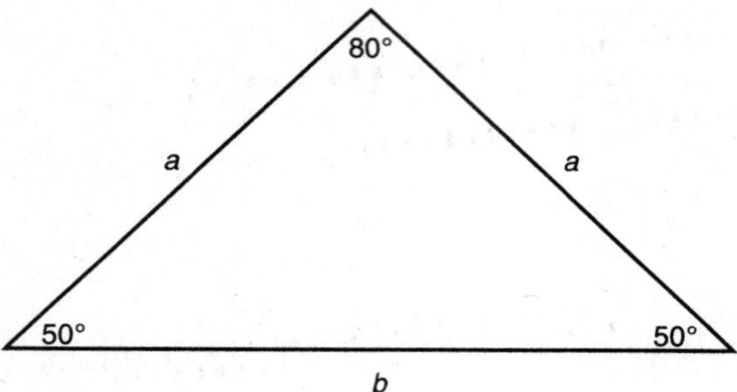

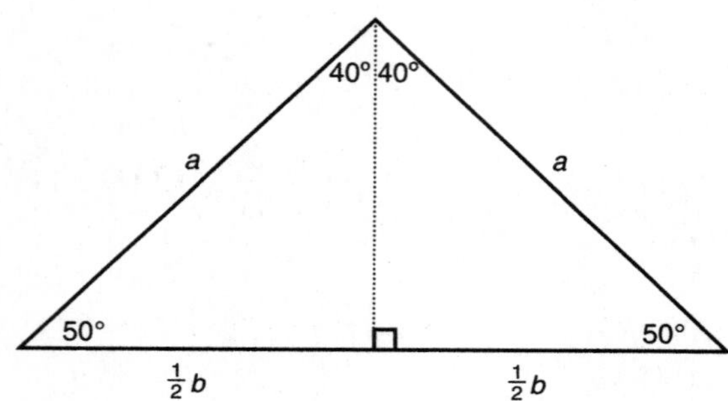

FIGURE 47.9 Isosceles triangles.

A right triangle (shown in Figure 47.10) has one right (90°) angle. The Pythagorean Relationship allows you to determine the length of an unknown side of a right triangle using the lengths of the other two sides. (Using the Pythagorean Relationship is reviewed later in this chapter.) In right triangles, the side opposite the right angle is called the hypotenuse, and the other two sides are called legs.

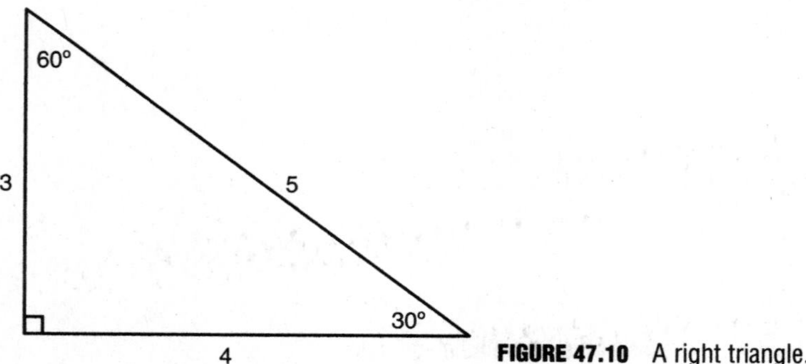

FIGURE 47.10 A right triangle.

The height of a triangle is defined as the vertical distance between the base and the opposite vertex, as shown in Figure 47.11.

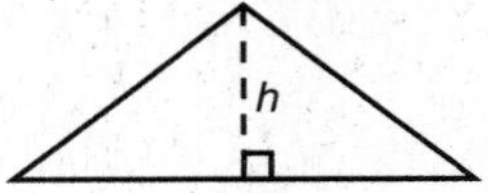

FIGURE 47.11 Height (h) of a triangle.

Circles

A circle (shown in Figure 47.12) is the set of points a certain distance (called the *radius*) from a center point. Knowing a circle's radius allows you to compute other features of the circle, such as diameter (distance across the circle), circumference (distance around the circle), and area (space within the circle).

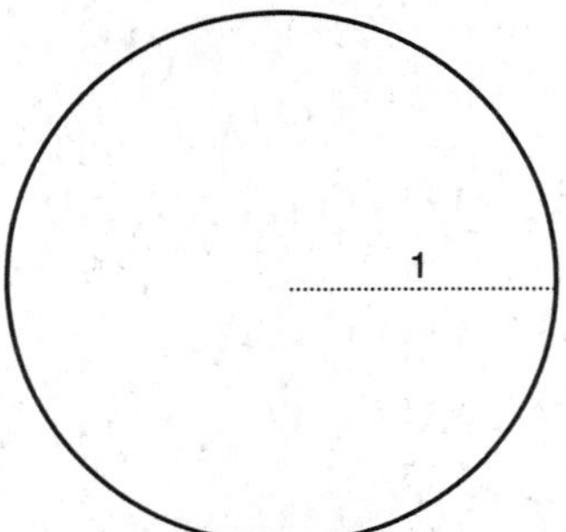

FIGURE 47.12 A circle of radius 1.

The following formulas show how you figure the various measurements of a circle and those values for the circle in Figure 47.12, which has a radius of 1:

$$\text{Diameter} = 2 \times \text{radius} = 2 \times 1 = 2$$

$$\text{Circumference} = \pi \times \text{diameter} = \pi \times 2 = 2\pi \approx 2 \times 3.14 \approx 6.26$$

$$\text{Area} = \pi \times (\text{radius})^2 = \pi \times 1^2 = \pi \times 1 = \pi \approx 3.14$$

Circle formulas use the number pi, represented by the Greek letter π, which equals approximately 3.14. Pi (π) is the ratio of circumference to diameter for all circles.

Derived 3-D Figures

The figures already presented in this chapter are said to be two-dimensional (2-D); they have lengths and height, but no depth. Three-dimensional (3-D) figures are derived by extending 2-D figures in the third dimension. For example, a shoebox shape (rectangular solid) is made by extending a rectangle in space. A cube is a special type of rectangular solid having equal edge lengths. A cylinder (for example, a roll of paper towel) is a circle extended in the third dimension. A cone is a right triangle rotated 360° about one of its legs. A square pyramid (as from Egypt) has a square base and sides extending toward a single point above the center of the square. Figure 47.13 shows some important three-dimensional figures.

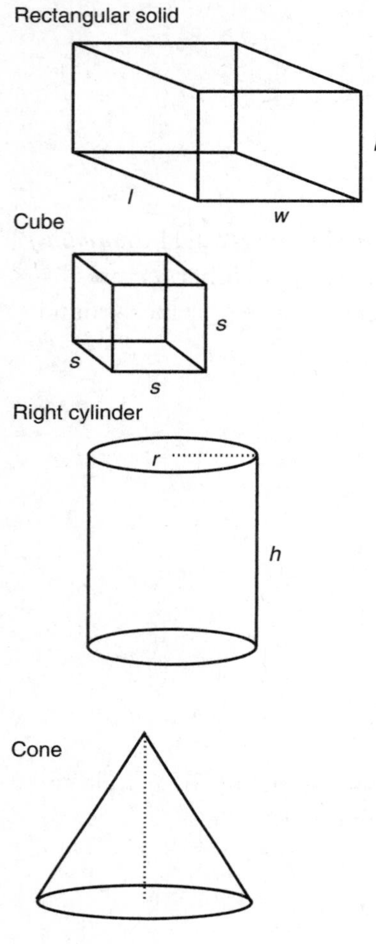

FIGURE 47.13 Important three-dimensional figures.

Side and Angle Relationships

In geometry, certain angle measures can be computed if you know other angle measures. Because straight lines measure 180°, the measures of all the angles on one side of a straight line add up to 180°. Consider the following example:

> To determine the value of x, subtract the measure of the other angle on the straight line (41°) from the total angle measure of the straight line (180°): $x = 180 - 41 = 139$.

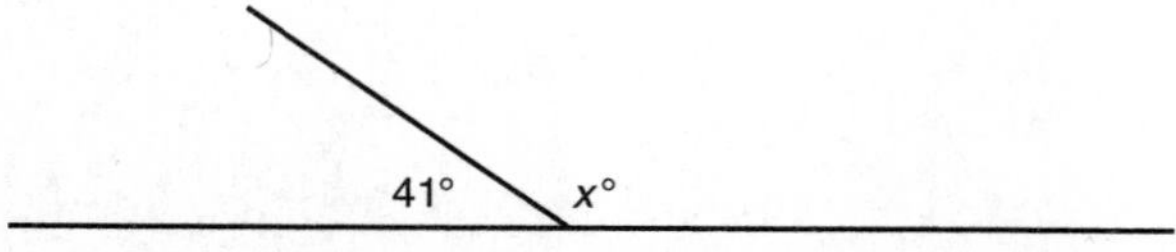

Pairs of congruent angles are created when lines intersect. These are called vertical angles. An angle measure equals the measure of the angle directly across the vertex (the intersection point of the lines) from it. Consider the following example:

> You can determine the values of a and b because each one's vertical angle is given to you. Angle a is across the vertex from the 120° angle, so a = 120°. Likewise, b = 60°.

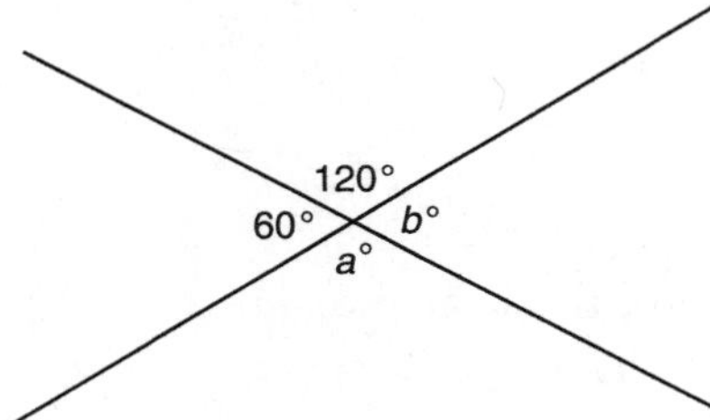

As stated earlier in the chapter, the sum of the angle measures within a triangle is 180°. For quadrilaterals, this sum is 360°. This means that if all but one angle measure is known, the remaining angle can be found by subtracting the known angle measures from the known sum.

Similarity and Congruency

The terms "similar" and "congruent" can describe two or more lines, line segments, angles, or figures.

Similar means proportional. Similar figures have the same angle measures and different but proportional side lengths.

The triangles in Figure 47.14 are similar because the angles are the same and the sides are proportional. To find the ratio of the side lengths, divide one side from the other corresponding side. Here, the ratio of lengths is 1.5 to 1 ($\frac{4.5}{3} = \frac{6}{4} = \frac{7.5}{5} = 1.5$).

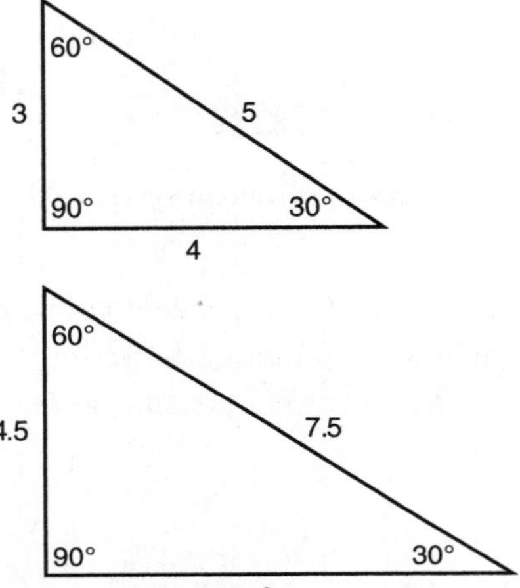

FIGURE 47.14 Similar triangles.

You can also determine similarity by calculating the ratios of side lengths within the triangles being compared. In the smaller triangle of Figure 47.14, there are three such ratios: 3/4, 4/5, 3/5. These ratios equal the corresponding ratios of the sides of the larger triangle in Figure 47.14:

$$\frac{3}{4} = \frac{4.5}{6}$$

$$\frac{4}{5} = \frac{6}{7.5}$$

$$\frac{3}{5} = \frac{4.5}{7.5}$$

Congruent means exactly equivalent. Congruent angles have the same measure. Congruent figures have the same angle measures and side lengths.

The triangles in Figure 47.15 are the same (congruent), although they are drawn facing different directions. Congruent figures have equal perimeters, areas, and in the case of 3-D figures, volumes.

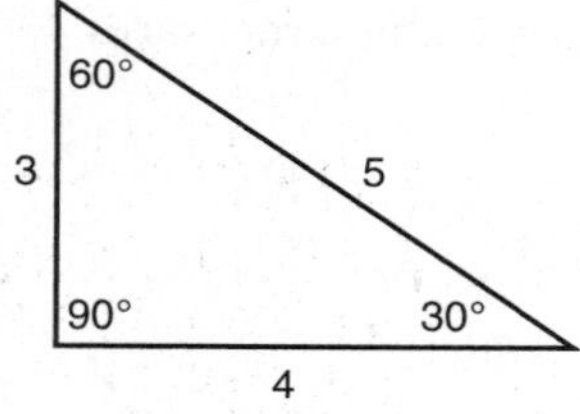

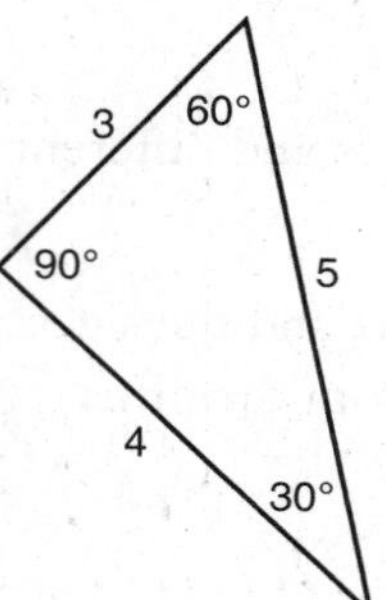

FIGURE 47.15 Congruent triangles.

Perimeter, Circumference, and Area

EXAM PREP Study TIP

You will be provided with a formulas page in your GED test booklet, but you should be familiar with how and when to use the formulas.

On the GED, you will need to apply specific formulas to compute dimensions of 2-D figures.

Perimeter is the sum of the side lengths of a 2-D figure. In circles, the equivalent concept is called circumference. Perimeter and circumference are lengths, and are, therefore, measured in linear (one-dimensional) units, such as inches, feet, centimeters, and so on:

Square: 4 × side

Rectangle: 2 × length + 2 × width

Triangle: $side_1 + side_2 + side_3$

Circumference of a circle: π × diameter; diameter is equal to 2 × radius, and pi (π) is an irrational number approximately equal to 3.14.

Area is the amount of space covered by a 2-D figure. Area is measured in two-dimensional units such as in^2 (square inches), ft^2 (square feet), acres, and so on:

Square: side^2

Rectangle: length × width

Parallelogram: base length × height

Triangle: $(\frac{1}{2})$ × base length × height

Trapezoid: $(\frac{1}{2})$ × (base length$_1$ + base length$_2$) × height

Circle: π × radius^2

Volume

The space occupied by a 3-D figure is called *volume*. Volume is measured in three-dimensional units, such as in^3 (cubic inches), ft^3 (cubic feet), L(liters) and so on:

Cube: edge^3

Rectangular solid: length × width × height

Square pyramid: $(\frac{1}{3})$ × (base edge length)^2 × height

Cylinder: π × radius^2 × height

Cone: $(\frac{1}{3})$ π × radius^2 × height

The Pythagorean Relationship

In a right triangle, the length of any side can be calculated from the lengths of the other two sides using the Pythagorean Relationship:

$$a^2 + b^2 = c^2$$

In the Pythagorean Relationship, *a* and *b* are the lengths of the legs (sides forming the right angle) and *c* is the length of the hypotenuse (side opposite the right angle).

To use this equation, make correct substitution of values for two of the variables and solve for the variable that remains. Consider the following example:

What is the length of the hypotenuse (c) of the right triangle below?

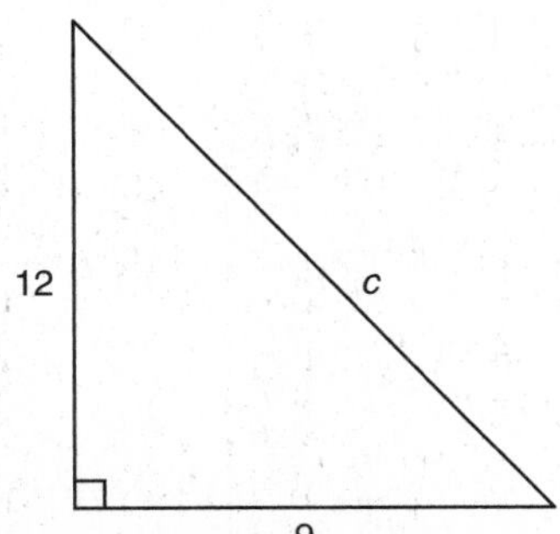

Substitute 9 and 12 for a and b, and then solve as follows:

$9^2 + 12^2 = c^2$

$81 + 144 = c^2$

$225 = c^2$

Take the square root of both sides.

$15 = c$

Therefore, the length of the hypotenuse is 15.

Remember that you can use the Pythagorean Relationship to find the length of any of the three sides of a right triangle. Consider the following example:

What is the length of a in the right triangle shown below?

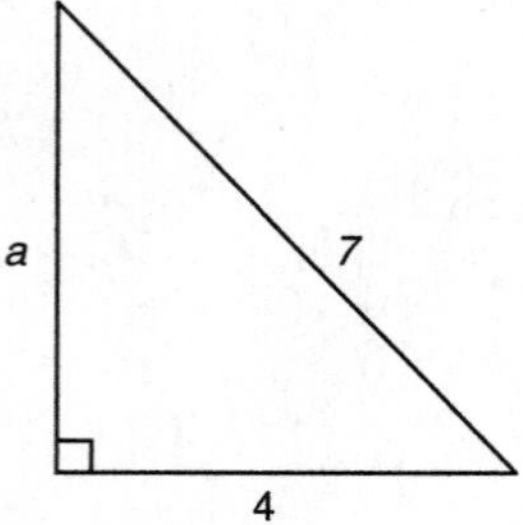

Substitute 4 for b and 7 for c in the Pythagorean Relationship, then solve as follows:

$a^2 + 4^2 = 7^2$

$a^2 + 16 = 49$

$a^2 = 33$

Take the square root of both sides.

$a = \sqrt{33}$ (This number is simplified.)

Therefore, the length of the second leg is $\sqrt{33}$.

Practice Questions

Complete the following geometry practice questions using a calculator as needed.

1. If angle A = 136°, calculate the value of angles *B*, *C*, and *D*.

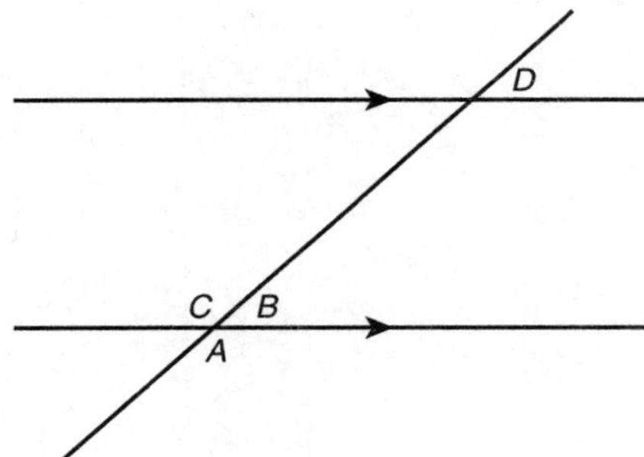

2. Calculate the measures of angles *A*, *B*, and *C*, and the length of side *X* of the parallelogram below. (Hint: Use congruency relationships of sides and angles, as well as the Pythagorean Relationship.)

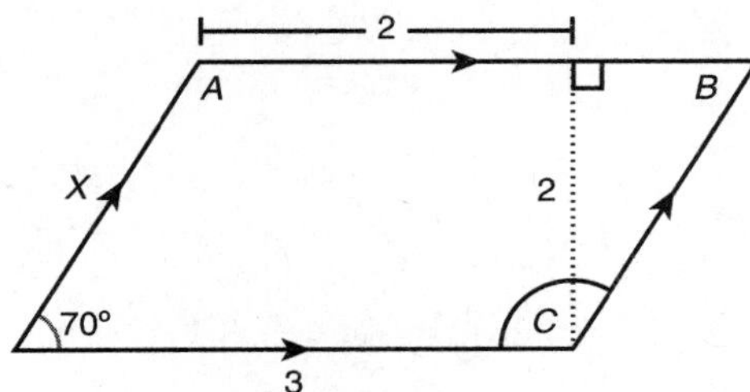

3. Calculate the measure of angle *A* and the length of side *B* in the figure below.

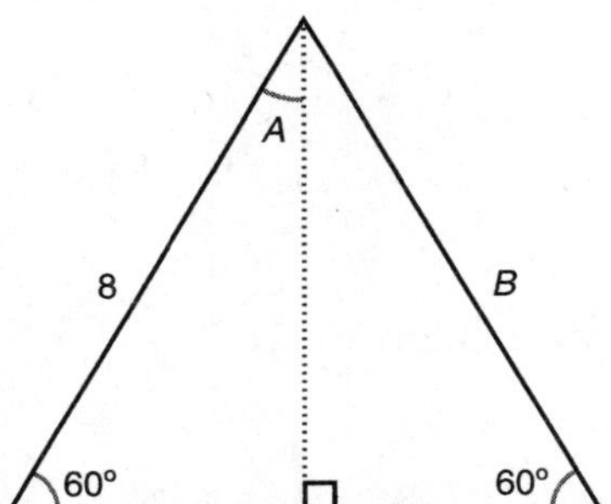

4. Are the figures below congruent, similar, or neither?

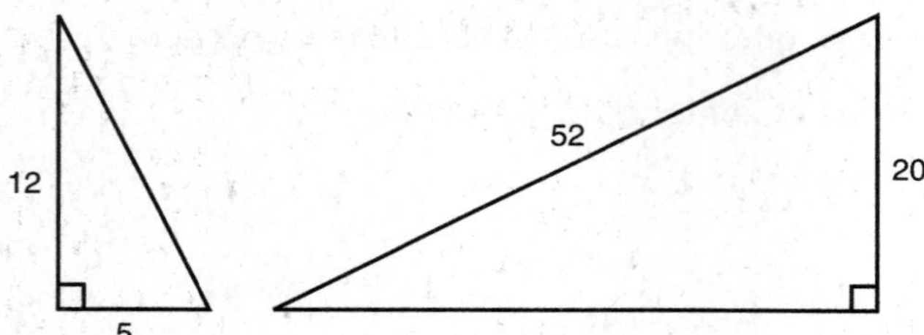

5. In triangle ABC below, angle A = 34°. What is B + C?

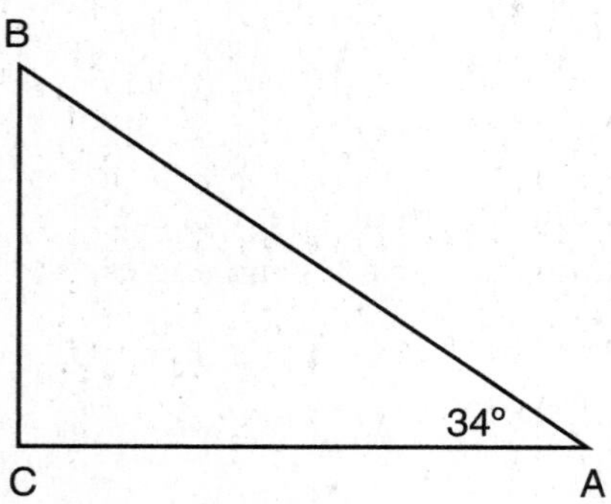

6. What is the value of x in the diagram below?

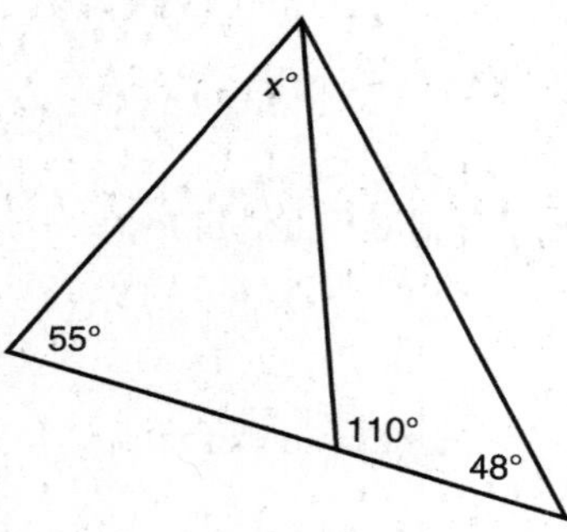

7. Calculate the radius, circumference, and area of the circle below.

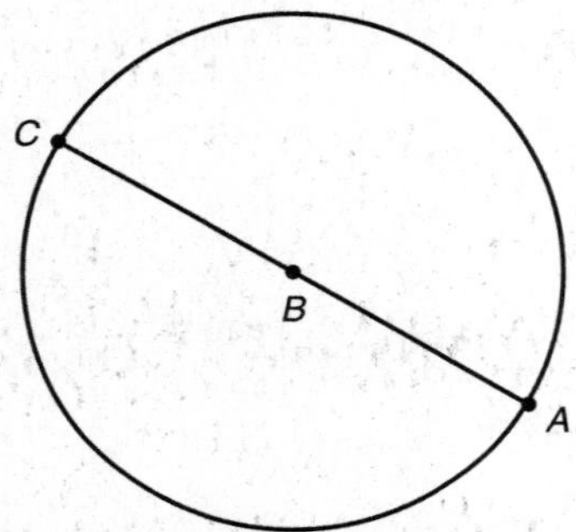

B is the center of the circle.

8. John is building a fence around his pasture shown in the diagram below. How many feet of fencing does John need to complete the project? (Hint: You will need to calculate a length and then use the Pythagorean Relationship.)

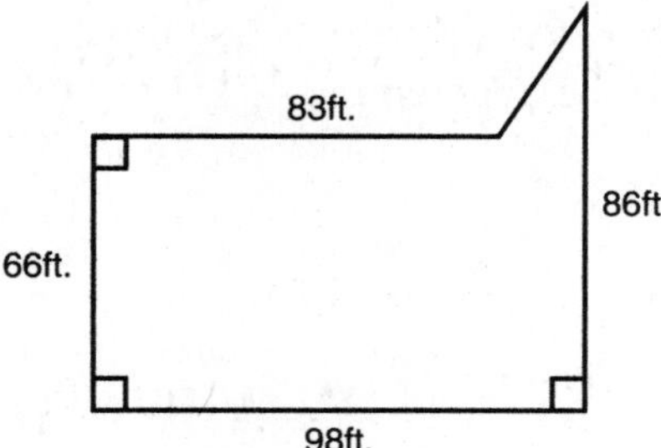

9. What is the area of John's pasture, in square feet?

10. Hillary was hired by a food company to oversee the opening of a new factory for canning evaporated milk. As part of her new job, she must decide on the type of can to be used. She has narrowed down the decision to two cans. Can A is a cylinder with a radius of 5cm and a height of 8cm. Can B is a cylinder with half of the radius and twice the height. Which of the two cans would hold more evaporated milk, and by how many cm^3?

Answers and Explanations

1. **The correct answers are *B* = 44°, *C* = 136°, and *D* = 44°.** A straight line measures 180°, so the measures of a pair of adjacent angles formed by an intersecting line must add up to 180°. Therefore, $180° - A = B$.

   $180° - 136° = B$

   $44° = B$

   A and *C* are vertical angles, so they are equal. Therefore, $C = 136°$. Because the horizontal lines are parallel, you know angles *D* and *B* are equal. Therefore, $B = 44°$.

2. **The correct answers are *A* = 110°, *B* = 70°, *C* = 110°, and *X* = $\sqrt{5}$.**

   Opposite sides and angles in a parallelogram are equal, so $B = 70°$. A quadrilateral's angles add up to 360°, so $A + C + 70 + 70 = 360$. Because *A* and *C* are opposite angles, they are equal; therefore, $2A = 360 - (70 + 70) = 220°$.

   $A = 110°$

   Therefore, $C = 110°$.

To find the length of side X, recognize that it is congruent to the opposite side. The opposite side forms the hypotenuse of a right triangle with one leg of length 2 and another leg of unknown length. Calculate the missing leg length. Because opposite sides are equal, if the bottom side = 3, then the top side = 3. The segment of the top side between the vertical line and B is, therefore, 3 – 2 = 1. Use the Pythagorean Relationship to calculate the length of the hypotenuse.

$a^2 + b^2 = c^2$

$1^2 + 2^2 = c^2$

$1 + 4 = c^2$

$5 = c^2$

$\sqrt{5} = c$

Therefore, $X = \sqrt{5}$.

3. **The correct answers are A = 30° and B = 8.** Because two angles are equal, the two sides forming the third angle will have the same length. This is a property of isosceles triangles. Therefore, $B = 8$.

   Because the triangle has two angles of 60°, and the sum of all angles in a triangle must be 180°, the third angle measures 60° (180 – 60 – 60 = 60). (As it turns out, all the angles of the triangle measure 60°, so the triangle is equilateral.) The vertical dashed line is perpendicular to the base of the triangle; therefore, the dashed line divides the top angle of the equilateral triangle exactly in half.

   $A = 60° \div 2 = 30°$

4. **The correct answer is "similar."** The triangles are clearly not congruent because they are different sizes. To determine whether the two triangles are similar, a ratio of two similar sides must be examined. Any two sides can be chosen as long as they are the same for both triangles. Begin with the short leg of the right triangles:

   $\frac{20}{5} = 4$. The ratio of the longer leg to the shorter leg is 4:1.

   Now you must choose whether to compare the other pair of corresponding legs or the pair of hypotenuses. In either case, you must use the Pythagorean Relationship.

   Option 1: Calculate the hypotenuse of the smaller triangle.

   $a^2 + b^2 = c^2$

   $12^2 + 5^2 = c^2$

   $144 + 25 = c^2$

   $169 = c^2$

   $13 = c$

Compare this length to the length of the other triangle's hypotenuse: $\frac{52}{13} = 4$. The ratio of the longer hypotenuse to the shorter hypotenuse is 4:1. The ratio matches the ratio of the short legs, so the triangles are similar.

Option 2: Calculate the long leg of the larger triangle.

$a^2 + b^2 = c^2$

$a^2 + 20^2 = 52^2$

$a^2 + 400 = 2704$

$a^2 = 2304$

$a = 48$

Compare this length to the length of the other triangle's long leg: $\frac{48}{12} = 4$. The ratio of the larger triangle's long leg to the corresponding leg of the smaller triangle is 4:1. The ratio matches the ratio of the short legs, so the triangles are similar.

5. **The correct answer is 146°.** Recall that the sum of the angles of a triangle is 180°. Therefore, in this case, $A + B + C = 180°$. You are given that $A = 34°$. So, $34 + B + C = 180°$. Solve for $B + C$ as follows:

   $34 + B + C = 180$

   $B + C = 180 - 34$

   $B + C = 146$

6. **The correct answer is 55.** Recall that the sum of the angles of any triangle is 180°. To determine x you must determine the measure of the other unknown angle within the interior triangle on the left. Notice how the unlabeled angle and the angle measuring 110° are supplementary—they add up to 180° because their nonshared sides form a line. Therefore, the unlabeled angle is 180° – 110° = 70°. Now calculate the difference of 180° and the two known angle measures, 55° and 70°: $x = 180° - 70° - 55° = 55°$.

7. **The correct answers are radius = 3, circumference = 6π, and area = 9π.** Radius of a circle, by definition, is half the diameter. Therefore, the radius is $6 \div 2 = 3$. Circumference is equal to pi times the diameter. Therefore, the circumference is $\pi \times 6 = 6\pi$. Area of a circle is equal to pi times the radius squared. Therefore, the area is $\pi \times 3^2 = 9\pi$. To compute decimal answers, substitute 3.14 for π above.

8. **The correct answer is 358.** The amount of fence is equal to the perimeter of the shape. The length of the shortest side is unknown. To figure out the length of this diagonal side, it is best to treat the entire shape as a combination of a rectangle and a triangle. Draw a line separating the two to help you to visualize the line segments.

The vertical leg of the triangle is 86 feet – 66 feet = 20 feet. The short leg of the triangle (which is not actually part of the perimeter) is equal to 98 feet – 83 feet, which equals 15 feet. Using the Pythagorean Relationship, calculate the hypotenuse:

$a^2 + b^2 = c^2$

$15^2 + 20^2 = c^2$

$225 + 400 = c^2$

$625 = c^2$

$25 = c$

Finally, add all sides together: 83 + 66 + 98 + 86 + 25 = 358.

9. **The correct answer is 6,618.** Consider the pasture a combination of a rectangle and a triangle, as you did in the previous problem. Area of a rectangle is equal to length times width. Therefore, the area of the rectangle portion of the shape is 66 feet × 98 feet = 6468 ft^2. Area of a triangle is equal to $\frac{1}{2}$ times base times height $\frac{1}{2}$(bh). Therefore, the area of the triangle portion of the shape is $\frac{1}{2}$(98 ft – 83 ft)(86 ft – 66 ft) = $\frac{1}{2}$(15 ft)(20 ft) = 150 ft^2.

   Find the total area of the pasture by adding the two partial areas you calculated: 6468 ft^2 + 150 ft^2 = 6,618 ft^2.

10. **The correct answer is that Can A holds 100cm³, or approximately 314cm³, more than Can B.** The volume of a cylinder is pi times radius-squared times height. Compare the volumes of the two cylindrical cans.

    Area = $\pi \times r^2 \times h$

    Can A:

    Area = $\pi \times 5^2 \times 8$

    Area = 200π

    Can B:

    Area = $\pi \times 2.5^2 \times 16$

    Area = 100π

    Can A has greater volume. Calculate the difference between the volumes of Cans A and B:

    $200\pi - 100\pi = 100\pi$

    (You may choose to approximate pi and multiply: $100\pi \approx 100 \times 3.14 = 314$)

What's Next?

The next chapters in this section include GED Mathematics practice questions and answers (Chapter 48) as well as a glossary of mathematic terms (Chapter 49). Review the glossary and attempt to answer all the practice questions, using your critical thinking skills and knowledge of mathematics concepts. Refer to Chapters 35 through 47 as necessary.

CHAPTER FORTY-EIGHT

Mathematics Practice Questions and Answer Explanations

This chapter includes 25 simulated mathematics questions. Carefully read the directions and answer the questions. Allow yourself a total of 45 minutes to complete these practice questions.

Use the answer sheet on the following page to mark your answers. Then compare your answers to the answers and explanations at the end of this chapter. Be sure to read through the explanations thoroughly. Identify and review topics you've consistently struggled with.

Please note that this chapter does not follow the precise format of the GED.

Answer Sheet

1. ① ② ③ ④ ⑤
2. ① ② ③ ④ ⑤
3.
4.
5. ① ② ③ ④ ⑤
6. ① ② ③ ④ ⑤
7. ① ② ③ ④ ⑤
8. ① ② ③ ④ ⑤
9. ① ② ③ ④ ⑤
10.
11. ① ② ③ ④ ⑤
12. ① ② ③ ④ ⑤
13. ① ② ③ ④ ⑤
14. ① ② ③ ④ ⑤
15. ① ② ③ ④ ⑤
16. ① ② ③ ④ ⑤
17. ① ② ③ ④ ⑤
18.

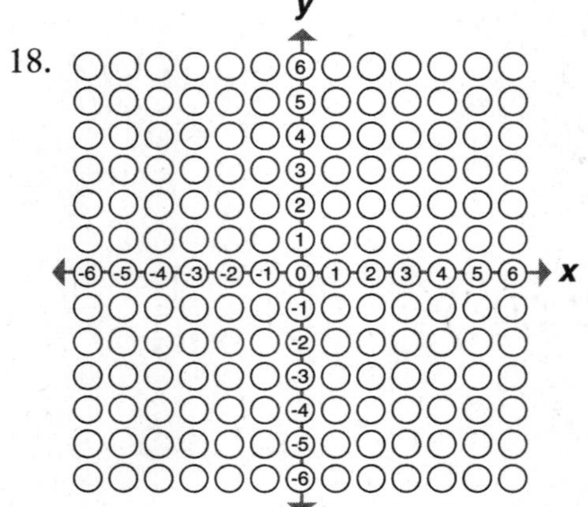

19. ① ② ③ ④ ⑤
20. ① ② ③ ④ ⑤
21. ① ② ③ ④ ⑤
22. ① ② ③ ④ ⑤
23. ① ② ③ ④ ⑤
24. ① ② ③ ④ ⑤
25. ① ② ③ ④ ⑤

Practice Questions

Directions: You will have 23 minutes to answer questions 1—13. You may use your calculator with these 13 questions only. Choose the one best answer to each question.

Questions 1 and 2 refer to the following information and table.

Aishah and her family planned a trip to Canada. Her local bank gave her the exchange rates for U.S. dollars (USD) and Canadian dollars (CAD) below.

Exchange Rates for USD and CAD

U.S. Dollars (USD)	Canadian Dollars (CAD)
1	1.13928
0.877751	1

1. While in Canada, Aishah bought a jacket that cost 40 CAD. Based on the exchange rate she received for her money, what was the approximate cost of the jacket in USD?

   (1) 45.00

   (2) 40.00

   (3) 37.00

   (4) 35.00

   (5) 33.00

2. Aishah exchanged 800 USD for CAD. How many CAD did she receive in return?

   (1) 1,038.36

   (2) 911.42

   (3) 702.20

   (4) 616.35

   (5) 209.22

3. Jordan can purchase a study guide from his biology instructor for $3.50, or he can borrow the study guide from a classmate and copy it at a cost of $0.05 per page. If the cost to purchase the study guide is exactly equal to the cost to copy it, then the study guide must have how many pages?

   Mark your answer in the circles in the grid on your answer sheet.

4. How many minutes would it take a car to travel 18 miles at a constant speed of 45 miles per hour?

   Mark your answer in the circles in the grid on your answer sheet.

5. Which equation could be used to find d, the height of the building in the diagram below?

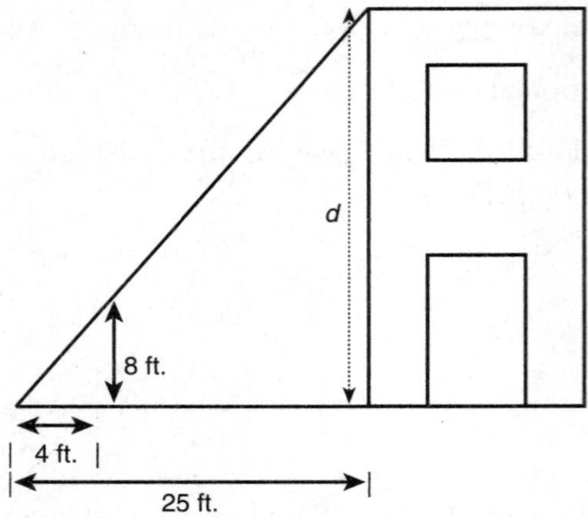

(1) $\frac{d}{25} = \frac{4}{8}$

(2) $\frac{d}{4} = \frac{8}{25}$

(3) $\frac{8}{4} = \frac{d}{25}$

(4) $\frac{8}{4} = \frac{25}{d}$

(5) $\frac{d}{25} = \frac{4}{8}$

6. A neighborhood home-improvement store is having a sale. The cost of ceramic tiles is now $0.49 each, and grout is 10% off the regular price of $4.50 per can. Traci wants to purchase 120 ceramic tiles and 1 can of grout. How much will she pay before tax?

(1) $4.99

(2) $49.00

(3) $58.80

(4) $62.85

(5) $124.50

Questions 7 through 9 refer to the following information and tables.

Andrew fitted an electric toy car with soft, smooth rubber wheels and placed the car on a smooth, flat surface. Andrew started the car and a stopwatch at the same time. Andrew stopped the stopwatch as the car crossed the 75-foot mark. He calculated the results of 3 separate trials, as shown in the table below.

Procedure 1

Trial Number	Time in Seconds
1	22.8
2	23.2
3	22.5

Andrew repeated the procedure, this time fitting the car with hard rubber wheels. The results are shown in the table below.

Procedure 2

Trial Number	Time in Seconds
1	57.0
2	56.4
3	56.7

7. What was the average time the car with the soft wheels took to cross the 75-foot mark when it was fitted with hard rubber wheels?

   (1) 22.8 seconds

   (2) 33.9 seconds

   (3) 39.8 seconds

   (4) 56.7 seconds

   (5) 170.1 seconds

8. Assuming that the car traveled at a constant speed, approximately how far had the car with soft wheels traveled in Trial 3 after 11.25 seconds?

   (1) 22.5 feet

   (2) 37.5 feet

   (3) 75.0 feet

   (4) 253.125 feet

   (5) Not enough information is given.

9. During which procedure and trial did the car travel at the highest speed?

   (1) Procedure 1, Trial 1

   (2) Procedure 1, Trial 2

   (3) Procedure 1, Trial 3

   (4) Procedure 2, Trial 1

   (5) Procedure 2, Trial 3

10. At a bottling plant, 10,000 liters of carbonated water are needed to produce 1,500 cases of soda. How many liters of carbonated water are needed to produce 300 cases of soda?

    Mark your answer in the circles in the grid on your answer sheet.

11. The greeting card racks that Carlos is building for the local bookstore are designed to hold 26 boxes of greeting cards on each shelf. Each rack will have 5 shelves. How many racks will Carlos need to hold a total of 520 boxes of greeting cards?

    (1) 4

    (2) 5

    (3) 21

    (4) 26

    (5) 31

12. To make a cleaning solution, Amanda added 2 quarts of concentrated soap to 2.5 gallons of water. How many gallons of cleaning solution did Amanda make?

    (1 gallon = 4 quarts)

    (1) 2.5

    (2) 3.0

    (3) 4.5

    (4) 5.0

    (5) 10.0

13. Frank is a billing clerk in a doctor's office. Three patients owe $125.00 each for exams. Their insurance companies pay for 20% of the cost of doctor visits. What is the total amount that Frank will bill to all three of the patients directly?

    (1) $75.00

    (2) $100.00

    (3) $125.00

    (4) $150.00

    (5) $300.00

Mathematics Part II

Directions: You will have 22 minutes to answer questions 14—25. You may *not* use a calculator with these 13 questions. Choose the one best answer to each question.

Questions 14 and 15 refer to the following information and graph.

Franklin measured the visibility of a basketball placed 300 meters away at different times during the day. He asked 30 classmates to say whether or not they could see the basketball. The results of his survey are shown in the graph below.

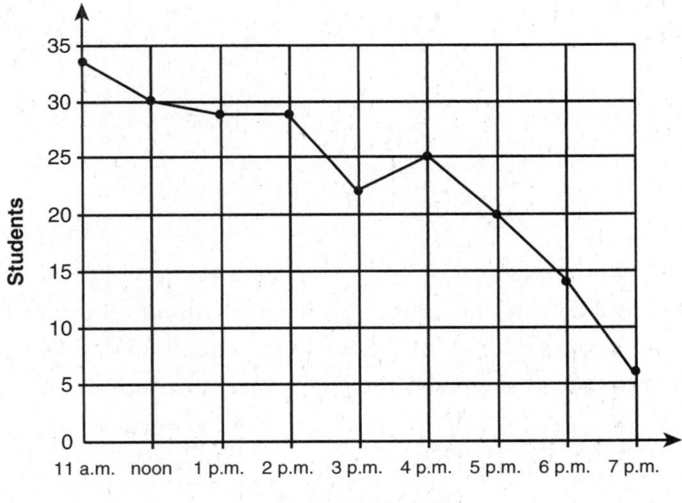

14. During the afternoon, cloud cover dispersed, causing the visibility of the basketball to increase for an hour. According to the graph, when did the cloud cover begin to disperse?

    (1) noon

    (2) 1 p.m.

    (3) 2 p.m.

    (4) 3 p.m.

    (5) 4 p.m.

15. After how many hours could only $\frac{2}{3}$ of Franklin's classmates see the basketball?

    (1) 3

    (2) 4

    (3) 5

    (4) 6

    (5) 7

16. The positive square root of 80 lies between what pair of integers?

    (1) 4 and 5

    (2) 5 and 6

    (3) 6 and 7

    (4) 7 and 8

    (5) 8 and 9

17. A total of t singers join the school chorus. The director divides them into 4 groups of s singers and one group of 5 singers. Which of the following equations expresses the relationship between the number of singers in the chorus and the number of singers in each group?

    (1) $t = 5s + 4$

    (2) $t = 4s + 5$

    (3) $t = 4(s - 5)$

    (4) $t = 5(s - 5)$

    (5) $t = 4(5s + 1)$

18. Three vertices of rectangle RSTV are shown on the graph.

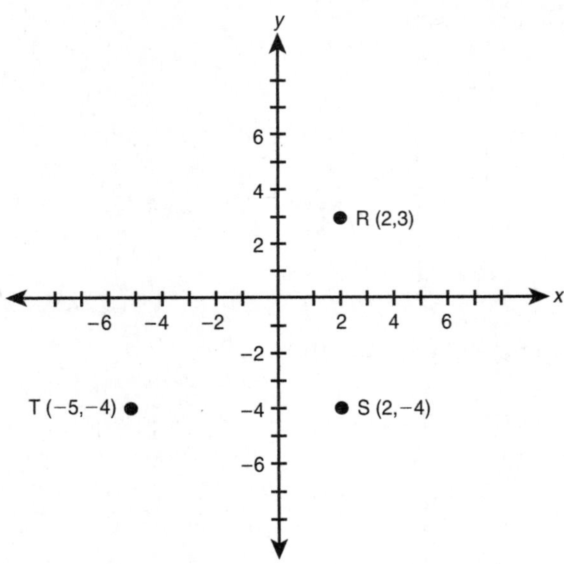

What is the location of point V, the fourth vertex of the rectangle?

DO NOT MARK YOUR ANSWER ON THE GRAPH ABOVE.

Mark your answer on the coordinate plane grid on your answer sheet.

19. In the diagram below, triangle *FGJ* and triangle *HJG* are congruent (the same shape and size).

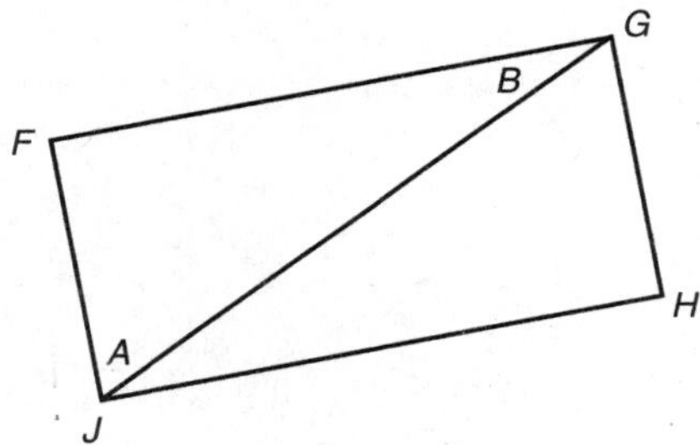

Which of the following must be true?

(1) Segment *FJ* is parallel to segment *GH*.

(2) The measure of angle *A* equals the measure of angle *B*.

(3) Segment *FG* equals segment *JG*.

(4) The measure of angle *FJG* equals the measure of angle *GHJ*.

(5) Segment *JH* is perpendicular to segment *FJ*.

20. Last week, Althea delivered 250 newspapers. This week she delivered half as many newspapers as she delivered last week. What is the total number of newspapers Althea delivered last week and this week?

    (1) 125
    (2) 150
    (3) 250
    (4) 375
    (5) 500

21. What is the fourth term in the arithmetic sequence 13, 10, 7, …?

    (1) 14
    (2) 9
    (3) 4
    (4) 0
    (5) –7

22. The graph below shows the increase in the number of students enrolled at the local high school.

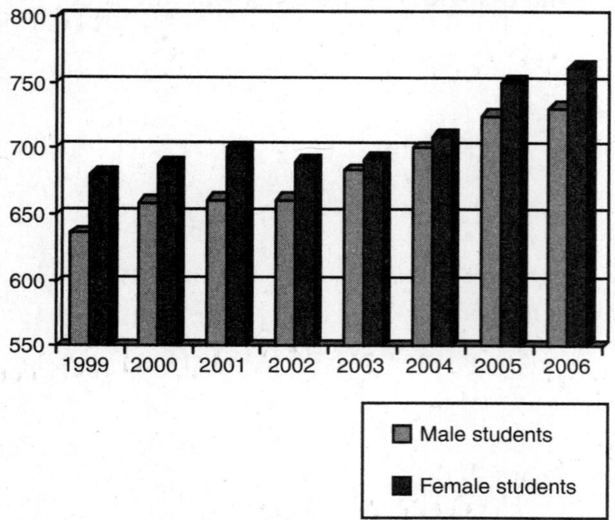

Between which two years did the number of enrollments increase the least?

    (1) 1999 and 2000
    (2) 2000 and 2001
    (3) 2001 and 2002
    (4) 2002 and 2003
    (5) 2005 and 2006

23. Which of the following is the complete solution to the equation (x + 7)(x – 3) = 0?

 (1) –7 only

 (2) 3 only

 (3) 3 or –7

 (4) 7 or –3

 (5) 7 or 3

24. The following statements about the diagram below are true:

 Angle *FJK* is a straight angle.

 The measure of ∠ *IJK* is 20°.

 Angle *FJH* is a right angle.

 The measure of ∠ *GJI* = 135°.

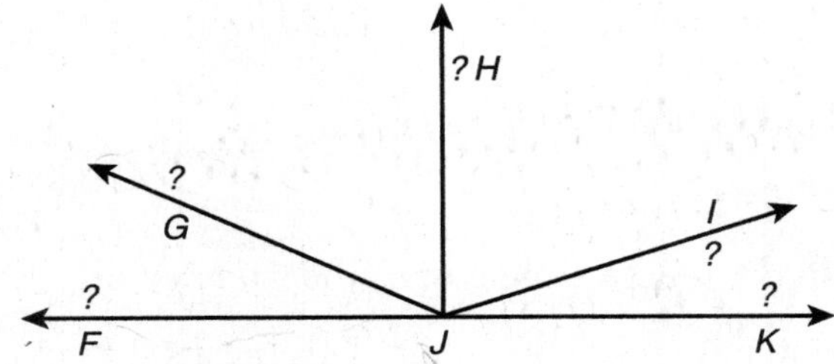

 What is the measure of ∠ *FJG*?

 (1) 15°

 (2) 20°

 (3) 25°

 (4) 30°

 (5) 35°

25. The normal temperature of a chest freezer is –5° F. Recently, Barbara has noticed that the temperature has dropped x° F. Which expression represents the new temperature of the chest freezer?

 (1) $-5 - x$

 (2) $-5 + x$

 (3) –5

 (4) $-5x$

 (5) 5

Answers and Explanations

1. **The correct answer is (4).** The chart indicates that Aishah received 1 Canadian dollar for every 0.877751 U.S. dollars she exchanged. Therefore, convert from CAD to USD by multiplying CAD by 0.877751.

   $40 \times 0.877751 = 35.11004$

   Therefore, the approximate cost in USD is 35.00.

2. **The correct answer is (2).** The chart indicates that Aishah received 1.13928 CAD for every 1 USD she exchanged. Therefore, convert USD to CAD by multiplying by 1.13928.

   $800 \times 1.13928 = 911.424$ (Because this problem deals with money, round down or truncate the number to 911.42.)

3. **The correct answer is 70.** To solve this problem, set up an equation where p is the number of pages in the study guide.

   $0.05p = 3.50$

   Solve for p by dividing both sides of the equation by 0.05.

   $p = 70$

   Therefore, photocopying 70 pages costs $3.50, the same cost as the study guide.

4. **The correct answer is 24.** There are 60 minutes in one hour. This means that the car is traveling at a constant speed of 45 miles per 60 minutes. Set up a proportion to calculate the number of minutes it would take the car to travel 18 miles:

   $$\frac{18 \text{ miles}}{x \text{ minutes}} = \frac{45 \text{ miles}}{60 \text{ minutes}}$$

   Cross-multiply and solve for x.

   $45x = 60 \times 18$

   $45x = 1{,}080$

   $x = 24$

5. **The correct answer is (3).** You are asked to select the proportion that correctly compares corresponding ratios. Answer choice (3) is the only answer choice that is a possible option. The ratio of the vertical leg of the small triangle to the horizontal leg of the small triangle is $\frac{8}{4}$. This equals the corresponding ratio (vertical leg to horizontal leg) in the larger similar triangle: $\frac{d}{25}$.

6. **The correct answer is (4).** The first step you should take in solving this problem is to determine the cost of each item. Because the customer is purchasing 120 ceramic tiles at a cost of $0.49 per tile, multiply the number of tiles by the cost of each tile:

   $120 \times \$0.49 = \$58.80$

   Traci will pay $58.80 for the ceramic tiles. According to information in the problem, she is also purchasing one can of grout. Because the grout is 10% off, the cost will be 100% – 10%, or 90% of the original price ($4.50). Multiply $4.50 by 0.90:

   $\$4.50 \times .90 = \$4.05$

   Traci will pay $4.05 for the can of grout. Now, calculate the total charges for the ceramic tiles and the grout:

   $\$58.80 + \$4.05 = \$62.85$

   Traci will pay $62.85 before tax.

7. **The correct answer is (4).** The hard wheels data is in the second table so you can ignore the data in the first table. Calculate the average of those three times: $(57.0 + 56.4 + 56.7) \div 3 = 56.7$

8. **The correct answer is (2).** Because the car traveled at a constant speed, you can set up a proportion between the time and distance of the whole run and the time and distance of the partial run.

   $$\frac{22.5 \text{ seconds}}{75 \text{ ft}} = \frac{11.25 \text{ seconds}}{x \text{ ft}}$$

   $75 \times 11.25 = 22.5x$

   $843.75 = 22.5x$

   $37.5 = x$

   Therefore, the car traveled 37.5 feet in 11.25 seconds.

9. **The correct answer is (3).** The data in the tables reflects the amount of time the cars took to travel a constant distance. Therefore, the car that finished in the least amount of time traveled at the highest speed.

10. **The correct answer is 2,000.** To solve this problem, set up a proportion:

    $$\frac{10{,}000 \text{ L}}{1{,}500 \text{ cases}} = \frac{x \text{ L}}{300 \text{ cases}}$$

    Cross-multiply, and then solve.

    $1{,}500x = 10{,}000 \times 300$

    $1{,}500x = 3{,}000{,}000$

    $x = 2{,}000$

11. **The correct answer is (1).** To determine the total number of racks that Carlos will need to hold 520 boxes of greeting cards, first calculate the number of boxes that one rack will hold. Multiply the number of boxes that one shelf on a rack will hold (26) by the number of shelves on each rack (5):

    $26 \times 5 = 130$

    One rack will hold 130 boxes of greeting cards.

    Because Carlos needs to build enough racks to hold 520 boxes, divide 520 by the number of boxes that one rack will hold (130):

    $520 \div 130 = 4$

    Carlos will need to build 4 racks to hold 520 boxes of greeting cards.

12. **The correct answer is (2).** To solve this problem, first divide the number of quarts (2) by the number of quarts per gallon (4): $\frac{2}{4} = \frac{1}{2}$. The fraction $\frac{1}{2} = 0.5$; therefore, two quarts of concentrate is equal to .5 gallons of concentrate. Now add the number of gallons of concentrate (.5) to the number of gallons of water (2.5) to show that Amanda made 3.0 gallons of concentrate.

13. **The correct answer is (5).** Your first step is to determine the total amount that the 3 patients owe. Multiply the amount of money that each patient owes ($125.00) by the number of patients (3), to get $375.00.

    Because the insurance companies pay 20%, the patients are responsible for 100% – 20% = 80% of the cost. Calculate 80% of $375.

    $\$375.00 \times 0.80 = \$300.00$

14. **The correct answer is (4).** In this graph, visibility seemed to decrease as the day progressed. The hour from 3 to 4 p.m., however, shows an increase in the number of students who were able to see the basketball.

15. **The correct answer is (3).** The first step in solving this problem is to realize that $\frac{2}{3}$ of Franklin's 30 classmates is 20. The graph crosses the horizontal grid line for 20 students at the vertical grid line for 5 p.m. Therefore, because the survey began at noon, only $\frac{2}{3}$ of Franklin's classmates could see the basketball after 5 hours.

16. **The correct answer is (5).** Solve this problem using a guess-and-check strategy. In addition, work backward, squaring integers instead of attempting to calculate square roots of numbers around 80. For example, begin by determining the square of 10: $10 \times 10 = 100$. Guess lower: $9 \times 9 = 81$. This is very close to 80 and will constitute the greater integer you are looking for. Showing that $8 \times 8 = 64$ confirms that the square root of 80 is some number between 8 and 9.

17. **The correct answer is (2).** This question tests your ability to translate a word problem into an equation. If there are 4 groups of s singers and one group of 5 singers, then the total number of singers is $t = s + s + s + s + 5$, or $t = 4s + 5$.

18. **The correct answer is**

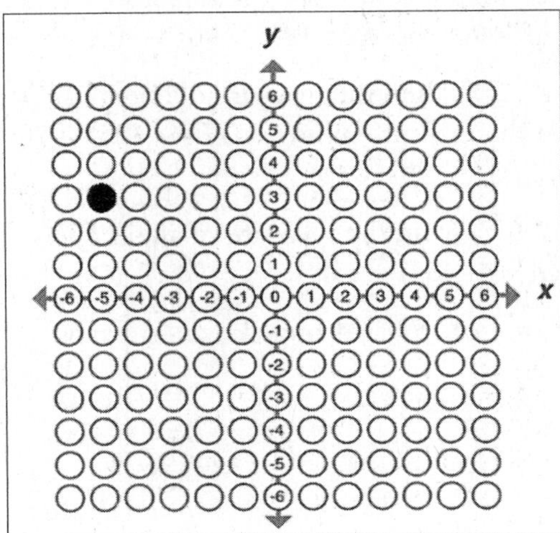

For the figure to be a rectangle, the fourth vertex must have the same x value as point T and the same y value as point R. Therefore, point V has the coordinates (–5, 3).

19. **The correct answer is (1).** Although the triangles appear to be right triangles, you can only assume that they are congruent to one another. Given this information, you know that quadrilateral *FGHJ* is a parallelogram. This means that segment *FJ* must be congruent and parallel to segment *GH*. No other answer choice must be true.

20. **The correct answer is (4).** The problem states that the total number of newspapers Althea delivered between last week and this week is 250 + .5(250) = 375.

21. **The correct answer is (3).** A term in the sequence is the previous term minus 3. Therefore, if the third term is 7, the fourth term is 4.

22. **The correct answer is (3).** To determine a two-year span with the least increase in student enrollment, first see if enrollment ever decreased. Between 2001 and 2002, the enrollment of male students appears to have stayed the same, whereas female enrollment dropped. This is the only two-year span on the graph that shows a decrease in enrollment of any size.

23. **The correct answer is (3).** Recall that any number multiplied by zero equals zero. Therefore, the complete answer to the equation is the set of numbers that would make either quantity zero:

Therefore, $x = -7$ or $x = 3$.

$-7 + 7 = 0$

$3 - 3 = 0$

24. **The correct answer is (3).** The conditions in the problem tell you that angle *FJK* is a straight angle, meaning it measures 180°. Angle *FJH* is a right angle, so it measures 90°. Therefore, angle *HJK* measures 90°, because 180° – 90° = 90°.

    If angle *HJK* measures 90° and *IJK* measures 20°, then the measure of angle *HJI* = 90° – 20° = 70°. If *GJI* measures 135°, then the measure of angle *GJH* = 135° – 70° = 65°.

    Finally, subtract the measure of angle *GJH* (65°) from the measure of angle *FJH* (90°) to compute the measure of angle *FJG*: 90° – 65° = 25°.

25. **The correct answer is (1).** If the temperature of –5 has dropped by x, the new temperature is x less than –5, or $-5 - x$.

What's Next?

Chapter 49, "Mathematics Terms," includes a list of math terms that might appear on your GED Mathematics Test. These terms have also likely been used throughout the chapters in Part VIII.

CHAPTER FORTY-NINE

49 Mathematics Terms

A

acute Describing an angle that is less than 90° or a triangle with angles that are all less than 90°.

adjacent angle Either of two angles having a common side and common vertex, for example, angles *a* and *b* in the following:

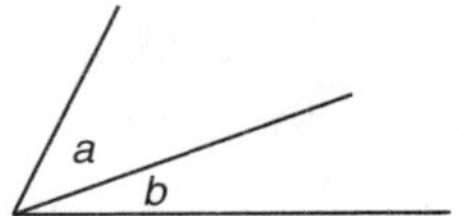

area Extent of two-dimensional size, measured in square units, of a geometric shape (see also Appendix D, "Mathematics Formulas").

average (See *mean*).

B

base In geometry: bottom side of a plane figure. For example, in the following right triangle, *AC* is the base:

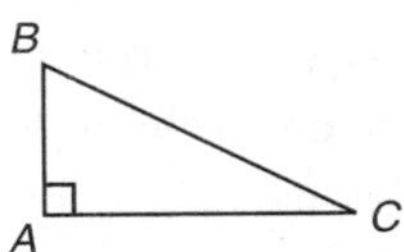

In algebra: the number that is raised to a power. For example, 2^3 represents the base 2 raised to the power of 3.

C

circumference The distance around a circle (see also Appendix D).

collinear Passing through or lying on the same straight line.

complementary angles Pair of angles whose measures sum 90°.

concentric Having a common center.

congruent Equal in length or measure.

coordinate plane *or* **Cartesian plane** Standard (x,y) plane defined by two axes at right angles to each other. The horizontal axis is the x-axis, and the vertical axis is the y-axis. Points on the coordinate plane are indicated by an ordered pair of numbers. The ordered pair (0, 0), where the x and y axes meet, is the origin.

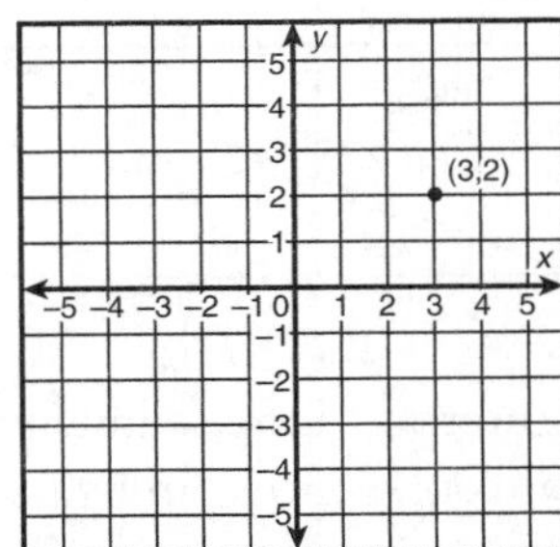

cube Term raised to the 3rd power; a regular solid having six congruent faces.

cubic inch Volume of a cube with edges that each measure one inch.

cylinder Solid with circular ends and straight sides.

D

decimal Describing the common number system in which digits can be placed to the left and right of a decimal point to indicate their place value. Place value refers to the value of a digit in a number relative to its position. Starting from the left of the decimal point, the values of the digits are ones, tens, hundreds, and so on. Starting to the right of the decimal point, the values of the digits are tenths, hundredths, thousandths, and so on.

denominator Bottom part of a fraction. For example, in the fraction $\frac{3}{4}$, 4 is the denominator.

determinant Difference between multiplied terms in a matrix.

diagonal Line segment that connects two nonadjacent vertices in any polygon. In the following rectangle, *AC* and *BD* are diagonals.

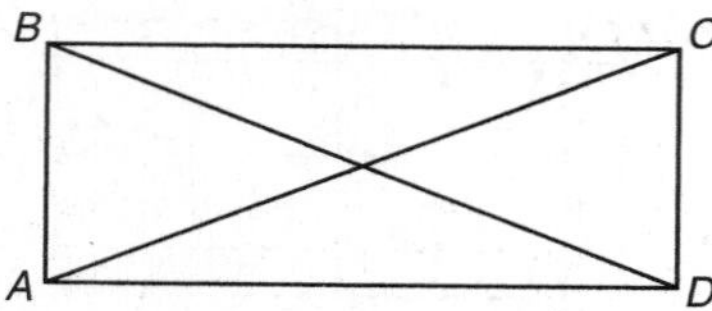

diameter Line segment that joins two points on a circle and passes through the center of the circle, as follows, where *AB* is the diameter.

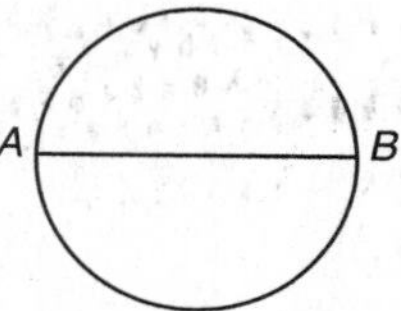

difference Result of subtraction.

directly proportional Increasing or decreasing together or with the same ratio.

divisibility Ability to be divided, usually meaning with no remainder. For example, 6 is divisible by 2 because the result is 3 with no remainder.

E

endpoint Either of two points defining a line segment.

equilateral triangle Triangle in which all sides are congruent and each of the angles measures 60°.

exponent Number that indicates the operation of repeated multiplication. A number with an exponent is said to be "raised to the power" of that exponent. For example, 2^3 indicates 2 raised to the power of 3, which translates into $2 \times 2 \times 2$. In this instance, 3 is the exponent. Likewise, 3^4 indicates 3 raised to the power of 4, which translates into $3 \times 3 \times 3 \times 3$. In this instance, 4 is the exponent.

F–G

factor One of two or more expressions that are multiplied together to get a product: in the equation [$2 \times 3 = 6$], 2 and 3 are factors of 6. Likewise, in the equation [$x^2 + 5x + 6$], $(x + 2)$ and $(x + 3)$ are factors.

fraction Expression that indicates the quotient of two quantities: $\frac{2}{3}$ is a fraction, where 2 is the numerator and 3 is the denominator.

greatest common factor Largest number that will divide evenly into any two or more numbers: 1, 2, 4, and 8 are all factors of 8; likewise, 1, 2, 3, and 6 are all factors of 6. Therefore, the greatest common factor of 8 and 6 is 2.

H–I

hexagon Six-sided figure.

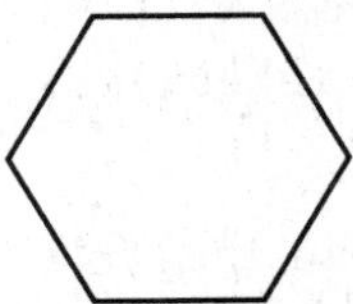

hypotenuse Longest side of a right-angle triangle, which is always the side opposite the right angle. In the following right triangle, *AB* is the hypotenuse:

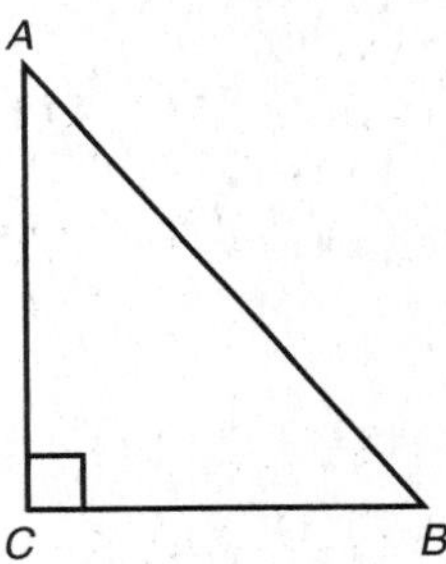

inequality Mathematical expression that shows that two quantities are not equal. For example, $(2 + x) < 8$ is an inequality, which means that 2 plus x is less than 8. Likewise, $a > 17$ is an inequality, which means that a is greater than 17.

integer One of all the positive and negative whole numbers and zero.

interior angle Angle inside a shape. The sum of the interior angles of a geometric figure can be found by multiplying 180° by 2 less than the number of sides. For example, a rectangle has 4 sides: $180° \times (4 - 2) = 360°$.

isosceles triangle Triangle with two congruent sides and two congruent angles.

J–L

least common denominator (LCD) The smallest number (other than 0) that is a multiple of a set of denominators (for example, the LCD of $\frac{1}{4}$ and $\frac{1}{6}$ is 12).

least common multiple (LCM) Smallest number (other than 0) that is a multiple of a set of numbers (for example, the LCM of 6 and 9 is 18).

line Straight set of points that extends into infinity in both directions, as follows:

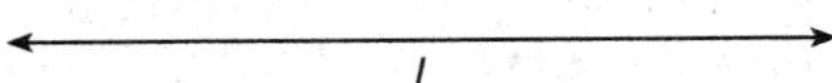

line segment Two points and all the points on a line in between:

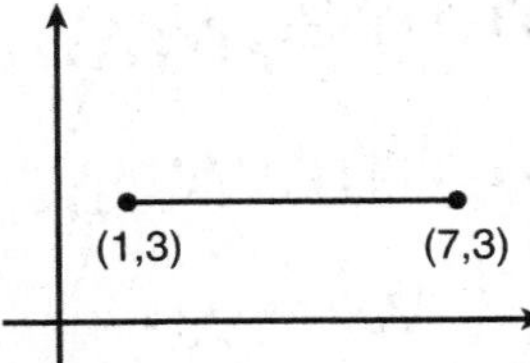

linear Relating to, or existing as, a line.

M–N

matrix Rows and columns of elements arranged in a rectangle.

mean Average, found by adding all the terms in a set and dividing by the number of terms (see also Appendix D).

median Middle value of a series of numbers in ascending or descending order. In the series {2, 4, 6, 8, 10}, the median is 6. To find the median in an even set of data, find the average of the middle two numbers. In the series {3, 4, 5, 6}, the median is 4.5 (see also Appendix D).

midpoint Point that divides a line segment into two equal segments (see also Appendix D).

numerator Top part of a fraction: 3 is the numerator of the fraction $\frac{3}{4}$.

O

oblong Deviating from a square, circular, or spherical form by being slightly longer in one area.

obtuse Describing an angle with a measure greater than 90°.

octagon Eight-sided figure:

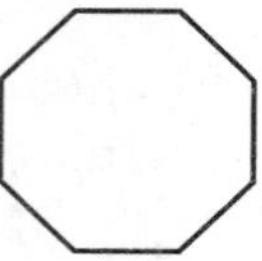

P

parallel Describing lines in the same plane that do not intersect each other; in a coordinate plane, noncollinear lines or segments having the same slope as one another (see also *parallel* in Chapter 28, "Social Studies Terms").

parallelogram Quadrilateral with opposite sides that are parallel and congruent and opposite angles that are congruent:

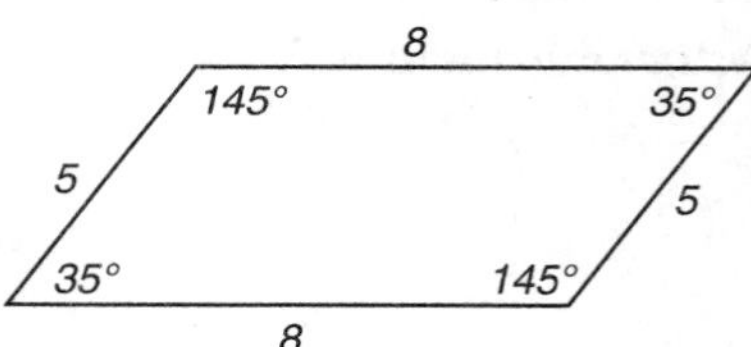

PEMDAS Acronym of the correct order in which to perform mathematical operations:

1. Do the operations within the *parentheses*, obeying the order of operations.
2. Do the *exponents*, if any.
3. Do the *multiplication and division*, in order from left to right.
4. Do the *addition and subtraction*, in order from left to right.

pentagon Five-sided figure:

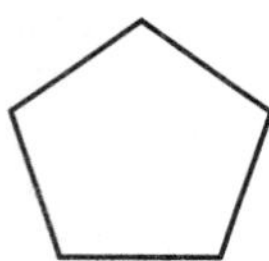

percent Fraction whose denominator is 100: the fraction $\frac{25}{100}$ is equal to 25%.

perimeter Distance around a figure (see also Appendix D).

perpendicular Property of lines that intersect and form 90° angles.

point Location in a plane or in space that has no dimensions.

polygon Closed plane figure made up of several line segments that are joined together. For example, a triangle, a rectangle, and an octagon are polygons.

positive slope Characteristic of upward slant (from left to right) of a line on a coordinate plane due to the positive coefficient of x. Slope is m in the traditional definition of a line: $y = mx + b$, where x and y are the horizontal and vertical values, respectively, and b is the y-intercept, the point on the y-axis that the line intersects.

prime number Positive integer that can be evenly divided only by 1 and itself: 1, 3, 5, 7, 11, 13, 17, and so on.

probability Likelihood that an event will occur. For example, Jeff has three striped and four solid ties in his closet; therefore, he has a total of seven ties in his closet. He has three chances to grab a striped tie out of the seven ties he has in total. So, the likelihood of Jeff grabbing a striped tie is 3 out of 7, which can also be expressed as the ratio 3:7 or the fraction $\frac{3}{7}$.

product Result of multiplication.

proportion Statement of equality between two ratios, for example, $\frac{a}{b} = \frac{c}{d}$.

Pythagorean relationship Property of right triangles that allows prediction of the length of the third side from the lengths of the other two sides (see also Appendix D).

Q–R

quadrilateral Any four-sided polygon having four angles: parallelogram, rectangle, square, trapezoid, and so on.

quotient Result of division.

radius (pl. radii) Line segment with endpoints at the center of the circle and on the perimeter of the circle, measuring one-half the length of the diameter:

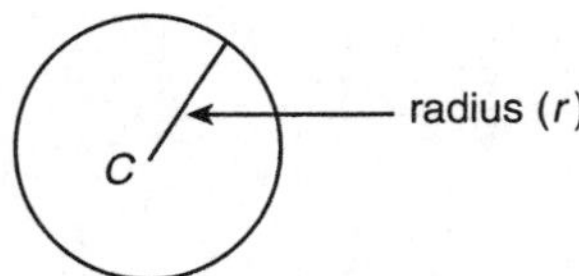

ratio Comparison between two quantities, often indicated using a colon or a fraction. For example, the ratio of girls to boys in a certain class could be shown as 1 to 2, 1:2, or $\frac{1}{2}$.

real number Any number that can be associated with points on a number line, that is, between positive and negative infinity.

real number line Infinite line of real numbers represented on a one-dimensional graph. Numbers that correspond to points to the right of zero are positive, and numbers that correspond to points to the left of zero are negative. For any two numbers on the number line, the number to the left is less than the number to the right.

rectangle Polygon with two sets of congruent sides (therefore all rectangles are parallelograms) and four right angles.

regular (polygon) Having congruent sides and angles.

right (angle) Measuring 90°.

S

set Defined group of numbers or objects: {2, 4, 6, 8} is the set of positive even whole numbers less than 10.

similar (figures) Describing figures in which the measures of corresponding angles are equal and the corresponding sides are in proportion. For example, two similar triangles:

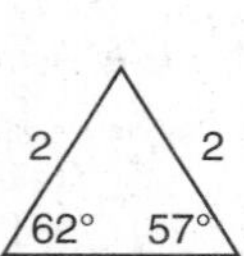

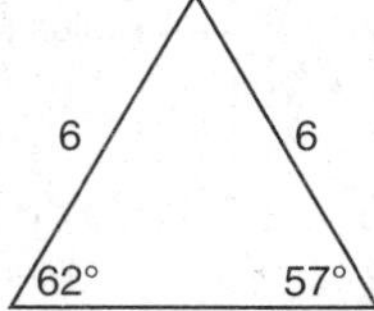

slope Value of the rate of change of *y* relative to *x* of a line on a coordinate plane (see also Appendix D).

solution set Set of values that makes an equation true.

special triangles Cases of triangles having predictable side and angle measures, which are proportional to these values:

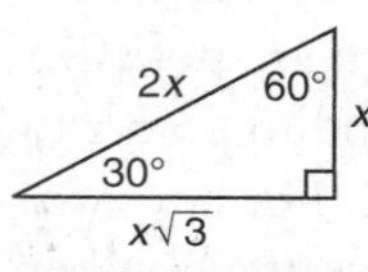

30-60-90 Triangle

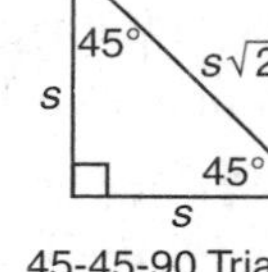

45-45-90 Triangle

The sides of a 3-4-5 Special Right Triangle have the ratio 3:4:5.

sphere Surface consisting of all points the same distance from a center point.

square Any number multiplied by itself. Squaring a negative number yields a positive result: $(-2)^2 = 4$.

square root Inverse of the square. The square root of a number, *n*, is written as $\sqrt{n}$, which equals the nonnegative value *a* that fulfills the expression $a^2 = n$. For example, the square root of 5 is expressed as $\sqrt{5}$, and $(\sqrt{5})^2 = 5$.

sum Result of addition.

T–Z

transversal Line that intersects two or more lines; for example, *n* is a transversal in the following:

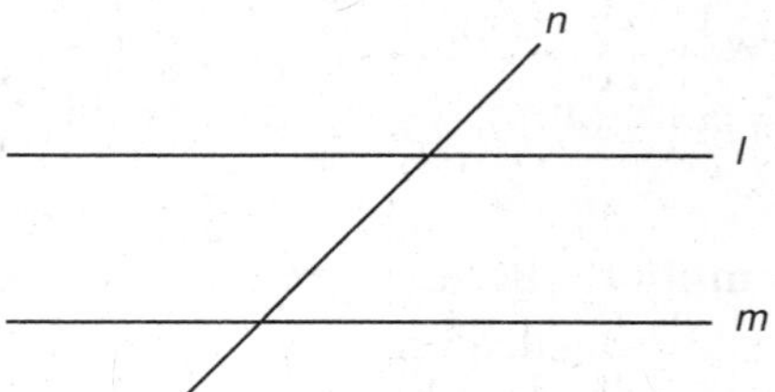

trapezoid Quadrilateral with only two parallel sides, as follows:

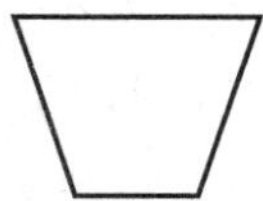

vertex (pl. vertices) Point of intersection, also specifically a point where two sides meet in a geometric figure or where two line segments meet to form an angle, as follows:

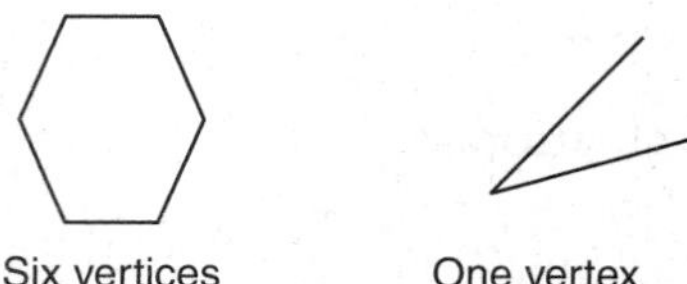
Six vertices One vertex

vertical angle One of two opposite angles that are formed by intersecting lines. Vertical angles are congruent. In the following, angles *a* and *b* are vertical angles:

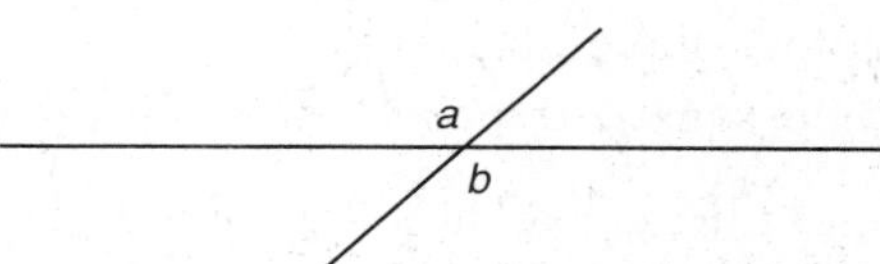

volume Measure of space or capacity of a three-dimensional object (see also Appendix D).

PART IX
Full-Length Practice Tests

The two sets of practice GED tests in this part of the book were prepared to simulate a real set of tests. Be sure to take at least one set of tests under realistic conditions. This is the best way to practice handling the mental and physical fatigue that comes from extended periods of concentration.

Part IX includes the following chapters:

Chapter 50 Practice Test 1 with Answers and Explanations

Chapter 51 Practice Test 2 with Answers and Explanations

CHAPTER FIFTY

Practice Test 1 with Answers and Explanations

This chapter includes a full-length, simulated GED practice test that should help you evaluate your progress in preparing for the GED. Make an honest effort to answer each question, then review the explanations that follow.

There are five separate sections on this test, including

- Language Arts, Writing
- Language Arts, Reading
- Social Studies
- Science
- Mathematics, Part I and Part II

Work on only one section at a time, and make every attempt to complete each section in the time allowed for that particular section. Carefully mark only one answer on your answer sheet for each question.

Mark your answers on the answer sheets on the following pages. Then compare your answers to the answers and explanations at the end of this chapter. Be sure to read through the explanations thoroughly. Identify and review topics you've consistently struggled with.

Answer Sheets

Language Arts, Writing Test

1. ① ② ③ ④ ⑤
2. ① ② ③ ④ ⑤
3. ① ② ③ ④ ⑤
4. ① ② ③ ④ ⑤
5. ① ② ③ ④ ⑤
6. ① ② ③ ④ ⑤
7. ① ② ③ ④ ⑤
8. ① ② ③ ④ ⑤
9. ① ② ③ ④ ⑤
10. ① ② ③ ④ ⑤
11. ① ② ③ ④ ⑤
12. ① ② ③ ④ ⑤
13. ① ② ③ ④ ⑤
14. ① ② ③ ④ ⑤
15. ① ② ③ ④ ⑤
16. ① ② ③ ④ ⑤
17. ① ② ③ ④ ⑤
18. ① ② ③ ④ ⑤
19. ① ② ③ ④ ⑤
20. ① ② ③ ④ ⑤
21. ① ② ③ ④ ⑤
22. ① ② ③ ④ ⑤
23. ① ② ③ ④ ⑤
24. ① ② ③ ④ ⑤
25. ① ② ③ ④ ⑤
26. ① ② ③ ④ ⑤
27. ① ② ③ ④ ⑤
28. ① ② ③ ④ ⑤
29. ① ② ③ ④ ⑤
30. ① ② ③ ④ ⑤
31. ① ② ③ ④ ⑤
32. ① ② ③ ④ ⑤
33. ① ② ③ ④ ⑤
34. ① ② ③ ④ ⑤
35. ① ② ③ ④ ⑤
36. ① ② ③ ④ ⑤
37. ① ② ③ ④ ⑤
38. ① ② ③ ④ ⑤
39. ① ② ③ ④ ⑤
40. ① ② ③ ④ ⑤
41. ① ② ③ ④ ⑤
42. ① ② ③ ④ ⑤
43. ① ② ③ ④ ⑤
44. ① ② ③ ④ ⑤
45. ① ② ③ ④ ⑤
46. ① ② ③ ④ ⑤
47. ① ② ③ ④ ⑤
48. ① ② ③ ④ ⑤
49. ① ② ③ ④ ⑤
50. ① ② ③ ④ ⑤

Language Arts, Reading Test

1. ① ② ③ ④ ⑤
2. ① ② ③ ④ ⑤
3. ① ② ③ ④ ⑤
4. ① ② ③ ④ ⑤
5. ① ② ③ ④ ⑤
6. ① ② ③ ④ ⑤
7. ① ② ③ ④ ⑤
8. ① ② ③ ④ ⑤
9. ① ② ③ ④ ⑤
10. ① ② ③ ④ ⑤
11. ① ② ③ ④ ⑤
12. ① ② ③ ④ ⑤
13. ① ② ③ ④ ⑤
14. ① ② ③ ④ ⑤
15. ① ② ③ ④ ⑤
16. ① ② ③ ④ ⑤
17. ① ② ③ ④ ⑤
18. ① ② ③ ④ ⑤
19. ① ② ③ ④ ⑤
20. ① ② ③ ④ ⑤
21. ① ② ③ ④ ⑤
22. ① ② ③ ④ ⑤
23. ① ② ③ ④ ⑤
24. ① ② ③ ④ ⑤
25. ① ② ③ ④ ⑤
26. ① ② ③ ④ ⑤
27. ① ② ③ ④ ⑤
28. ① ② ③ ④ ⑤
29. ① ② ③ ④ ⑤
30. ① ② ③ ④ ⑤
31. ① ② ③ ④ ⑤
32. ① ② ③ ④ ⑤
33. ① ② ③ ④ ⑤
34. ① ② ③ ④ ⑤
35. ① ② ③ ④ ⑤
36. ① ② ③ ④ ⑤
37. ① ② ③ ④ ⑤
38. ① ② ③ ④ ⑤
39. ① ② ③ ④ ⑤
40. ① ② ③ ④ ⑤

Social Studies Test

1. ① ② ③ ④ ⑤
2. ① ② ③ ④ ⑤
3. ① ② ③ ④ ⑤
4. ① ② ③ ④ ⑤
5. ① ② ③ ④ ⑤
6. ① ② ③ ④ ⑤
7. ① ② ③ ④ ⑤
8. ① ② ③ ④ ⑤
9. ① ② ③ ④ ⑤
10. ① ② ③ ④ ⑤
11. ① ② ③ ④ ⑤
12. ① ② ③ ④ ⑤
13. ① ② ③ ④ ⑤
14. ① ② ③ ④ ⑤
15. ① ② ③ ④ ⑤
16. ① ② ③ ④ ⑤
17. ① ② ③ ④ ⑤
18. ① ② ③ ④ ⑤
19. ① ② ③ ④ ⑤
20. ① ② ③ ④ ⑤
21. ① ② ③ ④ ⑤
22. ① ② ③ ④ ⑤
23. ① ② ③ ④ ⑤
24. ① ② ③ ④ ⑤
25. ① ② ③ ④ ⑤
26. ① ② ③ ④ ⑤
27. ① ② ③ ④ ⑤
28. ① ② ③ ④ ⑤
29. ① ② ③ ④ ⑤
30. ① ② ③ ④ ⑤
31. ① ② ③ ④ ⑤
32. ① ② ③ ④ ⑤
33. ① ② ③ ④ ⑤
34. ① ② ③ ④ ⑤
35. ① ② ③ ④ ⑤
36. ① ② ③ ④ ⑤
37. ① ② ③ ④ ⑤
38. ① ② ③ ④ ⑤
39. ① ② ③ ④ ⑤
40. ① ② ③ ④ ⑤
41. ① ② ③ ④ ⑤
42. ① ② ③ ④ ⑤
43. ① ② ③ ④ ⑤
44. ① ② ③ ④ ⑤
45. ① ② ③ ④ ⑤
46. ① ② ③ ④ ⑤
47. ① ② ③ ④ ⑤
48. ① ② ③ ④ ⑤
49. ① ② ③ ④ ⑤
50. ① ② ③ ④ ⑤

Science Test

1. ① ② ③ ④ ⑤
2. ① ② ③ ④ ⑤
3. ① ② ③ ④ ⑤
4. ① ② ③ ④ ⑤
5. ① ② ③ ④ ⑤
6. ① ② ③ ④ ⑤
7. ① ② ③ ④ ⑤
8. ① ② ③ ④ ⑤
9. ① ② ③ ④ ⑤
10. ① ② ③ ④ ⑤
11. ① ② ③ ④ ⑤
12. ① ② ③ ④ ⑤
13. ① ② ③ ④ ⑤
14. ① ② ③ ④ ⑤
15. ① ② ③ ④ ⑤
16. ① ② ③ ④ ⑤
17. ① ② ③ ④ ⑤
18. ① ② ③ ④ ⑤
19. ① ② ③ ④ ⑤
20. ① ② ③ ④ ⑤
21. ① ② ③ ④ ⑤
22. ① ② ③ ④ ⑤
23. ① ② ③ ④ ⑤
24. ① ② ③ ④ ⑤
25. ① ② ③ ④ ⑤
26. ① ② ③ ④ ⑤
27. ① ② ③ ④ ⑤
28. ① ② ③ ④ ⑤
29. ① ② ③ ④ ⑤
30. ① ② ③ ④ ⑤
31. ① ② ③ ④ ⑤
32. ① ② ③ ④ ⑤
33. ① ② ③ ④ ⑤
34. ① ② ③ ④ ⑤
35. ① ② ③ ④ ⑤
36. ① ② ③ ④ ⑤
37. ① ② ③ ④ ⑤
38. ① ② ③ ④ ⑤
39. ① ② ③ ④ ⑤
40. ① ② ③ ④ ⑤
41. ① ② ③ ④ ⑤
42. ① ② ③ ④ ⑤
43. ① ② ③ ④ ⑤
44. ① ② ③ ④ ⑤
45. ① ② ③ ④ ⑤
46. ① ② ③ ④ ⑤
47. ① ② ③ ④ ⑤
48. ① ② ③ ④ ⑤
49. ① ② ③ ④ ⑤
50. ① ② ③ ④ ⑤

Mathematics Test

1. ① ② ③ ④ ⑤

2.

	○	○	○	
⊙	⊙	⊙	⊙	⊙
⓪	⓪	⓪	⓪	⓪
①	①	①	①	①
②	②	②	②	②
③	③	③	③	③
④	④	④	④	④
⑤	⑤	⑤	⑤	⑤
⑥	⑥	⑥	⑥	⑥
⑦	⑦	⑦	⑦	⑦
⑧	⑧	⑧	⑧	⑧
⑨	⑨	⑨	⑨	⑨

3. ① ② ③ ④ ⑤
4. ① ② ③ ④ ⑤
5. ① ② ③ ④ ⑤
6. ① ② ③ ④ ⑤
7. ① ② ③ ④ ⑤
8. ① ② ③ ④ ⑤
9. ① ② ③ ④ ⑤
10. ① ② ③ ④ ⑤

11.

	○	○	○	
⊙	⊙	⊙	⊙	⊙
⓪	⓪	⓪	⓪	⓪
①	①	①	①	①
②	②	②	②	②
③	③	③	③	③
④	④	④	④	④
⑤	⑤	⑤	⑤	⑤
⑥	⑥	⑥	⑥	⑥
⑦	⑦	⑦	⑦	⑦
⑧	⑧	⑧	⑧	⑧
⑨	⑨	⑨	⑨	⑨

12. ① ② ③ ④ ⑤
13. ① ② ③ ④ ⑤
14. ① ② ③ ④ ⑤
15. ① ② ③ ④ ⑤

16.

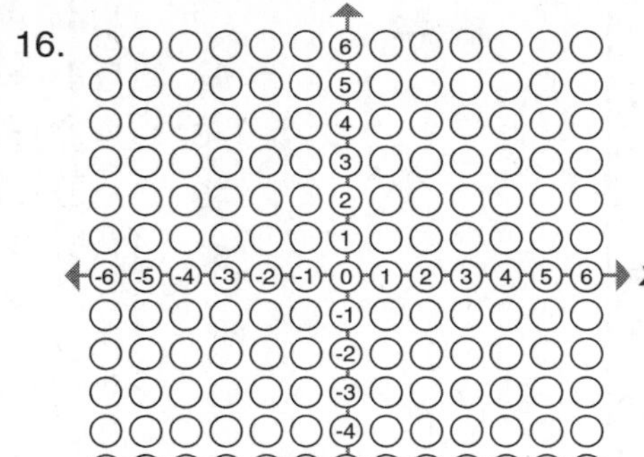

17. ① ② ③ ④ ⑤

18.

	○	○	○	
⊙	⊙	⊙	⊙	⊙
⓪	⓪	⓪	⓪	⓪
①	①	①	①	①
②	②	②	②	②
③	③	③	③	③
④	④	④	④	④
⑤	⑤	⑤	⑤	⑤
⑥	⑥	⑥	⑥	⑥
⑦	⑦	⑦	⑦	⑦
⑧	⑧	⑧	⑧	⑧
⑨	⑨	⑨	⑨	⑨

19. ① ② ③ ④ ⑤
20. ① ② ③ ④ ⑤
21. ① ② ③ ④ ⑤
22. ① ② ③ ④ ⑤
23. ① ② ③ ④ ⑤
24. ① ② ③ ④ ⑤
25. ① ② ③ ④ ⑤
26. ① ② ③ ④ ⑤
27. ① ② ③ ④ ⑤
28. ① ② ③ ④ ⑤
29. ① ② ③ ④ ⑤

Mathematics Test (continued)

30.

	○	○	○	
⊙	⊙	⊙	⊙	⊙
⓪	⓪	⓪	⓪	⓪
①	①	①	①	①
②	②	②	②	②
③	③	③	③	③
④	④	④	④	④
⑤	⑤	⑤	⑤	⑤
⑥	⑥	⑥	⑥	⑥
⑦	⑦	⑦	⑦	⑦
⑧	⑧	⑧	⑧	⑧
⑨	⑨	⑨	⑨	⑨

31. (coordinate plane grid: x from -6 to 6, y from -6 to 6)

y

6
5
4
3
2
1
-6 -5 -4 -3 -2 -1 0 1 2 3 4 5 6 x
-1
-2
-3
-4
-5
-6

32. ① ② ③ ④ ⑤
33. ① ② ③ ④ ⑤
34. ① ② ③ ④ ⑤
35. ① ② ③ ④ ⑤
36. ① ② ③ ④ ⑤
37. ① ② ③ ④ ⑤
38. ① ② ③ ④ ⑤
39. ① ② ③ ④ ⑤
40. ① ② ③ ④ ⑤
41. ① ② ③ ④ ⑤
42. ① ② ③ ④ ⑤
43. ① ② ③ ④ ⑤
44. ① ② ③ ④ ⑤
45. ① ② ③ ④ ⑤
46. ① ② ③ ④ ⑤
47. ① ② ③ ④ ⑤
48. ① ② ③ ④ ⑤
49. ① ② ③ ④ ⑤
50. ① ② ③ ④ ⑤

Language Arts, Writing Test

Directions: Read all directions and questions carefully. Pick the single best answer, and answer every question. You will not be penalized for wrong answers.

The GED Language Arts, Writing Test has two parts, which must be taken consecutively. Part I consists of 50 multiple-choice questions for which you will be given 75 minutes to answer. Part II tests your ability to write an essay about a topic of general interest. You will have 45 minutes to plan, write, and revise your essay. The GED does permit you to take advantage of all 120 minutes, though. If you finish Part I early, you may move on to Part II with the remaining time; likewise, if you finish your essay with time to spare, you may return to Part I.

GO ON TO THE NEXT PAGE

Questions 1–10 are based on the following letter.

WE DO BASEMENTS, Inc.
P.O. Box 890
Bay City, Michigan 48706

Dear Mr. and Mrs. Conroy:

(A)

(1) Recently I want to thank you for your inquiry regarding the condition of your basement. (2) We were very familiar with the kinds of problems you described in your phone message of 4/02/2006. (3) As you may be aware, the wall and floor dampness that you are having experiencing particularly in the early spring months are very common complaints of Michigan residents.

(B)

(4) Our company has spent many years developing a foolproof system to help alleviate these problems. (5) In the past decade, we have installed many basement systems, and with great success. (6) These systems take into account the specific conditions of each residents, such as wall and floor construction, landscaping surrounding the structure, and any system already in place to keep the basement dry, such as a sump pump.

(C)

(7) We need to assist you. (8) It is important for us to visit the premises and assess the current condition of your basement. (9) One of our associates will then sit down together with the both of you and outline our recommendations. (10) We may also recommend the installation of our proprietary system, which we call The Base Gravel Solution. (11) It is possible that a rather simple sealing procedure will solve the problems you are having with moisture in your basement. (12) This innovative design, requires the construction of a gravel trench around the perimeter of the basement floor. (13) When completed, basement moisture and wetness will be virtually eliminated forever.

(D)

(14) Whatever the recommendation, we are assured a quick, clean process of installation as well as effective results. (15) Enclosed is a brochure that explains the many options that our company can provide you in order to solve your problem with a wet basement. (16) We will be contacting you in the near future to set up an appointment with you.

Sincerely,

Jason Carpenter

Jason Carpenter, President

GO ON TO THE NEXT PAGE

1. Sentence 1: **Recently I want to thank you for your inquiry regarding the condition of your basement.**

   The most effective revision of Sentence 1 would begin with which group of words?

   (1) As you had been recently inquired
   (2) Recently, as you had inquired
   (3) Thank you for your recent inquiry
   (4) You had inquired, recently, and I thank you
   (5) Inquiring recently, I thank you

2. Sentence 2: **We were very familiar with the kinds of problems you described in your phone message of 4/02/2006.**

   Which correction should be made to Sentence 2?

   (1) change We were to We are
   (2) insert a comma after described
   (3) remove very
   (4) change described to had described
   (5) replace your with you're

3. Sentence 3: **As you may be aware, the wall and floor dampness that you are having experiencing, particularly in the early spring months, are very common complaints of Michigan residents.**

   Which is the best way to write the underlined portion of this sentence? If the original is the best way, choose option (1).

   (1) are having experiencing
   (2) had been experiencing
   (3) had experienced
   (4) had experiencing
   (5) are experiencing

4. Sentence 5: **In the past decade, we have installed many basement systems, and with great success.**

   Which is the best way to write the underlined portion of this sentence? If the original is the best way, choose option (1).

   (1) systems, and with
   (2) systems, with
   (3) systems and with
   (4) systems, but with
   (5) systems with

5. Sentence 6: **These systems take into account the specific conditions of each residents, such as wall and floor construction, landscaping surrounding the structure, and any system already in place to keep the basement dry, such as a sump pump.**

   Which correction should be made to sentence 6?

   (1) replace residents with residence
   (2) insert a comma after landscaping
   (3) remove the comma after structure
   (4) replace presence with presents
   (5) remove the comma after dry

6. Sentences 7 and 8: **We need to assist you. It is important for us to visit the premises and assess the current condition of your basement.**

   Which is the most effective combination of sentences 7 and 8?

   (1) In order to assist you, it is important for us to visit the premises and assess the current condition of your basement.
   (2) Assisting you, it is important to visit your premises and assess the current condition of your basement.
   (3) To assist you, in order to assess the current condition of your basement, it is important to visit.
   (4) Assisting you and visiting your premises is important to assess the current condition of your basement.
   (5) To assist you, and to assess the current condition of your basement, it is important for us to visit the premises.

7. Sentence 9: **One of our associates will then sit down together with the both of you and outline our recommendations.**

   Which is the best way to write the underlined portion of this sentence? If the original is the best way, choose option (1).

   (1) together with the both of you
   (2) with the both of you together
   (3) with you
   (4) with you both together
   (5) together with both of you

GO ON TO THE NEXT PAGE

The letter has been repeated for your use in answering the remaining questions.

WE DO BASEMENTS, Inc.
P.O. Box 890
Bay City, Michigan 48706

Dear Mr. and Mrs. Conroy:

(A)

(1) Recently I want to thank you for your inquiry regarding the condition of your basement. (2) We were very familiar with the kinds of problems you described in your phone message of 4/02/2006. (3) As you may be aware, the wall and floor dampness that you are having experiencing particularly in the early spring months are very common complaints of Michigan residents.

(B)

(4) Our company has spent many years developing a foolproof system to help alleviate these problems. (5) In the past decade, we have installed many basement systems, and with great success. (6) These systems take into account the specific conditions of each residents, such as wall and floor construction, landscaping surrounding the structure, and any system already in place to keep the basement dry, such as a sump pump.

(C)

(7) We need to assist you. (8) It is important for us to visit the premises and assess the current condition of your basement. (9) One of our associates will then sit down together with the both of you and outline our recommendations. (10) We may also recommend the installation of our proprietary system, which we call The Base Gravel Solution. (11) It is possible that a rather simple sealing procedure will solve the problems you are having with moisture in your basement. (12) This innovative design, requires the construction of a gravel trench around the perimeter of the basement floor. (13) When completed, basement moisture and wetness will be virtually eliminated forever.

(D)

(14) Whatever the recommendation, we are assured a quick, clean process of installation as well as effective results. (15) Enclosed is a brochure that explains the many options that our company can provide you in order to solve your problem with a wet basement. (16) We will be contacting you in the near future to set up an appointment with you.

Sincerely,

Jason Carpenter

Jason Carpenter, President

8. Sentence 11: **It is possible that a rather simple sealing procedure will solve the problems you are having with moisture in your basement.**

Which revision should be made to the placement of sentence 11?

(1) remove sentence 11
(2) move sentence 11 to follow sentence 13
(3) move sentence 11 to follow sentence 9
(4) begin the paragraph with sentence 11
(5) move sentence 11 to the end of the paragraph

9. Sentence 12: **<u>This innovative design, requires</u> the construction of a gravel trench around the perimeter of the basement floor.**

Which is the best way to write the underlined portion of this sentence? If the original is the best way, choose option (1).

(1) This innovative design, requires
(2) This innovative design requires
(3) This, innovative design, requires
(4) This innovative, design, requires
(5) This innovative design requires,

10. Sentence 14: **Whatever the recommendation, we are assured a quick, clean process of installation as well as effective results.**

Which correction should be made to sentence 14?

(1) replace <u>recommendation</u> with <u>having recommended</u>
(2) remove the comma after <u>recommendation</u>
(3) replace <u>we are assured</u> with <u>we assure</u>
(4) replace <u>effective results</u> with <u>results that are effective</u>
(5) no correction is necessary

GO ON TO THE NEXT PAGE

Questions 11–18 are based on the following letter.

Thousand Oaks Bank
4219 Ascot Place
Evergreen, Missouri 00989

Dear Mr. Bellingham:

(A)

(1) Upon reviewing our records, we found that you have attained Gold Star status here at Thousand Oaks Bank! (2) Because of your continued patronage, we would like to extend an exciting offer to you. (3) Please review the enclosed information about loans available to you that are interest-free for 3 years. (4) If either of the options interests you, come into the bank any time during the week to complete the paperwork. (5) This would take only a few moments of your time.

(B)

(6) Once again, remember, there is NO INTEREST charged for three years under either option! (7) And now let me explain this once-in-a-lifetime offer. (8) For a very short period, we are offering you a three-year, no-interest auto loan for up to $20,000! (9) However, if you are not currently in the market for a new automobile, we were also offering the same terms for a home equity loan. (10) Perhaps you would like to remodel your kitchen, or build a new deck. (11) A Home Equity Line of Credit would certainly help you in this endeavor. (12) A home equity line of credit actually allows you to do anything you want. (13) There are no stipulations for its use.

(C)

(14) We need to reiterate to you that this offer has a deadline, which you will find in the enclosed information. (15) If you have any questions or concerns, you should contact our Special Services Department at 800-555-0176. (16) Once you complete the letter of acceptance, it should take about three days for the amount requested to appear in your account.

(D)

(17) So, why are we extending such an incredible offer? (18) This is our way to thank you for your loyalty to Thousand Oaks Bank, and to extend our deep appreciation for your business.

Sincerely,

Contessa Markley

Contessa Markley, Special Services

GO ON TO THE NEXT PAGE

11. Sentence 3: **Please review the enclosed information about loans available to you that are interest-free for 3 years.**

Which correction should be made to sentence 3?

(1) insert a comma after information
(2) replace you with your
(3) insert a comma after interest-free
(4) remove to after available
(5) no correction is necessary

12. Sentences 4 and 5: **If either of the options interests you, come into the bank any time during the week to complete the paperwork. This would take only a few moments of your time.**

Which is the best way to write the underlined portion of these sentences? If the original is the best way, choose option (1).

(1) the paperwork. This would take
(2) the paperwork this would take
(3) the paperwork, that would take
(4) the paperwork to take
(5) a letter of acceptance, found

13. Sentence 6: **Once again, remember there is NO INTEREST charged for three years under either option!**

Which revision should be made to the placement of sentence 6?

(1) move sentence 6 to the beginning of paragraph A
(2) move sentence 6 to the end of paragraph A
(3) move sentence 6 to follow sentence 12
(4) move sentence 6 to the beginning of paragraph C
(5) move sentence 6 to the end of paragraph B

14. Sentence 9: **However, if you are not currently in the market for a new automobile, we were also offering the same terms for a home equity loan.**

Which correction should be made to sentence 9?

(1) replace are with is
(2) change offering to offer
(3) replace we were with we was
(4) change terms with term
(5) replace we were with we are

15. Sentence 10: **Perhaps you would like to remodel your kitchen, or build a new deck.**

Which correction should be made to sentence 10?

(1) change remodel to remodeling
(2) insert a comma after Perhaps
(3) replace build with built
(4) remove the comma after kitchen
(5) replace new with knew

16. Sentences 12 and 13: **A home equity line of credit actually allows you to do anything you want. There are no stipulations for its use.**

Which is the best way to write the underlined portion of these sentences? If the original is the best way, choose option (1).

(1) anything you want. There are no
(2) anything you want, there aren't any
(3) anything, there aren't
(4) anything you want in addition there are no
(5) anything you want, no

GO ON TO THE NEXT PAGE

The letter has been repeated for your use in answering the remaining questions.

Thousand Oaks Bank
4219 Ascot Place
Evergreen, Missouri 00989

Dear Mr. Bellingham:

(A)

(1) Upon reviewing our records, we found that you have attained Gold Star status here at Thousand Oaks Bank! (2) Because of your continued patronage, we would like to extend an exciting offer to you. (3) Please review the enclosed information about loans available to you that are interest-free for 3 years. (4) If either of the options interests you, come into the bank any time during the week to complete the paperwork. (5) This would take only a few moments of your time.

(B)

(6) Once again, remember, there is NO INTEREST charged for three years under either option! (7) And now let me explain this once-in-a-lifetime offer. (8) For a very short period, we are offering you a three-year, no-interest auto loan for up to $20,000! (9) However, if you are not currently in the market for a new automobile, we were also offering the same terms for a home equity loan. (10) Perhaps you would like to remodel your kitchen, or build a new deck. (11) A Home Equity Line of Credit would certainly help you in this endeavor. (12) A home equity line of credit actually allows you to do anything you want. (13) There are no stipulations for its use.

(C)

(14) We need to reiterate to you that this offer has a deadline, which you will find in the enclosed information. (15) If you have any questions or concerns, you should contact our Special Services Department at 800-555-0176. (16) Once you complete the letter of acceptance, it should take about three days for the amount requested to appear in your account.

(D)

(17) So, why are we extending such an incredible offer? (18) This is our way to thank you for your loyalty to Thousand Oaks Bank, and to extend our deep appreciation for your business.

Sincerely,

Contessa Markley

Contessa Markley, Special Services

GO ON TO THE NEXT PAGE

17. Sentence 14: **We need to reiterate to you that this offer has a deadline, which you will find in the enclosed information.**

    The most effective revision of sentence 14 would begin with which group of words?

    (1) In the enclosed information where you will find
    (2) As the enclosed information indicates,
    (3) As we said before, you should find a deadline
    (4) In explaining the enclosed information to you
    (5) You will see, as we have said previously, that

18. Sentence 17: **So, why are we extending such an incredible offer?**

    Which correction should be made to sentence 17?

    (1) replace we with you
    (2) replace offer? with offer.
    (3) insert a comma after why
    (4) change extending to extended
    (5) no correction is necessary

Questions 19–25 are based on the following notice.

PROBLEM DOGS

(A)

(1) Nearly everyone knows that dogs were man's best friends. (2) The assumption behind that statement is that dogs are easy to get along with and truly can be pals or buddies. (3) Like a friend, however, most dogs have distinct personalities, which may include odd habits or mannerisms. (4) These quirks need to be understood and must be accepted if one is to be a true and loyal friend.

(B)

(5) One dog I know is an escape artist. (6) Time and time, again he has broken out of his home in order to look for his owner. (7) While this may seem funny at first, it isn't so funny when considering that the owner lives in a second story apartment. (8) This dog has been strongly attached to his owner and also hates thunderstorms. (9) If the owner has left the dog in the house alone during a thunderstorm, the dog will no doubt attempt to escape, even if it means crashing through the glass of a window. (10) This is very upsetting to the owner, especially when he returns to find his dog has been injured or his apartment damaged. (11) The owner of this dog has taken many measures to help his dog with these anxieties, and slowly the dog is calming down. (12) The owner has gone through a great deal of expense and worry over his dog, but the dog remains his "best friend."

(C)

(13) Another friend has a dog that weighs 75 pounds and is all bone and muscle with very little fat on his body. (14) He has long legs and loves to gallop around, chasing balls and catching plastic saucers. (15) During a raucous game of catch, this dog had ended up banging his head into his owner's nose, breaking it. (16) While the owner continues to love her pet, she has endured a great deal of pain while waiting for nasal surgery, and then again after the surgery itself. (17) She will no doubt, however, go back to playing with her dog. (18) Beginning when her nose is healed, she will want to play with her dog again. (20) In both of these cases, the dogs continue to be greatly loved by their masters, even with their wild natures and unpredictable behavior.

(D)

(21) Their owners have adapted their lives and experienced their own pain and anxiety over their pets. (22) Nevertheless, they prove the adage that dog is man's best friend.

GO ON TO THE NEXT PAGE

19. Sentence 1: **Nearly everyone knows that dogs were man's best friends.**

    Which correction should be made to sentence 1?

    (1) replace Nearly with Almost
    (2) place a comma after knows
    (3) replace were with are
    (4) replace knows with known
    (5) no correction is necessary

20. Sentence 4: **These quirks need to be understood and must be accepted if one is to be a true and loyal friend.**

    Which correction should be made to sentence 4?

    (1) replace to be understood with understanding
    (2) insert to before need
    (3) change accepted to accepting
    (4) replace and must with also must
    (5) remove must be

21. Sentence 6: **Time and time, again he has broken out of his home in order to look for his owner.**

    Which is the best way to write the underlined portion of this sentence? If the original is the best way, choose option (1).

    (1) time, again he has broken
    (2) time again he has been breaking
    (3) time again, he has broken
    (4) time again, he had broken
    (5) time again he had been breaking

22. Sentence 8: **This dog has been strongly attached to his owner and also hates thunderstorms.**

    Which is the best way to write the underlined portion of the sentence? If the original is the best way, choose option (1).

    (1) has been strongly
    (2) is strongly
    (3) had become strongly
    (4) had strongly
    (5) will have strongly

23. Sentence 15: **During a raucous game of catch, this dog had ended up banging his head into his owner's nose, breaking it.**

    Which correction should be made to sentence 12?

    (1) change had ended to ended
    (2) remove the comma after catch
    (3) change banging to banged
    (4) replace owner's with owners
    (5) insert a comma after head

24. Sentences 17 and 18: **She will no doubt, however, go back to playing with her dog. Beginning when her nose is healed, she will want to play with her dog again.**

    The most effective combination of sentences 17 and 18 would include which group of words?

    (1) her dog, of course once her nose is healed
    (2) with her dog once her nose is healed
    (3) playing with her dog, her nose healing
    (4) healing and then playing with her dog again
    (5) her nose healing and playing with her dog

25. Which revision would improve the effectiveness of the document?

    Begin a new paragraph with

    (1) sentence 4
    (2) sentence 6
    (3) sentence 12
    (4) sentence 20
    (5) sentence 22

GO ON TO THE NEXT PAGE

Questions 26–33 are based on the following letter.

Happy Acres USA
789 Browntree Rd
Buffalo, NY 29176

Dear Mr. Atchison:

(A)

(1) We have tested the soil sample which you had sent to us two weeks ago and have the results. (2) You had indicated on Your Sample form that you are interested in growing a vegetable garden in the area where the soil sample was extracted. (3) As you will see from the results of our tests, with proper amending, you should be able to start your garden next spring with ease and assurance of good growth.

(B)

(4) The person who handled your soil sample for this fall, Joe Schwartz, one of our lead technicians who specializes in soil treatments. (5) First of all, he determined a substantial amount of dolomitic lime is required to amend your soil. (6) Half of the required lime should be tilled into the soil this fall. (7) However, the other half should be added in the spring, two weeks before planting.

(C)

(8) As you will also note, the soil at this particular site is lacking in several needed minerals, such as phosphorus and potassium. (9) The appropriate pre-measured fertilizer is circled on the attached sheet. (10) This fertilizer need to be added to the soil 7 to 10 days prior to planting. (11) Using a rake, incorporate these additions. (12) To a depth of at least three inches. (13) Six to eight weeks after planting, add urea to the soil and water in.

(D)

(14) You also indicated that you were having problems keeping ferns out of your growing area. (15) Ferns are difficult to eradicate because of their unique root system. (16) There are several products to try however, and you will see those listed at the bottom of the report. (17) Thank you for letting us serve you, and do not hesitate to contact us with any questions or concerns.

Grow Happy!,

Anna Harden

Anna Harden

26. Sentence 1: **We have tested the soil sample which you had sent to us two weeks ago and have the results.**

Which is the best way to write the underlined portion of this sentence? If the original is the best way, choose option (1).

(1) which you had sent
(2) which had been sent
(3) you have sent
(4) you sent
(5) which you have sent

27. Sentence 2: **You had indicated on Your Sample form that you are interested in growing a vegetable garden in the area where the soil sample was extracted.**

Which correction should be made to Sentence 2?

(1) change Your Sample to your sample
(2) insert a comma after indicated
(3) replace on with as
(4) replace a with an
(5) no correction is necessary

28. Sentence 4: **The person who handled your soil sample for this fall, Joe Schwartz, one of our lead technicians who specializes in soil treatments.**

Which correction should be made to sentence 4?

(1) change sample to samples
(2) change person to people
(3) replace fall, with fall is
(4) insert and after Schwartz
(5) change handled to handles

29. Sentences 6 and 7: **Half of the required lime should be tilled into the soil this fall. However, the other half should be added in the spring, two weeks before planting.**

Which is the best way to write the underlined portion of this sentence? If the original is the best way, choose option (1).

(1) this fall. However, the
(2) this fall. Then the
(3) this fall, while the
(4) this fall and yet the
(5) this fall, however, the

30. Sentence 8: **As you will also note, the soil at this particular site is lacking in several needed minerals such as phosphorus and potassium.**

Which correction should be made to sentence 8?

(1) replace will with would
(2) replace is with are
(3) insert and after lacking
(4) replace minerals with mineral
(5) no correction is necessary

31. Sentence 10: **This fertilizer need to be added to the soil 7 to 10 days prior to planting.**

Which correction should be made to sentence 10?

(1) change need to be to needs to be
(2) change added to have added
(3) replace 7 to 10 days with 7, 10 days
(4) change prior to priority
(5) change planting to have planted

32. Sentences 11 and 12: **Using a rake, incorporate these additions. To a depth of at least three inches.**

The most effective combination of sentences 11 and 12 would include which group of words?

(1) additions, at least to a depth of
(2) additions, and doing this to a depth of
(3) additions to a depth of
(4) additions, you should do this to a depth of
(5) to a depth these additions

33. Sentence 16: **There are several products to try however, and you will see those listed at the bottom of the report.**

Which correction should be made to sentence 16?

(1) replace There with They're
(2) replace several with many other
(3) insert a comma after try
(4) remove of the report
(5) no correction is necessary

GO ON TO THE NEXT PAGE

Questions 34–43 are based on the following memorandum.

MEMO

TO: All Bigelow Elementary School teaching staff
FROM: Hidden Lake Senior Center
RE: Volunteer Opportunities

(A)

(1) Welcome back, to school, teachers! (2) We hope you will seriously consider that we at Hidden Lake Senior Center are offering an exciting opportunity.

(B)

(3) As many of you know, our facility is located within walking range of nearly every school in the district. (4) Bigelow Elementary School is, unfortunately, out of the walking range. (5) However, staff and students still have been able to participate in one or more of the activities we wish to share with you.

(C)

(6) Studies have proven over and over again the mutual benefit. (7) Senior citizens and youth achieve work and play together. (8)In this light, we would like to invite you and your class to participate in either a regular weekly or monthly activity, or perhaps even a seasonal one (once per season).

(D)

(9) The possibilities are really endless, requiring only some creativity on your part. (10) Some ideas for activities include performing a short play or concert, sharing art projects, putting together jigsaw puzzles, or reading books to a senior citizen. (11) Perhaps brainstorming with your students would be beneficial so that they are more likely to taken ownership of their activity.

(E)

(12) We have found that some children are timid and even frightened of the elderly. (13) Projects such as the ones we are suggesting, however, tend to help young people understand and accept seniors. (14) Their are also many children who are very comfortable with older people and they can be great resources for ideas. (15) We hope you will share your ideas with us, when we visit your school. (16) We visit all the schools in the district. (17) We would like to get this program started as soon as possible!

Sincerely,

Anabella Scott

Anabella Scott, Activities Director

34. Sentence 1: **Welcome, back to school, teachers!**

Which correction should be made to sentence 1?

(1) remove the comma after Welcome
(2) remove the comma after school
(3) insert a comma after back
(4) change school to School
(5) no correction is necessary

35. Sentence 2: **We hope you will seriously consider that we at Hidden Lake Senior Center are offering an exciting opportunity.**

If you rewrote sentence 2 beginning with We at Hidden Lake Senior Center the next word should be

(1) offering
(2) exciting
(3) we
(4) are
(5) opportunity

36. Sentence 4: **Bigelow Elementary School is, unfortunately, out of the walking range.**

Which is the best way to write the underlined portion of this sentence? If the original is the best way, choose option (1).

(1) out of the walking
(2) out of walking
(3) out
(4) walking
(5) having walked

37. Sentence 5: **However, staff and students still have been able to participate in one or more of the activities we wish to share with you.**

Which correction should be made to sentence 5?

(1) replace or with and
(2) change have been to are
(3) replace wish to wished
(4) change share to shared
(5) change you to us

38. Sentences 6 and 7: **Studies have proven over and over again the mutual benefit. Senior citizens and youth achieve work and play together.**

The most effective combination of sentences 6 and 7 would include which group of words?

(1) Although it has been proven
(2) While proof is there
(3) benefit, for the senior citizens
(4) achieve to work and play
(5) achieve by working and playing

39. Sentence 9: **The possibilities are really endless, requiring only some creativity on your part.**

Which revision should be made to the placement of sentence 9?

(1) move sentence 9 to follow sentence 10
(2) move sentence 9 to the end of paragraph A
(3) remove sentence 9
(4) move sentence 9 to the beginning of paragraph B
(5) move sentence 9 to the end of paragraph E

40. Sentence 11: **Perhaps brainstorming with your students would be beneficial so that they are more likely to taken ownership of their activity.**

Which is the best way to write the underlined portion of this sentence? If the original is the best way, choose option (1).

(1) taken ownership
(2) takes ownership
(3) take ownership
(4) have taken ownership
(5) taking on ownership

The letter has been repeated for your use in answering the remaining questions.

MEMO

TO: All Bigelow Elementary School teaching staff
FROM: Hidden Lake Senior Center
RE: Volunteer Opportunities

(A)

(1) Welcome back, to school, teachers! (2) We hope you will seriously consider that we at Hidden Lake Senior Center are offering an exciting opportunity.

(B)

(3) As many of you know, our facility is located within walking range of nearly every school in the district. (4) Bigelow Elementary School is, unfortunately, out of the walking range. (5) However, staff and students still have been able to participate in one or more of the activities we wish to share with you.

(C)

(6) Studies have proven over and over again the mutual benefit. (7) Senior citizens and youth achieve work and play together. (8)In this light, we would like to invite you and your class to participate in either a regular weekly or monthly activity, or perhaps even a seasonal one (once per season).

(D)

(9) The possibilities are really endless, requiring only some creativity on your part. (10) Some ideas for activities include performing a short play or concert, sharing art projects, putting together jigsaw puzzles, or reading books to a senior citizen. (11) Perhaps brainstorming with your students would be beneficial so that they are more likely to taken ownership of their activity.

(E)

(12) We have found that some children are timid and even frightened of the elderly. (13) Projects such as the ones we are suggesting, however, tend to help young people understand and accept seniors. (14) Their are also many children who are very comfortable with older people and they can be great resources for ideas. (15) We hope you will share your ideas with us, when we visit your school. (16) We visit all the schools in the district. (17) We would like to get this program started as soon as possible!

Sincerely,

Anabella Scott

Anabella Scott, Activities Director

41. Sentence 14: **Their are also many children who are very comfortable with older people and they can be great resources for ideas.**

    Which correction should be made to sentence 14?

    (1) replace Their with There
    (2) replace Their with They're
    (3) change who are to who is
    (4) change can be to have been
    (5) insert a comma after resources

42. Sentence 15: **We hope you will share your ideas with us, when we visit your school.**

    Which is the best way to write the underlined portion of this sentence? If the original is the best way, choose option (1).

    (1) ideas with us, when
    (2) ideas, with us when
    (3) ideas with us when,
    (4) ideas, with us, when
    (5) ideas with us when

43. Which revision would improve the effectiveness of paragraph E?

    (1) remove sentence 17
    (2) remove sentence 16
    (3) move sentence 17 to the beginning of paragraph E
    (4) move sentence 15 to follow sentence 17
    (5) no revision is necessary

GO ON TO THE NEXT PAGE

Questions 44–50 are based on the following consumer pamphlet.

Identifying Birds

(A)

(1) Bird identification can be anything from a hobby you don't know you already have to a full-blown obsession you've cultivated over the years. (2) Most people fall somewhere in the middle, sitting at their breakfast tables and casually commented, "Oh, look what just landed on the feeder!"

(B)

(3) Very often it is a rare bird that hooks a person into buying a bird book and some binoculars for the first time. (4) There is something intriguing about the differentiation of bird species, then that compels birders to learn more. (5) While it can be frustrating to try to identify a new bird, it is always gratifying to find a perfect match to that glossy photo in a bird book. (6) Some birds like to eat oiled sunflower seeds, while others prefer nuts and berries.

(C)

(7) If a person has a bird book, you can bet he has a bird feeder or two. (8) If not, he'll soon learn all about them and the right kinds of feed for the local population. (9) Woodpeckers take every opportunity to poke with their large beaks, and so they enjoy a block of suet. (10) Some birds are extremely cautious as they search for food and eat at a feeder, while others seem to be almost tame. (11) Some birds, like pigeons, will even eat out of a person's hand!

(D)

(12) One of the most exciting parts of bird identification and enjoyment is the variety of bird songs and noises that different species make. (13) Listening to the black crow can be annoying with his blaring, sharp caw. (14) On the other hand, hearing the mating song of a lone brown thrasher in the deep woods is probably the best lullaby that there's. (15) Bird books often describe the songs of each bird, and recordings can be bought or even downloaded from the Internet. (16) It is important to remember, however, that a single species of bird potentially have hundreds of different songs. (17) Your cardinal may not sound like the cardinal on the recording!

(E)

(18) Bird identification is a relatively inexpensive hobby. (19) A good pair of binoculars and a bird book are probably all that is needed to launch oneself into this gratifying pastime. (20)There are also field trips offered in most communities. (21) They are lead by bird experts. (22) Bird watching and identification can bring families and friends together, or satisfy the need for solitude. (23) And, it's all right outside your window!

GO ON TO THE NEXT PAGE

44. Sentence 2: **Most people fall somewhere in the middle, sitting at their breakfast tables and casually commented, "Oh, look what just landed on the feeder!"**

Which correction should be made to sentence 2?

(1) replace sitting with sat
(2) remove the comma after middle
(3) replace sitting at their with sat at their
(4) change commented to commenting
(5) no correction is necessary

45. Sentences 4: **There is something about the differentiation of bird species, then that compels birders to learn more.**

Which is the best way to write the underlined portion of the sentence? If the original is the best way, choose option (1).

(1) species, then that
(2) species, and then that
(3) species that
(4) species. Then that
(5) species. That

46. Sentence 6: **Some birds like to eat oiled sunflower seeds, while others prefer nuts and berries.**

Which revision should be made to the placement of sentence 6?

(1) move sentence 6 to the beginning of paragraph A
(2) move sentence 6 to the end of paragraph A
(3) move sentence 6 to follow sentence 8
(4) move sentence 6 to the beginning of paragraph B
(5) move sentence 6 to the end of paragraph D

47. Sentence 13: **Listening to the black crow can be annoying with his blaring, sharp caw.**

If you rewrote sentence 13 beginning with The black crow can be, the next words should be

(1) listened to annoyingly
(2) annoyingly listening to
(3) annoying with his
(4) listened to and annoying
(5) annoying and listening

48. Sentence 14: **On the other hand, hearing the mating song of a lone brown thrasher in the deep woods is probably the best lullaby that there's.**

Which is the best way to write the underlined portion of the sentence? If the original is the best way, choose option (1).

(1) there's
(2) theirs
(3) there are
(4) there is
(5) they're

49. Sentences 16: **It is important to remember, however, that a single species of bird potentially have hundreds of different songs.**

Which correction should be made to sentence 16?

(1) replace however with how ever
(2) remove the comma after remember
(3) replace bird with birds
(4) replace have with has
(5) change hundreds to hundred

50. Sentences 20 and 21: **There are also field trips offered in most communities. They are led by bird experts.**

The most effective combination of sentences 20 and 21 would include which group of words?

(1) communities, and they are led by
(2) communities, and led by
(3) communities that led by
(4) Led by bird experts, there are
(5) Most communities offer

Answers and explanations for this test begin on page 684.

GO ON TO: LANGUAGE ARTS, WRITING PART II

Writing, Part II

The box on page 623 contains your assigned topic.

You must write on the assigned topic ONLY.

You will have 45 minutes to write on the assigned essay topic. If you have time remaining in this test period after you complete your essay, you may return to Part I of the Writing Test.

Evaluation of your essay will be based on the following features:

- Well-focused main ideas
- Clear organization
- Specific development of your ideas
- Control of sentence structure, punctuation, grammar, word choice, and spelling

REMEMBER, YOU MUST COMPLETE BOTH THE MULTIPLE-CHOICE QUESTIONS (PART I) AND THE ESSAY (PART II) TO RECEIVE A SCORE ON THE LANGUAGE ARTS, WRITING TEST. To avoid having to repeat both parts of the test, be sure to do the following:

- Do not leave the pages blank.
- Write legibly in ink so that the essay readers will be able to read your handwriting.
- Write on the assigned topic. If you write on a topic other than the one assigned, you will not receive a score for the Language Arts, Writing Test.
- Write your essay on the lined pages of the answer sheet. Only the writing on these pages will be scored.

GO ON TO THE NEXT PAGE

Topic

Compromise is important for maintaining civility in society and reaching team, family, and work goals.

Identify a compromise you once reached. Write an essay explaining how and why the compromise was reached and how it affected you. Use your personal observations, experience, and knowledge to support your essay.

Part II is a test to determine how well you can use written language to explain your ideas.

In preparing your essay, you should take the following steps:

- Read the **DIRECTIONS** and the **TOPIC** carefully.
- Plan your essay before you write. Use the scratch paper provided to make any notes and to organize your ideas. These notes will be collected but not scored.
- Before you finish your essay, reread what you have written and make any changes that will improve your essay.

Your essay should be long enough to develop the topic adequately.

An explanation of how to evaluate your writing on this test is found on page 687.

GO ON TO: LANGUAGE ARTS, READING

Language Arts, Reading Test

The GED Language Arts, Reading Test consists of 40 multiple-choice questions that you will be given 65 minutes to answer. The questions assess your ability to analyze various short reading passages. These may be whole works or excerpts from larger works.

Each passage begins with a "purpose question" printed in all capital letters. These are not titles. They are intended to focus your reading and may help you grasp the meaning of the passages.

Some questions will reference certain lines of the passage by their numbers. For these, use the line numbers along the left side of the passage. Every fifth line is indicated, so find the number nearest the one you want and count up or down.

Directions: Read all directions and questions carefully. Pick the single best answer, and answer every question. You will not be penalized for wrong answers.

Questions 1 through 5 refer to the following excerpt from a novel.

HOW IS THE WILD PORTRAYED?

Dark spruce forest frowned on either side the frozen waterway. The trees had been stripped by a recent wind of their white covering of frost, and they seemed to lean towards each other, black and ominous, in the fading light. A vast silence reigned over the land. The land itself was a desolation, lifeless, without movement, so lone and cold that the spirit of it was not even that of sadness. There was a hint in it of laughter, but of a laughter more terrible than any sadness—a laughter that was mirthless as the smile of the sphinx, a laughter cold as the frost and partaking of the grimness of infallibility. It was the masterful and incommunicable wisdom of eternity laughing at the futility of life and the effort of life. It was the Wild, the savage, frozen-hearted Northland Wild.

But there was life, abroad in the land and defiant. Down the frozen waterway toiled a string of wolfish dogs. Their bristly fur was rimed with frost. Their breath froze in the air as it left their mouths, spouting forth in spumes of vapour that settled upon the hair of their bodies and formed into crystals of frost. Leather harness was on the dogs, and leather traces attached them to a sled which dragged along behind. The sled was without runners. It was made of stout birch-bark, and its full surface rested on the snow. The front end of the sled was turned up, like a scroll, in order to force down and under the bore of soft snow that surged like a wave before it. On the sled, securely lashed, was a long and narrow oblong box. There were other things on the sled—blankets, an axe, and a coffee-pot and frying-pan; but prominent, occupying most of the space, was the long and narrow oblong box.

In advance of the dogs, on wide snow-shoes, toiled a man. At the rear of the sled toiled a second man. On the sled, in the box, lay a third man whose toil was over,—a man whom the Wild had conquered and beaten down until he would never move nor struggle again. It is not the way of the Wild to like movement. Life is an offence to it, for life is movement; and the Wild aims always to destroy movement. It freezes the water to prevent it running to the sea; it drives the sap out of the trees till they are frozen to their mighty hearts; and most ferociously and terribly of all does the Wild harry and crush into submission man—man who is the most restless of life, ever in revolt against the dictum that all movement must in the end come to the cessation of movement.

But at front and rear, unawed and indomitable, toiled the two men who were not yet dead. Their bodies were covered with fur and soft-tanned leather. Eyelashes and cheeks and lips were so coated with the crystals from their frozen breath that their faces were not discernible. This gave them the seeming of ghostly masques, undertakers in a spectral world at the funeral of some ghost. But under it all they were men, penetrating the land of desolation and mockery and silence, puny adventurers bent on colossal adventure, pitting themselves against the might of a world as remote and alien and pulseless as the abysses of space.

Jack London, excerpted from *White Fang*, ©1906.

1. When the narrator says that in the box "lay a third man whose toil was over,—a man whom the Wild had conquered and beaten down until he would never move nor struggle again" (lines 43–46), he is implying which of the following?

   (1) The third man was too tired to walk with the others.
   (2) The third man had decided the expedition was too much trouble.
   (3) The third man had died of exposure.
   (4) The third man was not necessary for the expedition to continue.
   (5) The other two men thought the third man was weak.

2. On the basis of the passage's description of the Wild, what kind of person would the narrator think is most likely to succeed there?

   The person would probably be

   (1) good with dogs
   (2) tolerant of change
   (3) easily swayed by others
   (4) stubborn and determined
   (5) accustomed to cold weather

3. When the narrator says, "There was a hint in it of laughter, but of a laughter more terrible than any sadness—a laughter that was mirthless as the smile of the sphinx, a laughter cold as the frost and partaking of the grimness of infallibility" (lines 9–14), what is he suggesting about the Wild?

   The spirit of the Wild

   (1) is impersonal and distant
   (2) is cold but happy
   (3) is inscrutable
   (4) is sinister and uncaring
   (5) is strange and mysterious

4 The narrator would probably identify which one of the following traits as an essential characteristic of the Wild?

   (1) movement
   (2) stillness
   (3) despair
   (4) anger
   (5) hatred

5. Which of the following phrases is closest in meaning to the phrase "ghostly masques" in line 65?

   (1) cardboard disguises
   (2) costumes
   (3) supernatural actors
   (4) winter demons
   (5) nature demons

GO ON TO THE NEXT PAGE

Questions 6 through 11 refer to the following poem.

WHAT DOES THE SPEAKER SAY ABOUT WORK?

I Hear America Singing

I hear America singing, the varied carols I hear;
Those of mechanics—each one singing his, as it should be, blithe and strong;
The carpenter singing his, as he measures his plank or beam,
The mason singing his, as he makes ready for work, or leaves off work;
The boatman singing what belongs to him in his boat—the deckhand singing on the steamboat deck;
The shoemaker singing as he sits on his bench—the hatter singing as he stands;
The wood-cutter's song—the ploughboy's, on his way in the morning, or at the noon intermission, or at sundown;
The delicious singing of the mother—or of the young wife at work—or of the
girl sewing or washing—Each singing what belongs to her, and to none else;
The day what belongs to the day—At night, the party of young fellows, robust, friendly,
Singing, with open mouths, their strong melodious songs.

"I Hear America Singing" from *Leaves of Grass* by Walt Whitman, ©1855.

GO ON TO THE NEXT PAGE

6. What might the speaker mean when he speaks of the women, "Each singing what belongs to her, and to none else" in line 11?
   (1) Each woman has her own melody.
   (2) Each job has a different melody.
   (3) Women's work is more solitary than men's.
   (4) The women are inherently selfish.
   (5) The women have ownership of their lives and that gives them happiness.

7. What characteristic of the songs is evident in line 2: "each one singing his, as it should be, blithe and strong"?

   The songs are
   (1) quiet but harmonious
   (2) distant
   (3) beautiful and fragile
   (4) vigorous and happy
   (5) independent

8. How might the speaker react if he observed a mother rocking her child?

   The speaker might
   (1) worry that the child had been hurt
   (2) wonder what song she was singing
   (3) disapprove of a mother not doing her job
   (4) question if the child could sing
   (5) sense the love of the mother and the comfort of the child

9. The word "strong" appears at both the beginning and the end of the poem (lines 2 and 14). What is the main effect of the image of strong songs?
   (1) to emphasize the pride of the average American worker
   (2) to indicate that the workers have loud voices
   (3) to indicate that the songs have powerful themes
   (4) to imply that only the strong can sing
   (5) to insist that poetry can be powerful

10. Consider the date of the poem and the types of activities it celebrates. Which of the following occupations could be added to the poem while maintaining its imagery?
    (1) professor
    (2) blacksmith
    (3) lawyer
    (4) architect
    (5) banker

11. In the first edition of *Leaves of Grass*, Walt Whitman, the author of the poem, appeared on the inside of the front cover, dressed in work clothes and a tipped hat. From the content of this poem and this image of Whitman, which qualities are most likely to best describe him?
    (1) loving and sincere
    (2) sincere and unpretentious
    (3) serious and strong
    (4) shy and mischievous
    (5) pompous and solitary

GO ON TO THE NEXT PAGE

Questions 12 through 17 refer to the following excerpt from a speech.

HOW DOES THE PRESIDENT FEEL ABOUT THE ATTACK?

My Fellow Americans:

The sudden criminal attacks perpetrated by the Japanese in the Pacific provide the climax of a decade of international immorality. Powerful and resourceful gangsters have banded together to make war upon the whole human race. Their challenge has now been flung at the United States of America. The Japanese have treacherously violated the long-standing peace between us. Many American soldiers and sailors have been killed by enemy action. American ships have been sunk; American airplanes have been destroyed. The Congress and the people of the United States have accepted that challenge.

Together with other free peoples, we are now fighting to maintain our right to live among our world neighbors in freedom, in common decency, without fear of assault.

I have prepared the full record of our past relations with Japan, and it will be submitted to the Congress. It begins with the visit of Commodore Perry to Japan eighty-eight years ago. It ends with the visit of two Japanese emissaries to the Secretary of State last Sunday, an hour after Japanese forces had loosed their bombs and machine guns against our flag, our forces and our citizens.

I can say with utmost confidence that no Americans, today or a thousand years hence, need feel anything but pride in our patience and in our efforts through all the years toward achieving a peace in the Pacific which would be fair and honorable to every nation, large or small. And no honest person, today or a thousand years hence, will be able to suppress a sense of indignation and horror at the treachery committed by the military dictators of Japan, under the very shadow of the flag of peace borne by their special envoys in our midst.

The course that Japan has followed for the past ten years in Asia has paralleled the course of Hitler and Mussolini in Europe and in Africa. Today, it has become far more than a parallel. It is actual collaboration so well calculated that all the continents of the world, and all the oceans, are now considered by the Axis strategists as one gigantic battlefield.

In 1931, ten years ago, Japan invaded Manchukuo—without warning.

In 1935, Italy invaded Ethiopia—without warning. In 1938, Hitler occupied Austria—without warning.

In 1939, Hitler invaded Czechoslovakia—without warning.

Later in '39, Hitler invaded Poland—without warning.

In 1940, Hitler invaded Norway, Denmark, the Netherlands, Belgium and Luxembourg—without warning.

In 1940, Italy attacked France and later Greece—without warning.

And this year, in 1941, the Axis Powers attacked Yugoslavia and Greece and they dominated the Balkans—without warning.

In 1941, also, Hitler invaded Russia—without warning.

And now Japan has attacked Malaya and Thailand—and the United States—without warning.

It is all of one pattern.

We are now in this war. We are all in it—all the way. Every single man, woman and child is a partner in the most tremendous undertaking of our American history. We must share together the bad news and the good news, the defeats and the victories—the changing fortunes of war.

President Franklin D. Roosevelt, *Fireside Chats*, December 9, 1941.

GO ON TO THE NEXT PAGE

12. Why does Franklin Roosevelt list the Axis leaders' military offenses between 1931 and 1941 (lines 51–69)?

    The list will

    (1) excuse Japan's actions by showing other countries acting similarly
    (2) provide a history lesson for listeners
    (3) provide evidence to support a declaration of war
    (4) induce people to stop buying products made in Axis countries
    (5) imply the Axis leaders conferred with each other from the beginning

13. Why does Roosevelt repeat the phrase "without warning" in his list of military offenses (lines 51–69)?

    (1) to describe the beginnings of World War II
    (2) to create a poem for rhetorical effect
    (3) to explain the rules of war to his listeners
    (4) to emphasize through repetition the terrible nature of the attacks
    (5) to imply that it is acceptable to attack another country with warning

14. What is the most likely reason Roosevelt refers to Japan's leaders as "military dictators" (line 39)?

    (1) He didn't know Japan had an emperor.
    (2) He confused Japan's government with Germany's.
    (3) He misunderstood Japan's system of government.
    (4) He wanted to imply a contrast with America's peaceful democracy.
    (5) He was using the same terminology as the Japanese.

15. What is the meaning of "emissaries" (line 26)?

    (1) diplomats
    (2) spies
    (3) residents
    (4) lawyers
    (5) administrators

16. When Roosevelt declares that the United States has joined World War II, what is the main reason he says, "We are all in it—all the way" (lines 74–75)?

    (1) to prepare the country for women soldiers
    (2) to reassure U.S. allies
    (3) to impress Congress
    (4) to unify the country and prepare it for coming sacrifices
    (5) to challenge the Axis countries

17. Who was the primary audience for this speech?

    (1) Business leaders visiting the White House
    (2) The U.S. Congress
    (3) The government of Germany
    (4) The Japanese embassy
    (5) The American people

GO ON TO THE NEXT PAGE

Questions 18 through 22 refer to the following excerpt from a review.

HOW DID THE AUDIENCE REACT TO THE PLAY?

The new melodrama that came to town last evening is another play that has drawn its scenarios and inspiration from the excitement which took possession of Europe in midsummer of the year just past. It is called "Inside the Lines," and its first New York presentation was made at the Longacre Theatre.

It is another spy play. The road of battle may be all very well for so roomy a theatre as the Manhattan Opera House down in Thirty-fourth Street, but the more stealthy conflicts of the secret missions are better suited to the smaller auditoriums of the playhouses along Broadway. Like "The White Feather," the new English war play now established at the Comedy Theatre, "Inside the Lines" deals with the haunting horror of the German Secret Service. Like "The White Feather," it has to do with a plot from German headquarters to attack the British power at sea in August, 1914.

Unlike the English war play, the new melodrama at the Longacre has nothing to do with the apparently placid interior of a modest seacoast hotel, but gains some advantage from its highly romantic settings on the rock of Gibraltar. The fretful old tourist from Illinois expressed his doubts as to the general usefulness of anyone who would reside on an insurance advertisement, but from this comfortable distance Gibraltar seems a very promising spot for melodramatic shocks. The not infrequent moments of wild and careless improbability into which "Inside the Lines" lapses are further covered over by some competent acting done in the company assembled for its presentation. So it is that the new play at the Longacre provides a moderately interesting evening in the theatre.

"Inside the Lines" is from the pen of Earl Derr Biggers, who is widely known as the author of the story from which George Cohan fashioned "Seven Keys to Baldpate." And in writing this melodrama of his own, he has not neglected to take a leaf from Mr. Cohan's wide-open book. He, too, has written a play with a secret. Like the mysterious Mr. Denby of "Under Cover," the scheming secret agent seemingly sent from Berlin to work destruction at Gibraltar, and represented at the Longacre by Lewis S. Stone, turns out in the end to be somebody very, very different.

This twist to the story comes at the very close of the play, but it was not an overwhelming surprise last evening. Most of those out front must have been inclined to the belief that neither would the British felt be blown up nor so entirely personable and popular a player as Mr. Stone be shot at sunrise. Furthermore, it is becoming so altogether fashionable in melodrama for things to be other than they seem that there must have been a widespread suspicion that just this thing was going to happen at the end. Thus is the trick of the secret losing some of its force by repetition.

"War Melodrama at the Longacre," *New York Times*, ©1915.

GO ON TO THE NEXT PAGE

18. Which of the following best explains why the play was well-suited to the Longacre Theatre?
    (1) Its subject matter, "secret missions," is best produced in a smaller theatre like the Longacre.
    (2) It was a war play that needed a very large stage.
    (3) The play had only one set.
    (4) The play could expect only very small audiences.
    (5) The Longacre Theatre specializes in melodramas.

19. What can the reader conclude about how the reviewer reacted to the play?

    The reviewer
    (1) disliked the play intensely
    (2) felt sorry for the audience
    (3) could not understand the plot
    (4) thought the play was a great success
    (5) thought the play was flawed but interesting

20. What reason best explains why the reviewer describes an audience member as a "fretful old tourist from Illinois" (line 27)?

    The reviewer wanted to indicate that
    (1) the man was old and from the Midwest
    (2) he didn't know the tourist's name
    (3) the tourist had a thick accent
    (4) the tourist was unsophisticated and didn't understand Broadway theater
    (5) people travel hundreds of miles to see Broadway plays

21. When the reviewer writes, "it is becoming so altogether fashionable in melodrama for things to be other than they seem that there must have been a widespread suspicion that just this thing was going to happen," (lines 60–64) what does he mean?
    (1) The play was not original.
    (2) The audience could predict the ending of the play.
    (3) The play was very confusing to the audience.
    (4) The play would be financially unsuccessful.
    (5) The costume department created excellent disguises.

22. This review was published in *The New York Times* in 1915. What was the event that caused "the excitement which took possession of Europe in midsummer of the year just past" (lines 3–5)?

    The event was
    (1) the debut of a blockbuster new play
    (2) the development of motion pictures
    (3) the development of new technology for special effects on stage
    (4) a change in the political structure of Europe
    (5) the start of World War I

GO ON TO THE NEXT PAGE

Questions 23 through 28 refer to the following excerpt from a play.

DOES THE WOODCUTTER RESPECT THE PRINCESS?

[The woodcutter is discovered singing at his work, in a glade of the forest outside his hut. He is tall and strong, and brave and handsome; all that a woodcutter ought to be. Now it happened that the princess was passing, and as soon as his song is finished, sure enough, on she comes.]

PRINCESS: Good morning, Woodcutter.

WOODCUTTER: Good morning. *(But he goes on with his work.)*

PRINCESS: *(After a pause)* Good morning, Woodcutter.

WOODCUTTER: Good morning.

PRINCESS: Don't you ever say anything except good morning?

WOODCUTTER: Sometimes I say good-bye.

PRINCESS: You *are* a cross woodcutter today.

WOODCUTTER: I have work to do.

PRINCESS: You are still cutting wood? Don't you ever do anything else?

WOODCUTTER: Well, you are still a Princess; don't *you* ever do anything else?

PRINCESS: *(Reproachfully)* Now, that's not fair, Woodcutter. You can't say I was a Princess yesterday, when I came and helped you stack your wood. Or the day before, when I tied up your hand where you had cut it. Or the day before that, when we had our meal together on the grass. Was I a Princess then?

WOODCUTTER: Somehow I think you were. Somehow I think you were saying to yourself, "Isn't it sweet of a Princess to treat a mere woodcutter like this?"

PRINCESS: I think you're perfectly horrid. I've a good mind never to speak to you again. And—and I would, if only I could be sure that you would notice I wasn't speaking to you.

WOODCUTTER: After all, I'm just as bad as you. Only yesterday I was thinking to myself how unselfish I was to interrupt my work in order to talk to a mere Princess.

PRINCESS: Yes, but the trouble is that you *don't* interrupt your work.

WOODCUTTER: *(Interrupting it and going up to her with a smile)* Madam, I am at your service.

PRINCESS: I wish I thought you were.

WOODCUTTER: Surely you have enough people at your service already. Princes and Chancellors and Chamberlains and Waiting Maids.

PRINCESS: Yes, that's just it. That's why I want your help. Particularly in the matter of the Princes.

WOODCUTTER: Why, has a suitor come for the hand of her Royal Highness?

PRINCESS: Three suitors. And I hate them all.

WOODCUTTER: And which are you going to marry?

PRINCESS: I don't know. Father hasn't made up his mind yet.

WOODCUTTER: And this is a matter which father—which His Majesty decides for himself?

PRINCESS: Why, of course! You should read the History Books, Woodcutter. The suitors to the hand of a Princess are always set some trial of strength or test of quality by the King, and the winner marries his daughter.

WOODCUTTER: Well, I don't live in a Palace, and I think my own thoughts about these things. I'd better get back to my work. *(He goes on with his chopping.)*

A. A. Milne, excerpted from *Make-Believe*, ©1918.

GO ON TO THE NEXT PAGE

23. Which of the following best explains why the Princess likes speaking to the Woodcutter?
    (1) He doesn't treat her like others do.
    (2) She enjoys the special treatment she receives from him.
    (3) They have similar hobbies.
    (4) She enjoys woodworking.
    (5) She enjoys the outdoors.

24. What can the reader conclude about the Princess from her statements in this excerpt?

    She is

    (1) sullen and disagreeable
    (2) condescending and haughty
    (3) melancholy and sad
    (4) superficial and vain
    (5) proud but caring

25. Which of the following best describes the Princess and the Woodcutter?
    (1) ruler and subject
    (2) close friends
    (3) brother and sister
    (4) potential romantic partners
    (5) co-workers

26. In this excerpt, how does the author use the topic of the three suitors?

    To suggest that

    (1) the princess relies too much upon her father
    (2) the woodcutter disagrees with how a husband is chosen for the princess
    (3) three is the traditional number of suitors in a fairy tale
    (4) the princess doesn't like many men
    (5) the princess would make an excellent wife

27. When the Princess says, "I wish I thought you were" (line 48), what does it indicate about her feelings?

    She

    (1) wants more courtiers
    (2) needs constant attention from admirers
    (3) wishes the woodcutter were a prince
    (4) is dismissive of the woodcutter
    (5) wishes she had more of the woodcutter's personal attention

28. Which of the following best explains why the woodcutter is described as "tall and strong, and brave and handsome; all that a woodcutter ought to be" (lines 3–4)?
    (1) The description is the same as for a prince. The woodcutter will probably end up as a suitor for the princess.
    (2) Woodcutters are generally strong young men in good health.
    (3) Everyone is handsome in fairy tales.
    (4) It explains the interest of the princess. The Woodcutter is a desirable person.
    (5) The play is idealistic.

GO ON TO THE NEXT PAGE

Questions 29 through 34 refer to the following excerpt.

HOW DO THE TOWNSPEOPLE FEEL ABOUT JOHN DOLITTLE?

"Yon crittur's got a broken leg," he said—"and another badly cut an' all. I can mend you your boats, Tom, but I haven't the tools nor the learning to make a broken squirrel seaworthy. This is a job for a surgeon—and for a right smart one an' all. There be only one man I know who could save yon crittur's life. And that's John Dolittle."

"Who is John Dolittle?" I asked. "Is he a vet?"

"No," said the mussel-man. "He's no vet. Doctor Dolittle is a nacheralist."

"What's a nacheralist?"

"A nacheralist," said Joe, putting away his glasses and starting to fill his pipe, "is a man who knows all about animals and butterflies and plants and rocks an' all. John Dolittle is a very great nacheralist. I'm surprised you never heard of him—and you daft over animals. He knows a whole lot about shellfish—that I know from my own knowledge. He's a quiet man and don't talk much; but there's folks who do say he's the greatest nacheralist in the world."

"Where does he live?" I asked.

"Over on the Oxenthorpe Road, t'other side the town. Don't know just which house it is, but 'most anyone 'cross there could tell you, I reckon. Go and see him. He's a great man."

So I thanked the mussel-man, took up my squirrel again and started off towards the Oxenthorpe Road.

The first thing I heard as I came into the marketplace was some one calling "Meat! M-E-A-T!"

"There's Matthew Mugg," I said to myself. "He'll know where this Doctor lives. Matthew knows everyone."

So I hurried across the market-place and caught him up.

"Matthew," I said, "do you know Doctor Dolittle?"

"Do I know John Dolittle!" said he. "Well, I should think I do! I know him as well as I know my own wife—better, I sometimes think. He's a great man—a very great man."

"Can you show me where he lives?" I asked. "I want to take this squirrel to him. It has a broken leg."

"Certainly," said the cat's-meat-man. "I'll be going right by his house directly. Come along and I'll show you."

So off we went together.

"Oh, I've known John Dolittle for years and years," said Matthew as we made our way out of the market-place. "But I'm pretty sure he ain't home just now. He's away on a voyage. But he's liable to be back any day. I'll show you his house and then you'll know where to find him."

All the way down the Oxenthorpe Road Matthew hardly stopped talking about his great friend, Doctor John Dolittle—"M. D." He talked so much that he forgot all about calling out "Meat!" until we both suddenly noticed that we had a whole procession of dogs following us patiently.

"Where did the Doctor go to on this voyage?" I asked as Matthew handed round the meat to them.

"I couldn't tell you," he answered. "Nobody never knows where he goes, nor when he's going, nor when he's coming back. He lives all alone except for his pets. He's made some great voyages and some wonderful discoveries. Last time he came back he told me he'd found a tribe of Red Indians in the Pacific Ocean—lived on two islands, they did. The husbands lived on one island and the wives lived on the other. Sensible people, some of them savages. They only met once a year, when the husbands came over to visit the wives for a great feast—Christmas-time, most likely. Yes, he's a wonderful man is the Doctor. And as for animals, well, there ain't no one knows as much about 'em as what he does."

Hugh Lofting, excerpted from *The Voyages of Doctor Dolittle*, ©1922.

GO ON TO THE NEXT PAGE

29. When describing John Dolittle, the musselman says, "He's no vet. Doctor Dolittle is a nacheralist" (lines 10–11). He is implying which of the following?

(1) Dr. Dolittle isn't trained in the treatment of sick animals.
(2) Dr. Dolittle only studies plants.
(3) Dr. Dolittle is an expert in all areas of nature.
(4) Dr. Dolittle has not had any formal education.
(5) Dr. Dolittle prefers botany to zoology.

30. What is the general tone of the passage?

(1) serious and dark
(2) morbid and depressed
(3) mocking and sarcastic
(4) humorous and lightly ironic
(5) lighthearted and carefree

31. When the narrator says, "we both suddenly noticed that we had a whole procession of dogs following us patiently" (lines 63–65), why are the dogs following him and Matthew Mugg?

The dogs

(1) belong to Dr. Dolittle
(2) belong to Matthew Mugg
(3) are interested in Matthew Mugg's description of Dr. Dolittle
(4) are waiting for Matthew Mugg's meat
(5) always gather in the market-place

32. How do the neighborhood people feel about Dr. Dolittle?

They think he is

(1) eccentric and dangerous
(2) wonderfully talented and slightly mysterious
(3) arrogant and aloof
(4) outgoing and friendly
(5) knowledgeable but unneighborly

33. Which of the following phrases is closest in meaning to the phrase "daft over" in line 18?

(1) admiring of
(2) indifferent to
(3) crazy about
(4) afraid of
(5) interested in

34. When Matthew describes the "Red Indians" by saying that "The husbands lived on one island and the wives lived on the other. Sensible people, some of them savages" (lines 76–79), he is implying which of the following?

(1) Married couples never live apart.
(2) It is barbaric to live apart from one's spouse.
(3) Men and women do not coexist well.
(4) Foreign cultures are fascinating.
(5) Small islands foster marital harmony.

GO ON TO THE NEXT PAGE

Questions 35 through 40 refer to the following excerpt from a novel.

WHAT DOES THE NARRATOR LIKE ABOUT THE RESTAURANT?

A few blocks south of the apartment I'm renting, Joe's Lunch Bucket serves up amazing sandwiches. The owner runs the place, so he stays open as late as he has customers, usually until some time after midnight. The restaurant is at the end of an alley. If you sit on the last stool by the window, you can see the big public fountain in the adjacent square. There are usually swarms of children and teenagers milling around the area; no one really enforces the curfew, especially in the summer when the nights are warm and families stroll around the shops and public spaces downtown.

Joe has a menu stuck to the front window with masking tape that is yellowed and cracked from years in the sun. I've never stopped to read it and, as far as I can tell, neither have the other regulars. Never mind the dingy interior, noisy kitchen, and lack of parking. I just go there for the food. I like to sit at the bar along the window and relax with the sinful deliciousness of Joe's Special Rueben. Newcomers to Joe's marvel at the stack of corned beef and sauerkraut spilling from the bread onto my paper plate.

Good food is the key to Joe's fortune. The sign outside is hardly eye-catching and the restaurant always appears to be dimly lit. One can't help but notice the large smiley face decal affixed to the front door that reads "Keep Smiling!" The sandwiches certainly make me smile, but I can't say they do the same for Joe himself. His constant ugly expression belies the care that he takes with his meats, breads, and cheeses. So, too, does his quirky restaurant. The counters are dented and scratched from years of knife abuse. The old refrigerator case clicks and whines constantly. As I savor my sandwich, my gaze always drifts toward the caulk along the windowpanes, once white, which is slowly deteriorating with the rest of the place. In fact, I've often thought to offer Joe my painting services in exchange for some sustenance. Regardless of the appearance of the place, I still enjoy my delicious sandwich. The food is, after all, the only charm this little place needs.

A lot of people pay daily visits to the sandwich shop. I know many of their faces by now, but I could more easily recall their tastes in sandwiches. Older people like the stand-bys—chicken salad, corned beef, and the like. Kids come in after school for grilled cheeses or Joe's tuna salad. When I am back home and reminiscing, I picture all these people with their favorite meals. Perhaps it's the familiarity that secures Joe's as my favorite sandwich shop. I know that I can come in whenever I please and someone would look away from their savory sandwich and offer a friendly hello. It's nice to know that Joe's Lunch Bucket and its neighborly ambience are just a short walk away.

35. What is the effect of indicating that Joe's Lunch Bucket is located at the end of an alley?
    (1) to indicate the type of city in which the restaurant is located
    (2) to provide a contrast with the success of the restaurant
    (3) to create an image of dirty city streets
    (4) to make the city seem less intimidating
    (5) to foreshadow a negative critique of the restaurant

36. How does the narrator respond to the menu posted in the window?
    (1) The narrator reads it carefully.
    (2) The narrator disregards it.
    (3) The narrator is the only person who reads it.
    (4) The narrator thinks the restaurant owner should remove it.
    (5) The narrator relies on the menu for choosing a sandwich.

37. According to the passage, what is the main reason customers come to Joe's Lunch Bucket?
    (1) To enjoy an elegant lunch in beautiful surroundings
    (2) To entertain friends and family on special occasions
    (3) To eat large homemade sandwiches in a familiar atmosphere
    (4) To chat with the friendly owner
    (5) To find some peace and quiet

38. Which one of the following words is closest in meaning to the word "fortune" in line 27?
    (1) wealth
    (2) success
    (3) luck
    (5) status

39. Which of the following is implied by the phrase "stand-bys" in line 52?
    (1) plainness
    (2) reliability
    (3) wait time
    (4) substitution
    (5) backup

40. The author of the excerpt would probably identify which one of the following as being essential to a restaurant's survival?
    (1) a visible location
    (2) cleanliness
    (3) pleasant workers
    (4) appealing food
    (5) low prices

Answers and explanations for this test begin on page 688.

GO ON TO: SOCIAL STUDIES

Social Studies Test

The GED Social Studies Test consists of 50 multiple-choice questions that you will be given 70 minutes to answer. You will have to draw upon some prior knowledge of history, civics and government, economics, and geography; however, you will not have to recall facts.

Directions: Choose the one best answer to each question.

GO ON TO THE NEXT PAGE

Question 1 refers to the following graph.

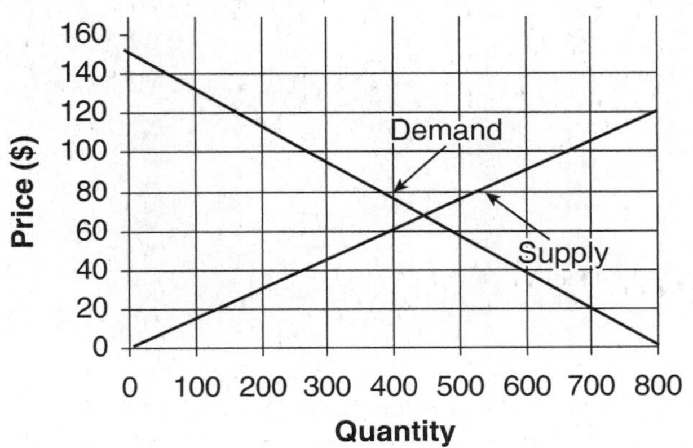

1. Which question about one-way tickets on Train #6 can be answered by using information in the graph?
   (1) Why are one-way tickets on Train #6 so expensive?
   (2) At which price would the train company maximize its income from sales of one-way tickets on Train #6?
   (3) To what extent has the price of one-way tickets on Train #6 changed over time?
   (4) How many people want to buy one-way tickets on Train #6 but do not because of the price?
   (5) Which of the company's train routes operates most efficiently?

Question 2 refers to the following table.

Median U.S. Rental Vacancy Rates

	1970	1980	1990	2004	2005
1st Quarter	5.4%	5.2%	7.5%	10.4%	10.1%
2nd Quarter	5.4%	5.6%	7.0%	10.2%	9.8%
3rd Quarter	5.3%	5.7%	7.2%	10.1%	9.9%
4th Quarter	5.2%	5.0%	7.2%	10.0%	9.6%

Source: U.S. Census Bureau

2. Which of the following is a possible explanation for the significant increase in median rental vacancy rates starting in 1990?
   (1) Median rent began decreasing around 1990.
   (2) Quality of rental housing has steadily improved over time.
   (3) Owning a home has become a better value than renting for many people.
   (4) U.S. population growth has exceeded projections.
   (5) Reduction in median income has further limited the money available for home purchases.

---

3. The first immigration from Cuba to the United States dates from the sixteenth century, before the formation of either country. In the late nineteenth century, many Cubans followed the example of Vicente Martinez-Ybor by setting up small cigar factories in Tampa, Florida. The most recent wave of Cuban immigrants to the United States began in 1959 following the Cuban Revolution led by Fidel Castro.

   What attracted most Cuban immigrants to the United States in 1960?
   (1) temperate climate
   (2) higher tax rates
   (3) political freedom
   (4) improved sanitation
   (5) environmental quality

GO ON TO THE NEXT PAGE

4. "Jim Crow" laws were state and local laws enacted soon after the Civil War in Southern and border states of America that required racial segregation in all public spaces. Most public places, including schools and public transportation, were required to have separate facilities for whites. When were the Jim Crow laws finally repealed?

   Most Jim Crow laws

   (1) were repealed by the Civil Rights Act of 1964
   (2) were repealed by the *Plessy v. Ferguson* decision of 1896
   (3) were repealed because of the Scopes Trial of 1925
   (4) were repealed by constitutional amendment
   (5) are still in effect

Questions 5 and 6 refer to the following painting and information.

Washington Crossing the Delaware (Emanuel Leutze, 1851) commemorates George Washington's crossing of the Delaware River on December 25, 1776, during the American Revolutionary War.

5. The crossing was the first move in a surprise attack against British forces and came when morale was especially low. What is the message implied in the painting?

   (1) The winter of 1776 was especially cold.
   (2) Washington and his troops would overcome tremendous odds to win the war.
   (3) Washington was arrogant and cared little for his troops.
   (4) American troops were poorly equipped for naval warfare.
   (5) It is always difficult to fight battles in winter.

6. In which of the following documents would the soldiers in the painting have found specific justification for their fight against Great Britain?

   (1) the Bill of Rights
   (2) the Declaration of Independence
   (3) the Constitution
   (4) the *Roe v. Wade* decision
   (5) the Civil Rights Act

Question 7 refers to the following cartoon.

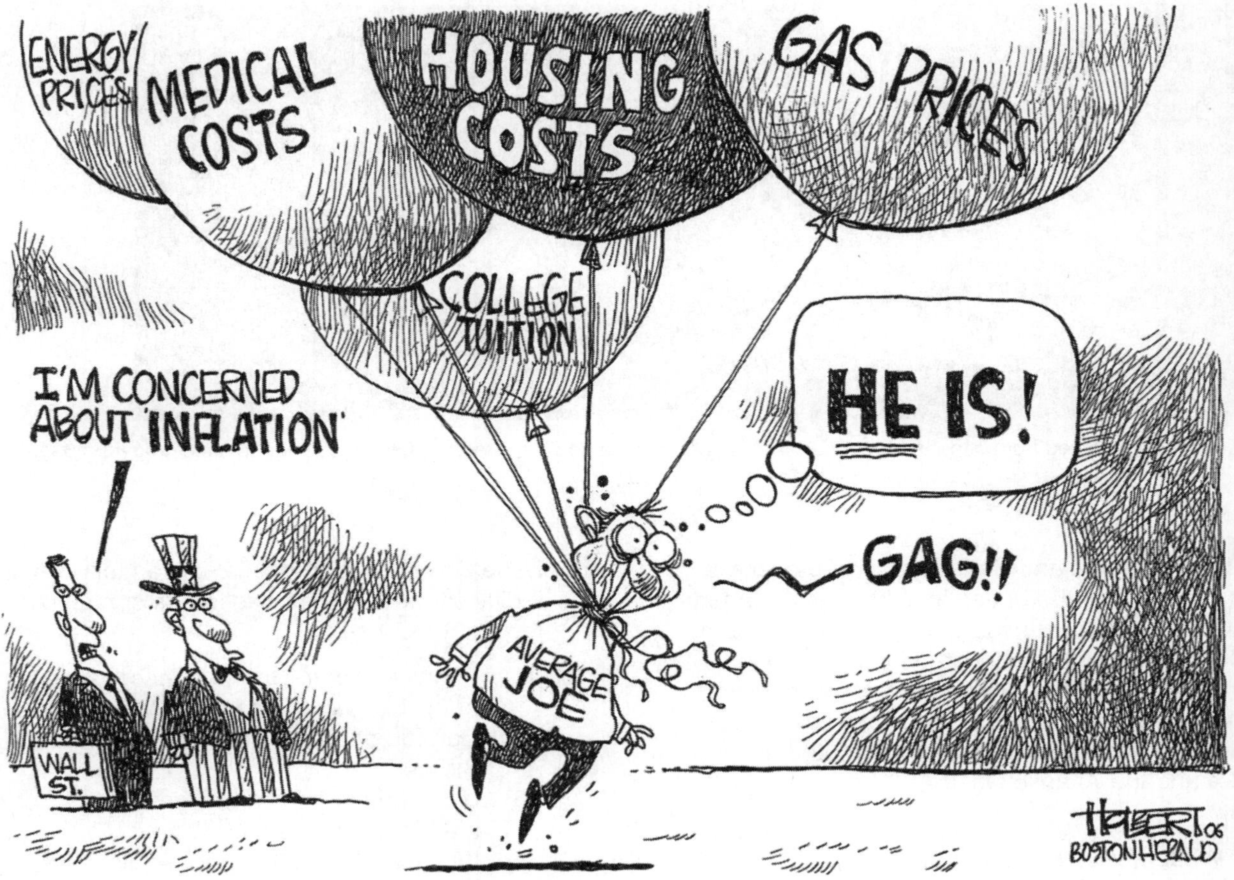

Source: Jerry Holbert: ©Boston Herald/dist. by Newspaper Enterprise Association, Inc.

7. Inflation is an economic term that describes a general rise in prices. What irony about inflation is depicted in this cartoon?
   (1) Inflation is a problem that affects all classes equally.
   (2) Despite the wealth of the upper class, they are the most hurt by inflation.
   (3) While government and financial institutions appear concerned about inflation, it is the middle class who suffers.
   (4) The American government doesn't care about inflation, but citizens do.
   (5) While stock market investors complain about inflation, it is American business practices that cause it.

Questions 8 and 9 refer to the following map and information.

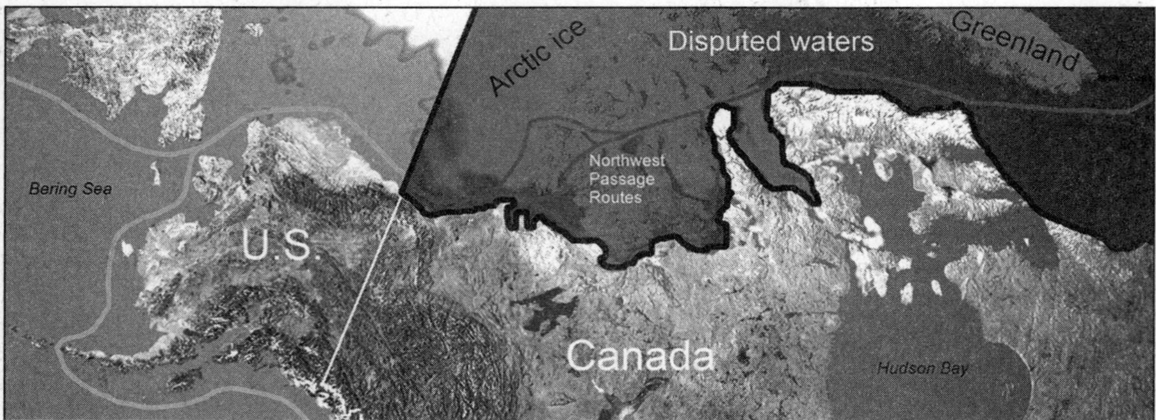

Source: NASA, adapted from images at http://earthobservatory.nasa.gov/Newsroom/NewImages/images.php3?img_id=16340

The United States and Canada disagree over the status of much of the ocean in far northern Canada. The U.S. government asserts that the routes of the Northwest Passage are located in international waters, whereas the Canadian government claims that the routes lie within Canadian territory. The Northwest Passage is an important route between Alaska and the Atlantic Ocean.

8. What conclusion about the status of the Northwest Passage can be drawn from the map and the information?

   (1) The United States does not recognize exclusive national rights to any area of the oceans.
   (2) The United States recognizes Canada's claim to remote arctic areas.
   (3) The United States would prefer that operations in the Northwest Passage remain uncontrolled by Canada.
   (4) The United States claims the waters of the Northwest Passage as its own.
   (5) The United States and Canada dispute U.S. ownership of Alaska.

9. Based on the information and the map, why is it difficult for Canada to assert its control over the disputed waters?

   (1) The U.S. Coast Guard is responsible for patrolling Canadian waters.
   (2) Canada does not trade with the United States.
   (3) U.S. territory lies on the western end of the Northwest Passage.
   (4) It is difficult to patrol and regulate a vast region of arctic islands.
   (5) Very few merchant ships operate in the Northwest Passage.

GO ON TO THE NEXT PAGE

Questions 10 through 13 refer to the following information.

The Statute of Frauds has its origins in pre-17th century England and states that certain contracts need to be in writing. Almost all wealth in medieval England was based on land ownership. Therefore, documenting the sale of land was very important. This was complicated when neither the buyer nor the seller could read or write. Instead, they would gather some nearby residents to witness a ceremony called a *livery of seisin*. During the ceremony, the seller would pick up a stone or twig and hand it to the buyer in exchange for the purchase price. If a dispute over ownership later arose, the witnesses could be called forward to testify that they had seen the transfer of ownership take place.

Soon after the livery of seisin became widespread, some landowners realized they could steal more land by showing up at funerals with a few well-armed "witnesses." The "witnesses" would claim that the dead landowner had sold his land to their employer and that they had witnessed the ceremony. There were rarely any serious protests and when there were, they were usually resolved violently. By the late seventieth century, some of these landowners had become very powerful and were even able to raise private armies. To maintain political stability, the Statute of Frauds was enacted in 1679.

10. The livery of seisin was a legal practice in medieval England. When was this time period?
    (1) Approximately 800 B.C.–100 A.D.
    (2) Approximately 500 A.D.–1600 A.D.
    (3) Approximately 1700 A.D.–1900 A.D.
    (4) Approximately 1900 A.D.–1950 A.D.
    (5) Approximately 1950 A.D.–2000 A.D.

11. What does the passage imply about private armies?
    (1) They were usually very small.
    (2) They were often manned by foreign soldiers.
    (3) They were used to intimidate mourners at funerals.
    (4) They often fought with stones and sticks.
    (5) They could be used to challenge the government.

12. Why did medieval land sellers give buyers a stone or twig?
    (1) The stone or twig symbolized the land being sold.
    (2) Stones and twigs were used as money in medieval England.
    (3) Stones and twigs had religious significance for medieval English people.
    (4) The stones and twigs had the details of the sale written on them.
    (5) Exchanging stones and twigs was seen as a gesture of kindness.

13. What does the author think about the importance of literacy for property law?

    Literacy is
    (1) unnecessary because people find other ways to document property sales
    (2) unnecessary because, in medieval England, all land was communally owned
    (3) very important because it reduces the opportunity for fraud
    (4) important for raising private armies
    (5) unnecessary under a monarchy government

---

14. Daylight Saving Time is an energy conservation measure where clocks are set forward one hour in the spring and back one hour in the fall. Beginning in March 2007, the United States government will increase the duration of Daylight Saving Time by approximately one month in order to conserve more energy. Which of the following would be evidence that increasing the duration of Daylight Saving Time succeeded in conserving energy?
    (1) an increase in traffic accidents in March 2007 over the previous year
    (2) an increase in daylight for Halloween trick-or-treaters
    (3) an increase in total oil consumption in March 2007 over the previous year
    (4) a decrease in total oil consumption in March 2007 over the previous year
    (5) an increase in crop production in 2007 over the previous year

GO ON TO THE NEXT PAGE

Questions 15 and 16 refer to the following chart.

U.S. presidential line of succession as established by the Presidential Succession Act of 1947.

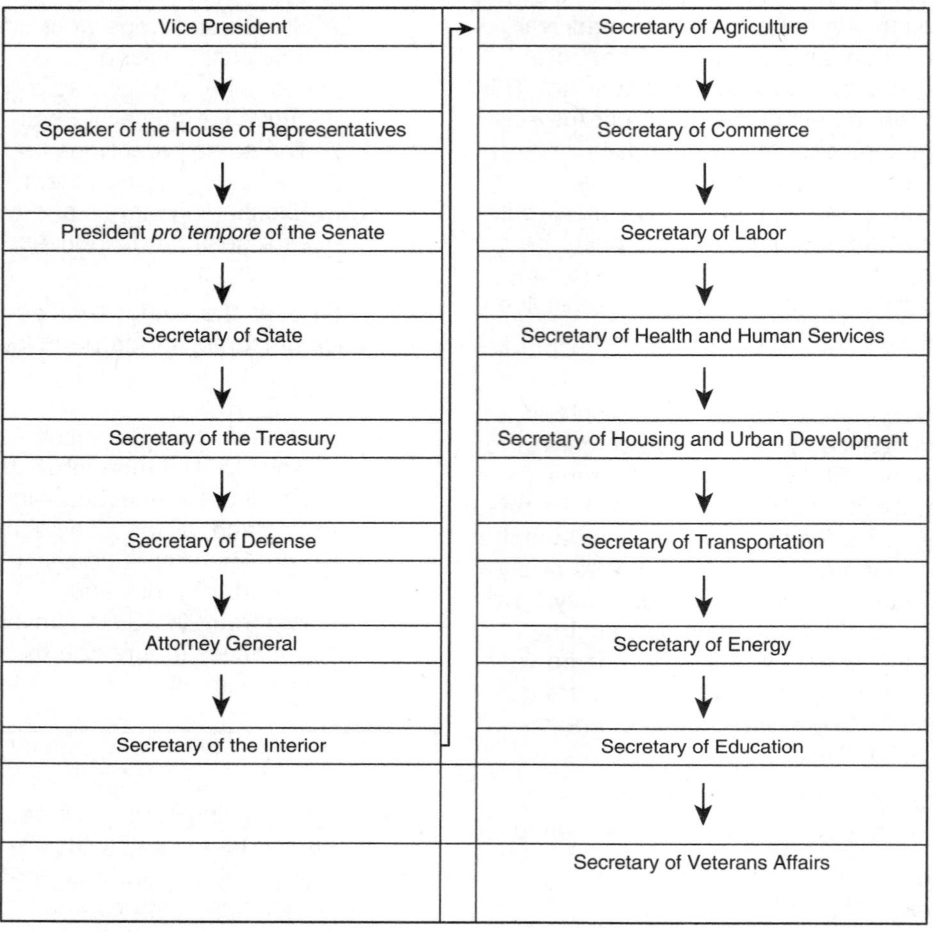

15. Under which of the following circumstances would it not be necessary to invoke the presidential line of succession?
    (1) the president's death
    (2) the president's resignation
    (3) the president's impeachment and subsequent conviction
    (4) the president's incapacity
    (5) the president's election defeat

16. For the president's annual State of the Union address, why is one member of the cabinet always secured in a secret location away from the Capitol?
    (1) to fulfill the duties of the president during the long speech
    (2) to supervise national security operations while government is in recess for the speech
    (3) to prevent exhaustion of the entire line of succession in the event of a catastrophe
    (4) to ensure that one member of the cabinet remains uninfluenced by the speech
    (5) to simulate Washington, D.C. evacuation procedures for training purposes

GO ON TO THE NEXT PAGE

Questions 17 through 19 refer to the following information.

In March 1867, an agreement known as "Seward's Folly" was made between Russia and Secretary of State William H. Seward to transfer ownership of the Alaska Territory to the United States for a mere $7.2 million. As the pact's name suggests, many Americans marveled at Seward's foolishness. What, after all, did this place called Alaska have to offer America?

The first answer came with the Klondike Gold Rush in 1897. For over a decade, miners, fishermen, and trappers entered the territory and developed a colonial economy where Alaska's rich land and water resources were extracted and exported for the profit of a few entrepreneurs. Alaskan residents soon sought to gain control over their assets by acquiring official territory status. Official status gave Alaskans some say over their government; however, most of the political power remained with the federal government. The federal government also maintained control over Alaska's vast resources.

Things changed with Japan's 1941 attack on Pearl Harbor and subsequent occupation of two of the Aleutian Islands. A frightened Congress immediately provided Alaska with billions of dollars for military defense and construction of the Alaska Highway (originally a supply road during World War II). Finally, resources poured into Alaska, rather than the other way around. By 1943, three quarters of Alaska's 233,000 residents were part of the military. And in 1959, after years of public and political pressure, Alaska gained its statehood.

17. Why does the author end the first paragraph with a rhetorical question?

    The author

    (1) questions the value of Alaska to the United States
    (2) doubts that Seward made a wise decision in buying the Alaskan territory
    (3) expects the reader to answer her question
    (4) uses the question to introduce the main idea of her essay
    (5) is critical of American expansion in the 19th century

18. According to the passage, why did Alaska become important to the U.S. government during World War II?

    (1) Japan had invaded the Aleutian islands.
    (2) Large reserves of oil were discovered in Alaska.
    (3) Russia asked to buy back the territory.
    (4) Alaska's gold reserves became important during World War II.
    (5) Thousands of soldiers were stationed in Alaska.

19. What were the primary resources exported from Alaska in the late nineteenth and early twentieth centuries?

    (1) fur, seafood, and gold
    (2) grain and vegetables
    (3) petroleum products
    (4) timber and paper products
    (5) whale blubber and native art

GO ON TO THE NEXT PAGE

Questions 20 and 21 refer to the following graph and information.

Employment in Profession and Business Servers

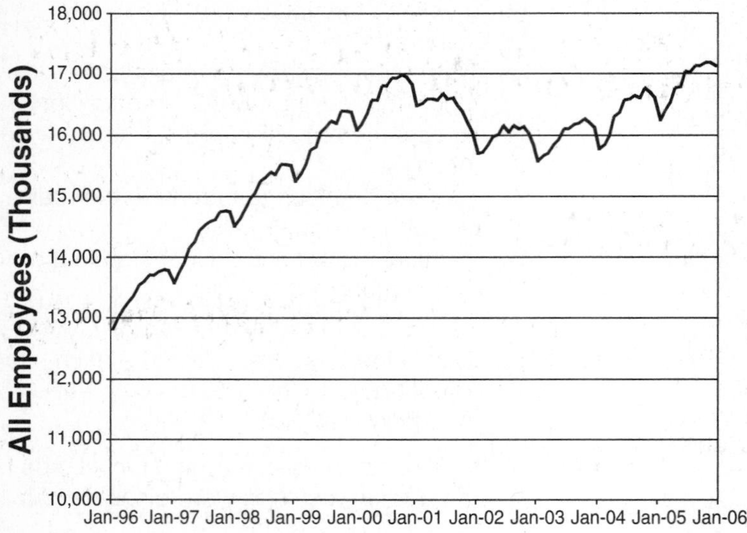

The U.S. Department of Labor divides the "professional and business services supersector" into three parts: the "professional, scientific, and technical services sector" (for example, lawyers, architects, accountants, photographers, researchers); the "management of companies and enterprises sector" (for example, venture capital firms); and the "administrative and support and waste management and remediation services sector" (for example, secretaries, human resources managers, security guards, maintenance workers, office managers). The Department of Labor forecasts that employment in professional and business services will increase significantly in the future.

20. What conclusion about employment in professional and business services is confirmed by clear evidence in the graph?

    (1) Employment has continuously increased.
    (2) The majority of employees are paid an hourly wage.
    (3) Employment declines slightly every winter.
    (4) Accountants have larger salaries than photographers.
    (5) Employment peaked in the year 2000.

21. Which government policy to increase employment in professional and business services would likely be most acceptable to employers and the public?

    (1) making professional and business services exempt from taxes
    (2) removing people from other sectors to work in professional and business services
    (3) prohibiting seasonal employee layoffs
    (4) strengthening job training programs and incentives for pursuing higher education
    (5) dismantling the business and professional services sector and distributing employees to other sectors

GO ON TO THE NEXT PAGE

Questions 22 and 23 refer to the following information.

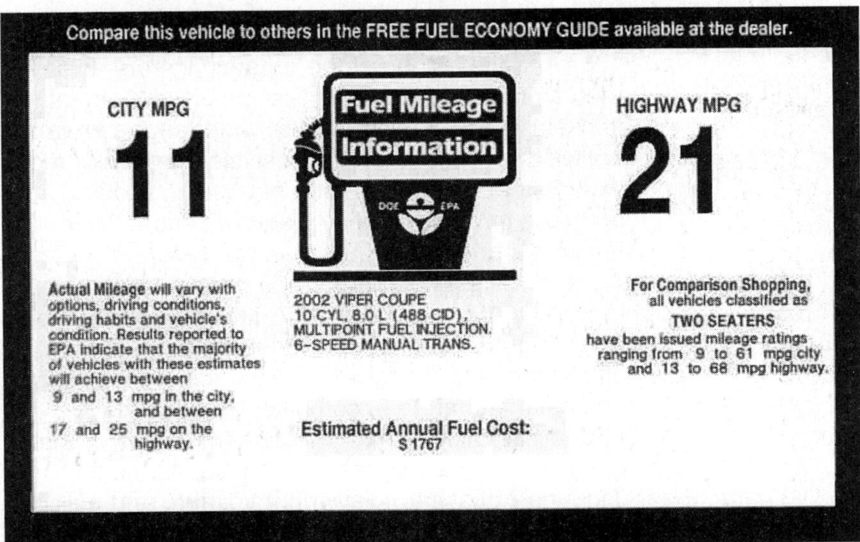

22. How is this vehicle fuel economy window sticker useful to U.S. consumers?

    The sticker

    (1) shows consumers the total cost of owning the vehicle
    (2) is too technical to be of any use to most consumers
    (3) quickly goes out of date as gasoline prices change
    (4) can give information for comparison shopping
    (5) shows how to operate the vehicle

23. Which of the following best explains why the U.S. government would require the use of the vehicle fuel economy window stickers?

    (1) to discourage new vehicle sales
    (2) to monitor new vehicle inventories
    (3) to increase taxes for polluters
    (4) to encourage the conservation of gasoline
    (5) to ensure that many different types of vehicles are available to buy

24. Contrary to popular usage, the Internet and the World Wide Web are not synonymous. The Internet is a collection of interconnected computer networks, linked by physical and wireless connections. The Web is a collection of interconnected documents with text and other types of media, all organized using hyperlinks and web addresses. Based on this definition, which of the following would be an example of using the Internet but not the World Wide Web?

    (1) discussing car repair in a chat room
    (2) reading news and weather reports
    (3) browsing pictures of your friend's new baby
    (4) shopping for clothes and shoes
    (5) watching instructional videos

25. The World Health Organization is a specialized agency of the United Nations whose mission is to combat disease, especially key infectious diseases, and to promote the general health of people around the world.

    Based on this information, which of the following would be a primary interest of the World Health Organization?

    (1) Research and development of nonfossil fuels
    (2) Antiterrorism investigations
    (3) Research and development of genetically modified crops
    (4) Research and development of antimalaria vaccines
    (5) Political stability in developing nations

26. According to the law of supply and demand, which of the following is most likely to occur when there is a reduction in gasoline production, but people decide to buy more gasoline than they did last year?

    (1) The price of gasoline will increase.
    (2) The incomes of gasoline producers will decrease.
    (3) The number of gasoline producers will decrease.
    (4) Gasoline producers will demand government price caps on gasoline.
    (5) The cost of producing gasoline will increase.

<u>Questions 27 through 30</u> refer to the following information.

The publication of the *Encyclopédie*, beginning in 1751, stands as one of the greatest literary achievements of the 18th century. French Enlightenment thinkers sought to compile the wide range of human knowledge in a concise, accessible form. Their motivation stemmed from a fervent belief in social progress through rationality and not superstition, religiosity, and tyranny, as was the case in the Dark Ages. Writer Denis Diderot and mathematician Jean le Rond d'Alambert undertook the challenging task of editing the masterwork. Together they sought to create a comprehensive encyclopedia with entirely original material. To accomplish this feat, they enlisted the help of many prominent figures of the enlightenment, most notably philosopher Jean-Jacques Rousseau, playwright Voltaire, and political theorist Montesquieu. By its completion in 1780, the *Encyclopédie* comprised 35 volumes containing more than 70,000 articles by nearly 30 authors.

Publication of such a massive work was costly, so France's affluent cultural elite formed the main subscriber base. When each volume left the press, it was delivered to its buyer. Though only the rich could afford the books, the authors intended the collections of articles for the masses. After all, an essential goal of the Enlightenment was the diffusion of human knowledge and the dispelling of superstitions.

27. According to the information, what was true about publishing books in the 18th century?

    Publishing books

    (1) was a simple and fast process because of the printing press
    (2) became illegal for Enlightenment thinkers
    (3) was so expensive that it restricted the market for books
    (4) caused people to cling tightly to their old-fashioned beliefs
    (5) encouraged political upheaval

28. What conclusion about the Enlightenment is most strongly supported in the information?
    (1) The Enlightenment was a philosophical reaction to the freethinking of the Dark Ages.
    (2) The Enlightenment caused conflicts between rich people and poor people in France.
    (3) Enlightenment thinkers believed in education for all people.
    (4) If the Enlightenment had not occurred, there would be not encyclopedias today.
    (5) Distribution of the *Encyclopédie* caused the intellectual revival known as the Enlightenment.

29. According to the information presented, when would a buyer receive a copy of a single *Encyclopédie* volume?

    When

    (1) an entire set of volumes is finished being printed
    (2) the buyer meets with the publishers in secret
    (3) the greater public was able to afford the *Encyclopédie*
    (4) the buyer swore allegiance to the Enlightenment movement
    (5) the volume was finished being printed

30. Based on the information presented, when would a person have superstitions about a phenomenon?

    When the person

    (1) has not learned the rational explanation of the phenomenon
    (2) is an Enlightenment thinker
    (3) is not a member of the cultural elite
    (4) has read many important books
    (5) believes in social progress through education

Question 31 refers to the following graph.

Number of People in the United States Age 65 and Over and 85 and Over, Selected Years 1900–2000 and Projected 2010–2050.

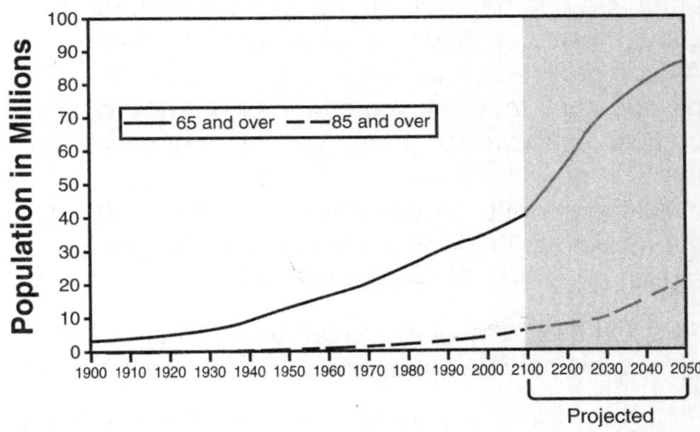

Source: U.S. Census Bureau, Decennial Census and Projections in Older Americans Update 2006: Key Indicators of Well-Being, Federal Interagency Forum on Aging Related Statistics

31. On the basis of the projections in the graph, how is the total U.S. population likely to change in the coming decades?
    (1) The total population will stay constant.
    (2) The total population will increase.
    (3) The total population will decrease.
    (4) The average age of the population will decrease.
    (5) People age 65 and over will eventually outnumber younger people.

Question 32 refers to the following information.

In 1995, the U.S. Environmental Protection Agency (EPA) began the allowance-trading component of the Acid Rain Program to control sulfur dioxide pollution. Under the program, companies must purchase one permit from the EPA for each ton of sulfur dioxide emissions they will emit in a year. As companies develop ways to emit less sulfur dioxide, they may sell some of their permits to other companies that need them. At the end of every year, the EPA buys a certain number of available permits, permanently taking them off the market. In this way, the national sulfur dioxide emissions limit is lowered every year.

32. On the basis of this information, which best explains EPA's reasoning?

    (1) Placing pollution limits on every company is the best way to control acid rain.
    (2) Using a market system for pollution rights is the most efficient way to control acid rain.
    (3) Experts should develop a uniform pollution control technology for all companies.
    (4) Polluters will always find ways to circumvent regulations.
    (5) Acid rain can be eliminated immediately.

Questions 33 and 34 are based on the following diagram and information.

U.S. Federal Highway Administration functional classification system.

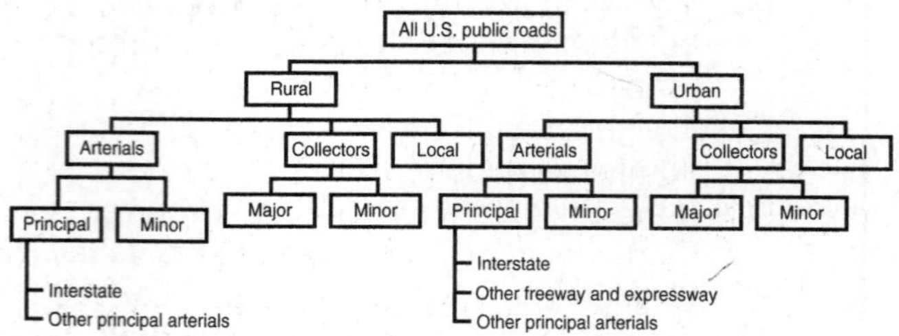

The Federal Highway Administration classifies roads according to the type of service provided and the type of area (urban or rural). There are three main types of roads:

Arterials, which provide the highest level of mobility for longer, uninterrupted trips

Collectors, which collect and distribute traffic from the arterial network and connect with local roads

Local roads, which provide direct access to residences and businesses

SOURCES: U.S. Department of Transportation (USDOT), Federal Highway Administration (FHWA) and Federal Transit Administration.

33. What is a possible functional classification of a freeway from Montana to Washington?

    (1) major collector
    (2) minor arterial
    (3) local
    (4) interstate
    (5) minor collector

34. Which of the following conclusions about transportation in the United States is supported by the information?

    (1) Traffic on major collectors is not controlled by traffic lights.
    (2) Principal arterials frequently intersect local roads.
    (3) Interstate highways are the most efficient routes between major cities.
    (4) Automobiles are a secondary form of transportation in spite of the extensive road network.
    (5) Minor arterials typically go around urban areas.

GO ON TO THE NEXT PAGE

Questions 35 and 36 refer to the following graph.

U.S. corporate profits before and after taxes, 1998–2005.

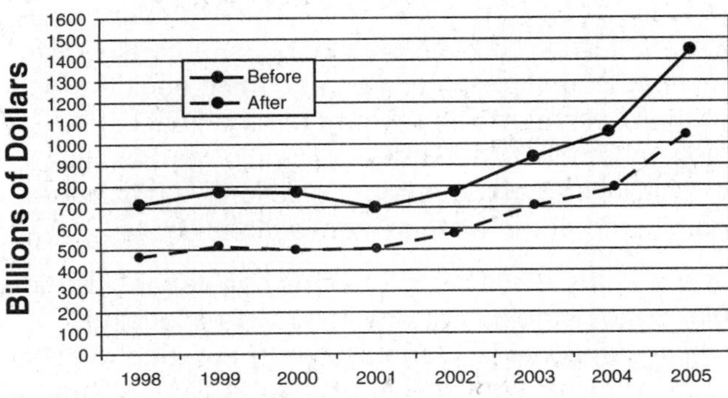

Source: Department of Commerce, Bureau of Economic Analysis

35. Which question about corporate profits can be answered by using information in the graph?
    (1) Why did corporate profits before taxes decrease between 2000 and 2001?
    (2) Which corporations paid the most in taxes from 1998 to 2005?
    (3) How many corporations did not make a taxable profit during any year from 1998 to 2005?
    (4) For which year from 1998 to 2005 did corporations pay the most taxes?
    (5) How much did individuals, compared with corporations, pay in taxes from 1998 to 2005?

36. Which of the following best describes the trends shown in the graph?
    (1) Profits before taxes increased, then decreased, and then increased again.
    (2) Profits before taxes remained constant.
    (3) Profits before taxes increased at a constant rate.
    (4) Profits after taxes increased at a constant rate.
    (5) Profits after taxes decreased, then increased, and then decreased again

Question 37 refers to the following information.

Beginning in 1773, the British East India Company assumed monopoly control over the opium trade in the Bengal region of India. China, where opium was popular, banned imports of the drug. Nevertheless, smuggling of opium into China by agents of the British East India Company was already widespread and continued to expand. Revenue from opium sales in China funded the purchase of tea from China that would be exported to Great Britain. In 1838, China imposed a death penalty on opium smuggling. The final result of increased enforcement was the First Opium War between China and Great Britain.

37. Which conclusion about the opium trade between the British East India Company and China can be drawn from the information?
    (1) Chinese people thought opium prices were excessive.
    (2) Opium use was having a destructive effect on Chinese people.
    (3) Chinese rulers thought the opium trade would lead to further unwanted involvement with Great Britain.
    (4) People who smuggled opium also committed other crimes while in China.
    (5) The First Opium War resulted from a dispute over control of the opium production.

GO ON TO THE NEXT PAGE

Questions 38 refers to the following graph.

Distribution of U.S. small businesses by start year, 1992.

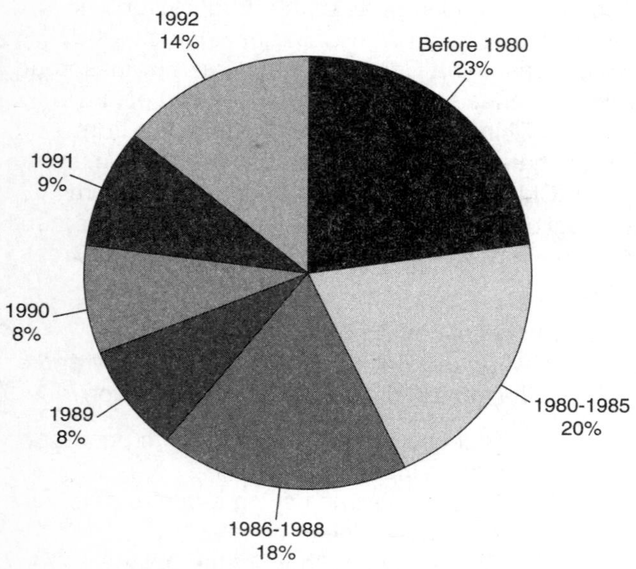

Source: U.S. Small Business Administration, Office of Advocacy, from data provided by the U.S. Department of Commerce and Bureau of the Census.

38. What conclusion about small businesses in 1992 is confirmed by the graph?

    (1) Less than half of small businesses were more than seven years old.
    (2) Nearly half of new small businesses failed within one year.
    (3) More businesses started in 1989 than 1991.
    (4) Fewer businesses started in 1992 than 1991.
    (5) More businesses started in the period from 1991 to 1992 than in the period from 1986 to 1989.

Questions 39 and 40 are based on the following information.

The series of primary presidential elections in the United States is one of the first stages in the long process of electing a president. The two major political parties and certain smaller ones generally have multiple potential candidates and must decide which of them will represent the party in the final November election. For the two major parties, the overall winner of the primary elections is officially nominated at the national convention.

In a primary election, voters cast ballots for a particular candidate. In actuality, voters are choosing which candidate's delegates from their state to send to the national convention, where the final vote for nomination takes place. The qualifications for voting in a primary vary from state to state. In some states, anyone may vote, but in others only registered party members may vote.

The first primary election in which candidates can win delegates is held in New Hampshire in the first months of an election year. The New Hampshire primary election is so important to the race for president that candidates who do poorly usually have to drop out of the running entirely. The results of the New Hampshire primary election also have important consequences for candidates' continued media exposure and financial support. In every presidential election since 1952, New Hampshire has held the first primary election, a crucial landmark on the road to the White House.

39. According to the information, a presidential candidate would most likely drop out of the race for party nomination in which of the following circumstances?

    The candidate

    (1) received extensive media coverage
    (2) was a member of a smaller political party
    (3) received few votes in early primary elections
    (4) was not from New Hampshire
    (5) did not participate in the New Hampshire primary election

GO ON TO THE NEXT PAGE

40. An election monitor is a person who observes the casting and counting of ballots to ensure the fairness of the process.

    Which of the following is a likely example of an action that would be taken by an election monitor during a primary election?

    (1) making political speeches
    (2) distributing campaign pamphlets
    (3) preventing people from voting twice
    (4) debating the candidates' policies
    (5) cleaning the voting machines

---

41. The United Nations Convention on Law of the Sea refers to several diplomatic meetings and one treaty concerning the national ownership of territorial, resource, and pollution rights and responsibilities in the world's oceans. One aspect of the Law of the Sea is the establishment of an Exclusive Economic Zone (EEZ) extending 200 nautical miles offshore. A nation has exclusive rights to the natural resources within its EEZ.

    Which of the following would be resolved by applying the Law of the Sea?

    (1) conflicts in overseas air traffic control systems
    (2) questions about ownership of uninhabited islands in the South Pacific
    (3) flooding caused by melting of polar ice
    (4) disputes over fishing by Norwegian vessels near the coast of Iceland
    (5) disagreement between Washington and Oregon over shipping lanes

42. In March 1932, the toddler son of famed aviator Charles Lindbergh Jr. was abducted from the family's home in Hopewell, New Jersey. Many historians claim the investigation was handled poorly in the crucial first days. Physical evidence such as footprints and fingerprints was destroyed by the disorganized presence of local and state police. Shortly after the boy was taken, ransom letters postmarked in Brooklyn, New York, arrived. The investigation also extended to Virginia, Washington, D.C., Maryland, South Carolina, Texas, Illinois, and Minnesota. Although kidnapping was not a federal matter, Lindbergh's status as a national hero made President Herbert Hoover bend the rules to allow federal law-enforcement agencies to take up the investigation. The search for the boy ended in failure when a truck driver discovered his corpse along a road. In response to the kidnapping and murder, the U.S. Congress established the Federal Kidnapping Act to help find victims of kidnappings.

    On the basis of the information, what did the act most likely do?

    (1) grant kidnapping investigation oversight rights to local police agencies
    (2) limit the length of kidnapping investigations
    (3) authorize federal agencies to conduct kidnapping investigations across state lines
    (4) grant local police agencies rights to conduct kidnapping investigations in other states
    (5) ban payment of ransom demands in kidnapping cases

Questions 43 through 45 refer to the following information.

The Louvre, in Paris, France, is the largest art museum in the world. It has almost 275,000 works of art, which are displayed in more than 140 exhibition rooms. The Louvre houses a priceless continuum of French artistic heritage containing remnants from the Capetian Kings as early as 987 through the empire of Napoleon and beyond. The collection at the Louvre has some of the most famous works of art in the world, including the *Mona Lisa* by Leonardo da Vinci and the *Venus de Milo* by Michelangelo.

The Louvre not only contains a vast collection of artwork, but also has a long and interesting history. It was originally a fort built by King Phillip sometime around 1200. In the 1300s it became a royal residence for Charles V, who had it renovated to accommodate his royal taste. Although he did have his own collection of art there, everything was dispersed when he died.

This majestic building remained empty until 1527, when François I decided that he wanted to live there. François I was a collector of early Italian Renaissance art and already owned the *Mona Lisa*, as well as paintings by Titian and Raphael, when he moved into the Louvre. However, he would not move into it until a project was started to again revamp it and make it even more grandiose than it had been during the reign of Charles V.

François I died before the work was complete, but it continued on until the death of the head architect. Several generations of French royalty lived in the palatial residence until Louis XIV left in 1682 to reside full time at Versailles. The Louvre, however, was far from abandoned. The art collection grew from about 200 paintings in 1643 to about 2,500 works of art in 1715. For about 30 years after Louis XIV's death in 1715, the Louvre became the home of various artists and intellectuals. It was a hub of creativity and elitism until the public began to be admitted in 1749.

During the past 100 years, art academies have been established at the Louvre, and some of the artwork has been moved to specialized museums. Changes are still being made to the Louvre, and it remains a marvelous place in which to visit and see some of the most glorious works of art of all time.

43. What is the best explanation for the various collections of art that were displayed in the Louvre prior to it becoming a public museum?

    (1) Decorators chose art for the interior of the royal palace based on qualities of the building.
    (2) The sitting king would display his personal collection in the palace where he lived.
    (3) The public had little interest in art before the Louvre became a public museum.
    (4) Many works of art would have been destroyed if not secured in a royal building.
    (5) All the art had religious significance for the various kings of France.

44. What is the basis for François I's initial refusal to move into the Louvre?

    (1) his preference for a different palace
    (2) his preoccupation with traveling
    (3) his desire for a more impressive palace
    (4) his dislike of Charles V
    (5) his recognition of the palace's safety hazards

45. In the 18th century, the Louvre ceased being a royal palace.

    Which of the following is a likely cause of the Louvre becoming a public museum?

    (1) King Louis XIV's financial difficulties
    (2) lack of suitable gallery space for France's art treasures
    (3) a sharp increase in interest in the visual arts
    (4) the transition of French society toward democracy
    (5) pressure from royal officials

GO ON TO THE NEXT PAGE

Questions 46 through 48 refer to the following graph.

Number of children in the United States by age, 1950–2004.

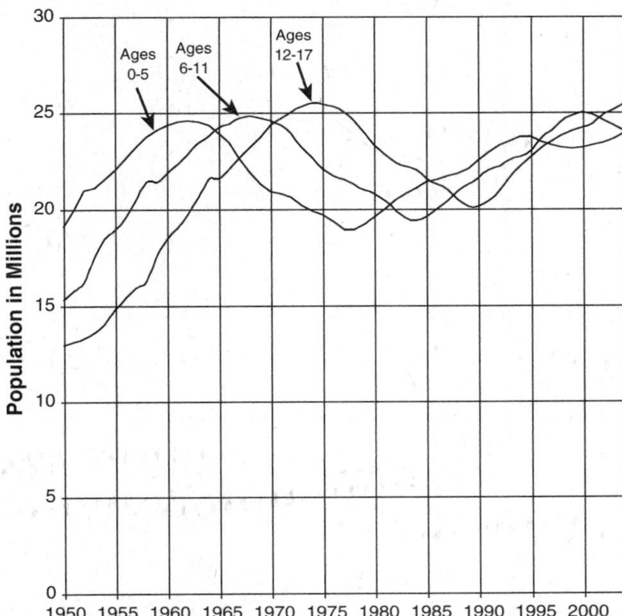

Source: U.S. Census Bureau.

46. Which of the following statements about the number of children in the United States is confirmed by the information above?
    (1) There were more children ages 12 through 17 than 6 through 11 for every year from 1950 to 2004.
    (2) The population of each age group declined for approximately 15 years during the period from 1950 to 2004.
    (3) The population of children ages 0 through 5 increased every year from 1950 to 2004.
    (4) The average annual birth rate in the United States has stayed approximately the same over the period from 1950 to 2004.
    (5) There were fewer children ages 6 through 11 than 0 through 5 for every year from 1970 to 1995.

47. What question about children in the United States can be answered by using the information in the graph?
    (1) On average, how many children were born to a woman in 1990?
    (2) During which 5-year period between 1950 and 2004 was the number of children ages 12 through 17 greatest?
    (3) How many adults, compared with children, were there in the United States in 1995?
    (4) Why did the number of children ages 12 through 17 decrease beginning in 1974?
    (5) What percentage of the total U.S. population in 1980 were children ages 0 through 17?

48. Which of the following is most likely to occur in the new century if trends in the graph continue?

    The population of children
    (1) will generally grow with some periods of decline
    (2) will grow at a steady rate
    (3) will grow at a gradually increasing rate
    (4) will slowly decline
    (5) will fluctuate only slightly

49. Which of the following is the most reasonable explanation for a shortage of a product on the market?

    (1) Most consumers find the product overpriced.
    (2) The product has many uses.
    (3) An inexpensive substitute for the product is available.
    (4) The producers underestimated the demand for the product.
    (5) Producers have supplied too much of the product.

50. The North American Free Trade Agreement (NAFTA) among Canada, Mexico, and the United States began in 1994 and will be fully implemented in 2008. The agreement lifts many barriers to trade, including certain tariffs, quotas, and licensing systems. Opponents of NAFTA fear the loss of U.S. and Canadian jobs to the cheaper Mexican labor market. In addition, agricultural subsidies in the United States make it harder for Mexican farms to compete for market share.

    According to this information, what was the main reason for implementing NAFTA?

    (1) It would make American manufactured goods more valuable.
    (2) It would simplify trade and make it less expensive.
    (3) It was crucial to continued peaceful relations among North American countries.
    (4) It was a fast solution to congestion at seaports and border crossings.
    (5) It would balance the U.S. and Mexican markets for agricultural products.

Answers and explanations for this test begin on page 692.

GO ON TO: SCIENCE

Science Test

The GED Science Test consists of 50 multiple-choice questions that you must answer in 80 minutes. You will have to draw upon some prior knowledge of life science, earth and space science, and physical science; however, you will not have to recall facts.

Directions: Choose the one best answer to each question.

GO ON TO THE NEXT PAGE

1. A chemist decides to extract the salt from a sample of seawater. Which of the following processes would be the most effective method of extracting salt from the seawater solution?

   (1) pouring the water through a sieve
   (2) freezing the water
   (3) bubbling oxygen through the water
   (4) allowing the water to evaporate
   (5) slowly dripping the water from a tube

2. Different animals use their senses in different ways. Dolphins, in particular, have weak eyesight but a heightened sense of hearing compared to humans. Dolphins use echolocation to navigate. Calls to their surroundings echo back to dolphins, who interpret from the sound waves information about location and the distance and shape of objects.

   Which of the following would dolphins use echolocation for?

   (1) to recognize the taste of a certain type of fish
   (2) to smell out the distance of the object
   (3) to interpret the distance to a rock using sound waves
   (4) to determine their location from the taste of the water
   (5) to discourage predators by irritating them

3. An adaptation can be a physical change or behavioral trait of an organism. Adaptations occur to increase the survivability and reproductive success of a species.

   Which of the following would most likely not be an adaptation of polar bears?

   (1) thick white fur allowing for camouflage and warmth
   (2) superior sense of smell
   (3) excellent swimming ability
   (4) summer fur that absorbs UV light
   (5) preference for human food waste

4. As a climber continually increases his altitude, he starts to breathe heavily, eventually experiencing a headache and nausea.

   These symptoms are most probably the result of which of the following?

   (1) The climber is not in shape and should not be exerting himself.
   (2) The climber is closer to the ozone layer and its harmful gases.
   (3) The climber is closer to the sun and his body temperature is rising.
   (4) There is less oxygen at higher altitude than lower altitude.
   (5) The climber has acquired pneumonia because of the colder climate.

5. In an experiment, a student tried to mix oil and water. The following result occurred:

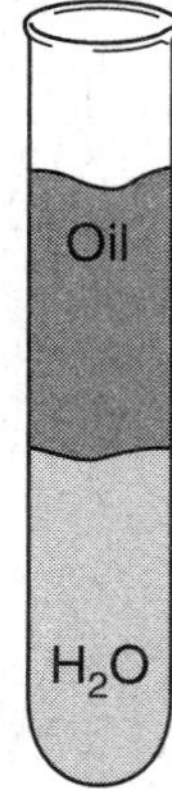

   What is the best explanation for why the results shown occurred?

   (1) Water is heavier than oil, so it sinks.
   (2) Oil is heavier than water, so it sinks.
   (3) Oil is not soluble in water.
   (4) Oil evaporates faster than water.
   (5) Oil is too greasy to mix with any other substance.

GO ON TO THE NEXT PAGE

6. Food chains display the feeding relationships between species. In the food chain below, bacteria is the decomposer. What do decomposers do?

(1) eat only plants and vegetation
(2) break down organic material for nutrients and energy
(3) eat only meat of dead animals
(4) eat the food that the animal does not eat
(5) eat only predator animals

7. Sea water is denser than fresh water.

Which of the following pictures would represent what would occur when equal volumes of sea water and fresh water are placed together on a balance?

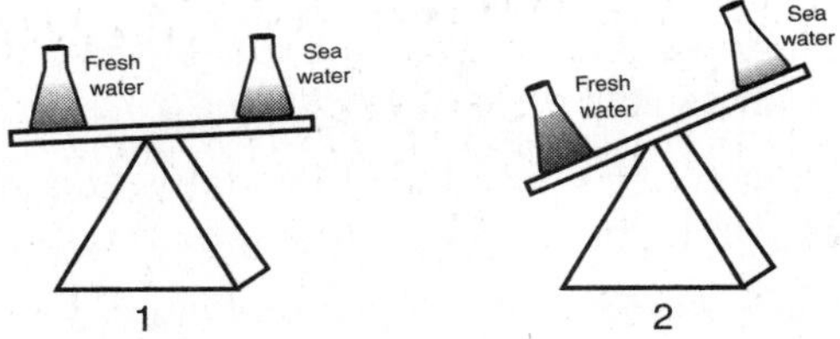

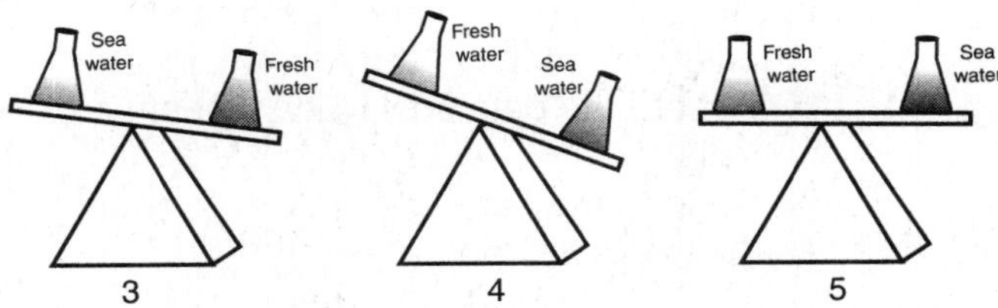

(1) 1
(2) 2
(3) 3
(4) 4
(5) 5

8. Over a period of 500 years, a particular land formation changes from a jagged, exposed rock to a smoother, grass-covered hill.

Which of the following would best explain the change?

(1) Falling rocks rounded the edges of the jagged rock.
(2) The jagged rock was weathered by water, wind, or chemicals.
(3) Rocks were deposited on the formation.
(4) The heat from the sun partially melted the rock, making it smoother.
(5) Humans started to climb the mountainous region.

9. There are billions of stars in the universe, with the sun being one of them.

What is the best explanation for why the Earth revolves around the sun and not any other star?

(1) The other stars exist only at night.
(2) The other stars are much smaller than the sun.
(3) The other stars are much further from Earth than the sun is.
(4) The other stars are much bigger than the sun.
(5) The other stars are too bright and would be harmful to life on Earth.

10. In the figure shown below, as temperature increases, what happens to density?

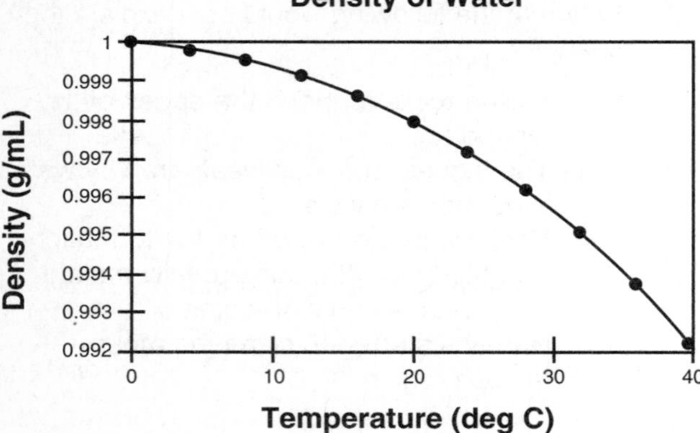

(1) The density also increases.
(2) The density stays the same.
(3) The density decreases.
(4) The density decreases and then increases.
(5) The density increases and then decreases.

11. As an airplane ascends from low to high altitudes, many passengers complain about "popping ears."

What is the best explanation for this observation?

(1) Air pressure decreases sharply as an airplane makes its initial ascent.
(2) Air pressure increases sharply as an airplane makes its initial ascent.
(3) The gravitational force between the earth and the passengers' eardrums decreases.
(4) The eardrums are sensitive to rapid acceleration.
(5) Changing altitude changes the mixture of gases in the airplane's cabin.

12. Two identical ice cube trays are filled with an equal amount of water. Tray A is placed in a freezer and Tray B is left at room temperature. After a few hours, the water in Tray A has undergone freezing.

Assuming no water is lost to spillage or evaporation, which of the statements below regarding Tray A is true?

(1) The ice in Tray A has greater mass than the water in Tray B.
(2) The ice in Tray A has the same mass as the water in Tray B.
(3) The ice in Tray A has less mass than the water in Tray B.
(4) The ice in Tray A has undergone a chemical change.
(5) The mass of the ice in Tray A depends on how fast the freezing occurred.

13. A group of four students wanted to study the growth of mice from birth. They planned to measure the length and mass of the mice every other day and record the data in a table. Their goal is to obtain the most valid results with as little error as possible.

Which of the following should the students do to attain the most accurate growth data?

(1) Measure the length and mass every 6 days.
(2) Feed certain mice more than others.
(3) Repeat the experiment with many different groups of mice.
(4) Record the data only when it seems valid.
(5) Change the results slightly to fit better their hypotheses.

GO ON TO THE NEXT PAGE

14. In a particular home, every time the hair dryer is put into a plug and used, all the appliances in the same room stop working.

What is the best explanation for this?

(1) There is not enough electric current in the house to supply all of the appliances.
(2) The capacity of the fuse regulating electric current supplied to the room needs to be increased.
(3) The capacity of the fuse regulating electric current supplied to the room needs to be decreased.
(4) There are too many appliances in use in a particular room and the fuse performed as designed.
(5) The wire supplying electricity was cut.

15. Skin cancer is a growing threat in America, and 90% of skin cancers are caused by exposure to sunlight and UV rays.

Which of the following would not be a logical preventive measure against skin cancer?

(1) Stay out of the sun when the sun is the brightest.
(2) Apply sunscreen often to block UV rays.
(3) Use a big umbrella when out on the beach.
(4) Apply a lot of sun tanning oil.
(5) Cover up with light clothing.

16. Asthma is a chronic respiratory system disease that is most prevalent in children. The rate of asthma among the general population is constantly growing, and the incidence rate is growing among younger children. Asthma can be controlled, but not cured. Inhalers containing various kinds of medication are the most common treatment for asthma. The following graph plots the prevalence of asthma over a period of 16 years.

Asthma prevalence among children, 1980-1996

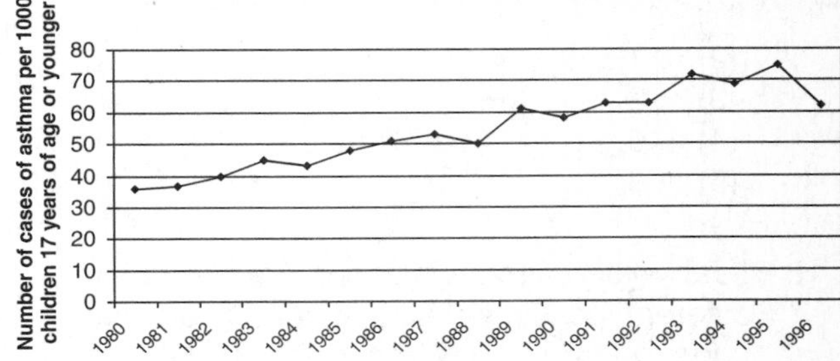

Source: National Health Interview Survey, National Center for Health Statistics (http://www.cdc.gov/asthma/slides/prevalence06.ppt)

Which of the following is the best conclusion about asthma?

(1) Asthma was most prevalent among children in 1996.
(2) Asthma prevalence has been decreasing since 1980.
(3) Between 1991 and 1992, asthma prevalence among children changed significantly.
(4) Asthma prevalence has been constantly increasing since 1980.
(5) Asthma prevalence in children was lower in 1990 than in 1996.

GO ON TO THE NEXT PAGE

17. A chromosome is a unit of DNA that determines genetic characteristics of an individual. Somatic cells, which are normal body cells, contain 23 chromosomes each. Gametes contain double the number of chromosomes that somatic cells contain. In meiosis, a diploid gamete divides into haploid cells, each of which has half the number of chromosomes of the diploid cell.

    At the end of meiosis, how many chromosomes does a haploid cell have?

    (1) 6
    (2) 11.5
    (3) 23
    (4) 46
    (5) 68

18. In an experiment, two seeds are planted in different locations. The first seed is planted under a large tree with rich soil, and the other seed is planted in grassland. At the end of three months, the plant in the grassland had grown to a height of about 12 inches, whereas the plant underneath the tree had grown to a height of only about 6 inches.

    What is the best explanation of why the plant in the grassland grew more than the plant underneath the tree?

    (1) The area underneath the tree had less oxygen supply.
    (2) The plant in the grassland received more sunlight.
    (3) There was less carbon dioxide under the tree.
    (4) The area under the tree did not receive sufficient water supply.
    (5) The tree stole all of the plant's nutrients and water supply, so it did not grow as much as the grassland plant.

19. Mental, physical, and emotional stress can have adverse effects on an individual's body. One of the consequences of chronic stress is the decrease in the effectiveness of the immune system.

    Which of the following is most likely to happen to an individual experiencing chronic stress?

    (1) suffering a car accident
    (2) frequent back pain
    (3) catching a cold
    (4) being completely healthy
    (5) breaking an arm while playing sports

20. Seasonal Affective Disorder (SAD) occurs when the weather is dreary and an individual is not exposed to enough natural sunlight. The symptoms of this disorder are excessive fatigue, mood swings, irritability, and depression.

    In which of these locations in SAD most likely?

    (1) Alaska
    (2) Florida
    (3) India
    (4) Italy
    (5) Mexico

21. A cold glass of lemonade is placed outside by a swimming pool on a hot, sunny day. As time passes, water droplets start to appear on the outside of the glass.

    By what process is the water appearing on the outside of the glass?

    (1) evaporation
    (2) condensation
    (3) precipitation
    (4) sublimation
    (5) None of these processes is possible; water from the pool must have splashed onto the glass.

GO ON TO THE NEXT PAGE

22. A positively charged ion is in an electric field with a negatively charged source, as shown in the following figure.

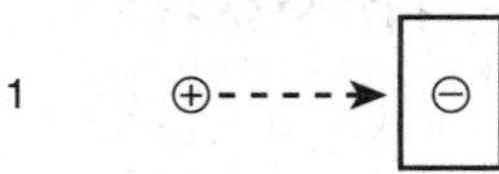

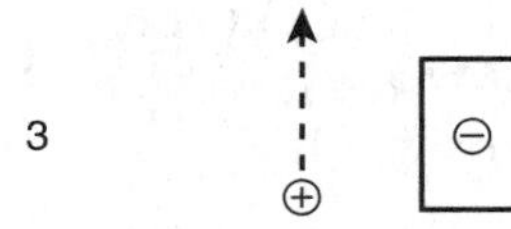

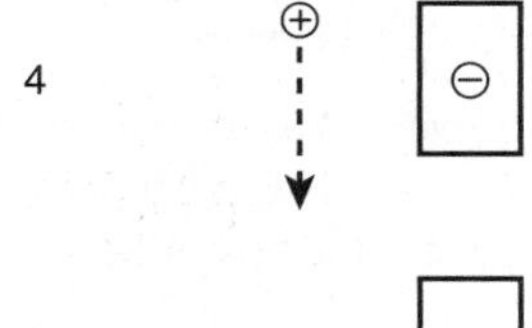

5 ⊕ No movement ⊖

In which direction does the ion travel?

(1) 1
(2) 2
(3) 3
(4) 4
(5) 5

23. A tumor in a patient's body is growing and begins to impede normal functioning. Tumors are abnormal growths composed of cells that may be cancerous. Chemotherapy can be used to attempt to decrease the size of the tumor, or the tumor can be removed by surgery.

By which of these processes do the cells of a tumor reproduce?

(1) meiosis
(2) transpiration
(3) mitosis
(4) osmosis
(5) transcription

24. In a lab, a student is warned not to light a match near the sign for a flammable chemical.

Which of the signs should the student look for?

(1)

(2)

(3)

(4)

(5)

GO ON TO THE NEXT PAGE

25. Two types of sleep-wake cycles in animals are diurnal and nocturnal. Diurnal animals are active during the daytime and asleep at night. Nocturnal animals are active during the nighttime when no sunlight is present and asleep during the day. Humans are considered diurnal animals.

Which of the following would not be an evolutionary adaptation of nocturnal animals?

(1) ability to detect heat
(2) long-range hearing ability
(3) enhanced sense of smell
(4) skin resistant to sun damage
(5) larger, more sensitive eyes

26. A ship traveling at full speed is 50 miles away from an iceberg that is predominately below the surface of the water.

Which of the following would be the best method for the ship's crew to locate icebergs in their path?

(1) Conduct constant surveillance using binoculars.
(2) Monitor the radio for warnings from other ships.
(3) Review nautical charts for known hazards.
(4) Use sound waves to detect objects in the water.
(5) There is no way to detect the iceberg.

Questions 27 through 29 refer to the following information.

New species are continually introduced into the population while old species that are greatly valued become extinct. There are many endangered species around the world, including the snow leopard, lemurs, and different varieties of parrot, that will become extinct without human intervention. Many factors are involved in a species becoming endangered. Following are five factors that contribute to the endangerment of species:

Habitat destruction—Changes to species' native environments that occur so rapidly that the species have no time to adapt.

Introduction of exotic species—Intentional or accidental entry of new species into ecosystems to which they are not native.

Overexploitation—Species are consumed at an excessive rate (examples: trapping wild felines for their pelts, hunting elephants for their ivory).

Disease—Pathogens infecting species that have no natural immunity to them.

Pollution—Human activity produces chemicals toxic to species.

27. Which of the following human activities should be continued to save endangered species such as tigers?

(1) creating conservation parks in tigers' natural habitat to keep tigers and humans separated
(2) promoting economic activity in wilderness areas
(3) creating a new habitat for tigers by placing all the endangered species in zoos
(4) rescuing the tigers from their current habitat and placing them on a new continent
(5) encouraging new types of plants for tigers to feed on

GO ON TO THE NEXT PAGE

28. In the 18th and 19th centuries, European settlers released rabbits on their properties in Australia so they could later hunt the small animal. The rabbits quickly multiplied. Over more than 100 years, the results have included widespread erosion damage and the extinction of numerous native species.

From the choices above, what is the endangerment factor displayed here?

(1) habitat destruction
(2) introduction of exotic species
(3) overexploitation
(4) disease
(5) pollution

29. The Houston toad is an endangered species because of conversion of its wetland habitat for urban and agricultural use. Human activity in Houston toad habitat also exposes the animal to automobile exhaust and drought.

Which of the following seems to be the major threat to the Houston toad?

(1) habitat destruction
(2) introduction of exotic species
(3) overexploitation
(4) disease
(5) pollution

---

30. When an individual is faced with fear, the "fight or flight" reflex is triggered by the release of certain hormones into the body by the endocrine system. These hormones stimulate the heart, lungs, muscles, and the nervous system.

Which of the following body systems causes the stimulation of other body systems associated with this reflex?

(1) the respiratory system
(2) the endocrine system
(3) the reproductive system
(4) the digestive system
(5) the skeletal system

31. A 50-pound block of concrete and a 100-pound block of concrete are both dropped from the top of a 10-story building at the same time to test the effects of gravity.

Which of the following is most likely to occur?

(1) The 50-pound block will hit the ground first.
(2) The 100-pound block will hit the ground first.
(3) The two blocks will hit the ground at the same time.
(4) The 50-pound block will take twice the amount of time to reach the ground as the 100-pound block will take.
(5) The 100-pound block will take twice the amount of time to reach the ground as the 50-pound block will take.

32. Evolution has allowed animals to adapt and develop characteristics that better fit the environment that they inhabit. The following diagram displays the adaptations of bird feet.

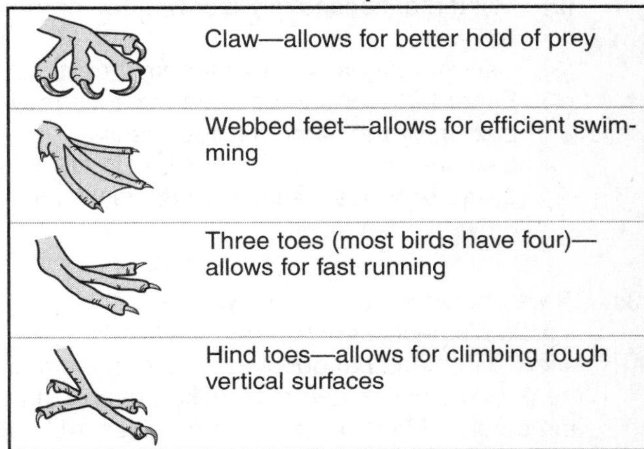

Which feet adaptation would be the best for a bird, such as a woodpecker, that scales tree trunks while searching for insect larvae to eat?

(1) the claw only
(2) webbed feet only
(3) hind toes only
(4) hind toes or three toes
(5) hind toes or the claw

GO ON TO THE NEXT PAGE

33. Two seeds of the same plant were treated with a normal fertilizer and an enhanced fertilizer to compare the differences in leaf size. The two seeds were placed in separate pots with the different fertilizers. The results are graphed below.

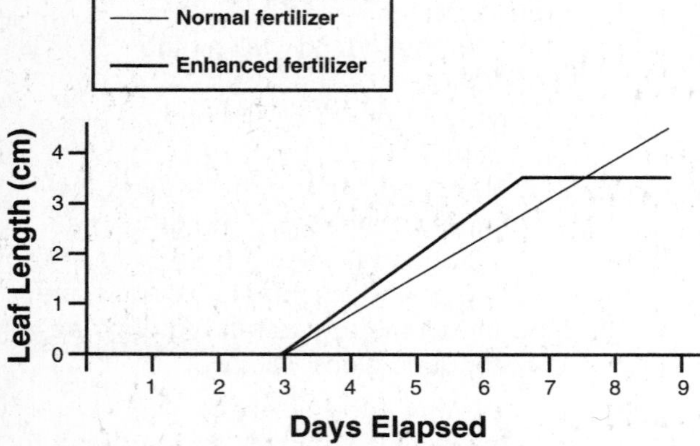

According to the data, if you wanted leaves 4 cm long, what would be the best way to achieve these results?

(1) Use the enhanced fertilizer for eight days.
(2) Mix the enhanced fertilizer with the normal fertilizer.
(3) Use the normal fertilizer for eight days.
(4) Either fertilizer can be used because they both have the same desired results.
(5) Use only the enhanced fertilizer in all cases because it allows for the leaves to grow at a faster rate.

34. "A well-balanced diet along with regular exercise is necessary to keep healthy. Protein is found in meat, but good sources of protein for meat-eaters and vegetarians alike are tofu, nuts, and cereals. Many fruits and vegetables are also a good source of protein."

Of the following, who is most likely to make the statement made above?

(1) dietitian
(2) chemist
(3) geneticist
(4) cattle rancher
(5) health code inspector

35. A certain city is situated in western Australia. The country of Australia lies in the Southern Hemisphere and is surrounded by the Indian Ocean, the Pacific Ocean, and the Southern Ocean. The following graph represents the average monthly temperatures of the certain city in western Australia.

Average Temperature for a Certain City in Australia

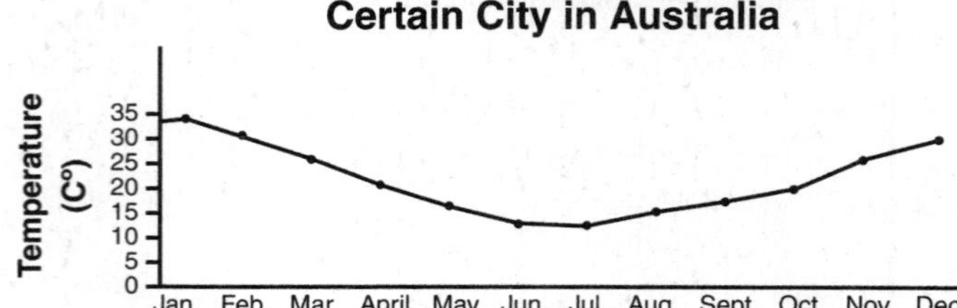

According to the graph, which of the following months would be considered summer months?

(1) March, April, May, June
(2) May, June, July, August
(3) June, July, August, September
(4) July, August, September, October
(5) November, December, January, February

36. A piece of ice is observed floating in liquid water.

What is the best explanation for the ice floating and not sinking?

(1) The piece of ice is heavier than the water.
(2) Ice contains more hydrogen than water.
(3) Ice has a lower density than water.
(4) Ice has a greater density than water.
(5) All objects float in water.

GO ON TO THE NEXT PAGE

37. Emma is preparing a large beef roast for dinner and is using her mother's recipe. The recipe would normally serve eight people, but since Emma is cooking for only four people, she wants to reduce all the ingredients by half.

Mom's Beef Roast (serves 8)

4 pounds beef chuck roast
4 cups whole canned tomatoes
8 carrots
8 stalks of celery
3 pounds potatoes
4 cups beef stock
2 onions
4 cloves of garlic
salt
pepper
parsley

For 4 people, what would be the quantities of the ingredients?

(1) 2 pounds of beef chuck roast and 2 carrots
(2) 2 pounds of beef chuck roast and 4 cups whole canned tomatoes
(3) 8 stalks of celery and $1\frac{1}{2}$ pounds potatoes
(4) 1 onion and 2 cloves of garlic
(5) 2 cups of beef stock and 4 cloves of garlic

38. Lunar eclipses occur when there is a full moon. Total eclipses occur when no sunlight is able to reach the moon.

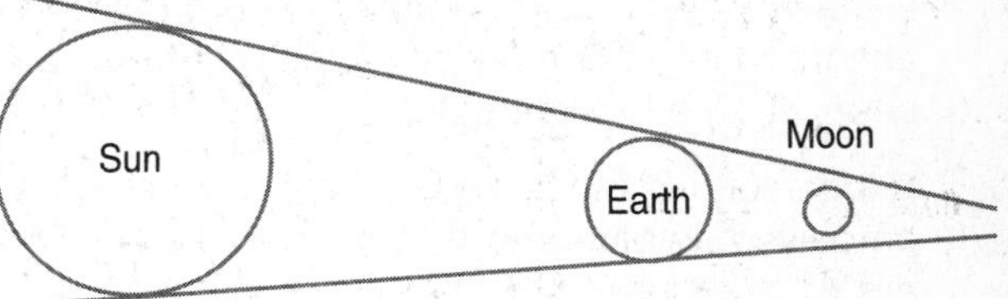

What is the best explanation for why no sunlight reaches the moon?

(1) The sun is in the earth's shadow.
(2) The moon is in the earth's shadow.
(3) The moon is too far from the sun to reach any sunlight.
(4) The sun comes in between the moon and the earth.
(5) The moon disappears momentarily.

39. There are two different species of plant in a garden. Both types of plant are exposed to the same soil, the same amount of light, and the same amount of water. One of the plants shows little growth compared to the other plant, which flourishes.

Which of the following is the best explanation for why there could be a difference in growth?

(1) The soil that was used was heavily polluted.
(2) The two plants require different amounts of water.
(3) The two plants receive different wavelengths of light.
(4) One plant is watered on Mondays, and the other plant is watered on Thursdays.
(5) The garden is habitat for many kinds of insects.

GO ON TO THE NEXT PAGE

40. When light hits an object, some wavelengths are absorbed while others are reflected. What humans perceive as color is the wavelength of light reflected off an object and into the eye. Black is observed when all wavelengths are absorbed and none are reflected. White is seen when all wavelengths are reflected.

Which color is most likely observed when light perceived as blue and light perceived as yellow are both absorbed by an object?

(1) red
(2) light blue
(3) purple
(4) pink
(5) green

41. Contrary to popular belief, a camel's hump holds fat, not water. This fat store is consumed when food and water are scarce.

After a long, strenuous journey across the desert, what would most likely be the condition of a camel's hump?

(1) firm, upright, full
(2) showing no sign of ever having existed
(3) sagging and not as full as before the journey
(4) There would be two humps present where one hump was present before the journey.
(5) The hump would be bigger after the journey than it was before the journey.

42. In science experiments to simulate a volcanic eruption, students mix baking soda with vinegar. This reaction produces carbon dioxide bubbles that provide the effect of lava.

How is this simulated eruption similar to a real volcanic eruption?

(1) Gases are released as products.
(2) Magma forms.
(3) Water is formed.
(4) Baking soda is a reactant.
(5) The products of both can be very harmful to humans.

43. Calcium is a nutrient that is essential for the body's functioning. It has an important role in promoting healthy bones and many bodily functions.

Which of the following is not a calcium-providing dairy product?

(1) milk
(2) mozzarella cheese
(3) eggs
(4) yogurt
(5) ice cream

44. The chart below is for children over 4 years old and adults in a 2,000-calorie-per-day diet. Reference Daily Intake values are considered sufficient to meet the nutritional requirements of nearly all individuals.

Food Component	Reference Daily Intake
Fat	65g
Cholesterol	300mg
Carbohydrates	300g
Fiber	25g
Sodium	2400mg
Potassium	3500mg
Protein	50g

Of which of the following food components does the body require the greatest mass on a daily basis?

(1) cholesterol
(2) carbohydrates
(3) fiber
(4) sodium
(5) potassium

GO ON TO THE NEXT PAGE

45. Caitlin has a container of a solute completely dissolved in a solvent. She would like to extract all the dissolved solute from the solvent.

What would be the best way for her to obtain her desired results?

(1) Filter the mixture to separate the components.
(2) Add water to the mixture.
(3) Boil the mixture to evaporate the liquid and leave only the solute present.
(4) Condense the mixture to evaporate the liquid and leave only the solute present.
(5) Add more solute to promote precipitation.

46. Surfing requires the ability to balance one's center of mass while also taking into consideration other physics concepts.

Which aspect of physics does a surfer not use?

(1) buoyancy
(2) gravity
(3) magnetism
(4) friction
(5) energy

47. Paul needs to change the oil in his car. His car can hold 1.25 gallons of oil, and the gas station sells oil by the quart. There are four quarts in a gallon. How many quarts must Paul buy to have enough to fill his car with oil?

(1) 4
(2) 5
(3) 6
(4) 7
(5) 8

48. In reproduction, each male gamete contains either an X or a Y chromosome, and each female gamete contains only the X chromosome. The gamete from the father that implants in the female gamete (the egg) is essentially random. During fertilization, the X or Y chromosome from the father fuses with the X chromosome from the mother to determine the sex of the child.

If the child were a male, what would the genotype be?

(1) XX
(2) XY
(3) YY
(4) X
(5) Y

49. On Earth, golf balls fall back to the ground shortly after they have been hit.

Which of the following best explains how astronaut Alan Sheppard was able to hit a golf ball hundreds of yards with a slow, one-handed swing during the Apollo 14 moon landing?

The moon

(1) has no breathable air
(2) has no wind
(3) is extremely barren compared with Earth
(4) is much smaller than Earth and has less gravity
(5) is covered in fine dust

50. A hurricane is a system of clouds, winds, and thunderstorms that forms over tropical areas of the oceans.

Which of the following observations is an indication that a hurricane may be approaching?

(1) Air temperatures increase.
(2) Gusty winds become calm.
(3) Sea level drops.
(4) The sunlight is intense.
(5) The sky is darkening in the distance.

Answers and explanations for this test begin on page 697.

GO ON TO: MATHEMATICS

Mathematics Formulas

Area		
	Square	s^2
	Rectangle	$l \times w$
	Parallelogram	$b \times h$
	Triangle	$\frac{1}{2} \times b \times h$
	Trapezoid	$\frac{1}{2} \times (b_1 \times b_2) \times h$
	Circle	$\pi \times r^2$
Perimeter		
	Square	$4 \times s$
	Rectangle	$2 \times l + 2 \times w$
	Triangle	$\text{side}_1 + \text{side}_2 + \text{side}_3$
Circumference		
	Circle only	$2 \times \pi \times r$ OR $\pi \times$ diameter (diameter is two times the radius)
Volume		
	Cube [each face is a square]	s^3
	Rectangular solid	$l \times w \times h$
	Square pyramid [base is a square]	$\frac{1}{3} \times s^2 \times h$
	Cylinder [base is a circle]	$\pi \times r^2 \times h$
	Cone [base is a circle]	$\frac{1}{3} \times \pi \times r^2 \times h$
Coordinate Geometry		
	Distance between points; (x_1,y_1) and (x_2,y_2) are two points in a plane.	$\sqrt{(x_2 - x_1)^2 + (y_2 - y_1)^2}$
	Slope of a line; (x_1,y_1) and (x_2,y_2) are two points on the line.	$\frac{y_2 - y_1}{x_2 - x_1}$
Pythagorean Theorem		
	Determine the length of one side of a right triangle using the lengths of the other two sides; *a and b are legs; c is the hypotenuse (the side opposite the right angle).*	$a^2 + b^2 = c^2$
Measures of Central Tendency		
	Mean (average): *x* is a value and *n* is the total number of values for which you want a mean.	$\frac{x_1 + x_2 + \ldots + x_n}{n}$
	Median: begin with a set of values in numerical order.	The median is the middle value in a set with an odd number of values, halfway between (the average of) the two middle values in a set with an even number of values.
Rates		
	Simple Interest	principal (starting amount) $\times$ rate $\times$ time
	Distance	rate $\times$ time
	Total Cost	(number of units) $\times$ (price per unit)

GO ON TO THE NEXT PAGE

Mathematics Test

The GED Mathematics Test consists of 50 questions that you will be given 90 minutes to complete. The test is divided into two parts. On Part I, Questions 1–25, you may use a calculator. On Part II, Questions 26–50, you may not use a calculator.

Directions: Choose the one best answer to each question.

1. Mark received a loan from his bank, which he must repay plus 7% interest in one year. Julia received a loan of $500 more than Mark did, and in one year she must repay it plus 6% interest. After one year, what was the difference between the amount of interest Mark paid and the amount of interest Julia paid?

   (1) $30.00

   (2) $60.00

   (3) $72.00

   (4) $150.00

   (5) Not enough information is given.

2. If $2x - 9 = 13$, what is the value of x?

   Mark your answer in the circles on the grid on your answer sheet.

3. Soccer Super Store is having a sale. All clothing is 20% off. A customer wants to purchase a T-shirt that regularly costs $15.10 and a pair of shorts that regularly costs $24.95. Approximately how much does the customer save by purchasing both items during the sale?

   (1) $7.00

   (2) $8.00

   (3) $9.00

   (4) $10.00

   (5) $11.00

Questions 4 and 5 refer to the following graph and information.

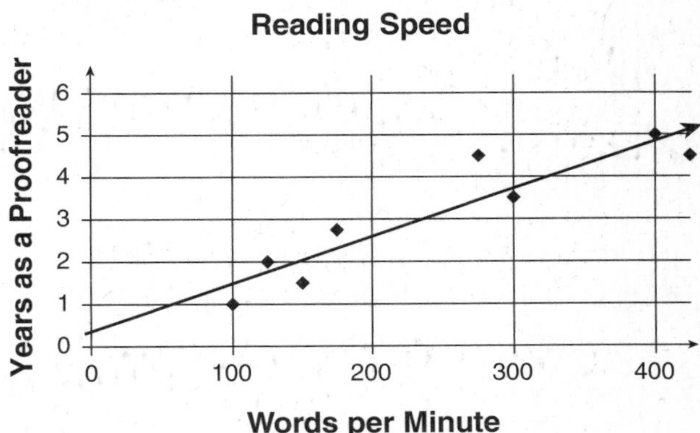

Pliskin Publishing pays its proofreaders based on the number of manuscripts they can read during the week. The graph above shows the reading speed in words per minute of 8 proofreaders, as well as the line of best fit for those speeds. The line of best fit can be used to make predictions for how much more an experienced proofreader can earn when compared to inexperienced proofreaders.

4. Based on the line of best fit, what would be the approximate reading speed, in words per minute, of a person who has worked 7 years as a proofreader?

   (1) 500

   (2) 400

   (3) 300

   (4) 200

   (5) 100

5. What does the line of best fit predict the reading speed, in words per minute, will be for a person who has been a proofreader for less than 1 year?

   (1) Less than 100

   (2) Equal to 100

   (3) Between 100 and 200

   (4) Greater than 200

   (5) Not enough information is given.

GO ON TO THE NEXT PAGE

6. Steve works at a greenhouse. The ideal conditions for a particular type of flowering plant include temperatures between 57° F to 65° F. Steve notices that the temperature gauge in the greenhouse reads 72° F. What is the difference, in degrees F, between the midpoint of the ideal temperature range and the current temperature in the greenhouse?

   (1) 7
   (2) 8
   (3) 11
   (4) 15
   (5) 50

7. Leg FG of the right triangle shown in the diagram below is half as long as leg FH.

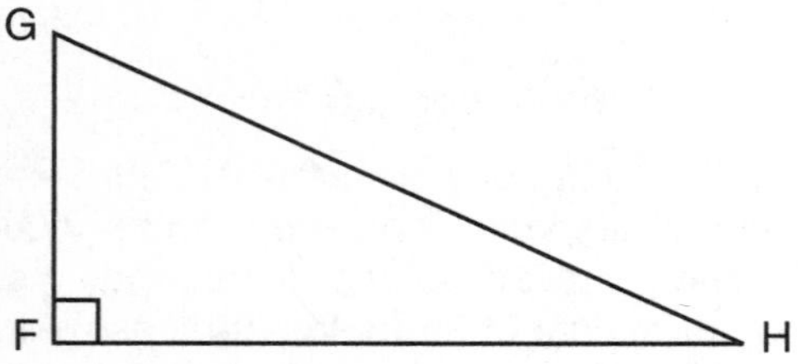

   If the area of the triangle is 25 in^2, what is the length, in inches, of leg FG?

   (1) 3
   (2) 4
   (3) 5
   (4) 8
   (5) 10

8. The mean (average) age of 7 girls is 9. If five of the girls are 8, 8, 9, 10 and 11 years old, respectively, which of the following could be the ages, in years, of the 2 other girls?

   (1) 7 and 13
   (2) 9 and 12
   (3) 10 and 11
   (4) 11 and 6
   (5) 13 and 5

Questions 9 and 10 refer to the following information and table.

Richard planned to meet a friend in York, England. His local bank gave him the exchange rates for U.S. Dollars (USD) and British Pounds (GBP), listed below.

Exchange Rates for USD and GBP

US Dollars (USD)	British Pounds (GBP)
1	0.537634
1.86	1

9. Richard exchanged 800 USD for GBP. How many GBP did he receive in return?

   (1) 43.01
   (2) 148.8
   (3) 430.10
   (4) 1,488
   (5) 4,301

10. While Richard was in England, he bought a wheel of cheese that cost 47 GBP. Based on the exchange rate he received for his money, what was the approximate cost of the wheel of cheese in USD?

   (1) 70
   (2) 80
   (3) 90
   (4) 100
   (5) 110

---

11. The school cafeteria is receiving a shipment of 504 frozen pizzas that were packed in boxes of 12 pizzas each. How many boxes should the cafeteria receive?

   Mark your answer in the circles on the grid on your answer sheet.

GO ON TO THE NEXT PAGE

12. What is the volume, in cubic centimeters, of a cube that measures 8.5 centimeters on one edge?

    (1) 25.500

    (2) 72.250

    (3) 102.125

    (4) 545.500

    (5) 614.125

Question 13 refers to the rectangle below.

13. Marcia wants to protect the top of her rectangular desk with a piece of glass. How many square inches of glass would she need to cover the top of her desk?

    (1) 117

    (2) 234

    (3) 468

    (4) 1,521

    (5) 3,042

---

14. The expression $-6(-x + 4) - 2(x - 3)$ is equal to which of the following expressions?

    (1) $-8x - 18$

    (2) $-8x - 30$

    (3) $-4x + 18$

    (4) $4x + 30$

    (5) $4x - 18$

15. A circle has a diameter of 13 inches. Which of the following is the best estimate of the circumference of the circle in inches?

    (1) 26

    (2) 31

    (3) 41

    (4) 82

    (5) 133

16. Show the location of the *y*-intercept for line $3x + y = 5$.

    Mark your answer on the coordinate plane grid on your answer sheet.

17. You manage a small record store and must track expenses. Each month you spend $1,500.00 on rent and $3,000.00 on payroll expenses. Utilities and miscellaneous expenses total about $10.00 per day. Payroll accounted for what proportion of your total expenses last month? (assume that there are 30 days in one month)

    (1) $\frac{1}{30}$

    (2) $\frac{1}{3}$

    (3) $\frac{5}{9}$

    (4) $\frac{5}{8}$

    (5) $\frac{8}{5}$

18. What is the value of the expression $2(201 + 13 - 49) \div 15 - 5$?

    Mark your answer in the circles in the grid on your answer sheet.

GO ON TO THE NEXT PAGE

19. Jane works as a special events coordinator. A client has hired Jane to plan a one-night event at a local hotel. The hotel charges a flat fee of \$450.00 per night for use of the room, plus \$18.00 per person for food and beverages. There will be 200 people at the event. How much will Jane's client pay the hotel for this one-night event?

    (1) \$468.00

    (2) \$668.00

    (3) \$2,018.00

    (4) \$3,600.00

    (5) \$4,050.00

20. Which of the following expresses the product of 2,200 and 13,000 in scientific notation?

    (1) 2.86×10^8

    (2) 2.86×10^7

    (3) 2.86×10^6

    (4) 28.6×10^7

    (5) 28.6×10^8

21. The dimensions of the rectangle shown below are 3s and 4s.

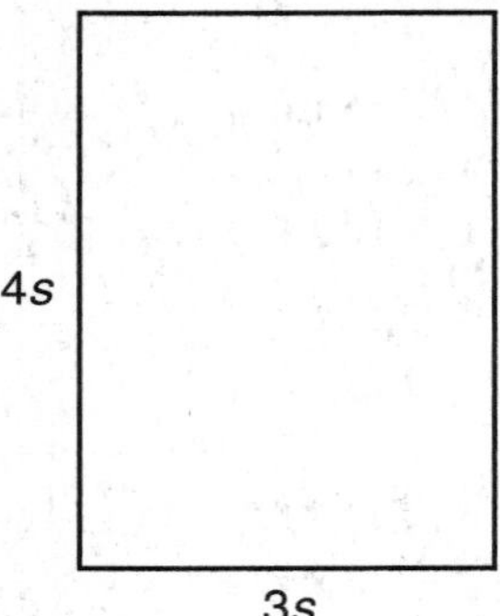

How many square units are in its area?

(1) 12

(2) $7s$

(3) $12s$

(4) $7s^2$

(5) $12s^2$

GO ON TO THE NEXT PAGE

Questions 22–25 refer to the following table.

Approximate Walking Times (minutes)

	AUD	BUS	CAF	CFM	HOS	POL	WAT	YOU	ZOO
AUD Auditorium	0	25	22	26	12	9	17	20	15
BUS Business District	25	0	2	13	16	10	24	11	8
CAF Café District	22	2	0	17	15	8	21	13	8
CFM Central Farmers' Market	26	13	17	0	12	20	23	17	21
HOS University Hospital	12	16	15	12	0	18	25	23	22
POL Police Headquarters	9	10	8	20	18	0	13	20	16
WAT Municipal Waterworks	17	24	21	23	25	13	0	14	6
YOU Youth Center	20	11	13	17	23	20	14	0	5
ZOO City Zoo	15	8	8	21	22	16	6	5	0

The table above shows approximate walking times between various important locations within a city. Each location is designated by a three-letter code. For example, the walk from AUD to YOU takes approximately 20 minutes.

22. Approximately how long, in minutes, would it take to walk from CAF to POL?

    (1) 8

    (2) 10

    (3) 15

    (4) 20

    (5) 21

23. Ryan is planning to walk from BUS to CFM to ZOO. Approximately how many minutes will Ryan take to complete the walk?

    (1) 8

    (2) 16

    (3) 21

    (4) 34

    (5) 42

24. Starting from WAT, to how many of the 8 other attractions given in the table could you walk within 15 minutes?

    (1) 0

    (2) 2

    (3) 3

    (4) 4

    (5) 5

25. A bus trip between HOS and ZOO takes 9 minutes each way. How much time would be saved by taking the bus instead of walking from HOS to ZOO and then back to HOS?

    (1) 13

    (2) 18

    (3) 21

    (4) 26

    (5) 46

GO ON TO: MATHEMATICS, PART II

Mathematics, Part II

Choose the one best answer to each question. You may **NOT** use a calculator for these questions.

26. Roberto starts with $513 in his savings account. If he withdraws $225, which of the following equations could be used to find out how much he has remaining in his savings account?

    (1) $513 \div 225$

    (2) $513 - 225$

    (3) 225×513

    (4) $225 - 513$

    (5) $225 + 513$

27. Sides AB and BC of $\angle ABC$ each measure 4 inches. If $\angle A = 60°$ and $\angle C = 60°$, what is the length in inches of side AC?

    (1) 2

    (2) 4

    (3) 8

    (4) 12

    (5) Not enough information is given.

28. Which of the following is the value of 127,523 rounded to the nearest thousand?

    (1) 127,000

    (2) 127,500

    (3) 128,000

    (4) 128,500

    (5) 128,600

Question 29 refers to the following graph.

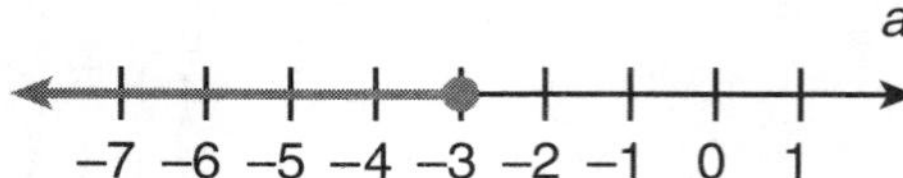

29. Which inequality is graphed on the number line?

    (1) $a > -3$

    (2) $a \geq -3$

    (3) $a < -3$

    (4) $a \leq 3$

    (5) $a < 3$

---

30. The cost of Jordan's dinner totaled $18.00. He wants to leave a 15% tip. In dollars, how much money should he leave as a tip?

    Mark your answer in the circles in the grid on your answer sheet.

31. The graph of a circle is shown on the grid below.

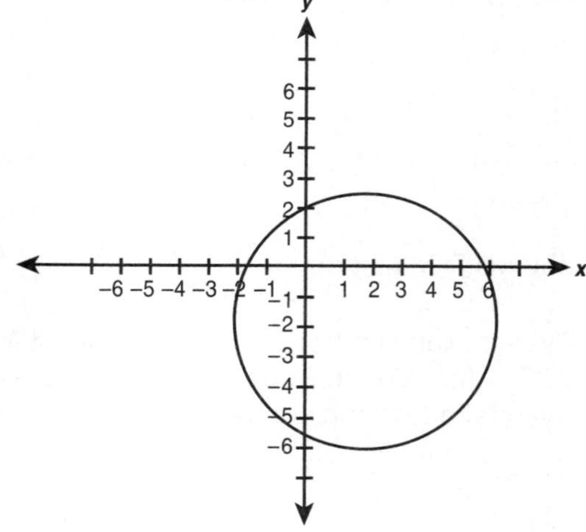

What point is the location of the center of the circle?

Mark your answer on the coordinate plane grid on your answer sheet.

32. The Gold 'n Crusty Pretzels factory can produce 400 cases of pretzels per hour when workers are on duty. The workday begins at 9 a.m. and ends at 6:45 p.m. If the factory closes for lunch from 12:30 p.m. to 1:15 p.m., how many cases of pretzels can the factory produce in one workday?

(1) 2,400
(2) 2,800
(3) 3,200
(4) 3,600
(5) 4,000

33. If $\frac{(14 - n)}{n} \times 8.5 = 8.5$, what is the value of n?

(1) 1
(2) 2
(3) 7
(4) 8
(5) 14

34. West Bay municipal harbor determines the cost of mooring a boat overnight with the following formula.

$$C = 5 + \frac{x^2}{100}$$

C is the cost (in dollars) for mooring, and x is the largest dimension (in feet) of the boat to be moored. If Mary has a boat that is 30 feet by 10 feet, what is the total amount she would pay to moor her boat overnight at the West Bay municipal harbor?

(1) $5
(2) $6
(3) $14
(4) $21
(5) $905

Questions 35 and 36 refer to the following graph.

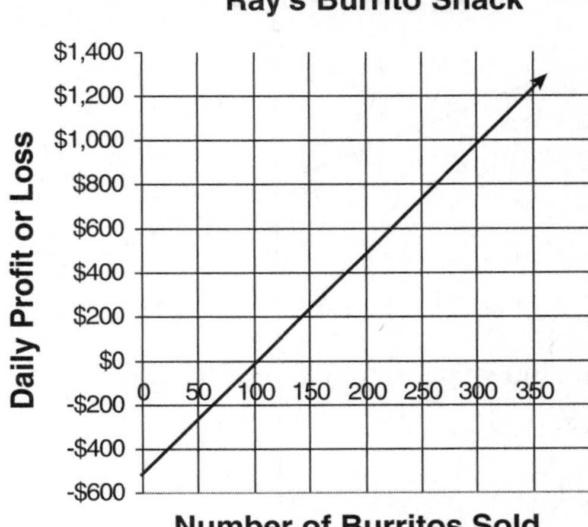

The expected daily profit (or loss) that Ray's Burrito Shack makes as a function of the number of burritos sold that day is shown in the graph above.

35. What is the approximate daily profit or loss (if negative) for Ray's Burrito Shack if 125 burritos were sold today?

(1) a loss of $400
(2) a loss of $200
(3) a profit of $100
(4) a profit of $200
(5) a profit of $600

36. Ray's Burrito Shack sold 400 burritos in one day. Based on the trends shown in the graph, approximately how much profit was made during that day?

(1) $1,500
(2) $1,200
(3) $1,100
(4) $1,000
(5) $900

GO ON TO THE NEXT PAGE

37. In the diagram below, the measure of angle ACB is 115°.

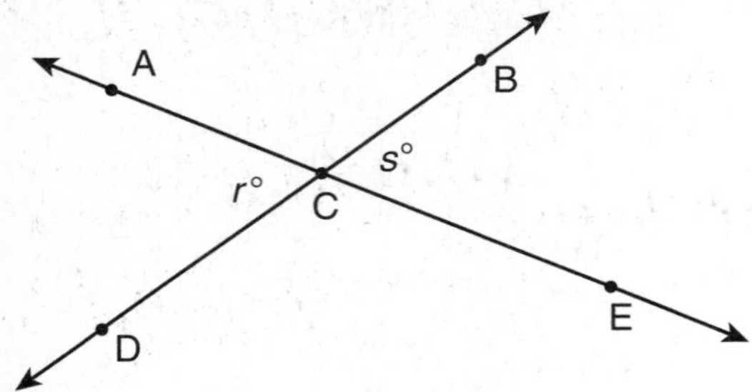

What is the value in degrees of $(r + s)$?

(1) 65

(2) 115

(3) 130

(4) 180

(5) Not enough information is given.

38. A jet aircraft cruises at a speed of 680 miles per hour. Which of the following would be the best estimate of the distance the aircraft cruises in 10.39 hours?

(1) 1,000

(2) 3,000

(3) 6,000

(4) 7,000

(5) 10,000

39. A bicycle shop advertises a closeout sale that offers, "Take an additional 20% off the lowest price." A helmet that was originally $80.00 is on sale for $50.00. What is the closeout price?

(1) $45.00

(2) $40.00

(3) $35.00

(4) $20.00

(5) $10.00

40. A total of k red peppers were harvested. Workers place them into j bags of 6 peppers each, but 2 peppers are left over. Which of the following equations expresses the relationship between the numbers of peppers harvested and the number of bags of peppers?

(1) $k = 6j + 2$

(2) $k = 2j + 6$

(3) $k = 6j - 2$

(4) $k = 2(j + 6)$

(5) $k = 6(2j + 1)$

41. Which of the following is the complete solution to the equation $(x + 9)(x - 5) = 0$?

(1) –9 only

(2) 5 only

(3) 9 and –5

(4) –9 and 5

(5) 5 and 9

42. Philip weighed 225 pounds when he began exercising regularly. After 90 days, he weighed x pounds less. Which expression represents his weight after 90 days?

(1) $225 + x$

(2) $225 - x$

(3) x

(4) $225x$

(5) $-x$

43. A used car costs $2,500. If Joel has $1,050 saved, how much more does he need to purchase the car?

(1) $3,550

(2) $1,450

(3) $1,050

(4) $1,000

(5) $450

GO ON TO THE NEXT PAGE

44. Briana wants to rent a dumpster to dispose of construction waste while she and her husband renovate their home. The dumpster rental company charges $75 for delivery of the dumpster and one haul-away of garbage. Each additional haul-away of garbage costs $50. What would Briana pay to have a dumpster delivered and then fill it three times?

(1) $100

(2) $150

(3) $175

(4) $200

(5) $225

45. Sarah is wearing an airspeed-measuring device that approximates her speed as she skis down a mountainside. During the run, her speed starts at 0, then increases at a constant rate to 40 miles per hour. When it reaches 40 miles per hour, it begins dropping at the same rate at which it increased. Which of the following graphs best represents the correct speed cycle?

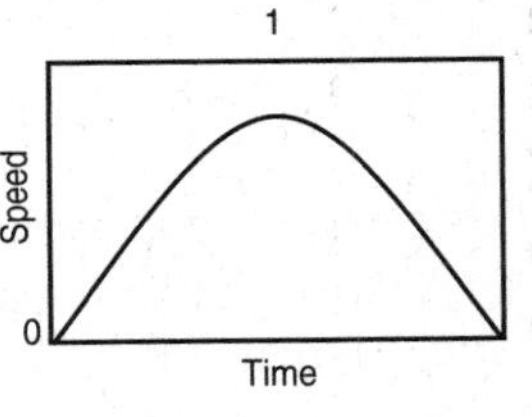

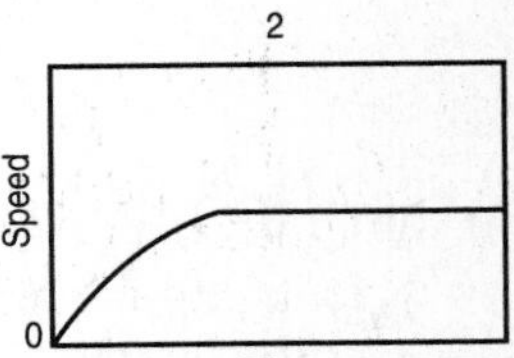

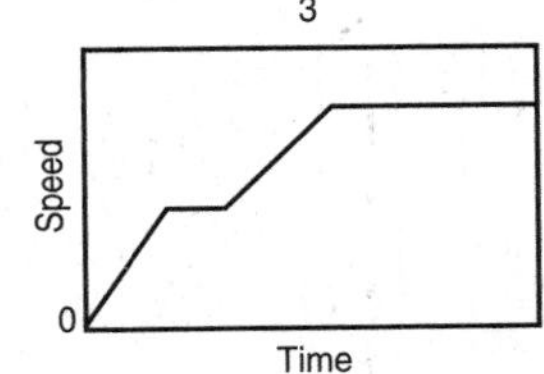

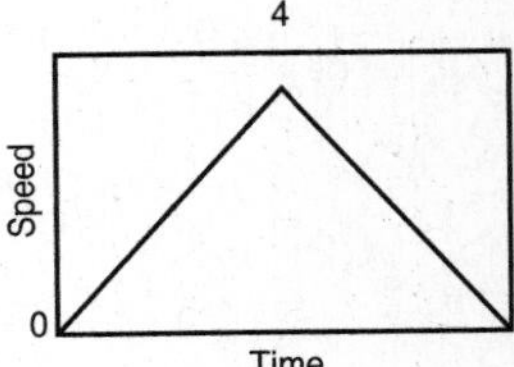

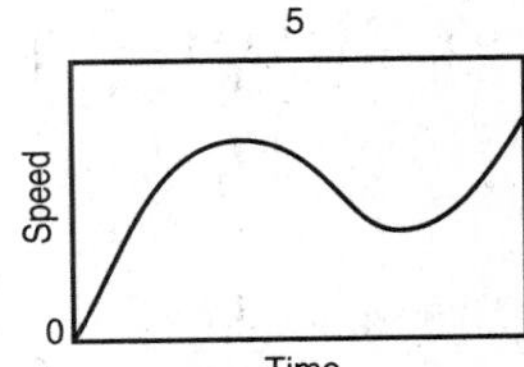

(1) 1

(2) 2

(3) 3

(4) 4

(5) 5

46. The cost of paving a 4-ft. by 5-ft. rectangular patio is \$100.

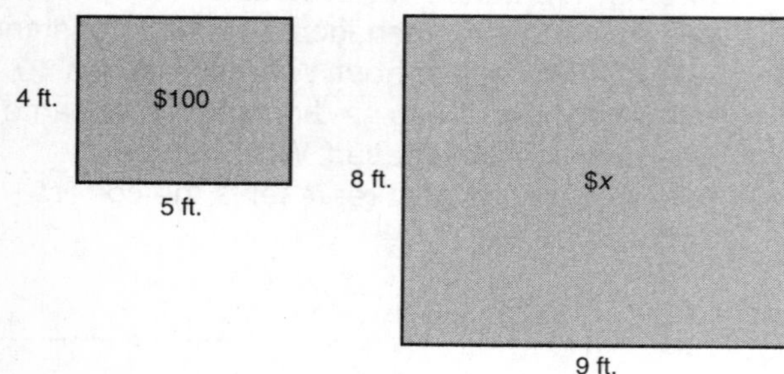

If the cost (x) of paving a patio is proportional to its area, which of the following expressions correctly determines the price (x) for an 8-foot by 9-foot patio?

(1) $\frac{9}{17} = \frac{100}{x}$

(2) $\frac{20}{72} = \frac{100}{x}$

(3) $\frac{20}{x} = \frac{72}{100}$

(4) $\frac{18}{34} = \frac{100}{x}$

(5) $\frac{18}{x} = \frac{34}{100}$

47. Supervisors earn an average of \$940 more per month than other employees at a fast-food restaurant in Danbury. The restaurant employs 4 supervisors and 23 other employees. Let x represent the average monthly pay of a nonsupervisor.

Which of the following functions correctly shows the relationship between the monthly payroll (P) and the wages of these employees?

(1) $P = 4(x + 940) + 23x$

(2) $P = 4x + 23(x + 940)$

(3) $P = 4(x + 940) + 23(x + 940)$

(4) $P = 4 + x + 23 + (x + 940)$

(5) $P = 4(x)(23)(x + 940)$

48. A square piece of paper has an area of 125 square inches. What is the approximate length of one side of the piece of paper?

(1) Between 14 and 15 inches

(2) Between 13 and 14 inches

(3) Between 12 and 13 inches

(4) Between 11 and 12 inches

(5) Between 10 and 11 inches

49. What is the slope of the line that passes through the points at (2,1) and (–4,3)?

(1) -3

(2) -1

(3) $-\frac{1}{3}$

(4) $\frac{1}{3}$

(5) 3

GO ON TO THE NEXT PAGE

Question 50 refers to the following drawing.

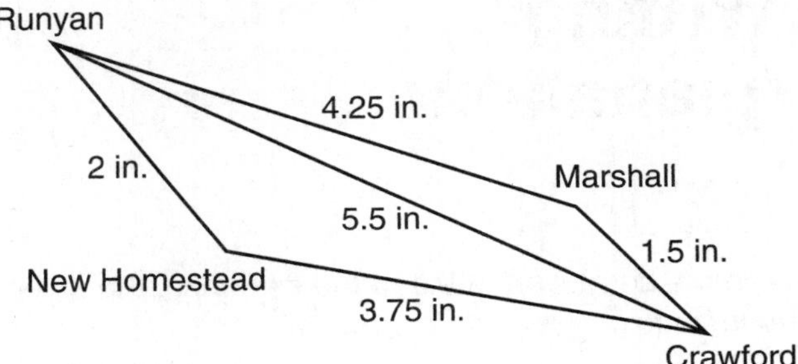

Scale: 1 in. = 80 mi

50. The map distances between towns are shown on the diagram. What is the actual distance in miles between Runyan and Marshall?

   (1) 120

   (2) 320

   (3) 340

   (4) 400

   (5) 440

Answers and explanations for this test begin on page 702.

END OF EXAMINATION

Language Arts, Writing Answers and Explanations

Part I

1. **The best answer is (3).** To achieve the correct meaning of the sentence, the adjective "recent" should modify the noun "inquiry."
2. **The best answer is (1).** The past verb "were" should be changed to the present verb "are" because the company is familiar with the problems at the time the letter was written.
3. **The best answer is (5).** Answer choice (1) is not a tense in English. Answer choices (2), (3), and (4) would indicate that the dampness has stopped. Only answer choice (5) would indicate that the problem is ongoing.
4. **The best answer is (5).** The phrase "with great success" modifies the verb phrase "have installed many basement systems" and therefore does not require "and," "but," or separation by a comma.
5. **The best answer is (1).** The plural noun "residents" refers to people. The singular noun "residence" refers to the place where the "residents" live—that is, the place where the dampness control system would be installed.
6. **The best answer is (1).** As written, sentence 7 is not very informative. Answer choice (1) clearly indicates what must be done to assist the customer. The other answer choices are awkward.
7. **The best answer is (3).** This question requires you to identify wordiness and choose the most concise revision. In previous sentences, Mr. and Mrs. Conroy were called "you" without "both." Remember that "you" can be both singular and plural. Secondly, the word "together" is not necessary because togetherness is implied when people sit down to discuss something.
8. **The best answer is (3).** Sentence 11 explains a possible simple solution, so it should be placed before the sentence that contrasts it by explaining a more complicated process. Furthermore, removing sentence 11 from its present location allows sentence 12 to follow sentence 10 immediately, which is important to the logical order of the paragraph.
9. **The best answer is (2).** The subject "This innovative design" must not be separated from its verb "requires" by any punctuation. Therefore, eliminate answer choices 1, 3, and 4. Answer choice (5) is incorrect because the object "the construction..." must not be separated from its verb "requires" by any punctuation.
10. **The best answer is (3).** The sentence as written contains incorrect usage of the passive voice. The correct meaning of the sentence would have "we" (the company) assuring the customers; therefore, the active voice is appropriate.
11. **The best answer is (5).** This sentence is clear and grammatically correct as written.
12. **The best answer is (3).** The most effective combination of these sentences uses a comma and a nonrestrictive clause beginning with "which" to modify the verb phrase "complete the paperwork."

13. **The best answer is (5).** Sentence 6 concludes the information presented in paragraph B about the two loan offers.

14. **The best answer is (5).** The present verb "are" should be used because the offers are ongoing at the time the letter was written.

15. **The best answer is (4).** No comma is necessary when the conjunction "or" combines two parallel items in a series. (The comma is appropriate before "or" when the series has three items or more.)

16. **The best answer is (1).** The two sentences are clearest and most concise when they stand apart as separate sentences. A dash or a semicolon would be correct, but these options are not given to you.

17. **The best answer is (2).** The revision would begin the clearest form of this sentence: "As the enclosed information indicates, this offer has a deadline."

18. **The best answer is (5).** The sentence does not require any correction.

19. **The best answer is (3).** The popular expression "Dogs are man's best friend" should remain as it is, in present tense.

20. **The best answer is (5).** The past participle "accepted" should stand alone to be conjoined by "and" with the past participle "understood." The verb "to be" would then link with both participles. As written, the sentence is wordy because "need to" and "must" have the same meaning.

21. **The best answer is (3).** "Time and time again" is an expression that can be an introductory phrase in this sentence. Therefore, a comma is needed after "again." Of answer choices 3 and 4, choose answer choice (3) to match the other present-perfect sentences within the paragraph.

22. **The best answer is (2).** The sentence describes the present characteristics of the dog. In addition, the simple present verb "is" maintains parallelism with the simple present verb "hates."

23. **The best answer is (1).** The sentence describes an event that occurred once in the past and is finished. Therefore, the simple present tense is appropriate.

24. **The best answer is (2).** This group of words would end the clearest combination of the two sentences: "She will no doubt, however, go back to playing with her dog once her nose is healed."

25. **The best answer is (4).** Sentence 20 refers to the stories from paragraphs B and C and introduces the ideas in paragraph D.

26. **The best answer is (4).** The act of sending the soil sample is in the past and completed. Therefore, the simple past form "you sent" is appropriate.

27. **The best answer is (1).** "Your Sample" is not a proper name or a title of any kind, so it does not need to be capitalized.

28. **The best answer is (3).** The sentence is a fragment as written; it lacks a main verb. As written, the sentence now refers Joe to the fall, which is incorrect. The rest of the sentence is correct as is.

29. **The best answer is (3).** The best revision would combine the two sentences because they essentially describe one procedure. Answer choice (3) is the clearest and most concise way to combine the sentences.

30. **The best answer is (5).** The sentence is clear and grammatically correct.
31. **The best answer is (1).** The verb "need" must agree in number with the singular subject "fertilizer." Therefore, the form "needs" is necessary.
32. **The best answer is (3).** This group of words would be included in the clearest way to express the meaning of the sentence: "Using a rake, incorporate these additions to a depth of at least three inches." This is a combination of the two sentences with no added words or punctuation.
33. **The best answer is (3).** When used in the middle of a sentence, "however" must be set apart with a comma on each side.
34. **The best answer is (1).** No comma is normally necessary after "Welcome." For example, "Welcome to the show" or "Welcome back to Florida."
35. **The best answer is (4).** If you rewrote the sentence with the subject "We at Hidden Lake Senior Center" at the beginning, it would be clearest to put the verb "are" next, as in "We at Hidden Lake Senior Center are offering an exciting opportunity that we hope you will seriously consider."
36. **The best answer is (2).** The phrase "out of range" is idiomatic, so "range" must not have an article like "the" before it. However, modification of "range" is possible, for example "out of hearing range" and "out of sight range."
37. **The best answer is (2).** The sentence should refer to the current opportunity for staff and students to participate in activities. Therefore, the simple present verb "are" should replace the present perfect verb phrase "have been."
38. **The best answer is (5).** This group of words is part of the clearest combination of these sentences: "Studies have proven over and over again the mutual benefit senior citizens and youth achieve by working and playing together."
39. **The best answer is (1).** This sentence follows logically from sentence 10, which contains many examples of possible activities.
40. **The best answer is (3).** The base form "take" is appropriate following the particle "to." Together, they form the infinitive verb "to take." Answer choice (4) passes this test, but the present perfect form is not appropriate in the sentence.
41. **The best answer is (1).** "There is" and "There are" are common ways to begin sentences in English. The word "their" is the third-person plural possessive pronoun. "They're" is the contraction of the subject pronoun "they" and the verb "are."
42. **The best answer is (5).** No comma is necessary before a clause introduced by the conjunction "when."
43. **The best answer is (2).** This letter addresses one school in particular. The information in sentence 16 does not affect the school in question and should, therefore, be eliminated.
44. **The best answer is (4).** The past form "commented" should be the gerund to maintain parallelism with the gerund "sitting."
45. **The best answer is (3).** This sentence is clearest and most concise when "then" and the comma are eliminated. The conjunction "that" introduces the restrictive clause that modifies the noun phrase "something about the differentiation of bird species."

46. **The best answer is (3).** Sentence 6 follows sentence 8 logically. Both sentences discuss the different feed preferences of birds.
47. **The best answer is (3).** The adjective "annoying" should follow the verb "be." Answer choice (3) represents the most concise revision because it eliminates the verb "listen," the act of which is implied in the sentence: "The black crow can be annoying with his blaring, sharp caw."
48. **The best answer is (4).** Use of the contraction "there's" is inappropriate at the end of a sentence; use "there is" instead. Answer choices 2 and 5 may be eliminated because they include an incorrect homonym of "there." Answer choice (3) may be eliminated because it includes the plural verb "are" when the subject with which it must agree is the singular noun "lullaby."
49. **The best answer is (4).** The subject "a single species of bird" is singular, so the plural verb "have" must be changed to the singular verb "has."
50. **The best answer is (5).** The modifier phrases "offered in most communities" and "led by bird experts" both modify "field trips." To avoid ambiguity over whether one modifier phrase modifies the other, it would be best to separate the two phrases within the sentence. Answer choice (5) is the revision that accomplishes this and leads to a clear, concise sentence: "Most communities offer field trips led by bird experts."

Part II

Because grading the essay is subjective, we've chosen not to include any "graded" essays here. Your best bet is to have someone you trust, such as your personal tutor, read your essays and give you an honest critique. Make the scoring rubric mentioned in Chapter 11, "GED Essay," available to whoever grades your essays. If you plan on grading your own essays, review the grading criteria and be as honest as possible regarding the structure, development, organization, technique, and word choice of your writing. Be sure to address the essay prompt you'll be given on test day, because failing to do so could result in a failing grade on the essay. Focus on your weak areas and continue to practice to improve your writing skills.

Language Arts, Reading Answers and Explanations

1. **The best answer is (3).** The clear implication of the text is that the man in the box is dead. The emphasis on the cold, unforgiving weather further implies that the man died of exposure.
2. **The best answer is (4).** The main point of the passage is to emphasize the harsh, even hostile climate in the North and how it assumes a personality of its own that actively hates living things. Although being good with dogs and accustomed to cold weather would be useful, a strong and determined personality would be necessary to endure such conditions.
3. **The best answer is (4).** Use of the word "laughter" personifies the Wild and indicates that it seems to take pleasure in causing ill to living things.
4. **The best answer is (2).** The passage reiterates in several places how the Wild seeks to destroy movement, as it did with the dead traveler in the box.
5. **The best answer is (3).** This question asks you to interpret figurative language. "Masque" in this case refers to a pantomime or masquerade, and "ghostly" is meant literally. The two men look like ghosts in a ritual performance, acting as undertakers at the supernatural funeral of another ghost.
6. **The best answer is (5).** The poem portrays people happily working. Each person has his or her job to do. Each controls his or her destiny. This is expressed in line 11: "...what belongs to her, and to none else."
7. **The best answer is (4).** All the professions are active ones. These are songs of people in motion. The songs reflect vigor and happiness.
8. **The best answer is (5).** All the songs in the poem speak to the author about the love of the singer for his or her occupation and the pride that he or she takes in it. Clearly, the author would likewise sense the love of the mother for her child. In addition, the extended metaphor of song in this poem shows that the speaker is pleased by work joyfully done. Music is often a symbol for joyful expression, happiness, and love.
9. **The best answer is (1).** Recognize that the metaphor of song is not meant to be taken literally. Therefore, eliminate answer choices (2), (3), and (4), which refer to singing. Answer choice (5) is not supported by the poem. Answer choice (1) is correct because it refers to the concept of workers' pride symbolized by their singing.
10. **The best answer is (2).** This question requires you to identify who exactly composes the America the poet Whitman describes. All the male workers have jobs performing physical labor. The female professions describe domestic tasks, which still constitute physical labor. The poem mentions no "office jobs," so to speak. A physical laborer such as a blacksmith would be most appropriately added.
11. **The best answer is (2).** This question requires you to extrapolate probable qualities of the author from a description of his picture and the content of the poem. As noted previously, the topic of the poem is not just Americans, but working-class laborers who enjoy their lives and take pride in their efforts. The style of Whitman's clothing in the picture would indicate that he wants to be seen as being like them: sincere and unpretentious (not marked by an assumption of importance).

12. **The best answer is (3).** In this synthesis question, the reader is asked to understand the structure of Roosevelt's argument for war. Listing the Axis offenses creates a pattern of behavior that seems likely to continue unless action is taken to stop it. Roosevelt wants his audience to understand that the attacks themselves amount to declaration of war against the United States and, therefore, that U.S. military retaliation is justified.

13. **The best answer is (4).** Repetition in speech or writing can be an extremely effective stylistic device because it allows the author to reinforce an idea. In this question, the reader is asked to identify what idea Roosevelt is trying to reinforce to his audience. The fact that all the attacks came without warning and in some cases without even a declaration of war emphasizes the illegal and unethical nature of the attacks and helps build a case for military retaliation.

14. **The best answer is (4).** This question requires that you identify the contrast Roosevelt makes between Japan and the United States. Japan, he says, is run by "military dictators," whereas the U.S. audience already knows that their government is a nonmilitary democracy. This contrast furthers Roosevelt's aim to create a division between the two countries that will further justify a declaration of war.

15. **The best answer is (1).** This question tests the reader's vocabulary. Based on the context, "diplomats" is the best choice. Of all the answer choices, only diplomats are likely to hold meetings with the secretary of state.

16. **The best answer is (4).** World War II was a time of great sacrifice in the United States. It's not necessary to know that to answer this analysis question, but the idea of coming sacrifice and the need for national unity certainly must have influenced the author of this passage. Roosevelt states that the war will take the total efforts of all Americans. That is why he feels the need to present such a strong argument for war.

17. **The best answer is (5).** Roosevelt's "Fireside Chats" were weekly radio addresses to the entire nation. Several clues to Roosevelt's audience can be found in the passage. First, he begins it with an address to "my fellow Americans." The word "Americans" often reappears in the passage. In the last paragraph, he repeatedly uses the word "we" to reinforce the collective nature of the task ahead. All these clues tell the reader that Roosevelt's audience is the American people.

18. **The best answer is (1).** The answer to this question is found in the second paragraph. The reviewer contrasts the large auditorium of the Manhattan Opera House with the smaller auditorium of the Longacre Theatre. He argues that great battle scenes need a larger venue, but that the "secret missions" of a spy play, such as "Inside the Lines," are better on smaller stages.

19. **The best answer is (5).** This question asks the reader to find clues as to the reviewer's impression of "Inside the Lines." Admittedly, the reviewer spends more time establishing his own credentials than reviewing the play. However, he tips his hat with the line, "So it is that the new play at the Longacre provides a moderately interesting evening in the theatre." He also writes that plot flaws are covered up by competent acting. These lines support answer choice (5).

20. **The best answer is (4).** This analysis question asks the reader to grasp the tone of the passage. The author is very interested in presenting himself as a sophisticated viewer who is best able to critique New York theater productions. One device he uses to establish himself in this role is to contrast himself with less-able viewers. In his opinion, the "fretful old tourist from Illinois" clearly can't appreciate the strengths and weaknesses of the play. Therefore, the tourist's opinions should be ignored.

21. **The best answer is (2).** This question requires you to identify the meaning of a rather complex sentence. The author states that because so many plays now use the same plot device, the audience was not surprised by the ending of this particular play.

22. **The best answer is (5).** This question requires you to make the connection between the subject matter of the play (military espionage) and the time period. The year 1915 followed the outbreak of World War I in Europe. The author is using understatement (by calling the war "the excitement") to describe violent military conflict.

23. **The best answer is (1).** This question requires you to draw inferences from different parts of the passage. The Princess tells the reader that she visits the Woodcutter regularly and that she has done such diverse things as help him with his work and eat lunch with him. In return, he gently makes fun of her by saying such things as, "Only yesterday I was thinking to myself how unselfish I was to interrupt my work in order to talk to a mere Princess." They both acknowledge he is not "at her service" in the traditional sense. Still, she continues to visit him. Clearly she enjoys the unique relationship they have.

24. **The best answer is (5).** This question requires you to characterize the Princess in the passage. While she is clearly aware of her elevated status in society and, therefore, a bit proud, she continues trying to establish a friendship with the Woodcutter. Furthermore, her attention to the Woodcutter, the way she helped him with his work and bandaged his injured hand, indicates she is a caring person.

25. **The best answer is (4).** This question requires you to make connections among different parts of the text. Although the Princess and the Woodcutter are, in fact, ruler and subject, the main idea of the passage hints that these roles do not define their relationship. The way that they discuss their roles indicates that they would like to break free of them. In all, they act like partners at the beginning of a potential romance. Although answer choice (1) is likely correct and answer choice (2) is one possible interpretation of the text, both are insufficient to describe the full extent of the two people's relationship.

26. **The best answer is (2).** The Woodcutter's last line reveals that he has his own opinions about how suitors are chosen for the princess. The author uses this topic to foreshadow a change in the relationship between the Woodcutter and the Princess.

27. **The best answer is (5).** The passage indicates that the Princess has spent quite a bit of time visiting the Woodcutter. She has eaten with him, helped him with his work, and bandaged his injuries. Moreover, she says she would stop speaking to him, except she's afraid he wouldn't notice. All this indicates that she is fond of him but she doesn't think he feels the same way about her. In other words, as this line further shows, she does not think she has enough of his personal attention.

28. **The best answer is (1).** This question requires you to consider the theme of the passage. Based on the characters and dialogue, the passage clearly sets up a modern fairy tale in a play called *Make-Believe*. Therefore, the reader should expect the author to play with fairy tale conventions. One convention is the worthy commoner who earns the right to marry royalty. *Cinderella* is one example, as is *Beauty and the Beast*. The Woodcutter is described with the type of language usually reserved for princes: he is tall and strong and brave and handsome. All this implies that, despite his occupation, he is a worthy suitor for the Princess.

29. **The best answer is (3).** The mussel-man defines “nacheralist” (actually spelled “naturalist”) in his own terms in the next paragraph.

30. **The best answer is (4).** This question requires you to determine the tone of the passage. Many of the details point to a humorous but slightly dark view of daily life. Several of the details—such as handing out cat’s meat to the dogs—are simply absurd. Therefore, the overall tone is humorous and lightly ironic.

31. **The best answer is (4).** The answer is given directly in the text near the end of the passage. When Matthew notices the dogs waiting patiently, he hands his cat meat out to them.

32. **The best answer is (2).** This synthesis question asks the reader to make connections among parts of the text to create a complete picture of Dr. Dolittle. Matthew Mugg and the mussel-man greatly admire Dolittle for his knowledge and experience. However, they admit they don’t know very much about his daily life because Dolittle keeps to himself and doesn’t talk much. These facts support answer choice (2).

33. **The best answer is (3).** This question tests your ability to understand vocabulary from its context. Tom is searching for Dr. Dolittle because he has a squirrel with a broken leg. Clearly, he is a man who loves animals and wants to care for them. In that sense, he is compared to Dr. Dolittle himself. Both men are crazy about, or “daft over,” animals.

34. **The best answer is (3).** By describing the Indians as “sensible people,” Matthew Mugg indicates his approval of their marital practice of living apart. He has also already indicated that he doesn’t understand his own wife very well. In short, he probably believes that men and women can’t live together peacefully.

35. **The best answer is (2).** The poor location of the restaurant is one aspect that stands in contrast to its good food and popularity. The passage also mentions seemingly negative qualities of the restaurant’s décor, owner, and equipment.

36. **The best answer is (2).** The narrator says he has never read the menu. Therefore, you can eliminate answer choices (1), (3), and (5). Answer choice (4) is not supported by the passage.

37. **The best answer is (3).** The passage focuses on the unrefined look of Joe’s and its (perhaps unexpectedly) excellent sandwiches. The narrator also mentions that Joe’s has a significant number of regular customers, which would reinforce the notion of a “familiar atmosphere.”

38. **The best answer is (2).** The passage describes Joe’s Lunch Bucket as a restaurant in which the owner works hard and keeps customers coming back for good sandwiches. Of the answer choices, only “success” could replace “fortune” in the text. The word “wealth” seems possible, but the isolated location and poor appearance of Joe’s would indicate that the owner is not earning an abundance of money from the business.

39. **The best answer is (2).** The narrator gives two examples of “stand-bys.” They are sandwiches: “chicken salad” and “corned beef.” In context, the narrator is referring to the usual sandwich choices of regular customers. If a regular customer often gets one particular type of sandwich, then that sandwich must be a “reliable” choice, meaning it is always satisfying.

40. **The best answer is (4).** The narrator states that “The food is, after all, the only charm this little place needs.” Joe’s succeeds without answer choices (1), (2), and (3). Answer choice (5) is not addressed in the passage.

Social Studies Answers and Explanations

1. **The best answer is (2).** Supply and demand curves show the equilibrium price for a product (in this case, a one-way train ticket). The equilibrium price is defined as the price at which the supplier makes the most money in total. For this graph, the equilibrium price is about $68 and the equilibrium quantity is about 450.
2. **The best answer is (3).** One fundamental of economics is that consumers will choose the cheaper of two equivalent products. In the case of housing, if buying is a better value than renting, more people will choose to buy, resulting in more empty rental units.
3. **The best answer is (3).** The key word in the information is "revolution," which is political upheaval in a country. Many Cubans came to the United States to escape adverse political circumstances that arose when Castro took power.
4. **The best answer is (1).** This question requires some basic knowledge of American history. Segregation was ended during the civil rights movement of the 1950s and 1960s. Specifically, most Jim Crow laws were repealed by the Civil Rights Act of 1964.
5. **The best answer is (2).** This question asks about the theme of the painting. Washington stands in a heroic pose as he moves across the icy river. The information before the question indicates that the river crossing was the first move in a surprise attack against the British when American troops' morale was low. The painting is strongly patriotic because in spite of great adversity, Washington and his men continued the fight and were eventually victorious.
6. **The best answer is (2).** The Declaration of Independence stated the reasons why the American states wanted to separate from Great Britain. The painting captures a scene from the Revolutionary War that took place on December 25, 1776. The Declaration of Independence was approved earlier that year on July 4, now known as Independence Day.
7. **The best answer is (3).** In the cartoon, the representative of Wall Street expresses concern about inflation, but the rising costs (represented by the hot air balloons) are actually choking the "Average Joe." The irony is the discrepancy between those who complain about inflation and those who are most harmed by it.
8. **The best answer is (3).** The information explains that the United States *does not* recognize Canada's claim to the arctic waters. It also mentions that the waters are important for ship traffic between the Atlantic Ocean and the state of Alaska. The best conclusion is that the United States would like Canada to stay out of American affairs in the far-northern ocean route.
9. **The best answer is (4).** The map shows that the disputed area is extremely large (many times larger than Alaska, the largest U.S. state) and largely covered in ice. These reasons and the adverse weather conditions typical of the arctic would make policing the disputed region very difficult.

10. **The best answer is (2).** The passage states that the Livery of Seisin was popular in pre-17th century medieval England. It was brought to an end in 1679. Therefore, the only reasonable answer is that medieval England existed approximately between 500 and 1600.

11. **The best answer is (5).** The passage states that powerful landowners were raising private armies and that the Statute of Frauds was enacted to maintain political stability. This implies a causal link, with the private armies ultimately threatening the government.

12. **The best answer is (1).** The stone or twig was handed to the buyer in exchange for the purchase price of the land because the stone or twig symbolized, or represented, the property for sale. The witnesses were then able to testify to this act of transmission.

13. **The best answer is (3).** While people do, in fact, find ways other than writing to document property sales, the methods under the Livery of Seisin were particularly vulnerable to intimidation and fraud. Therefore, literacy is important because it reduces the chance of fraud.

14. **The best answer is (4).** A decrease in oil consumption would indicate that total energy consumption had gone down. This would support the conclusion that the Daylight Saving Time program was successful.

15. **The best answer is (5).** The line of succession is in place in case the president can no longer fulfill his or her duties. For example, when President Kennedy was assassinated, then-Vice President Johnson was soon sworn in as president. Answer choice (5) would not invoke the line of succession because presidential election cycles are a normal part of the political process in the United States. The circumstances of answer choices (1), (2), (3), and (4) could all arise during a president's term.

16. **The best answer is (3).** The purpose of having so many people in the line of succession is to be absolutely certain that the country will never be without a president. As an added safeguard, the entire line of succession is never in the same place at the same time. The catastrophe referred to in answer choice (3) could be a bombing of the House Chamber during a State of the Union address, for example, in which the president, vice president, and all but one person down the line of succession are killed. In that case, the hidden member of the line of succession would be sworn in as president.

17. **The best answer is (4).** The author's rhetorical question introduces the topics of her next two paragraphs. The main idea of her essay is the answer to this question.

18. **The best answer is (1).** As the passage states, Japan invaded part of Alaska at the beginning of World War II. The author implies that this prompted Congress to increase military presence in Alaska to defend the country.

19. **The best answer is (1).** During the Gold Rush, Alaska's resources were first developed by "miners, fishermen and trappers." This implies that Alaska's resources were gold, fish, and fur.

20. **The best answer is (3).** The line graph shows that employment decreases beginning just before January of each year and then increases again in the new year.

21. **The best answer is (4).** The choice represents the least drastic policy decision. Answer choices (1), (2), (3), and (5) represent strong control of business by the government, which would not be acceptable to employers.

22. **The best answer is (4).** Fuel economy window stickers are required to be displayed on all new vehicles because the federal government wants consumers to know how much gasoline the vehicle uses. The major expense associated with owning a car or truck is filling its tank with gas. For many people, fuel economy is one of the most important factors in choosing among cars to buy.
23. **The best answer is (4).** By declaring vehicle fuel economy, some customers will decline to purchase certain vehicles because fuel economy is too low. On a large scale, this encourages manufacturers to make more efficient vehicles. The ultimate goal is a reduction in gasoline consumption for the sake of the economy and the environment.
24. **The best answer is (1).** According to the information, the World Wide Web is "a collection of interconnected documents with text and other types of media..." Answer choices (2), (3), (4), and (5) fall into this category. Answer choice (1) involves Internet chat, which does not involve "interconnected documents" containing text and media.
25. **The best answer is (4).** Malaria is a major infectious disease with tremendous impact on worldwide public health. Therefore, it is an area of primary interest to the World Health Organization.
26. **The best answer is (1).** According to the law of supply and demand, if the supply of gasoline decreases and demand for the gasoline increases, the price of the gasoline increases.
27. **The best answer is (3).** The beginning of the second paragraph states that publishing the *Encyclopédie* was so expensive that only the "affluent [rich] cultural elite" could buy them.
28. **The best answer is (3).** The second sentence of the information states that "Enlightenment thinkers sought to compile the wide range of human knowledge in a concise, accessible form." The word "accessible" means easy to approach, read, and so on. French-speaking enlightenment thinkers wanted to educated all the people, whose mindset they thought was stuck in the Dark Ages.
29. **The best answer is (5).** This answer comes directly from the second sentence of the second paragraph: "When each volume left the press, it was delivered to its buyer."
30. **The best answer is (1).** Enlightenment thinkers believed in rational, scientific thought. The *Encyclopédie* was intended to educate people on many different topics, and by doing so, old-fashioned, superstitious notions of the "how" and "why" of the universe would be dispelled.
31. **The best answer is (2).** This graph clearly shows that the population of people age 65 or over has been increasing since 1900 and will continue to do so through 2050. Using this fact as evidence and your own knowledge about global and national increases in population, answer choice (2) is the best conclusion.
32. **The best answer is (2).** The buying and selling of goods according to your demand for them is fundamental to a market system. The EPA has designed a market system for pollution rights because it believes it is the most efficient way to reduce pollution in the U.S. open market economy.

33. **The best answer is (4).** Montana and Washington are different states. With this information alone, you could choose “interstate,” which means “between states.” Otherwise, you would refer to the description of arterials: “...for longer, uninterrupted trips,” which accurately describes traveling from Montana to Washington. Interstates are classified as arterials.

34. **The best answer is (3).** The key word supporting this answer choice is “uninterrupted” in the description of arterials. The fastest route between cities is the one with the highest speeds and fewest interruptions at traffic lights and intersections. None of the other answer choices are supported by facts in the chart or the information.

35. **The best answer is (4).** The lines on the graph show profits before taxes and profits after taxes. This means that the distance between the lines at any one time along the horizontal axis equals the amount of taxes paid. To find out for which year from 1998 to 2005 corporations paid the most taxes, look for when in that time period the lines are furthest apart (use the gridline for help). This is 2005.

36. **The best answer is (1).** The trend in both lines is an increase for one or two years, then a decrease for one or two years, and then an increase for four years.

37. **The best answer is (2).** The information mentions that China first banned opium imports and then eventually imposed a death penalty for smuggling it into the country. A reasonable conclusion is that the opium-smuggling problem was worsening in the eyes of Chinese decision makers. Opium, a highly addictive drug, was certainly having a negative effect on Chinese society.

38. **The best answer is (1).** Businesses more than seven years old in 1992 are businesses started in 1985 or earlier. This means that, at most, the percentage of businesses seven years old or older in 1992 is the sum of the percentages for start years “1980–1985” and “Before 1980” (20% + 23% = 43%). Forty-three percent is less than half (50%).

39. **The best answer is (3).** The second sentence of the third paragraph states that candidates who do poorly in the first (New Hampshire) primary usually have to drop out of the race.

40. **The best answer is (3).** Voting twice constitutes election fraud; therefore it is one situation that an election monitor would try to prevent.

41. **The best answer is (4).** It is reasonable to assume that the phrase “near the coast of Iceland” implies within Iceland’s Exclusive Economic Zone. Under the Law of the Sea, Norwegian vessels would not be allowed to fish there (which is the harvesting of a natural resource) without permission from Iceland.

42. **The best answer is (3).** The information emphasizes the extent of the territory covered during the investigation of the kidnapping. It also states that local law enforcement may have hurt the chances of finding the child. It is implied in the passage that federal investigators would have done a better job with the case. Therefore, the Federal Kidnapping Act would have been intended to improve the handling of interstate kidnapping cases by authorizing federal investigators to deal with them.

43. **The best answer is (2).** The passage states that the Louvre was a royal residence for various kings of France. Historically, works of art were commissioned or purchased by wealthy, powerful people such as royalty. The kings would have wanted to display their art collections for their own enjoyment and as a sign of good taste, power, and wealth.

44. **The best answer is (3).** This question is directly answered by the third paragraph, which states that François would not move into the Louvre until it was renovated to be “even more grandiose.”

45. **The best answer is (4).** Without knowing much French history, you would need to recall that the end of the 18th century is marked by the French and American revolutions, which were rejections of royal domination in favor of democratic systems of government. With the fall of the monarchy and the aristocracy, many of the grand palaces in France came under public ownership. Today, as in the case of the Louvre, many are museums open to the public.

46. **The best answer is (2).** The three lines in the graph are nearly the same, just shifted horizontally. This makes sense because the difference between each age range is six years, and the lines each appear shifted about six years. All three lines have a period of decline. By counting the vertical gridlines, which are five years apart, you can see that the periods of decline are just about 15 years.

47. **The best answer is (2).** By looking for the highest point on the graph, you can determine if you have enough information to answer the question. Conveniently, the “Ages 12–17” line has a nearly five-year point above the gridline for “25.” No other five-year period on the line is above that gridline, so you know that the number of children ages 12 through 17 from 1950 to 2004 was highest during that period.

48. **The best answer is (1).** The graph shows periods of increase and decrease, but over the long term the graph increases. This follows with the basic increasing trend in population of the United States and the world that you may already know.

49. **The best answer is (4).** A shortage of a product means that there is more product demanded than product supplied. This means that producers have not been making enough of the product, perhaps because they anticipated demand being lower than it actually turned out to be.

50. **The best answer is (2).** The information specifically states that “the agreement lifts many barriers to trade.” This implies a simplification of trade. Also, eliminating “tariffs” specifically means a direct reduction in the cost of trade.

Science Answers and Explanations

1. **The best answer is (4).** The process of evaporation will convert the water from a liquid to a gaseous state and leave behind any salt that was dissolved in the water. The process of removing excess salt from water through evaporation is known as desalination.
2. **The best answer is (3).** The paragraph indicates that echolocation is a navigation adaptation that involves the use of sounds waves.
3. **The best answer is (5).** The other answer choices are adaptations developed over the evolutionary history of the polar bear in response to natural circumstances. Bears' affinity for human trash is not an adaptation, because it actually poses a risk to the animal. The waste may be unhealthy, and bears that become unphased by humans often have to be euthanized to ensure human safety.
4. **The best answer is (4).** As altitude increases, air pressure, and therefore air density, decreases. This means every inhalation contains less oxygen, the gas essential to sustain animal life. Climbers who ascend too quickly do not allow their bodies to increase the density of red blood cells to maximize each breath. Initial symptoms of oxygen deprivation include headache and nausea.
5. **The best answer is (5).** Oil does not stay mixed with water. The word "soluble" means "able to be dissolved." The other answer choices do not explain why oil and water do not mix.
6. **The best answer is (2).** "Decompose" means "break down." In an ecosystem, decomposers consume dead plants and animals, eventually helping return the nutrients to the soil.
7. **The best answer is (4).** Density is the measure of mass per unit volume. Because equal volumes of sea water and fresh water are being compared, and because sea water is denser than fresh water, the sea water has more mass. Therefore, the balance will tip down on the sea water side.
8. **The best answer is (2).** Over a long period of time, rock can be weathered (broken down) into finer particles like sand, silt, and clay. The process of weathering smoothes sharp rocks. The product of weathering is the accumulation of finer particles such as sand, silt, and clay. These particles make up the nonliving components of soil, which would be necessary to support a covering of grass.
9. **The best answer is (3).** Gravitation increases as objects draw nearer. Compared to the sun, the other stars in the universe are extremely far from Earth. The effect of their gravitation is so insignificant that it is undetectable.
10. **The best answer is (3).** As a general rule, when the temperature of a substance increases, its density decreases. This is supported by the graph; as the temperature scale increases from left to right, the curve moves from higher to lower density.
11. **The best answer is (1).** Air pressure decreases as altitude increases. The eardrum is a thin piece of tissue surrounded by fluid that detects the compression and decompression of sounds waves in air or water. Eardrums are sensitive to air pressure fluctuations because air within the middle ear may remain at the original pressure as the external air pressure changes.

12. **The best answer is (2).** Freezing is an example of phase change, which is a physical (not chemical) change. In phase change, mass is conserved, meaning it does not change. (Density and volume, however, do change.)

13. **The best answer is (3).** Error is reduced in the results of experimentation when the sample size (in this case, how many mice are observed) is increased. When sample size is too small, a few unusual subjects can distort the trends in the data.

14. **The best answer is (4).** Fuses are small safety devices through which electric current may pass only when the current is below a designed limit. When current reaches the limit, the metal wire inside the fuse melts and the circuit is broken. Homes are fitted with fuses or circuit breakers to ensure that only a safe amount of electricity can pass through the wires inside the walls. This helps prevent electric shock and fire. It is never a good decision to alter the capacity of fuses that were specifically selected by an electrician for a particular installation.

15. **The best answer is (4).** Tanning is the skin's reaction to damage caused by UV rays. Sunscreen is a lotion that deflects and absorbs some of the UV rays before they penetrate the skin. Sun tanning oil, on the other hand, may not contain any sunscreen and is designed to maximize the tanning effects of sun exposure.

16. **The best answer is (5).** The data point for 1990 is just below 60, and the data point for 1996 is just above 60. None of the other answer choices is supported by the graph.

17. **The best answer is (3).** This question requires careful reading. The question stem indicates that somatic cells contain 23 chromosomes. Gametes contain double this amount, or 46. In the next sentence, gametes are identified as diploid cells. Haploid cells have half the chromosomes of diploid cells: $46 \div 2 = 23$.

18. **The best answer is (2).** Although the soil under the tree is described as "rich," the seed planted in it did not grow as well as the seed planted in the grassland. The major factor that affects plant growth, and which is different between the two locations, would be sun exposure. Large trees prevent much direct sunlight from reaching the ground below them, but grasslands are largely treeless landscapes.

19. **The best answer is (3).** The question stem tells you that stress can decrease the effectiveness of the immune system, the body system that fights infection. Only answer choice (3) involves infection.

20. **The best answer is (1).** Alaska is located in and near the arctic. Regions as far north as Alaska experience harsh winters and long periods of little or no sunlight during the day.

21. **The best answer is (2).** *Condensation* is the process by which water vapor *condenses* into a liquid, often because of decreased temperature. In the case of the cold glass of lemonade, when warmer water vapor makes contact with the cold glass, some of it condenses into water droplets that adhere to the glass.

22. **The best answer is (1).** Particles with opposite electric charges attract one another. Therefore, the positively charged ion will be attracted to the negatively charged source of the electric field.

23. **The best answer is (3).** Mitosis is the process of ordinary cell division. (Meiosis is reproductive cell division.) A tumor grows as its population of cells increases through division.

24. **The best answer is (2).** These signs are standard warning signs used throughout the United States. Sign 1 means "poison," sign 2 means "flammable," sign 3 means "explosive," sign 4 means "radiation," and sign 5 means "biohazard." Even if you did not know the meaning of the signs beforehand, you can tell from the large flame that sign 2 is warning of a risk of fire.

25. **The best answer is (4).** The question asks which answer choice would not be an adaptation of nocturnal animals—those awake at night. Answer choice (4) describes an adaptation to the sun, which would not be important to animals that are not active and that remain hidden during the day.

26. **The best answer is (4).** This answer choice describes sonar, or "sound navigation and ranging," the technology that uses sound to detect objects and vessels in the water long distances from a ship. You've probably heard the distinct "ping" of active sonar in a submarine movie. Sounds waves emitted from a sonar system travel through the water (which is actually a better medium for sound than air is) and bounce off objects, sending sound waves back to the sonar device. The results are interpreted by a computer and displayed as a map (today, a very detailed one) showing objects, their depths, and their ranges. This technology would be the superior choice for locating icebergs. It doesn't rely on possibly outdated maps, the advice of other ships, or daylight to function.

27. **The best answer is (1).** Creating conservation parks assures that human activity will have minimal effect on the tigers. Each of the other answer choices violates one of the five factors given in the information.

28. **The best answer is (2).** The environmental damage was the result of introducing rabbits into an area where they had not existed before. The ecosystem could not support the rapidly increasing population of rabbits.

29. **The best answer is (1).** In general, humans cannot conduct economic activity (and thus pollute) in wetlands. These areas are normally drained or filled in before buildings can go up or farm fields can be planted. Therefore, the major threat the Houston toad faces is habitat destruction.

30. **The best answer is (2).** The endocrine system is the system of glands and other organs responsible for all the chemical signals, or hormones, in the body. The main hormone associated with fear responses is adrenaline, sometimes called epinephrine. This hormone is released by the adrenal gland into the bloodstream and has many effects on the various organs of the body.

31. **The best answer is (3).** The force of gravity affects the two blocks equally. They will hit the ground at nearly the same time. The only factor affecting their rate of fall is air resistance, which depends on surface area. The difference in surface area between the two blocks is unlikely to be significant, however, and therefore is insignificant to the rate of fall.

32. **The best answer is (3).** The chart indicates that hind toes are an adaptation for climbing rough vertical surfaces, which describes tree trunks.

33. **The best answer is (3).** The normal fertilizer shows a steady increase in leaf size over time. The enhanced fertilizer begins by increasing the leaf size faster than the normal fertilizer does, but this effect eventually levels off to where leaf size barely increases over days six through nine. Using only the normal fertilizer will render 4-cm-long leaves in the shortest period of time.

34. **The best answer is (1).** Dieticians are experts in human foods and nutrition. They would also recommend exercise as a step toward better health.

35. **The best answer is (5).** The seasons are determined by the tilt of the earth, which affects the angle at which light and heat energy from the sun strikes the different parts of the earth. In the United States, which lies in the Northern Hemisphere, winter comes when the Northern Hemisphere is tilted away from the sun. At that time, the Southern Hemisphere is tilted toward the sun, and that hemisphere experiences summer. Therefore, the seasons in the two hemispheres (Northern and Southern) can be described as opposites of each other at any given time. The graph shows that the months Americans know as winter months are the hottest months in the certain city in Australia. November, December, January, and February are the summer months there.

36. **The best answer is (3).** Objects float in water when they are less dense than water. Ice is less dense than water, as is oil and dry wood, for example.

37. **The best answer is (4).** This answer choice includes two amounts that are half the original amounts found in the information in the box. In each of the other answer choices, only one amount is half its original amount.

38. **The best answer is (2).** The diagram shows the extent of the shadow the Earth casts on the moon. During a total lunar eclipse, no sunlight reaches the moon because the moon is entirely blocked from sun exposure by the Earth.

39. **The best answer is (2).** Plants all have different water, light, soil, and climate requirements. Only answer choice (2) identifies one of these requirements. Answer choice (1) is wrong because heavily polluted soil would not let either of the plants flourish. Answer choice (3) is wrong because the sunlight reaching one plant is the same as the sunlight reaching the other. Answer choice (4) is wrong because the days the plants are watered would not affect the long-term growth of the plants. Answer choice (5) is wrong because the impact of the insects is unspecified; in fact, most insects are beneficial to gardens.

40. **The best answer is (1).** Red, yellow, and blue are the primary colors, meaning the fundamental colors on which all other colors are based. If blue and yellow light are absorbed by an object, then only red light is reflected.

41. **The best answer is (3).** The information before the question indicates that the fat that makes up the camel's hump is consumed when food and water are scarce, exactly the conditions one would expect during a "long, strenuous journey across the desert." With some of the fat being consumed during the journey, the camel's hump would be "not as full as before," as answer choice (3) indicates.

42. **The best answer is (1).** Volcanic eruptions release large concentrations of different gases into the atmosphere. The simulation produces carbon dioxide bubbles. Therefore, answer choice (1) is correct. The other answer choices are incorrect because they do not describe both "eruptions."

43. **The best answer is (3).** "Dairy products" means "milk products." Among the answer choices, only eggs are not a milk product.

44. **The best answer is (2).** The question asks for the food component with the greatest mass. Remember that the values in the table have two different units, grams and milligrams. Divide milligrams by 1,000 or shift the decimal point three places to the left to convert milligrams to grams. Clearly, 300 grams is the largest value in the table.

45. **The best answer is (3).** All the answer choices describe physical changes to the solution. When a solute is completely dissolved in a solvent, the solute is dispersed on the molecular level. Therefore, filtering would be impractical or impossible. Eliminate answer choice (1). Answer choices (2) and (5) would clearly have no effect on extracting the solute. Answer choice (4) is contradictory: condensation and evaporation are opposite actions. Only answer choice (3) is a means to remove the solvent, leaving the solute behind.

46. **The best answer is (3).** Magnetism is a property of certain metals and not relevant to surfing. Buoyancy keeps the board afloat. Gravity keeps the water and the surfer on the earth. Friction keeps the surfer from sliding off the board. Energy is transferred all the time in any situation.

47. **The best answer is (2).** There are four quarts in a gallon. Paul needs 1.25 gallons. Convert what Paul needs to quarts, using a proportion:

$$\frac{4\text{ qt}}{1\text{ gal}} = \frac{9x\text{ qt}}{1.25\text{ gal}}$$

(Cross-multiply)

$4 \times 1.25 = x$

$5 = x$

Therefore, Paul needs 5 quarts of oil.

48. **The best answer is (2).** Begin by eliminating answer choices (4) and (5) because they have only one chromosome; remember that the chromosome from the male fuses with the chromosome from the female. Of the three remaining answer choices, only XY is possible as the genotype for the male because every male can pass on X or Y to his offspring. (As an aside, females have the genotype XX.)

49. **The best answer is (4).** Gravity is the force that causes objects to fall to Earth. The moon also has gravity, but because the moon is much less massive than Earth, its gravitational force is much less, too (one sixth of Earth's, in fact). This means that any object above the surface of the moon would take much longer to land than it would on Earth. In his spacesuit, Sheppard could manage only a weak swing, yet he hit the ball hundreds of yards (a substantial golf shot by any measure).

50. **The best answer is (5).** The information before the question indicates that a hurricane comprises clouds, winds, and thunderstorms. If a hurricane was approaching, you would be able to see the characteristic dark sky of storm clouds in the distance. None of the other answer choices are supported by the information given.

Mathematics Answers and Explanations

Part I

1. **The correct answer is (5).** This question asks for the difference in a real amount (not a percentage) of interest. Without knowing the actual amount of Mark's loan, you cannot determine the interest he paid. Therefore, there is not enough information to answer this question.

2. **The correct answer is 11.** Solve the equation for x, as follows:

   $2x - 9 = 13$

   Add 9 to both sides.

   $2x = 22$

   Divide both sides by 2.

   $x = 11$

3. **The correct answer is (2).** Because the problem asks "approximately how much," begin by rounding the two prices: $\$15.10 \approx \$15$ and $\$24.95 \approx \$25$. Next, calculate the sum of the amount the customer would save on the T-shirt and the shorts. Use proportions to calculate 20% of the prices.

   Savings on T-shirt (represented by the variable a):

   $$\frac{20}{100} = \frac{a}{15}$$

   (Cross-multiply)

   $100a = 300$

   Divide both sides by 100.

   $a = 3$

   Savings on shorts (represented by the variable b):

   $$\frac{20}{100} = \frac{b}{25}$$

   (Cross-multiply)

   $100b = 500$

   Divide both sides by 100.

   $b = 5$

   Therefore, the total savings is $a + b = 3 + 5 = 8$.

4. **The correct answer is (1).** The question says "based on the line of best fit," so ignore the individual data points. Imagine the line extending beyond the area of the graph. When the line reaches 7 on the vertical axis, it will be closer to 500 than any of the other answer choices that lie in the domain of the graph.

5. **The correct answer is (1).** When the best-fit line crosses the one-year gridline, it has the value of about 50 words per minute. Therefore, a proofreader with less than one year of experience would be predicted to read fewer than 100 words per minute.

6. **The correct answer is (3).** First determine the midpoint of 57 and 65. Do this by counting or by calculating the average.

   Counting: Count 8 from 57 to 65. Take half of 8, which is 4, and count back that amount: 61.

   Average: $\frac{57 + 65}{2} = \frac{122}{2} = 61$

   Next, calculate the difference of 72 and 61: 72 – 61 = 11.

7. **The correct answer is (3).** Set up an equation for the area of a triangle:

   $\frac{1}{2} \times \text{base length} \times \text{height} = 25$

   Because you are given that the height (FG) is half the base length (FH), you can use one variable for the base length.

   $\frac{1}{2} \times b \times \left(\frac{1}{2}b\right) = 25$

   Simplify.

   $\frac{1}{4}b^2 = 25$

   $b^2 = 100$

   $b = 10$

   From the question, you know that the height (FG) is half of this base, so the answer is 5.

8. **The correct answer is (4).** Set up an equation to calculate the average. Use variables to represent the unknown ages of the two girls.

   $\frac{(8 + 8 + 9 + 10 + 11 + a + b)}{7} = 9$

   Simplify, and then multiply both sides by 7.

   $46 + a + b = 63$

   Subtract 46 from both sides.

   $a + b = 17$

   Therefore, you must choose the answer choice that is a pair of numbers which sums 17. Among the answer choices, only 11 and 6 sum 17.

9. **The correct answer is (3).** Set up a proportion to calculate the value of 800 USD in GBP.

   $\frac{1.86 \text{ dollars}}{1 \text{ pound}} = \frac{800 \text{ dollars}}{x \text{ pounds}}$

(Cross-multiply)

$800 = 1.86x$

Divide both sides by 1.86.

$430.10 = x$

10. **The correct answer is (3).** Set up a proportion to calculate the value of 47 GBP in USD. Use the conversion factor of 1:1.86 because it is the simplest of the two factors given in the table.

$$\frac{1.86 \text{ dollars}}{1 \text{ pound}} = \frac{x \text{ dollars}}{47 \text{ pounds}}$$

(Cross-multiply)

$x = 47 \times 1.86$

$x = 87.42$ or approximately 90

11. **The correct answer is 42.** Divide the number of pizzas by the number of pizzas in each box to determine the number of boxes: $502 \div 12 = 42$.

12. **The correct answer is (5).** The area formula for a cube is s^3, where s is the length of one edge of the cube: $s^3 = s \times s \times s = 8.5 \times 8.5 \times 8.5 = 614.125$.

    Alternatively, you can use the calculator: Enter 8.5, press the exponent key (X^y), enter 3, and then press the equals key (=).

13. **The correct answer is (5).** Calculate the area of the desk. The area formula for a rectangle is length times width: $39 \times 78 = 3{,}042$.

14. **The correct answer is (5).** Simplify the expression following the order of operations.

    $-6(-x + 4) - 2(x - 3)$

    Perform the multiplication, being careful about sign change.

    $-6 \times -x + -6 \times 4 - 2 \times x - 2 \times -3$

    $6x - 24 - 2x + 6$

    Combine like terms.

    $4x - 18$

15. **The correct answer is (3).** Remember that the formula for circumference of a circle is pi times diameter. Pi is approximately 3.14, or slightly greater than 3. Approximate pi times 13:

    $3 \times 13 = 39$.

    Therefore, the closest approximation among the answer choices is 41.

16. **The correct answer is**

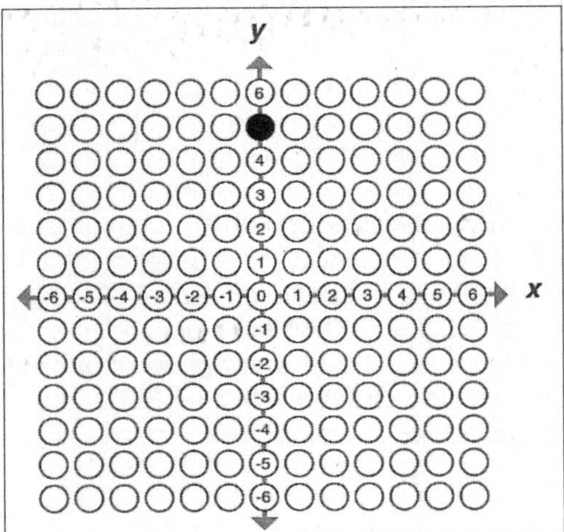

Remember that the y-intercept of a line is the y-value of the line where it intersects the y-axis. In the standard slope-intercept form of a linear equation, $y = mx + b$, m is the slope of the line and b is the y-intercept. Set the given equation in slope-intercept form and determine b: $3x + y = 5$ is equivalent to $y = -3x + 5$. Therefore, b (the y-intercept) is 5. Fill in the bubble for the point (0,5).

17. **The correct answer is (4).** Begin by calculating total monthly expenses. Remember that the daily $10 expense must be multiplied by 30 (the assumed number of days in a month).

$1{,}500 + 3{,}000 + (10 \times 30)$
$= 1{,}500 + 3{,}000 + 300 = 4{,}800$

The proportion of payroll expenses (3,000) to total expenses (4,800) can be expressed as $\frac{3{,}000}{4{,}800}$. Simplify the fraction. The greatest common factor of 3,000 and 4,800 is 600. Divide the numerator and the denominator by 600: 5/8.

18. **The correct answer is 17.** Simplify the expression following the order of operations.

$2(201 + 13 - 49) \div 15 - 5$

Perform operations in parentheses first.

$= 2(165) \div 15 - 5$

Multiply.

$= 330 \div 15 - 5$

Divide.

$= 22 - 5$

Subtract.

$= 17$

Alternatively, you can enter the whole expression into the calculator as written; however, be very careful because the more operations you enter at once, the greater your chance of making a mistake.

19. **The correct answer is (5).** Set up an equation for the total cost (C) of the event based on the flat fee of $450 and the per-guest fee of $18: $C = 450 + 18g$, where g is the number of guests. If 200 people are attending, substitute 200 for g and compute:

    $C = 450 + 18 \times 200$

    $C = 450 + 3{,}600$

    $C = 4{,}050$

20. **The correct answer is (2).** Remember that scientific notation is the expression of a number as a number between 1 and 10 times a power of 10. Therefore, you can eliminate answer choices (4) and (5) because 28.6 is not between 1 and 10. Note that 2.86 is the product of 2.2 and 1.3. The number 2.2 is 2,200 with the decimal point shifted 3 places to the left. The number 1.3 is the number 13,000 with the decimal point shifted 4 places to the left. Therefore, scientific notation of the product of 2,200 and 13,000 is the product of 2.2 and 1.3 times 10 to the power of 3 plus 4:

    $2.2 \times 1.3 \times 10^{(3+4)} =$

    2.86×10^7

21. **The correct answer is (5).** The area of a rectangle is length times width: $4s \times 3s = 12s^2$.

22. **The correct answer is (1).** The table gives approximate walking times in minutes. Determine the value at the intersection of the column CAF and the row POL (or the row CAF and the column POL).

23. **The correct answer is (4).** Calculate the sum of the walking time from BUS to CFM and the walking time from CFM to ZOO: 13 + 21 = 34.

24. **The correct answer is (3).** Count the number of attractions whose walking time from WAT is 15 minutes or less. Remember not to include the value at the intersection of the WAT row and the WAT column. Only POL, YOU, and ZOO are within 15 minutes of walking from WAT.

25. **The correct answer is (4).** Calculate the difference between the round-trip riding time and the round-trip walking time. The one-way walking time between HOS and ZOO is 22; therefore, the round-trip walking time is 44. The one-way riding time is 9 minutes; therefore, the round-trip riding time is 18. Time saved is the difference between 44 and 18: 44 – 18 = 26.

Part II

26. **The correct answer is (2).** The word “withdraws” means “takes out.” Therefore, you must subtract the amount withdrawn from the starting amount to calculate the amount remaining: 513 – 225.

27. **The correct answer is (2).** If two angles of a triangle each measure 60 degrees, then the third angle of the triangle must also measure 60 degrees because the sum of the angle measures of a triangle is 180 degrees. If all angles of a triangle are equal, then the triangle is equilateral. Equilateral triangles also have equal side lengths; therefore, the length of the third side, like the lengths of the other two sides, is 4.

28. **The correct answer is (3).** The thousands place is 4 places left of the decimal point. (Think “ones, tens, hundreds, thousands…”) To round to the nearest thousand, see whether the hundreds digit is less than 5 or greater than or equal to 5. Because the hundreds digit of 127,523 is 5, you round the thousands digit up to 8: 128,000.

29. **The correct answer is (3).** The number line shows an open point on –3 and a line extending indefinitely to the left. (Eliminate the answer choices with positive 3: 4 and 5) The open point means that the solution set does not include –3. Therefore, you may eliminate the "greater than or equal to" and "less than or equal to" choices: 2 and 4. The line extended to the left means "less than," so answer choice (3) is correct.

30. **The correct answer is 2.7 or 2.70 or 2.700.** The simplest way to calculate 15% of a number is to calculate the sum of 10% of the number and 5% of the number. (5% is half of 10%.)

    10% of \$18.00: $\frac{10}{100} = \frac{x}{18}$

    (Cross-multiply)

    $100x = 180$

    $x = 1.8$ (You could also have gotten this answer by simply shifting the decimal point in 18.00 one place to the left.)

    5% of \$18.00 (Half of 10%): $1.8 \div 2 = 0.9$

    Add the two percentages together: $1.8 + 0.9 = 2.7$

31. **The correct answer is**

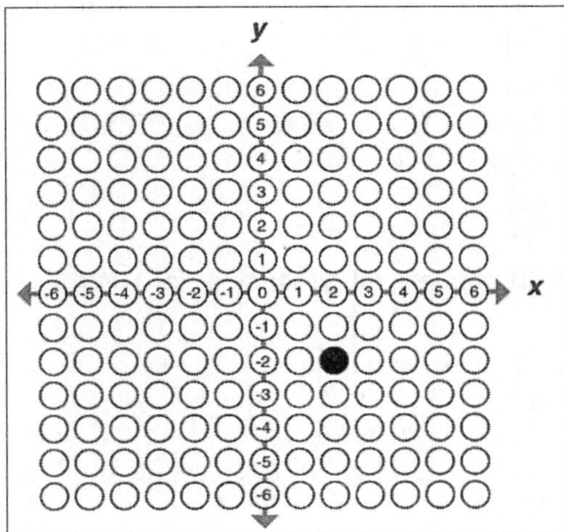

The center of the circle is the point that is an equal distance from all points on the circle. The easiest way to locate the center is to determine which point has the *x* value exactly halfway between the least and greatest *x* values on the circle and the *y* value exactly halfway between the least and greatest *y* values on the circle. In this circle, the least *x* value is –2 and the greatest *x* value is 6. Therefore, the diameter is 8 (6 – –2 = 8). Halfway across the circle horizontally has the *x* value of 2 (4 away from –2 and 6). The least *y* value of the circle is –6 and the greatest *y* value is 2. (We already know that the diameter is 8.) Therefore, the *y* value of the center of the circle is 4 down from 2 or 4 up from –6 (–2). The center point is (2,–2).

32. **The correct answer is (4).** Begin by determining how many hours the factory operates during the workday. Remember to account for the 12-hour clock.

    The time from 9 a.m. to 12 p.m. is $12 - 9 = 3$ hours. The time from 12 p.m. to 6:45 p.m. is 6 hours 45 minutes. Therefore, there are 3 hours + 6 hours 45 minutes = 9 hours 45 minutes between the start and the end of the workday.

    Next, subtract the lunch period. The time from 12:30 p.m. to 1:15 p.m. is 45 minutes. Therefore, the total working time during the day is 9 hours 45 minutes – 45 minutes = 9 hours.

    If 400 cases are made per hour, multiply 400 by the number of hours to calculate the total number of cases produced: $400 \times 9 = 3{,}600$.

33. **The correct answer is (3).** Solve the equation for n.

    $$\frac{(14 - n)}{n} \times 8.5 = 8.5$$

    Divide both sides by 8.5.

    $$\frac{(14 - n)}{n} = 1$$

    Multiply both sides by n.

    $14 - n = n$

    Add n to both sides.

    $14 = 2n$

    Divide both sides by 2.

    $7 = n$

34. **The correct answer is (3).** Substitute 30, the largest dimension, for x in the formula and solve for C:

    $$C = 5 + \frac{30^2}{100}$$

    $$C = 5 + \frac{900}{100}$$

    $C = 5 + 9$

    $C = 14$

35. **The correct answer is (3).** First locate 125 on the horizontal axis. This is halfway between the 100 and 150 gridlines. Next, approximate the height of the line at the point: about \$100.

36. **The correct answer is (1).** This question requires you to extrapolate information outside the domain of the graph from trends observed within the domain of the graph. The point on the line for 400 burritos would be just off the graph, so look at the trends before that point. Because the graph is a line with constant positive slope, you can assume that profit increases proportionately with an increase in burritos sold. Selling 350 burritos generates slightly more than \$1,200 in profit. Between 300 and 350, the profit increases by more than 200. You can assume this same increase will occur between 350 and 400. The sum of slightly more than 1,200 and slightly more than 200 is best estimated as 1,500.

37. **The correct answer is (3).** You are given that angle ACB measures 115°. This angle and angle DCE are vertical angles; therefore, angle DCE also measures 115°. Recall than the sum of all the angles formed by two intersecting lines is 360°:

$115 + 115 + r + s = 360$

$230 + r + s = 360$

$r + s = 130$

38. **The correct answer is (4).** This question assesses your estimating skills. Notice that 680 and 10.39 are very close to round numbers that are easy to use in calculations: 680 is about 700 and 10.39 is about 10: $700 \times 10 = 7{,}000$.

39. **The correct answer is (2).** This question requires you to apply the 20% discount to the lowest price of $50. There are two ways to approach this percentage problem: (1) finding the amount of the discount and subtracting it from the sale price, or (2) calculating the percentage that would remain after the discount first.

Method 1: $\frac{20}{100} = \frac{x}{50}$

Cross-multiply and divide.

$100x = 1{,}000$

$x = 10$

Subtract the discount amount, $10, from the sale price, $50, to determine the closeout price: $50 - 10 = 40$.

Method 2: When 20% is taken away, that means that 100% – 20% = 80% remains.

Calculate 80% of the sale price: $\frac{80}{100} = \frac{x}{50}$ Cross-multiply and divide.

$100x = 4{,}000$

$x = 40$ [the closeout price]

40. **The correct answer is (1).** If 6 peppers go in each bag, the total number of peppers in all the bags is 6 times the number of bags, or $6j$. The 2 peppers left over must be added to this total to equal the total number of peppers harvested.

41. **The correct answer is (4).** Remember that any number multiplied by 0 equals 0. Therefore, the solution set to this equation includes the values of x that would make one quantity or the other equal 0:

$-9 + 9 = 0$, so -9 is one solution.

$5 - 5 = 0$, so 5 is one solution.

42. **The correct answer is (2).** This question requires careful reading. The variable x represents the weight Philip lost. Therefore, his new weight is the original weight, 225 pounds, minus the weight he lost, x.

43. **The correct answer is (2).** Calculate the difference between the cost of the car and the amount Joel has saved: $2{,}500 - 1{,}050 = 1{,}450$.

44. **The correct answer is (3).** To answer this question, you must be careful to remember that one haul-away of garbage is included in the initial cost of $75. This means Briana will need to buy 2 additional haul-aways, which cost $50 each. Total cost $= 75 + 2 \times 50 = 75 + 100 = 175$.

45. **The correct answer is (4).** The key phrase is the information given before the question—"increases at a constant rate." On the graph, this would be represented by a straight line. Next, the information says that Sarah's speed peaks and then begins decreasing at the same rate as it increased. This means there will be a cusp (sharp point) at the peak of the graph and a second segment with opposite (negative) slope of the first segment.

46. **The correct answer is (2).** The key word in this question is "proportional." To solve for the paving cost of the larger patio, set up a proportion with the area and paving cost of the smaller patio:

    Begin by computing the areas of the patios, as follows:

    Small patio: $4 \times 5 = 20$

    Large patio: $8 \times 9 = 72$

    Now set up the proportion:

    $$\frac{20}{100} = \frac{72}{x}$$

    This arrangement of the proportion isn't among the answer choices, so you should check to see if you can rewrite in an equivalent way.

    The simplest change is to set the top terms in proportion to the bottom terms:

    $$\frac{20}{72} = \frac{100}{x}$$

47. **The correct answer is (1).** It is given that x represents the average monthly pay of a nonsupervisor. There are 23 nonsupervisors, so the total payroll of nonsupervisors is found by multiplying 23 by x. Supervisors earn an average of \$940 more per month than nonsupervisors, so their average monthly earnings can be expressed as x + \$940. There are 4 supervisors, so the total payroll of supervisors is found by multiplying 4 by the quantity (x + \$940). Therefore, the total payroll is $P = 4(x + 940) + 23x$

48. **The correct answer is (4).** Recall that the area formula for a square is $A = s^2$. Therefore, $125 = s^2$ and $\sqrt{125} = s$. You must estimate the square root of 125. Use the guess-and-check method. Begin with a round number, such as 10, for example.

    $10^2 = 100$

    Check higher.

    $11^2 = 121$

    This is just less than 125, but the answer choices show a pair of integers the square root must fall between. Check higher.

    $12^2 = 144$.

    This is greater than 125, so the square root of 125 is between 11 and 12.

49. **The correct answer is (3).** Recall that the slope is defined as the change in y value divided by the change in x value. You can subtract the two pairs of values in either order and get the same result.

Order #1:

$$\frac{(3 - 1)}{(-4 - 2)} = \frac{2}{-6} = -\frac{1}{3}$$

Order #2:

$$\frac{(1 - 3)}{(2 - -4)} = \frac{-2}{6} = -\frac{1}{3}$$

50. **The correct answer is (3).** Set up a proportion using the map distance between Runyan and Marshall and the scale of the map:

$$\frac{1 \text{ inch}}{80 \text{ miles}} = \frac{4.25 \text{ inches}}{x \text{ miles}}$$

(Cross-multiply)

$80(4.25) = x$

$340 = x$

CHAPTER FIFTY-ONE

Practice Test 2 with Answers and Explanations

This chapter includes a full-length, simulated GED practice test that should help you evaluate your progress in preparing for the GED. Make an honest effort to answer each question, then review the explanations that follow.

There are five separate sections on this test, including

- Language Arts, Writing
- Language Arts, Reading
- Social Studies
- Science
- Mathematics, Part I and Part II

Work on only one section at a time, and make every attempt to complete each section in the time allowed for that particular section. Carefully mark only one answer on your answer sheet for each question.

Mark your answers on the answer sheets on the following pages. Then compare your answers to the answers and explanations at the end of this chapter. Be sure to read through the explanations thoroughly. Identify and review topics you've consistently struggled with.

Answer Sheets

Language Arts, Writing Test

1. ① ② ③ ④ ⑤
2. ① ② ③ ④ ⑤
3. ① ② ③ ④ ⑤
4. ① ② ③ ④ ⑤
5. ① ② ③ ④ ⑤
6. ① ② ③ ④ ⑤
7. ① ② ③ ④ ⑤
8. ① ② ③ ④ ⑤
9. ① ② ③ ④ ⑤
10. ① ② ③ ④ ⑤
11. ① ② ③ ④ ⑤
12. ① ② ③ ④ ⑤
13. ① ② ③ ④ ⑤
14. ① ② ③ ④ ⑤
15. ① ② ③ ④ ⑤
16. ① ② ③ ④ ⑤
17. ① ② ③ ④ ⑤
18. ① ② ③ ④ ⑤
19. ① ② ③ ④ ⑤
20. ① ② ③ ④ ⑤
21. ① ② ③ ④ ⑤
22. ① ② ③ ④ ⑤
23. ① ② ③ ④ ⑤
24. ① ② ③ ④ ⑤
25. ① ② ③ ④ ⑤
26. ① ② ③ ④ ⑤
27. ① ② ③ ④ ⑤
28. ① ② ③ ④ ⑤
29. ① ② ③ ④ ⑤
30. ① ② ③ ④ ⑤
31. ① ② ③ ④ ⑤
32. ① ② ③ ④ ⑤
33. ① ② ③ ④ ⑤
34. ① ② ③ ④ ⑤
35. ① ② ③ ④ ⑤
36. ① ② ③ ④ ⑤
37. ① ② ③ ④ ⑤
38. ① ② ③ ④ ⑤
39. ① ② ③ ④ ⑤
40. ① ② ③ ④ ⑤
41. ① ② ③ ④ ⑤
42. ① ② ③ ④ ⑤
43. ① ② ③ ④ ⑤
44. ① ② ③ ④ ⑤
45. ① ② ③ ④ ⑤
46. ① ② ③ ④ ⑤
47. ① ② ③ ④ ⑤
48. ① ② ③ ④ ⑤
49. ① ② ③ ④ ⑤
50. ① ② ③ ④ ⑤

Language Arts, Reading Test

1. ① ② ③ ④ ⑤
2. ① ② ③ ④ ⑤
3. ① ② ③ ④ ⑤
4. ① ② ③ ④ ⑤
5. ① ② ③ ④ ⑤
6. ① ② ③ ④ ⑤
7. ① ② ③ ④ ⑤
8. ① ② ③ ④ ⑤
9. ① ② ③ ④ ⑤
10. ① ② ③ ④ ⑤
11. ① ② ③ ④ ⑤
12. ① ② ③ ④ ⑤
13. ① ② ③ ④ ⑤
14. ① ② ③ ④ ⑤
15. ① ② ③ ④ ⑤
16. ① ② ③ ④ ⑤
17. ① ② ③ ④ ⑤
18. ① ② ③ ④ ⑤
19. ① ② ③ ④ ⑤
20. ① ② ③ ④ ⑤
21. ① ② ③ ④ ⑤
22. ① ② ③ ④ ⑤
23. ① ② ③ ④ ⑤
24. ① ② ③ ④ ⑤
25. ① ② ③ ④ ⑤
26. ① ② ③ ④ ⑤
27. ① ② ③ ④ ⑤
28. ① ② ③ ④ ⑤
29. ① ② ③ ④ ⑤
30. ① ② ③ ④ ⑤
31. ① ② ③ ④ ⑤
32. ① ② ③ ④ ⑤
33. ① ② ③ ④ ⑤
34. ① ② ③ ④ ⑤
35. ① ② ③ ④ ⑤
36. ① ② ③ ④ ⑤
37. ① ② ③ ④ ⑤
38. ① ② ③ ④ ⑤
39. ① ② ③ ④ ⑤
40. ① ② ③ ④ ⑤

Social Studies Test

1. ① ② ③ ④ ⑤
2. ① ② ③ ④ ⑤
3. ① ② ③ ④ ⑤
4. ① ② ③ ④ ⑤
5. ① ② ③ ④ ⑤
6. ① ② ③ ④ ⑤
7. ① ② ③ ④ ⑤
8. ① ② ③ ④ ⑤
9. ① ② ③ ④ ⑤
10. ① ② ③ ④ ⑤
11. ① ② ③ ④ ⑤
12. ① ② ③ ④ ⑤
13. ① ② ③ ④ ⑤
14. ① ② ③ ④ ⑤
15. ① ② ③ ④ ⑤
16. ① ② ③ ④ ⑤
17. ① ② ③ ④ ⑤
18. ① ② ③ ④ ⑤
19. ① ② ③ ④ ⑤
20. ① ② ③ ④ ⑤
21. ① ② ③ ④ ⑤
22. ① ② ③ ④ ⑤
23. ① ② ③ ④ ⑤
24. ① ② ③ ④ ⑤
25. ① ② ③ ④ ⑤
26. ① ② ③ ④ ⑤
27. ① ② ③ ④ ⑤
28. ① ② ③ ④ ⑤
29. ① ② ③ ④ ⑤
30. ① ② ③ ④ ⑤
31. ① ② ③ ④ ⑤
32. ① ② ③ ④ ⑤
33. ① ② ③ ④ ⑤
34. ① ② ③ ④ ⑤
35. ① ② ③ ④ ⑤
36. ① ② ③ ④ ⑤
37. ① ② ③ ④ ⑤
38. ① ② ③ ④ ⑤
39. ① ② ③ ④ ⑤
40. ① ② ③ ④ ⑤
41. ① ② ③ ④ ⑤
42. ① ② ③ ④ ⑤
43. ① ② ③ ④ ⑤
44. ① ② ③ ④ ⑤
45. ① ② ③ ④ ⑤
46. ① ② ③ ④ ⑤
47. ① ② ③ ④ ⑤
48. ① ② ③ ④ ⑤
49. ① ② ③ ④ ⑤
50. ① ② ③ ④ ⑤

Science Test

1. ① ② ③ ④ ⑤
2. ① ② ③ ④ ⑤
3. ① ② ③ ④ ⑤
4. ① ② ③ ④ ⑤
5. ① ② ③ ④ ⑤
6. ① ② ③ ④ ⑤
7. ① ② ③ ④ ⑤
8. ① ② ③ ④ ⑤
9. ① ② ③ ④ ⑤
10. ① ② ③ ④ ⑤
11. ① ② ③ ④ ⑤
12. ① ② ③ ④ ⑤
13. ① ② ③ ④ ⑤
14. ① ② ③ ④ ⑤
15. ① ② ③ ④ ⑤
16. ① ② ③ ④ ⑤
17. ① ② ③ ④ ⑤
18. ① ② ③ ④ ⑤
19. ① ② ③ ④ ⑤
20. ① ② ③ ④ ⑤
21. ① ② ③ ④ ⑤
22. ① ② ③ ④ ⑤
23. ① ② ③ ④ ⑤
24. ① ② ③ ④ ⑤
25. ① ② ③ ④ ⑤
26. ① ② ③ ④ ⑤
27. ① ② ③ ④ ⑤
28. ① ② ③ ④ ⑤
29. ① ② ③ ④ ⑤
30. ① ② ③ ④ ⑤
31. ① ② ③ ④ ⑤
32. ① ② ③ ④ ⑤
33. ① ② ③ ④ ⑤
34. ① ② ③ ④ ⑤
35. ① ② ③ ④ ⑤
36. ① ② ③ ④ ⑤
37. ① ② ③ ④ ⑤
38. ① ② ③ ④ ⑤
39. ① ② ③ ④ ⑤
40. ① ② ③ ④ ⑤
41. ① ② ③ ④ ⑤
42. ① ② ③ ④ ⑤
43. ① ② ③ ④ ⑤
44. ① ② ③ ④ ⑤
45. ① ② ③ ④ ⑤
46. ① ② ③ ④ ⑤
47. ① ② ③ ④ ⑤
48. ① ② ③ ④ ⑤
49. ① ② ③ ④ ⑤
50. ① ② ③ ④ ⑤

Mathematics Test

1. ① ② ③ ④ ⑤
2. ① ② ③ ④ ⑤
3. ① ② ③ ④ ⑤
4. ① ② ③ ④ ⑤
5. ① ② ③ ④ ⑤
6.

7. ① ② ③ ④ ⑤
8. ① ② ③ ④ ⑤
9.

10. ① ② ③ ④ ⑤
11. ① ② ③ ④ ⑤
12.

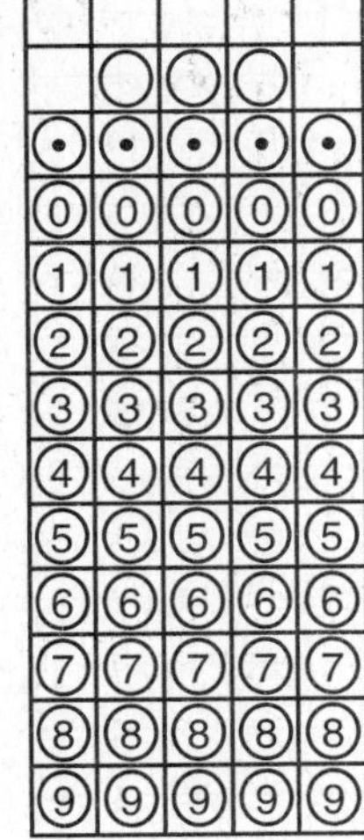

13. ① ② ③ ④ ⑤
14. ① ② ③ ④ ⑤
15. ① ② ③ ④ ⑤
16.

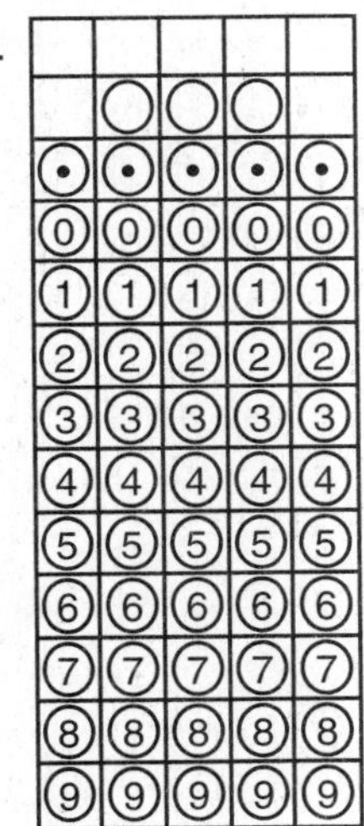

17. ① ② ③ ④ ⑤
18. ① ② ③ ④ ⑤
19. ① ② ③ ④ ⑤
20. ① ② ③ ④ ⑤
21. ① ② ③ ④ ⑤
22. ① ② ③ ④ ⑤
23. ① ② ③ ④ ⑤
24. ① ② ③ ④ ⑤
25.

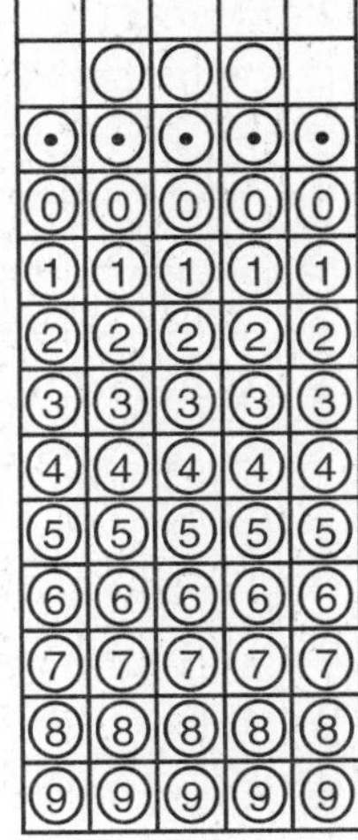

26. ① ② ③ ④ ⑤
27. ① ② ③ ④ ⑤
28. ① ② ③ ④ ⑤
29.

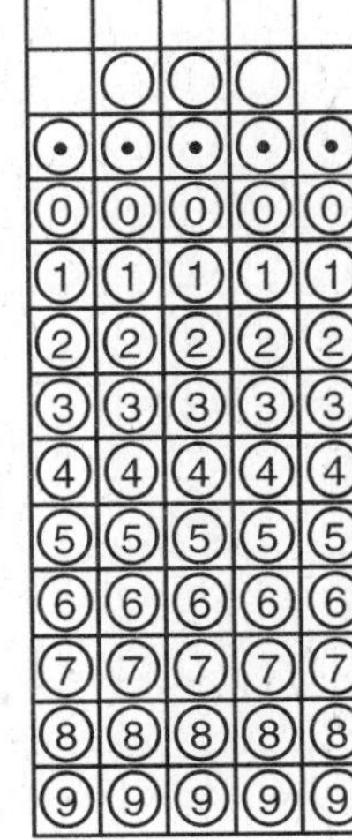

30. ① ② ③ ④ ⑤
31. ① ② ③ ④ ⑤
32. ① ② ③ ④ ⑤
33. ① ② ③ ④ ⑤

Mathematics Test (continued)

34.

	○	○	○	
⊙	⊙	⊙	⊙	⊙
⓪	⓪	⓪	⓪	⓪
①	①	①	①	①
②	②	②	②	②
③	③	③	③	③
④	④	④	④	④
⑤	⑤	⑤	⑤	⑤
⑥	⑥	⑥	⑥	⑥
⑦	⑦	⑦	⑦	⑦
⑧	⑧	⑧	⑧	⑧
⑨	⑨	⑨	⑨	⑨

35. ① ② ③ ④ ⑤

36. ① ② ③ ④ ⑤

37.

	○	○	○	
⊙	⊙	⊙	⊙	⊙
⓪	⓪	⓪	⓪	⓪
①	①	①	①	①
②	②	②	②	②
③	③	③	③	③
④	④	④	④	④
⑤	⑤	⑤	⑤	⑤
⑥	⑥	⑥	⑥	⑥
⑦	⑦	⑦	⑦	⑦
⑧	⑧	⑧	⑧	⑧
⑨	⑨	⑨	⑨	⑨

38. ① ② ③ ④ ⑤

39. ① ② ③ ④ ⑤

40. ① ② ③ ④ ⑤

41.

	○	○	○	
⊙	⊙	⊙	⊙	⊙
⓪	⓪	⓪	⓪	⓪
①	①	①	①	①
②	②	②	②	②
③	③	③	③	③
④	④	④	④	④
⑤	⑤	⑤	⑤	⑤
⑥	⑥	⑥	⑥	⑥
⑦	⑦	⑦	⑦	⑦
⑧	⑧	⑧	⑧	⑧
⑨	⑨	⑨	⑨	⑨

42. ① ② ③ ④ ⑤

43. ① ② ③ ④ ⑤

44. ① ② ③ ④ ⑤

45. ① ② ③ ④ ⑤

46. ① ② ③ ④ ⑤

47. ① ② ③ ④ ⑤

48. ① ② ③ ④ ⑤

49. ① ② ③ ④ ⑤

50. ① ② ③ ④ ⑤

Language Arts, Writing Test

Directions: Read all directions and questions carefully. Pick the single best answer, and answer every question. You will not be penalized for wrong answers.

The GED Language Arts, Writing Test has two parts, which must be taken consecutively. Part I consists of 50 multiple-choice questions for which you will be given 75 minutes to answer. Part II tests your ability to write an essay about a topic of general interest. You will have 45 minutes to plan, write, and revise your essay. The GED does permit you to take advantage of all 120 minutes, though. If you finish Part I early, you may move on to Part II with the remaining time; likewise, if you finish your essay with time to spare, you may return to Part I.

GO ON TO THE NEXT PAGE

Questions 1–8 are based on the following letter.

Continental Homes, Inc.
789 Ashton Court, Suite 2
Wilkes-Barre, Pennsylvania 18702

Dear Miss Stranton:

(A)

(1) Thank you for taken time visiting with us last week. (2) As we discussed, we are very interested in selling our home and also finding the appropriate Agent to help us. (3) We feel we have spent enough time trying to sell our home which is for sale ourselves, which has proven more difficult than we originally estimated. (4) Clearly, it is time to call in the experts.

(B)

(5) As you can imagine, we have been shopping around for the best agency to represent us. (6) Many of our friends have had adverse experiences with real estate firms. (7) And so many agents offer promises that never come to fruition while the home sits empty and unattended. (8) We've also heard of agents that squander chances to sell houses by failing to give clients enough time to clean up before a potential buyer comes for a tour. (9) Both of these scenarios are unacceptable to us, along with some others.

(C)

(10) After much deliberation, we have elected you to representing us for the next three months. (11) After that time period, if our home is not sold, we will reevaluate our situation and determine our next step. (12) We are under a timeline that requires us to be in our new home by the end of the year. (13) It is impossible for us to afford two mortgages. (14) So we need to sell our present home as soon as possible.

(D)

(15) We would like to meet with you again to go over terms of our contract with you and your agency. (16) There may be some additional items, that we would like to include in that contract. (17) Thank you again for your time and understanding, and we look forward to hearing from you.

Sincerely,

John and Mary Addison

1. Sentence 1: **Thank you for taken time visiting with us last week.**

   Which is the best way to write the underlined portion of this sentence? If the original is the best way, choose option (1).

   (1) taken time visiting
   (2) taken the time to visit
   (3) have taking time visiting
   (4) taking time to visit
   (5) having taking time to visit

2. Sentence 2: **As we discussed, we are very interested in selling our home and also finding the appropriate Agent to help us.**

   Which correction should be made to sentence 2?

   (1) change discussed to discussing
   (2) insert a comma after interested
   (3) replace are with were
   (4) change Agent to agent
   (5) no correction is necessary

3. Sentence 3: **We feel we have spent enough time trying to sell our home which is for sale ourselves, which has proven more difficult than we originally estimated.**

   Which correction should be made to sentence 3?

   (1) change feel to felt
   (2) change have to has
   (3) remove which is for sale
   (4) insert and after ourselves
   (5) change ours to his

4. Sentences 6 and 7: **Many of our friends have had adverse experiences with real estate firms. And so many agents offer promises that never come to fruition while the home sits empty and unattended.**

   Which is the best way to write the underlined portion of these sentences? If the original is the best way, choose option (1).

   (1) real estate firms. And so many agents offer
   (2) real estate firms, many agents offering
   (3) real estate firms, and then many agents are offering
   (4) real estate firms and also many agents offer
   (5) real estate firms. And many agents have offered

5. Sentence 8: **We've also heard of agents that squander chances to sell houses by failing to give clients enough time to clean up before a potential buyer comes for a tour.**

   Which correction should be made to sentence 8?

   (1) replace failing with fail
   (2) replace agents with agent
   (3) insert and after houses
   (4) replace heard with herd
   (5) no correction is necessary

6. Sentence 10: **After much deliberation, we have elected you to representing us for the next three months.**

   Which correction should be made to sentence 10?

   (1) change we have to we had
   (2) change elected to elect
   (3) replace representing with represent
   (4) change us to we
   (5) change the next to next

7. Sentences 13 and 14: **It is impossible for us to afford two mortgages. So we need to sell our present home quickly.**

   The most effective combination of sentences 13 and 14 would include which group of words?

   (1) two mortgages, so quickly
   (2) two mortgages and so quickly
   (3) two mortgages, so we need
   (4) to sell our home, the two mortgages
   (5) need to sell quickly our present home

8. Sentence 16: **There may be some additional items, that we would like to include in that contract.**

   Which correction should be made to the placement of sentence 16?

   (1) replace There with They're
   (2) replace additional with additionally
   (3) remove the comma after items
   (4) remove in that contract
   (5) no correction is necessary

GO ON TO THE NEXT PAGE

Questions 9–18 are based on the following notice.

POSTED, FYI, IMPORTANT!

To: All Homeowners
From: Green Lakes Association

(A)

(1) We are having a busy, summer this year, with many guests coming and going. (2) There has been much fine weather this season for people's enjoyment using the lake, having barbecues at the park, and riding their all-terrain vehicles (ATVs).

(B)

(3) It has come to our attention that some people may not be aware of the rules of ATV riding, particularly as it relates to private property. (4) For example, driving off the road and onto the shoulder is NOT an acceptable or even legal practice. (5) Many riders were encroaching on private property, making trails on someone else's land. (6) This is not only considered trespassing, but it is also creating other problems.

(C)

(7) Deep ruts and wide paths are made alongside the roadway. (8) The stability of our roads is undermined. (9) As everyone is aware, our road system is in a constant state of disrepair and needs continuous grading. (10) The ATV trail system that is forming in our community causes further erosion and washing away of the road gravel. (11) There are also many ATV riders who are not observing basic safety laws.

(D)

(12) These include, but were not limited to, not wearing a helmet, riding double, and speeding. (13) Riders: all of these infractions and more are subject to appropriate fines and penalties, so we urge use caution when operating you're vehicles!

(E)

(14) We do not wish to be punitive in this matter, but feel it is absolutely necessary that all ATV owners in our development become aware of the problems we are experiencing. (15) We have asked local law enforcement officials to monitor our area more frequently and issue warnings and/or citations as necessary. (16) We are not out to punish anyone. (17) Thank you for your cooperation in these matters, and have a wonderful fall season as nature begins her show!

Sincerely,

Hugh Longstreet

Hugh Longstreet, Grounds Maintenance

9. Sentence 1: **We are having a busy, summer this year, with many guests coming and going.**

   Which correction should be made to sentence 1?

   (1) remove the comma after busy
   (2) remove the comma after year
   (3) insert a comma after guests
   (4) change guests to Guests
   (5) no correction is necessary

10. Sentence 2: **There has been much fine weather this season for people's enjoyment using the lake, having barbecues at the park, and riding their all-terrain vehicles (ATVs).**

    If you rewrote sentence 2 beginning with

    Many people have enjoyed the fine weather this season

    the next word should be

    (1) having
    (2) barbecues
    (3) at
    (4) by
    (5) and

11. Sentence 3: **It has come to our attention that some people may not be aware of the rules of ATV riding, particularly as it relates to private property.**

    Which is the best way to write the underlined portion of this sentence? If the original is the best way, choose option (1).

    (1) it relates
    (2) relating
    (3) it related
    (4) related
    (5) they relate

12. Sentence 5: **Many riders were encroaching on private property, making trails on someone else's land.**

    Which correction should be made to sentence 5?

    (1) replace were with are
    (2) change on to of
    (3) replace making to having made
    (4) change someone to someone's
    (5) change else's to else

13. Sentences 7 and 8: **Deep ruts and wide paths are made alongside the roadway. The stability of our roads is undermined.**

    The most effective combination of sentences 7 and 8 would include which group of words?

    (1) deep ruts and wide paths, our roads
    (2) alongside the roadway, undermining
    (3) undermined whenever there are deep ruts
    (4) alongside the roadway the stability
    (5) the stability, undermining

14. Sentence 11: **There are also many ATV riders who are not observing basic safety laws.**

    Which revision should be made to the placement of sentence 11?

    (1) move sentence 11 to the end of paragraph A
    (2) move sentence 11 to the beginning of paragraph B
    (3) move sentence 11 to the beginning of paragraph D
    (4) move sentence 11 to the end of paragraph D
    (5) move sentence 11 to the end of paragraph E

GO ON TO THE NEXT PAGE

The letter has been repeated for your use in answering the remaining questions.

POSTED, FYI, IMPORTANT!

To: All Homeowners
From: Green Lakes Association

(A)

(1) We are having a busy, summer this year, with many guests coming and going. (2) There has been much fine weather this season for people's enjoyment using the lake, having barbecues at the park, and riding their all-terrain vehicles (ATVs).

(B)

(3) It has come to our attention that some people may not be aware of the rules of ATV riding, particularly as it relates to private property. (4) For example, driving off the road and onto the shoulder is NOT an acceptable or even legal practice. (5) Many riders were encroaching on private property, making trails on someone else's land. (6) This is not only considered trespassing, but it is also creating other problems.

(C)

(7) Deep ruts and wide paths are made alongside the roadway. (8) The stability of our roads is undermined. (9) As everyone is aware, our road system is in a constant state of disrepair and needs continuous grading. (10) The ATV trail system that is forming in our community causes further erosion and washing away of the road gravel. (11) There are also many ATV riders who are not observing basic safety laws.

(D)

(12) These include, but were not limited to, not wearing a helmet, riding double, and speeding. (13) Riders: all of these infractions and more are subject to appropriate fines and penalties, so we urge use caution when operating you're vehicles!

(E)

(14) We do not wish to be punitive in this matter, but feel it is absolutely necessary that all ATV owners in our development become aware of the problems we are experiencing. (15) We have asked local law enforcement officials to monitor our area more frequently and issue warnings and/or citations as necessary. (16) We are not out to punish anyone. (17) Thank you for your cooperation in these matters, and have a wonderful fall season as nature begins her show!

Sincerely,

Hugh Longstreet

Hugh Longstreet, Grounds Maintenance

15. Sentence 12: **These include, but were not limited to, not wearing a helmet, riding double, and speeding.**

    Which is the best way to write the underlined portion of this sentence? If the original is the best way, choose option (1).

    (1) were not limited to
    (2) are limited to
    (3) have been limited to
    (4) are not limited to
    (5) are being limited to

16. Sentence 13: **Riders: all of these infractions and more are subject to appropriate fines and penalties, and we urge caution when operating you're vehicles.**

    Which correction should be made to sentence 13?

    (1) replace subject with subjected
    (2) replace urge with are urged
    (3) change to become to became
    (4) change you're to your
    (5) insert a comma after owners

17. Sentence 14: **We do not wish to be punitive in this matter, but feel it is absolutely necessary, that all ATV owners in our development become aware of the problems we are experiencing.**

    Which is the best way to write the underlined portion of this sentence? If the original is the best way, choose option (1).

    (1) matter, but feel it is absolutely necessary,
    (2) matter but feel it is absolutely necessary
    (3) matter, but feel, it is absolutely necessary
    (4) matter but feel, it is absolutely necessary
    (5) matter, but feel it is absolutely, necessary

18. Which revision would improve the effectiveness of paragraph E?

    (1) remove sentence 16
    (2) remove sentence 17
    (3) move sentence 17 to the beginning of paragraph E
    (4) move sentence 15 to follow sentence 17
    (5) no revision is necessary

GO ON TO THE NEXT PAGE

Questions 19–25 are based on the following memo.

Growing Flowers

(A)

(1) Growing flowers can be a literally beautiful experience. (2) Unfortunately, it can also be a disappointing one if approaching with the wrong attitude. (3) Gardening as a whole is strictly a trial-and-error endeavor, and it is often, at the mercy of uncontrollable forces, such as the weather. (4) The mind's eye can make a much more colorful, symmetrical and bug-free flower garden than most real gardens are able to produce.

(B)

(5) Annuals are flowers that need to be planted with each new growing season as they are subject to cold temperatures and last only for one season. (6) One of the first things a new flower gardener learns is the difference between annuals and perennials. (7) Generally, however, they will continue to produce blossoms during the entire growing season. (8) Perennials, on the other hand, bloom on their own every year, but often their blossoms will last for only two weeks. (9) Because of these differences, most gardeners use both annuals and perennials in their flower gardens.

(C)

(10) Flowers also vary in there need for sunlight. (11) Some plants, like sunflowers, require bright sunlight for most of each day in order to produce the best blossoms. (12) Impatiens are a shade-loving flower and will wilt under too much strong sunshine. (13) Therefore, it is very important to know before planting what type of sunlight a particular variety prefers.

(D)

(14) Another factor to consider when planting flowers is the amount of water the plant prefers. (15) Some plants prefer to stay moist at all times while others will develop root rot and eventually perish. (16) Russian sage is an example of a plant that prefers dry soil, while hydrangeas enjoy moisture soil. (17) The gardener must also pay attention to the soil and its properties. (18) The healthiest garden flowers are those that can develop a strong root system. (19) Strong root systems depend on healthy soil.

(E)

(19) Even considering all of these elements to successful gardening, one is still at the mercy of powers that are unpredictable and uncontrollable. (20) These include daily weather patterns, such as an abundance of cloudy days, or an infestation of a particularly damaging insect. (21) Most seasoned gardeners learn to live by the motto, "There's always next year!"

GO ON TO THE NEXT PAGE

19. Sentence 2: **Unfortunately, it can also be a disappointing one if approaching with the wrong attitude.**

    Which correction should be made to sentence 2?

    (1) replace Unfortunately with Fortunately
    (2) remove the comma after Unfortunately
    (3) replace a disappointing one with a disappointed one
    (4) change approaching to approached
    (5) no correction is necessary

20. Sentence 3: **Gardening as a whole is strictly a trial-and-error endeavor, and it is often, at the mercy of uncontrollable forces, such as the weather.**

    Which is the best way to write the underlined portion of the sentence? If the original is the best way, choose option (1).

    (1) endeavor, and it is often,
    (2) endeavor, and it is often
    (3) endeavor,
    (4) endeavor and it is often,
    (5) endeavor. It is often,

21. Sentence 6: **One of the first things a new flower gardener learns is the difference between annuals and perennials.**

    Which revision should be made to the placement of sentence 6?

    (1) move sentence 6 to the end of paragraph A
    (2) move sentence 6 to the beginning of paragraph B
    (3) move sentence 6 to follow sentence 8
    (4) move sentence 6 to the beginning of paragraph C
    (5) move sentence 6 to the end of paragraph D

22. Sentence 8: **Perennials, on the other hand, bloom on their own every year, but often their blossoms will last for only two weeks.**

    If you rewrote sentence 13 beginning with

    On the other hand,

    the next words should be

    (1) perennial blooming
    (2) bloom perennially
    (3) perennials bloom
    (4) blooming perennial
    (5) blooms that reproduce perennials

23. Sentence 10: **Flowers also vary in there need for sunlight.**

    Which is the best way to write the underlined portion of the sentence? If the original is the best way, choose option (1).

    (1) there
    (2) their
    (3) there are
    (4) there is
    (5) they're

24. Sentence 16: **Russian sage is an example of a plant that prefers dry soil, while hydrangeas enjoy moisture soil.**

    Which correction should be made to sentence 16?

    (1) replace an with a
    (2) remove the comma after soil
    (3) insert a comma after while
    (4) replace enjoy with enjoys
    (5) change moisture to moist

25. Sentences 18 and 19: **The healthiest garden flowers are those that can develop a strong root system. Strong root systems depend on healthy soil.**

    The most effective combination of sentences 18 and 19 would include which group of words?

    (1) root system, and this depends
    (2) root system, depends
    (3) root system, which depends
    (4) root system, which healthy soil
    (5) root system, which it depends

GO ON TO THE NEXT PAGE

Questions 26–34 are based on the following letter.

Right'n Ready Car Shop
Coeur d'Alene, Idaho

Dear Mr. Amtry:

(A)

(1) We appreciate, your correspondence, dated January 13, 2006. (2) It is always a pleasure to have received positive comments from a valued customer. (3) As you can imagine, a company such as ours is much more accustomed to complaints and criticism. (4) We know that we have many satisfied customers but few take the time to express themselves as you have done.

(B)

(5) You mentioned our Head Mechanic, Rocco Marx. (6) He has worked for our company for nearly 30 years now. (7) He took it upon himself to stay current with the many updated features of today's automobiles, such as the complex computerized electrical systems. (8) He also does an excellent job training the other mechanics, both in direct work with the vehicles themselves and also with our customers. (9) Rocco always tells the other workers that every vehicle has an owner, and that owner needs to be made happy.

(C)

(10) You also mentioned the recent renovations that we make to our Customer Lounge. (11) We know that waiting for a car repair can be lengthy and extremely boring. (12) Also, some customers have children that need to be kept entertained during this period of time, usually young. (13) This is why we installed the bookshelf and the indoor play equipment. (14) We are pleased, as Right 'n Ready employees, to know that our customers are already benefiting from these upgrades, which you mentioned in your letter.

(D)

(15) If you have a problem, please call us. (16) I have included in this letter a coupon for $50 off your next car repair. (17) Thank you again for being such a great customer of Right 'n Ready!

Sincerely,

Carl Wolfe

Carl Wolfe
President

26. Sentence 1: **We appreciate, your correspondence, dated January 13, 2006.**

Which correction should be made to sentence 1?

(1) insert a comma after dated
(2) remove the comma after appreciate
(3) insert a comma after January
(4) remove the comma after 13
(5) no correction is necessary

27. Sentence 2: **It is always a pleasure to have received positive comments from a valued customer.**

Which correction should be made to sentence 2?

(1) replace always a pleasure with always, the pleasure
(2) change have received to receive
(3) insert a comma after received
(4) change positive comments to positively commented
(5) change valued to value

28. Sentence 4: **We know that we have many satisfied customers but few take the time to express themselves as you have done.**

Which is the best way to write the underlined portion of the sentence? If the original is the best way, choose option (1).

(1) satisfied customers but few
(2) satisfied customers, but few
(3) satisfied, customers but few
(4) satisfied, customers, but few
(5) satisfied customers, but, few

29. Sentences 5 and 6: **You mentioned our Head Mechanic, Rocco Marx. He has worked for our company for nearly 30 years now.**

Which is the best way to write the underlined portion of these sentences? If the original is the best way, choose option (1).

(1) Rocco Marx. He has worked
(2) Rocco Marx, and he has worked
(3) Rocco Marx, and he had been working
(4) Rocco Marx, who has worked
(5) Rocco Marx, who had been working

30. Sentence 7: **He took it upon himself to stay current with the many updated features of today's automobiles, such as the complex computerized electrical systems.**

Which correction should be made to sentence 7?

(1) replace took with takes
(2) replace stay with stays
(3) remove the comma after automobiles
(4) replace such as with such is
(5) no correction is necessary

31. Sentence 10: **You also mentioned the recent renovations that we make to our Customer Lounge.**

Which correction should be made to sentence 10?

(1) change mentioned to had mentioned
(2) change make to have made
(3) insert a comma after our
(4) change make to did make
(5) no correction is necessary

The letter has been repeated for your use in answering the remaining questions.

Right'n Ready Car Shop
Coeur d'Alene, Idaho

Dear Mr. Amtry:

(A)

(1) We appreciate, your correspondence, dated January 13, 2006. (2) It is always a pleasure to have received positive comments from a valued customer. (3) As you can imagine, a company such as ours is much more accustomed to complaints and criticism. (4) We know that we have many satisfied customers but few take the time to express themselves as you have done.

(B)

(5) You mentioned our Head Mechanic, Rocco Marx. (6) He has worked for our company for nearly 30 years now. (7) He took it upon himself to stay current with the many updated features of today's automobiles, such as the complex computerized electrical systems. (8) He also does an excellent job training the other mechanics, both in direct work with the vehicles themselves and also with our customers. (9) Rocco always tells the other workers that every vehicle has an owner, and that owner needs to be made happy.

(C)

(10) You also mentioned the recent renovations that we make to our Customer Lounge. (11) We know that waiting for a car repair can be lengthy and extremely boring. (12) Also, some customers have children that need to be kept entertained during this period of time, usually young. (13) This is why we installed the bookshelf and the indoor play equipment. (14) We are pleased, as Right 'n Ready employees, to know that our customers are already benefiting from these upgrades, which you mentioned in your letter.

(D)

(15) If you have a problem, please call us. (16) I have included in this letter a coupon for $50 off your next car repair. (17) Thank you again for being such a great customer of Right 'n Ready!

Sincerely,

Carl Wolfe

Carl Wolfe
President

GO ON TO THE NEXT PAGE

32. Sentence 12: **Also, some customers have children that need to be kept entertained during this period of time, usually young.**

Which correction should be made to sentence 12?

(1) change have to had
(2) replace kept with keeping
(3) change entertained to had entertained
(4) replace this with that
(5) remove usually young

33. Sentence 14: **We are pleased, as Right 'n Ready employees, to know that our customers are already benefiting from these upgrades, which you mentioned in your letter.**

The most effective revision of sentence 14 would begin with which group of words?

(1) As Right 'n Ready employees, we are pleased
(2) We are Right 'n Ready employees who are pleased
(3) We know that our customers, as Right 'n Ready employees
(4) Our customers, as Right 'n Ready employees, we are pleased
(5) Right 'n Ready employees are pleased as employees

34. Which revision would improve the effectiveness of the letter?

(1) move sentence 10 to the end of paragraph C
(2) move sentence 14 to the beginning of paragraph B
(3) remove sentence 15
(4) move sentence 17 to the end of paragraph C
(5) move sentence 17 to the beginning of paragraph D

GO ON TO THE NEXT PAGE

Questions 35–42 are based on the following memo.

ONLINE AUCTIONS

(A)

(1) Most people have objects sitting around that they could sell if only they could find a willing buyer. (2) Which can be done in a variety of ways. (3) Some people have garage sales, others are putting ads in newspapers, and still others choose online auctions to clean out their basements.

(B)

(4) Selling an item online requires at least some knowledge of how a particular auction system runs. (5) Most online auction companies make it as simple as possible to put an item up for auction from books to clothing to even boats! (6) Basically, the seller has only to type in pertinent information such as a description of the item being sold, the desired length of the auction and the asking price. (7) If a photo is included, it is always helpful so potential buyers have a clear idea of what they're bidding on.

(C)

(8) Through this system, no physical money passes from one person to another, and individual accounts are accessed similarly to online banking. (9) Most online auction companies are very concerned about the security of their systems. (10) Ensuring that neither the seller nor the buyer is going to be jeopardized in any way is an important feature of a good online auctioneer. (11) Most companies have separate banking systems whereby a seller's fees are automatically deducted from his or her account. (12) By the same token, the buyer can deposit the cost of the item into that same account.

(D)

(13) Once an item has been put up for auction, the real fun begins for both the seller and buyer. (14) For the length of the auction, potential buyers will bid on the item, and frequently bidding war ensue. (15) This is when several people are interested in the same item. (16) Watching the price rise is, of course, more fun for the seller than the hopeful bidders, but a bidder can quit bidding at any time.

(E)

(17) Of course there were times when the item for sale has no bidders whatsoever.
(18) The seller still has fees to pay, with no money coming in. (19) Generally, however, online selling is a fun and often lucrative way to bring in a little extra cash.

GO ON TO THE NEXT PAGE

35. Sentence 2: **Which can be done in a variety of ways.**

Which correction should be made to sentence 2?

(1) replace Which with This
(2) insert a comma after can
(3) change done to doing
(4) change ways to way
(5) no correction is necessary

36. Sentence 3: **Some people have garage sales, others are putting ads in newspapers, and still others choose online auctions to clean out their basements.**

Which is the best way to write the underlined portion of this sentence? If the original is the best way, choose option (1).

(1) are putting ads in newspapers
(2) are putting in newspapers, ads
(3) will have put ads in newspapers
(4) will be putting ads, in newspapers
(5) put ads in newspapers

37. Sentence 5: **Most online auction companies make it as simple as possible to put items up for auction from books to clothing to even boats!**

Which is the best way to write the underlined portion of the sentence? If the original is the best way, choose option (1).

(1) up for auction from books to clothing to even boats!
(2) auction, from books, to clothing, or even boats!
(3) auctioning books, clothing, and boats!
(4) from books to clothing to even boats up for auction!
(5) books, clothing, and boats to be auctioned!

38. Sentence 7: **If a photo is included, it is always helpful so potential buyers have a clear idea of what they're bidding on.**

If you rewrote sentence 7 beginning with

Including a photo

the next words should be

(1) that can be the most helpful
(2) it is always helpful
(3) is always helpful
(4) will always be the most helpful
(5) helps always

39. Sentence 8: **Through this system, no physical money passes from one person to another, and individual accounts are accessed similarly to online banking.**

Which revision should be made to the placement of sentence 8?

(1) remove sentence 8
(2) move sentence 8 to follow sentence 3
(3) move sentence 8 to follow sentence 6
(4) move sentence 8 to follow sentence 12
(5) no revision is necessary

40. Sentence 11: **Most companies have separate banking systems whereby a seller's fees are automatically deducted from his or her account.**

Which revision should be made to the placement of sentence 11?

(1) move sentence 11 to the end of paragraph B
(2) move sentence 11 to follow sentence 9
(3) move sentence 11 to the beginning of paragraph E
(4) remove sentence 11
(5) no revision is necessary

GO ON TO THE NEXT PAGE

The letter has been repeated for your use in answering the remaining questions.

ONLINE AUCTIONS

(A)

(1) Most people have objects sitting around that they could sell if only they could find a willing buyer. (2) Which can be done in a variety of ways. (3) Some people have garage sales, others are putting ads in newspapers, and still others choose online auctions to clean out their basements.

(B)

(4) Selling an item online requires at least some knowledge of how a particular auction system runs. (5) Most online auction companies make it as simple as possible to put an item up for auction from books to clothing to even boats! (6) Basically, the seller has only to type in pertinent information such as a description of the item being sold, the desired length of the auction and the asking price. (7) If a photo is included, it is always helpful so potential buyers have a clear idea of what they're bidding on.

(C)

(8) Through this system, no physical money passes from one person to another, and individual accounts are accessed similarly to online banking. (9) Most online auction companies are very concerned about the security of their systems. (10) Ensuring that neither the seller nor the buyer is going to be jeopardized in any way is an important feature of a good online auctioneer. (11) Most companies have separate banking systems whereby a seller's fees are automatically deducted from his or her account. (12) By the same token, the buyer can deposit the cost of the item into that same account.

(D)

(13) Once an item has been put up for auction, the real fun begins for both the seller and buyer. (14) For the length of the auction, potential buyers will bid on the item, and frequently bidding war ensue. (15) This is when several people are interested in the same item. (16) Watching the price rise is, of course, more fun for the seller than the hopeful bidders, but a bidder can quit bidding at any time.

(E)

(17) Of course there were times when the item for sale has no bidders whatsoever. (18) The seller still has fees to pay, with no money coming in. (19) Generally, however, online selling is a fun and often lucrative way to bring in a little extra cash.

41. Sentence 14: **For the length of the auction, potential buyers bid on the item, and frequently bidding war ensue.**

Which correction should be made to sentence 14?

(1) replace length with lengths
(2) change bid to would have bid
(3) change bid to bidded
(4) replace item with items
(5) change bidding war to bidding wars

42. Sentence 17: **Of course there were times when the item for sale has no bidders whatsoever.**

Which is the best way to write the underlined portion of this sentence? If the original is the best way, choose option (1).

(1) Of course there were
(2) Of course there have been
(3) Generally there are times
(4) Of course there are times
(5) Then there are sometimes those times

GO ON TO THE NEXT PAGE

Questions 43–50 are based on the following memorandum.

MEMORANDUM

To: All Rosie's Diner Employees
From: Markie Smythe, General Mgr.

Re: Employee Input

(A)

(1) With employees from all shifts, management has formed a committee, in an effort to improve our restaurant. (2) The names for this committee were literally drawn out of a hat. (3) Meaning that they were not selected by management. (4) We selected names from each employee group (waitstaff, host station, cooks, etc.) (5) We felt it was important to get a random, broad spectrum of feedback from all areas of our operation.

(B)

(6) This committee will focus on improvement rather than criticism. (7) Therefore, we have been expecting each committee member to bring positive ideas for improvement to the table at every meeting, or at least be willing to brainstorm positively with the group.

(C)

(8) We are aware that some rumors have been going around about changes to the diner. (9) We would like, to dispel these rumors and invite all employees to contribute to the focus of this committee in the following way. (10) We will have written forms available asking for input in specific areas such as wait times uniforms, and food quality.

(D)

(11) There is no need to sign your name on the form, and there is a wooden box in the employee lounge in which to deposit your completed form. (12) At the beginning of each meeting, we will have read several of these evaluations and base our discussions on those, as well as the comments of group members.

(E)

(13) We are proud of Rosie's Diner and we are proud of you. (14) Our regular diners continue to praise their dining experience and, by word of mouth, new customers are visiting us for the first time. (15) Just as any business does, we know, that there is always room for improvement to our operations, and that is the focus of this endeavor. (16) Thank you for your continued support and cooperation!

GO ON TO THE NEXT PAGE

43. Sentence 1: **With employees from all shifts, management has formed a committee, in an effort to improve our restaurant.**

The most effective revision of sentence 1 would begin with which group of words?

(1) Management has formed
(2) They have formed
(3) For improving our
(4) As a committee
(5) We are improving

44. Sentences 2 and 3: **The names for this committee were literally drawn out of a hat. Meaning that they were not selected by management.**

The most effective combination of sentences 2 and 3 would include which group of words?

(1) hat. This means
(2) hat. And this means
(3) hat and were
(4) hat and while this means
(5) hat; meaning

45. Sentence 6: **This committee will focus on improvement rather than criticism.**

Which is the best way to write the underlined portion of the sentence? If the original is the best way, choose option (1).

(1) committee will focus
(2) committee focusing
(3) committee, by focusing
(4) focusing by the committee
(5) committee focused

46. Sentence 7: **Therefore, we have been expecting each committee member to bring positive ideas for improvement to the table at every meeting, or at least be willing to brainstorm positively with the group.**

Which is the best way to write the underlined portion of the sentence? If the original is the best way, choose option (1).

(1) Therefore, we have been expecting
(2) Therefore, we expect
(3) Therefore, we have expected
(4) Therefore, we had expected
(5) We have been expecting

47. Sentence 9: **We would like, to dispel these rumors and invite all employees to contribute to the focus of this committee in the following way.**

Which correction should be made to sentence 9?

(1) remove the comma after like
(2) insert a comma after rumors
(3) insert you after all
(4) change committee in to committee. In
(5) no correction is necessary

48. Sentence 10: **We will have written forms available asking for input in specific areas such as wait times uniforms, and food quality.**

Which correction should be made to sentence 10?

(1) change will have to will have had
(2) replace for with four
(3) replace We with They
(4) insert a comma after times
(5) remove the comma after uniforms

49. Sentence 12: **At the beginning of each meeting, we will have read several of these evaluations and base our discussions on those, as well as the comments of group members.**

Which is the best way to write the underlined portion of the sentence? If the original is the best way, choose option (1).

(1) we will have read
(2) we will read
(3) we have read
(4) we have been reading
(5) we had read

50. Sentence 15: **Just as any business does, we know, that there is always room for improvement to our operations, and that is the focus of this endeavor.**

Which correction should be made to sentence 15?

(1) replace any with the
(2) remove the comma after does
(3) remove the comma after know
(4) replace that is with those are
(5) change does to do

Answers and explanations for this test begin on page 808.

GO ON TO: LANGUAGE ARTS, WRITING, PART II

Writing, Part II

The box on page 741 contains your assigned topic.

You must write on the assigned topic ONLY.

You will have 45 minutes to write on the assigned essay topic. If you have time remaining in this test period after you complete your essay, you may return to Part I of the Writing Test.

Evaluation of your essay will be based on the following features:

- Well-focused main ideas
- Clear organization
- Specific development of your ideas
- Control of sentence structure, punctuation, grammar, word choice, and spelling

REMEMBER, YOU MUST COMPLETE BOTH THE MULTIPLE-CHOICE QUESTIONS (PART I) AND THE ESSAY (PART II) TO RECEIVE A SCORE ON THE LANGUAGE ARTS, WRITING TEST. To avoid having to repeat both parts of the test, be sure to do the following:

- Do not leave the pages blank.
- Write legibly in ink so that the essay readers will be able to read your handwriting.
- Write on the assigned topic. If you write on a topic other than the one assigned, you will not receive a score for the Language Arts, Writing Test.
- Write your essay on the lined pages of the answer sheet. Only the writing on these pages will be scored.

GO ON TO THE NEXT PAGE

Topic

An important characteristic of leaders is their ability to make sound decisions and judgments under pressure. What was one situation in the past where you demonstrated leadership under pressure?

Part II is a test to determine how well you can use written language to explain your ideas.

In preparing your essay, you should take the following steps:

- Read the **DIRECTIONS** and the **TOPIC** carefully.
- Plan your essay before you write. Use the scratch paper provided to make any notes and to organize your ideas. These notes will be collected but not scored.
- Before you finish your essay, reread what you have written and make any changes that will improve your essay.

Your essay should be long enough to develop the topic adequately.

An explanation of how to evaluate your writing on this test is found on page 811.

GO ON TO: LANGUAGE ARTS, READING

Language Arts, Reading Test

The GED Language Arts, Reading Test consists of 40 multiple-choice questions that you will be given 65 minutes to answer. The questions assess your ability to analyze various short reading passages. These may be whole works or excerpts from larger works.

Each passage begins with a "purpose question" printed in all capital letters. These are not titles. They are intended to focus your reading and may help you grasp the meaning of the passages.

Some questions will reference certain lines of the passage by their numbers. For these, use the line numbers along the left side of the passage. Every fifth line is indicated, so find the number nearest the one you want and count up or down.

Directions: Read all directions and questions carefully. Pick the single best answer, and answer every question. You will not be penalized for wrong answers.

GO ON TO THE NEXT PAGE

Questions 1 through 5 refer to the following excerpt from a short story.

WHAT ARE THE NARRATOR'S FEELINGS ABOUT HIS SON?

I had seen the Magic Shop from afar several times; I had passed it once or twice, a shop window of alluring little objects, magic balls, magic hens, wonderful cones, ventriloquist dolls, the basket trick, packs of cards that LOOKED all right, and all that sort of thing, but never had I thought of going in, until one day, almost without warning, Gip hauled me by my finger right up to the window, and so conducted himself that there was nothing for it but to take him in. I had not even been sure that the place was there, to tell the truth.

I had fancied it was down nearer the Circus, or round the corner in Oxford Street, or even in Holborn; always over the way and a little inaccessible it had been, with something of the mirage in its position; but here it was now quite indisputably, and the fat end of Gip's pointing finger made a noise upon the glass. "If I was rich," said Gip, dabbing a finger at the Disappearing Egg, "I'd buy myself that. And that"—which was The Crying Baby, Very Human— "and that," which was a mystery, and called, so a neat card asserted, "Buy One and Astonish Your Friends." "Anything," said Gip, "will disappear under one of those cones. I have read about it in a book. And there, dadda, is the Vanishing Halfpenny, only they've put it this way up so's we can't see how it's done." Gip, dear boy, inherits his mother's breeding, and he did not propose to enter the shop or worry in any way; only, you know, quite unconsciously he lugged my finger doorward, and he made his interest clear. "That," he said, and pointed to the Magic Bottle. "If you had that?" I said; at which promising inquiry he looked up with a sudden radiance. "I could show it to Jessie," he said, thoughtful as ever of others.

"It's less than a hundred days to your birthday, Gibbles," I said, and laid my hand on the door handle. Gip made no answer, but his grip tightened on my finger, and so we came into the shop. It was no common shop this; it was a magic shop, and all the prancing precedence Gip would have taken in the matter of mere toys was wanting. He left the burden of the conversation to me. It was a little, narrow shop, not very well lit, and the doorbell pinged again with a plaintive note as we closed it behind us. For a moment or so, we were alone and could glance about us. There was a tiger in papier-mache on the glass case that covered the low counter—a grave, kind-eyed tiger that waggled his head in a methodical manner; there were several crystal spheres, a china hand holding magic cards, a stock of magic fish-bowls in various sizes, and an immodest magic hat that shamelessly displayed its springs. On the floor were magic mirrors; one to draw you out long and thin, one to swell your head and vanish your legs, and one to make you short and fat; and while we were laughing at these, the shopman came in.

This passage is adapted from *The Magic Shop* by H. G. Wells ©1903.

GO ON TO THE NEXT PAGE

1. When the narrator says, "Gip, dear boy, inherits his mother's breeding, and he did not propose to enter the shop or worry in any way" (lines 30–33), what is he suggesting about Gip?

   Gip is

   (1) worried that his father doesn't want to go into the shop
   (2) trying not to worry about his mother
   (3) worried that he will not get any presents from the shop
   (4) trying not to be a bother, even though he is curious
   (5) afraid to enter the shop, despite his curiosity

2. On the basis of the narrator's character as revealed in this excerpt, what relationship is he likely to have with Gip in the future?

   He will

   (1) never buy Gip another birthday present
   (2) continue to spend time with Gip and enjoy his company
   (3) purchase presents for Gip from a toy store
   (4) continue to ignore Gip's suggestions
   (5) resent Gip for his kindness

3. Which of the following best expresses the main idea of the excerpt?

   (1) A child begs for expensive birthday gifts.
   (2) A father and son spend time together in the park.
   (3) A father mourns the loss of a loved one.
   (4) A rude child refuses to go outside with his father.
   (5) A father encourages his well-mannered son's interests.

4. What is the main effect of the narrator's use of phrases such as "at which promising inquiry he looked up with a sudden radiance" (lines 37–38) and "thoughtful as ever of others" (line 39)?

   (1) It suggests that Gip was an impulsive child.
   (2) It shows that Gip was a greedy child.
   (3) It suggests that Gip was a caring and considerate child.
   (4) It shows that Gip was a daring and bright child.
   (5) It suggests that Gip was a very moody child.

5. Based on information in this excerpt, which of the following words would best describe the narrator's impression of the location of the magic shop?

   (1) obvious
   (2) obscure
   (3) fancy
   (4) forbidden
   (5) secure

GO ON TO THE NEXT PAGE

Questions 6 through 10 refer to the following poem.

HOW DO LIFE'S DREAMS DIFFER FROM REALITY?

Dreams

What dreams we have and how they fly
Like rosy clouds across the sky;
Of wealth, of fame, of sure success,
Of love that comes to cheer and bless;
And how they wither, how they fade,
The waning wealth, the jilting jade—
The fame that for a moment gleams,
Then flies forever,—dreams, ah—dreams!
O burning doubt and long regret,
O tears with which our eyes are wet,
Heart-throbs, heart-aches, the glut of pain,
The somber cloud, the bitter rain,
You were not of those dreams—ah! well,
Your full fruition who can tell?
Wealth, fame, and love, ah! love that beams
Upon our souls, all dreams—ah! dreams.

Paul Laurence Dunbar, *The Complete Poems of Paul Laurence Dunbar* ©1922

6. What feeling is the speaker attributing to dreams in lines 1–2: "What dreams we have and how they fly/Like rosy clouds across the sky;"?
   (1) distaste
   (2) optimism
   (3) concentration
   (4) deception
   (5) leisure

7. Which of the following phrases best describes the overall mood of the poem?
   (1) eager contemplation
   (2) wistful longing
   (3) intense sorrow
   (4) misplaced anger
   (5) awkward peace

8. Which advice would the speaker most likely give to a child?
   (1) to expect all dreams to come true
   (2) to make lofty goals because they are easy to achieve
   (3) to limit dreams to those which are impossible to fail
   (4) to live solely in the present without regard for the future
   (5) to be prepared for dreams to fail

9. Paul Laurence Dunbar was born in the nineteenth century in Dayton, Ohio, to parents who had escaped slavery. From his message in the poem and knowing Dunbar's origins, which of the following did he most likely experience?
   (1) widespread achievement of all his goals
   (2) great success beginning at an early age
   (3) long periods of boredom during his childhood
   (4) literary success despite challenging circumstances
   (5) ridicule because of his sensitive nature

10. Notice that the exclamation "ah" (line 8) is repeated three times in the second stanza. What effect does this repetition have on the speaker's message?

    The repetition
    (1) makes analyzing the elements of dreams more difficult
    (2) fills gaps in the rhythm of the poem
    (3) reflects the speaker's exclamatory tone
    (4) mocks dreams
    (5) completes the rhyme scheme of the poem

GO ON TO THE NEXT PAGE

Questions 11 through 15 refer to the following excerpt from an article.

WHAT IS THE FUTURE OF ENERGY GENERATION?

Industrialized countries have long had an insatiable thirst for power. Nowadays, power means energy. Although we may still use some fuel oil for heating in northern areas, and even wood in a smaller proportion, nearly all new developments rely on electrical power to keep warm during winter. Summer offers little reprieve because air conditioning is increasingly popular and uses as much energy as heating.

You might think we could control the situation with stable increases in supply and strategic programs for reducing consumption, but you would be mistaken. Demand is on the verge of exploding in several developing countries, with some 2 billion potential new consumers. In short, we could be in for a massive power failure.

Necessity is the mother of the wildest inventions. We have burned coal for decades and continue to do so in order to generate electricity. But Mother Nature suffers from the emissions and looks towards the Kyoto [pollution control] Protocol to produce viable alternatives. When implemented properly, nuclear energy is more efficient and cleaner than coal. But this technology is not very popular because of the risk of accidents, radioactive waste disposal issues and the fall-out of contentious applications. Furthermore the preparation and enrichment of uranium and the disposal of radioactive waste all represent energy intensive operations.

Renewable energy is available from modern hydroelectric facilities, which originate from watermills equipped with paddle wheels—an invention discovered before the Christian era. These facilities are the envy of many nations without the necessary natural resources to operate them. Solar and geothermal energy are valued for their ecological properties but have limited concrete potential. Finally, there is wind power: a technology to which we are turning in the hope it will provide the ultimate answer to our energy needs.

Excerpt from "Wind Energy: Building a Better Blade for Tomorrow" by Daniel Bertrand in *The Textile Journal*, Vol.123, No. 3, May-June 2006.

GO ON TO THE NEXT PAGE

11. Which of the following best describes the majority of devices used to heat new developments in northern areas?

    They are

    (1) fuel oil heaters
    (2) wood burning stoves
    (3) solar panels
    (4) geothermal pipes
    (5) electric forced-air furnaces

12. What is the primary purpose of this passage?

    (1) to explain the risks associated with nuclear power
    (2) to discuss the main types of power used in the United States
    (3) to explain the need for new types of energy
    (4) to discuss the increasing cost of energy worldwide
    (5) to increase awareness of global warming

13. What is the main benefit of nuclear energy according to the passage?

    (1) It is only slightly more expensive than burning coal.
    (2) There are no emissions from fossil fuel combustion.
    (3) Radioactive waste does not require special disposal.
    (4) There is no risk of radiation leakage.
    (5) Accidents are likely to happen only in remote areas.

14. Which of the following is thought by the author to be the final solution to global energy concerns?

    (1) nuclear power
    (2) wind power
    (3) hydroelectric power
    (4) solar power
    (5) geothermal power

15. The author discusses the Kyoto Protocol in order to do which of the following?

    (1) highlight a global failure of research into new energy
    (2) prove that hydroelectric power is a potentially dangerous source of energy
    (3) explain the United States' increasing need for electricity
    (4) show a global commitment to finding nonpolluting sources of energy
    (5) demonstrate the safety of nuclear power

GO ON TO THE NEXT PAGE

Questions 16 through 20 refer to the following excerpt from a business document.

HOW MUST EMPLOYEES RESPOND TO COMPLAINTS?

Guide to Handling Tenant Complaints

Beacon Property Management Company recognizes the importance of maintaining good relationships with the tenants who live in its apartment communities. Sometimes it is necessary to deal with an unhappy tenant. The following guidelines must be followed by all employees of Beacon Property Management when dealing with tenant complaints:

- Complaints about others

  If the complaint is regarding an emergency or civil disturbance (such as noise violations), ask the tenant to contact the police immediately. Be careful about dealing with disturbances yourself; the police are much better suited to handle these situations. In addition, the proper authorities will most likely know and understand any local ordinances or safety codes that tenants and others may be violating. It is the job of these authorities to enforce laws and other rules established by state or local governments.

  If the tenant complains about a nonemergency situation pertaining to others, ask for the complaint in writing. When you receive the written complaint, schedule a visit with the offending tenant and attempt to settle the complaint.

- Complaints about the apartment

  If the complaint is regarding a maintenance or repair request (such as a broken window or problems with the utilities), schedule a maintenance person to visit the apartment and, if possible, fix the problem within 24 hours. Make sure that a *written service request* is completed, and a copy is left for the tenant.

GO ON TO THE NEXT PAGE

16. According to the document, which one of the following requires contacting the "proper authorities" (line 10)?
    (1) a complaint about an employee who was impolite
    (2) a complaint about smoke coming from a basement storeroom
    (3) a complaint about a broken window
    (4) a complaint regarding a letter from the management company
    (5) a complaint about a tenant whose car is parked in the wrong space

17. What is the main purpose of Beacon Property Management's "Guide to Handling Tenant Complaints"?
    (1) to prevent tenants from violating the rules
    (2) to protect employees in emergency situations
    (3) to make clear to the employees the procedures for dealing with complaints
    (4) to enforce good relationships between tenants of the apartment communities
    (5) to inform tenants of the local ordinances regarding filing a complaint

18. Which of the following would be an example of a "civil disturbance" (line 7)?

    A tenant

    (1) fails to notify an employee of a broken pipe and water damage occurs
    (2) consistently pays her rent two weeks late
    (3) has pets in the apartment
    (4) fails to remove his or her garbage promptly
    (5) is playing music so loudly that it can be heard throughout the entire building

19. When an employee receives a complaint about a maintenance problem, what is the first step the employee should take in handling the complaint?
    (1) Call the proper authorities.
    (2) Wait 24 hours.
    (3) Schedule a maintenance visit.
    (4) Leave a written service request with the tenant.
    (5) Schedule a visit with the complaining tenant.

20. What is the reason for requiring nonemergency complaints to be made in writing?
    (1) Verbal complaints are often inaccurate.
    (2) Beacon Property Management will be able to discipline employees.
    (3) Written complaints are less confusing.
    (4) Beacon Property Management will have a record of the complaint.
    (5) Most problems cannot be corrected within 24 hours.

GO ON TO THE NEXT PAGE

Questions 21 through 25 refer to the following excerpt from a play.

WHAT IS THE RELATIONSHIP BETWEEN THE MOTHER AND HER SON?

[It is between four and five in the afternoon. The door is opened violently; and Higgins enters with his hat on.]

MRS. HIGGINS: (*Dismayed*) Henry! (*Scolding him*) What are you doing here today? It is my at-home day: you promised not to come. (*As he bends to kiss her, she takes his hat off, and presents it to him.*)

HIGGINS: Oh bother! (*He throws the hat down on the table.*)

MRS. HIGGINS: Go home at once.

HIGGINS: (*Kissing her*) I know, mother. I came on purpose.

MRS. HIGGINS: But you mustn't. I'm serious, Henry. You offend all my friends: they stop coming whenever they meet you.

HIGGINS: Nonsense! I know I have no small talk; but people don't mind. (*He sits on the settee.*)

MRS. HIGGINS: Oh! Don't they? Small talk indeed! What about your large talk? Really, dear, you mustn't stay.

HIGGINS: I must. I've a job for you. A phonetic job.

MRS. HIGGINS: No use, dear. I'm sorry; but I can't get round your vowels; and though I like to get pretty postcards in your patent shorthand, I always have to read the copies in ordinary writing you so thoughtfully send me.

HIGGINS: Well, this isn't a phonetic job.

MRS. HIGGINS: You said it was.

HIGGINS: Not your part of it. I've picked up a girl.

MRS. HIGGINS: Does that mean that some girl has picked you up?

HIGGINS: Not at all. I don't mean a love affair.

MRS. HIGGINS: What a pity!

HIGGINS: Why?

MRS. HIGGINS: Well, you never fall in love with anyone under forty-five. When will you discover that there are some rather nice-looking young women about?

HIGGINS: Oh, I can't be bothered with young women. My idea of a loveable woman is something as like you as possible. I shall never get into the way of seriously liking young women: some habits lie too deep to be changed. (*Rising abruptly and walking about, jingling his money and his keys in his trouser pockets*) Besides, they're all idiots.

MRS. HIGGINS: Do you know what you would do if you really loved me, Henry?

HIGGINS: Oh bother! What? Marry, I suppose?

MRS. HIGGINS: No. Stop fidgeting and take your hands out of your pockets. (*With a gesture of despair, he obeys and sits down again.*) That's a good boy. Now tell me about the girl.

Bernard Shaw, *Pygmalion* ©1916

GO ON TO THE NEXT PAGE

21. Which of the following phrases <u>best</u> describes Mrs. Higgins?

    (1) highly skeptical
    (2) easy to please
    (3) mean and heartless
    (4) even-tempered
    (5) exceedingly friendly

22. Based on the information in this excerpt, how would Higgins <u>most likely</u> behave around his mother's friends?

    He would

    (1) listen attentively
    (2) dominate the conversation
    (3) remain completely silent
    (4) talk only about his work
    (5) amuse them

23. Which of the following <u>best</u> describes the mood created in this scene?

    (1) anxious
    (2) despairing
    (3) joyful
    (4) soothing
    (5) neglected

24. What can be inferred from Higgins saying "Oh, I can't be bothered... they're all idiots" (lines 43–50)?

    (1) Higgins dislikes his mother's friends.
    (2) Higgins will never be happy.
    (3) Higgins thinks young women are immature.
    (4) Higgins lives with his mother.
    (5) Higgins has begun a new love affair.

25. Why does Higgins enter his mother's house?

    (1) He has a present for her.
    (2) She asked him to fix something.
    (3) He wants to meet her friends.
    (4) She made him dinner.
    (5) He needs a favor.

GO ON TO THE NEXT PAGE

Questions 26 through 30 refer to the following review.

DID THE AUTHOR ENJOY THE EXHIBITION?

Art spectators both new and seasoned are sure to be inspired by the colors and shapes in the Detroit Institute of Arts exhibition "Murano: Glass from the Olnick Spanu Collection." The special show, which opened last Sunday, continues through February 27. While the museum remains under renovation, the price of admission to the glass exhibition ($10 for adults, $5 for kids 6–17, free for younger ones and DIA members) includes general admission to the rearranged galleries of the museum. Before and after eyeing the glass, visitors can expect a generally enjoyable—albeit abbreviated—tour of what the DIA calls its "Greatest Hits." Works are "remixed" into theme groups like "Animals as Symbols" and "The Individual," instead of regionally and chronologically as patrons may be used to. The galleries appear somewhat cluttered, but the mishmash of things has the added effect of inspiring deeper reflection on the human condition.

On my visit to the Murano exhibition, there were many children and their parents ogling the brightly tinted glass objects, some functional and others wildly sculptural. "Cool" was a word on many lips. For families, the exhibition presents an important opportunity to introduce young people to the joys of owning and cherishing art objects. In addition, the size of the exhibition and the limited gallery space make a visit wholly manageable for visitors with little ones or who have difficultly spending much of the day standing and walking.

Murano describes a group of islands in the lagoon of Venice that has been an important center of glass production since Roman times. For centuries, Murano glassmakers held tightly their accumulation of trade secrets, but the inevitable market reaction of cheaper glass—in both price and quality—did take its toll on Murano artisans. Thankfully, however, Murano was given a kickstart when new furnaces were installed in the nineteenth century. By the twentieth century, glassmakers began playing with traditional forms and collaborating with progressive artists and designers. Today, Murano glass is loved the world over for its unabashed liveliness. Things so shiny and red or royal blue or lemon yellow bring out the widest smiles in even the most austere critics. Kids yearn to touch the bulbous creations. (Everything is in display cases.) I particularly enjoyed the many glass bottles with pointed or round glass stoppers. Streaks of many shades of blue, green, or red run thinly and discretely from the base to the top. There are parallels between the action of glassblowing and, say, pulling taffy. And Murano glass does indeed look good enough to eat.

Take an extra moment to consider the many designs of Carlo Scarpa, one of the most influential Italian architects of the twentieth century. His work is a major focus of the Olnick Spanu Collection. According to the visitor guide I was given upon entering the exhibition gallery, Scarpa's designs focus on textures, clarity, and form. Some objects are polished, others etched. Some are clear, while others are completely opaque, strangely mimicking pottery. Much of the glass is translucent with milky white swirls. Scarpa's shapes are remarkably spare and uncomplicated; however, the artist appears not to have been preoccupied with strict adherence to geometry.

First and foremost, the exhibition is a feast for the eyes, but it is also a chance to ponder the marvelous human application of physics and chemistry. You'll want to remember your visit with photographs, but they are not allowed to be taken in the exhibition gallery. As an alternative, you may consider the beautiful full-color catalog of the show, offered by the exhibition shop in softcover for $45.

26. Which of the following is the main idea of the excerpt?

    The author

    (1) thinks the museum is not worth visiting during the renovation
    (2) would prefer to see an exhibition of pottery instead of glass
    (3) doesn't like the bright colors and geometric shapes of Murano glass
    (4) wishes more people shared his taste in art
    (5) considers visiting the glass exhibition to be worthwhile

27. Which statement best expresses the author's thoughts on the museum's "Greatest Hits"?

    (1) They are not works of art the author would have chosen to display.
    (2) They are thoughtfully arranged considering the limited space available during the renovation.
    (3) They are not worthwhile to visit.
    (4) They are arranged in no certain way.
    (5) They are spread too far apart in the museum.

28. Which of the following <u>best</u> describes the tone of this excerpt?

    (1) humorous
    (2) angry
    (3) informative
    (4) joyful
    (5) unconcerned

29. Which of the following <u>best</u> describes the style in which this review is written?

    (1) frugal
    (2) methodical
    (3) formal
    (4) technical
    (5) ironic

30. According to the author, which of the following words <u>best</u> describes the glass exhibition?

    (1) superficial
    (2) unorganized
    (3) confusing
    (4) pleasing
    (5) crowded

GO ON TO THE NEXT PAGE

Questions 31 through 35 refer to the following excerpt from a short story.

HOW DOES THE NARRATOR REACT TO THE NEWS ABOUT HIS CHILDHOOD FRIEND?

It seems to me now that Fanshawe was always there. He is the place where everything begins for me, and without him I would hardly know who I am. We met before we could talk, babies crawling through the grass in diapers, and by the time we were seven we had pricked our fingers with pins and made ourselves blood brothers for life. Whenever I think of my childhood, I think of Fanshawe. He was the one who was with me, the one who shared my thoughts, the one I saw whenever I looked up from myself.

But that was a long time ago. We grew up, went off to different places, drifted apart. None of that is very strange, I think. Our lives carry us along in ways we cannot control, and almost nothing stays with us. It dies when we do, and death is something that happens to us every day. Seven years ago this November, I received a letter from a woman named Sophie Fanshawe. "You don't know me," the letter began, "and I apologize for writing to you like this out of the blue. But things have happened, and under the circumstances I don't have much choice." It turned out that she was Fanshawe's wife. She knew that I had grown up with her husband, and she also knew that I lived in New York, since she had read many of the articles I had published in magazines.

The explanation came in the second paragraph, very bluntly, without any preamble. Fanshawe had disappeared, she wrote, and it was more than six months since she had last seen him. Not a word in all that time, not the slightest clue as to where he might be. The police had found no trace of him, and the private detective she hired to look for him had come up empty-handed. Nothing was sure, but the facts seemed to speak for themselves. Fanshawe was probably dead; it was pointless to think he would be coming back. In the light of all this, there was something important she needed to discuss with me, and she wondered if I would agree to see her.

This letter caused a series of little shocks in me. There was too much information to absorb all at once; too many forces were pulling me in different directions. Out of nowhere, Fanshawe had mentioned that he had vanished again. He was married, he had been living in New York—and I knew nothing about him anymore. Selfishly, I felt hurt that he had not bothered to get in touch with me.

31. When does the scene in this excerpt take place?
    (1) before the narrator was born
    (2) during the narrator's childhood
    (3) during the narrator's adulthood
    (4) after the narrator's death
    (5) during the narrator's adolescence

32. From what is stated in the passage, which of the following can be inferred about why Sophie wrote to the narrator?
    (1) Sophie was concerned about the narrator.
    (2) The narrator was her childhood friend.
    (3) Fanshawe often sent the narrator letters.
    (4) The narrator may have heard from Fanshawe.
    (5) Fanshawe had recently spent time with the narrator.

33. Based on the passage, how does the narrator feel about his lost friendship?
    (1) resentful
    (2) conflicted
    (3) happy
    (4) understanding
    (5) devastated

34. Which of the following best represents the author's tone?
    (1) nostalgic
    (2) outraged
    (3) unsettled
    (4) excited
    (5) humorous

35. The relationship between the narrator and Fanshawe in lines (4–12) can best be described as one of
    (1) two very close friends
    (2) two complete strangers
    (3) two actual brothers
    (4) two former friends
    (5) two acquaintances

GO ON TO THE NEXT PAGE

Questions 36 through 40 refer to the following product warranty statement.

HOW DOES THIS WARRANTY PROTECT YOU?

STATEMENT OF LIMITED WARRANTY

FATHER AND SON SOFTWARE AND COMPUTING ACCESSORIES ("the Company") warrants to you for the Warranty Period that there are no defects in the materials and workmanship of this Product. The Warranty Period is One Year from the date you purchased this product. Repair or replacement is your only remedy if this Product if defective. The Company is not responsible for damage to or loss of any equipment, media, programs, or data related to the use of this Product. Except for repair or replacement, the Company is not liable for any other relief. You may be expected to send the Product to the Company with a photocopy of this warranty and your receipt of purchase.

This Limited Warranty is the only warranty that the Company is giving for this Product. It is the ultimate and sole statement of the Company's obligations to you. It replaces all other agreements and understandings that you may have with representatives of the Company. This Limited Warranty may not be changed at all unless both you and the Company agree to the change in a signed document outlining your specific Product, the date purchased, and the exact changes.

Exceptions: This warranty is VOID if: 1) this Product has been serviced or altered in any way by an individual who is not an Authorized Representative of the Company, 2) this Product was not purchased from a U.S. reseller authorized by the Company, 3) the serial number of this Product has been changed, removed, or otherwise modified, 4) there has been any accidental or intentional damage done to this Product, or 5) any non-Father and Son brand accessories, power cords, or replacement parts have been added to or used with this Product.

36. Which of the following best expresses the main idea of the third paragraph?
    (1) If the product cannot be fixed, the warranty is valid.
    (2) The warranty applies only if the product is fixed by the owner.
    (3) If the problem is not Father and Son's fault, the company will fix it.
    (4) If the owner caused the problem, the warranty is void.
    (5) Buy Father and Son's products at your own risk.

37. For the company to honor the warranty, which of the following will the owner most likely be asked to do?
    (1) Produce a copy of the product's bar code.
    (2) Dispose of the defective parts of the product.
    (3) Find someone to complete the labor on the product.
    (4) Ship the product back to the company with proper documentation.
    (5) Submit a request for reimbursement after the product is fixed.

38. What is the purpose of this warranty?
    (1) to deny Father and Son's responsibilities to the owner
    (2) to promise purchasers total satisfaction with any product they have bought
    (3) to highlight the fact that no replacements or refunds will be given for any reason
    (4) to outline the specific circumstances under which Father and Son will repair or replace the product
    (5) to document the level of quality that all products made by Father and Son must meet

39. Which of the following would not void the warranty?
    (1) dropping a Father and Son brand printer down the stairs
    (2) the owner opening up a Father and Son brand typewriter to replace a broken key
    (3) using Father and Son brand cleaning solution on a DVD player
    (4) having your uncle, who is a photographer, fix your Father and Son brand camera
    (5) scratching off the serial number on a Father and Son computer

40. Which words best describe the tone of this document?
    (1) informal and friendly
    (2) unclear and misleading
    (3) mean and spiteful
    (4) precise and official
    (5) dull and tedious

Answers and explanations for this test begin on page 812.

GO ON TO: SOCIAL STUDIES

Social Studies Test

The GED Social Studies Test consists of 50 multiple-choice questions that you will be given 70 minutes to answer. You will have to draw upon some prior knowledge of history, civics and government, economics, and geography; however, you will not have to recall facts.

Directions: Choose the one best answer to each question.

GO ON TO THE NEXT PAGE

Question 1 refers to the following graph.

Supply and Demand Curves for Evenheat Premium Series Barbecue Grill.

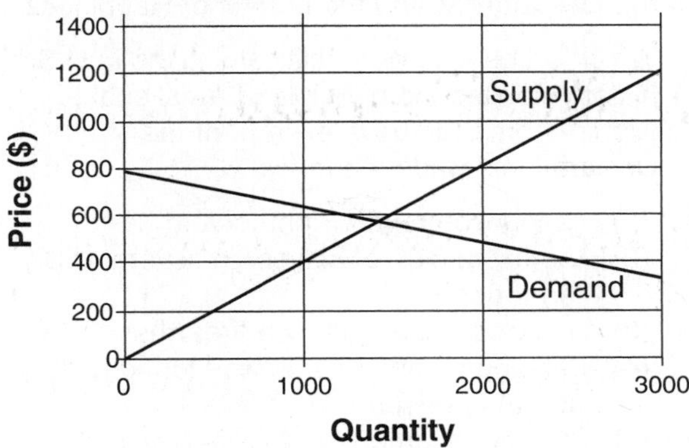

1. Which conclusion about the Evenheat Premium Series barbecue grill can be drawn from information in the graph?

   (1) The grill is expensive compared to other similar grills.
   (2) No grills would sell at a price of $800.
   (3) The company would maximize its income by selling the grill for more than $600.
   (4) No grills would sell at any price.
   (5) More than 2,000 grills would sell at the equilibrium price.

Question 2 refers to the following table.

Number of Active Duty U.S. Military Personnel

	Army	Navy	Marine Corps	Air Force
1951	1,531,774	736,596	192,620	788,381
1961	858,622	626,223	176,909	821,151
1971	1,123,810	621,565	212,369	755,300
1981	781,419	540,219	190,620	570,302
1991	710,821	570,262	194,040	510,432
2001	480,801	377,810	172,934	353,571

Source: U.S. Department of Defense (http://siadapp.dior.whs.mil/personnel/MILITARY/ms9.pdf)

2. Which of the following is a likely explanation for the significant decrease in active duty military personnel between 1971 and 2001?

   (1) The military became an all-volunteer force after the draft ended in the 1970s.
   (2) U.S. military power was severely weakened after World War II ended in the 1940s.
   (3) Congress has gradually reduced military funding since the 1950s.
   (4) Most personnel wounded or killed in battle are not replaced.
   (5) Most military employees are civilians not on active duty.

3. In 1906, novelist Upton Sinclair published a novel titled *The Jungle* that depicted the horrific working conditions of Chicago's meatpacking plants. The author detailed the unsanitary and disturbing practices that went on in these very plants, such as the slaughtering and packaging of diseased cattle. The reaction among Americans led president Theodore Roosevelt to pass the Pure Food and Drug Act, which is still used today.

   On the basis of the information, what did the new laws most likely require?

   (1) an increase in the minimum wage of factory workers
   (2) the closing of many Chicago meatpacking plants
   (3) federal inspection of meatpacking plants and products
   (4) that everyone at the White House become vegetarians
   (5) a reduction in the price of meat products

4. "We hold these Truths to be self-evident, that all Men are created equal, that they are endowed by their Creator with certain unalienable Rights, that among these rights are Life, Liberty, and the pursuit of Happiness."

   Which of the following political actions in U.S. history violates the principle of "unalienable Rights" from the above excerpt of the Declaration of Independence?

   (1) giving women the right to vote
   (2) the expansion of slavery in several U.S. territories
   (3) allowing citizens to own firearms
   (4) sending someone who was found guilty at trial to prison
   (5) the impeachment of a president for treason

GO ON TO THE NEXT PAGE

Questions 5 through 7 refer to the following posters.

Sources: (left) Office of Defense Transportation, 1943 (right) Office of War Information, 1943, United States Department of Defense.

5. Which of the following statements about major wars is factually supported by the posters?

   Major wars

   (1) require sacrifices on the part of civilians as well as soldiers
   (2) cause civilians to consume goods and services excessively
   (3) result in a surplus of consumer goods
   (4) hurt the economy by removing millions of consumers from the marketplace
   (5) cause congestion in stores and transportation systems

6. According to the posters, what did the U.S. government ask civilians to do?

   (1) stop spending money
   (2) conserve resources crucial to the war effort
   (3) stay at home as much as possible
   (4) donate train tickets and new clothes to the military
   (5) ensure that men in their family are properly dressed

7. According to the U.S. government's point of view, what was the reason civilians needed to consider the messages in the posters?

   (1) Many people were unaware of U.S. involvement in World War II.
   (2) World War II was fought in many U.S. towns and cities.
   (3) Adult civilians are better able to cope with the stress of war by staying at home.
   (4) Civilian overspending could result in collapse of the U.S. economy.
   (5) The U.S. military during World War II relied on maximizing economic efficiency.

GO ON TO THE NEXT PAGE

Questions 8 and 9 refer to the following map and information.

Reapportionment of U.S. Representatives after the year 2000 census.

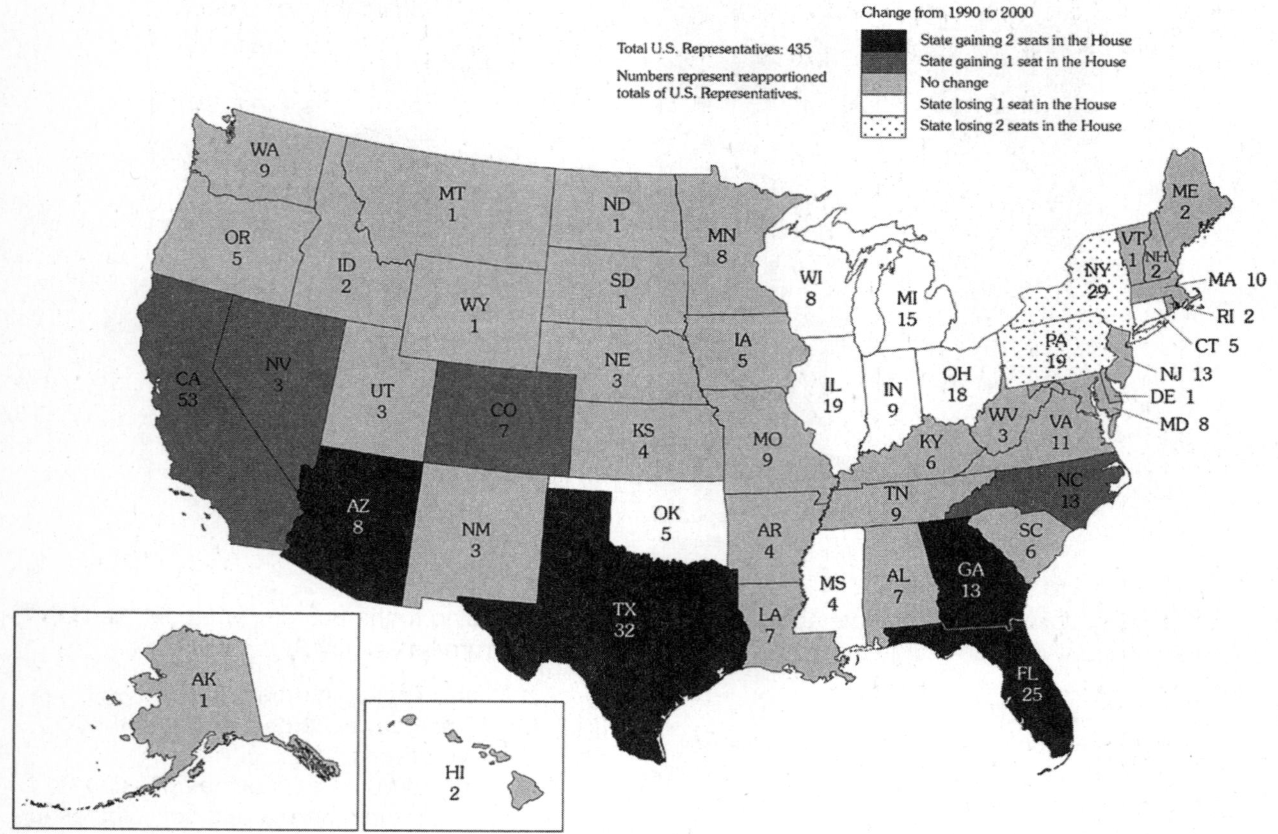

Source: U.S. Census Bureau

One of the fundamental reasons for conducting the U.S. Census of population every 10 years is to reapportion the U.S. House of Representatives. Apportionment is the process of dividing the 435 memberships, or seats, in the U.S. House of Representatives among the 50 states. An apportionment has been made on the basis of each decennial census from 1790 to 2000, except following the 1920 census.

The number of representatives or seats in the U.S. House of Representatives has remained constant at 435 since 1911, except for a temporary increase to 437 at the time of admission of Alaska and Hawaii as states in 1959. However, the apportionment based on the 1960 census, which took effect for the Congressional election in 1962, reverted to 435 seats. The average size of a congressional district based on the Census 2000 apportionment population is 646,952, more than triple the average district size of 193,167 based on the 1900 census apportionment, and about 74,486 more than the average size based on the 1990 census (572,466).

Source: U.S. Census Bureau (http://www.census.gov/prod/2001pubs/c2kbr01-7.pdf)

8. What conclusion about reapportionment of U.S. representatives can be drawn from the map and the information?

   (1) Most Northwest states neither lost nor gained seats because their populations stayed approximately the same between 1990 and 2000.
   (2) The reapportionment system favors states with small land areas.
   (3) The reapportionment system favors states with smaller populations.
   (4) Most Great Lakes states lost seats because their rates of population growth between 1990 and 2000 were below the national average.
   (5) The total number of seats fluctuates every 10 years after the census.

9. Based on the information and the map, why did Texas gain two seats in the House of Representatives?

   (1) It experienced population growth well above the national average.
   (2) It experienced population growth at about the national average.
   (3) It experienced population growth below the national average.
   (4) More people migrated out of Texas than into Texas.
   (5) Fewer people voted in congressional elections in other states than voted in congressional elections in Texas.

GO ON TO THE NEXT PAGE

Questions 10–13 refer to the following information.

The ancient Vikings of Scandinavia (what is now Norway, Sweden, and Denmark) led what would today be considered by most to be a crude existence. In many ways, however, they were far more advanced than their contemporaries.

The Vikings, also known as *Norsemen* (meaning men from the north), were among the first international seafaring traders with purpose-built, wooden trading ships. Vikings sailed from Norway through the Straits of Gibraltar to the eastern Mediterranean. Vikings also crossed the Atlantic Ocean, settling in Iceland and Greenland (a frozen land given the inviting name of Greenland in an effort to entice Viking settlers to emigrate). From there, the Vikings crossed a much shorter distance over to the North American continent where archaeological evidence of their presence has been found in what is now northern Newfoundland, Canada. Whether they arrived in North America centuries before Christopher Columbus or not, their far-reaching travel from the 9th through the 12th centuries is, nevertheless, remarkable.

One way in which the Vikings were certainly behind their contemporaries was in reading and writing. Very few Vikings could read or write, so those who could were considered valuable and important people. Vikings did not have books as we think of them; instead, records of brave deeds were etched on large standing stones. These *runes* were made up of an alphabet of only 16 different symbols. Because so few Vikings could read, they believed that runes were magical and could be used to cast spells. Because they wrote down very little of their history or beliefs, most of what is known of the Vikings today is the result of archaeologists' discoveries and written records and oral histories of people who met them, such as their Christian neighbors (and victims) and the Arabs with whom they traded. In fact, a children's bedtime prayer, still in use in parts of northern Great Britain, including Ireland, includes the phrase, "…and save us from the wrath of the Norsemen."

10. According to the passage, how were the Vikings more advanced than their contemporaries?

    (1) The Vikings were able to read and write well.
    (2) Equipped with well-built ships, the Vikings were among the first to engage in far-reaching travel.
    (3) Seeing the importance in establishing good relationships, the Vikings were cordial toward their Christian neighbors.
    (4) The Vikings knew the ways of the sea better than most modern-day sailors.
    (5) The Vikings published books centuries before contemporary printers.

11. According to the passage, what is interesting about the country of Greenland?

    (1) Greenland was the major settling ground of the Vikings.
    (2) Just like its name indicates, Greenland is lush with vegetation.
    (3) The Vikings originated in Greenland.
    (4) Actually a frozen land, Greenland was given its name in an effort to entice emigration.
    (5) It is the one northern country that the Vikings didn't inhabit.

12. From where was today's knowledge of the Vikings acquired?

    (1) It was acquired from the books and well-preserved documents of the Vikings.
    (2) It was acquired from runes.
    (3) It was acquired from archaeologists' discoveries and Viking books.
    (4) It was acquired from archaeologists' discoveries, written records, and oral histories.
    (5) It was acquired from the Greenland treasury.

GO ON TO THE NEXT PAGE

13. The children's prayer, which includes the phrase, "...and save us from the wrath of the Norsemen," is an example of which of the following?

 (1) It is an example of a written history.
 (2) It is an example of a rune.
 (3) It is an example of an oral history.
 (4) It is an example of an archaeologist's discovery.
 (5) It is an example of a preserved document.

---

14. The Environmental Protection Agency (EPA) is revising the standards for determining the miles per gallon (MPG) estimates that are displayed on new vehicles. The agency is putting these new standards into practice in 2008 in the hope of helping consumers better understand the possible cost for fueling their new vehicles, while also helping the environment by more efficiently using oil resources.

 Which of the following would be evidence that the new MPG standards fulfilled the EPA's goals?

 (1) an increase in total new vehicle sales
 (2) a decrease in oil consumption for 2008 from previous years
 (3) a decrease in the sales of vehicles with low MPG estimates
 (4) an increase in oil consumption for 2008 from previous years
 (5) an increase in use of public transportation

Questions 15 and 16 refer to the following chart.

Appeals process for the U.S. Supreme Court

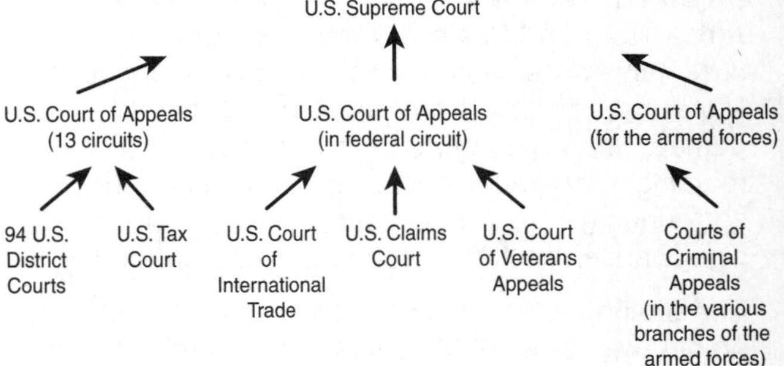

15. Which of the following is a possible order of courts by which a case could be appealed?

 (1) U.S. Supreme Court, U.S. Court of International Trade, U.S. Court of Appeals
 (2) U.S. Court of Appeals, U.S. Claims Court, U.S. Court of Veterans Appeals
 (3) U.S. Tax Court, U.S. Court of Appeals, U.S. Supreme Court
 (4) Court of Criminal Appeals, U.S. Court of Appeals, U.S. Court of International Trade
 (5) U.S. District Court, U.S. Court of Appeals, U.S. Tax Court

16. The appeals process is an example of which concept from the Constitution?

 (1) majority rule
 (2) freedom of assembly
 (3) freedom of speech
 (4) checks and balances
 (5) executive powers

Questions 17–19 refer to the following information.

The reign of Justinian (527–565) marked the final end of the Roman Empire. During Justinian's reign, his military recovered former Roman territories in Africa, Italy, and Spain. However, throughout Justinian's wars, Roman citizens faced many hardships: the aqueducts around Rome suffered damage, returning parts of the countryside to marshland; marauding enemies devastated the surrounding countryside; and probably of most significance, the Italian economy suffered greatly.

The prolonged wars' impact on the treasury of the empire was a result of several factors. For instance, Justinian appeared to have difficulty establishing priorities. He would put military plans into action before he had the means to provide his commander with enough troops to do the job effectively. In addition to insufficient troop strength, problems also resulted because of inadequate supplies and compensation for those troops. To feed and pay the troops, money traditionally was raised by collecting property taxes from the citizens of Constantinople in the eastern part of the empire. Reportedly, only about a third of those taxes due the empire were actually collected, which added to the funding problems.

17. Why does the author begin the passage with an account of the success experienced by Justinian during his reign?

    The author

    (1) wanted to give some history about the fall of the Roman Empire
    (2) wanted to point out that Justinian did have some success as a leader
    (3) felt the information was important to the reader's understanding of the passage as a whole
    (4) thought it was important to include Africa, Italy, and Spain in the passage
    (5) wanted to contrast Justinian's outward success with the turmoil and hardship of the Roman citizens

18. According to the passage, which of the following is an example of Justinian's difficulty establishing priorities?

    (1) He allowed the aqueducts to suffer significant damage.
    (2) He worked to meet his own needs, rather than the needs of his people.
    (3) He allowed enemies to destroy the countryside.
    (4) He failed to provide sufficient troop strength, both physically and monetarily.
    (5) He found it unnecessary to financially support the troops.

19. Which of the following best describes the method of ruling practiced by Justinian and his empire?

    (1) disorganized
    (2) powerful
    (3) insightful
    (4) structured
    (5) decisive

Questions 20 and 21 refer to the following map.

Busiest ports of entry to the United States from Canada, by passengers in personal vehicles, 2005

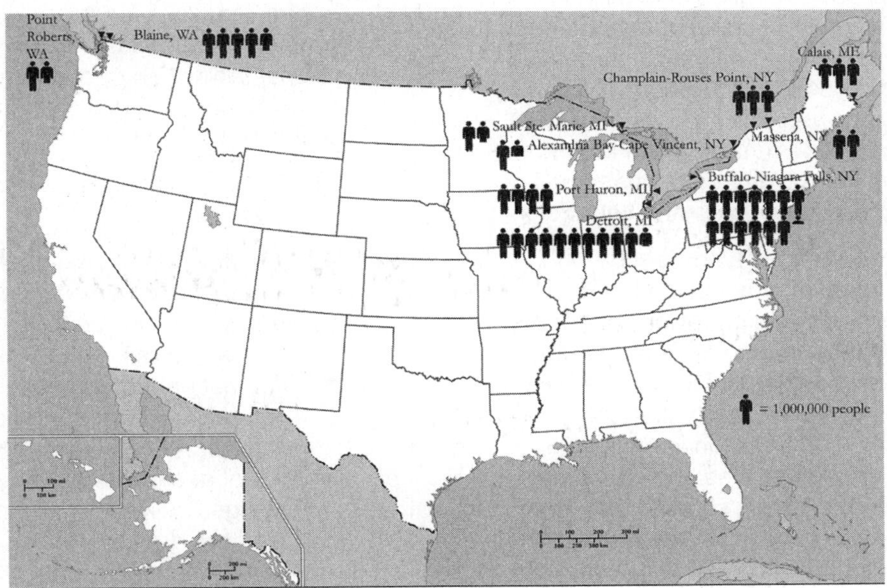

Adapted from U.S. Department of Transportation, Research and Innovative Technology Administration, Bureau of Transportation Statistics, Border Crossing/Entry Data; based on data from U.S. Department of Homeland Security, Customs and Border Protection, OMR database.

20. Which conclusion about the population density along the United States–Canada border is confirmed by clear evidence in the map?
    (1) The majority of people entering the United States from Canada do so in personal vehicles.
    (2) Few people in Canada have business in the United States.
    (3) Population density is highest in the eastern half of the border.
    (4) No personal vehicles cross the border between Canada and Michigan.
    (5) Population density is highest in the western half of the border.

21. What is the main purpose of recording when people enter the United States from Canada?
    (1) to encourage travel between the two countries
    (2) to protect domestic security and help enforce laws
    (3) to make it possible to measure the popularity of vacation destinations
    (4) to ensure visitors are pleased with their experience in the United States
    (5) to discourage people from traveling across the border

Questions 22 and 23 refer to the following information.

Antilock braking systems (ABS) were first researched as early as the 1930s and were introduced in the 1950s, primarily for use in airplanes. The technology, in a purely mechanical form, was first used in automobiles in the 1960s in a few race cars and experimental vehicles. The modern ABS became a common option in production automobiles during the 1990s. It is now offered as standard equipment in most models of cars and light trucks.

ABS activation causes a pulsating "feedback" through the brake pedal that is noticeable to the vehicle operator. If a driver is not aware of this phenomenon, he or she may release the brake pedal during an emergency stop, losing the benefit of the ABS and thereby increasing stopping distance. Therefore, familiarization is critical for drivers of ABS-equipped vehicles. In fact, some studies done during the 1990s showed that there was practically no difference in fatality rates between autos equipped with ABS and those that were not so equipped.

22. The passage specifically mentions that ABS is used in all the following *except*

    (1) race cars
    (2) airplanes
    (3) light trucks
    (4) trains
    (5) experimental vehicles

23. Which of the following best explains why "there was practically no difference in fatality rates between autos equipped with ABS and those that were not so equipped"?

    (1) More times than not, ABS doesn't work.
    (2) Drivers unfamiliar with ABS are at just as great of a risk for fatality in a motor vehicle accident as a driver operating a vehicle without ABS.
    (3) ABS is a useless product.
    (4) Many ABS are improperly installed, which leads to their malfunction.
    (5) Vehicles without ABS are easier to operate than ABS-equipped vehicles.

---

24. Brazil is the fifth largest country in the world by both population and area. In 1960, the newly built interior city of Brasilia became its capital, replacing the Atlantic coast city of Rio de Janeiro. Reasons for the move include the improvement of relationships with bordering nations, promotion of economic development in the interior, and unification of all the distant regions of the country.

    These facts best support which generalization about national capitals?

    (1) Location of national capitals is not important to economic success.
    (2) Unification of a country is only possible in the capital city.
    (3) Population and economic activity naturally grow in and near national capitals.
    (4) National capitals are never attacked by foreign armies.
    (5) Workers are more efficient in cities away from the coast.

25. The Center for Disease Control and Prevention is one of the main components of the Department of Health and Human Services, whose goal it is to promote a healthy lifestyle among all Americans. Which of the following *does not* show their dedication to ensuring that people make healthier lifestyle choices?

    (1) a strong opposition to tobacco use among people of any age
    (2) focus on the importance of regular exercise
    (3) efforts to defend against terrorist attacks
    (4) concern about increasing prevalence of high blood pressure
    (5) advice that pregnant women should not drink alcohol

GO ON TO THE NEXT PAGE

26. The production of high-definition televisions by a company has recently decreased, whereas the demand for them has risen. According to the law of supply and demand, what will the company most likely do to provide the greatest possible benefit for themselves?

    (1) produce fewer televisions and lower the price
    (2) produce fewer televisions and keep the price the same
    (3) go out of business because they cannot satisfy consumer demand
    (4) begin producing a new product that is less popular than the television
    (5) produce more televisions and raise the price

GO ON TO THE NEXT PAGE

Questions 27 through 30 refer to the following information.

Although some claim that modern society infringes on the environment, others believe that environmentalism and environmental management can go hand in hand. According to the latter, a hands-off approach isn't always the best one. For example, nature itself uses fire as a part of maintaining the proper balance of underbrush, new-growth trees, and other vegetation, but that hands-off approach can be devastating to both humans and wildlife when conditions are such that a fire can burn out of control. In addition to the immediate damage to property and loss of life, there can be subsequent devastating consequences as well. Landslides can accompany heavy rains when hillsides have been stripped of trees by fire, something that also impacts local water sources and results in the loss of the topsoil necessary to support immediate renewed growth.

Controlled burning as a way to contain such fires cannot be done on land with dense underbrush and an overabundance of small, new-growth trees. To do a controlled burn, such vegetation must be thinned out, and "ladder" fuels, by which wildfire may climb to the tree canopy, must be reduced before fire is introduced. Otherwise, a fire will likely burn uncontrollably.

One California landowner said, "Sometimes current environmental laws don't make sense to me. If I failed to get rid of the trash on my property, I'd be in violation of zoning regulations. To my way of thinking, underbrush and excess new-growth trees are nature's garbage, yet many want us to let it just pile up."

Regional Forester Jack Blackwell, first appointed a regional forester under former Democratic President Clinton and now working for the Republican Bush administration, was quoted in a November 2004 Associated Press article as having said that he approved logging plans for 11 Sierra national forests because he believes "it would be a betrayal of our national forests to let them burn up." Blackwell said the logging plans will prevent a repeat of catastrophic wildfires, such as those that devastated Southern California in 2003, and will improve wildlife habitat while reducing the danger of fire around mountain communities. Environmentalists claim that any logging disrupts the ecological balance, arguing that fire is nature's way of controlling dense underbrush and turning mulch into topsoil.

27. According to the information, what is true about the proper way to conduct controlled burning?

(1) Controlled burning is any fire that abides by zoning regulations.
(2) It is impossible to do controlled burning.
(3) In controlled burning, it is necessary to thin out much of the underbrush and many new-growth trees.
(4) Controlled burning works best when the fuel load is piled up just before fire is introduced.
(5) It is best to take a hands-off approach, allowing nature to control the fire.

28. What conclusion about the relationship between humans and the environment is most strongly supported by the information?

(1) By committing to care for the environment, while at the same time acknowledging the importance of its natural processes, humans can live in harmony with the environment.
(2) History has shown that humans have done nothing but harm to the environment; therefore, the relationship between humans and the environment is one of harm.
(3) The relationship between humans and the environment is strictly political; most activism is confined to the politician's realm.
(4) The relationship between humans and the environment is conditional; humans will protect the parts of the environment that are of benefit to them.
(5) Humans and the environment have always had an amiable relationship; humans work to promote environmentally friendly causes.

GO ON TO THE NEXT PAGE

29. According to the information presented, what is the purpose of logging the national forests mentioned in the last paragraph?

    The purpose is

    (1) to downsize the forests; they are beginning to overtake nearby towns.
    (2) to provide more lumber for developmental housing projects.
    (3) to protect the forests by preventing catastrophic wildfires.
    (4) to make room for industrial projects.
    (5) to reduce threatening wildlife in the area.

30. Based on the information presented, when would wildfire officials choose to conduct controlled burning?

    When fire officials

    (1) record an unusually high amount of rainfall
    (2) believe that the density of a forest has become too low
    (3) observe an excess of ground-level plant material
    (4) expect reduced instances of wildfire during the upcoming season
    (5) are attempting to prevent accidental wild-fires

Question 31 refers to the following graph.

Gross federal debt as a percentage of gross domestic product at the end of year, 1940–2000

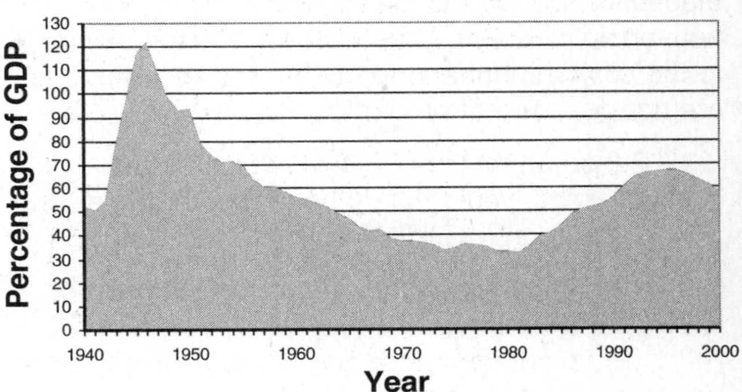

31. Which question about federal debt can be answered by using information in the graph?

    (1) At the end of which years was gross federal debt greater than gross domestic product?
    (2) Why did gross federal debt decrease during the middle of the twentieth century?
    (3) Which areas of government spending create the greatest amount of federal debt?
    (4) How can government reduce federal debt while increasing gross domestic product?
    (5) What percentage of gross federal debt at the end of 1965 resulted from defense spending during that year?

<u>Question 32</u> refers to the following information.

A large amount of pollution comes from hazardous household waste (HHW). HHW includes materials such as paint thinners, oil, discarded pharmaceuticals, gasoline, pesticides, and household cleaners. These pose a serious threat to the environment and to human health if they are not disposed of properly.

32. Based on this information, which of the following would *not* be beneficial in decreasing the amount of HHW?
   (1) reusing hazardous products instead of buying more
   (2) painting with oil-based paints instead of latex (water-based) paints
   (3) using a plunger instead of drain cleaner
   (4) recycling food scraps and yard trimmings to make compost
   (5) using sandpaper instead of chemical paint strippers

<u>Questions 33 and 34</u> are based on the following advertisement.

HILL's LIGHT DIVISION GOLD EDITION

2005 Digirealms Interactive presents the upgraded and expanded Gold Edition of their hit Civil War battlefield simulation *Hill's Light Division.* Control troop movements and assignments, build fortifications and encampments, and respond to unexpected enemy activity with the new Backup Plan feature as you lead Confederate General A.P. Hill and his men into battle against the Union Army of the Potomac. *The Gold Edition contains expanded analysis of each battle scenario and over 60 minutes of documentary material on the eastern theater of the Civil War!*

#FK2412 2 DVD-ROM Package $20

33. Based on the advertisement, what does Digirealms Interactive appear to assume about its video-game player market?
   (1) Players know a great deal about the Eastern Theater of the Civil War.
   (2) Players prefer older editions of war simulation games.
   (3) Players are attracted to upgrades and reduced prices.
   (4) Players no longer consider the Civil War an interesting topic.
   (5) Players would have enjoyed life during the Civil War.

34. Which of the following conclusions about the Civil War is supported by the information?
   (1) The unpredictable nature of Civil War battles meant commanding officers had to make many quick decisions during fighting.
   (2) Confederate General A. P. Hill was not a successful commander of soldiers.
   (3) There was only one theater of combat during the Civil War.
   (4) Hill's Light Brigade defeated the Union Army of the Potomac.
   (5) The frequent movement of camps made finding enemy forces difficult.

GO ON TO THE NEXT PAGE

Questions 35 and 36 refer to the following graphs.

Percentage of U.S. Population by Age Group and Sex, 1950

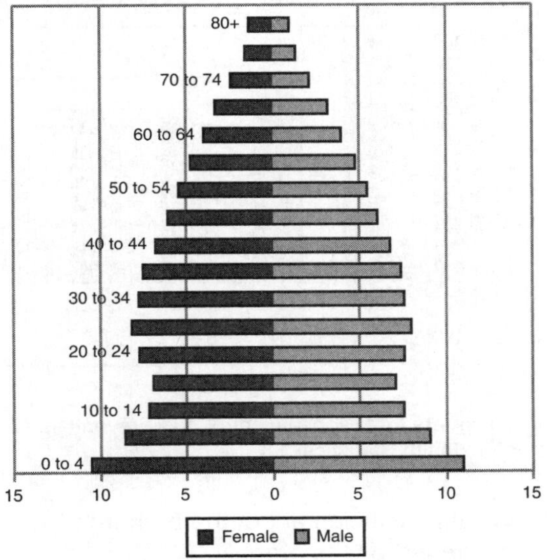

Percentage of U.S. Population by Age Group and Sex, 2000

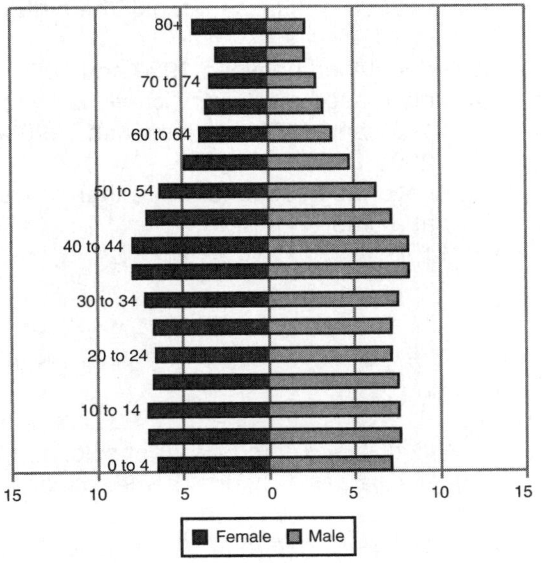

Source: U.S. Census Bureau, Population Division/International Programs Center

35. Which question about the U.S. population can be answered by using information in the graph?

    (1) Approximately what percentage of the population was age 50 or older in 2000?
    (2) Approximately how many people were age 24 or younger in 1950?
    (3) What caused the growth of the 40- to 44-year-old age group between 1950 and 2000?
    (4) In what year did the population of 30- to 34-year-olds first exceed the population of 25- to 29-year-olds?
    (5) How many people were born between 1950 and 2000?

36. Which of the following describes a trend shown in the graphs?

    Between 1950 and 2000,

    (1) the population became more evenly distributed across age groups
    (2) the percentage of people age 60 or older decreased
    (3) the largest age group of the population remained people age 4 or younger
    (4) the population remained approximately the same
    (5) the population decreased, then increased, and then decreased again

GO ON TO THE NEXT PAGE

Question 37 refers to the following information.

For many decades, drug trafficking has been a huge problem in Colombia. Every year there are thousands of kidnappings and homicides related to the drug trade. Many attempts at reform have been made, with a large amount of financial support coming from the United States. More than 2 million Colombians have fled their country in recent years because of the violence. Though enforcement and penalties have been made stricter in the past few years, Colombian traffickers still manage to supply the United States with 90% of its cocaine and 50% of its heroin.

37. From this information, what is the best explanation for the continued dominance of the illegal drug trade in Colombia?

    (1) The traffickers do not fear imprisonment or death.
    (2) Many people have fled the country, so there is more room to grow the drugs.
    (3) Demand from the United States for the drugs is so high that traffickers are willing to take the risks involved with smuggling them.
    (4) The government in Colombia is doing little to curb the efforts of traffickers.
    (5) Production of cocaine and heroin is actually legal in Colombia.

Questions 38 refers to the following graph.

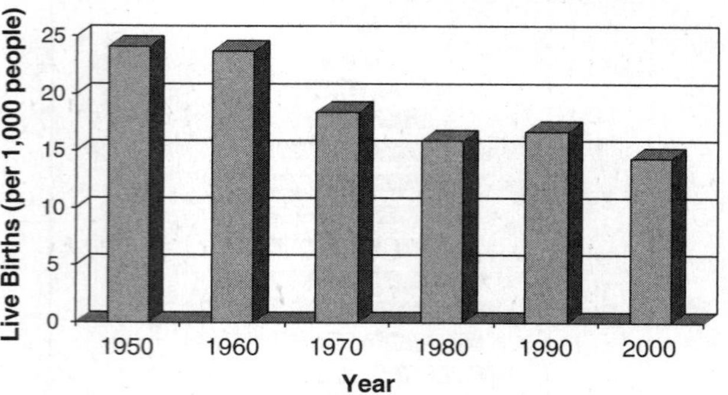

Source: Centers for Disease Control and Prevention, National Center for Health Statistics

38. What conclusion about the birth rate is confirmed by the graph?

    The birth rate

    (1) never increased between 1950 and 2000
    (2) in 2000 was less than half the birth rate in 1950
    (3) decreased between 1980 and 1990
    (4) decreased more significantly between 1960 and 1970 than between 1990 and 2000
    (5) never decreased for more than 10 years at a time

GO ON TO THE NEXT PAGE

Questions 39 and 40 are based on the following information.

The theory that people first arrived in North America 11,000 years ago has been popularly accepted since the 1930s. It has been hypothesized that these first Americans were people of Asian descent, who crossed over a land bridge that once linked Russia and Alaska. The land bridge existed in the area that is now the Bering Strait and is evidenced by the modern Aleutian Islands. In recent years, however, this view has been challenged.

A site in Chile that was first studied in 1977, called "Monte Verde," suggests that people were living there 12,500 years ago, which was 1,500 years prior to the Asian people crossing the land bridge. The traditional view of people walking over the land bridge has also been challenged by ideas such as people arriving by boat from unexpected places all over the world. There is much controversy over the topic, and dates for the arrival of the first Americans have been stretched to 15,000 years ago, 40,000 years ago, and, in according to some researchers, even 100,000 and 200,000 years ago.

39. Which conclusion regarding who was the first to arrive in North America is best supported by the information in the passage?

(1) People of Asian descent weren't the first to arrive in North America.
(2) Much controversy surrounds the issue, and no absolute conclusion has been made.
(3) The first people to arrive in North American arrived 200,000 years ago.
(4) People of Asian descent were the first people to arrive in North America.
(5) Although some argue that people could have arrived by boat, the land bridge was the only possible means by which people arrived in North America.

40. According to the passage, why has the popularly accepted hypothesis that people of Asian descent were the first to arrive in North America via the land bridge been challenged?

(1) Instead of migrating to North America via the land bridge, people migrated via boat.
(2) Scientists have discovered that people arrived in North America 200,000 years ago.
(3) It has been discovered that the land bridge never existed.
(4) Christopher Columbus was the first to arrive in North America.
(5) "Monte Verde" in Chile suggests that people lived in North America 1,500 years prior to the Asian land bridge crossing.

GO ON TO THE NEXT PAGE

41. In 1620, 102 passengers plus crew left Plymouth, England, aboard the sailing vessel *Mayflower* bound for North America. These Pilgrims, as they have come to be called, were united by a common belief in the Separatist religious movement, which held that their views were irreconcilable with those of the Church of England. The Pilgrims desired a place where they could live without fear of repression by other groups.

    What mostly attracted the Pilgrims to North America in 1620?

    (1) economic opportunity
    (2) recreation
    (3) military conquest
    (4) religious freedom
    (5) easy access

42. U.S. Census data can be used to calculate the location of the mean (average) center of U.S. population. This is the center of population according to physical distribution and density. In 1790, the mean center of population was in Kent County, Maryland. Every 10 years since, the mean center of population has moved between one and three counties west. By 1980, the mean center of population had moved west of the Mississippi River to Jefferson County, Missouri.

    On the basis of the information, which of the following could be a reason for the change in the mean center of population since 1790?

    (1) a significant migration from the west to the east
    (2) a steady migration from the east to the west
    (3) an increase in birth rates throughout the country
    (4) a decline in the population of Maryland
    (5) a slowing of migration among different regions of the country

GO ON TO THE NEXT PAGE

Questions 43 through 45 refer to the following information.

During the 20th century, as a result of the over-hunting of whales by commercial whaling ships, many whale species became endangered—some nearly to the point of extinction. As a result, the motto "Save the Whales" became a common phrase in many western industrialized cultures. The thought of killing this large mammal for human consumption was appalling to many policy makers. And so, in 1977, the International Whaling Committee (IWC) imposed an outright ban on all whaling. Almost immediately, a great cry sounded from the Inuit (sometimes called Eskimos), the indigenous people of the Arctic Circle who rely on the whale for their very survival.

For more than a thousand years, Inuit whalers have hunted bowhead whales. Whaling songs date back nearly as far. The whale has many uses for the Inuit people, and no part of the animal is wasted. The baleen (whalebone) is cut into strips and is used like wire for fastening objects or in boots for insulation. The huge vertebrae are used for seats. The stomach and bladder are used for drums. The remainder, including the tongue, skin, and other organs, is used for food.

This food is very nutritious. A typical serving of whale meat is 95% protein. The meat is also rich in iron, niacin, vitamin E, and phosphorus. A favorite snack, *maktaaq* (whale skin) is rich in calcium, selenium, and omega-3 fatty acids. A study of Inuit eating habits found that those who consumed primarily traditional Inuit food (60–70% whale meat) were less likely to be obese than Inuit who consumed a more Westernized diet.

43. Why did the Inuit protest the ban on whaling?

    (1) They felt the ban was too broad reaching.
    (2) They thought the ban was unjustly imposed.
    (3) They didn't care about the fate of the whales.
    (4) They feared that a ban would damage the ecosystem.
    (5) They rely on the whale for survival.

44. According to the passage, which of the following combinations is found in *maktaaq*?

    (1) calcium, selenium, and niacin
    (2) iron, niacin, and phosphorus
    (3) vitamin E, selenium, and omega-3 fatty acids
    (4) calcium, selenium, and vitamin E
    (5) calcium, selenium, and omega-3 fatty acids

45. Which of the following is a likely cause of the endangering of whales?

    (1) Inuit hunting
    (2) overhunting by commercial whaling ships
    (3) oil spills
    (4) human consumption
    (5) the "Save the Whale" campaign

GO ON TO THE NEXT PAGE

Questions 46 through 48 refer to the following map and information.

Credit: Data courtesy Marc Imhoff of NASA GSFC and Christopher Elvidge of NOAA NGDC. Image by Craig Mayhew and Robert Simmon, NASA GSFC.

The brightest areas of the Earth are the most urbanized but not necessarily the most populated. (Compare western Europe with China and India.) Cities tend to grow along coastlines and transportation networks. Even without the underlying map, the outlines of many continents would still be visible. The U.S. interstate highway system appears as a lattice connecting the brighter dots of city centers. In Russia, the Trans-Siberian Railroad is a thin line stretching from Moscow through the center of Asia to the Sea of Japan. The Nile River in North Africa, from the Aswan Dam to the Mediterranean Sea, is another bright thread through an otherwise dark region.

Even more than 100 years after the invention of the electric light, some regions remain thinly populated and unlit. Antarctica is entirely dark. The interior jungles of Africa and South America are mostly dark, but lights are beginning to appear there. Deserts in Africa, Arabia, Australia, Mongolia, and the United States are poorly lit as well (except along the coast), along with the boreal forests of Canada, Russia, and the great mountains of the Himalaya.

Source: NASA *Visible Earth* (http://visibleearth.nasa.gov/view_rec.php?id=1438)

46. According to the map and information, what comparison can be made among the continents?

    (1) population growth rates
    (2) religious beliefs
    (3) level of urbanization
    (4) distribution of natural resources
    (5) variety of cultural groups

47. What is the most probable reason for an increase in light use at night?

    (1) Many cultures keep outdoor fires burning throughout the night.
    (2) Lately, people are going to bed later.
    (3) Roads and urban centers continue to spread and grow.
    (4) The cost of electricity is decreasing.
    (5) Populations are shifting toward regions with decreased sun exposure.

48. Which statement would be supported by the fact that light use at night is increasing in the interior jungles of Africa and South America?

    (1) People living in jungles are migrating to the cities.
    (2) Jungles are expanding worldwide.
    (3) Flooding rivers are impeding jungle industries.
    (4) Governments are increasing restrictions on industrial activities in jungles.
    (5) The harvesting of wood and other jungle resources is increasing.

GO ON TO THE NEXT PAGE

49. What would be the best explanation for a surplus of a product on the market?

    (1) An insufficient amount of the product is available to meet the public demand.
    (2) The product has gotten great reviews in the media.
    (3) The costs of labor in producing the product have increased.
    (4) A more expensive alternative to the product has recently become available.
    (5) An excess amount has been produced in relation to the demand.

50. The Asia-Pacific Economic Cooperation (APEC) is a group of 21 Pacific Rim countries that meet every year to improve economic and political ties. Included in APEC are countries such as Australia, Canada, China, the United States, New Zealand, and Mexico. Their mission is to peacefully advance economic cooperation among one another through measures such as reducing tariffs and other trade barriers. The group has recently criticized North Korea, whom they feel is posing a serious threat to the world.

    According to this information, what is the most logical explanation for APEC's recent criticism of North Korea?

    It is because North Korea

    (1) does not have much to offer in terms of trade
    (2) has very high tariffs
    (3) has been developing and testing nuclear arms
    (4) does not get along very well with Canada
    (5) refused to join APEC when they were asked

Answers and explanations for this test begin on page 815.

GO ON TO: SCIENCE

Science Test

The GED Science Test consists of 50 multiple-choice questions that you must answer in 80 minutes. You will have to draw upon some prior knowledge of life science, earth and space science, and physical science; however, you will not have to recall facts.

Directions: Choose the one best answer to each question.

GO ON TO THE NEXT PAGE

1. Folic acid has been found to reduce the risk of neural tube birth defects if taken by pregnant women early in their pregnancy. Folic acid can be found in leafy vegetables, fortified cereals, and vitamin B tablets.

   Based on this information, what would be the best advice a doctor could give a woman who wants to become pregnant and wants to avoid neural tube birth defects?

   (1) avoid spinach during pregnancy
   (2) eat eggs for breakfast to increase the protein in her diet
   (3) take a vitamin B tablet daily before and during pregnancy
   (4) increase the amount of dairy in her diet
   (5) Avoid strenuous exercise during pregnancy

2. Earth has experienced many periods of flourishing life followed by states of extinction. The following figure shows the arrangement of layers in which various species' fossils are found. More recent species' fossils are found in the layers above older species' fossils. The layers correspond to time periods designated by the letters A, B, C, D, and E.

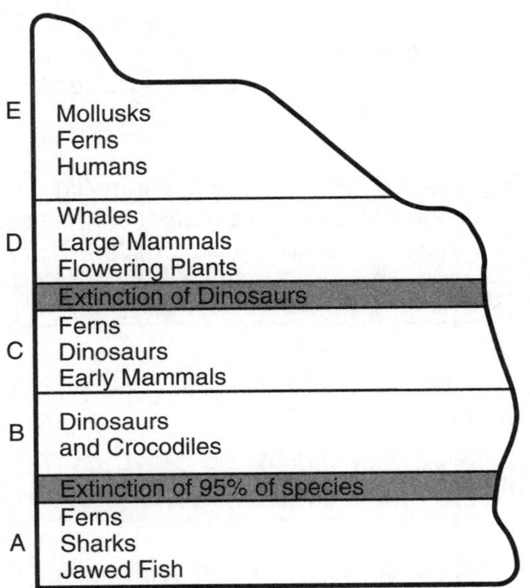

   During which period did mammals first exist?

   (1) A
   (2) B
   (3) C
   (4) D
   (5) E

3. Many countries around the world observe Daylight Saving Time. Clocks are set an hour ahead in the spring and an hour behind in the fall. What is the reason for Daylight Saving Time?

   (1) The earth turns slower in the summer, so clocks must be adjusted to accommodate this change.
   (2) The earth's axis tilts more toward the sun during the summer months, causing the earth to warm up.
   (3) The change is observed in areas that benefit from having more sunlight during hours of activity.
   (4) The clocks control the earth's turn rate.
   (5) Daylight Saving Time changes the amount of hours in the day from 24 hours to 25 hours.

4. Global warming theories predict that the earth is moving toward a warmer climate and higher temperatures. The change could cause polar ice caps and glaciers to melt. The populations of organisms in these areas would be threatened. Which of the following biomes would be the most endangered by melting polar ice?

   (1) grassland
   (2) desert
   (3) rain forest
   (4) tundra
   (5) aquatic

GO ON TO THE NEXT PAGE

5. The pH scale measures how acidic or basic a substance is. According to the scale, 7 is neutral. Values lower than 7 are acidic, and values higher than 7 are basic. The following table lists different pH values.

Substance	pH Value
Lemon juice	2.4
Orange juice	3.5
Milk	6.5
Pure water	7
Human blood	7.4
Household bleach	12.5

According to the table, which of the following substance is the most basic?

(1) lemon juice
(2) milk
(3) pure water
(4) human blood
(5) household bleach

6. The state of a substance can change as its temperature changes. Phase changes depend on the temperature and pressure of the surrounding atmosphere. Shown next is a phase change as pressure is held constant, but temperature is increased.

SOLID → LIQUID → GAS
A B

Following the direction indicated by the arrows, which of the following would describe point A?

(1) melting
(2) freezing
(3) evaporation
(4) condensation
(5) sublimation

7. Ocean tides are produced by gravitational effects exerted on the earth by the sun and the moon. Tides go through cycles of high versus low tides, as well as lunar versus solar tides. The solar tide is exactly 12 hours long. If the solar tide begins at 12-noon, at what time will it end and the lunar tide begin?

(1) 11 a.m.
(2) 12 midnight
(3) 1 a.m.
(4) 10 p.m.
(5) 11 p.m.

8. Water pressure is different at different depths. Scuba divers are warned not to come to the surface too quickly because dissolved nitrogen in their blood can create bubbles, which leads to a painful condition known as "the bends." This condition can cause serious injury or death. Which of the following causes the nitrogen to form bubbles?

(1) decreasing pressure as the diver is ascending
(2) increasing pressure as the diver is ascending
(3) constant pressure as the diver is ascending
(4) the ample temperature difference of the water
(5) more air bubbles at the surface of the water

9. As a part of an experiment, the melting points of different metals were measured. The results are recorded in the following table.

Metal	Melting Point (°C)
Bismuth	251.50
Copper	1084.62
Nickel	1455.00
Silver	961.78
Tin	231.93

Which metal has a melting point between 500°C and 1000°C?

(1) bismuth
(2) copper
(3) nickel
(4) silver
(5) tin

GO ON TO THE NEXT PAGE

10. Leila noticed that when she eats certain foods, she has a severe allergic reaction. Her symptoms are an itchy nose, eyes, and skin, congestion, and diarrhea. On four occasions, she compiled a list of the foods that she ate before an allergic reaction occurred. Her findings are recorded in the following table.

Meal	Components
1	cereal with skim milk and a banana
2	grilled cheese sandwich, tomato soup, and a glass of water
3	pepperoni pizza and a cola
4	grilled chicken, a potato, broccoli, an ice cream bar, and a glass of tomato juice

Eating which of the following most likely causes Leila's allergic reactions?

(1) tomato products
(2) grilled foods
(3) bread products
(4) meat products
(5) dairy products

11. Damien wanted to see what objects would slide down the steep driveway in front of his house. He used an ice cube, a peanut covered in vegetable oil, and a rock. The ice cube and peanut slid down, but the rock did not. Which of the following explains why the rock remained stationary while the other objects slid?

(1) The ice cube and the peanut have more friction between them than the rock and the hill have between them.
(2) The rock is experiencing buoyant force and the other objects are not.
(3) The ice cube and the peanut are heavier than the rock.
(4) Cold objects slide better than hot objects.
(5) The rock and the hill have more friction between them than the sliding objects and the hill have.

12. Wave technologies transmit information or energy from one location to another without the use of wires. Which of the following devices does not use wave technology?

(1) cell phones
(2) television
(3) hybrid car engines
(4) radio
(5) satellites

13. Perspiration is an essential function that helps the body stay cool. Because perspiration is the body's natural way of regulating temperature, people perspire more when it's hot outside and when they are exerting themselves. When are you most likely to experience the process of perspiration?

(1) while sitting at a desk
(2) during a long-distance race
(3) in the winter on a sunny day
(4) while drinking water
(5) while swimming laps in the pool

14. Vestigial organs are anatomical structures in organisms that have lost their function as a result of evolution. Which of the following is *not* an example of a vestigial organ?

(1) human appendix
(2) undeveloped hind-leg bones in whales
(3) ostrich wings
(4) malformed human hand
(5) human coccyx, or "tailbone"

GO ON TO THE NEXT PAGE

Questions 15–17 refer to the following passage.

Diabetes mellitus is a serious disease on the rise in America. There are two types: type I and type II. Type I diabetes is often called "insulin dependent diabetes," and type II is often called "insulin independent diabetes." Both are marked by the body's inability to regulate the concentrations of glucose in the blood. The result is hyperglycemia, or high levels of blood glucose.

Type I diabetes usually manifests during early childhood. It is an autoimmune disease, meaning that the individual's own immune system is the cause. The cells in the pancreas responsible for producing insulin, the hormone responsible for regulating blood glucose concentrations, are specifically attacked and killed. Therapy for this type of diabetes usually involves daily insulin injections, an exercise program, and stringent monitoring of diet.

Type II diabetes typically occurs later in life. It is not an autoimmune disorder, but rather is caused by an inability to successfully use insulin. There are several factors leading to type II diabetes, but the most common is obesity. Obese individuals slowly develop a resistance to insulin. Usually these diabetics can control their condition with an exercise program and strict diet.

15. Which of the following is an opinion rather than a fact?
    (1) Daily insulin injections are a hassle.
    (2) Type I diabetes is caused by the immune system.
    (3) Hyperglycemia is seen in both types of diabetes.
    (4) A young child with diabetes probably does not have type II.
    (5) A strictly monitored diet is a treatment used in both types of diabetes.

16. Which of the following facts would support the argument that type I diabetes is a more serious condition than type II diabetes?
    (1) Hyperglycemia can result in kidney disease.
    (2) Insulin injections are relatively inexpensive.
    (3) Obesity acts to further aggravate diabetic complications.
    (4) The pancreas has many important functions.
    (5) The longer people have diabetes, the more likely they are to face life-threatening complications.

17. Which person most likely has type I diabetes?
    (1) John is 8 years old. He is not allowed to have candy because the sugar makes him ill.
    (2) Rita is a 43-year-old mother. She often gets hyperglycemia if she does not adhere to the strict diet her doctor recommended for her.
    (3) Barbara is a 67-year-old nurse. She began taking insulin injections 25 years ago and has worked very hard since then to lose weight and maintain a healthy lifestyle.
    (4) Theodore is a 38-year-old who takes insulin injections. His friends call him a "pole" because of his lean build. He has suffered from the condition and has required injections since age 30.
    (5) Jean is 26 years old. She is very overweight, and her doctor has placed her on a strict diet.

GO ON TO THE NEXT PAGE

18. Mutualism describes the relationship between two organisms in which both benefit from their interaction. Which of the following is an example of mutualism?

(1) Fleas live in the coats of many animals and obtain nourishment from the host's blood.
(2) Bees collecting nectar to make honey pollinate flowers in the process.
(3) A vine uses a tree for structural support.
(4) Carpenter ants carve nests into trees and compromise the health of the trees.
(5) A tapeworm in the digestive tract of a dog absorbs nutrients before they enter the dog's bloodstream.

19. In order to lift heavy objects, pulleys are often used. Increasing the number of pulleys in a system increases the weight one person can lift. The efficiency of a system of pulleys is represented by the ratio of the amount of work performed to the amount of effort put in. A perfect machine has an efficiency of 1 because no effort is lost because of friction.

A worker notices that if he uses a smooth rope instead of a coarse rope, his pulley system has a higher efficiency. Which of the following explains why?

(1) decreased friction between the rope and the pulley
(2) increased friction between the rope and the pulley
(3) decreased friction between the rope and the object being lifted
(4) increased friction between the rope and the object being lifted
(5) smooth ropes are stronger than coarse ropes

20. Nicotinamide adenine dinucleotide (NAD+) is an electron transporter chemical involved in aerobic respiration. NAD+ has an initial charge of +1. If NAD+ were to gain 2 electrons and 1 proton (H+), what would be the resulting charge of the molecule?

(1) –2
(2) –1
(3) 0 (neutral)
(4) +1
(5) +2

21. Blood type is controlled by three genes: A, B, and O. However, a person has only two of these genes. Each one of the genes is inherited separately from each parent. The table below shows the different combinations of genes and the resulting blood type.

Genes	Blood Type
AA	A
AO	A
BB	B
BO	B
AB	AB
OO	O

If a man who is AB and a woman who is BO have a child, which blood type would be impossible for the child to have?

(1) A
(2) B
(3) AB
(4) O
(5) All are possible

22. The Richter scale measures the intensity of an earthquake. It is based on a logarithmic scale with a base of 10. This means that each integer on the scale represents 10 times greater intensity than the previous integer. If earthquake A measures 2 on the Richter scale, and earthquake B measures 4 on the Richter scale, earthquake B is how many times more intense than earthquake A?

(1) 2
(2) 10
(3) 20
(4) 100
(5) 200

GO ON TO THE NEXT PAGE

23. The cuff used to measure blood pressure is called a sphygmomanometer. Blood pressure measurements are given as two numbers. One is the systolic pressure, or the pressure generated by a heartbeat, and the other is diastolic pressure, or the pressure while the heart is in between beats. Based on this information, which of the following can be assumed?

(1) Systolic pressure is less than that of diastolic pressure.
(2) Diastolic pressure is less than that of systolic pressure.
(3) High blood pressure can be effectively treated with a sphygmomanometer.
(4) Only a trained professional should measure blood pressure.
(5) Diastolic pressure is more important to know than systolic pressure.

24. Commercial radio in the United States is broadcast using frequency modulation (FM) or amplitude modulation (AM). With FM, the amplitude, or strength, of the radio wave remains constant while its frequency fluctuates around a "carrier frequency." FM receivers compensate for amplitude fluctuations. With AM, the frequency remains constant while the sound information is conveyed by changing the amplitude of the radio wave. Lightning in the atmosphere has the affect of altering the amplitude of radio waves.

Based on the information, which of the following can be assumed?

(1) FM radio has poorer sound quality than AM radio.
(2) There are more commercial AM radio stations in the United States than commercial FM radio stations.
(3) AM radio is more affected by lightning storms than FM radio is.
(4) FM radio is more affected by lightning storms than AM radio is.
(5) Neither FM nor AM radio can be broadcast during heavy lightning storms.

25. *E. coli* bacteria in your large intestine are so numerous and competitive that they prevent other types of bacteria from establishing colonies. Which of the following is the most likely result of this action?

(1) *E. coli* are harmful to humans because they can damage the large intestine.
(2) Disease-causing bacteria will not be able to enter the large intestine.
(3) Disease-causing bacteria will enter the large intestine but will be unable to multiply and do damage.
(4) Bacteria can enter the large intestine and thrive off of the surplus of nutrients.
(5) Antibiotics used to clear the intestine of bacteria would prevent bacterial infection.

26. Both bats and dolphins use echolocation to perceive the world around them. To do this, they make a very high-pitched sound. The sound bounces off of objects and returns to the animal. Using echolocation, dolphins are able to detect objects in their path faster than bats can. Which of the following offers the best explanation for this?

(1) Sound travels faster in water than it does in air.
(2) Dolphins are more intelligent.
(3) Bats are nocturnal, and it is difficult for them to perceive the world around them.
(4) Sound travels faster in air than it does in water.
(5) Fish, a dolphin's source of food, move faster than moths, a bat's source of food.

27. If the Gibbs energy of a chemical reaction is negative, the reaction is said to be spontaneous. Gibbs energy is given by the following equation:

Gibbs energy = H – ST

Which of the following scenarios would produce a spontaneous chemical reaction?

(1) H is negative and ST is positive.
(2) H is positive and large, and ST is positive and small.
(3) H is positive and ST is negative.
(4) H is zero and ST is negative.
(5) H is positive and ST is zero.

GO ON TO THE NEXT PAGE

28. Chefs observe that cooking the same type of rice in boiling water takes significantly longer at high elevation than at low elevation.

    Which of the following is the MOST LIKELY explanation for this?

    (1) Water quality varies geographically.
    (2) The chefs are using pans made of different metals.
    (3) The boiling temperature of water varies with atmospheric pressure.
    (4) Propane, natural gas, and other cooking fuels burn hotter at lower elevations.
    (5) Kitchens at high elevation receive less solar radiation than those at low elevation.

GO ON TO THE NEXT PAGE

Questions 29–31 refer to the following passage and graph.

Populations of different species in a particular ecosystem are heavily dependent on each other. With limited resources, populations cannot expand indefinitely. In fact, research has shown that populations actually fluctuate over time. They rise and fall in response to the availability of resources. To examine this, a group of ecologists decide to study the fluctuating numbers in the populations of squirrels and hawks over time. The results of the experiment are shown below.

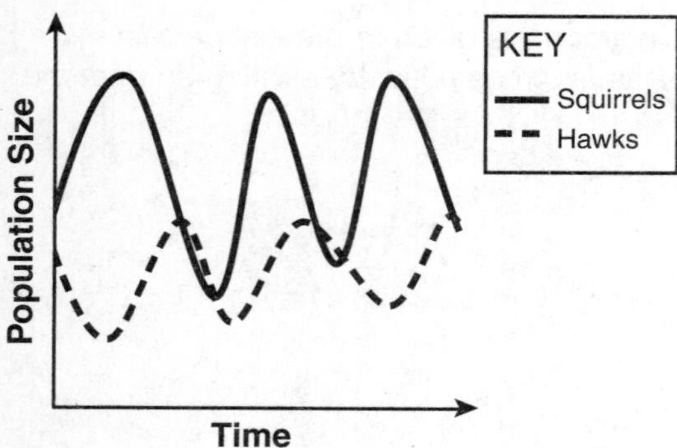

29. Which of the following is the best possible conclusion that can be made from the data?
    (1) Squirrels reach sexual maturity faster than hawks.
    (2) When the squirrel population is highest, the hawk population is lowest.
    (3) When the squirrel population is highest, the hawk population is highest.
    (4) A growing hawk population is a good indicator for a decline in the squirrel population.
    (5) Eventually, the hawks will permanently outnumber the squirrels.

30. A population of foxes is introduced into this ecosystem and heavily relies on squirrels as a source of food. Which of the following is the best prediction of the effect the foxes will have over time?
    (1) The two curves would both flatten out and fluctuate less.
    (2) The squirrel population would be hunted into extinction.
    (3) The average squirrel population would drastically reduce, but the hawk population will remain unaffected because foxes don't hunt hawks.
    (4) Hawks will become extinct.
    (5) The average hawk population will be reduced.

31. Which of the following is an unstated assumption suggested by the passage?
    (1) Populations of different species are dependent on each other.
    (2) The availability of resources directly affects populations in an ecosystem.
    (3) Hawks hunt squirrels as a source of food.
    (4) The population of squirrels is expected to fluctuate.
    (5) The population of hawks is expected to fluctuate.

GO ON TO THE NEXT PAGE

32. Coronary heart disease is often cause by deposits of cholesterol blocking coronary arteries. Recent research has shown that omega-3 fatty acids reduce cholesterol's ability to block arteries. This type of fatty acid is found primarily in fish. Which of the following can be assumed from the information given?

    (1) Living near a body of water can reduce the risk of coronary heart disease.
    (2) Eating fish is the only way to prevent coronary heart disease.
    (3) The only type of fat people should eat is omega-3 fatty acids.
    (4) All of the above
    (5) None of the above

33. The light-year is a unit often used in astronomy. It is defined as the distance light travels in one year. Which of the following units could be used to represent a light year?

    (1) meter
    (2) second
    (3) kilometers
    (4) gram
    (5) ampere

Question 34 refers to the passage below.

The immune system has a remarkable memory. After it has come into contact with a particular disease-causing organism, it elicits an immune response. As part of the response, millions of cells, specific to fighting organisms, are produced. After the threat is eliminated, most of the cells die. However, some survive and reproduce. These memory cells remain in the body for extended periods of time, often throughout a person's entire life. If the same organism attempts to infect again, the memory cells eliminate the threat before it can ever pose a problem.

34. Vaccinations are given to prevent certain illnesses, such as polio, by eliciting an immune response. Which of the following is the most likely mechanism by which vaccinations work?

    (1) Vaccinations involve infecting a person with a disease so they will not get it in the future.
    (2) Vaccinations are injections of memory cells.
    (3) Vaccinations are never effective throughout a person's life.
    (4) Vaccinations involve making the body respond as if infected by introducing damaged or nonfunctional disease-causing organisms into the body.
    (5) Vaccinations prevent certain disease-causing organisms from entering the body.

GO ON TO THE NEXT PAGE

<u>Question 35</u> refers to the following passage and diagram.

All cells have a plasma membrane, which regulates what enters and exits the cells. The membrane is composed of two layers of phospholipids. Each phospholipid is composed of a polar head (typically a phosphate) and a nonpolar tail (a fatty acid). Polar molecules, such as water, travel through the membrane unassisted in a process called simple diffusion. However, nonpolar molecules must move through the membrane with the help of transport proteins.

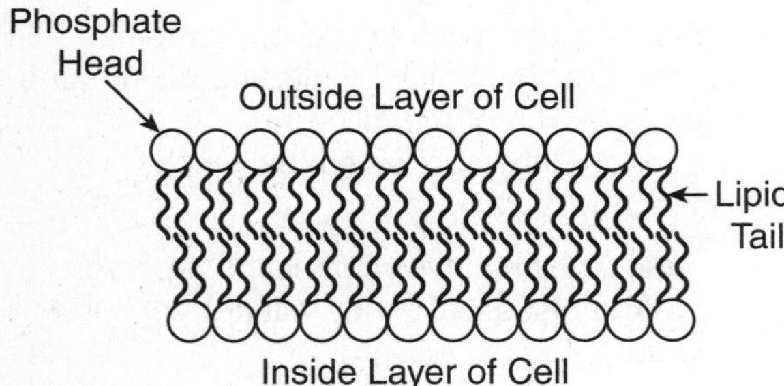

35. Based on the information, which of the following is required to transport nonpolar molecules through the plasma membrane?
    (1) a heavy concentration of nonpolar molecules exerting pressure on the plasma membrane
    (2) water molecules
    (3) a rupture in the plasma membrane
    (4) removal of the polar head of a phospholipid
    (5) transport proteins

---

36. A turbofan is a type of airplane engine that uses a large fan-shaped compressor to pressurize air, which is then mixed with jet fuel and ignited, propelling the airplane. Which of the following best explains why the space shuttle must use rocket engines instead of turbofans?
    (1) The air high in the atmosphere is too cold to ignite in a turbofan.
    (2) There is not enough air high in the atmosphere to be pressurized in a turbofan.
    (3) The space shuttle travels too slowly to use turbofans.
    (4) The space shuttle could not carry enough jet fuel to power turbofans.
    (5) Rocket engines are safer to operate than turbofans.

37. The formula for glucose is $C_6H_{12}O_6$. For every molecule of glucose that is metabolized, four carbon dioxide (CO_2) molecules are released as a waste product, and the rest is further metabolized to generate energy. One of the oxygen atoms in each CO_2 molecule comes from a source other than the glucose. The other two atoms in each CO_2 molecule come from the glucose. After all 4 CO_2 molecules are released as waste, how many total atoms from the original glucose molecule are left?
    (1) 8
    (2) 12
    (3) 16
    (4) 20
    (5) 24

<u>Questions 38 and 39</u> refer to the following passage.

Friction is the force that works against motion. Friction can be determined mathematically as the product of an object's mass and the coefficient of friction. The coefficient of friction depends on the two surfaces interacting. For example, a coin sliding across a carpet has a greater coefficient of friction than a coin sliding across a smooth marble floor, because the carpet is a rougher surface.

38. Which of the following statements explains why box A, which rests on a smooth surface, can actually be harder to push than box B, which rests on a rough surface?

    (1) Box B has a smaller coefficient of friction than box A.
    (2) Box B has a greater coefficient of friction than box A.
    (3) Box A has a smaller mass than box B.
    (4) Box A has a greater mass than box B.
    (5) Box A has a smaller mass and a greater coefficient of friction than box B.

39. Which of the following best explains the dangers of driving in icy conditions?

    (1) Ice on the pavement has a very low coefficient of friction.
    (2) The frigid temperatures reduce the coefficient of friction of the road surface.
    (3) Ice on the pavement has a very high coefficient of friction.
    (4) Ice on the pavement has greater mass.
    (5) Ice on the pavement has less mass.

<u>Questions 40 and 41</u> refer to the following passage.

T-cells are a type of white blood cell in the human body. They patrol the body looking for infected or damaged cells. Usually, when a cell is infected with a virus, changes occur to sugars on the outer membrane. T-cells are programmed to recognize sugars on the outer membrane of cells that do not match "self" sugars. When a "non-self" sugar is detected, the T-cell destroys the cell.

40. Which of the following is an unstated assumption based on the passage?

    (1) Healthy cells don't produce "non-self" sugars.
    (2) T-cells never attack healthy cells.
    (3) White blood cells are larger than red blood cells.
    (4) T-cells attack cells indiscriminately.
    (5) The abbreviation "T," in T-cell, stands for thymus.

41. AIDS is a disease that selectively destroys T-cells. Which of the following is most likely a danger of having AIDS?

    (1) AIDS destroys all the white blood cells.
    (2) The body is much less able to fight infection.
    (3) AIDS kills all of a person's blood cells.
    (4) AIDS-infected T-cells cannot be recognized by other T-cells.
    (5) All immune function is gone, and the body is incapable of fighting any infection.

GO ON TO THE NEXT PAGE

42. Pressure inside a cylinder of gas is determined by the frequency and force of gas molecules colliding with the cylinder walls. Increasing temperature causes the gas molecules to move faster. Which of the following can be assumed from the given data?

    (1) Gas molecules are more affected by temperature than any other environmental factor.
    (2) Increasing temperature always causes pressurized cylinders to explode.
    (3) Increasing temperature will decrease the pressure inside a cylinder of gas.
    (4) Decreasing temperature will decrease the pressure inside a cylinder of gas.
    (5) Pressure inside a cylinder of gas is constant because the amount of gas is constant.

43. Glycogen is a polymer of glucose, a sugar found in many foods. The liver takes excess glucose and stores it in the form of glycogen. Muscles also have glycogen stores. Under which condition would you expect glycogen formation?

    (1) after a meal
    (2) while fasting
    (3) while running
    (4) while sleeping
    (5) while playing basketball

Questions 44 and 45 refer to the following information and graph.

The peaks of mountains often lose sediment because of wind erosion. The height in meters (m) of two mountain peak sections, C and D, was observed at different times over a period of one year. The erosion rate in meters per year of mountain peak sections C and D and the percentage of the year that they were exposed to wind erosion is recorded in the following graph:

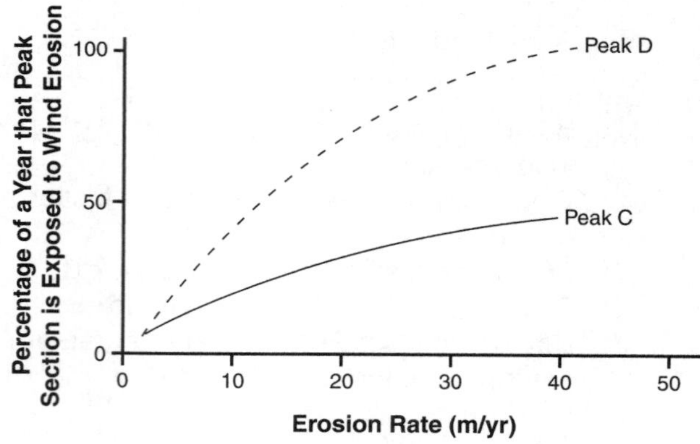

44. Based on the graph, when peak section D is exposed to wind erosion 75% of the year, what is the approximate peak-erosion rate, in meters per year?

    (1) 25
    (2) 40
    (3) 45
    (4) 75
    (5) The erosion rate cannot be measured.

45. Which of the following statements is supported by the graph?

    (1) Peak section C was exposed to more wind erosion than peak section D.
    (2) Peak section D was exposed to more wind erosion than peak section C.
    (3) Sediment loss was the same for both sections.
    (4) Peak section C had a faster erosion rate than peak section D.
    (5) Peak section D had a slower erosion rate than peak section C.

GO ON TO THE NEXT PAGE

46. Sally wants to set up an experiment to test the effectiveness of different types of plant food (fertilizer) on a certain type of rose bush. Her goal is to determine which fertilizer produces the tallest rose bushes with the greatest number of flowers. Which of the following is a dependent variable in Sally's experiment?

    (1) the type of fertilizer she uses
    (2) the number of flowers produced
    (3) the time of day she waters the bushes
    (4) the type of rose bushes she uses
    (5) the starting height of the rose bushes

47. Which of the following statements best explains why plants in the Northern Hemisphere experience more growth in the spring and summer than in the winter?

    (1) The tilt of the Earth on its axis provides longer days and more direct sunlight during the summer.
    (2) The tilt of the Earth on its axis provides longer days and more direct sunlight during the winter.
    (3) The position of the moon affects the length of day during the winter.
    (4) There are 365 days in a year.
    (5) The moon is closer to the Earth in the spring and summer.

48. Monarch butterflies have many adaptations for survival. They have very short life spans and are well known for their migration pattern. Their wings are also widely recognized for their bright orange-reddish hue with black stripes and white spots, all serving to suggest that monarch butterflies are either poisonous or very foul-tasting. Which of the following is an adaptation of the monarch butterfly essential in warning off potential predators?

    (1) their flight to Mexico for the winter
    (2) their bright wing coloration
    (3) their foul taste
    (4) their long tongues
    (5) their diet of milkweed

49. A white ball, a gray ball, and a black ball are all placed on a windowsill during bright sunlight hours. Dark color is associated with increased absorption of infrared radiation. After two hours in the sun, which ball should feel the hottest?

    (1) the black ball
    (2) the gray ball
    (3) the white ball
    (4) They all feel the same.
    (5) There is not enough information to answer the question.

50. Air pollution has become a major problem on our planet. The composition of the atmosphere is changing, affecting weather patterns and the habitats of all animals, including humans. Which of the following would *not* be a good way to clean the air?

    (1) buying gas-efficient vehicles
    (2) the use of smoke stacks
    (3) the use of public transportation
    (4) the use of nonaerosol cans
    (5) planting a tree

Answers and explanations for this test begin on page 820.

GO ON TO: MATHEMATICS

Mathematics Formulas

Area		
	Square	s^2
	Rectangle	$l \times w$
	Parallelogram	$b \times h$
	Triangle	$\frac{1}{2} \times b \times h$
	Trapezoid	$\frac{1}{2} \times (b_1 \times b_2) \times h$
	Circle	$\pi \times r^2$
Perimeter		
	Square	$4 \times s$
	Rectangle	$2 \times l + 2 \times w$
	Triangle	$\text{side}_1 + \text{side}_2 + \text{side}_3$
Circumference		
	Circle only	$2 \times \pi \times r$ OR $\pi \times$ diameter (diameter is two times the radius)
Volume		
	Cube [each face is a square]	s^3
	Rectangular solid	$l \times w \times h$
	Square pyramid [base is a square]	$\frac{1}{3} \times s^2 \times h$
	Cylinder [base is a circle]	$\pi \times r^2 \times h$
	Cone [base is a circle]	$\frac{1}{3} \times \pi \times r^2 \times h$
Coordinate Geometry		
	Distance between points; (x_1,y_1) and (x_2,y_2) are two points in a plane.	$\sqrt{(x_2 - x_1)^2 + (y_2 - y_1)^2}$
	Slope of a line; (x_1,y_1) and (x_2,y_2) are two points on the line.	$\frac{y_2 - y_1}{x_2 - x_1}$
Pythagorean Theorem		
	Determine the length of one side of a right triangle using the lengths of the other two sides; *a and b are legs; c is the hypotenuse (the side opposite the right angle).*	$a^2 + b^2 = c^2$
Measures of Central Tendency		
	Mean (average): *x* is a value and *n* is the total number of values for which you want a mean.	$\frac{x_1 + x_2 + \ldots + x_n}{n}$
	Median: begin with a set of values in numerical order.	The median is the middle value in a set with an odd number of values, halfway between (the average of) the two middle values in a set with an even number of values.
Rates		
	Simple Interest	principal (starting amount) × rate × time
	Distance	rate × time
	Total Cost	(number of units) × (price per unit)

GO ON TO THE NEXT PAGE

Mathematics Test

The GED Mathematics Test consists of 50 questions that you will be given 90 minutes to complete. The test is divided into two parts. On Part I, Questions 1–25, you may use a calculator. On Part II, Questions 26–50, you may not use a calculator.

Directions: Choose the one best answer to each question.

1. Elise works in a carpet store. Carpet that is normally priced at $19.50 per square yard is reduced to $15.60 per square yard. Installation is billed separately at $1.95 per square yard. How much will Elise's customer pay to have 50 square yards of carpet installed during the sale?

   (1) $1,072.50
   (2) $922.00
   (3) $884.90
   (4) $877.50
   (5) $655.00

2. Joey, who works at Terrific T-Shirts, can produce 40 T-shirts with the same design in one hour. One day at 11 a.m., he receives an order for a club that needs 180 shirts. If he works with a 30-minute lunch break, at what time will he have the order complete?

   (1) 1:30 p.m.
   (2) 5 p.m.
   (3) 4 p.m.
   (4) 6:15 p.m.
   (5) 3:30 p.m.

3. The base of the triangle below is 16 units long.

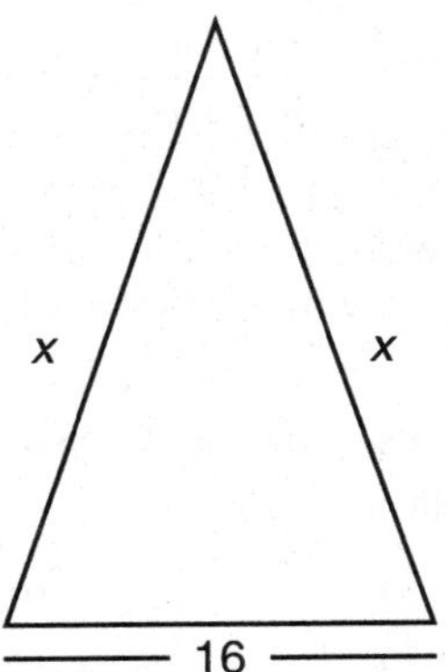

   If the length of x is $1\frac{1}{2}$ times the base, what is the perimeter of the triangle?

   (1) 78
   (2) 64
   (3) 56
   (4) 48
   (5) 32

4. As a camp counselor, Marcus needs to make sure that everyone drinks enough water on a hike. Marcus will accompany 24 campers on a hike. Each of the hikers (including Marcus) should drink at least $\frac{1}{2}$ gallon of water every hour. The hike will last for 1.5 hours. Approximately how much water, in gallons, should Marcus bring on the hike?

   (1) 19
   (2) 24
   (3) 25
   (4) 50
   (5) 75

GO ON TO THE NEXT PAGE

5. If $\frac{12 - x}{x} + 7 = 9$, what is the value of x?

(1) 2

(2) 4

(3) 8

(4) 12

(5) 17

6. A man earns $8 per hour of work for a standard, 40-hour workweek. He is also paid $11 per hour for overtime work. If he is paid $419 for one week at work, how many hours of overtime did he work?

Mark your answer in the circles on the grid on your answer sheet.

Questions 7 and 8 refer to the following information and table.

John planned a trip to Italy over the summer. His local exchange bank gave him the exchange rates for U.S. Dollars (USD) and Euro (EUR), which are listed below.

Exchange Rates for USD and EUR

US Dollars (USD)	Euro (EUR)
1	.752
1.329	1

7. Before leaving, John exchanged 350 USD for EUR. How many EUR did he receive in return?

(1) 410.00

(2) 375.00

(3) 290.40

(4) 263.20

(5) 185.60

8. While staying in Rome, John's hostel cost him 25 EUR per night. If he stayed there for three nights, what was the approximate cost of his stay in USD?

(1) 75.00

(2) 80.00

(3) 100.00

(4) 125.00

(5) 250.00

GO ON TO THE NEXT PAGE

9. Julie was in a minor car accident and had to have her entire driver's side door replaced at a cost of \$475. After a \$50 deductible is applied (that is, Julie pays the first \$50), her insurance company agrees to pay 70% of the remaining balance. How much, in dollars, will the insurance company pay?

   Mark your answer in the circles on the grid on your answer sheet.

10. Dave is a used car salesman. He currently has five four-door sedans on the car lot, priced at \$7,000; \$8,750; \$6,500; \$8,000; and \$9,300. What is the median price of the five sedans?

    (1) \$6,500
    (2) \$7,910
    (3) \$8,000
    (4) \$8,750
    (5) \$9,300

Question 11 refers to the circle below.

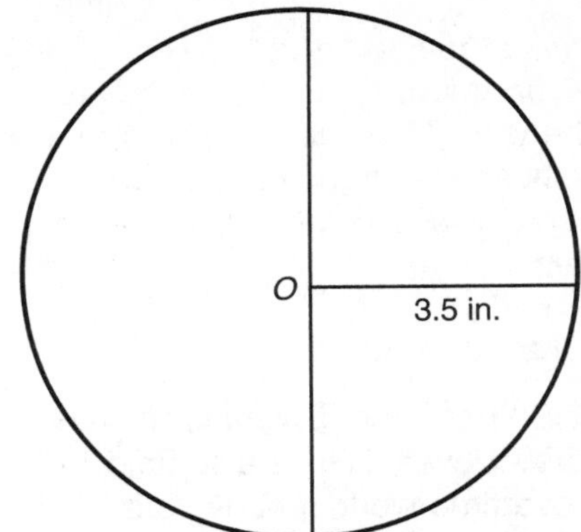

O is the center of the circle.

11. What is the circumference of the circle?

    (1) 3.5π
    (2) 7π
    (3) 12.25π
    (4) 14π
    (5) 35π

---

12. Body mass index (BMI) can be defined as BMI = $705w \div h^2$ where w is a person's weight in pounds and h is the person's height in inches. If Reggie weighs 215 pounds and is 73 inches tall, what is his BMI?

    Mark your answer in the circles on the grid on your answer sheet.

13. You have been hired for 3 hours to take pictures at a wedding reception. It takes you about 7 minutes to take a group picture and about 3 minutes to take a picture of an individual. The bride has requested that you take a total of 20 group pictures and as many individual pictures as you can in the time remaining. What is the maximum number of individual pictures that you can take at the reception?

    (1) 3
    (2) 13
    (3) 14
    (4) 20
    (5) 40

GO ON TO THE NEXT PAGE

<u>Question 14</u> refers to the following information and graph.

A local business has a goal to finish the year strong, averaging $55,000 per month in sales for the last three months of the year. The sales numbers for October and November are already in and are shown on the graph below. Sales numbers are in thousands of dollars.

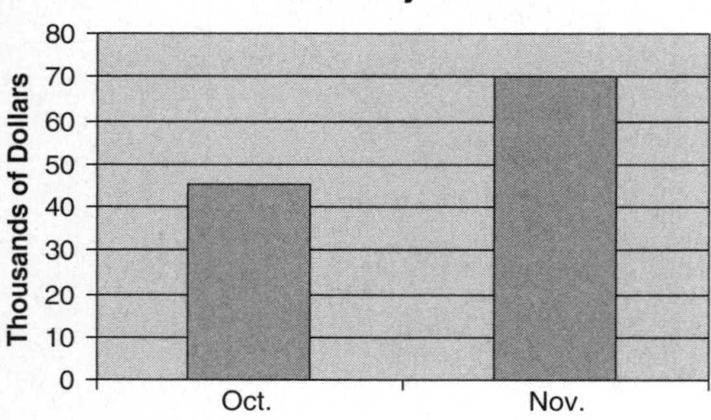

14. To reach its goal, what is the minimum dollar amount in sales that the business must make in December?

    (1) $30,500

    (2) $40,000

    (3) $50,000

    (4) $58,275

    (5) $75,000

15. Leg AB of the right triangle shown below is three times as long as leg BC.

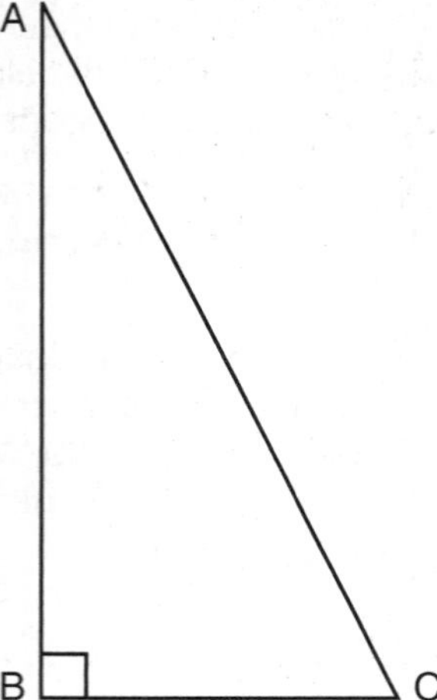

If the area of the triangle is 96 cm^2, what is the length, in cm, of leg AB?

    (1) 16

    (2) 24

    (3) 32

    (4) 40

    (5) 64

16. For her history course, Mary can purchase the required reading materials for $18.00, or she can borrow them from a friend and photocopy them at a cost of $.12 per page. If the cost to purchase the reading materials is the same as the cost to copy them, how many pages are there?

    Mark your answer in the circles on the grid on your answer sheet.

17. If $2.5(x + 4) = 30$, what is the value of x?

    (1) 8

    (2) 10

    (3) 12.5

    (4) 15

    (5) 23.5

Question 18 refers to the following table and information.

Five department stores are advertising the new XP10 MP3 player at sale prices shown in the table below.

Store A	Store B	Store C	Store D	Store E
40% off	$200	$160 off	1/2 price	30% off and $30 mail-in rebate

18. If the original price in each store was $300, which store is offering the lowest price?

    (1) A

    (2) B

    (3) C

    (4) D

    (5) E

---

19. Kim has been hired to tile a rectangular kitchen floor that is 10.5 feet wide and 11 feet long. Each of the floor tiles that Kim will use measures 6 inches by 6 inches. Approximately how many tiles will Kim need to complete the job?

    (1) 36

    (2) 45

    (3) 79

    (4) 288

    (5) 462

20. Wilson left $450 in a savings account for two years. At the end of each year, he received an interest credit of 6%. If he withdraws $300 and also pays a service charge of $2.25, how much will he have left in his savings account?

    (1) $164

    (2) $203.37

    (3) $225

    (4) $335.75

    (5) $480

21. The man in charge of a company's warehouse is expecting a delivery of 864 cameras. The cameras were packed in boxes of 27 cameras each. How many boxes should he be receiving?

    (1) 19

    (2) 25

    (3) 32

    (4) 38

    (5) 47

GO ON TO THE NEXT PAGE

Questions 22 and 23 refer to the following information and graph.

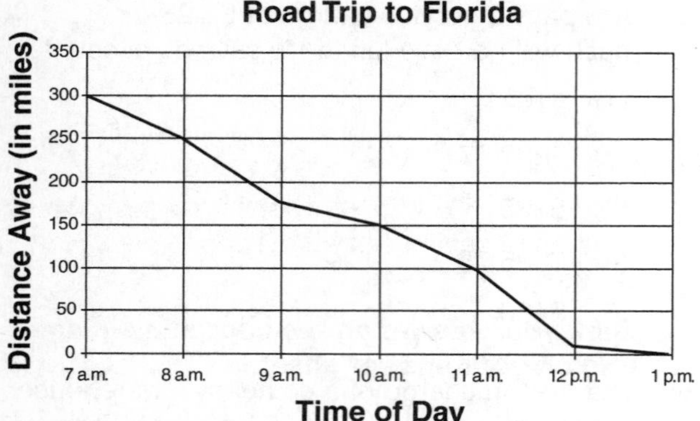

Several college students decided to take a road trip to Florida. The graph above represents their distance from their destination at various times during the trip.

22. During which one-hour time interval did the students travel at the fastest speed?

    (1) 7:00 a.m. to 8:00 a.m.

    (2) 8:00 a.m. to 9:00 a.m.

    (3) 10:00 a.m. to 11:00 a.m.

    (4) 11:00 a.m. to 12:00 p.m.

    (5) 12:00 p.m. to 1:00 p.m.

23. At what average speed, in miles per hour did the students travel between 7:00 a.m. and 10:00 a.m.?

    (1) 25

    (2) 40

    (3) 50

    (4) 65

    (5) 75

24. Which equation could be used to find x, the length of the ramp in the following diagram?

Loading Dock

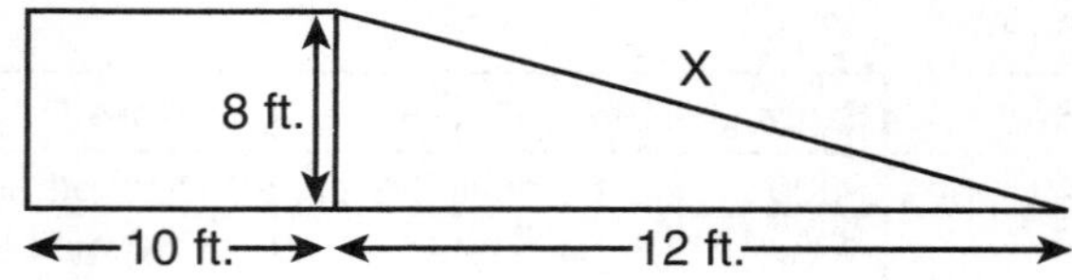

    (1) $(10 + 12)^2 = x^2$

    (2) $\left(\frac{8}{22}\right)^2 = x^2$

    (3) $\sqrt{8^2 + 12^2} = x$

    (4) $\sqrt{8^2 + 22^2} = x$

    (5) $8(10 + 12) = x$

25. If $4y - 3 = 25$, what is the value of y?

    Mark your answer in the circles on the grid on your answer sheet.

GO ON TO: MATHEMATICS, PART II

Mathematics, Part II

Choose the one best answer to each question. You may **NOT** use a calculator for these questions.

26. Which of the following is the complete solution to the equation $(x + 7)(x - 9) = 0$?

    (1) -9 and 7

    (2) -7 and 9

    (3) -7 only

    (4) 9 only

    (5) 7 and 9

27. A group wants to rent an ice skating rink for a party. The cost is \$250 plus \$3 per person. If x people are attending the party, which equation can be used to find T, the total cost for renting the rink?

    (1) $T = 250x + 3$

    (2) $T = x(250 + 3)$

    (3) $T = \frac{250}{3x}$

    (4) $T = 250 + 3x$

    (5) $T = (250)(3x)$

28. The temperature outside was 8°C at 3 p.m. By 9 p.m., the temperature was x degrees more than half of what it had been at 3 p.m. Which expression represents the temperature reading at 9 p.m.?

    (1) $8 - \frac{1}{2}x$

    (2) $8 + 2x$

    (3) $\frac{1}{2}(8) + x$

    (4) $x - 8$

    (5) $\frac{8}{x}$

29. Nancy is hoping to sell her computer by placing a classified ad in her local newspaper. The newspaper charges \$5 for the first 10 words, and 36 cents per word thereafter. What would she pay for her ad if it contained 27 words?

    Mark your answer on the coordinate plane grid on your answer sheet.

30. The following statements about the diagram below are true:

    Angle UYZ is a straight angle.

    Angle UYW is a right angle.

    The measure of angle VYX is 80°.

    The measure of angle XYZ is 35°.

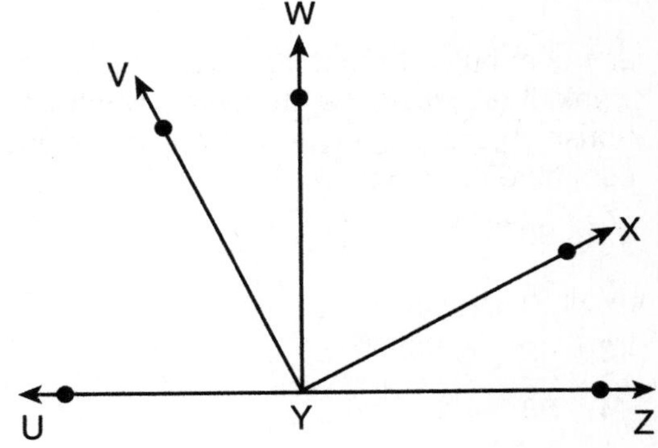

What is the measure of angle UYV?

(1) 30°

(2) 50°

(3) 65°

(4) 70°

(5) 110°

GO ON TO THE NEXT PAGE

31. Brian is moving and needs to rent a truck. The company he chooses charges $45 per day and an additional $.50 per mile. If Brian rents the truck for 2 days and drives a total of 80 miles, how much will he be charged?

(1) $90
(2) $130
(3) $150
(4) $175
(5) $210

32. Two points on a line are (2,3) and (5,12). Given these points, what is the slope of this particular line?

(1) 6
(2) 4
(3) 3
(4) 1
(5) $\frac{1}{2}$

33. Jim commutes to and from class three days per week. If his class is 9.65 miles away from his house, approximately how many miles does he commute each week?

(1) 96
(2) 74
(3) 62
(4) 58
(5) 43

34. Elizabeth took a friend out for dinner and their bill totaled $35. If she wants to leave a 20% tip, how much money should she leave for the tip?

Mark your answer in the circles on the grid on your answer sheet.

35. A case of water containing 12 bottles costs $3.99. Approximately how much would 5 cases of water cost?

(1) $20.00
(2) $36.00
(3) $48.00
(4) $52.00
(5) $60.00

Question 36 refers to the square below.

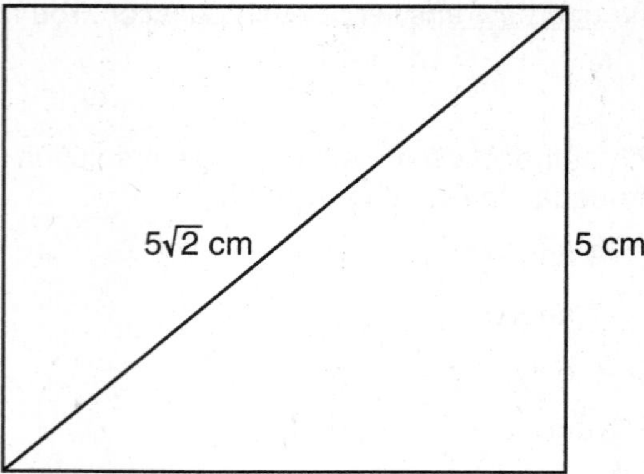

36. What is the perimeter of the square?

(1) 10 cm
(2) $10\sqrt{2}$ cm
(3) 20 cm
(4) 25 cm
(5) $30\sqrt{2}$ cm

37. Mandy drove 128 miles in 2 hours. At the same rate, how many miles could she drive in 3.5 hours?

Mark your answer in the circles on the grid on your answer sheet.

GO ON TO THE NEXT PAGE

Question 38 refers to the following graph.

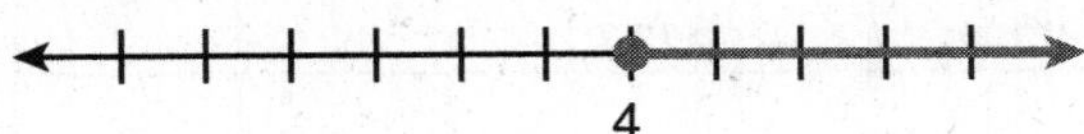

38. Which inequality is graphed on the number line?

    (1) $x \leq 4$

    (2) $4 < x$

    (3) $x = 4$

    (4) $x < 4$

    (5) $x \geq 4$

39. At a bookstore, part-time booksellers earn an average of $250 less per week than the managers. The store has 17 part-time booksellers and 4 managers. Let x represent the average weekly pay of a manager. Which of the following equations shows the weekly payroll (P) of all the bookstore employees?

    (1) $P = 4x + 17x$

    (2) $P = 4(x - 250) + 17(x - 250)$

    (3) $P = 4x + 17(x - 250)$

    (4) $P = 250x$

    (5) $P = 17x + 4(250 - x)$

40. In the diagram shown below, the measure of angle YZV is 65°. Angles VX and WY are straight angles.

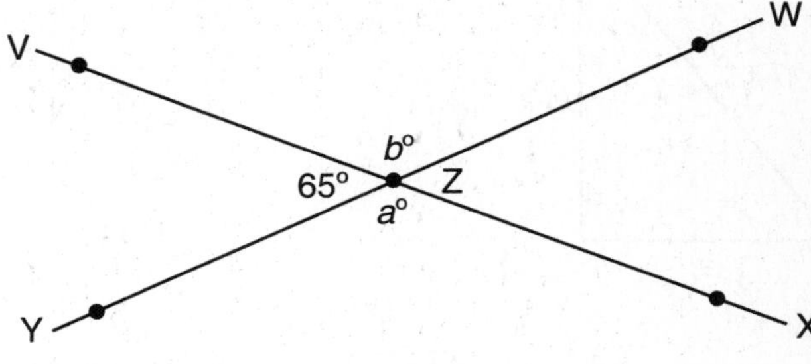

What is the value in degrees of $(a + b)$?

    (1) 280

    (2) 230

    (3) 180

    (4) 130

    (5) 100

41. Gene is driving to visit a friend. The scale on his map states that 1 inch = 6 miles. On the map, his friend's house is 3 inches away. What is the actual distance, in miles, between where Gene is now and his friend's house?

    Mark your answer in the circles on the grid on your answer sheet.

42. Paul must write four papers for his English class. He expects that the first one will take him 30 minutes, the second one will take half as much time as the first, the third will take 25 minutes, and the fourth will take the same amount of time as the second. What is the latest he can begin working if he needs to finish all of the papers by 3 p.m.?

    (1) 11:30 a.m.

    (2) 12 noon

    (3) 12:40 p.m.

    (4) 1:15 p.m.

    (5) 1:35 p.m.

Question 43 refers to the following figure.

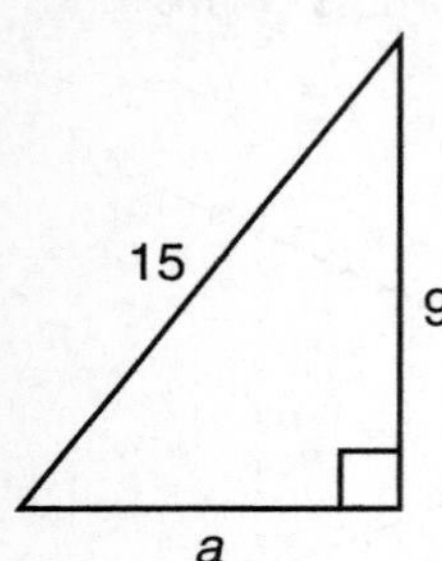

43. The hypotenuse of a right triangle measures 15 cm. If one leg measures 9 cm, which of the following expressions could be used to find the length of the other leg?

(1) $\sqrt{15^2 - 9^2}$

(2) $15^2 + 9^2$

(3) $\sqrt{15^2 + 9^2}$

(4) $15^2 \times 9^2$

(5) $15^2 - 9^2$

44. A furniture store is having a year-end clearance sale and is offering customers "30% off the sale price." A couch that was originally $800.00 is currently on sale for $600.00. What is the clearance price?

(1) $200.00

(2) $373.50

(3) $420.00

(4) $450.75

(5) $570.00

45. The height of a triangle is 3 times the base. The area of the triangle must be at least 85 feet^2. Which inequality can be solved to find the base (x)?

(1) $\frac{1}{2}(3x^2) \geq 85$

(2) $\frac{1}{2}(3x + x) \geq 85$

(3) $3x^2 < \frac{1}{2}(85)$

(4) $3x\left(\frac{1}{2x}\right) \geq 85$

(5) $3x + x > 85$

Question 46 refers to the following table.

Test Number	Score
1	75
2	65
3	80
4	95
5	—

46. If Michelle needs a mean score of 81 to earn a B in her class, what is the minimum that she must score on the fifth test to earn this grade?

(1) 70

(2) 80

(3) 85

(4) 90

(5) 100

47. A door-to-door vacuum salesman earns a weekly salary of $175 plus an additional $8 for every vacuum he sells. If in one week he earns $303, how many vacuums did he sell in that week?

(1) 6

(2) 9

(3) 12

(4) 16

(5) 42

GO ON TO THE NEXT PAGE

Questions 48–50 refer to the following information and graph.

Mike's Weight as a Function of Calorie Intake

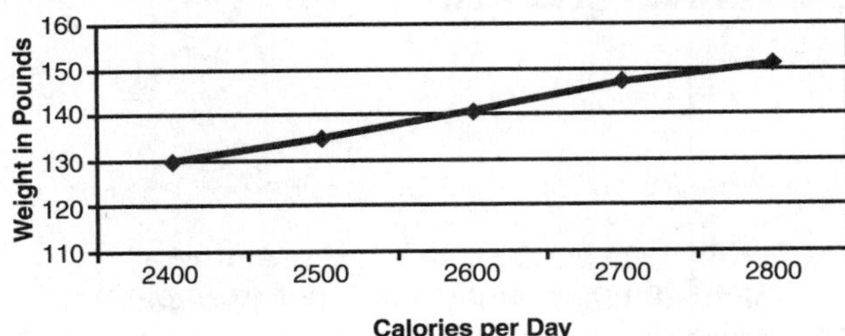

48. Mike is on the wrestling team and hopes to make the 132-pound weight class for the team's next meet. According to the graph, approximately how many calories per day should he eat to make his desired weight class?

    (1) 2,400
    (2) 2,450
    (3) 2,500
    (4) 2,550
    (5) 2,700

49. If Mike consumes 2,650 calories per day, approximately how much will he weigh?

    (1) Between 135 and 145 pounds
    (2) Between 140 and 150 pounds
    (3) Between 145 and 160 pounds
    (4) Between 150 and 160 pounds
    (5) Between 155 and 165 pounds

50. If Mike consumes 2,800 calories per day, approximately how many calories per pound of body weight is Mike consuming?

    (1) 7
    (2) 10
    (3) 12
    (4) 16
    (5) 19

Answers and explanations for this test begin on page 824.

END OF EXAMINATION

Language Arts, Writing Answers and Explanations

Part I

1. **The best answer is (4).** The phrase "thank you for" must be followed by a noun phrase or, as in this case, a verb in the gerund ("-ing") form.
2. **The best answer is (4).** The word "agent" is not a proper noun (for example, a person's name) and must not be capitalized.
3. **The best answer is (3).** The phrase "which is for sale" is redundant. The sentence makes clear that the home is for sale without including that phrase.
4. **The best answer is (2).** By not using the conjunction "and," the second part of the sentence is more clearly a modifier phrase of the noun phrase "adverse experiences with real estate firms." The verb "offer" would then be the gerund form "offering" so the modifier phrase does not have tense.
5. **The best answer is (5).** The sentence is grammatically correct and needs no changes.
6. **The best answer is (3).** When the phrase "elected to" is followed by a verb, that verb must be in the base form: "elected to represent."
7. **The best answer is (3).** These two sentences describe a cause-effect relationship; therefore, they can be joined with a comma and "so" (used as a conjunction).
8. **The best answer is (3).** Relative clauses beginning with "that" must not be separated from the main clause with a comma.
9. **The best answer is (1).** The adjective "busy" modifies the noun "summer," so the words should not be separated with a comma.
10. **The best answer is (4).** The preposition "by" correctly introduces the phrases beginning with the gerunds "using," "having," and "riding" and clearly conveys *how* the people have enjoyed the weather.
11. **The best answer is (5).** The verb "relate" refers to the plural noun "rules," so the plural subject pronoun is necessary.
12. **The best answer is (1).** This sentence should be written in the present tense to maintain parallelism with the rest of the letter. (The ATV problem is ongoing.)
13. **The best answer is (2).** These two sentences have a cause-effect relationship. Linking them in the simplest way results in the following sentence: "Wide ruts and paths are made alongside the roadway, undermining its stability." This new sentence also leaves out the second instance of "road," which could be considered redundant, or repetitive.
14. **The best answer is (3).** Sentence 11 would provide a complete introduction to the information in paragraph D; therefore, it should be moved to the beginning of that paragraph.
15. **The best answer is (4).** This sentence should be written in the present tense to maintain parallelism with the rest of the letter.

16. **The best answer is (4).** As used in the sentence, the contraction "you're" is incorrect. The correct homonym is "your," the possessive adjective. Notice how the sentence is a statement directed to "riders." The phrase "your vehicles" means "the vehicles that belong to you (the riders)."

17. **The best answer is (2).** No comma is necessary after the conjunction "but" and no comma must divide "necessary" from the relative clause beginning with "that." Answer choices (3) and (4) have a comma after "feel," which incorrectly separates that verb from its relative clause beginning with "it." Answer choice (5) has a comma incorrectly dividing the adverb "absolutely" from the adjective "necessary," which it modifies.

18. **The best answer is (1).** Sentence 16 repeats the notion from the first part of the first sentence of the paragraph. Therefore, it should be eliminated.

19. **The best answer is (4).** The proper form of "approach" is "approached." The verb itself refers to no one in particular, but it definitely does not refer to the subject "growing flowers" from the previous sentence. The "growing" is being *approached*. The "growing" is not *approaching* anything. (This should remind you of the concepts of passive and active voice in grammar.)

20. **The best answer is (2).** The comma is correctly placed before the conjunction "and," which links two independent clauses.

21. **The best answer is (2).** Sentence 6 is a good introductory sentence for the rest of the sentences in the paragraph. Therefore, it should be the first sentence in the paragraph.

22. **The best answer is (3).** This is the clearest and simplest choice. The resulting sentence is: "On the other hand, perennials bloom on their own every year, but often their blossoms will last for only two weeks."

23. **The best answer is (2).** The correct homonym is the possessive determiner "their," which indicates possession. In a sense, the "need" belongs to the "flowers."

24. **The best answer is (5).** The word "moisture" is a noun that appears to be modifying the noun "soil." An adjective such as "moist" is needed instead.

25. **The best answer is (3).** It is the simplest way to combine sentences 18 and 19. Using a comma and "which" is a clear way to introduce a relative clause, and it allows you to avoid repeating the long noun phrase "strong root systems."

26. **The best answer is (2).** A comma in this position breaks the flow of the complete sentence by separating the verb "appreciate" from its object "your correspondence."

27. **The best answer is (2).** The act of receiving positive comments is ongoing at the time of writing the letter, so it should be described using the simple present tense.

28. **The best answer is (2).** The noun phrase "satisfied customers" must not have an intervening comma. The conjunction "but" is used to join the two independent clauses in the sentence, so it requires a comma before it. No comma should be included between "but" and the start of the second clause.

29. **The best answer is (4).** These sentences are best combined using the personal relative subject pronoun "who." The present perfect tense is appropriate because the sentence describes the duration of Rocco's employment up to the present time.

30. **The best answer is (1).** The verb "take" should be in the present tense so that it makes sense logically (Rocco is still staying current) and maintains parallelism with the rest of the paragraph.

31. **The best answer is (2).** The "recent renovations" have already been made and are, therefore, in the past. The present form "make" should be replaced by the present perfect form, as in answer choice (2), or the simple past form.

32. **The best answer is (5).** The modifier phrase "usually young" does not make sense in its position, where it seems to modify (strangely) "time." The concept of "young" is already established by the word "children," so "usually young" is best omitted.

33. **The best answer is (1).** By moving "as Right 'n Ready employees" to the beginning of the sentence, the main clause ("we are pleased to know that") is not divided.

34. **The best answer is (3).** This sentence does not follow the topic of the thank-you letter.

35. **The best answer is (1).** The relative pronoun "which" cannot be the subject of a sentence.

36. **The best answer is (5).** The simple present tense maintains parallelism with the other verbs "have" and "choose."

37. **The best answer is (4).** The underlined portion should begin with the phrase "from books to clothing to even boats" because it modifies the preceding noun "items."

38. **The best answer is (3).** This is the simplest and clearest way to begin the sentence. "Including a photo" acts like a noun and is the subject of the sentence.

39. **The best answer is (4).** The description of the electronic banking system is found in sentences 11 and 12. Sentence 8 would provide an effective end to paragraph C.

40. **The best answer is (5).** Sentence 11 is effectively linked to sentences 10 and 12.

41. **The best answer is (5).** The singular noun "war" does not agree in number with the verb form "ensue." One way to fix the sentence is to make "war" plural.

42. **The best answer is (4).** The sentence describes a general phenomenon associated with online auctions, so the simple present tense is appropriate.

43. **The best answer is (1).** The best revision to this sentence places the subject first to conform with standard word order. In addition, using an expressed subject ("management") and not a pronoun ("we" or "they") is appropriate, especially in the first sentence of a paragraph or entire written work.

44. **The best answer is (3).** This choice correctly combines the phrase with the sentence, making one complete sentence. The sentence could be rewritten with a comma, not a period, before "meaning," but that correction is not among the answer choices.

45. **The best answer is (1).** The committee has not yet convened, so the future tense is appropriate in this case. Answer choices (2), (3), and (4) can be eliminated because they use the gerund form "focusing," which does not have tense properties. Answer choice (5) is in the past tense.

46. **The best answer is (2).** The expectations are ongoing at the time of writing the memo, so the simple present form "expect" is most appropriate.
47. **The best answer is (1).** The phrase beginning with "to dispel" is the object of the verb "like" and should, therefore, be joined to it without punctuation.
48. **The best answer is (4).** Commas are used to separate items in a series.
49. **The best answer is (2).** The sentence describes what will happen at future meetings. Therefore, the simple future tense is appropriate.
50. **The best answer is (3).** The clause beginning with "that there is" is the object of the verb "know" and should, therefore, be joined to it without punctuation.

Part II

Because grading the essay is subjective, we've chosen not to include any "graded" essays here. Your best bet is to have someone you trust, such as your personal tutor, read your essays and give you an honest critique. Make the scoring rubric mentioned in Chapter 11, "GED Essay," available to whomever grades your essays. If you plan to grade your own essays, review the grading criteria and be as honest as possible regarding the structure, development, organization, technique, and word choice of your writing. Be sure to address the essay prompt you'll be given on test day, because failing to do so could result in a failing grade on the essay. Focus on your weak areas and continue to practice to improve your writing skills.

Language Arts, Reading Answers and Explanations

1. **The best answer is (4).** The context of the passage suggests that Gip is thoughtful of others and would not want to be a bother or make his father worry in any way.
2. **The best answer is (2).** The pleasant tone of the passage suggests that the narrator enjoys Gip's company and will continue to want to spend time with him.
3. **The best answer is (5).** Gip is very well behaved, and the narrator treats him to a visit inside the fascinating magic shop.
4. **The best answer is (3).** This answer choice matches the positive tone of the phrases given in the question.
5. **The best answer is (2).** The first sentence of the second paragraph details how the author was somewhat unsure about the location of the magic shop. The word "obscure" is similar to "hidden."
6. **The best answer is (2).** The notion of dreams flying as "rosy clouds" is a positive, optimistic image.
7. **The best answer is (1).** The speaker makes an excited series of utterances about dreams and how they fail to come true. Answer choices (2), (3), and (4) can be eliminated because it is not clear that the speaker is bothered by the reality of dreams. For instance, the speaker does not curse dreams, which would indicate strong opinions. Rather, the speaker is making impassioned statements about dreams without adding his opinion.
8. **The best answer is (5).** The poem reminds the reader that as children, humans have lofty ideas about how the future will turn out for them. Naturally, many such dreams fail to come true. Answer choice (5) is a warning to anticipate such failures. The suggestions in answer choices (1) through (4) are not supported by the poem.
9. **The best answer is (4).** The practice of slavery in the United States continued through most of the nineteenth century; however, racism and the restriction of civil rights were major issues that continued to negatively affect descendents of slaves. That Dunbar had his poetry published was an important accomplishment.
10. **The best answer is (3).** The word "ah!" with or without the exclamation point is called an exclamation, or an excited utterance.
11. **The best answer is (5).** The first paragraph indicates that "nearly all new developments rely on electrical power to keep warm."
12. **The best answer is (3).** The passage reviews the various forms of energy in use today and considers the future of electricity-generating technology. The final sentence of the passage shows that the author considers wind to be a promising energy source for our future "energy needs."
13. **The best answer is (2).** The third paragraph says, "When implemented properly, nuclear energy is more efficient and cleaner than coal." The cleanliness refers to the negative byproducts of burning coal, such as ash and various harmful gases.
14. **The best answer is (2).** The last sentence of the passage suggests that wind power may be "the ultimate answer to our energy needs."

15. **The best answer is (4).** Bracketed descriptive detail identifies the Kyoto Protocol as a pollution-control measure. In the same sentence, the author mentions "viable alternatives," which refers to alternatives from energy sources associated with high pollution.

16. **The best answer is (2).** Smoke emanating from a storeroom would qualify as an "emergency," which the document says is a matter to be referred to "the police."

17. **The best answer is (3).** The "Guide" is an instructional document for employees. It describes in detail the procedure for handling complaints.

18. **The best answer is (5).** The passage specifically mentions "noise violations" as a type of "civil disturbance."

19. **The best answer is (3).** Making a maintenance appointment is the first action given in the paragraph titled "Complaints about the apartment."

20. **The best answer is (4).** The last sentence of the document indicates that "a copy is left for the tenant." Logically, this means that the original is kept by the company for its records.

21. **The best answer is (1).** Most of Mrs. Higgins' statements indicate that she is doubtful of her son's intentions.

22. **The best answer is (2).** The dialogue indicates that Mrs. Higgins is highly concerned with appearances. Higgins claims that he has no small talk for his mother's friends. Mrs. Higgins replies, "What about your large talk?" This suggests that she does not want her son involved in conversation with her friends.

23. **The best answer is (1).** There is a measured amount of conflict in this scene, so a good description of the mood could be "anxious."

24. **The best answer is (3).** Mrs. Higgins would like her son to find a young woman, but Higgins' comment shows that he does not think young women are suitably smart or mature for his taste.

25. **The best answer is (5).** Higgins says to his mother, "I've a job for you." This means he will ask her to do something for him, which could be called a favor.

26. **The best answer is (5).** The overall tone of the passage is upbeat and pleasant. The author has many positive comments about the exhibition and would encourage people to browse it.

27. **The best answer is (2).** The author thinks that although the temporary arrangement of art work (known as the "Greatest Hits") makes the galleries appear somewhat cluttered, their arrangement by theme provides a uniquely meaningful experience.

28. **The best answer is (3).** The author maintains a journalistic, informative tone throughout the review.

29. **The best answer is (3).** The author uses precise vocabulary and imagery. Diction and sentence structure are carefully prepared, indicating a "formal" writing style.

30. **The best answer is (4).** The review indicates that the glass exhibition made the author happy.

31. **The best answer is (3).** The excerpt specifically includes the clause "We grew up," showing that the author is a grown man.

32. **The best answer is (4).** Sophie is Fanshawe's wife, and she contacted the narrator in hopes that he may know where to find her missing husband.

33. **The best answer is (2).** The final paragraph of the passage indicates that the narrator has mixed feelings about his lost friendship with Fanshawe. He struggles to comprehend how a man who once vanished from the narrator's life seems to have vanished again.

34. **The best answer is (3).** The author's tone hints at regrets about falling out of touch with Fanshawe. The effect is sadness, so the author's tone could be described as "unsettled."

35. **The best answer is (1).** The concept of becoming "blood brothers" is a ritualistic act of bonding friends closer together.

36. **The best answer is (4).** The third paragraph gives "exceptions" to the warranty protection. They include ways the defect may be the fault of the customer and, therefore, not covered under the warranty.

37. **The best answer is (4).** This answer choice essentially repeats the last sentence of the first paragraph.

38. **The best answer is (4).** The warranty statement is a declaration of the company's liability for product defects. It is very specific about what is and what is not covered by the warranty.

39. **The best answer is (3).** The other answer choices describe altering or damaging the product in some way that is expressly forbidden in the warranty statement. Answer choice (3) describes putting a product to normal use.

40. **The best answer is (4).** This warranty statement has a legal tone and uses words sparingly and carefully.

Social Studies Answers and Explanations

1. **The best answer is (2).** The demand line crosses the price axis below $800. At this price, a quantity of zero grills is demanded.
2. **The best answer is (1).** The last military draft took place during the Vietnam War. Today's military increasingly relies on technology and not manpower to remain as strong as necessary.
3. **The best answer is (3).** The information indicates that the reaction to the meat-packing images in *The Jungle* was at least partially responsible for the passage of the Pure Food and Drug Act. This suggests that the federal government took steps to increase the healthfulness of meatpacking operations.
4. **The best answer is (2).** Slavery violates the "unalienable Right" of "Liberty," which means freedom.
5. **The best answer is (1).** Such limitations constitute sacrifices on the part of civilians.
6. **The best answer is (2).** The posters are appeals to residents of the United States to limit their consumption of train travel and clothing. These are examples of resources important to the war effort.
7. **The best answer is (5).** These posters suggest that conserving resources such as train travel and clothing is important to the war effort, as evidenced by the images of soldiers on the left and the line "our labor and our goods are fighting" on the right. Such conservation of resources would increase the efficiency of their use in the economy.
8. **The best answer is (4).** Total U.S. population steadily increases in all states, so answer choice (1) cannot be correct. Land area does not affect reapportionment of House seats, so answer choice (2) can be eliminated. Answer choice (3) can be eliminated because House seats are directly related to population. Answer choice (4) is confirmed because the Great Lakes States, which are nearly all white or dotted, lost seats. The written information indicates that with every census, the average congressional district population size increases. Losing seats means that a state did not keep pace with the national average population increase. Answer choice (5) is not supported by the passage, which confirms that the House seats are held constant by federal law.
9. **The best answer is (1).** According to the information, gaining seats in the House indicates that a state's population growth outpaced the national average.
10. **The best answer is (2).** According to the passage, the Vikings "were among the first international seafaring traders with purpose-built, wooden trading ships," and "their far-reaching travel from the ninth through the twelfth centuries is, nevertheless, remarkable." Therefore, answer choice (2) is the best answer.
11. **The best answer is (4).** According to the passage, Greenland was a frozen land given its name "in an effort to entice Viking settlers to emigrate." Therefore, answer choice (4) is the best answer.

12. **The best answer is (4).** The passage states that “most of what is known of the Vikings today is the result of archaeologists’ discoveries and written records and oral histories of people who met them.”

13. **The best answer is (3).** An oral history is a spoken story or series of facts passed from one generation to the next. Because the prayer is referred to as something “still used in part of northern Great Britain,” one can assume that the spoken prayer was passed from one generation to the next, making it an oral history.

14. **The best answer is (2).** According to the passage, one of the goals of the Environmental Protective Agency (EPA) when revising the process used to determine the miles per gallon estimates was to help the environment by “more efficiently using oil resources.” Because the question asks for the answer that serves as evidence of the fulfillment of the EPA’s goals, one can assume that the decrease in the oil consumption for 2008 from previous years, as found in answer choice (2), fulfills the EPA’s goal of the more efficient use of oil resources.

15. **The best answer is (3).** The order of courts demonstrated by answer choice (3) is the only answer that follows correctly the flow of the courts demonstrated by the diagram.

16. **The best answer is (4).** The appeals process adheres to the principal of checks and balances because no one court is making all the decisions.

17. **The best answer is (5).** By beginning the passage with a highlight from Justinian’s reign, and then following it with the less-pleasant circumstances, the author sets up a contrast between good and bad.

18. **The best answer is (4).** According to the passage, Justinian established priorities poorly for several reasons. These reasons included failing to provide sufficient troop strength, as well as failing to provide adequate supplies and compensation for those troops.

19. **The best answer is (1).** The passage frequently points to Justinian’s disorganized method of ruling. For example, “he would put military plans into action before he had the means to provide his commander with enough troops to do the job effectively.” He also failed to provide enough financial support for the troops because only about a third of the taxes due the empire to support the troops were actually collected, which added to the funding problem. These factors support the statement that Justinian was disorganized, which makes answer choice (1) the best answer.

20. **The best answer is (3).** As seen in the graph, population density is greatest in the eastern half of the border.

21. **The best answer is (2).** Recording the entrance of people into the United States from Canada helps to protect domestic security, and help enforce laws. Therefore, answer choice (2) is the best answer.

22. **The best answer is (4).** The passage states that airplanes, racecars, experimental vehicles, and light trucks all make use of ABS. Of all the answer choices, the train is the only mode of transportation not mentioned by the passage, making answer choice (4) best.

23. **The best answer is (2).** According to the passage, "familiarization is critical for drivers of ABS-equipped vehicles. In fact, some studies done during the 1990s showed that there was practically no difference in fatality rates between autos equipped with ABS and those that were not so equipped." By evaluating this statement, one can see that drivers unfamiliar with ABS are at risk for fatality in vehicle accidents.

24. **The best answer is (3).** As found in the passage, Brasilia replaced Sao Paolo as the capital of Brazil to promote economic development in the interior of the country, as well as to encourage population unification. These facts support the statement that population and economic activity naturally grow in and near national capitals.

25. **The best answer is (3).** Although defending against terrorist attacks may promote the safety and prosperity of Americans, it does not directly relate to making healthier lifestyle choices, unlike the other answer choices.

26. **The best answer is (5).** According to the law of supply and demand, when the demand for a product is greater than the supply of that product, the price of the product goes up. For the company in question to produce the greatest possible profit, it should produce more televisions and raise the price.

27. **The best answer is (3).** The passage states that "controlled burning as a way to contain such fires cannot be done on land with dense underbrush and an overabundance of small, new-growth trees. In order to do a controlled burn, such vegetation must be thinned out and ladder fuels reduced prior to a fire taking place."

28. **The best answer is (1).** To answer this question, one must evaluate the passage as a whole. Because the passage indicates that human interaction with the environment is necessary, one can assume that a relationship between humans and the environment can in fact exist. Furthermore, the passage goes on to illustrate how "good stewardship of the earth and environmentalism can go hand in hand." Based on this information, answer choice (1) is best.

29. **The best answer is (3).** According to the passage, the logging plans will prevent catastrophic wildfires so that the national forests don't just "burn up."

30. **The best answer is (5).** According to the passage, controlled burning is done to attempt to control accidental wildfires.

31. **The best answer is (1).** By looking at the graph, you can see that when the federal debt is greater than 50% of the gross domestic product at the end of any given year, the debt is greater than the product.

32. **The best answer is (2).** According to the passage, HHW includes oil, which is found in oil-based paints. Therefore, using oil-based paints instead of latex (water-based) paints wouldn't be beneficial to reducing HHW, which makes answer choice (2) best.

33. **The best answer is (3).** By reading the advertisement, you can see that the product is an upgraded version of an original product. Because of the presence of a price reduction banner, as well as the advertisement of an upgrade, you can assume that Digirealms Interactive assumes that members of its video-game player market are attracted to upgrades and reduced prices.

34. **The best answer is (1).** As stated in the advertisement, the upgraded game offers a new feature that allows the player to "respond to unexpected army activity." Based on this statement, it can be assumed that the Civil War was unpredictable, and commanding officers had to make quick decisions.

35. **The best answer is (1).** Because the graphs focus on age distribution, it is possible to add up the individual bars of a specific age range to determine what percentage of the total population that age range occupies. This process is alluded to in answer (1).

36. **The best answer is (1).** As shown by the graphs, the age distribution in 2000 is much more even than it was in 1950.

37. **The best answer is (3).** The paragraph indicates that Colombian drug enforcement, penalties, and enforcement funding have been strengthened. Despite this, the incentive to smuggle drugs still remains. This is because of the market demand (albeit illegal) for drugs.

38. **The best answer is (4).** As shown by the graphs, the difference in the heights of the 1960 and 1970 bars is significantly greater than the difference in the heights of the 1990 and 2000 bars.

39. **The best answer is (2).** To answer this question, one must evaluate the passage as a whole. Although the author does give time to the various hypotheses associated with the first visitors to America, the authors concludes "there is much controversy over the topic."

40. **The best answer is (5).** The passage states that the popular hypothesis has been challenged because "a site in Chile that was first studied in 1977 called 'Monte Verde' suggests that people were living there 12,500 years ago, which was 1,500 years prior to the Asian people crossing the land bridge."

41. **The best answer is (4).** The passage states that the Pilgrims desired to live in a place where they wouldn't have to fear religious repression.

42. **The best answer is (2).** According to the passage, "the mean center of population has moved between 1 and 3 counties west," which means that the population steadily moved from the east to the west between 1790 and 1980.

43. **The best answer is (5).** The passage states that "a great cry sounded from the Inuit (sometimes called Eskimos), the indigenous people of the Arctic Circle who rely on the whale for their very survival."

44. **The best answer is (5).** According to the passage, "a favorite snack, *maktaaq* (whale skin) is rich in calcium, selenium, and omega-3 fatty acids."

45. **The best answer is (2).** The passage states that "during the twentieth century, as a result of the overhunting of whales by commercial whaling ships, many whale species became endangered—some nearly to the point of extinction."

46. **The best answer is (3).** Because the map and information given illustrate and describe the most-lit places in the world and then draws a direct relationship between the population and light distribution of an area, it can be inferred that a comparison of the level of urbanization can be made between different areas on the map.

47. **The best answer is (2).** Lately, people have moved toward going to bed later and later at night. As they stay active late into the night, they continue to use light. This trend of going to bed later has led to an increase in the overall use of light.

48. **The best answer is (5).** The use of machinery and other tools to harvest various jungle resources will play a part in the increase in the use of light during the evening.

49. **The best answer is (5).** If a company produces more of a given product than was demanded, a surplus will result.

50. **The best answer is (2).** According to the passage, APEC promotes the peaceful advance of economic cooperation among its members through measures such as reducing tariffs. North Korea's high tariffs oppose these goals.

Science Answers and Explanations

1. **The best answer is (3).** The information preceding the question indicates that "folic acid has been found to reduce the risk of neural tube birth defects" and that the nutrient can be found in "vitamin B tablets." Therefore, it makes sense that a doctor would advise a woman to take vitamin B tablets before and during her pregnancy.
2. **The best answer is (3).** According to the figure, mammals *first* appeared during period C. Although mammals are also listed in period D, "early mammals" show up in period C.
3. **The best answer is (3).** The main purpose of daylight saving time is to make better use of daylight during times of activity, which best supports answer choice (3).
4. **The best answer is (4).** "Polar" ice caps and glaciers are found in and near the tundra, answer choice (4).
5. **The best answer is (5).** According to the information, "values above 7 are basic." To answer the question, you must locate the substances in the table with a pH higher than 7. Although human blood and household bleach both have a pH higher than 7, the question asks for the most basic substance, which is household bleach, answer choice (5), with a pH of 12.5.
6. **The best answer is (1).** For a substance to change from a solid to a liquid, it must first melt. Therefore, answer (1) is the best answer.
7. **The best answer is (2).** According to the information, "the solar tide is exactly 12 hours long." Because the solar tide began at 12 noon, it would end 12 hours later, at 12 midnight.
8. **The best answer is (1).** According to the information, nitrogen forms bubbles if a scuba diver ascends too quickly. To answer the question, one must know that as water depth increases, water pressure also increases. When a scuba diver ascends, he or she is heading upward toward the water's surface, which means that the water depth and pressure are decreasing. It is during this time that nitrogen may form bubbles, making answer choice (1) best.
9. **The best answer is (4).** The table shows the melting points of different metals. To answer the question, indicate the metal whose melting point falls between 500° C and 1000° C. Silver, with a melting point of 961.78° C, is the only metal that qualifies, making answer choice (4) best.
10. **The best answer is (5).** To answer the question, you must evaluate the findings presented in the table, looking for repeating food components in the meals. Although all the answer choices appear in at least one of the meals, dairy products are part of every recorded meal.
11. **The best answer is (5).** Friction acting on an object causes the object to slow down or even stop moving altogether. Because the rock didn't slide down the hill and the other objects did, you can assume that more friction was acting on the rock than the other objects, making answer choice (5) best.
12. **The best answer is (3).** Hybrid car engines are not powered by wave technology; rather, they are powered by both electricity and gasoline.
13. **The best answer is (2).** Because people perspire when they exert themselves, you will most likely perspire during a long-distance race. "Running" is a better choice than "swimming" because the water helps cool the body much like sweat does.

14. **The best answer is (4).** Unlike the other answer choices, a malformed human hand or foot, answer choice (4), isn't a vestigial organ, because it hasn't lost its function due to evolution. Instead, malformation often results from a genetic defect or complications during pregnancy.

15. **The best answer is (1).** Unlike the other answer choices, "daily insulin injections are a hassle," answer choice (1) is an opinion. The other answers were identified as fact by the preceding passage.

16. **The best answer is (5).** This answer refers to the seriousness of diabetes, which makes it the best choice.

17. **The best answer is (4).** According to the passage, type I diabetes is typically treated with insulin injections. Even though answer choice (1) includes information about a young boy, there is not enough evidence to support the notion that he has diabetes at all, only that he is sensitive to sugar.

18. **The best answer is (2).** The relationship demonstrated between the bees and the flowers is beneficial to both parties, making it symbiotic.

19. **The best answer is (1).** The smooth rope contributes to less friction between the rope and the pulley, which means that less effort is lost because of friction, making the machine more efficient.

20. **The best answer is (3).** To answer this question, you must understand the following things: NAD+ has a positive charge, electrons carry a negative charge, and protons carry a positive charge. When two negative electrons and one positive proton are added to the positive NAD+, the resulting charge is neutral because the combination of two positive charges plus two negative charges cancel each other out, making the combined charge neutral.

21. **The best answer is (4).** All the answer choices are possible resulting blood types except blood type O, making answer choice (4) the best answer.

22. **The best answer is (4).** According to the information, earthquake A measures 2 on the Richter scale, and earthquake B measures 4 on the Richter scale. Because each consecutive integer is 10 times larger than the previous integer, and earthquake A and earthquake B measure two integers apart, you must find the value of 10×10, which is 100.

23. **The best answer is (2).** The heart's pressure output is higher on heartbeats (systolic pressure) than it is in between heartbeats (diastolic pressure).

24. **The best answer is (3).** The information specifically indicates that "FM receivers compensate for amplitude fluctuations," while AM operates on amplitude fluctuations. The information also says that lightning "has the affect of altering the amplitude of radio waves." Therefore, it is reasonable to assume that lightning has a great effect on AM radio but not on FM radio.

25. **The best answer is (3).** According to the information, E. coli bacteria prevent other types of bacteria from establishing colonies. Therefore, any bacteria that enter the large intestine will be unable to multiply and survive, making answer choice (3) best.

26. **The best answer is (1).** Although both dolphins and bats use echolocation, dolphins do it more quickly than bats do. This is because sound travels faster through water than it does in air, making answer choice (1) best.

27. **The best answer is (1).** According to the information, "if the Gibbs energy of a chemical reaction is negative, the reaction is said to be spontaneous." If H is negative and ST is positive, then according to math rules, a negative value minus a positive value gives a negative result. Therefore, the chemical reaction would be spontaneous.

28. **The best answer is (3).** Boiling point (temperature) is a function of atmospheric pressure. As elevation increases, boiling point decreases. This means that the rice boiling at high elevation is cooking at a lower temperature than the rice at low elevation; therefore, it will take longer to cook. If you were not fully aware of this concept, you might recall the high-altitude directions on many boxed baked goods. Often, these call for higher oven temperatures and longer baking times.

29. **The best answer is (4).** By evaluating the graph, you can see that the relationship between the population of the squirrels and the population of the hawks tends to be inversely related; as the hawk population grows, the squirrel population declines, and vice versa.

30. **The best answer is (5).** As shown in the graph, hawks rely heavily on squirrels as a source of food. If foxes, which also rely heavily on squirrels for food, were introduced into the ecosystem, you can assume that, because of the new shortage in the food supply because of the foxes, the hawk population would decrease.

31. **The best answer is (3).** Although the passage never explicitly states the relationship between squirrels and hawks, its reference to the graph, which does demonstrate this relationship, makes an unstated assumption that hawks hunt squirrels as a source of food.

32. **The best answer is (5).** None of the answers can be assumed from the information given, making answer choice (5) the best answer.

33. **The best answer is (1).** The light-year is used to measure distance. If a unit is to be used to represent the light-year, it must also measure distance. The meter is the only answer choice that is used to measure distance, making answer choice (1) best.

34. **The best answer is (4).** Eliciting a response like the one described in the passage, a vaccination urges the body to produce the memory cells used to fight various diseases.

35. **The best answer is (5).** The last sentence of the information states, "non-polar molecules must move through the membrane with the help of transport proteins."

36. **The best answer is (2).** The sentence before the question says that turbofans need to pressurize air in order to operate. Recall that as altitude increases, air pressure decreases. The air is said to be "thinner," meaning there is less of it to enter a turbofan. With increasing altitude, eventually a turbofan will fail. The space shuttle must be propelled in regions of the atmosphere where pressure is a mere fraction of what it is comparatively close to the surface.

37. **The best answer is (3).** According to the information, for every molecule of glucose that is metabolized, four carbon dioxide (CO_2) molecules are released as a waste product. Of each of these CO_2 molecules, one carbon atom and one oxygen atom come from the original glucose model. This means that, because four CO_2 molecules are released as waste, a total of four carbon atoms and four oxygen atoms are lost from the original glucose molecule. The original glucose model began with 24 atoms. It then loses 8 of these atoms to the CO_2 waste, which leaves behind 16 of the original glucose molecules.

38. **The best answer is (4).** Friction is determined by finding the product of an object's mass and coefficient of friction. Box A, which rests on a smooth surface, has a smaller coefficient of friction than box B, which rests on a rough surface. Still, box A was harder to move than box B, which means that the overall friction of box A must be greater than the overall friction of box B. This is possible if the mass of box A is greater than the mass of box B, making answer choice (4) best.

39. **The best answer is (1).** Ice, being a slippery surface, has a very low coefficient of friction, which can make driving conditions dangerous.

40. **The best answer is (1).** Based on the passage, T-cells attack virus-infected cells after detecting "non-self" sugars. These sugars indicate infected cells, so their presence in uninfected cells would cause T-cells to attack those uninfected cells, too.

41. **The best answer is (2).** According to the passage, T-cells fight infections. If AIDS destroys T-cells, then the body is much less able to fight infection.

42. **The best answer is (4).** According to the information given, increasing the temperature of the gas molecules inside a container will cause the gas molecules to move faster and therefore cause the pressure to increase. It can then be safely assumed that decreasing the temperature would decrease the pressure, making answer choice (4) best.

43. **The best answer is (1).** According to the passage, glycogen synthesis occurs when excess glucose is stored in the form of glycogen. Because glucose is found in many foods, it can be assumed that glycogen synthesis would take place after eating a meal.

44. **The best answer is (1).** According to the graph, peak D's erosion rate at an exposure percentage of 75% is approximately 25m/yr, making answer choice (1) best.

45. **The best answer is (2).** According to the graph, a greater percentage of peak D is exposed to wind erosion throughout the year, which supports answer choice (2).

46. **The best answer is (2).** A dependent variable is one of the variables being tested for; it is a variable that is dependent on, or affected by, one or more of any independent variables. The number of flowers produced will likely be affected by the fertilizer, the type of rose bush, and so on.

47. **The best answer is (1).** An understanding of how the tilt of the Earth's axis and its position around the sun impacts the Earth is needed. During the spring and summer, the Northern Hemisphere is tilted toward the sun. It receives more hours of light per day; in addition, the rays reach the surface more directly. As a result, more energy is available to plants during those seasons.

48. **The best answer is (2).** The monarch butterfly's bright wing coloration is used to a warn off potential predators, making answer choice (2) best.

49. **The best answer is (1).** Dark colors absorb more heat than light colors. Therefore, the black ball would feel the hottest after being left in the sun, making answer choice (1) correct.

50. **The best answer is (2).** All the answer choices except the use of smoke stacks would help to clean the air, making answer choice (2) best.

Mathematics Answers and Explanations

Part I

1. **The correct answer is (4).** To solve this problem, you must consider the relationship between all given values, as well as determine their bearing on the final sale price. You are told that the price of carpet has been reduced from $19.50 to $15.60 per square yard. The original price has no impact on your answer here, so ignore the $19.50. If a customer wants 50 square yards of carpet installed, she must first pay 50 × $15.60, which equals $780. Because there is also a charge for installation, you need to add 50 × $1.95, which is $97.50, to the cost. Therefore, the final sale price is $97.50 + $780, which equals $877.50.

2. **The correct answer is (3).** To solve this problem, you need to figure out how long it will take Joey to make the shirts. If he can produce 40 shirts in one hour, and he needs to make 180 shirts total, it will take him 4.5 hours to finish ($\frac{180}{40} = 4.5$). Next, you must take into account his 30-minute lunch break. With this in mind, it will take him a total of 5 hours to have the shirts ready. Having started at 11 a.m., he will be finished by 4 p.m., which is answer choice (3).

3. **The correct answer is (2).** To solve this problem, you must first understand the concept of finding the perimeter of an object. The perimeter of the triangle is found by adding together the lengths of each side. Here you are given that x is $1\frac{1}{2}$ times the base, which is 16. Therefore, x is 16 × 1.5, which equals 24. Because two of the sides are labeled x and the base length is given, you add 24 + 24 + 16 to find the triangle's perimeter, which equals 64.

4. **The correct answer is (1).** To solve this problem, you must determine how much water each hiker will drink over the span of the hike, and then multiply that value times the total number of hikers. Because each hiker should drink at least one-$\frac{1}{2}$ gallon of water every hour, and the hike lasts for 1.5 hours, you must multiply these values to determine the amount of water each hiker will consume over the course of the hike: $\frac{1}{2} \times \frac{3}{2}$ equals $\frac{3}{4}$ gallons of water per hiker. Then multiply $\frac{3}{4}$ gallons by the 25 hikers (24 campers plus Marcus) for a grand total of 18.75 gallons. Because 18.75 gallons is approximately 19 gallons, answer choice (1) is correct.

5. **The correct answer is (2).** To solve this problem, you first need to isolate the unknown on one side of the equation. The best way to do this is to subtract 7 from both sides.

$$\left(\frac{12-x}{x}\right) + 7 - 7 = 9 - 7$$

$$\left(\frac{12-x}{x}\right) = 2$$

Next, multiply both sides by x to get rid of the fraction.

$$\left(\frac{12-x}{x}\right) \times x = 2 \times x$$

$12 - x = 2x$

Now, add an x to both sides.

$12 - x + x = 2x + x$

$12 = 3x$

Finally, divide both sides by 3 to solve for x:

$$\frac{12}{3} = \frac{3x}{3}$$

$4 = x$

6. **The correct answer is 9.** To solve this problem, you need to find out how many hours the man worked in addition to his typical 40-hour workweek. For 40 hours, he would receive \$320 (40 × \$8 = \$320). Next, you must find the difference between the \$419 he was paid and the \$320 he earned for his normal hours (\$419 – \$320 = \$99). Finally, because you know that he earned \$99 for his overtime, you can divide this by his overtime hourly pay to find out how many extra hours he put in ($\frac{\$99}{\$11} = 9$). The man worked 9 hours of overtime.

7. **The correct answer is (4).** To solve this problem, you need to multiply the amount of USD John exchanged (350) by the current exchange rate for USD in relation to EUR (.752). After exchanging his money, John had 350 × .752 = 263.2 EUR.

8. **The correct answer is (3).** To solve this problem, you must first find out how much John's stay at the hostel totaled in EUR (25 EUR per night × 3 nights = 75 EUR). Next, you have to convert the 75 EUR into USD. You do so by multiplying the cost of the hostel in EUR (75) by the current exchange rate for EUR in relation to USD (1.329). This gives you an answer of 99.675, so the closest answer would be 100.

9. **The correct answer is 297.5.** To solve this problem, you must first subtract Julie's deductible from the total cost, which is \$425 (\$475 – \$50 = \$425). Because the insurance company offered to pay 70% of the remaining cost, you need to multiply \$425 by .7, which equals \$297.50.

   The answer grid has only five spaces (one must be used for the decimal point), so omit the final zero when you record the answer.

10. **The correct answer is (3).** To solve this problem, you must first understand that a median is defined as the middle of a set of numbers. It divides the lower half from the upper half. In this problem, there are five possible prices for the type of car that the customer is interested in. The median is the number located in the middle of the order. You should arrange the prices from lowest to highest:

    $6,500; $7,000; $8,000; $8,750; $9,300

    After doing this, it is clear that the median is $8,000.

11. **The correct answer is (2).** To solve this problem, you must use the formula for the circumference of a circle, which is $C = 2\pi r$. In this problem, radius (r) = 3.5 inches. So, $2\pi r = 2(3.5) = 7$. To find the circle's circumference, substitute 3.5 inches into the circumference equation. $C = 2(3.5)\pi = 7\pi$.

12. **The correct answer is 28.44.** To solve this problem, you must input the given numbers into the body mass index (BMI) equation.

    $$\text{BMI} = \frac{(705)(215)}{73^2}$$

    $$\text{BMI} = \frac{151{,}575}{5{,}329}$$

    BMI = 28.44

13. **The correct answer is (2).** To solve this problem, you must first determine the amount of time it will take for the 20 group pictures to be taken. Because it takes 7 minutes per group picture, and the bride has asked for 20 group pictures, multiply 7 by 20 to find the total number of minutes needed, which is 140.

    It will take you about 140 minutes to take the group pictures. You have been hired to take pictures for 3 hours. Convert these hours (3) into minutes. There are 60 minutes in 1 hour, so multiply 60 by 3 to get 180 minutes.

    You will spend a total of 180 minutes taking pictures. Next, subtract the number of minutes you will spend taking the 20 group pictures (140) from the total number of minutes (180), to get 180 – 140, or 40 minutes.

    You have 40 minutes in which to take individual pictures. Because it takes 3 minutes per individual picture, divide 40 minutes by 3 minutes to determine the number of individual pictures you can take:

    $40 \div 3 = 13.3$

    Because you cannot take part of a picture, you will only be able to take a maximum of 13 individual pictures.

14. **The correct answer is (3).** To solve this problem, you must determine the December sales amount needed to bring the three-month sales average to $55,000. Because you are given the numbers for October and November, the first step is to add these two together ($45,000 + $70,000 = $115,000). The next step is to multiply $55,000 by 3, which gives you $165,000. The minimum sales for December must be a number that, when added to $115,000, will give you an answer of $165,000 (because $165,000 divided by 3 will give you an average of $55,000 for each month). Because $165,000 minus $115,000 equals $50,000, this is the minimum amount of sales needed in December to achieve a monthly average of $55,000.

15. **The correct answer is (2).** To solve this problem, you must know how to find the area of a triangle. The area is equal to $\frac{1}{2}$ base $\times$ height ($\frac{1}{2}bh$). For this right triangle, BC is the base, and AB is the height. You are given that AB is 3 times the length of BC and that the area is 96 cm^2. Therefore, your equation should look like this:

$$\frac{1}{2}(x)(3x) = 96$$

$$\frac{1}{2}3x^2 = 96$$

To begin solving, first multiply both sides by 2 to eliminate the fraction.

$$\frac{1}{2}3x^2 \times 2 = 96 \times 2$$

$$3x^2 = 192$$

Now, divide both sides by 3 to get the x^2 alone:

$$\frac{3x^2}{3} = \frac{192}{3}$$

$$x^2 = 64$$

To solve for x, take the square root of 64:

$$x = 8$$

You are not quite done yet. When setting up the equation, we had x as the value for BC. Because you are looking for the length of AB, which is three times the length of BC, the answer is 3(8), which is 24.

16. **The correct answer is 150.** To solve this problem, you must determine the number of pages that Mary will copy. If the cost of the purchased course pack and the reprinted version are the same, then Mary must be copying $18.00 worth of pages at a rate of $0.12 each. The total number of pages can be determined by dividing $18 by $0.12, which equals 150 pages.

17. **The correct answer is (1).** To solve this problem, you must solve for x. Begin by first dividing each side of the equation by 2.5.

$$\frac{2.5(x + 4)}{2.5} = \frac{30}{2.5}$$

$$x + 4 = 12$$

Then, subtract 4 from both sides to find x.

$$x + 4 - 4 = 12 - 4$$

$$x = 8$$

18. **The correct answer is (3).** To solve this problem, you must find each store's sale price to determine which offers the best deal.

    Store A is selling the player at 40% off. Therefore, it is selling for 60% of its original value. $300 × .6 = $180

    Store B is offering the player for $200.

    Store C is offering a $160 discount. $300 – $160 = $140

    Store D is offering the player at 1/2 price. $300 × .5 = $150

    Store E is offering the player at 30% off. Therefore, it is selling for 70% of its original value. $300 × .7 = $210. Store E also offers a $30 mail in rebate. $210 – $30 = $180

    After examining all five stores' prices, it is clear that store C has the lowest price, which is answer choice (3).

19. **The correct answer is (5).** To solve this problem, you must first calculate the area of the floor. The area of a rectangle is calculated by multiplying the length (11 feet) by the width (10.5 feet):

    $11 \times 10.5 = 115.5$

    The area of the kitchen floor is 115.5 square feet. Next, calculate the area of each of the tiles. The area of a square is equal to the length of one side squared. One side is 6 inches, which equals $\frac{1}{2}$ foot. Therefore, the area in squared feet of a tile is $(\frac{1}{2})(\frac{1}{2}) = \frac{1}{4}$, which is equivalent to .25.

    Each tile measures .25 square feet. Now, divide the total number of square feet in the kitchen (115.5) by the number of square feet in each tile (.25) to find the number of tiles you will need to cover the kitchen floor:

    $\frac{115.5}{.25} = 462$. Kim will need about 462 tiles to complete the job.

20. **The correct answer is (2).** To solve this problem, you must first find out how much money he had in the bank at the end of the first year. If he earned 6% interest on $450, his total at the end of the year can be expressed as $450 × 1.06, which equals $477. Now, you must repeat for the second year. $477 × 1.06 equals $505.62. If he takes out $300 and also pays a charge of $2.25, his final balance is $505.62 – $300.00 – $2.25 = $203.37.

21. **The correct answer is (3).** To solve this problem, you must divide the total number of cameras by the number of cameras packaged per box. Because there are 864 total cameras, which will be boxed at 27 cameras per box, simply divide 864 cameras by 27 cameras to determine the total number of boxes the man will receive: 864 ÷ 27 = 32.

22. **The correct answer is (4).** To solve this problem, you must determine during which hour of the trip the students traveled the fastest. The easiest way to do this is to look at the slope of the line in between the various hours of the trip. The point with the steepest slope between consecutive hours will show you the hour during which they traveled the fastest. In viewing the graph, the slope is steepest between 11:00 a.m. and 12:00 p.m., which is answer choice (4).

23. **The correct answer is (3).** To solve this problem, you need to find the average speed at which the students traveled during a stretch of their trip. At 7:00 a.m., they were 300 miles away from their destination, and at 10:00 a.m., they were 150 miles away. This means that they traveled 150 miles within that time interval (300 – 150 = 150). Because they were traveling for 3 hours in this particular stretch, their average speed was 150 miles ÷ 3 hours, or 50 miles per hour.

24. **The correct answer is (3).** To solve this problem, you need to use the Pythagorean Relationship. The Pythagorean Relationship is $a^2 + b^2 = c^2$, with a representing the height of the triangle, b representing the base length of the triangle, and c representing the hypotenuse length of the triangle. To find the value of x, which is the hypotenuse of the triangle in the diagram, input the triangle's values into the Pythagorean Relationship, then take the square root of both sides:

    $8^2 + 12^2 = x^2$

    $\sqrt{8^2 + 12^2} = x$

25. **The correct answer is 7.** You must first isolate the variable term on one side of the equation by adding 3 to both sides of the equation as shown below.

    $4y - 3 + 3 = 25 + 3$

    $4y = 28$

    To solve for y, you must divide both sides by 4.

    $\frac{4y}{4} = \frac{28}{4}$

    You are left with the answer, which is $y = 7$.

Part II

26. **The correct answer is (2).** To solve this problem, you must determine which value(s) for x will set the equation to 0. This equation has two solutions, so you can immediately eliminate answers (3) and (4). To get the correct solutions, you must set each part of the equation equal to zero:

    $x + 7 = 0$ and $x - 9 = 0$

    $x = -7$ and $x = 9$

27. **The correct answer is (4).** To solve this problem, you must determine the formula needed to find the total cost for renting the ice rink. The cost for renting the rink can be expressed as the basic fee (250) plus 3 times the number of people attending ($3x$). The only answer that expresses the equation correctly is $T = 250 + 3x$, which is answer choice (4).

28. **The correct answer is (3).** To solve this problem, you must represent mathematically the relationship between the temperature at 3 p.m. and at 9 p.m. You know that the temperature at 3 p.m. was 8° C and are told that at 9 p.m. the temperature is one half of this, plus x degrees. Therefore, the expression that represents the temperature at 9 p.m. is $\frac{1}{2}(8) + x$, which is answer choice (3).

29. **The correct answer is 11.12.** To solve this problem, you must determine the total cost for Nancy to run her ad in the newspaper. You know that Nancy will pay $5 for the first 10 words of her ad. Because her ad is 27 words long, she needs to pay for an additional 17 words on top of the 10 original words. If each extra word costs 36 cents, she will be paying an extra $6.12 (17 × $0.36). So the total cost of her add will be $5 + $6.12, or $11.12.

30. **The correct answer is (3).** To solve this problem, you must find the measure of angle UYV. Because UYZ is a straight angle, it measures 180° by definition. You are given that VYX equals 80°, and XYZ is 35°. Therefore, UYV must equal 180° – 80° – 35° to complete the straight angle. The answer is 65°, which is answer choice (3).

31. **The correct answer is (2).** To solve this problem, you must determine the final cost of Brian's rental by adding the charges per mile to the charges per day. If Brian is using the truck for two days, he will have to pay the daily fee ($45) twice, which totals $90. If he drives 80 miles, he has to pay an additional $40 (80 miles times $.50 per mile). Therefore, his total cost is $90 + $40, which equals $130, which is answer choice 2.

32. **The correct answer is (3).** To solve this problem, you must know the formula for the slope of a line between two given points. The formula is

    $\frac{y_2 - y_1}{x_2 - x_1}$; where (x_1, y_1) and (x_2, y_2) are two points on the line.

    Using the two points given in this problem, the slope of the line is $\frac{12 - 3}{5 - 2}$, which equals 3.

33. **The correct answer is (4).** To find an approximate solution, round 9.65 miles up to 10 miles and multiply by 6 (3 days × 2 driving legs per day):

    $6 \times 10 = 60$

    At this point, notice that answer choices (3) and (4) are close to 60. Answer choice (4) is best because it is less than 60, just as 9.65 is less than its rounded value of 10.

34. **The correct answer is 7.** To solve this problem, you must determine how much tip Elizabeth should leave if she wants to leave a tip equal to 20% of the total bill. Use proportions to be certain of your percentage calculations:

    $\frac{20}{100} = \frac{\text{tip}}{\$35\text{(total bill)}}$

    $20 \times 35 = 100 \times \text{tip}$

    $700 = 100 \times \text{tip}$

    $\frac{700}{100} = \text{tip}$

    $7 = \text{tip}$

35. **The correct answer is (1).** To approximate the answer, substitute $4 for $3.99 (the price per case). Therefore, 5 cases cost approximately $4 × 5 = $20.

36. **The correct answer is (3).** To solve this problem, you must know the formula used to find the perimeter of a square. Because all sides of a square are the same length, by definition, then the perimeter of a square is found by the equation $P = 4s$. In this problem, $s = 5$ cm. Input 5 cm into the equation for s to find the perimeter, which is 20 cm.

37. **The correct answer is 224 miles.** To solve this problem, use a proportion:

$$\frac{128 \text{ miles}}{2 \text{ hours}} = \frac{x \text{ miles}}{3.5 \text{ hours}}$$

$$128 \times 3.5 = 2x$$

$$448 = 2x$$

$$224 = x$$

38. **The correct answer is (5).** To solve this problem, you must understand how inequalities are graphed on a number line. On this number line, there is a point at 4 that is filled in and is going to the right on the line. This means that x is equal to (because of the point being filled in) or greater than (because of the line going to the right) 4. In mathematical expression, $x \geq 4$.

39. **The correct answer is (3).** To solve this problem, you must first understand that a monthly payroll is the total amount that the bookstore pays its workers. Because x is the average salary of managers and there are 4 managers in the store, part of the equation must be $4x$. Also, you are given that regular employees make, on average, $250 less than managers each month. There are 17 regular employees, and their total monthly cost can be expressed as $17(x - 250)$. Therefore, the final equation is $P = 4x + 17(x - 250)$.

40. **The correct answer is (2).** To solve this problem, you must first understand that the total degrees for one side of a straight line must add up to 180. Here you are given that one of the angles equals 65°. Therefore, angles a and b must both equal 115°, as they can both be combined with the given angle to create a straight line. The sum of a and b is 115° + 115°, which equals 230°.

41. **The correct answer is 18.** To solve this problem, you must apply the map's scale to the distance between Gene and his friend's house, as measured on the map. You are given that the scale on the map shows 1 inch is equal to 6 miles. If Gene is 3 inches from his destination on the map, you can figure out how far he actually is by multiplying 6 by 3, which gives you 18 miles.

42. **The correct answer is (5).** To solve this problem, you must add up the total amount of time it is going to take Paul to write the four papers. You are given that the first will take 30 minutes. The second one will take half the time of the first ($30 \times .5$), or 15 minutes. The third will take 25 minutes, and the fourth will take the same amount of time as the second, 15 minutes. The total amount of time it will take him is: $30 + 15 + 25 + 15 = 85$ minutes. If he has to be finished by 3 p.m., the latest he can start is 1:35 p.m.

43. **The correct answer is (1).** To solve this problem, you must use the Pythagorean Relationship. For right triangles, the Pythagorean Relationship states that $a^2 + b^2 = c^2$, where c is the length of the hypotenuse and a and b are the other sides. In this problem you are given the values of b and c, so your equation would look like this:

$a^2 + 9^2 = 15^2$

$a^2 = 15^2 - 9^2$

$a = \sqrt{15^2 - 9^2}$

44. **The correct answer is (3).** To solve this problem, you must determine what value results when 30% is taken off the sale price. The original price has no effect on the answer in this problem. Because the store is offering an additional 30% off the sale price of $600, they are selling the couch for 70% of its sale price. Use a proportion to determine the clearance price:

$\frac{70}{100} = \frac{c}{600}$

$42{,}000 = 100c$

$420 = c$

45. **The correct answer is (1).** To solve this problem, you must know the formula used to find the area of a triangle. The formula for the area of a triangle is $area = \frac{1}{2}(base)(height)$. In this problem, you are told that the height is 3 times the base, so you should use x for the base and $3x$ for the height. Because the area is <u>at least</u> 85 cm², you must use the greater than or equal to sign (≥). The inequality that matches this information is given by $\frac{1}{2}(3x^2) \geq 85$.

46. **The correct answer is (4).** To solve this problem, one must understand the concept of the mean of a set of numbers. A mean is the average of a set of numbers and is given by the following:

$\frac{x_1 + x_2 + \ldots + x_n}{n}$

The variables (denoted by x) are the values for which a mean is desired, and n is the total number of values for x.

In this problem, you are given four test scores and asked to find the fifth that will result in the desired mean score of 81. The equation can be set up like this:

$\frac{75 + 65 + 80 + 95 + x}{5} = 81$

Solve for x:

$\frac{315 + x}{5} = 81$

$5 \times \frac{315 + x}{5} = 5 \times 81$

$315 + x = 405$

$315 + x - 315 = 405 - 315$

$x = 90$

So, Michelle must get a 90% on the next test to get a B in class.

47. **The correct answer is (4).** To solve this problem, you must first figure out how much the salesman made from his sales. Because he is paid a weekly salary of $175 and he made $303 in this week, he made $128 from his sales ($303 – $175). Because he makes $8 for every vacuum he sells, divide $128 by $8 to figure out how many vacuums he sold. The salesman sold 16 vacuums, which is answer choice (4).
48. **The correct answer is (2).** To solve this problem, you must locate 132 lbs on the graph and find how many calories Mike should eat to reach that weight class. In looking at the graph, it is clear that Mike's weight is at 130 when he consumes 1,400 calories per day and is at 135 when he consumes 1,500. From these numbers, it can be deduced that the best chance he would have of making the 132-pound class would be to eat about 1,450 calories per day.
49. **The correct answer is (2).** To solve this problem, you must determine within what weight range a wrestler will fall when consuming 2,650 calories per day. According to the graph, a wrestler who consumes 2,650 calories per day will weigh between 140 and 150 pounds, which is answer choice (2).
50. **The correct answer is (5).** To solve this problem, you must first determine Mike's approximate body weight when he is consuming 2,800 calories per day. According to the graph, when Mike consumes 2,800 calories per day, his weight will be approximately 150 pounds. To find how many calories per pound he consumes, divide 2,800 calories by 150 pounds: which $2{,}800 \div 150 = 12$ calories per pound.

PART X
Appendixes

Use the information in these appendixes as a reference while you read the chapters in this book. Consult the additional resources for added help. Also, the "GED Quick Review" sheet in the front of the book is a concise summary of the test information and skills included in this book. Refer to it shortly before testing to help you stay relaxed and confident about the GED.

Part X includes the following appendixes:

Appendix A What's Next?

Appendix B Calculator Directions

Appendix C General Vocabulary List

Appendix D Mathematics Formulas

Appendix E Additional GED Resources

APPENDIX A

What's Next?

This appendix contains information about how the GED can help you get into college or get a better job.

GED and Employment

Many jobs, particularly high-paying jobs, require a high school diploma or equivalency credential. In addition, without proof of high school–level academic skills, you may be held back for promotion in your current job. A great way to advance in the workplace is to move along the educational track, which begins with finishing high school or, for adults, succeeding on the GED.

The GED is sometimes called a "high school equivalency test" and for good reason. The GED Testing Service (of the American Council of Education) works very hard to ensure that the skills tested on each edition of the GED conform to those found in a typical high school program. Passing the GED means you have proven that you have the skills expected of graduating high school students. In fact, the GED Testing Service administered the current version of the test to groups of high school graduates and found that about 42% of them would fail the GED, proving that passing it is an important accomplishment. Passing the GED as an adult shows that your learning has not ceased since you left school. Earning your high school equivalency reflects well on you by showing employers—current and future—that you are willing to make the time and effort necessary to further your education and expand your workplace skills.

Employers take the GED seriously. The GED Testing Service reports that more than 90% of U.S. employers view passing the GED as equivalent to a traditional high school diploma with regard to hiring, salary, and opportunity for advancement. Many employers, both large and small, have programs to help employees practice, pay for, and pass the GED. The GED Testing Service also maintains a program called "Employers of Choice," which supports corporations in their efforts to move employees through the high school equivalency process.

Ask your current employer about whether the company will support your taking the GED and whether passing it will improve your chances for advancement. The worst answer you could receive is "no," but you will probably find your employer is very supportive of people who work to further their education.

GED and College

Today, more than ever, the GED credential is accepted in place of a traditional high school diploma in higher education admission consideration. Recent estimations show that about 93% of colleges and universities across the 50 U.S. states and the District of Columbia, 9 U.S. territories, and 13 Canadian provinces and territories accept a passing GED score instead of a diploma for admission consideration. In fact, the GED Testing Service reports that people with GED credentials perform as well as new high school graduates in higher education and training.

Earning the GED credential means you can enter technical or vocational school, as well as a community college or a four-year college or university.

Technical schools can be public or private institutions. Their mission is to train students in a specific field of work. This is why they're often called "trade schools" or "vocational schools." You can find programs in plumbing, auto repair, and other technical disciplines at technical schools.

Community colleges tend to offer a broad range of academic programs. In your area of the United States or Canada, community colleges might be called "city colleges," "county colleges," or simply "colleges" (in contrast to universities). The term "junior college" could describe a public community college but is typically reserved for private two-year schools.

Community colleges are an excellent option for many learners new to higher education. The course offerings are generally broad, the schools tend to be local, and tuition is significantly lower than at four-year schools. Community colleges offer diplomas and certificates for specialty programs and two-year associate's degrees in a variety of subject areas. Many students choose to transfer from a community college to a four-year college or university after earning credit in introductory coursework or earning an associate's degree.

After passing the GED, some learners choose to begin study at a four-year college or university. Four-year colleges and universities have more intensive application procedures than do community colleges. You will need to apply well in advance of the semester you want to enter. Contact any schools you might consider to learn about their admissions process and requirements. You will also have to submit scores from at least one more standardized test (such as the ACT or SAT).

It takes most students four to five years of full-time study to attain a bachelor's degree. These degrees are available in nearly any discipline you can imagine. Some students enter college or university with a clear idea of what they want to study. Others arrive at their preferred "major" after some trial and error in choosing classes. Earning a bachelor's degree at a college or university in the United States or Canada is very expensive, but the return on the investment can be great. College graduates generally earn significantly more than do their counterparts without degrees.

When evaluating colleges, consider more than just the academic reputation. What are the costs? Do you qualify for reduced tuition based on your residency? Are scholarships available for nontraditional (adult) students? Is the campus urban, suburban, or rural? Who makes up the student body? Where would you live? Would you work and go to school at the same time? These are all questions college admissions counselors can help you answer.

GED and You

Remember that taking the GED is an important step toward improving yourself and increasing your opportunities. Congratulate yourself on making a smart decision about your future.

B

APPENDIX B

Calculator Directions

You will be provided with a calculator at the testing center for optional use on Part I of the Mathematics Test. Part II must be completed without the use of the calculator.

All GED testing centers use the Casio fx-260 calculator. Check out a picture at http://www.casio.com/products/images/FX-260Solar/xlarge to familiarize yourself with the layout of the buttons. You might also consider purchasing the calculator (for about $10) so you can practice with it.

See also the Kentucky Educational Television (KET) GED Prep website listed in Appendix E, "Additional GED Resources," for interactive calculator practice.

Start the calculator:

The Casio fx-260 is a solar calculator, so in a bright testing room you will have no problems turning the unit on. Press On in the upper-right corner. The screen will display 0 and DEG, which indicates you are making calculations in the proper format for the GED.

Clear the calculator:

To clear your calculations and start over, press ON or the red AC (all clear) key.

Enter the expression as written to perform *arithmetic*. Pressing the = (equals) key displays the result.

Example: 10 + 7.5 + 3.3

1. Power on or clear: ON or AC
2. Enter the expression: 10 + 7.5 + 3.3 =
3. The calculator displays the correct answer: 20.8

Expressions might include *multiplication of a quantity* (terms in parentheses) by a number. As shown in the following example, there might not be an explicit multiplication sign, but the parentheses indicate multiplication is necessary.

$2(x + y)$

Although no multiplication sign is written, one *must* be used with the calculator.

Example: 4(15 – 8)

1. Power on or clear: ON or AC
2. Enter the expression: 4 × (15 – 8) =
3. The calculator displays the correct answer: 28

The *square root* function is the second function of the x^2 key. You must be careful to use the SHIFT key correctly.

Example: $\sqrt{121}$

1. Power on or clear: ON or AC.
2. Enter the number or expression for which you want the square root: 121.
3. Press (but do not hold) Shift. The word SHIFT will appear at the top-left of the screen.
4. Press x^2. The square root symbol is printed in orange above the button.
5. The calculator displays the correct answer: 11

Use +/- (the "sign change" key) to make a positive number negative or a negative number positive. Any arithmetic can be performed with both positive and negative numbers.

Example: –2 – –16

1. Power on or clear: ON or AC
2. Enter the expression, applying the sign change after entering the digits: 2 +/- –16 +/- =

   Note: When you press the +/- key, the negative sign appears on the far left of the display screen. When you press the key again, the negative sign will disappear.
3. The calculator displays the correct answer: 14

Use [a b/c] (the fraction key) to enter a proper or improper fraction.

Example: 2/6

1. Power on or clear: ON or AC
2. Enter the numerator, then press the fraction key, and then enter the denominator: 2 a b/c 6
3. The calculator displays the fraction using a special fraction symbol: 2 [a b/c] (the bottom and right sides of a square) 6.
4. Pressing = displays the reduced fraction: 1 [a b/c] 3.
5. Pressing a b/c displays the decimal equivalent of the fraction: .3333333333

Use a b/c (the fraction key) to enter a mixed number.

Example: 3 1/2

1. Power on or clear: ON or AC
2. Enter the whole number, then the fraction key, then the numerator, then the fraction key, then the denominator: 3 a b/c 2 a b/c 4
3. The calculator displays the mixed number using a special fraction symbol: 3 a b/c 2 a b/c 4.
4. Press = to display the reduced mixed number: 3 a b/c 1 a b/c 2.
5. Press SHIFT then the d/c (this is the second function of the fraction key) to convert the mixed number to an improper fraction: 7 a b/c 2
6. Press a b/c to convert the improper fraction to its decimal equivalent: 3.5

APPENDIX C

General Vocabulary List

Some of these words have been asked about by former students. Many are terms used in the book, and some are included here because they have been selected by experienced instructors as representative of the vocabulary level that is expected on the GED. The definitions given might not be exhaustive; words can have many meanings. Buy a thorough college dictionary if you don't have one—it is an essential tool for any learner.

A

abound Be well supplied; have great quantities.

absence State of being away or lacking something; inattentiveness.

absurd Extremely ridiculous or completely lacking reason.

abundance A great supply; more than plenty.

accommodate Adapt or adjust in a way that makes someone else comfortable; make room.

accusation Statement blaming someone for a crime or error.

acrid Harsh or bitter taste or smell.

acute Sharp; quick and precise; intense.

adapt Change or modify to suit a particular purpose.

adjacent Near or close (to something); adjoining.

adolescence Stage of development between puberty and maturity.

affiliation Connection between groups of people, organizations, or establishments.

agility Quality of being quick and nimble.

alienate Isolate oneself from others or another person from oneself.

align Adjust parts so that they fit together correctly, usually in a straight line.

allegiance Loyalty to a person, group, country, or cause.

ambiguous Unclear or capable of having more than one meaning.

ample More than sufficient amount; roomy.

analogous Similar and comparable in some way; serving a similar function.

anew Starting again in a new or different way.

anomaly Something that is different from the norm.

anticipate Look forward to, expect.

apathy Lack of any emotion, interest, or concern.

aperture Opening or hole, usually in an optical instrument, such as a camera, that limits the amount of light passing through a lens.

apocalypse Great or total devastation; approximating the end of the world.

apparatus Group of materials or devices used for a specific purpose.

appealing Attractive or inviting; the act of making a request for a decision or help.

arisen State of being up after sitting or lying.

articulate (v.) Clearly explain; (adj.) quality of being able to speak clearly.

aspect Certain part of something; the side of an object that faces in a certain direction.

assert Demonstrate power; defend a statement as true.

assumption Something believed to be true without proof; unsupported evidence.

astonishing Amazing or bewildering.

atrium Area of a building, usually a courtyard, that has skylights or is open to the sky and often contains plants.

B

bacteria Single-celled, sometimes infectious, microorganisms.

banish Force to leave; exile.

bemoan Express grief; deplore.

beneficiary Recipient of benefits, especially funds or property from an insurance policy or will.

binge Duration of excessive and uncontrolled self-indulgence.

brood Dwell over past misfortune (see also *brood* in Chapter 34, "Science Terms").

C

calamity Horrible event that results in extreme loss.

calligraphy Stylized, artistic handwriting.

carbohydrate Sugars and starches that serve as a major energy source for animals.

catalog Systematic list of items, such as books in a library or goods for sale at a store.

cause Anything producing an effect or result.

chaos State of complete disarray.

characteristics Distinguishing attributes or qualities of a person or thing.

chronology List of events arranged by time of occurrence.

circumscribe Enclose a shape with lines or curves so that every vertex of the enclosed object touches part of the enclosing configuration; encircle.

coherent Quality of being logical and clear.

cohesiveness Quality of sticking together.

coincidental Occurring by chance.

commendable Worthy of praise.

compare Describe similarities or differences between two things.

competence Quality of having adequate skill, knowledge, and experience.

compose Form by placing parts or elements together; bring oneself to a state of calm.

comprehensive All-inclusive.

compressibility Ease with which pressure can alter the volume of matter.

concede Admit or reluctantly yield; surrender.

concentration Amount of one substance contained within another; intense mental effort or focus.

concerto Composition for an orchestra and one or more solo instruments, typically in three movements.

concoct Prepare by mixing ingredients together; devise a plan.

condense Become more compact; to change from a vapor to a liquid.

conducive Tending to cause or bring about.

conjure Bring to mind; to produce as if by magic.

conscience Mental sense that guides moral decisions.

consecutive Uninterrupted sequence.

consent (n.) Permission; (v.) to agree.

consequence Result of an action.

conservatory Fine arts school; greenhouse of plants aesthetically arranged.

constant Quality of being unchanging; marked by firm resolution or loyalty.

contemplate Carefully consider.

contemporary (adj.) Current, modern people or things of the same time, era, or age.

contradict Assert the opposite.

contrast (v.) Set in opposition to show differences; (n.) difference or differences, often strong, between two things.

contrive Clearly plan; cleverly devise.

controversial Characterized by dispute or controversy.

cordial Sincere; courteous.

correlate Have corresponding characteristics.

credulity Tendency to trust too easily.

crimson Deep red color.

criterion Requirements on which judgment can be based.

crucial Extremely important.

cuisine Food prepared by a style of cooking; for example, “Italian cuisine.”

D

decipher Interpret the meaning, usually of a code or hard-to-read handwriting.

decompose Disintegrate into components.

de-emphasize Minimize the importance.

defection Withdrawal of support; act of joining another party to a conflict or war.

deform Disfigure; ruin the shape of an object.

degree One in a series of steps in a process or scale; one of various units of measurement.

delegate (v.) Transfer responsibilities to another; (n.) personal representative.

deliberate (adj.) Carefully planned out; (v.) consider carefully.

delve Deeply and thoroughly search.

demean Reduce in worth.

demise End of existence.

demur Express opposition.

derive Infer certain knowledge; trace the origin or development of something.

descend Come from a particular origin; move down from a higher point.

descendant Person, animal, or plant that can be traced back to a certain origin; future or subsequent generations.

deter Prevent from taking a particular course of action.

deviation Divergence from a certain path.

devise (v.) Design or create (often confused with the noun *device*, which means "tool that fulfils a certain purpose").

diligent Continuously putting in great, careful effort.

dilute Weaken the strength of a solution.

diminish Make smaller, decrease, or lessen.

disavow Deny knowledge of, responsibility for, or association with.

discern Differentiate or distinguish; to perceive.

discomforting Embarrassing.

disconcerting Unsettling.

discriminatory Showing bias.

disdainful Scornful and sneering.

dispel Rid one's mind of; drive out.

disperse Scatter or spread out.

disquieting Lacking peace of mind; causing mental unrest.

dissolution Process of dissolving or disintegrating.

dissolve Pass into and become part of; terminate.

distinct Easily distinguishable from others.

dominant Most prominent; exuding authority.

drastic Extreme.

durable Resistant to wear.

E

effect Result of a cause.

elaborate (adj.) Rich with detail and well developed; (v.) expand on the idea of something.

eloquent Very clear and precise; being skilled in clear and precise speech.

embalm Preserve a dead body by treating it with chemical preservatives.

embrace Enclose in one's arms; become accepting of other ideas or people.

emissions Things that are discharged (often gases into the air).

emit Release particular things such as liquid, heat, and gasses.

empowered Possessing the necessary abilities for a particular task; given power or authority.

emulate Follow an admirable example; imitate.

endorsement A guarantee to support; a signature on a document such as a check.

endow Give a positive trait; to provide monetary funds by donation.

endure Continue despite difficulty; tolerate.

enormity A horrible wrong; tremendous size.

enrich Improve.

entangle Twist and tie up in a complicated manner.

enumerate State things in a list.

envision Picture a mental image.

eon Duration of time so long it cannot be measured (see also *eon* in science terms).

epic (adj.) Very impressive and extraordinary (see also *epic* [n.] in Chapter 20, "Language Arts, Reading Terms").

error Mistake; difference between a computed value and the correct value.

escapist One who mentally leaves the real world for a world of fantasy.

essence Important characteristics that help differentiate something; key element of an idea; something spiritual; a scent.

essential Indispensable or necessary.

essentially At the very core.

establish Create a foundation.

ethical In line with what is right and wrong.

evaporate Draw away moisture and convert into vapor.

exceed Go far beyond a limit; excel.

exceptional Rare due to uncommonly great qualities.

exhibit (v.) Display; (n.) something displayed; piece of evidence submitted to a court during a trial.

expertise Skill or knowledge in a certain area or field.

exquisite Characterized by great beauty and intricacy.

extensive Detailed and far reaching.

extrapolate Guess by inferring from known information.

extravagant Lavish beyond the norm.

exultant Gleeful because of success.

F

feign Fabricate or deceive.

fickle Constantly changing one's mind.

fledgling A young bird that has just acquired feathers; an inexperienced newcomer.

flourish (v.) Abound plentifully; thrive; (n.) dramatic gesture; written embellishment.

foil (n.) Character whose traits exemplify the opposite traits of another character when they are compared; weapon used in the sport of fencing; (v.) prevent an action, often by ruining a plan.

forecast Predict future events, such as the weather.

foresee Know beforehand.

foreshadow Suggest or hint at future occurrences.

forgo Refrain from doing something previously planned.

formalize Make something official or valid.

franchise Right given to an individual or group to operate a branch of a business and sell the business's products; the right to vote.

frenzied In a temporary crazed state.

friction Force resistant to motion between two objects in contact.

frivolous Unnecessary and silly.

G

gable Triangular section of a wall that fills the space between the two slopes of a roof.

gaudy Tastelessly flashy.

glib Showing ease and slickness of action but lacking thought or concern.

H

haggle Bargain in an annoying manner; harass.

harbinger Sign that foreshadows upcoming events; a messenger.

herbivorous Plant-eating organism.

hoist Lift up.

hue Color.

I

idiosyncrasy Peculiar characteristic.

imminent Close to happening; impending.

imply Indirectly suggest (often confused with *infer*, which means "to conclude").

improvise Do or perform without preparation; create something only from readily available materials.

incarcerate To imprison.

inclined Disposed to a certain path of thought; sloping angle.

inconstant Not following a pattern; varying.

incorporate To bring two things or certain aspects of two things together.

indifference Total lack of concern or interest.

indignation Anger due to unfairness.

indulge Freely partake in; yield to the wish or desire of oneself or others.

inevitable Bound to happen; unavoidable.

inexhaustible Plentiful; impossible to use up completely.

inexplicable Impossible to give the reason for; unexplainable.

infirmary Small hospital, often in an institution, used to provide care for the sick.

infuse Permeate: garlic-infused olive oil.

ingenious Brilliant and clever.

inherent Naturally occurring and permanent.

inscribe Write or engrave words on a surface; write one's name on something.

insinuate Subtly imply.

institute (v.) Enact or establish; (n.) organization, especially an academic one.

interpret Translate; explain or draw conclusions.

interpretation Personal explanation for another's creation, such as a play or poem.

intricacy Detail of something complex.

invaluable Priceless.

involuntary Done without one's consent or free will.

irreconcilable Impossible to adjust or compromise.

irrelevant Not relevant or pertinent; outside the scope of a discussion or argument.

irrevocable Impossible to reverse.

J

juxtaposition Act of placing things next to each other, usually for comparing or contrasting.

K–L

languish Become weak; become disenchanted.

lavish (adj.) Elaborate and luxurious; (v.) freely and boundlessly bestow.

liberally Done in a manner that is generous (for example, liberally applying sunscreen).

lumbering Lethargically walking around with clumsiness.

M

manifest (adj.) Clearly recognizable; (v.) make clear; (n.) list of transported goods or passengers used for record keeping.

mediocre Lacking any special qualities, even inferior.

melancholy Glumness; deep, usually sad, contemplative thought.

mere Small; slight; being nothing more than what is stated: *He earns a mere $7 per hour.*

meteorite Meteor that reaches the surface of the earth before it is entirely vaporized.

meticulous Devoting a high amount of attention to detail.

minuscule Extremely small; unimportant.

moral (adj.) Based on standards of good and bad; (n.) a rule of proper behavior (see also *moral* [n.] in Chapter 20, "Language Arts, Reading Terms").

morale Mental well being; mood.

mortar Wood or stone bowl in which substances are ground by a pestle; cement mixture used to bond bricks or stones; military weapon similar for firing shells.

mutability Ability to transform.

N

negligible Meaningless; insignificant.

nostalgia Sentimental yearning for the past.

notion Belief, sometimes without much conviction; idea or concept.

numerous Existing in great numbers of units or persons.

O

offal Wasted trimmings of an animal carcass; trash or rubbish.

onus Burden of responsibility.

opus Major creative composition, usually in classical music.

oracle Future-telling deity or prophet; shrine devoted to a future-telling deity or prophet.

overt Obvious and clearly shown.

P

paragon Example of excellence.

pathetic Deserves pity or sympathy.

peculiarity Unusual quality or characteristic.

pendulum Device that is suspended in such a way to allow it to swing back and forth using gravity.

perceive Become aware of something, usually through the senses.

periphery Outermost boundary of an area.

phantom (adj.) Exists only in the mind, illusionary; (n.) ghost.

plagiarism Fraud consisting of copying another's work and presenting it as original.

powwow Meeting or gathering.

preceding Coming before.

precipitate Cause something to happen very suddenly.

predominant Having superior strength; paramount.

preliminary Precedes or comes prior to.

prerequisite (adj.) Required as a prior condition; (n.) something prerequisite.

prestigious Having honor or respect from others.

prevail Triumph; overcome adversity.

prevalent Commonly used or occurring.

prototype Original or draft form of something.

protract Lengthen or prolong.

prowess Great skill in something.

pseudoscience Irrational or unfounded beliefs masquerading as science (for example, astrology).

pyrotechnics Display of fireworks.

Q

quadrant One part of a larger object that has been divided into four parts.

quasi (*used as a prefix*) Resembling to some degree.

quintessential Being the most typical: "Judy is the quintessential cheerleader—athletic, pretty, and spirited."

R

rapid Fast.

rapt Completely occupied by, or focused on, something.

recount Describe the facts or details of a past event; to retell a story or repeat testimony.

recurrent Taking place over and over.

redeem Pay off a debt or fulfill an obligation; to make good.

redirect Alter the course or direction.

rediscover Learn about or see something as though for the first time.

relevant Logically connected; pertinent.

reluctant Unwilling and resistant.

reparation Compensation given to make amends.

respectively In the order given.

retention Ability to hold things in or retain.

rifling Spiral grooves on the inside of a gun barrel; gerund of *rifle* [v.]: search through hastily.

rudimentary Very basic or not fully developed.

S

sacrilege Misuse something that is sacred.

sanctuary Sacred place; refuge (for people, animals, and so on); main room of a Christian church used for worship services.

saturation State of being completely full or soaked.

scrutiny Very close examination.

seminal Forming the basis for future development; at the beginning; original.

simultaneous Happening or existing at the same time.

skepticism Attitude of doubt or disbelief.

solace Comfort; safety.

sovereign (adj.) Having supreme power; self-governing; (n.) ruler or king.

span Distance between two things.

speculation Conclusions based on uncertain evidence; purchase of something with the hope of reselling it later at a profit.

stagnant Not moving or changing; stale.

straddle Having one leg on each side of something.

subcontractor Someone who agrees to perform one part of a larger commitment or contract.

subjective Depending on a person's attitudes or opinions.

subsequent Coming next or later.

sustenance Things that provide nourishment for survival.

T

tenet Belief that is held to be true by a certain group.

transcend Go above and beyond; rise above.

U

uniform (adj.) Always the same; consistent; (n.) identical clothing worn by members of a certain group.

unilateral Performed in a one-sided manner.

unparalleled Without equal or comparison.

unprecedented Having no previous example.

unsolicited Unwanted, not asked for.

V–Z

variable In science: an element of an experiment that is changed to produce significant results (contrast with "constant"); in math: elements of formulas and other expressions (usually represented by letters of the alphabet) that may be substituted for by a real number when applying a function (commonly called "plugging in" values for variables).

various Of differing kinds.

vindication Act of clearing someone or something from blame.

virtually In almost all instances; simulated as by a computer.

visionary (adj.) Characterized by dreams or illusions; (n.) person with vision or foresight.

APPENDIX D

Mathematics Formulas

This appendix contains the important math formulas that you will be required to understand for the GED. The list of formulas will be repeated at the beginning of each Math Section on your actual GED.

The following are definitions for the formulas in Table D.1:

- *s* is the length of a side of a square
- *b* is the length of the base
- *h* is height
- *w* is width
- *l* is length
- *r* is radius
- π (pi) is approximately equal to 3.14

TABLE D.1 Math Formulas

Area	
Square	s^2
Rectangle	$l \times w$
Parallelogram	$b \times h$
Triangle	$\frac{1}{2} \times b \times h$
Trapezoid	$\frac{1}{2} \times (b_1 \times b_2) \times h$
Circle	$\pi \times r^2$
Perimeter	
Square	$4 \times s$
Rectangle	$2 \times l + 2 \times w$
Triangle	$side_1 + side_2 + side_3$
Circumference	
Circle *only*	$2 \times \pi \times r$ OR $\pi \times$ diameter (diameter is two times the radius)
Volume	
Cube [each face is a square]	s^3
Rectangular solid	$l \times w \times h$
Square pyramid [base is a square]	$\frac{1}{3} \times s^2 \times h$
Cylinder [base is a circle]	$\pi \times r^2 \times h$
Cone [base is a circle]	$\frac{1}{3} \times \pi \times r^2 \times h$

(continues)

TABLE D.1 Math Formulas

Coordinate Geometry	
Distance between points; (x_1,y_1) and (x_2,y_2) are two points in a plane.	$\sqrt{(x_2 - x_1)^2 + (y_2 - y_1)^2}$
Slope of a line; (x_1,y_1) and (x_2,y_2) are two points on the line.	$\frac{y_2 - y_1}{x_2 - x_1}$
Pythagorean Theorem	
Determine the length of one side of a right triangle using the lengths of the other two sides; *a and b are legs; c is the hypotenuse (the side opposite the right angle).*	$a^2 + b^2 = c^2$
Measures of Central Tendency	
Mean (average); *x* is a value and *n* is the total number of values for which you want a mean.	$\frac{x_1 + x_2 + ... + x_n}{n}$
Median; begin with a set of values in numerical order.	The middle value in a set with an odd number of values; halfway between (the average of) the two middle values in a set with an even number of values.
Rates	
Simple Interest	principal (starting amount) × rate × time
Distance	rate × time
Total Cost	(number of units) × (price per unit)

APPENDIX E

Additional GED Resources

The purpose of this book is to help you prepare for the GED. Although this book provides you with useful information about the tests and realistic practice materials to get you ready for the real thing, we suggest the following additional resources—websites and books—to aid you in your GED preparation.

General GED Information

http://www.gedtest.org—The official website of the GED Testing Service.

http://www.gedpractice.com—Practice material from Steck-Vaughn.

http://www.ket.org/ged2002—Test information and practice from Kentucky Educational Television (KET).

http://www.floridatechnet.org/GED/LessonPlans/Lessons.htm—GED teacher lesson plans from Florida Atlantic University.

http://www.AdvantageEd.com—Advantage Education GED individual tutoring services.

Language Arts Information

http://www.wsu.edu/~brians/errors—Common errors in English usage.

http://www.literacyworks.org/learningresources—Interesting news articles with vocabulary lists and various types of interactive questions.

Corbeil, Jean-Claude, and Ariane Archambault. *The Firefly Visual Dictionary*. Richmond Hill, Ontario, Canada: Firefly Books Ltd., 2002.

Swan, Michael. *Practical English Usage*. Oxford: Oxford University Press, 1995.

Science Information

http://www.exploratorium.edu—Lots of interesting activities from the San Francisco Science Museum.

http://www.wikidchem.org—"The Free Chemistry Archive."

http://education.usgs.gov/common/secondary.htm—U.S. Geological Survey educational resources in biology, geology, and geography.

http://www.actionbioscience.org—Educational website to promote bioscience literacy.

Social Studies Information

http://www.hyperhistory.com/online_n2/History_n2/a.html—An excellent historical timeline.

http://www.si.edu/RESOURCE/FAQ/nmah/timeline.htm—Encyclopedia Smithsonian: American History Timeline.

http://www.nationmaster.com—Explore geographic statistics, charts, maps, and articles.

Math Information

http://www.math.com—Lots of good math review and practice.

http://www.mathforum.org/students—Math resources from Drexel University.

Additional Practice Tests

Official U.S. Edition GED Practice Tests from Steck-Vaughn in the U.S.: English, Spanish, and French editions in standard, large-print, and audio cassette formats are available for purchase.

Phone: 1-800-531-5015

Online: http://steckvaughn.harcourtachieve.com

Official Canadian Edition GED Practice Tests in English or French are available for purchase directly from Thomson Nelson in Canada.

Phone: 1-800-268-2222

Online: http://www.nelson.com/nelson/highered/ged/

Index

Symbols

‘ (apostrophe), 163

: (colon), 165

, (comma), 161-163

“ (double quotation marks), 163-164

... (ellipses), 166

∞ (infinity symbol), 461

A

absolute value, 462-463

acids, 416

active voice, 136-137

acts (drama), 231

addition, 465
  adding decimals, 479
  adding fractions, 487

adjectives, 114

administration (GED), 10

adrenaline, 87
  and anxiety, 88

adverbs, 114

affective domain, Taxonomy of Educational Objectives, 95

Age of Discovery, 277
  New World explorers, 278

Age of Enlightenment, 280

agreement (noun/verb), 116-122

algebra
  coordinate plane, 536
    distance between points, calculating, 538-540
    exercises, 542-544
    linear equations, 540
    slope, calculating, 541
  equations, 531, 545
    expressions, multiplying, 544
    word problems, 532-533

expressions, simplifying, 533-534
factoring, 545-548
inequalities, 535-536
patterns, representing, 534-535
alkali metals, 413
alleles, 387
alliteration (poetry), 223
amendments to U.S. Constitution, 327-328
American Revolution, 295
amplitude, 424
analysis level (Taxonomy of Educational Objectives), 96
ancient China, 274
ancient Egypt, 268-269
ancient Greece, 270-271
ancient Rome, 271-273
angles, 554
vertical, 559
answers
answer sheet, managing, 91
changing, 92
guessing, 92
to Language Arts, Reading tests
diagnostic test, 72-73
practice test, 597, 688-691, 715, 812-814
to Language Arts, Writing tests
diagnostic test, 70-71
practice test, 597, 684-687, 715, 808-811
to mathematics tests
diagnostic test, 79-81
practice test, 599, 702-710, 717, 824-832
to science tests
diagnostic test, 76-78
practice test, 598, 697-701, 716, 820-823
to social studies tests
diagnostic test, 74-75
practice test, 598, 692-696, 716, 815-819
application level (Taxonomy of Educational Objectives), 96
applied forces, 418
aqueous solutions, 415
area, 561
formulas, 855
articles, 114
Articles of Confederation, 299
Articles of the Constitution
Article One, 322
Article Three, 325-326
Article Two, 323-324
artificial stressors, 87
artistic commentary as form of nonfiction, 233
atmosphere, 404
cloud formations, 405
meteorology, 404-405
atomic theory, 411
atomic weight, 412
atoms
chemical bonding, 415
ions, 416
autocracy, 321
average. *See* mean

B

b/c (fraction key), calculators, 842
bases, 416
basic operations, practice questions and answers, 468-469
big bang theory, 399
biology
cells, 383
classification of organisms, 393-395
evolution, 395
genetic mutations, 389
mitosis, 385
organ systems, 389
digestive system, 391
endocrine system, 392-393
muscular system, 392
nervous system, 389
respiratory system, 390
skeletal system, 392
urinary system, 391
reproduction
meiosis, 386
spermatozoon, 386
biosphere, 406
black holes, 400
Bloom, Benjamin
Taxonomy of Educational Objectives, 95
analysis level, 96
application level, 96

comprehension level, 96
evaluation level, 96
knowledge level, 95
synthesis level, 96
Bolshevik Revolution, 287-288
brain stem, 390
branches of U.S. government
checks and balances, 326-327
executive branch of U.S. government, 323
judicial branch of U.S. government, 325-326
legislative branch of U.S. government, 322
breaks, taking, 90
breathing as relaxation technique, 90
BTUs (British Thermal Units), 422
bubonic plague, 276
Buddhism, 274
Bush, George H. W., 317
Bush, George W., 318-319

C

calculating
median, 511
total cost, 525
work, 418-419
calculators, testing center-provided
arithmetic, performing, 841
b/c (fraction key), 842
clearing calculations, 841
multiplication of a quantity, 841
positive/negative numbers, 842
square root function, 842
starting, 841
usage example, 843
web resources, 841
capitalism, 339
capitalization, 160
cardiac muscle, 392
Carter, Jimmy, 316
cartilage, 392
Casio fx-260 calculators
arithmetic, performing, 841
b/c (fraction key), 842
clearing calculations, 841
multiplication of a quantity, 841
positive/negative numbers, 842
square root function, 842
starting, 841
usage example, 843
web resources, 841
cause and effect, relating in nonfiction, 235-237
Celsius temperature scale, 421
cells, 99, 383
organelles, 384
Central American independence, 283
central nervous system, 389
cerebellum, 390
cerebrum, 390
Ceres, 403
Ch'in Dynasty, 274
Champollion, Jean, 269
changing answers, 92
character analysis (drama), 231-232
characterization, 210, 215
characters, 215
charts, 512
checks and balances, 326-327
chemical bonding, 415
chemical equations, 414
chemical reactions, 414
chemistry
atomic theory, 411
chemical changes, 414
compounds, 415
acids, 416
bases, 416
electrons, 415
endothermic reactions, 414
ions, 416
Law of Conservation of Matter, 414
mixtures, 415
periodic table, 412
pollutants, 416-417
solutes, 415
solutions, 415
solvents, 415
Christianity, 273
circle graphs
interpreting, 101
exercise, 101-102
circles, 557

circumference, 560
formula, 855
citizenship (U.S.), 329
obtaining, 330
Civil War, 301-302
classification of organisms, 393-395
clauses, 126
non-restrictive, 140
run-on sentences, 128-129
climate, 349
climax, 213
Clinton, Bill, 317-318
cloning, 389
cloud formations, 405
cluster diagrams, 174
cognitive (knowledge, comprehension, reasoning) domain, Taxonomy of Educational Objectives, 95
cognitive endurance, 86
college, importance of GED in, 838
colonization of the U.S., 294
commissioners, 331
common mistakes on the Language Arts, Writing multiple-choice test, 148
complicated sentences, 148
illogical statements, 150
inappropriate vocabulary, 149
lack of specificity, 148
opinionated/emotional statements, 148
poor penmanship, 149
too conversational, 150
unsafe assumptions, 150
communism, 339
comparative analysis, 237-238
comparing
decimals, 477
fractions, 486
knowledge and skills, 85-86
complex sentences, 120
compounds, 415-416
comprehension level (Taxonomy of Educational Objectives), 96
concise language as element of effective writing, 145-147
conduction, 422
conductivity, 428
conflict, 212
Confucianism, 274
congruency, 560
conjugation, 116-118, 131, 135-136
future tense, 133
past tense, 132
present perfect forms, 119
present tense, 133
simple past forms, 119
unreal conditional, 134
conjunctions, 114, 129-131
in sentence subject, 121
connection shift questions, writing test, 109
constituency, 126
Constitution, U.S., 322
amendments, 323, 327-328
Article One, 322
Article Three, 325-326
Article Two, 323-324
Consumer Expenditure Survey (2004), 341-342
continental drift, 407
continents, 343
contour lines, 347-349
contractions, 158-159
contrasting ideas in nonfiction, 237-238
controlling suspense and surprise, 88
convection, 422
converting
fractions
to decimal, 486
to mixed numbers, 486
hours to minutes, 526
minutes to hours, 526
mixed numbers to fractions, 486
percentages to decimal, 499
units of measurement, 523-524
coordinate geometry formula (mathematics), 856
coordinate plane, 536
distance between points, calculating, 538-540
exercises, 542-544
linear equations, 540
slope, calculating, 541
coordinating conjunctions, 129
correction questions, Writing Test, 108
correlative conjunctions, 129-130
correspondence as form of nonfiction, 234

council-manager municipal government, 331
counties, 331
couplets (poetry), 222
covalent bonding, 415
creationism, 395
currency, 340
cytoplasm, 385

D

Da Vinci, Leonardo, 277
dangling modifiers, 140-141
Darwin, Charles, 395
data analysis
  charts, 512
  graphs, 513
  practice questions and answers, 514, 517-519
  tables, 512
decimals, 477
  adding, 479
  comparing, 477
  dividing, 479-481
  multiplying, 479-481
  practice questions and answers, 482-484
  rounding, 478
  scientific notation, 478-479
  subtracting, 479
Declaration of Independence, 296-299
demand, 334-336
democracy, 321
demographic maps, 97
demographics, 350
demonstratives, 114
dependent probability, 506
derived 3D figures, 557
descriptivism, 111
determiners, 114
  common errors, 123
  possessive, 122
dew point, 350
diagnostic tests
  Language Arts, Reading, 36-43
    answers and explanations, 72-73
  Language Arts, Writing Part I, 25-31
    answers and explanations, 70-71
  Language Arts, Writing Part II, 32-33, 623, 741
  mathematics, 64-67
    answers and explanations, 79-81
  science, 54-60
    answers and explanations, 76-78
  social studies, 45-50
    answers and explanations, 74-75
dialect, 125
dialogue (drama), 229
diction, 216
diet as stressor, 89
digestive system, 391
direct objects, 126-128
disabilities, accommodating (GED testing), 14-15
distance formula (mathematics), 856
divergent plate boundaries, 407
division
  dividing decimals, 479, 481
  dividing fractions, 488
  quotient, 466
DNA (deoxyribonucleic acid), genes, 387
dominant alleles, 387
Doppler effect, 425
drama
  acts, 231
  character analysis, 231-232
  dialogue, 229
  dramatic structure, 230
  prologues/epilogues, 231
  protagonists, 230
  scenes, 231
  stage direction, 229-230
Dust Bowl, 306
dwarf planets, 401

E

EAE (Edited American English), 125
  versus Standard English, 111
early civilizations
  China, 274
  Egypt, 268-269
  Greece, 270-271
  Rome, 271-273

Earth, 403. *See also* Earth and space science
atmosphere, 404
meteorology, 404-405
biosphere, 406
climate, 349
continents, 343
demographics, 350
equator, 345
hemispheres, 345
hydrosphere, 405
lithosphere, 407
measuring, 345
oceans, 343
overpopulation, 351
pedosphere, 408
time zones, 346-347
Earth and space science
big bang theory, 399
galaxies, 400
scale of observations, 400
solar system, 401
planets, 401-403
space exploration, 403-404
stars, 400
earthquakes, 407
ecology, 396-397
economic systems
capitalism, 339
communism, 339
socialism, 339
economics, 333
Consumer Expenditure Survey (2004), 341-342
economic growth, 336
measuring, 337-338
equilibrium price, 335
fiscal policy, 340
GDP, 337
inflation, 337
money systems, 340
recession, 336
supply and demand, 334-336
editing your GED essay, 175
editorial cartoons, interpreting, 102-104
effective essays, writing, 172-175
effective writing, elements of
concise language, 145-147
logical sentence order, 143-144
pronoun use, 146
relationship between paragraphs, 147-148
word choice, 144-145
Einstein, Albert, 426
Eisenhower, Dwight D., 310-312
Electoral College, 328-329
electricity, 427
conductors, 428
power generation companies, 428-429
static electricity, 428
electromagnetic radiation, 425
electrons, 412, 415
elements, periodic table, 412
elevation, 347
embryos, 389
employment, importance of GED in, 837
end rhymes, 222
endocrine system, 392-393
endoskeleton, 392
endothermic reactions, 414
energy, 419
heat, 421
measuring, 422
transfer methods, 422
epics, 222
epilogues/prologues (drama), 231
epinephrine, 87
equations, 531, 545
chemical equations, 414
word problems, 532-533
Equator, 345
equilibrium price, 335
Eris, 403
erosion, 408
essays, Writing Test, 110. *See also* Language Arts, Writing test
estimation, 481-482
euphemisms, 217
European Middle Ages. *See* Middle Ages
evaluation level (Taxonomy of Educational Objectives), 96

evolution, 395
example GED essays, 176-178
exams
practice exams, web resources, 858
reading
exam-taking strategies, 207
format of, 205
scoring, 206-207
writing
construction shift questions, 109
correction questions, 108
essays, 110
multiple choice questions, 107
revision questions, 108
executive branch of U.S. government, 323
checks and balances, 326-327
exoskeleton, 392
exothermic reactions, 414
exponents, 471-472
practice questions and answers, 473-475
exposition, 212

F

factoring, 545-548
Fahrenheit temperature scale, 421
falling action, 213
Federal Reserve, 337
federalism, 322
Fertile Crescent, 270
feudal system, 275
fiction
characterization, 215
climax, 213
conflict, types of, 212
imagery, 220
plot, 214
climax, 213
resolution, 213
point of view, 215
resolution, 213
setting, 211
third-person narration, 215-216
tone, 218-219
fight or flight response, 87
figures of speech, 218
finishing exam, incentives for, 92
first person, 118
fiscal policy, 340
food as stressor, 89
Ford, Gerald, 316
forms of government, 321
formulas, 473
fossils, 406
fraction key (b/c), calculators, 842
fractions, 485
adding, 487
comparing, 486
converting to decimal, 486
converting to mixed numbers, 486
dividing, 488
equivalent, 485
mixed numbers, 485
multiplying, 488
practice questions and answers, 489-492
simplifying, 486
subtracting, 487
word problems, solving, 489
fragments, 127
French Revolution, 281-282
frequency, 424
friction, 418

G

galaxies, 400
GDP (Gross Domestic Product), 337
GED
administration, 10
authors of, 9
disabilities, accommodating, 14-15
elements of, 9
purpose of, 10
registration, 9
scoring
general guidelines, 10-11
passing scores, 11
reporting scores, 11
testing agencies
Canadian agencies, 14
local agencies, 11-13

U.S. federal prisons, 13
U.S. government, 13
U.S. military, 13
U.S. territories, 13
web resources, 857-858
gender-neutral pronouns, 123
genetics
alleles, 387
cloning, 389
mutations, 389
geography, 343
continents, 343
Earth, measuring, 345
topographical maps, contour lines, 347-349
geology, 343
geometry, 553
angles, 554
area, 561
circles, 557
circumference, 560
congruency, 560
coordinate geometry formula, 856
derived 3D figures, 557
perimeter, 560
practice questions and answers, 563, 566-568
Pythagorean Relationship, 561-562
quadrilaterals, 554-555
similarity, 559
triangles, 555
vertical angles, 559
volume, 561
Gettysburg Address, 302
globalization, 290
glucose, 393
Golgi apparatus, 385
grammar, 125
modification, 139-141
morphology, 125
parts of speech
adjectives, 114
adverbs, 114
agreement, 118
conjunctions, 114
determiners, 114
interjections, 114
nouns, 114-116
number, 118
prepositions, 114
pronouns, 114, 122-124
verbs, 114-117
syntax, 125
graphs, 513
circle graphs, interpreting, 101-102
correlations, 513
interpolation, 513
line graphs, 513
interpreting, 100
negative correlation, 514
gravitation, 417
Great Depression, 306
New Deal, 307-308
guessing on the GED exam, 92
Gutenberg's press, 277

H

haiku (poetry), 222
Haitian independence, 283
Han Dynasty, 274
heat, 421
measuring, 422
transfer methods, 422
hemispheres, 345
hieroglyphics, 268
Hinduism, 274
holistic scoring, 170
homonyms, 153-157
homophones, 153
Hooke, Robert, 383
hours, converting to minutes, 526
House of Representatives, 322
hurricanes, 405
Huygens, Christiaan, 426
hydroelectric power generation, 428
hydrosphere, 405
hyphen (-), 166

I

identifying fact versus opinion in nonfiction, 235
igneous rocks, 408
imagery, 211, 220, 225
improper fractions, 485
incentives for finishing exam, 92
inclined plane, 419
income tax, 341
indefinite pronouns, 122-123
Indian Citizenship Act of 1924, 294
indirect objects, 126, 128
Industrial Revolution, 283-284
industrialization, 304-305
inequalities, 535-536
inertia, 418
inference, 238-239
infinitives, 131
inflation, 337
infrasound, 424
interest, 501
interest rates formula, 856
interjections, 114
interpolation, 513
interpreting
  editorial cartoons, 102, 104
  graphs
    circle graphs, 101-102
    line graphs, 100
  Language Arts, Writing essay score, 171
  maps, exercise, 97
  tables, 99
ionic bonds, 415
ions, 416
irregular past forms of verbs, 119
irrelevant language, avoiding, 145
Islam, 273
isotopes, 412
italics versus underline, 167-168

J

Joan of Arc, 276
jobs, importance of GED in obtaining, 837
journalism as form of nonfiction, 233
Judaism, 273
judicial branch of U.S. government, 325-326
  checks and balances, 326-327
Jupiter, 403

K

Kennedy, John F., 312-314
kinetic energy, 419
knowledge versus skills, 85-86
knowledge level (Taxonomy of Educational Objectives), 95
Korean War, 310
KSA (knowledge, skills, and abilities), 85

L

language arts
  descriptivism, 111
  drama
    acts, 231
    character analysis, 231-232
    dialogue, 229
    dramatic structure, 230
    prologues/epilogues, 231
    protagonists, 230
    scenes, 231
    stage direction, 229-230
  poetry, 221
    alliteration, 223
    couplets, 222
    end rhymes, 222
    epics, 222
    haiku, 222
    hearing, 222
    imagery, 225
    limericks, 222
    metaphors, 223-224
    mood, 227
    odes, 222
    personification, 223-224
    quatrains, 222
    rhyme schemes, 223
    similes, 223-224
    slant rhymes, 223

sonnets, 222
symbolism, 225-226
themes, 226
prescriptivism, 111
reading terms, 257-261
web resources, 857
Language Arts, Reading test
diagnostic test, 36-43
answers and explanations, 72-73
format of, 205
multiple choice practice questions, 245-256
practice test, 625-639, 743, 746-759
scoring, 206-207
test-taking strategies, 207
Language Arts, Writing test
common mistakes, 148
lack of specificity, 148
complicated sentences, 148
illogical statements, 150
inappropriate vocabulary, 149
opinionated/emotional statements, 148
poor penmanship, 149
too conversational, 150
unsafe assumptions, 150
interpreting, 171
Part I, diagnostic test, 25-31
answers and explanations, 70-71
Part II essay
diagnostic test, 32-33, 623, 741
effective essays, writing, 172-175
example essays, 176-178
preparing for, 169
prompt, 169
revising and editing, 175
scoring, 170
practice questions, 183-197, 603-621, 721-741
rubric, 170-171
terms, 199-201
latitude, 345
Law of Conservation of Energy, 419
Law of Conservation of Matter, 414
laws of motion, 417
applied forces, 418
equal and opposite reaction, 418
inertia, 418
universal gravitation, 417
learning techniques, Taxonomy of Educational Objectives, 95
analysis level, 96
application level, 96
comprehension level, 96
evaluation level, 96
knowledge level, 95
synthesis level, 96
legend, 97
legislative branch of U.S. government, 322
checks and balances, 326-327
levers, 420
life sciences. *See* biology
light waves, 426
light years, 400
limericks (poetry), 222
Lincoln, Abraham, 302
line graphs, 513
interpreting, 100
linear equations, 540
Linnaeus, Carolus, 393
literary nonfiction, 233
lithosphere, 407
longitude, 345
longitudinal wave particles, 423
lysosomes, 384

M

machines, 419-420
Magna Carta, 275
magnetic field, 427
magnetism, 427
managing time during exam, 91
maps, 97
Mars, 403
mathematics. *See also* mathematics test; statistics
addition, 465
algebra
coordinate plane, 536-544
equations, 531-533, 545
expressions, multiplying, 544
expressions, simplifying, 533-534
factoring, 545-548

inequalities, 535-536
patterns, representing in equations, 534-535
decimals, 477
adding, 479
comparing, 477
dividing, 479-481
multiplying, 479-481
practice questions and answers, 482-484
rounding, 478
subtracting, 479
diagnostic test, 64-67
answers and explanations, 79-81
division, 466
estimation, 481-482
exponents, 471-472
practice questions and answers, 473-475
formulas, 473
area, 855
circumference, 855
coordinate geometry, 856
distance, 856
mean, 856
Measures of Central Tendency, 856
median, 856
perimeter, 855
Pythagorean Theorem, 856
rates, 856
simple interest rates, 856
total cost, 856
volume, 855
fractions, 485
adding, 487
comparing, 486
converting to decimal, 486
converting to mixed numbers, 486
dividing, 488
equivalent, 485
multiplying, 488
practice questions and answers, 489-492
simplifying, 486
subtracting, 487
word problems, solving, 489
geometry, 553
angles, 554
area, 561
circles, 557
circumference, 560
congruency, 560
derived 3D figures, 557
perimeter, 560
practice questions and answers, 563, 566-568
Pythagorean Relationship, 561-562
quadrilaterals, 554-555
similarity, 559
triangles, 555
vertical angles, 559
volume, 561
multiplication, 465
order of operations, PEMDAS, 472
percentages, 499
converting to decimal, 499
interest calculations, 501
practice questions and answers, 504
solving problems, 500
place value, 461
subtraction, 465
web resources, 858
mathematics Test
calculators, testing center-provided
arithmetic, performing, 841
b/c (fraction key), 842
clearing calculations, 841
multiplication of a quantity, 841
positive/negative numbers, 842
square root function, 842
starting, 841
usage example, 843
content coverage areas, 459-460
formulas, 855
web resources, 841
practice questions and answers, 571-586, 673-682, 702-710, 717, 797-806, 824-832
problem-solving strategies, 466-467
mayor-council municipal government, 331
mean, calculating, 511, 856
Measures of Central Tendency (mathematics), 856
measuring
acid and base strength, pH scale, 416
Earth latitude and longitude, 345
economic growth, 337-338
heat, 422

mechanics, 417
- Law of Conservation of Energy, 419
- laws of motion
  - applied forces, 418
  - equal and opposite reaction, 418
  - inertia, 418
- machines, 419-420
- work, calculating, 418-419

median, 511, 856
meiosis, 386
Mendel, Gregor, 387
Mendeleev, Dmitri, 412
Mercury, 403
Mesolithic period, 268
metalloids, 413
metals, 413
metamorphic rocks, 408
metaphors, 223-224
meteorology, 404-405
- cloud formations, 405
- convection currents, 423

metric system, 522-524
Mexican-American War, 300
Middle Ages
- bubonic plague, 276
- feudal system, 275
- Magna Carta, 275
- Norman Conquest, 275

minerals, 408
minutes, converting to hours, 526
misplaced modifiers, 140
mitochondria, 384
mitosis, 385
mixed numbers, 485
- converting to fractions, 486

mixtures, 415
modification, 139-141
momentum, 418
monarchy, 321
Mondell (WY), Rep. Frank, 327
money, calculating total cost, 525
money systems, 340
Monroe Doctrine, 300
monumental Supreme Court cases, 325
mood (poetry), 227
morphology, 125
multiplication
- algebraic expressions, 544
- of decimals, 479, 481
- of fractions, 488
- product, 465
- quantities, 841

municipal government, 331
muscular system, 392
music and relaxation, 89
mutations, 389
mythology, 270

N

Napoleon, 281-282
neatness, effect on GED essay scoring, 171
nebulae, 400
negative correlations, 514
negative numbers, 461
- absolute value, 462-463
- practice questions, 463
- calculator functions, 842

Neptune, 403
nervous system, 389
neutron stars, 400
neutrons, 412
New Deal, 307-308
New World explorers, 278
Newton, Isaac
- laws of motion, 417
  - applied forces, 418
  - equal and opposite reaction, 418
  - inertia, 418
  - universal gravitation, 417

Nineteenth Amendment to the Constitution, 305
Nixon, Richard M., 315-316
non-restrictive clauses, 140
nonfiction, 233
- author's opinion, identifying, 234
- cause and effect, relating, 235-237
- comparative analysis, 237-238
- fact versus opinion, identifying, 235

ideas, comparing and contrasting, 237-238
inference, 238-239
summarizing, 239-240
types of, 233
noninterventionism, 303-304
nonmetals, 413
Norman Conquest, 275
nouns, 114-116
agreement, 119-122
number, 118
subject, 112
number line
∞ (infinity symbol), 461
absolute value, 462-463
numeric values
estimating, 481-482
mean, calculating, 511
median, calculating, 511

O

obtaining U.S. citizenship, 330
oceans of the Earth, 343
octet rule, 415
odes (poetry), 222
Old Stone Age, 268
oligarchy, 321
order of mathematical operations, PEMDAS, 472
organ systems, 389
digestive system, 391
endocrine system, 392-393
muscular system, 392
respiratory system, 390
skeletal system, 392
urinary system, 391
nervous system, 389
organelles, 384
overpopulation, 350

P

panic, 87
paragraphs, 143
concise language, 145-147
relationship between, 147-148
logical sentence order, 143-144
pronoun use, 144
transition words, 147
word choice, 144-145
parallel structure, 137-139
parentheses, 164
in mathematical expressions, 472
parts of speech, 113
adjectives, 114
adverbs, 114
conjunctions, 114, 129-131
in sentence subject, 121
determiners, 114
interjections, 114
nouns, 114-116
number, 118
prepositions, 114
pronouns, 114, 122-124
gender-neutral, 123
indefinite, 122-123
possessive determiner error, 123
usage in paragraphs, 144
verbs, 114, 116-117
agreement, 117-118
conjugation, 116-118
constituency, 126
irregular past forms, 119
tense, 132-136
passive determiners, 114
passive voice, 136-137
patterns, representing in algebraic equations, 534-535
pedosphere, 408
PEMDAS (Parentheses, Exponents, Multiplication, Division, Addition, Subtraction), order of mathematical operations, 472
percentages, 499. *See also* probability
converting to decimal, 499
interest calculations, 501
practice questions and answers, 504
solving problems, 500
perfectly internalized skills, 86
perimeter, 560
formulas, 855
periodic table, 412
peripheral nervous system, 389

personal pronouns, 122
personification, 223-224
pH scale, 416
photons, 426
photosynthesis, 393
physical changes, 414
physics
  electricity, 427
    conductors, 428
    power generation, 428-429
    static electricity, 428
  laws of motion, 418
  magnetism, 427
  mechanics, 417
    energy, 419
    machines, 419-420
  states of matter, 421
  wave-particle duality, 426
  waves, 423-424
    electromagnetic radiation, 425
    light, 426
    sound waves, 425
  work, calculating, 418-419
place, 210
place value, 461
placenta, 389
planets, 401-403
planning your GED essay, 173
plate tectonics, 407
plot, 210-214
plural noun forms, 115-116
Pluto, 403
poetry, 221
  alliteration, 223
  couplets, 222
  end rhymes, 222
  epics, 222
  haiku, 222
  hearing, 222
  imagery, 225
  limericks, 222
  metaphors, 223-224
  mood, 227
  odes, 222
  personification, 223-224
  quatrains, 222
  rhyme schemes, 223
  similes, 223-224
  slant rhymes, 223
  sonnets, 222
  symbolism, 225-226
  themes, 226
point of view, 210, 215
poles, 427
political cartoons, interpreting, 102-104
political maps, 97
pollution, chemistry of, 416-417
positive correlations, 513
positive numbers, 461
  absolute value, 462-463
  calculator functions, 842
  practice questions, 463
possessive determiners, 122
  common errors, 123
potential energy, 419
power, 418
practice questions and answers
  geometry, 563-568
  Language Arts, Reading multiple-choice section, 245-256
  Language Arts, Writing Part I, 183-197
  math, 571-586
  science, 431-448
  social studies, 353-369
practice tests
  Language Arts, Reading, 625-639, 743-759
    answers, 597, 688-691, 715, 812-814
  Language Arts, Writing, 603-621, 721-741
    answers, 597, 684-687, 715, 808-811
  mathematics, 673-682, 797-806
    answers, 599, 702-710, 717, 824-832
  science, 659, 661-671, 782-795
    answer sheet, 598, 716
    answers, 697-698, 700-701, 820-823
  social studies, 640-657, 760-780
    answer sheet, 598, 716
    answers, 692-696, 815-819
  web resources, 858

practicing
skills, 86
with time limits, 87
predicates, 112, 126
prehistory, 267
preparing for GED, 89, 169
plan of attack, formulating, 91
prepositions, 114
prescriptivism, 111
present perfect verb forms, conjugating, 119
prime meridian, 345
principal-interest rate, 501
Principia Mathematica, 417
probability, 505
dependent probability, 506
practice questions and answers, 507-510
problem-solving strategies for mathematics test, 466-467
product (multiplication), 465
Prohibition, 305
projection, 97
prologues/epilogues (drama), 231
pronouns, 122-124
agreement, 119-122
gender-neutral, 123
indefinite, 122-123
number, 118
possessive determiner error, 123
subject, 112
usage in paragraphs, 144
proper fractions, 485
proper names, capitalization, 160
proportion, 494
prose
fiction. *See* fiction
style, 216
euphemisms, 217
figures of speech, 218
protagonists (drama), 230
Protestant Reformation, 278
psychomotor (manipulation of objects) domain, Taxonomy of Educational Objectives, 95
publications, italicizing, 167-168
pulleys, 420
punctuation, 161
apostrophe, 163
colon, 165
comma, 161-163
dash, 167
ellipses, 166
hyphen, 166
parentheses, 164
quotation marks
double quotation marks, 163-164
single quotation marks, 164
semicolon, 165-166
Pythagorean Relationship, 539, 561-562
Pythagorean Theorem, 856

Q

quadrilaterals, 554-555
quantifiers, 114
quantities, 472
quasi-governmental enterprises, 339
quatrains (poetry), 222
questions, skipping, 90
quotation marks
double quotation marks, 163-164
single quotation marks, 164
quotient, 466

R

radiation, 422
rate, 493
formulas, 856
reading terms, 257-261
reading Test
format of, 205
scoring, 206-207
test-taking strategies, 207
Reagan, Ronald, 317
recession (economic), 336
recessive alleles, 387
Reconstruction, 302
redundant language, avoiding, 145
registering for GED exam, 9
relating cause and effect in nonfiction, 235-237

relaxation techniques, 88-89
breathing, 90
suspense and surprise, controlling, 88
taking breaks, 90
religion
Buddhism, 274
Christianity, 273
Confucianism, 274
Hinduism, 274
Islam, 273
Judaism, 273
Renaissance, 276
Age of Discovery, 277-278
Da Vinci, Leonardo, 277
Gutenberg's press, 277
Protestant Reformation, 278
reproduction
meiosis, 386
spermatozoon, 386
resolution, 213
respiratory system, 390
revising your GED essay, 175
Revolutionary War, 295, 299
rhyme schemes (poetry), 223
road maps, 97
Roosevelt, Franklin D.
New Deal, 307-308
rough endoplasmic reticulum, 385
rounding decimals, 478
rubrics, 170
run-on sentences, 128-129

S

Saturn, 403
scale, 97, 526
scenes (drama), 231
science test
content of, 381
diagnostic test, 54-60
answers and explanations, 76-78
format of, 381
practice questions and answers, 431-448
practice test, 659-671, 697-701, 782-795, 820-823
answers, 598, 716
terms list, 449-455
web resources, 857
scientific notation, 478-479
scoring GED exam
general guidelines, 10-11
Language Arts, Writing essay, 170
examples, 176-178
rubric, 170-171
passing scores, 11
Reading Test, 206-207
reporting scores, 11
screws, 420
second person, 118
sedimentary rocks, 408
sentence structure, 112. *See also* parts of speech
clauses, 126
non-restrictive, 140
complex sentences, 120
direct objects, 126-128
fragments, 127
indirect objects, 126-128
parallel structure, 137-139
predicate, 112, 126
punctuation, 161
apostrophe, 163
colon, 165
comma, 161-163
dash, 167
ellipses, 166
hyphen, 166
parentheses, 164
quotation marks, 163-164
semicolon, 165-166
run-ons, 128-129
subject, 112, 126
voice, 136-137
separation of powers, 326-327
setting, 210-211
Seward's Folly, 303
similes, 223-224
simple interest, 501
formula, 856
simple machines, 419-420
simple past verb forms, conjugating, 119

simplifying
- algebraic expressions, 533-534
- fractions, 486

singular/plural noun forms, 115-116
skeletal muscle, 392
skeletal system, 392
skills
- perfectly internalized skills, 86
- practicing, 86
- versus knowledge, 85-86

skipping difficult questions, 90
slant rhymes, 223
slavery, 295
sleep, 89
slope, calculating, 541
smooth endoplasmic reticulum, 384
smooth muscle, 392
social studies test
- covered content areas, 265-266
- diagnostic test, 45-50
  - answers and explanations, 74-75
- practice questions and answers, 353-369
- practice test, 640-657, 760-780
  - answers, 598, 692-696, 716, 815-819
- terms list, 371-378
- web resources, 858

socialism, 339
soil layer, 408
solar system, 401
- planets, 401-403

solutes, 415
solutions, 415
solvents, 415
solving
- percentage problems, 500
- word problems on mathematics test, 466

somatic cell nuclear transfer, 389
sonnets, 222
sound waves, 425
space exploration, 403-404
Spanish-American War, 304
spelling
- contractions, 158-159
- homonyms, 153-157

spermatozoon, 386
square root, 471-472
- calculator function, 842

stage direction, 229-230
Standard English, 125
- versus EAE, 111

stars, 400
state government, 330-331
static electricity, 428
statistics, 493
- practice questions and answers, 494, 497
- proportion, 494
- rate, 493
- ratio, 493

Stone Age, 267
strong-mayor municipal government, 331
strategic thinking, 86
style, 210, 216
- euphemisms, 217
- figures of speech, 218

subject, 112, 126
- agreement, conjugation, 118
- number, 118
- with conjunctions, 121

subordinating conjunctions, 129-130
subordinators, 129
subtracting
- decimals, 479
- fractions, 487

subtraction, 465
summarizing ideas in nonfiction, 239-240
supernova, 400
supply and demand, 334-336
- equilibrium price, 335

Supreme Court, 325
surprise, controlling, 88
suspense, controlling, 88
symbolism, 225-226
symbols, representing chemical reactions, 414
symptoms of panic, 87
syntax, 125
synthesis level (Taxonomy of Educational Objectives), 96

T

tables, 512
  interpreting, 99
taking breaks, 90
Taxonomy of Educational Objectives, 95
  analysis level, 96
  application level, 96
  comprehension level, 96
  evaluation level, 96
  knowledge level, 95
  synthesis level, 96
temperature scales, 421
tense, 131, 135-136
  future, 133
  past, 132
  present, 133
  unreal conditional, 134
test-taking strategies for reading test, 207
testing agencies
  Canadian agencies, 14
  local agencies, 11-13
  U.S. federal prisons, 13
  U.S. government, 13
  U.S. military, 13
  U.S. territories, 13
theme, 209-210, 226
third-person, 215-216
  narration, 118
time conversion, 526
time limits, practicing with, 87
time management, 91
time zones, 346-347
tone, 211, 218-219
topic sentences, 143
topographical maps, 97
  contour lines, 347-349
tornadoes, 405
total cost, calculating, 525
  formula, 856
town meeting municipal government, 331
Trail of Tears, 300
transform boundaries, 407
transition words, 147
transverse wave particles, 423
triangles, 555
triangular trade, 295
Twelfth Amendment (U.S. Constitution), 323

U

U.S. customary units of measurement, 522
U.S. Government
  Congress, 322
  Constitution
    amendments, 327-328
    Article One, 322
    Article Three, 325-326
    Article Two, 323-324
    Twelfth Amendment, 323
  Electoral College, 328-329
  executive branch, 323
  judicial branch, 325-326
  legislative branch, 322
  role of citizen, 329-330
  separation of powers, 326-327
U.S. history
  American Revolution, 295
  Articles of Confederation, 299
  Bush, George H. W, 317
  Bush, George W., 318-319
  Carter, Jimmy, 316
  Civil War, 301
    Gettysburg Address, 302
  Clinton, Bill, 317-318
  colonization, 294
  Declaration of Independence, 296-299
  Eisenhower, Dwight D., 310-312
  Ford, Gerald, 316
  Great Depression, 306
    New Deal, 307-308
  immigration, 304
  industrialization, 304-305
  Kennedy, John F., 312-314
  Korean War, 310
  native Americans, 293-294
  Nixon, Richard M., 315-316
  noninterventionism, 303-304
  Prohibition, 305
  Reagan, Ronald, 317
  Revolutionary War, 299

slavery, 295
thirteen colonies, 294
Vietnam War, 314-315
westward expansion, 300-301
Trail of Tears, 300
women's suffrage, 305
World War I, 305
World War II, 308-310
U.S. Senate, 322
ultrasound, 424
underline versus italics, 167-168
units of measurement, 521
converting, 523-524
metric system, 522-523
unit conversions, 524
U.S. customary units, 522
universal gravitation, 417-418
Uranus, 403
urinary system, 391

V

van Leeuwenhoek, Anton, 279, 384
Venus, 403
verbs, 114-117
agreement, 116-122
conjugation, 116-118
constituency, 126
infinitive form, 131
irregular past forms, 119
present perfect forms, 119
simple past forms, 119
tense, 131, 135-136
future, 133
past, 132
present, 133
unreal conditional, 134
vertical angles, 559
Vietnam War, 314-315
voice, 136-137
volume, 561
formulas, 855

W

wave-particle duality, 426
wavelength, 424
waves, 423-424
electromagnetic radiation, 425
light, 426
sound waves, 425
weak-mayor municipal government, 331
weather
climate, 349
convection currents, 423
meteorology, 404-405
webbing, 174
wedges, 420
wheel and axle, 420
word choice, 144-145
word problems, solving on mathematics test, 466
work
calculating, 418-419
simple machines, 419-420
world history
Age of Enlightenment, 280
Bolshevik Revolution, 287-288
Central American independence, 283
early civilizations
China, 274
Egypt, 268-269
Greece, 270-271
Rome, 271-273
European Middle Ages, 275
bubonic plague, 276
feudal system, 275
Magna Carta, 275
Norman Conquest, 275
French Revolution, 281-282
Haitian independence, 283
Industrial Revolution, 283-284
prehistory, 267
Stone Age, 267
religion
Buddhism, 274
Christianity, 273

Confucianism, 274
Hinduism, 274
Islam, 273
Judaism, 273
Renaissance, 276
Age of Discovery, 277-278
Da Vinci, Leonardo, 277
Gutenberg's press, 277
Protestant Reformation, 278
World War I, 285-287, 305
World War II, 288-290, 308-310
World War I, 285-287, 305
World War II, 288-290, 308-310
writing
creating effective essays, 172-175
reasons for, 175
terms, 199-201
writing test
capitalization, 160
construction shift questions, 109
correction questions, 108
essays, 110
italics versus underline, 167-168
multiple choice questions, 107
punctuation
apostrophe, 163
colon, 165
comma, 161-163
dash, 167
ellipses, 166
hyphen, 166
parentheses, 164
quotation marks, 163-164
semicolon, 165-166
revision questions, 108

X-Y-Z

x-axis, 513

y-axis, 513